Classics in
Environmental
Criminology

Classics in Environmental Criminology

Edited by

Martin A. Andresen
Paul J. Brantingham
J. Bryan Kinney

SIMON FRASER UNIVERSITY
PUBLICATIONS

CRC Press
Taylor & Francis Group
Boca Raton   London   New York

CRC Press is an imprint of the
Taylor & Francis Group, an **informa** business

Published with:
Simon Fraser University Publications
1300 West Mall Centre
8888 University Drive
Burnaby, British Columbia V5A 1S6
Canada
International Standard Book Number (SFU): 978-0-86491-309-8
Website: http://www.sfu.ca/sfupublications

CRC Press
Taylor & Francis Group
6000 Broken Sound Parkway NW, Suite 300
Boca Raton, FL 33487-2742

© 2010 by Simon Fraser University Publications
CRC Press is an imprint of Taylor & Francis Group, an Informa business

No claim to original U.S. Government works

Printed in the United States of America on acid-free paper
10 9 8 7 6 5 4 3 2 1

International Standard Book Number: 978-1-4398-1779-7 (Hardback)

Library of Congress Cataloging-in-Publication Data

Classics in environmental criminology / editors, Martin A. Andresen, Paul J. Brantingham,
    Bryan J. Kinney.
      p. cm.
    Includes bibliographical references and index.
    ISBN 978-1-4398-1779-7 (hardcover : alk. paper)
    1. Crime--Environmental aspects. 2. Criminology. I. Andresen, Martin A. II. Brantingham,
Paul J. III. Kinney, Bryan J. IV. Title.

HV6150.C55 2010
364--dc22
                                                        2010011685

Visit the Taylor & Francis Web site at
http://www.taylorandfrancis.com

and the CRC Press Web site at
http://www.crcpress.com

Acknowledgments

As with any work, this anthology could not have been completed without the work of a number of people. First and foremost, the staff at the various publishers who facilitated the process of our obtaining permissions was invaluable. We would like to thank Lawrence Cohen and Marcus Felson for providing explicit permission to reproduce their work here, and George Rengert for supplying us with the original figures from his co-authored book. We would also like to thank Nancy Earle for her editing and Robert McNevin for his design work on the anthology's manuscript. Last, but not least, we would like to thank Dr. John Whatley of SFU Publications for his tireless efforts in getting this anthology to press.

A Note on the Texts

These articles are derived from the most current versions; they stay true to the original idiom, Canadian, British, and U.S. variations in spelling, layout, and citation style used by the authors with the exception of correction of clear errors in punctuation or spelling. We have re-registered images used in the original when they were of low quality but only in cases where they were more readable as a result. The Consolidated References section is an alphabetized list of all works referenced in the articles.

Permissions

The following articles in this collection are in the public domain:

Burgess, E.W. 1916. Juvenile delinquency in a small city. *Journal of the American Institute of Criminal Law and Criminology* 6: 724–728.

Quetelet, L.A.J. 1842. *A Treatise on Man and the Development of His Faculties.* Edinburgh: W. and R. Chambers, pp. 82–96.

The articles in this collection not in the public domain have been reprinted with permission from the following sources:

Brantingham, P.J. and F.L. Faust. 1976. A conceptual model of crime-prevention. *Crime and Delinquency* 22, 284–296. Copyright © 1976 Sage Publications.

Brantingham, P.L. and P.J. Brantingham. 1981. Notes of the geometry of crime. In Brantingham, P.J. and P.L. Brantingham (eds.), *Environmental Criminology.* Beverly Hills, CA: Sage Publications, pp. 27–53. Copyright © 1981 Sage Publications.

Brantingham, P.L. and P.J. Brantingham. 1993. Environment, routine and situation: toward a pattern theory of crime. In R.V. Clarke and M. Felson (eds.), *Routine Activity and Rational Choice: Advances in Criminological Theory,* Volume 5. New Brunswick, NJ: Transaction Publishers, pp. 259–294. Copyright © 1993 Transaction Publishers.

Brantingham, P.L. and P.J. Brantingham. 1993. Nodes, paths and edges: considerations on the complexity of crime and the physical environment. *Journal of Environmental Psychology* 13, 3–28. Copyright © 1993 Elsevier B.V. *Journal of Environmental Psychology.*

Clarke, R.V.G. 1980. Situational crime prevention: theory and practice. *British Journal of Criminology* 20, 136–147. Copyright © 1980 British Journal of Criminology.

Clarke, R.V.G and D.B. Cornish. 1985. Modeling offenders' decisions: a framework for research and policy. *Crime and Justice: An Annual Review of Research* 6: 147–185. Copyright © 1985 University of Chicago Press.

Cohen, L.E. and M. Felson. 1979. Social change and crime rate trends: a routine activity approach. *American Sociological Review* 44, 588–608. Copyright © 1979 The American Sociological Association.

Cornish, D.B. and R.V.G. Clarke. 1987. Understanding crime displacement: an application of rational choice theory. *Criminology* 25, 933–947. Copyright © 1987 The American Society of Criminology.

About the Editors

Martin A. Andresen: BA, MA (S Fraser), PhD (Br Col); Assistant Professor, Simon Fraser University School of Criminology.
Areas of Interest: Spatial crime analysis; geography of crime, environmental criminology; applied spatial statistics and geographical information analysis; (critical) quantitative methods.

Paul J. Brantingham: AB, JD (Col), Dip Criminology (Cantab); Professor School of Criminology, Simon Fraser University, British Columbia, Canada. RCMP University Research Chair in Crime Analysis.
Areas of interest: Computational criminology; environmental criminology; ecology of crime; crime analysis; historical criminology; comparative criminal justice; legal aid and related matters.

J. Bryan Kinney: BA (UBC), MA, PhD (S Fraser); Assistant Professor, Simon Fraser University; Assistant Director, Institute for Canadian Urban Research Studies (ICURS).
Areas of Interest: Environmental criminology theory; geography of crime; police studies; crime prevention and crime reduction; quantitative research methods.

Table of Contents

Acknowledgments   v
A Note on the Texts   vii
Permissions   ix
About the Editors   xi

Section I

EARLY WORK ON THE ECOLOGY OF CRIME

**1   The Place of Environmental Criminology within
      Criminological Thought   5**

      M.A. ANDRESEN

**2   Of the Development of the Propensity to Crime
      (1842)   29**

      L.A.J. QUETELET

3   Localities of Crime in Suffolk (1856)   77

      J. GLYDE

4   Juvenile Delinquency in a Small City (1916)   83

      E.W. BURGESS

**5   Juvenile Delinquency and Urban Areas:
      A Study of Rates of Delinquency in Relation
      to Differential Characteristics of Local
      Communities in American Cities (1969)   87**

      C.R. SHAW AND H.D. MCKAY

6   **Urban Ecological Aspects of Crime in
        Akron (1974)**   **125**

        G.F. PYLE, E.W. HANTEN, P.G. WILLIAMS,
        A.L. PEARSON II, J.G. DOYLE, AND K. KWOFIE

7   **Intraurban Crime Patterns (1974)**   **155**

        K.D. HARRIES

Section II

CLASSICS IN ENVIRONMENTAL
CRIMINOLOGY

8   **Social Change and Crime Rate Trends: A Routine
        Activity Approach (1979)**   **187**

        L.E. COHEN AND M. FELSON

9   **Routine Activities and Crime: An Analysis of
        Victimization in Canada (1990)**   **217**

        L.W. KENNEDY AND D.R. FORDE

10 **Notes on the Geometry of Crime (1981)**   **231**

        P.L. BRANTINGHAM AND P.J. BRANTINGHAM

11 **The Use of Space in Burglary (1985)**   **257**

        G.F. RENGERT AND J. WASILCHICK

12 **Nodes, Paths, and Edges: Considerations on
        the Complexity of Crime and the Physical
        Environment (1993)**   **273**

        P.L. BRANTINGHAM AND P.J. BRANTINGHAM

13 **Modeling Offenders' Decisions: A Framework for
        Research and Policy (1985)**   **311**

        R.V.G. CLARKE AND D.B. CORNISH

14   **Linking Criminal Choices, Routine Activities, Informal Control, and Criminal Outcomes (1986)**   341

M. FELSON

15   **Understanding Crime Displacement: An Application of Rational Choice Theory (1987)**   351

D.B. CORNISH AND R.V.G. CLARKE

16   **Environment, Routine, and Situation: Toward a Pattern Theory of Crime (1993)**   365

P.L. BRANTINGHAM AND P.J BRANTINGHAM

Section III

ENVIRONMENTAL CRIMINOLOGY AND CRIME PREVENTION

17   **A Conceptual Model of Crime Prevention (1976)**   395

P.J. BRANTINGHAM AND F.L. FAUST

18   **Crime Prevention and Control through Environmental Engineering (1969)**   409

C.R. JEFFERY

19   **Criminal Behavior and the Physical Environment: A Perspective**   431

C.R. JEFFERY

20   **Situational Crime Prevention: Theory and Practice**   449

R.V.G CLARKE

21   **Routine Activities and Crime Prevention in the Developing Metropolis (1987)**   461

M. FELSON

22 **Future Spaces: Classics in Environmental
        Criminology—Where Do We Go from Here?**   **481**

        J.B. KINNEY

References   **489**

Index   **527**

Early Work on the Ecology of Crime

I

Environmental criminology, as a discipline, did not develop in a vacuum. Rather, as with all new developments in the (social) sciences, environmental criminology was born out of a particular approach to the study of crime that may be broadly described as spatial criminology. The purpose of the first part of this anthology is to highlight that development. Therefore, the chapters chosen for Part I were selected on the basis of two criteria: the significance and importance of the chapters based on their findings, and how they represent the change in the ecological scale of analysis through time.

As noted in Brantingham and Brantingham (1981a), this spatial approach to the study of crime has three distinct phases: the first, a European phenomenon, emerged in the early nineteenth century; the second, a North American phenomenon, emerged in the early twentieth century; and the third, a North American and British phenomenon, emerged in the late twentieth century. The early work on the ecology of crime consists of the first two phases of spatial criminology.

Early nineteenth century spatial criminology usually gives reference to two figures from France: Adolphe Quetelet and André-Michel Guerry. The work of Guerry in spatial criminology, *Essai sur la statistique morale de la France*, published in 1833, is often cited as preceding Quetelet because Quetelet's book, *A Treatise on Man and the Development of His Faculties*, was published in 1842. However, Quetelet actually began work in the field of spatial criminology before Guerry, publishing an earlier first work in 1831, *Research on the Propensity for Crime at Different Ages*. As such, the inclusion of Quetelet's work in this anthology is based on his status as the first "spatial criminologist," and a selection from *A Treatise on Man and the Development of His Faculties* is included here because of its availability relative to his earlier work.

Reading the work of Quetelet is actually a humbling experience because of the labor that was undertaken by him without the use of computers. The material included in this volume, from the third chapter in the third book, "Of the Development of the Propensity to Crime," discusses the impact of age, education, profession, climate, seasons, and gender on property and violent crime as it varies across the French departments. Each one of these topics has a tremendous literature today that only confirms what Quetelet found over 170 years ago. Needless to say, any anthology that includes early work on the ecology of crime and does not include the work of Quetelet is missing much of the foundation that modern (spatial) criminology is based on.

Though ground-breaking research at the time, French departments are rather coarse units of analysis that most certainly have just as much crime variation within them as between them—French departments are equivalent to a county in the United States or a district in England. The spatial criminological work that followed Quetelet and Guerry was undertaken in England and used cartographically larger (finer scale) units of analysis for crime. The work of John Glyde is one example—see Brantingham and Brantingham (1981a) for a thorough review of this literature. In Glyde's early article "Localities of Crime in Suffolk," taken from the 1856 version of the *Journal of the Statistical Society of London*, the finest resolution is the town. Glyde finds significant variation between towns in a county (Suffolk) in England. Aside from analyzing crime at a finer resolution than those of his contemporaries in France, Glyde finds that it is *where* the criminals *reside* that matters, not necessarily where the criminal events *occur*.

Turning to the early twentieth century, spatial criminology in the United States began with the early work of Ernest Burgess. Ernest Burgess's 1916. "Juvenile Delinquency in a Small City," builds on the work of John Glyde because it studies the delinquency of juveniles based on the location of their residence—six wards within a small city. Not only does the town of residence within a county impact the rate of delinquency, but so does the location within that town. This and other work by Ernest Burgess led to the development of the Chicago School that dominated (spatial) criminological thought for close to fifty years.

One of the most influential theoretical frameworks to come out of the Chicago School is that of social disorganization theory. Following the work of Glyde and Burgess, social disorganization theory explains criminal activity with reference to the characteristics of the community that delinquents live within. Sections from the *magnum opus* that defined social disorganization theory, *Juvenile Delinquency and Urban Areas: A Study of Rates of Delinquency in Relation to Differential Characteristics of Local Communities in American Cities* by Clifford Shaw and Henry McKay, are included in the collection because, once again, the scale of analysis became finer and further insight was gathered regarding the ecology of crime. In fact, the spatial unit of analysis in the work of Shaw and McKay was one-square-mile neighborhoods, approximately the size of a contemporary census tract; until very recently, this has been the standard unit of analysis in spatial criminology. It should be noted, however, that the nature of the analysis by Shaw and McKay is not fundamentally different from that of Quetelet because of the scale of analysis; Shaw and McKay employed more variables and performed more complex statistical analyses, but the essence is the same. The importance of the work, however, cannot be understated because little ground had been gained in this phase of spatial criminology for decades after the publication of Shaw and McKay's early work (see Cohen and Felson 1979a).

Most often, histories of spatial criminology move from social disorganization theory into environmental criminology proper. However, there was some work by geographers Gerald Pyle and Keith Harries in the 1970s that set the standard for research on the ecology of crime The first multivariate statistical analysis of the ecology of crime took place in Pyle's monograph, *The Spatial Dynamics of Crime*. This research did not change the spatial scale of analysis (census tract), but did advance the methodology used to analyze ecological crime patterns.

Keith Harries's "Intraurban Crime Patterns" (in *The Geography of Crime and Justice*) forms the last chapter in Section I. Harries' chapter is useful because he reviews much of the twentieth century ecology of crime literature we could not include in this anthology. He separates his review into *macroenvironments* and *microenvironments*: macroenvironments are those intracity studies already discussed, and microenvironments are the specific locations of criminal events. This latter section of the review provides a passage into Section II of the collection, because most often environmental criminology is concerned with the specific nature of crime in both time and space.

The Place of Environmental Criminology within Criminological Thought* 1

M.A. ANDRESEN

Contents

1.1	The Basics	6
1.2	Social Disorganization Theory	9
	1.2.1 Fundamental Concepts	10
	1.2.2 What Is Social Disorganization Theory and How Does It Relate to Crime?	11
	1.2.3 Testing Social Disorganization Theory	12
1.3	Routine Activity Theory	13
	1.3.1 Fundamental Concepts	14
	1.3.2 What Are Routine Activities and How Do They Relate to Crime?	15
	1.3.3 Testing Routine Activity Theory	17
1.4	Geometric Theory of Crime	18
	1.4.1 Fundamental Concepts	18
	1.4.2 The Geometry of Crime	19
	1.4.3 Applications and Testing of the Geometric Theory of Crime	20
1.5	Rational Choice Theory	22
	1.5.1 Fundamental Concepts	22
	1.5.2 What Is Rational Choice Theory?	24
	1.5.3 Applications of Rational Choice Theory	25
1.6	Pattern Theory of Crime	25
	1.6.1 Fundamental Concepts	26
	1.6.2 The Pattern Theory of Crime	26
	1.6.3 The Benefits of the Pattern Theory of Crime	27
1.7	The Organization of This Book	28

* The author would like to thank Paul J. Brantingham and Ronald V. Clarke for helpful comments on an earlier version of this chapter.

1.1 The Basics

There are four basic dimensions for understanding the phenomena of crime: the legal dimension, the offender dimension, the victim dimension, and the place (or situational) dimension (Brantingham and Brantingham 1981a). Those who investigate the legal dimension concern themselves with the creation and enforcement of laws; those who investigate the offender dimension, the dominant field of contemporary criminology, concern themselves with why individuals violate the law primarily along the lines of motivation; those who investigate the victim dimension are concerned with why particular targets (people or property) are victims of crime; and those who investigate the place dimension are concerned with the spatial and/or temporal component of crime (Brantingham and Brantingham 1981a). Consequently, the study of the fourth (place) dimension of crime is not particularly concerned with the first three dimensions. The first three dimensions are considered vital in the understanding of criminal events as they are all necessary for a criminal event to occur, but there are two reasons for the environmental criminologist's focus on the fourth dimension of space and time. First, pre-1970 criminological research is dominated by the study of the first three dimensions; as such, we know relatively little regarding the spatiotemporal components of crime; and, second, spatiotemporal patterns of crime are remarkably predictable. Therefore, there is much to be learned from this fourth dimension that can only complement the existing (and growing) knowledge of the first three dimensions.

Environmental criminology is an umbrella term that is used to encompass a variety of theoretical approaches, all focusing on the fourth dimension: routine activity theory, the geometric theory of crime, rational choice theory, and pattern theory—pattern theory is itself a meta-theory of the other three theoretical approaches.* On the last page of his seminal book, *Crime Prevention through Environmental Design*, C. Ray Jeffery (1971: 279) coined the term "environmental criminology" in a call for the establishment of a new school of thought in the field of criminology. This new school of thought was to retain the principles of the classical school of criminology (the deterrence of crime *before* it occurs), but the focus of this new school of thought was to be the environment within which crime occurs, not the individual offender.

Jeffery's call for a shift away from the focus on the individual offender emerges from his (and others') realization that past methods of addressing crime have failed: the deterrence-punishment model of criminal justice (police, courts, and prison) and the treatment-rehabilitation model (therapeutic treatment of the individual). Jeffery's claims of these failures were far from novel. Research and government studies repeatedly show the punishment is a

---

* See Brantingham and Brantingham (1998) for an outline of the various models and theories of environmental criminology.

failure in deterrence; despite the harsh treatments in the criminal justice system, recidivism remains high and most often unchanged—see Jeffery (1971; 1977) for extended discussions of the failures of these approaches to crime. So what is the environment that Jeffery spoke of?

The environment is to be conceptualized very broadly to include the physical design of places (architecture), the built environment (roadways, land use, types of buildings), as well as the legal and social institutions. Consequently, the environment that Jeffery believed should be modified is quite complex. Most importantly, we must consider ourselves as part of that environment. This is critical because we respond, adapt, and change as a result of the environment of which we are a part. As such, criminal behavior is merely one form of adaptation to an environment. For Jeffery, the most appropriate environment is one that has noncriminal behavior as the fittest adaptation, or optimal choice. This, of course, leads us to the next question: how is this environment to be attained?

The general model that Jeffery put forth was to make crime a high-risk and low-reward activity, to create environmental contingencies that control land use, travel paths, and access; and, in the long term, to create a society in which the existing laws are respected, potential offenders are busy (with jobs and/or education), citizens are given the knowledge to protect themselves through neighborhood organization and individual actions. But there was a problem. In order to (potentially) identify the specifics of this environment that could be created such that noncriminal adaptations are optimal, Jeffery called for the establishment of multiple research centers. These research centers would have significant government research funds operating on a five- to ten-year research program. Jeffery recognized that such research centers would be faced with resistance because people want a solution to crime problems today, not in a decade. His response was simple: you could allocate the appropriate resources into these research centers today and wait for ten years and (hopefully/potentially) get that money back many times over with what is learned, or you could spend that same money (tens of millions of dollars) on something you know will fail, the *status quo*. Though Jeffery's argument is persuasive, another author emerged literally months later with potential solutions that could be applied today.

Published on the heels of *Crime Prevention through Environmental Design* was Oscar Newman's (1972) *Defensible Space: Crime Prevention through Urban Design*. Oscar Newman's arguments are quite similar to those of Jeffery in that Newman believed that we need to build our neighborhoods in a manner that fosters the development of a social cohesion that acts against crime; that is, to create a defensible space. For Newman (1972), defensible space is a model of environments that inhibit crime through the creation of the physical expression of a social fabric that defends itself. This environment is dominantly created through changes in architecture. The result is an environment that exhibits territorial behavior and a sense of community, something that Newman argued has been the state of human settlements for centuries, but which was destroyed through modern urban design.

For Newman, this defensible space was created through the generation of territoriality, the provision of surveillance, the uniqueness of design to instil pride in ownership and awareness of the geographic placement of "safe" and "unsafe" areas. Territoriality is a term that captures a physical environment's ability to create perceived zones of "influence." Influence is used by Newman in a very specific way. Influence refers to our changing the physical environment (most often in modest ways) to express our territorial nature. Because of this influence, potential offenders recognize that the area they walk into is actively controlled by the individual(s) in residence. This provides an environmental cue that illegitimate actions in this geographic space will be recognized by others. Surveillance, specifically natural surveillance, is the creation of areas that allow the residents to watch over their property without having to make much effort to do so. For example, houses may be designed and placed such that their occupants can watch over their neighborhood. Uniqueness of design that instils pride in ownership, though listed as separate by Newman, is interdependent with the previous two concepts: if one does not take pride in ownership (or one's residence, more generally) then one is not likely to behave in a territorial manner or take advantage of the natural surveillance features of a property. This was particularly important for Newman because he was concerned with public housing that tends to have some stigma attached to it. And lastly, being aware of the geographic placement of safe and unsafe areas refers to placing a parking lot (an "unsafe" area because of the presence of many potential targets) in the unobstructed view of a store clerk (a "safe" area because of the surveillance of the parking lot). All four of these concepts are achieved through the appropriate architectural design of the neighborhood.

Jeffery (1977) criticized this focus on architecture to create defensible space in the second edition of his book. He believed that crime prevention through urban design was a subset of crime prevention through environmental design. As such, he felt Newman's approach was incomplete at best, and at worst detracted from the "real" research that needed to be performed. Jeffery's criticisms were likely in part due to the fact that Newman's approach was adopted almost immediately whereas Jeffery's approach was not (Robinson 1999).* The reason for this more rapid adoption is quite simple: Jeffery's approach involved a long-term research agenda that would necessarily involve long-term commitments of significant research funding

---

* Oscar Newman (1976) even wrote a comprehensive set of architect's guidelines for creating defensible space that was subsequently withdrawn because many of these guidelines did not work.

and Newman's approach could be applied immediately. In fact, *Defensible Space: Crime Prevention through Urban Design* contained a chapter titled "Modifying Existing Environments" (Chapter 7).

Regardless of their rate of adoption, both *Crime Prevention through Environmental Design* and *Defensible Space: Crime Prevention through Urban Design* emerged because of the recognition that the standard methods of crime prevention were failures in terms of both economic investment and recidivism. More importantly for the context here, both of these books spawned a large volume of literature that investigated the role of the environment in crime; these roles ranged from changes in social conditions, to the constraints imposed by the built environment, to choice of structures that are also constrained by the environment.

In what follows, the four environmental criminological theories, their fundamental concepts, and most notable tests and applications are discussed. Though the focus of Newman and Jeffery in particular was to prevent crime from occurring in the first place, much of what we call environmental criminology today seeks to understand crime through the perspective of our (ever changing) environment. However, crime prevention, in the spirit of Jeffery and Newman, is an integral component of the environmental criminology literature. As such, what we believe to be seminal contributions to crime prevention are also included in this anthology. Because of this environmental perspective, the theoretical understanding of the criminal event has advanced significantly since Jeffery first published his work. These later theoretical developments help understand *why* crime prevention works and we have thus decided to present them before the discussion of crime prevention.

We do this primarily for the new student of environmental criminology as it shows the place of environmental criminology within the broader criminological literature. Theoretical advancements, regardless of how significant they may be, do not drop from the sky—neither the work of Jeffery or Newman occurred in a vacuum. Thus, before the discussion moves into environmental criminology proper, we provide a similar discussion of social disorganization theory in order to uncover the context from which this fourth dimension of spatial criminology arose.

1.2 Social Disorganization Theory

Though focusing on the second dimension of criminal phenomena (investigating how neighborhoods influence *offenders*), social disorganization theory was the dominant form of spatial criminology before environmental criminology emerged. Because of the varying characteristics of neighborhoods, people who lived in different neighborhoods developed different dispositions toward committing crime. And more importantly, in the current context, the first environmental criminological theory discussed, routine activity theory, makes a distinct break in its fundamental concepts from social disorganization theory. Therefore, understanding social disorganization theory and its fundamental concepts is important in the understanding of how environmental criminology, in general, fits into criminological theory.

1.2.1 Fundamental Concepts

Social disorganization theory is not concerned with the individual characteristics of potential offenders, but the sociological influences on a person's delinquency. Specifically, social disorganization theory is the study of the relationship between neighborhood characteristics and crime, the strength of any relationship, whether or not any relationships are stable over time, and whether any relationships are related to the residents or the places in which they live. In order to completely understand any relationships that are found, one must also understand why neighborhoods are structured as they are. In order to do this, Clifford Shaw and Henry McKay invoked the social ecology of concentric zone theory, developed in Clifford Shaw's (1929) graduate work and based upon Burgess's (1925) model of city growth.

It was clear at the time the theory was adopted, (the early twentieth century) that certain areas within a city are dominated by particular land uses; some areas are residential, others for business, industry, and recreation. Within residential land use classifications, these areas can be further divided by economic status. Some areas have low socioeconomic status and others have high socioeconomic status. Indeed, most modern human settlements can be described along these lines.

In their most basic sense, turn of the twentieth century cities in North America were built around a central business and industrial district, bordered by residential areas differentiated by socioeconomic status. As one moves away from the central business and industrial district, the socioeconomic status of the residential zones increases. This pattern is most easily understood in the context of the turn of the twentieth century. Industrial districts at that time were dirty and polluted areas, not very desirable for residential housing. Consequently, those who could afford to moved away from the polluted industrial zone and moved into the more affluent residential zones. This is the essence of social ecology: space in society is limited and scarce, and we resolve that scarcity through economic means. As such, social ecology is a fundamental concept that considers the importance of space and revolves around competition.

The dynamics of this theory of competition over space are their most interesting for understanding crime. Because cities grow, the central business and industrial district also grows and that growth is typically a radial expansion outwards—geographic features such as mountains and water place restrictions on this growth pattern. Therefore, the central business and industrial district encroaches, or invades, the most immediate residential zone. This most immediate residential zone is then not only the most impoverished residential zone, but it is also in a constant state of transition; that is, it is a residential area being transformed into an industrial area. This transformation further impoverishes the area, decreasing its attractiveness as a residential area even more. Consequently, only the most impoverished of populations live in these areas. This time period was an era of rapid population growth through economic immigration in which impoverished immigrants settled in the undesirable and low-rent zone in transition simply because they could not afford anything else. Criminal enterprises also settled in the zone in transition because of low rent, customer access, and the inability of noncriminal residents to complain effectively to authorities about the criminals in their midst. Those who live in the zone in transition do so only for as long as necessary. This shows two properties of the zone in transition (and other relatively high crime areas) that lead to what Shaw and McKay (1942) referred to as social disorganization.

1.2.2 What Is Social Disorganization Theory and How Does It Relate to Crime?

Social disorganization theory arises from the application of the concept of social disorganization to the study of crime. Social disorganization is the inability of an area (neighborhood) to establish social cohesion that can prevent crime.* Social cohesion cannot be established in the zone in transition because of the high degree of population turnover and ethnic heterogeneity. Population turnover is present because of the undesirable nature of the zone in transition and ethnic heterogeneity is present because at the time of the development of social disorganization theory new immigrant populations tended to be impoverished and could not initially locate elsewhere. Therefore, multiple immigrant populations lived in the zone in transition. Incidentally, at the time of Shaw and McKay (1942), ethnically heterogeneous neighborhoods were composed of immigrants from different European countries. With multiple immigrant populations living in these ethnically diverse neighborhoods, they literally could not speak to each other. This leads to an area with a high degree of population turnover because of the socioeconomic conditions and a resident population that is unable to establish any

---

* Social cohesion is a term used to describe a neighborhood's ability to stand together, identify common interests, and carry out a (crime prevention) plan for the benefit of the community.

sense of community (social cohesion/organization) because of the inability to communicate.

Contemporary social disorganization theory focuses on social deprivation, economic deprivation, and family disruption as well as ethnic heterogeneity and population turnover (Cahill and Mulligan 2003; Linsky and Straus 1986; Sampson and Groves 1989; Stark 1996; Tseloni et al. 2002). Increases in any of these factors lead to increases in crime. The mechanism this operates through is simple: neighborhoods that are unable to establish social cohesion are conducive to criminal activity because they are places with few legitimate opportunities and a high degree of anonymity. Additionally, a low level of social cohesion results in the inaction on the part of residents when a problem develops: the police are not called when a car is being stolen or a house is being broken into, unless it is their own. The result is a neighborhood with a relative abundance of illegitimate opportunities and a citizen population that is not able to identify outsiders—a prime candidate for criminal activity.

1.2.3 Testing Social Disorganization Theory

Shaw and McKay (1942) undertook a series of empirical analyses to test their theory. By today's standards their empirical methods were quite simple, but their results are revealing. With regard to population turnover, Shaw and McKay (1942) found that small changes (decreases) in population lead to large changes (increases) in crime rates. However, large changes in population lead to very small changes in crime rates. This means that when an exodus begins (albeit on a small scale) the impact on crime is large, but once a neighborhood has deteriorated and has a high degree of crime further changes (reductions) in population have little impact.

With regard to ethnic heterogeneity, increases in the degree of foreign-born populations lead to increases in criminal activity. However, what Shaw and McKay (1942) are apt to point out is that it is not ethnicity, *per se*, that is related to crime. In high crime areas, over a period of time they remain places of high rates of crime, but the ethnic composition of those areas change. Consequently, it is not the ethnic group that is associated with crime, but the social conditions within that place. That is, it is the existence of ethnic (and presumably cultural) heterogeneity that is the problem; different ethnicities/cultures have different social expectations such that neighborhood residents are paralyzed because no one understands the limits of intervention within each group such that neighborhood feuds may be triggered. Two families that share some sociocultural characteristic may have different levels of tolerance for some behavior because they are culturally distinct along other lines—Old World battles may re-emerge in the New World. The trouble is that ethnic composition changes slowly over time, so it appears as though particular ethnic groups are particularly criminogenic.

One last relationship is worthy of discussion here: the relationship between unemployment and crime. It is commonly stated that increases in unemployment increase crime. This relationship exists because increases in unemployment lead to increases in motivation because of a decrease in legitimate opportunities. Indeed, Shaw and McKay (1942) find that the relationship between unemployment and crime rates across neighborhoods is the strongest of all relationships investigated. However, they also note that during the Great Depression when unemployment and welfare rates soared, there was little change in the level of crime across the city. Consequently, for Shaw and McKay (1942), the unemployment rate explained the overall spatial distribution of crime, but changes in the unemployment rate were not related to changes in the crime rate for *individual* neighborhoods.

However, this testing of their theory is problematic. Social disorganization theory states that socially disorganized places have high crime rates and social disorganization is measured by a lack of social cohesion. As such, population turnover, ethnic heterogeneity, social deprivation, economic deprivation, and family disruption leads to a lack (or breakdown) of social cohesion that leads to higher crime. Therefore, the causal relationship is between social cohesion/organization and crime, not the variables that lead to social cohesion (or lack thereof). The difference is at times subtle, but important. The causal relationship is often referred to as the structural relationship whereas the relationship between measures of social cohesion/organization and crime is often referred to as the reduced-form relationship. This means that if one tests a theory only with reduced-form relationships, any support (or lack thereof) may be purely circumstantial.

The first test of social disorganization theory that employed structural relationships was Sampson and Groves (1989), nearly sixty years after the work of Clifford Shaw and Henry McKay first emerged. Through the use of the British Crime Survey (which directly captured the presence of local friendship networks, the supervision of youth, and local organizational participation), Sampson and Groves (1989) were able to show that at a structural level, social disorganization theory bodes well for predicting crime. This and other work of Robert Sampson was responsible for the more recent re-emergence of social disorganization theory when investigating the ecological distribution of crime in urban contexts, most often used in conjunction with routine activity theory.

1.3 Routine Activity Theory

The first theory we need to discuss within environmental criminology is routine activity theory. This is for no other reason than that it was the first to be published as either a journal article or book chapter. Routine activity theory is also a natural topic to follow from social disorganization theory because it makes an explicit break from that literature. Rather than focusing on the neighborhood and its changing characteristics, routine activity theory focuses on the actions of individuals; routine activity theory also has different fundamental concepts than that of social disorganization theory.

1.3.1 Fundamental Concepts

The fundamental concept behind routine activity theory is *human ecology*. There are two primary differences between social ecology and human ecology that underline routine activity theory's break from its sociological past. First, social ecology has been criticized for focusing on competitive rather than cooperative relationships to understand the nature of human settlements. However, despite the existence of competitive relationships, much of our society can be understood through cooperative behavior. Second, though human ecology is similar to the social ecology of Clifford Shaw and Henry McKay through its emphasis on space, it also considers the importance of time. This lack of the incorporation of time into social ecology has been criticized by human ecologists. In fact, Amos Hawley's (1950) famous book, *Human Ecology*, includes a chapter that outlines such a criticism at length. We will look at each of these issues in turn.

Human ecology provides two concepts that allow us to think of how we humans adapt to our ever-changing environment in a noncompetitive way: symbiosis and commensalism (Hawley 1944, 1950). Symbiosis refers to the mutual dependence of organisms that have functional differences. Such relationships would include the birds that clean crocodile teeth or, in a human context, different people undertaking different jobs within one office. Commensalism, on the other hand, refers to the relationships between organisms that are based on functional similarity; two or more people who perform the same job, for example. These two concepts are then used by human ecologists to define a community in space and time that is based on noncompetitive behavior. The details of this community are not critical for understanding routine activity theory, but what is critical is the understanding that an environmental criminological theory seeks to understand crime from the perspective of noncompetitive legitimate activities across space and time. Marcus Felson's most recent book, *Crime and Nature* (2006), expands upon this ecological approach in the context of understanding crime.

In the context of time, human ecologists state that ecology is generally defined as understanding how a population (humans, for example) survives in an ever-changing environment. Therefore, the role of space is an important aspect of survival (where we live, work, and recreate), but it is only one aspect of that survival. For example, knowing *where* we spend our time is important, but also knowing *when* we are there is equally important. Consider a "high crime area" in a city's central business district. If the vast majority of the people who spend time in the central business district are there during the day and most of the crime in the area occurs at night, the vast majority of the denizens of the central business district are not at a high risk of criminal victimization. Only having the spatial component of criminal activity, therefore, misses extremely valuable information for the understanding of criminal events.

In order to consider the role of time, human ecologists invoke three concepts: rhythm, tempo, and timing. Rhythm is the regular periodicity in which events occur: every workday a person arrives in the office at eight o'clock; tempo is the number of events per unit of time, that is, the number of crimes per day in a given area; and timing is the coordination of interdependent activities, that is, the coordination of one's work rhythm with that of another. The important concept to get here is that there are spatial and temporal regularities with our noncompetitive legitimate activities and changes in those regularities change crime. If we change where we go, when we go there, how often we go there, and/or with whom we go, we alter the ways in which we can be victimized or victimize someone else.

1.3.2 What Are Routine Activities and How Do They Relate to Crime?

Lawrence Cohen and Marcus Felson define routine activities as "any recurrent and prevalent activities which provide for basic population and individual needs, whatever their biological or cultural origins" (1979: 593). Generally speaking, all of the activities that we undertake throughout our days, weeks, and months, to maintain ourselves (work, school, shopping, and recreation) are our routine activities. Routine activities are most often based on symbiosis and commensalism and involve the coordination of multiple people moving through space and time. As such, routine activities are, by and large, legal and commonplace.

Cohen and Felson go on to state that changes in routine activities over time can explain changes in crime rate trends. More generally, however, differences in routine activities, whether those differences are across time, across space, or between individuals, can be used to explain differences in crime rates. It is important to recognize that routine activity theory, as originally proposed, is not a general theory of crime—in later work, Marcus Felson (2002) has expanded the spectrum of crimes that routine activities can explain. The particular types of crimes that routine activity theory tries to explain are referred to as direct-contact predatory violations. Such violations involve at least one motivated offender, one suitable personal or property target, and the absence of a guardian capable of preventing such a violation—the minimal elements for a criminal event. And it is the convergence in time and space of these three elements that is necessary for a crime to occur; moreover, it is the changes in the nature of this convergence that change crime.

In the decades following the Second World War, incomes increased substantially, leading some scholars to refer to this period as the Golden Age of Capitalism (Webber and Rigby 1996). It was also a period of substantial increases in property and violent crime rates throughout the Western world. This is often referred to as the sociological paradox because increases in income were supposed to lead to decreases in crime. This is where routine activity theory has explanatory value. The substantial increases in income in the post-war era led to increased opportunities for more activities outside of the relatively protective environment of the home. With increases in income are increases in disposable income for eating out, shopping, and going to the movies. But there were other changes in society, sociocultural changes, that occurred at the same time: increased young populations, increased young people leaving home for (post-secondary) school, and increases in the number of women in the workforce. The importance in these changes is that with the changes in income and the corresponding changes in routine activities ever more people were drawn outside of the relatively protective environment of the home and this placed them at greater risk of criminal victimization and exposure to increased opportunities for crime. Therefore, as routine activities away from the home increased, crime increased.

The end result is that economic conditions, including income, do matter for understanding crime, but in a very particular way. It is not income that matters for crime, but how that income affects our behavior. In fact, the economic approach to crime put forth by Gary Becker, and subsequently by Isaac Ehrlich, predicts that increases in income lead to increases in crime because there are more items to be stolen; it is the relative payoffs for illegal and legal activities that dictate crime rates, not income levels (Becker 1968; Ehrlich 1973). This availability of items to be stolen is also critical for understanding the importance of routine activity theory in explaining crime.

The second minimal element of a direct-contact predatory crime, a suitable target, is also important for understanding the relationship between crime and the economy. Post-war changes in consumer products, namely the development of expensive lightweight electronic equipment, led to a massive increase in suitable targets simultaneously with increases in routine activities away from the relatively protective environment of the home—fewer people were home to protect their newly acquired property. The end result is an economy that increased routine activities outside the relatively protective environment of the home and created an abundance of suitable targets. As such, routine activity is able to explain why crime rates rose in the post-war era without invoking changes in criminal motivation.

1.3.3 Testing Routine Activity Theory

The first (macro level) test of routine activity theory was contained within the original article by Lawrence Cohen and Marcus Felson, with more testing in their immediately subsequent work (Felson and Cohen 1980; 1981). The most telling of their analyses was that of burglary rates in the United States, 1950 to 1972. In this analysis, the proportion of young populations, the proportion of those living alone, and the weight of property targets typically stolen in burglary were used to predict burglary rates; the former two were used to represent increased routine activities outside of the relatively protective environment of the home and the latter was used to represent target suitability. They found that the presence of young populations and single-person households increased burglary rates, whereas the weight of the lightest television in a department store's catalogue has a negative relationship with burglary rates. However, this latter relationship, though statistically significant, was the weakest among the three relationships tested. This implied that routine activities away from the relatively protective environment of the home were more important to how heavy the items were than inside the home.

Neighborhood (meso) level tests of routine activity theory are rather abundant using census boundary areas as the unit of analysis, commonly in conjunction with social disorganization theory (Andresen 2006). These studies assume that routine activities vary across space as well as time. For example, if increases in single-parent families over time are a good predictor of criminal activity and single-parent families also vary across space (the urban landscape), routine activity theory can be used to predict the spatial variations of criminal activity. In fact, routine activity theory has been found to be a better predictor than social disorganization theory in these analyses because unexpected results for "social disorganization theory variables" can be explained through routine activity theory (Andresen 2006).

Lastly, individual (micro) level tests of routine activity have also been undertaken, using victimization survey data to capture both criminal victimization and the routine activities of individuals. Kennedy and Forde (1990), investigating criminal victimization in Canada, is the most comprehensive of such individual-level tests of routine activity theory. Overall, Leslie Kennedy and David Forde found that unmarried young males with lower incomes and routine activities that take them to work, sporting events, drinking establishments, movies, restaurants, and simply walking or driving around have significantly higher rates of victimization than those who do not. Additionally, although individuals who live in socially disorganized neighborhoods are at greater risk of victimization, they find that the individual-level (routine activity theory) variables are more important, much like the neighborhood level analysis reported above. Consequently, our individual actions and the places we move through have been shown to impact criminal victimization.

1.4 Geometric Theory of Crime

Turning specifically to a geographical approach to the criminal event, the geometric theory of crime (commonly referred to as the geometry of crime), did not seek to place itself within the context of its contemporary criminological theories. Rather, the geometric theory of crime sought its explanation of the patterns of crime based on the geographic dimension of human activity patterns and focuses not on the motivation for crime but the perceived opportunities for crime that exist within the urban spatial structure.

1.4.1 Fundamental Concepts

The discipline of (human) geography has a long history of decision making in spatial contexts (Wolpert 1964; Horton and Reynolds 1971; Lowe and Moryadas 1975) and this history has relevance to understanding the criminal event, particularly *where* crime occurs. In particular there is the field of behavioral geography (see, for example, Rengert 1989) that investigates locational choices of individuals and how people move through space considering issues such as distance and direction. Specifically, individuals are active agents within their environment, choosing where to go and how to get there. Therefore, it is important to understand the role of the environment and, more importantly, what the environment is.

In the geometric theory of crime, the environment is conceptualized along the lines first put forward by Jeffery. One significant development from Jeffery's concept of the environment is found in the usage, "environmental backcloth." This environmental backcloth represents the built environment, social and cultural norms, institutions, the legal environment, and so on. The critical difference between Jeffery's depiction of the environment and the environmental backcloth is that the environmental backcloth explicitly recognizes the dynamic nature of our environment; hence, the use of "backcloth" instead of "context." Brantingham and Brantingham (1993) are very clear to emphasize the dynamic nature of our environment in ways similar to our use of the term "ecology" as it also refers to our ever-changing environment. The dynamic nature of the environment is sometimes described using the metaphor of a flag. The static context of the flag is its emblems and designs—the flag in two dimensions. But in recognition of the inherent dynamism of our environment, the *backcloth* includes a third dimension: the metaphorical flag blowing in the wind. Some parts of our environment are very slow to change, such as the road network in an established urban center.

Other parts of the environmental backcloth change rapidly: an area is safe in the day but not at night; or the sudden presence of an individual makes a once safe place very risky. Though we alter the environmental backcloth once we enter it, we must make choices of where to locate within it and how to move through it based on our perceptions of the environment that already exists. And because of the nature of urban (and rural) environments, we can only locate ourselves and move through the environmental backcloth in particular ways.

In his seminal 1960 book, *The Image of the City*, Kevin Lynch classified four elements of the city that were important, and which he invoked, for the subsequent development of the geometric theory of crime by Patricia and Paul Brantingham: nodes, paths, districts, and edges—Kevin Lynch also identified a further element, the landmark, but this element does not have significance for the geometric theory of crime. Nodes are places (conceptualized as points) within the city that a person travels to and from; paths are the channels that people move along, often circumscribed by streets, walkways, and public transit; districts are regions within the cities that are defined as areas that have commonalities and identifying features such that they are congruent spatial units such that any differences within the district must be smaller than the differences that exist between districts; and edges are the boundaries between districts that may be physical and distinct (literally crossing the tracks) or they may be subtle, such as the gradual change as one passes from one neighborhood to the next.

Nodes are places in which we spend most of our time: at home, work, recreation sites, entertainment, and shopping. In the context of a metropolis or large urban centers, these nodes may be business, entertainment, or industrial districts. Pathways are the channels that we use to move from node to node. Brantingham and Brantingham (1981b) use nodes and paths in order to generate maps of the places we spend our time and the pathways between them. These maps represent our activity spaces. With time our activity spaces also become our awareness spaces; this occurs because over time we develop knowledge and attachments to different locations such that we develop a sense of place, feeling comfortable in some areas and uncomfortable in other areas. The importance of our activity space is that if we are to be victims of crime, this victimization will most probably occur in our primary activity space simply because that is where we spend the majority of our time.

1.4.2 The Geometry of Crime

In order to understand the geometry of crime, the nodes, paths, activity space, and awareness space of offenders must be considered. Simply because it takes time and effort to overcome distance, offenders' primary search areas for criminal opportunities are going to coincide closely with their activity space. Consequently, Brantingham and Brantingham (1981b) mark the search areas of the immediate surroundings of activity nodes and the linear paths between them as high-intensity search areas, steadily decreasing that intensity with distance from the nodes and paths.

The important issue to understand here is that potential offenders have similar activity patterns as the rest of the population so understanding how one moves through, and becomes part of, an environment provides an understanding of how potential offenders move through, and become a part of, that same environment. Consequently, we become victims of crime when and where our activity spaces overlap with those of potential offenders. Unfortunately for the potential victims of crime this occurs quite often throughout the day, primarily because potential victims share nodes and pathways with potential offenders. This is simply because of the nature of urban environments largely dictating where people live, work, shop, and so on—we are *all* at the mercy of the urban planners of yesteryear. Also important in this context is the concept of the edge. By definition, an edge occurs at the boundary of two, or more, districts. Because this is a boundary between two or more districts, it is very difficult, if not impossible, to identify "insiders" and "outsiders." As a consequence, motivated offenders blend into the environment and are able to search for targets without the concern of residents with territorial behavior.

Primarily because of the (built) environment it is easy to see that the geometric theory of crime predicts specific patterns of crime: automotive theft (theft of and theft from) will be high at nodes and along paths that have a high degree of automotive theft opportunities, such as unguarded parking lots; likewise, assaults will be high at nodes that have a high degree of convergence of individuals—these geographic patterns are not necessarily going to be similar. Moreover, these nodes that have a high degree of crime will not have crime randomly or evenly dispersed within the node. Rather, crime tends to be concentrated in particular places within these high crime areas. Loosely speaking, these are the "edges" within the nodes—few automobiles are stolen in front of shopping mall entrances, for example. Lastly, the geometric theory of crime predicts that the vast majority of crime will occur within a small percentage of the available area within an urban center; for example, 80 percent of crimes may occur within 20 percent of the land area in a city.

1.4.3 Applications and Testing of the Geometric Theory of Crime

The geometric theory of crime is a type of theory that does not lend itself well to "standard" statistical tests because it does not have a list of independent variables that can be tested against a dependent variable—one could formulate such a test, but to the author's knowledge this has not been undertaken.

Rather, the geometric theory of crime has been used to understand geographic crime patterns or as a fundamental concept in a further application.

The most immediate application of the geometric theory of crime was in the context of burglary, undertaken by George Rengert and John Wasilchick in Delaware County, Pennsylvania. One of the dimensions that Rengert and Wasilchick (1985) investigated for burglary was the use of space. A common, though somewhat paradoxical, finding was the burglars typically chose targets in relatively low socioeconomic status neighborhoods. This is a common pattern of criminal activity across various time periods and locations, but it is paradoxical because there are more attractive targets in the higher socioeconomic status neighborhoods within Delaware County. However, this pattern is predictable within the geometric theory of crime, particularly through the concept of activity and awareness space. Generally speaking, the activity space of individuals is constrained because it takes time and effort to overcome distance: why travel 10 kilometers to purchase groceries when you can travel less than 1 kilometer? Consequently, the activity space for most individuals tends to be close to home—the travel to and from work is an exception to this rule, but the majority of activity space will be close to home, especially for youth. This is precisely what George Rengert and John Wasilchick found in their analysis. The search space of burglars, then, was within their activity space that was dominantly in the lower socioeconomic areas of the county. Additionally, there were social and cultural issues at work that defined the activity space of burglars. For example, in Delaware County a highway exists that divides its northern and southern neighborhoods. This edge could easily be crossed, but often was not; because of indicators of social status (clothing, cars, mannerisms) one set of residents may not be able to blend in within another neighborhood. Along more specific lines, African American burglars avoided white neighborhoods and white burglars avoided African American neighborhoods for similar reasons. In other words, one's social or ethnic status partly determined the activity space of an individual, restricting the areas in which one was willing to commit a burglary because of familiarity, or lack thereof.

The most well-known application of the geometric theory of crime is through the work of D. Kim Rossmo in geographic profiling. Geographic profiling is an investigative methodology that uses the locations of a connected series of crimes in order to determine the most probable area of offender residence. This methodology is most often applied to serial cases of murder, rape, arson, and robbery, but it may also be used for a string of crimes by one person that involves multiple scenes or other significant geographic characteristics—an automotive theft that leads to a robbery and an assault, for example. Such a series of locations allows a geographic profiler to interpret an offender's activity space and predict the most probable location of the offender's geographic anchor point; this anchor point is most often the offender's home, but may also be another current or former activity node such as work or another person's residence that is well known (see Wiles and Costello 2000). This methodology is based on years of research in criminology, geography, forensic psychology, cognitive mapping, mathematical modeling, statistical analysis, and investigative techniques by Rossmo (1999). Consequently, the basis of geographic profiling is the known spatial propensities of (serial) criminals in conjunction with the known spatial propensities of humans, in general. Most often, these propensities are the same.

1.5 Rational Choice Theory

Operating in the background of these spatial approaches to criminology is rationality: social disorganization theory is a theory of motivation that varies spatially, but routine activities are the outcome of rational choices as are our activity spaces. What we refer to as rational choice theory today stems from the work of Ronald Clarke and Derek Cornish, who consistently refer to rational choice as an approach rather than a theory—but the term "theory" will be used here for consistency.

The disciplines identified by Ronald Clarke and Derek Cornish (1985) were the sociology of deviance, criminology, economics, and cognitive psychology. Though instructive for the understanding of crime along certain dimensions, the theoretical frameworks of these disciplines is limited for the modeling of offenders' decisions. These frameworks are problematic along the lines of generalizability (sociology of deviance); they lack a coherent theoretical perspective (criminology), are too abstract and mathematical (economics), and are too general within the context of criminological decision making (cognitive psychology). Ronald Clarke and Derek Cornish recognized the common use of choice theory applied to criminological issues in these fields and their goal was to generate a general approach that dealt with crime as a sequence of rational choices that was not burdened by the theoretical baggage and modeling methods of these disciplines.

1.5.1 Fundamental Concepts

Before the discussion turns to how rational choice is used to understand the criminal event, it is important to understand the fundamental concept within rational choice theory—rationality. Invoking the concept of rationality in the context of crime tends to make some people rather uneasy. Most often, there is no difficulty in discussing property crimes (and violent property crimes, such as robbery) in the context of rationality because of an explicit monetary gain. Nonproperty violent crime, however, tends to cause some concern among people because they themselves do not see such crimes as rational. But what exactly is rationality?

Very simply put, something is considered rational if it is considered reasonable, meaning that a decision, for example, is the result of sound thought or judgement. Consequently, the rationality of one's actions or choices refers to whether or not a person's action or choices are made according to reason. However, it should be noted that rationality implies reasonableness from the offender's point of view, not the objective person's point of view or the average person's point of view (Cusson 1993). Therefore, a better way to assess rationality would be to consider what a choice is "worth" to someone versus other available options. In the discipline of economics, rationality has a very specific meaning. In order to make rational choices, a person must know all available alternatives, be able to assess their "value," rank all of these alternatives, and then make a choice.* Clearly, this "pure" form of rationality is not only complex, but rather unrealistic for the real world where we do not have perfect and complete information.

Such criticisms abound outside the discipline of economics, but also come from within the discipline. The general criticisms of the use of "pure" rationality (and the corresponding optimization of utility, or happiness) revolve around the following problems: the limitations of the human mind, particularly when a split-second decision must be made; the recognition that gathering and processing information is costly, particularly in terms of time; and the assumption that decision makers are supposed to know what they are trying to optimize. Herbert Simon (1957, 1982) hypothesized that we do not act rationally, but heuristically—this heuristic property has been shown to be present in offenders' decision processes in target selection (Cromwell et al. 1991). We act heuristically in our decision-making processes, seeking pleasure and avoiding pain, because situations are complex and we tend to be unable to process and compute every available option or action. This heuristic decision-making process has been termed "bounded rationality": we behave in a manner that is as optimal as possible. Or, in other words, we make the best decisions we can with the information available to us; when we know better, we do (optimize) better. Bounded rationality has the additional property of allowing "rational decision making" to be subjective, or at least individual specific: rationality is individual specific, not what "makes sense" to the rest of us. Of course, the more rigid models of rational choice do not force one person's rational choice to be the same as another person's rational choice, but the use of bounded rationality makes this distinction very clear to the student of rational choice.

---

* For an exhaustive list of the assumptions (often referred to as axioms by economists) of rationality see any intermediate microeconomics textbook.

1.5.2 What Is Rational Choice Theory?

Rational choice theory sets out as many as four primary choices that must be made for a potential offender: whether or not to commit crime at all, whether or not to select a particular target, how frequently to offend, and whether or not to desist from crime. Rational choice theory recognizes that there are a host of reasons why a person may commit a crime. The psychological, familial, social, and economic factors of a potential offender's life situation all play a role in that decision. But the important thing to recognize here is that crime is still a decision; we are not "forced" into a life of crime because of our family or the structure of the neighborhood we grew up in. Ronald Clarke and Derek Cornish make it clear that there is a conscious choice to become an offender: legitimate and illegitimate opportunities are considered and the "best" choice for that individual is made. Sometimes, the rational choice is to offend.

The second rational choice is in regard to particular targets. Potential offenders must interpret cues given off by the environment to decide upon what or whom to offend: Is the target valuable enough to risk getting caught? Is the area familiar to the offender? Are there potential guardians in close proximity?

The third rational choice is how often to offend. This choice is going to depend upon a number of factors such as the potential offender's social network, peer influences, monetary (or other) needs, and his or her ability to successfully avoid detection. Again, the key point here is that frequency is still a choice.

Lastly is the decision to desist from crime or continue. A potential offender may have internal issues that interfere with a life of crime such as getting detected (often on multiple occasions), exhausting targets, or aging out of crime; additionally, a potential offender may have external issues that interfere with a life of crime such as getting married, suffering an injury that creates difficulty with the commission of crime, or gets offered legitimate employment that can sufficiently replace the income from criminal activity.

Probably the most important component of this rational approach to criminal decision making is that this set of choices is specific for each crime. Simply because a person decides to commit burglaries does not mean that same person will commit a robbery or a sexual assault. The same is true for target selection choices because the environmental cues for a burglary are different than those for an automotive theft, and similarly for the frequency of offending and desistence from offending. As such, Ronald Clarke and Derek Cornish caution against any *general* rational choice theory of crime. If we are to understand and implement a rational choice theory of crime (particularly in the case of policy interventions for criminal justice), we must consider the rational choices for each type of crime as independent from all others.

1.5.3 Applications of Rational Choice Theory

As discussed above, rational choice theory uses choice structuring properties to better understand offender decision making. This theoretical approach is most famously used in situational crime prevention. Situational crime prevention is an approach to crime prevention that consists of measures to reduce criminal opportunities. This approach is directed at very specific crimes (specific not only in the crime classification, but the time and place of criminal activity), and seeks to modify the environment within which crime occurs, making crime more difficult, more risky, and less rewarding (Clarke 1997). As such, there is no panacea approach to preventing crime, just a set of principles to guide situational crime prevention activities:

1. Increase the perceived effort.
2. Increase the perceived risks.
3. Reduce the anticipated rewards.
4. Reduce provocations.
5. Remove the excuses for crime.

These five operating principles are further broken down into 25 techniques of situational crime prevention on the Web site of the Center for Problem-Oriented Policing (http://www.popcenter.org/25techniques/). And underlying all of these techniques is the assumption that potential offenders (or people, more generally) will respond to these activities in a heuristic fashion and reduce or, hopefully, eliminate their criminal activities.

More generally, rational choice theory is often used (not always explicitly) as a cost-benefit approach to criminal decision making. Consequently, it is not a theoretical approach that can be tested in the usual sense of the word. Rather, as will be shown in the discussion of crime pattern theory, below, rational choice theory is most often a fundamental concept in and of itself operating in the background, or it is used as a method of understanding why a crime occurred involving particular people at particular times and places.

1.6 Pattern Theory of Crime

The pattern theory of crime developed by Patricia and Paul Brantingham (1993) was the first attempt to develop a meta-theory within the field of environmental criminology. Patricia and Paul Brantingham recognized that this set of theories varied in its content and focus, but there were several aspects of these theories that were common.

Rationality operates in the background of all three theories. Of course rationality is behind rational choice theory, but it also plays an important role in routine activity theory and the geometric theory of crime. Our routine activities are the result of a set of choices that we make in order to carry out our lives. Where we go, how we get there, and when we go there are all the result of rational choices. Similarly, our activity nodes and pathways are chosen, at least partially, through rationality. Because it is expensive in terms of time and money to overcome distance, we tend to take the path of least resistance. This path is the rational choice because from a heuristic perspective it makes no sense to travel further than necessary to complete a task. And lastly, routine activities are always present within the geometric theory of crime, and vice versa. Nodes are the places we routinely visit, and we routinely travel the pathways between our nodes. In other words, our routine activities have a geometric component. Recognizing these similarities allows for the development of a common framework for understanding the criminal event.

1.6.1 Fundamental Concepts

In a trivial sense, all of the fundamental concepts of the previous environmental criminological theories are at work in the pattern theory of crime. At a more fundamental level, however, a pattern theory of crime must have something that can be used to unify the three different theories. That something is the crime template.

Developed by Paul and Patricia Brantingham (1978), the crime template is a concept for understanding crime site selection. Our environment sends out signals, or cues, that can be used by potential offenders to identify targets or victims. Over time, these environmental cues may be learned to indicate whether or not a target or victim is "good" or "bad" in the context of crime. This learned behavior can then be thought of as a template that is used for target or victim selection. Once a crime template is established, it is relatively fixed and influences future criminal behavior. Furthermore, we may have a number of crime templates, each specific to a particular crime classification or different locations.

The crime template may be thought of as a checklist that must be satisfied for a potential offender to undertake a particular criminal event. This checklist could be a set of conditions (environmental cues) that must be met for a crime to occur, a set of conditions that must not be present for a crime to occur, or some combination of both. Invoking the crime template the three environmental criminological theories can be integrated into a pattern theory of crime.

1.6.2 The Pattern Theory of Crime

A pattern is a recognizable interconnectedness of objects, processes, or ideas. This interconnectedness may be physical (on a map, for example) or it may be conceptual. Sometimes patterns are obvious, but at other times data must be scrutinized for the pattern to emerge. Patterns are particularly important for human activities (including crime) because we are creatures of habit and, therefore, have patterns to our daily lives. Consequently, the pattern theory of crime has a double meaning: first, there are the patterns of our lives to be understood and, second, there are the patterns that exist between the three environmental criminological theories.

The first commonality between the three environmental criminological theories, as well as with the work of Jeffery, is the importance of the environment in understanding the criminal event. All of our routine activities, the way we move through the urban mosaic (Kinney et al., 2008), and the decisions we make regarding those activities and movements are all partially determined by the physical, social, legal, and psychological environment. Within that environment are our routine activities that are undertaken within our activity space. Most often, because these activities are routine, they occur within our awareness space such that we are able to interpret the environmental cues that are emitted throughout our routine activities. Through this interpretation we develop a crime template that leads to the commission (or avoidance) of criminal events: the (rational) choice of whether or not to commit a crime. This commission or avoidance of a criminal event in turn reinforces our crime template or begins the process of changing that template, as well as modifying our routine activities, activity space, and awareness space to match our crime template. Rational choices are present at each and every stage of the pattern. The interconnectedness is complete.

In this brief summary of the pattern theory of crime it should be clear that this meta-theory becomes very complicated rather quickly. This is a cost to any crime analysis simply because of the number of factors that must be considered to get an understanding of the criminal event. The benefit of incurring this cost of complexity, however, is along two dimensions: the interconnectedness of the environmental criminological theories and the explicit dynamic nature of that interconnectedness.

1.6.3 The Benefits of the Pattern Theory of Crime

Showing that all of the three environmental criminological theories are connected is important for the understanding of the criminal event, but also for the cohesiveness of the field of environmental criminology. Each of the three environmental criminological theories is concerned with the environment within which crime occurs: routine activity theory is concerned with changes or variations in the social environment that lead to changes in crime rates, the geometric theory of crime is concerned with the built environment and how it shapes the geographic pattern of crime, and rational choice theory is concerned with the cognitive environment that governs the choice-structuring processes of potential offenders. Individually, each of these theories adds to our understanding of crime, but collectively they are able to provide a meaningful representation of the environment that crime occurs within.

The second dimension that reveals the benefits of the increased complexity within the pattern theory of crime is that it emphasizes the dynamic nature of the decision to offend at a particular time and place through feedback loops. The crime template affects and is affected by the commission (or avoidance) of crime, which in turn affects our routine activities, activity space, and awareness space. A change at any point within this interconnectedness sends a ripple through the decision-making processes that encompass environmental criminology. Therefore, because of this interconnectedness, at the heart of this spatiotemporal study of crime is the recognition that change or dynamism is inherent in the understanding of the criminal event. This recognition of change further legitimizes the place of environmental criminology within the broader criminological literature because it seeks not only to explain the old facts of criminal behavior, but new ones as well. As a result, it is important to understand where these theories came from so we can see where they are going and how they are changing. These are the goals of this book.

1.7 The Organization of This Book

This book is organized into three parts. Details of the various papers included in this anthology are provided at the beginning of each section, but a general outline of these sections is in order here. The first part includes early work on the ecology of crime. This research begins in the nineteenth century (France and England) and early twentieth century (United States) and is instructive to the study of environmental criminology because it allows for the reader to understand the nature of previous "environmental" approaches to crime. The second part includes the classics in environmental criminology. This includes the original papers for each of the four environmental criminological theories. Lastly, the third part includes the seminal papers that discuss environmental criminology and crime prevention. The anthology itself concludes with a chapter outlining how environmental criminology has evolved in recent years as well as where it is going.

Of the Development of the Propensity to Crime (1842)

2

L.A.J. QUETELET

From Quetelet, L.A.J. (1842). *A Treatise on Man and the Development of His Faculties* (pp. 82–96). Trans. Dr. R. Knox, FRSE. Edinburgh: W. and R. Chambers.

Contents

2.1 Of Crimes in General, and of the Repression of Them   29

2.2 Of the Influence of Knowledge, of Professions, and of Climate, on the Propensity to Crime   36

2.3 On the Influence of Seasons on the Propensity to Crime   55

2.4 On the Influence of Sex on the Propensity to Crime   57

2.5 Of the Influence of Age on the Propensity to Crime   63

2.6 Conclusions   72

2.1 Of Crimes in General, and of the Repression of Them

Supposing men to be placed in similar circumstances, I call the greater or less probability of committing crime, the *propensity to crime*. My object is more especially to investigate the influence of season, climate, sex, and age, on this propensity.

I have said that the circumstances in which men are placed ought to be similar, that is to say, equally favourable, both in the existence of objects likely to excite the propensity and in the facility of committing the crime. It is not enough that a man may merely have the intention to do evil, he must also have the opportunity and the means. Thus the propensity to crime may be the same in France as in England, without, on that account, the *morality* of the nations being the same. I think this distinction of importance.*

There is still another important distinction to be made; namely, that two individuals may have the same propensity to crime, without being equally *criminal*, if one, for example, were inclined to theft, and the other to assassination.†

Lastly, this is also the place to examine a difficulty which has not escaped M. Alphonse de Candolle in the work above mentioned: It is this, that our observations can only refer to *a certain number of known and tried offences, out of the unknown sum total of crimes committed*. Since this sum total of crimes committed will probably ever continue unknown, all the reasoning of which it is the basis will be more or less defective. I do not hesitate to say, that all the knowledge which we possess on the statistics of crimes and offences will be of no utility whatever, unless we admit without question that *there is a ratio, nearly invariably the same, between known and tried offences and the unknown sum total of crimes committed*. This ratio is necessary, and if it did not really exist, every thing which, until the present time, has been said on the statistical documents of crime, would be false and absurd. We are aware, then, how important it is to legitimate such a ratio, and we may be astonished that this has not been done before now. The ratio of which we speak necessarily varies according to the nature and seriousness of the crimes: in a well-organised society, where the police is active and justice is rightly administered, this ratio, for murders and assassinations, will be nearly equal to unity; that is to say, no individual will disappear from the

---

* This has been very clearly established by M. Alphonse de Candolle, in an article entitled Considerations sur la Statistique des Délits, inserted in the Bibliothèque Universelle de Genève, Feb. 1830. The author regards the propensity of individuals to crime as depending on their morality, the temptation to which they are exposed, and the greater or less facility they may find to commit offences. Of these three causes, the first belongs more especially to the man; the other two are, properly speaking, external to him. As it is with man that I am occupied, I have endeavoured, in the course of my researches, that the causes external to him might be constantly nearly equal, so that they might be left out of the computation. I have necessarily been obliged to take into account natural influencing causes, such as climate, seasons, sex, and age.

† In an article on Hygiène Morale, M. Villermé has fully shown how fatal the regime of prisons may become to the unfortunate person who is often confined for slight offences, and cast into the midst of a collection of wicked wretches, who corrupt him. "I have been told," says he, "by a person who accompanied Napoleon to the Isle of Elba, that, in the particular and at that time philosophical conversations of the ex-emperor, he has several times been heard to say, that under whatever relation we may view man, he is as much the result of his physical and moral atmosphere as of his own organisation. And the idea, now advanced by many others, which is contained in this phrase, is the most general as well as the most just that can be formed on the subject before us."—Annales d'Hygiene Publique, Oct. 1830.

society by murder or assassination, without its being known; this will not be precisely the case with poisonings. When we look to thefts and offences of smaller importance, the ratio will become very small, and a great number of offences will remain unknown, either because those against whom they are committed do not perceive them, or do not wish to prosecute the perpetrators, or because justice itself has not sufficient evidence to act upon. Thus, the greatness of this ratio, which will generally be different for different crimes and offences, will chiefly depend on the activity of justice in reaching the guilty, on the care with which the latter conceal themselves, on the repugnance which the individuals injured may have to complain, or perhaps on their not knowing that any injury has been committed against them. Now, if all the causes which influence the magnitude of the ratio remain the same, we may also assert that the effects will remain invariable. This result is confirmed in a curious manner by induction, and observing the surprising constancy with which the numbers of the statistics of crime are reproduced annually—a constancy which, no doubt, will be also reproduced in the numbers at which we cannot arrive: thus, although we do not know the criminals who escape justice, we very well know that every year between 7000 and 7300 persons are brought before the criminal courts, and that 61 are regularly condemned out of every 100; that 170,000 nearly are brought before courts of correction, and that 85 out of 100 are condemned; and that, if we pass to details, we find a no less alarming regularity; thus we find that between 100 and 150 individuals are annually condemned to death,* 280 condemned to perpetual hard labour, 1050 to hard labour for a time, 1220 to solitary confinement (à la delusion), &c.; so that this budget of the scaffold and the prisons is discharged by the French nation, with much greater regularity, no doubt, than the financial budget; and we might say, that what annually escapes the minister of justice is a more regular sum than the deficiency of revenue to the treasury.

I shall commence by considering, in a general manner, the propensity to crime in France, availing myself of the excellent documents contained in the *Comptes Généraux de l'Administration de la Justice* of this country; I shall afterwards endeavour to establish some comparisons with other countries, but with all the care and reserve which such comparisons require.

During the four years preceding 1830, 28,686 accused persons were set down as appearing before the courts of assize, that is to say, 7171 individuals annually nearly; which gives 1 accused person to 4463 inhabitants, taking

---

* The number of persons condemned to death has, however, diminished from year to year; is this owing to the increasing repugnance which tribunals feel to apply this punishment, for the abolition of which we have so many petitioners at the present day?

the population at 32,000,000 souls. Moreover, of 100 accused, 61 persons have been condemned to punishments of greater or less severity. From the remarks made above with respect to the crimes which remain unknown or unpunished and from mistakes which justice may make, we conceive that these numbers, although they furnish us with curious data for the past, do not give us any thing exact on the propensity to crime. However, if we consider that the two ratios which we have calculated have not sensibly varied from year to year, we shall be led to believe that they will not vary in a sensible manner for the succeeding years; and the probability that this variation will not take place is so much the greater, according as, all things being equal, the mean results of each year do not differ much from the general average, and these results have been taken from a great number of years. After these remarks, it becomes very probable that, for a Frenchman, there is 1 against 4462 chances that he will be an accused person during the course of the year; moreover, there are 61 to 39 chances, very nearly, that he will be condemned at the time that he is accused. These results are justified by the numbers shown in Table 2.1.

Thus, although we do not yet know the statistical documents for 1830, it is very probable that we shall again have 1 accused person in 4463 very nearly and 61 condemned in 100 accused persons; this probability is somewhat diminished for the year 1831 and still more for the succeeding years. We may, therefore, by the results of the past, estimate what will be realised in the future. This possibility of assigning beforehand the number of accused and condemned persons which any country will present, must give rise to serious reflections, since it concerns the fate of several thousand men, who are driven, as it were, in an irresistible manner, towards the tribunals, and the condemnations which await them.

These conclusions are deduced from the principle, already called in so frequently in this work, that effects are proportionate to their causes, and that the effects remain the same, if the causes which have produced them do not vary. If France, then, in the year 1830, had not undergone any apparent change, and if, contrary to my expectation, I found a sensible difference between the two ratios calculated beforehand for this year and the real ratios observed, I should conclude that some alteration had taken place in the causes, which had escaped my attention. On the other hand, if the state of France has changed, and if, consequently, the causes which influence the propensity to

crime have also undergone some change, I ought to expect to find an alteration in the two ratios which until that time remained nearly the same.*

It is proper to observe that the preceding numbers only show, strictly
speaking, the probability of being accused and afterwards condemned, without rendering us able to determine any thing very precise on the degree of the
propensity to crime; at least unless we admit, what is very likely, that justice
preserves the same activity, and the number of guilty persons who escape it
preserves the same proportion from year to year.†

In the latter columns of Table 2.1 is first made the distinction between
crimes against persons and crimes against property: it will be remarked, no
doubt, that the number of the former has diminished, whilst the latter has
increased; however, these variations are so small, that they do not sensibly

---

* After the preceding paragraphs were written, two new volumes of the Comptes Rendus
have appeared. As the results which they contain show how far my anticipations were
just, I thought it unnecessary to change the text, and shall merely give in a note the
numbers corresponding to those I availed myself of before.

Years	Accused Persons Present	Condemned Persons	Inhabitants to One Accused Person	Condemned in 100 Accused Persons	Accused of Crimes against		Ratio between the Numbers of the Two Kinds of Crime
					Persons	Property	
1830	6962	4130	4576	59	1666	5296	3.2
1831	7607	4098	4281	54	2046	5560	2.7
Aver.	7284	4114	4392	56	1856	5428	2.9

Thus, notwithstanding the changes of government, and the alterations in consequence of
it, the number of accused persons has not sensibly varied: "the slight increase observed
in 1831, may principally be attributed to the circumstance, that in consequence of reno-
vations in the criminal court arrangements, the operation of the judiciary police was
necessarily abated in the latter months of 1830; so that many cases belonging to this
period were not tried until 1831, which has increased the figure for this year."—Report
to the King [Rapport au Roi]. The number of acquittals is rather greater than in the preceding years; and the same remark will be made further on in the case of Belgium, the
government of which country was also changed. The number of accused persons absent
in 1830 was 787, and in 1831, 672; thus, the results of this year again agree with those of
the preceding years.

† If the letters A, A¹, A², &c., represent the numbers of individuals annually committed
for crimes, and a, a¹, a², &c., the corresponding numbers of individuals annually condemned; if we suppose, also, that the ratios &c., are sensibly equal to each other, that is
to say, if we shall also have . So that, if the number of the condemned A and A¹ is annually nearly the same, it will be the same with the number of those who are guilty; that
is to say, the propensity to crime will preserve the same value. It is thus that the almost
unchangeableness of the annual ratio of the accused to the condemned, allows us to
substitute for the ratio of the condemned of any two years the ratio of the accused for the
same two years.

Table 2.1   Ratios of Persons Accused, Condemned for France 1826–1829, by Persons or Property Offenses

Years	Accused Persons Present[a]	Condemned Persons	Inhabitants to One Accused Person	Condemned in 100 Accused Persons	Accused of Crimes against		Ratio between the Numbers of the Two Kinds of Crime
					Persons	Property	
1826	6988	4348	4557	62	1907	5081	2.7
1827	6929	4236	4593	61	1911	5018	2.6
1828	7396	4551	4307	61	1844	5552	3.0
1829	7373	4475	4321	61	1791	5582	3.1
Total	28686	17610	4463	61	7453	21233	2.8

[a] The number of accused persons absent was

In 1826	1827	1828	1829
603	845	776	746

I have taken the documents of 1826, 1827, 1828, and 1829 only, because the volume for 1825 did not contain the distinction of age or sex of which I make use further on. Moreover, in 1825 the number of accused was 1 to 4211 inhabitants, and 61 in 100 were condemned.

affect the annual ratio; and we see that we ought to reckon that three persons are accused of crimes against property to one for crimes against person.

Beside the preceding numbers I shall place those which correspond to them in the Low Countries, whilst the French code was still in force (Table 2.2).

Thus, the probability of being before a court of justice was almost the same for France and for the inhabitants of the Low Countries; at the same time the number of crimes against persons was fewer among the latter, but the repression of them was also greater, since 85 individuals were condemned out of 100 accused, which may be owing to the absence of a jury, their duties being fulfilled by the judges. This modification made in the French code should be taken into consideration. Indeed, it causes a very notable difference

Table 2.2   Ratios of Persons Accused, Condemned for Low Countries Using French Code, 1826–1827, by Persons or Property Offenses

Years	Accused Persons Present	Condemned Persons	Inhabitants to One Accused Person	Condemned in 100 Accused Persons	Accused of Crimes against		
					Persons	Property	Ratio
1826	1389	1166	4392	84	304	1085	3.5
1827	1488	1264	4100	85	314	1174	3.7

in the degree of repression; for when once accused, the Belgian had only 16 chances against 84, or 1 to 5, of being acquitted; whilst the Frenchman, in the same circumstances, had 39 chances to 61, or nearly 3 to 5, that is to say, thrice as many. This unfavourable position in which the accused person was placed with us, might be owing to the circumstance, that the judges before whom he appeared were indeed more severe than a jury, or perhaps that they were more circumspect in acquitting a person in the Low Countries. I shall not determine which of these was the case, but simply observe, that in courts of correction the French judges are even more severe than ours, and the same is the case in courts of police.

Thus, during the four years before 1830, in France, the reports gave 679,413 arraigned persons, or 1 to 188 inhabitants. Moreover, of this number, 103,032 individuals only were acquitted, or 15 in the 100 of those arraigned. There was then 1 chance against 187 that the Frenchman would be brought before a court of correction in the course of one year, and 85 chances to 15 that when there he would be condemned.

During the years 1826 and 1827, there were 61,670 persons arraigned, in the Low Countries, before courts of correction, of whom 13,499 were acquitted; and there was one arraigned person to 198 inhabitants. Therefore, the probability of a Frenchman being before a court is rather greater than for an inhabitant of the Low Countries, as also is the probability of his being subsequently condemned.

Setting aside the northern provinces of the ancient kingdom of the Low Countries from those which at the present time form the kingdom of Belgium, and which are more intimately connected with France, we find, for the latter provinces, during the years previous to 1831, the numbers shown in Table 2.3.

Each year, then, in Belgium, we have had, as an average, 1 person accused to 5031 inhabitants; and in France, 1 to 4400 inhabitants nearly. It is remarkable, that although these numbers do not differ much, yet the particular

Table 2.3   Ratios of Persons Accused, Condemned for Belgium, 1826–1830, by Persons or Property Offenses

Years	Accused Persons Present	Condemned Persons	Inhabitants to One Accused Person	Condemned in 100 Accused Persons	Accused of Crimes against		
					Persons	Property	Ratio
1826	725	611	5211	84	189	536	2.8
1827	800	682	4776	85	220	580	2.6
1828	814	677	4741	83	230	584	2.5
1829	753	612	5187	81	203	550	2.7
1830	741	541	5274	73	160	581	3.8
Aver.	767	625	5031	82	200	566	2.8

values for each year have not once given as great a number of accused persons
for Belgium as for France.

We may observe, that in Belgium, as in France, there was a slight diminution in the number of accused persons in 1830, which originated in the
same cause, namely, the closing of the tribunals for a certain period, in consequence of the revolution.

We see also that the repression of crime has sensibly diminished. This,
no doubt, is thus accounted for: after revolutions men are more circumspect
in their condemnations, since they are not always screened from personal
danger, even in the judgments which they pronounce.

The jury has been established in Belgium since 1831; we shall soon be
enabled to judge what influence this has had on the repression of crime, and
what are its most remarkable consequences.

2.2 Of the Influence of Knowledge, of Professions, and of Climate, on the Propensity to Crime

It may be interesting to examine the influence of the intellectual state of the
accused on the nature of crimes: the French documents on this subject are
such, that I am enabled to form the following table for the years 1828 and
1829;* to this table I have annexed the results of the years 1830 and 1831,
which were not known when the reflections which succeed were written
down (see Table 2.4).

Thus, all things being equal, the number of crimes against persons, compared with the number of crimes against property, during the years 1828 and
1829, was greater according as the intellectual state of the accused was more
highly developed; and this difference bore especially on murders, rapes, assassinations, blows, wounds, and other severe crimes. Must we thence conclude
that knowledge is injurious to society? I am far from thinking so. To establish
such an assertion, it would be necessary to commence by ascertaining how
many individuals of the French nation belong to each of the four divisions
which we have made above,† and to find out if, proportion being considered,
the individuals of that one of the divisions commit as many crimes as those
of the others. If this were really the case, I should not hesitate to say that, since
the most enlightened individuals commit as many crimes as those who have

---

* The intellectual state of 474 accused persons for the year 1828 has not been noted, as also
  4 for the year 1829, and 2 for 1831.
† See the Tableaux Sommaires faisant connaître l'Etat et les Besoins de l'Instruction
  Primaire dans le Département de la Seine. Paris: L. Colas; a pamphlet in 8vo, 1828, anon-
  ymous, but probably by M. Jomard. See also the Rapport Général sur la Situation et les
  Progrès de l'Enseignement Primaire en France et à l'Etranger, by the same person. 8vo.
  Paris: L. Colas, 1832.

Table 2.4   A Comparison of the Intellectual State of the Accused and Condemned Persons and Nature of Crime for 1828–1829 and 1830–1831

Intellectual State of the Persons Accused	1828–1829: Accused of Crimes against		Ratio of Crimes against Property to Crimes against Persons	1830–1831: Accused of Crimes against		Ratio of Crimes against Property to Crimes against Persons
	Persons	Property		Persons	Property	
Could not read or write	2072	6617	3.2	2134	6785	3.1
Could read and write but imperfectly	1001	2804	2.8	1033	2840	2.8
Could read and write well	400	1109	2.8	408	1047	2.6
Had received a superior education to his 1st degree	80	206	2.6	135[a]	184	1.4
Total	3553	10736	3.0 aver.	3710	10856	2.9 aver.

[a] The number of the accused of this class is increased in consequence of political events, and crimes against the safety of the state.

had less education, and since their crimes are more serious, they are necessarily more criminal; but from the little we know of the diffusion of knowledge in France, we cannot state any thing decisively on this point. Indeed, it may so happen, that individuals of the enlightened part of society, while committing fewer murders, assassinations, and other severe crimes, than individuals who have received no education, also commit much fewer crimes against property, and this would explain what we have remarked in the preceding numbers. This conjecture even becomes probable, when we consider that the enlightened classes are presupposed to possess more affluence, and consequently are less frequently under the necessity of having recourse to the different modes of theft, of which crimes against property almost entirely consist, whilst affluence and knowledge have not an equal power in subduing the fire of the passions and sentiments of hatred and vengeance. It must be remarked, on the other hand, that the results contained in the preceding table only belong to two years, and consequently present a smaller probability of expressing what really is the case, especially those results connected with the most enlightened class, and which are based on very small numbers. It seems to me, then, that at the most we can only say that the ratio of the number of crimes against persons to the number of crimes against property varies with the degree of knowledge; and generally, for 100 crimes against persons, we may reckon fewer crimes against property, according as the individuals belong to a class of greater or less enlightenment. In seeking

Table 2.5   A Comparison of Intellectual State of French Accused and Belgian Condemned Persons by Nature of Crime for Selected Time Periods

Intellectual State of the Persons Accused	Absolute Number			Relative Number		
	Accused in France		Condemned in Belgium:	Accused in France		Condemned in Belgium:
	1828–29	1830–31	1833	1828–29	1830–31	1833
Could not read or write	8689	8919	1972	61	61	19
Could read and write but imperfectly	3805	3873	472	27	27	15
Could read and write well	1509	1455	776	10	10	24
Had received a superior education to his 1st degree	286	319		2	2	
Total	14289	14566	3220	100	100	100

the relative annual proportion, we find the following numbers for France, to which I annex those furnished by the prisons in Belgium in 1833, according to the report of the inspector-general of prisons (see Table 2.5).

Thus, the results of the years 1828 and 1829 are again reproduced identically in 1830 and 1831, in France. Sixty-one out of one hundred persons accused could neither read nor write, which is exactly the same ratio as the Belgic prisons presented. The other numbers would also be probably the same, if the second class in Belgium took in, with the individuals *able to read only*, those who could write imperfectly.

The following details, which I extract from the *Report to the King* [*Rapport au Roi*] for the year 1829, will serve to illustrate what I advance:

> The new table, which points out the professions of the accused, divides them into nine principal classes, comprising,
> The *first*, individuals who work on the land, in vineyards, forests, mines, &c., 2453.
> The *second*, workmen engaged with wood, leather, iron, cotton, &c., 1932.
> The *third*, bakers, butchers, brewers, millers, &c, 253.
> The *fourth*, hatters, hairdressers, tailors, upholsterers, &c., 327.
> The *fifth*, bankers, agents, wholesale and retail merchants, hawkers, &c., 467.
> The *sixth*, contractors, porters, seamen, waggoners, &c., 289.
> The *seventh*, innkeepers, lemonade-sellers, servants, &c., 830.
> The *eighth*, artists, students, clerks, bailiffs, notaries, advocates, priests, physicians, soldiers, annuitants, &c., 449.
> The *ninth*, beggars, smugglers, strumpets, &c., 373.

Women who had no profession have been classed in those which their husbands pursued.

Comparing those who are included in each class with the total number of the accused, we see that the first furnishes 33 out of 100; the second, 26; the third, 4; the fourth, 5; the fifth, 6; the sixth, 4; the seventh, 11; the eighth, 6; the ninth, 5.

If, after that, we point out the accused in each class, according to the nature of their imputed crimes, and compare them with each other, we find the following proportions:

In the first class, 32 of the 100 accused were tried for crimes against persons, and 68 for crimes against property. These numbers are 21 and 79 for the second class; 22 and 78 for the third; 15 and 85 for the fourth and fifth; 26 and 74 for the sixth; 16 and 84 for the seventh; 37 and 63 for the eighth; 13 and 87 for the ninth.

Thus, the accused of the eighth class, who all exercised liberal professions, or enjoyed a fortune which presupposes some education, are those who, relatively, have committed the greatest number of crimes against persons; whilst 87-hundredths of the accused of the ninth class, composed of people without character, have scarcely attacked any thing but property.*

These results, which confirm the remark made before, deserve to be taken into consideration. I shall observe that, when we divide individuals into two classes, the one of liberal professions, and the other composed of journeymen, workmen, and servants, the difference is rendered still more conspicuous.

---

* See the Comptes Généraux, p. 9, 1830. The Comptes Généraux for 1830 and 1831 present the following results for each of the classes given in the text; here again we find the same constancy of numbers:

	For 1829	For 1830	For 1831
1st	2453	2240	2517
2d	1932	1813	1985
3d	253	225	272
4th	327	309	300
5th	467	455	426
6th	289	310	327
7th	830	848	320
8th	447	374	391
9th	373	388	469
Total	7373	6962	7006

Table 2.6 will assist us in arriving at the *influence of climate* on the propensity to crime;* it is formed from the documents of the *Comptes Généraux de l'Administration de la Justice* in France, for the five years previous to 1830. The second and the third columns give the numbers of those condemned for crimes against persons and property; the two following columns show the ratio of these numbers to the respective population of each department in 1827; a sixth column gives the ratio of crimes against property to crimes against persons; and the last column shows how many in 100 accused were unable to read or write; the numbers which are given there only relate to the years 1828 and 1829.

To the preceding documents I shall join those concerning the ancient kingdom of the Low Countries† and the dutchy of the Lower Rhine, where the French code is still in force, and allows comparisons to be still established (Table 2.7).

As it would be very difficult to form an idea of the whole of the results contained in the preceding tables, and as at the same time it would be impossible to embrace the whole at one glance, I have endeavoured to render them perceptible by shades of greater or less depth, placed on a map of France and the Low Countries, according to the greater or less number of crimes against persons or property, in proportion to the population (see Figure 2.1 and Figure 2.2). The first figurative map belongs to crimes against persons; it shows us at first, by the darkness of the shades, that the greatest number of crimes are committed in Corsica, in the South of France, and particularly in Languedoc and Provence, as well as Alsace and the Valley of the Seine. The southern part of the Low Countries, with the exception

---

* It has seemed to me that these numbers might give us a satisfactory idea of the state of knowledge in each department, especially of the lower classes, among whom the greatest number of crimes takes place. This method, by which we take for each department some hundred individuals whose intellectual state we can determine, appears to me to be more certain than that of M. Dupin, which is, to judge of the education of the province by the number of children sent to school. It may be that there is generally very little knowledge in those places where schools have been but recently established, and have not as yet been able to produce any appreciable effects. In order to render the results obtained by this method more comprehensible, ... Thus, the results, obtained by two different modes, nevertheless agree with each other in a very satisfactory manner. We may say that we find the greatest enlightenment where there is the greatest freedom of communication, and in the course of large rivers, such as the Rhine, the Seine, the Meuse, &c. In Southern France, the trading sea-coasts, and the banks of the Rhone, are also less obscure, whilst the absence of enlightenment is perceived chiefly in those parts of France which are not traversed by great commercial roads. We naturally look for instruction in those places where the need of it is greatest.

† The numbers for the Low Countries embrace the years 1826–1827, and for the dutchy of the Lower Rhine the years from 1822 to 1826, according to the Revue Encyclopedique for the month of August 1830. Since this summary gives us the number of crimes and not of the condemned, I have thought proper to give the number of crimes for France and the Low Countries, in order to render the results comparable.

Table 2.6 Influence of Climate on Propensity to Crime, France 1825–1829

Department	Condemned for Crimes against		Inhabitants to One Person Condemned for Crime against		Crimes against Property to One Crime against Persons	Accused Persons in the 100 Who Could Neither Read Nor Write
	Persons	Property	Persons	Property		
Corse	287	107	3224	8649	0.36	50
Haut-Rhin	144	295	14,192	6928	2.05	33
Lot	98	110	14,312	12,751	1.12	80
Ariège	82	78	15,118	15,893	0.95	83
Ardèche	108	99	15,205	16,587	0.92	67
Aveyron	99	160	17,677	10,938	1.62	69
Pyrenees-Orient	41	55	18,460	13,761	1.34	76
Seine-et-Oise	112	377	20,034	5953	3.36	56
Vaucluse	58	118	20,090	9875	2.03	65
Moselle	95	274	21,534	7466	2.88	49
Lozère	31	53	22,384	13,092	1.71	47
Var	67	117	23,216	13,295	1.75	71
Bas-Rhin	111	341	24,120	7851	3.07	31
Seine	197	2496	25,720	2030	12.67	34
Bouches-du-Rhin	63	208	25,897	7844	3.25	56
Eure	80	296	26,354	7123	3.70	63
Doubs	48	146	26,491	8909	3.04	35
Marne	61	244	26,643	6661	4.00	54
Tarne	59	169	27,767	9694	2.86	75
Seine-Inférieure	123	850	27,980	4049	6.91	59

Continued

Table 2.6 (Continued) Influence of Climate on Propensity to Crime, France 1825–1829

Department	Condemned for Crimes against		Inhabitants to One Person Condemned for Crime against		Crimes against Property to One Crime against Persons	Accused Persons in the 100 Who Could Neither Read Nor Write
	Persons	Property	Persons	Property		
Drôme	49	133	29,163	10,744	2.71	71
Calvados	84	394	29,819	6357	4.69	52
Hautes-Alpes	21	47	29,840	13,333	2.24	42
Landes	44	153	30,149	8690	3.48	86
Basses-Alpes	25	62	30,613	12,344	2.48	66
Vosges	62	132	30,632	14,388	2.13	45
Gard	53	129	32,788	13,471	2.43	67
Loiret	46	215	33,068	7075	4.67	70
Vienne	40	170	33,459	7873	4.25	81
Ille-et-Vilaine	82	318	33,747	8702	3.88	66
Hérault	50	92	33,956	18,454	1.84	62
Aude	39	75	34,102	17,733	2.42	72
Rhone	61	302	34,146	6895	4.95	51
FRANCE	4662	17543	34,168	9080	3.76	60
Puy-de-Dome	82	157	34,547	18,044	1.91	75
Loire-Inférieure	66	160	34,628	14,284	2.42	76
Aube	34	206	35,553	5868	6.06	54
Isère	73	220	36,026	11,958	3.01	62
Dordogne	64	149	36,256	15,573	2.33	76
Jura	33	123	37,344	12,613	2.96	50
Haute-Marne	32	94	38,254	13,023	2.93	46

Indre-et-Loire	37	131	39,211	11,075	3.54	79
Charente	45	92	39,295	19,220	2.05	60
Haute-Loire	36	35	39,677	40,810	0.97	75
Allier	35	124	40,757	11,504	3.54	91
Pas-de-Calais	76	568	41,751	5660	7.38	63
Basses-Pyrenees	47	142	43,880	14,524	3.02	73
Gers	35	91	43,943	16,901	2.60	70
Corrèze	32	56	44,513	25,430	1.75	77
Orne	48	183	45,248	11,868	3.81	66
Seine-et-Marne	35	167	45,459	9527	4.77	58
Maine-et-Loire	50	197	45,867	11,641	3.94	81
Haute-Vienne	30	120	46,058	11,515	4.00	79
Hautes-Pyrenees	24	64	46,263	17,349	2.67	71
Eure-et-Loire	30	231	46,592	6013	7.70	63
Ain	36	84	47,448	22,335	2.33	60
Deux-Sèvres	30	124	48,043	11,623	4.13	61
Charente-Inférieure	44	257	48,199	8252	5.84	66
Meurthe	52	249	48,788	10,189	4.79	42
Sarthe	45	177	49,613	12,614	3.93	87
Haute-Garonne	41	190	49,636	10,711	4.63	71
Haute-Saône	33	134	49,643	12,225	4.06	43
Mayenne	35	146	50,591	12,128	4.17	82
Morbihan	41	183	52,129	11,679	4.46	78
Cantal	25	75	52,403	17,468	3.00	61
Loir-et-Cher	22	142	52,424	8122	6.45	68

Continued

Table 2.6 (*Continued*) Influence of Climate on Propensity to Crime, France 1825–1829

Department	Condemned for Crimes against		Inhabitants to One Person Condemned for Crime against		Crimes against Property to One Crime against Persons	Accused Persons in the 100 Who Could Neither Read Nor Write
	Persons	Property	Persons	Property		
Nord	91	548	52,893	8783	6.02	71
Loire	34	104	55,252	18,063	3.06	54
Côte-d'Or	35	160	55,992	11,592	4.57	48
Nievre	24	109	56,620	12,467	4.54	65
Saone-et-Loire	45	168	57,308	15,350	3.73	74
Vendée	28	106	57,648	15,228	3.62	77
Lot-et-Garonne	29	111	58,084	15,181	3.83	68
Meuse	26	105	58,911	14,588	4.04	39
Yonne	29	140	58,986	12,219	4.83	45
Cher	21	98	59,188	12,683	4.67	86
Finistère	42	252	59,863	9977	6.00	79
Manche	51	247	59,922	12,373	4.84	62
Tarn-et-Garonne	20	89	60,397	13,572	4.45	88
Côtes-du-Nord	47	292	61,881	9960	6.21	90
Gironde	41	207	65,628	12,999	5.05	67
Aisne	36	259	67,995	9451	7.20	62
Oise	23	163	83,723	11,814	7.09	52
Somme	31	257	84,884	10,230	8.29	64
Ardennes	15	92	93,875	15,306	6.13	37
Indre	12	96	99,012	12,377	8.00	77
Creuse	6	40	210,777	31,617	6.67	80

Table 2.7 Influence of Climate on Propensity to Crime; for Low Countries (1826–1827) and Lower Rhine (1822–1826)

Provinces	Condemned for Crimes against		Inhabitants to One Person Condemned for Crime against		Crimes against Property to One Crime against Persons	Accused Persons in the 100 Who Could Neither Read Nor Write
	Persons	Property	Persons	Property		
Brabant, Southern	61	168	16,336	5932	2.75	13
Flanders, Eastern	82	154	17,100	9104	1.88	14
Limbourg	32	120	20,384	5436	3.75	15
Overyssel	16	42	20,385	7766	2.62	7
Brabant, Northern	30	66	22,031	10,014	2.20	9
Anvers	29	113	22,562	5800	3.90	12
Groningen and Drenthe	18	98	23,611	4296	5.44	7
Liege	26	82	25,107	7961	3.15	15
Flanders, Western	46	142	25,222	8171	3.09	15
Namur	14	66	27,433	5819	4.71	9
Gueldres	21	114	27,633	5090	2.20	9
Holland, Southern	28	216	32,000	4148	7.71	11
Holland, Northern, and Utrecht	23	263	37,560	4000	9.42	10
Luxembourg	14	47	42,208	12,572	3.34	8
Hainault	21	76	52,712	14,565	3.62	10
Zealand	5	86	53,450	3108	17.20	10
Friesland	3	103	132,248	3852	34.33	8
Low Countries	474	1956	25,747	6239	4.13	10
Low Countries (crimes)	424	1691	29,783	7217	4.00	10
Dutchy of the Lower Rhine	296	994	33,784	10,060	3.36	13
France	7160	20,308	21,648	7632	2.84	27

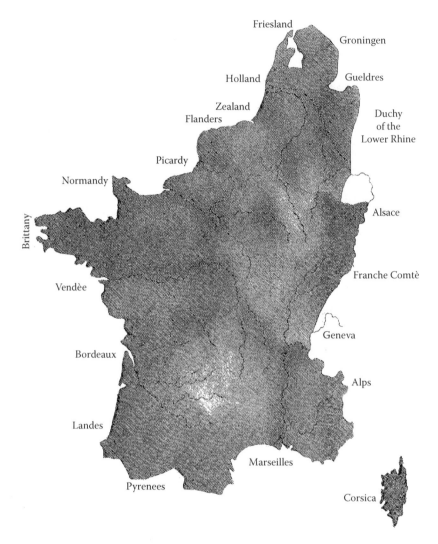

Figure 2.1 Map illustrative of the crimes against property.

of Hainault and Luxembourg, present also rather deep tints. However, it is proper to observe that the shades are perhaps more obscure than they ought to be, if we consider that they represent the number of condemned people, and that in general, in the Low Countries, the repression has been much stronger than in France, since in the latter country only 61 individuals are condemned in every 100 accused, whilst in the Low Countries, 85 is the proportion. On the contrary, Central France, Brittany, Maine, Picardy, as well as Zealand and Friesland, present much more satisfactory shades. If we compare this map with that which indicates the state of instruction, we shall be disposed to believe, at first, that crimes are in a measure in inverse ratio

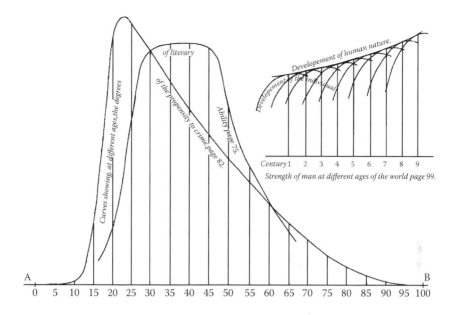

Figure 2.2 Crime propensity curves for age, literary ability, and development of human nature.

to the degree of knowledge. The figurative map of crimes against persons and those of crimes against property presents more analogy. In like manner, the departments which show themselves advantageously or disadvantageously on either side, may be arranged in the following manner, making three principal classes:

First Class—Departments where the number of those condemned for crimes against persons and property exceeds the average of France.
Corse, Landes, Rhône, Bouches-du-Rhône, Doubs, Haut-Rhin, Bas-Rhin, Moselle, Seine-Inférieure, Calvados, Eure, Seine-et-Oise, Seine, Marne, Loiret, Vienne, Ille-et-Vilaine—17 departments.
Second Class—Departments where the number of those condemned for crimes against property and persons has been less than the average of France.
Creuse, Indre, Cher, Nièvre, Saône-et-Loire, Jura, Ain, Isère, Loire, Haut-Loire, Cantal, Puy-de-Dôme, Allier, Corrèze, Haut-Vienne, Basses- Pyrénées, Hautes-Pyrénées, Haute-Garonne, Gers, Tarn-et-Garonne, Lot-et-Garonne, Gironde, Dordogne, Charente, Deux-Sèvres, Vendée, Loire-Inférieure, Maine-et-Loire, Sarthe, Orne, Mayenne, Manche, Finistère, Morbihan, Côtes-du-Nord, Somme, Oise, Aisne, Ardennes, Meuse, Meurthe, Haute-Saone, Haute-Marne, Côte- d'Or, Yonne, Seine-et-Marne—47 departments.

Third Class—Departments where the number of those condemned for crimes against persons only, or against property only, has been less than the average of France.

Var, Hautes-Alpes, Basses-Alpes, Drôme, Vaucluse, Gard, Ardèche, Lozère, Aveyron, Lot, Tarn, Hérault, Aude, Pyrénées-Orientales, Ariége, Charente-Inferieure, Loir-et-Cher, Eure-et-Loire, Nord, Pas-de-Calais, Aube, Vosges—22 departments.

In making the same distinction with regard to the provinces of the Low Countries,* we find:

First Class—Southern Brabant, Anvers, Limbourg, Groningen, and Drenthe—5 provinces.
Second Class—Hainault, Luxembourg—2 provinces.
Third Class—Namur, Liege, Western Flanders, Eastern Flanders, Zealand, Northern Brabant, Southern Holland, Northern Holland, Utrecht, Guelderland, Overyssel, Friesland—12 provinces.

Before endeavouring to deduce conclusions from the preceding calculations, I shall remark that certain ratios cannot be rigorously compared, on account of the defective valuation (or census) of the population, or from an unequal degree of repression in the different courts of justice. It will be difficult enough, to find out the errors arising from the first cause, as we have only, for the elements of verification, the relative numbers of births and deaths; as to the unequal degree of repression, such is not exactly the case, for, besides that we are led to believe that the activity of justice in finding out the authors of crimes is not every where the same, we see that acquittals are not always in the same ratio. Thus, according to the documents from 1825 to 1829, 61 individuals out of every 100 accused have been condemned in France, yet the degree of repression has generally been stronger in the northern than in the southern part of the country. The Court of Justice of Rouen has condemned the greatest number, and it has condemned 71 individuals out of 100 accused at the least; the courts of Dijon, Anjou, Douai, Nanci, Orleans, Caen, Paris, Rennes, have also exceeded the average; the courts of Metz, Colmar, Amiens, Bordeaux, Bourges, Besançon, Grenoble, Lyons, and La Corse, have presented nearly the same average as France; whilst the acquittals have been more numerous in the southern courts, such as Toulouse, Poitiers, Nismes, Aix, Riom, Pau, Argen, Limoges, and Montpellier—the two last courts having condemned, at an average, only 52 individuals of 100 accused. It yet remains

* See, for the most ample accounts, La Statistique des Tribunaux de la Belgique, pendant les Années 1826, 1827, 1828, 1829, and 1930, published by M.M. Quetelet and Smits. 4to. Brussels: 1832.

for examination, whether these decisive inequalities in the number of acquittals in the north and south of France are owing to a greater facility in bringing forward accusations, or to indulgence to the accused. It appears to me probable, that it may be in part owing to crimes against persons being more common, all things being equal, in the south, and crimes against property in the north; we know, also, that more acquittals take place in the first class of crimes than in the second. However the case may be, I think it will be proper not to lose sight of this double cause of error which I have just pointed out.

If we now cast our eyes over the departments of France which have exceeded the average of crimes against persons as well as of crimes against property, we shall first find Corsica and Landes to be, from their manners and customs, in peculiar circumstances, and which will scarcely permit of their being compared with the rest of France.

The Corsicans, indeed, impelled by cruel prejudices, and warmly embracing feelings of revenge, which are frequently transmitted from generation to generation, almost make a virtue of homicide, and commit the crime to excess. Offences against property are not frequent, and yet their number exceeds the average of France. We cannot attribute this state of things to want of instruction, since the number of accused who could neither read nor write was comparatively less than in France. This is not the case in Landes, where almost nine-tenths of the accused were in a state of complete ignorance. This department, where a poor and weak population live dispersed, as it were, in the midst of fogs, is one where civilisation has made the least progress. Although Landes is found in the most unfavourable class as regards crimes, it is nevertheless proper to say that it does not differ much from the average of France: we may make the same observations on the departments of Vienne and Ille-et-Vilaine. As to the other departments, we may observe that they are generally the most populous in France, in which we find four of the most important cities, Paris, Lyons, Marseilles, and Rouen; and that they also are the most industrious—those which present the greatest changes and intercourse with strangers. We may be surprised not to find with them the departments of the Gironde and Loire-Inférieure, which seem to be almost in the same circumstances as the departments of Bouches-du-Rhone and Seine-Inférieure, especially if we consider that, with respect to knowledge, they seem less favoured than these last, and the repression of crime also has generally been effective. This remark is particularly applicable to the department of the Gironde, for the Loire-Inférieure does not differ so much from the average of France. I shall not hesitate to attribute these differences to a greater morality in one part than the other. And this conjecture becomes more probable, if we observe that the whole of the departments of the south of France, which are on the shores of the sea from the Basses-Pyrenees to La Manche, except Landes and Ille-et-Vilaine which have already been mentioned, fall below the average of France for crimes against persons; and that, on the contrary, all the departments without exception, which are on the shores of the Mediterranean, as well as the ones adjacent to them, exceed this average. We may also remark, that the shores of the Atlantic, from Basses-Pyrenees to La Manche, generally fall below the average for crime against property.

The third class presents us with fifteen departments, on the border of the Mediterranean, and which all exceed the average of France in crimes against persons and are below the average in crimes against property. The districts on the Mediterranean appear, then, to have a very strong propensity to the first kind of crimes. Of seven other departments of the same class, one only exceeds the average for crimes against person, and that is Vosges in Alsace; the others exceed the average of crimes against property.

The departments of the second class, where the fewest condemnations for crimes against persons and property take place, are generally situated in the centre of France, on the shores of the Atlantic, from the Basses-Pyrenees to La Manche, and in the valleys watered by the Somme, the Oise, and the Meuse.

The following is a summary of what has been said:

1. The greatest number of crimes against persons and property take place in the departments which are crossed by or near to the Rhone, the Rhine, and the Seine, at least in their navigable portions.
2. The fewest crimes against persons and property are committed in the departments in the centre of France, in those which are situated in the west towards the Atlantic, from the Basses-Pyrenees to La Manche, and in those towards the north, which are traversed by the Somme, the Oise, and the Meuse.
3. The shores of the Mediterranean and the adjacent departments show, all things being equal, a stronger propensity to crimes against persons, and the northern parts of France to crimes against property.

After having established these facts, if we seek to go back to the causes which produce them, we are immediately stopped by numerous obstacles. And, indeed, the causes influencing crimes are so numerous and different, that it becomes almost impossible to assign to each its degree of importance. It also frequently happens, that causes which appear very influential, disappear before others of which we had scarcely thought at first, and this is what I have especially found in actual researches: and I confess that I have been probably too much occupied with the influence which we assign to education in abating the propensity to crime; it seems to me that this common error especially proceeds from our expecting to find fewer crimes in a country, because we find more children in it who attend school, and because there is in general a greater number of persons able to read and write. We ought rather to take notice of the degree of moral instruction, for very often the education received at school only facilitates the commission of crime.* We also consider poverty as generally conducing to crime; yet the department of Creuse, one of the poorest in France, is that which in every respect presents the greatest morality. Likewise, in the Low Countries, the most moral province is Luxembourg, where there is the greatest degree of poverty. It is proper, however, that we come to a right understanding of the meaning of the word poverty, which is here employed in an acceptation which may be considered improper. A province, indeed, is not poor because it possesses fewer riches than another, if its inhabitants, as in Luxembourg, are sober and active; if, by their labour, they can certainly obtain the means of relieving their wants, and gratifying tastes which are proportionally moderate; according as the inequality of fortune is less felt, and does not so much excite temptation; we should say, with more reason, that this province enjoys a moderate affluence. Poverty is felt the most in provinces where great riches have been amassed, as in Flanders, Holland, the department of the Seine, &c., and above all, in the manufacturing countries, where, by the least political commotion, by the least obstruction to the outlets of merchandise, thousands of individuals pass suddenly from a state of comfort to one of misery. These rapid changes from one state to another give rise to crime, particularly if those who suffer are surrounded by materials of temptation, and are irritated by the continual aspect of luxury and of the inequality of fortune, which renders them desperate.

It seems to me that one of the first distinctions to be made in our present inquiry, regards the different races of mankind who inhabit the countries which we are considering; as we shall shortly see, this point is of the greatest importance, although not the first which presents itself to the mind. "The population of France belongs to three different races—the *Celtic race*, which forms nearly three-fifths of its inhabitants; the *German race*, which comprehends those of the late provinces of Flanders, Alsace, and part of Lorraine; and the *Pelasgian race*, scattered along the shores of the Mediterranean and in Corsica. The changes of manners," adds Malte-Brun, "to which this division is exposed, may alter the character of a people, but cannot change it entirely."† If we cast our eyes over the figurative map of crimes against persons, this distinction of people is perceived in a remarkable manner. We shall see that the Pelasgian race, *scattered over the shores of the Mediterranean and in Corsica*, is particularly addicted to crimes against persons; among the Germanic race, which extends over Alsace, the dutchy of the Lower Rhine, a part of Lorraine, and the Low Countries, where the greater proportion of

---

* M. Guerry has arrived at conclusions similar to mine, and almost at the same time, in his Essai sur la Statistique Morale de la France, p. 51, and has expressed them almost in the same terms; the same results have also been obtained in England, Germany, and the United States.
† Précis de la Géographie Universelle, livre 159.

persons and of property gives rise to more occasions of committing crime, and where the frequent use of strong drinks leads more often to excesses, we have generally a great many crimes against property and persons. The Batavians and Frieslanders, who also belong to the Germanic race, are more especially prone to crimes against property. Lastly, the Celtic race appears the most moral of the three which we have considered, especially as regards crimes against persons; they occupy the greatest part of France and the Wallone of Belgium (*et la partie Wallone de la Belgique*). It would appear, moreover, that frontier countries, where the races are most crossed with each other, and where there is generally the most disturbance, and where the customhouses are established, are the most exposed to demoralisation.

After having admitted this distinction, based upon the differences of races, it remains to be examined what are the local anomalies which influence the morality of the people and modify their character.

The most remarkable anomaly which the Celtic race seems to present, is observed in the department of the valley of the Seine, especially below Paris; many causes contribute to this. We first observe that these departments, from their extent, contain the greatest proportion of persons and property, and consequently present more occasions for committing crimes; it is there that there are the greatest changes in the people, and the greatest influx of people from all countries without character, in a manner which must even have altered the primitive race more than any where else; lastly, it is there also where the greatest number of industrial establishments are found; and, as we have already had occasion to observe, these establishments maintain a dense population, whose means of subsistence are more precarious than in any other profession. The same remark is applicable to the valley of the Rhone, and with the more reason, as the Pelagian race has been able, in ascending this river, to penetrate farther into the interior of the country than any where else.

The commercial and industrious provinces of the Low Countries are likewise those in which the greatest number of crimes are committed.

As to the greater number of crimes against property to be observed as we advance towards the north, I think we may attribute it, in a great measure, to the inequality between riches and wants. The great cities, and the capitals especially, present an unfavourable subject, because they possess more allurements to passions of every kind, and because they attract people of bad character, who hope to mingle with impunity in the crowd.

It is remarkable that several of the poorest departments of France, and at the same time the least educated, such as Creuse, Indre, Cher, Haute-Vienne, Allier, &c., are at the same time the most moral, whilst the contrary is the case in most of the departments which have the greatest wealth and instruction. These apparent singularities are, I think, explained by the observations which have been made above. Morality increases with the degree of education in the late kingdom of the Low Countries, which would lead us to believe that the course of education was better.

The influence of climate is not very sensible here, as we may see by comparing Guienne and Gascoigne with Provence and Languedoc, and the inhabitants of the Hautes and Basses Pyrenees to the inhabitants of the Hautes and Basses Alpes, which, notwithstanding, are under the same latitudes. We may also say that the influence of knowledge and of climate partly disappears before more energetic influences; and that they are moreover far from effacing the moral character of the three races of men who inhabit the country which we are considering. Nevertheless, we cannot but allow, when bringing the ratios of the sixth column of our table together, that the number of crimes against property, in proportion to the number of crimes against persons, is increased considerably in advancing towards the north.

It is to be regretted that the documents of the courts of justice of other countries cannot be compared with those of France and the Low Countries. The difference in laws and the classifications of crime render direct comparisons impossible. Yet the countries of some extent, and which give the distinction of crimes against persons and crimes against property, allow at least of our drawing a comparison between their different provinces under this head. It perhaps will not be without some interest to our inquiry to compare the different parts of Prussia and Austria with one another. The data of criminal justice in Austria are extracted from the *Bulletin des Sciences* of M. de Férussac, for November 1829, and relate to the five years from 1819 to 1823; those of Prussia are extracted from *Revue Encyclopedique* for August 1830, and relate to the three years from 1824 to 1826 inclusive. I have followed the same form of the table as the above: nevertheless, I regret that I could not give the number of children in the schools of the different parts of Austria. For Prussia, I have taken the number of children in 1000 of those who attend the schools, according to the statement of the *Revue Encyclopedique* (Table 2.8).

It would be very difficult to point out the various races of men who have peopled the countries mentioned in Table 2.8, because they are so much mixed in certain parts, that their primitive character is almost lost. The German race predominates in the Prussian states, and is mixed with the northern Sclavonians, particularly along the shores of the Baltic and ancient Prussia, and with the western Sclavonians in the Grand-Dutchy of Posen and Silesia. In the Austrian states, and especially in the northern and eastern parts, the Sclavonian race is again mixed with the German; Malte-Brun even thinks that in Moravia the Sclavonians are three times as numerous as the Germans:* they are divided into several tribes, of which the most remarkable is the Wallachians; "they are brave in war, tolerant in religion,

---

* Précis de la Géographie Universelle, livre 145.

Table 2.8 Ratios of Crimes Against Persons and Property by School Participation for Austria and Russia

Arrondissements	Crimes against		Inhabitants to One Crime against		Crimes against Property to One Crime against Persons	Inhabitants to One Scholar
	Persons	Property	Persons	Property		
Austria						
Dalmatia	2986	2540	535	625	0.85	?
Gallicia & Bukovina	5234	14,105	3955	1470	2.70	?
Tyrol	658	2516	5707	1492	3.82	?
Moravia & Silesia	753	3545	12,662	2689	4.71	13
Gratz–Leibach & Trietz, or Internal Austria	589	2479[a]	13,311	3188	4.21	10
Lower Austria (or, Cotes de l'Ens)	573	7099	17,130	1382	12.37	10
Bohemia	737	7221[b]	18,437	1881	9.80	9
						Scholars in 1000 children
Prussia						
Prussia	249	8875	22,741	639	35.65	451
Saxony	147	5815	27,588	697	39.56	491
Posen	97	3481	31,440	875	35.88	490
Silesia	228	7077	33,714	1086	31.04	584
Westphalia	92	3383	38,436	1045	36.77	525
Brandenburg	112	5431	39,486	688	57.42	468
Pomerania	27	1622	92,131	1533	60.11	940

[a] The numbers for Bohemia and Internal Austria only relate to the four years 1819, 1820, 1822, and 1823.

[b] *Précis de la Géographie Universelle*, livre 145.

and scrupulously honest in their habits." The Tyrolese, formed of the ancient Rhoeti, would be, according to Pliny (book iii. chap. 19), originally from Etruria; the Dalmatians, of Sclavonic origin, are also mingled with Italians.

It will appear, then, also, from the table, that crimes are more numerous in Dalmatia, where the blood of the south is mixed with the blood of the people of the north. Among the Tyrolese, we find also the traces of more energetic passions than among the other people under the Austrian dominion, excepting, however, the inhabitants of Gallicia, descendants of the Rosniacks, who proceeded, together with the Croatians and Dalmatians, from the eastern Sclavonians.* Classing the people according to the degree of crime, it would appear that they are in the following order: Etruscans or Italians, Sclavonians, and Germans.† It would also appear that the eastern Sclavonians have a greater propensity to crime than the northern and western ones, who are more mixed with the Germans, and are in a more advanced state of civilisation. We see from Table 2.8 that the state of instruction in Prussia is in a direct ratio to the number of crimes; it appears to be nearly the same in the countries under the Austrian dominion.

2.3 On the Influence of Seasons on the Propensity to Crime

The seasons have a well-marked influence in augmenting and diminishing the number of crimes. We may form some idea from Table 2.9, which contains the number of crimes committed in France against persons and property, during each month, for three years, as well as the ratio of these numbers. We can also compare the numbers of this table with those which I have given to show the influence of seasons on the development of mental alienation, and we shall find the most remarkable coincidences, especially for crimes

---

* Ibid. 1.116.

† The western Sclavonians are composed, according to Malte-Brun, of Poles, Bohemians or Tcheches, of the Slovaqúes of Hungary, the Serbes in Lusatia.—Livre 116. "The distinctions between the Sclave (Sclavonian) and the German are, the care which the former takes of his property, and his constant desire to acquire more; he is not so industrious, not so capable of attachment and fidelity in his affections, and more disposed to seek for society and dissipation. He prides himself on greater prudence, and is generally distrustful, especially in his dealings with Germans, whom he always regards as a kind of enemy."—Livre 114. Malte-Brun also makes a distinction of Germans of the north and Germans of the south. "The Thuringerwald divides Germany into two regions—the north and the south. The German of the north, living on potatoes, butter, and cheese, deprived of beer and spirits, is the most robust, frugal, and intelligent: it is also with him that Protestantism has the most proselytes. Delicate in his mode of life, accustomed to wine, sometimes even given to drunkenness, the German of the south is more sprightly but also more superstitious."— Livre 148.

Table 2.9 Influence of Seasons on Propensity to Crime for France 1827–1828 and 1830–1831

Months	Crimes against Persons	Crimes against Property	Ratio: 1827–1828	Crimes against Persons	Crimes against Property	Ratio: 1830–1831
January	282	1,095	3.89	189	666	3.52
February	272	910	3.35	194	563	2.9
March	335	968	2.89	205	602	2.94
April	314	841	2.68	197	548	2.78
May	381	844	2.22	213	569	2.67
June	414	850	2.05	208	602	2.9
July	379	828	2.18	188	501	2.66
August	382	934	2.44	247	596	2.41
September	355	896	2.52	176	584	3.32
October	285	926	3.25	207	586	2.83
November	301	961	3.2	223	651	2.95
December	347	1,152	3.33	181	691	3.82
Total	3847	11,205	2.77	2428	7159	2.94

against persons, which would appear to be most usually dependent on failures of the reasoning powers.*

First, the epoch of maximum (June) in respect to the number of crimes against persons, coincides pretty nearly with the epoch of minimum in respect to crimes against property, and this takes place in summer; whilst, on the contrary, the minimum of the number of crimes against persons, and the maximum of the number of crimes against property, takes place in winter. Comparing these two kinds of crimes, we find that in the month of January nearly four crimes take place against property to one against persons, and in the month of June only two to three. These differences are readily explained by considering that during winter misery and want are more especially felt, and cause an increase of the number of crimes against property, whilst the violence of the passions predominating in summer, excites to more frequent personal collisions.

The periods of maxima and minima also coincide with those of the maxima and minima of births and deaths, as we have already shown.

The *Comptes Généraux* of France also contain data on the hours at which crimes have been committed, but only for thefts in Paris and the neighbour-

* The observations which we possess are neither so numerous nor so carefully compiled as to enable us to affirm that any direct ratio exists between the propensity to crimes against persons and the tendency to mental alienation; yet the existence of this ratio becomes more probable if we consider that we find again the same coincidence regarding the influence of age.

hood. These data are hitherto too few to draw any satisfactory conclusions from them.

2.4 On the Influence of Sex on the Propensity to Crime

We have already been considering the influence which climate, the degree of education, differences of the human race, seasons, &c., have on the propensity to crime; we shall now investigate the influence of sex.

At the commencement, we may observe that, out of 28,686 accused, who have appeared before the courts in France, during the four years before 1830, there were found 5416 women, and 23,270 men, that is to say, 23 women to 100 men. Thus, the propensity to crime in general gives the ratio of 23 to 100 for the sexes. This estimate supposes that justice exercises its duties as actively with regard to women as to men; and this is rendered probable by the fact, that the severity of repression is nearly the same in the case of both sexes; in other words, that women are treated with much the same severity as men.

We have just seen that, in general, the propensity to crime in men is about four times as great as in women, in France; but it will be important to examine further, if men are four times as criminal, which will be supposing that the crimes committed by the sexes are equally serious. We shall commence by making a distinction between crimes against property and crimes against persons. At the same time, we shall take the numbers obtained for each year, that we may see the limits in which they are comprised (Table 2.10).

Although the number of crimes against persons may have diminished slightly, whilst crimes against property have become rather more numerous, yet we see that the variations are not very great; they have but little modified the ratios between the numbers of the accused of the two sexes. We have 26 women to 100 men in the accusations for crimes against property, and for crimes against persons the ratio has been only 16 to 100.* In general, crimes against persons are of a more serious nature than those against property, so that our distinction 19 favourable to the women, and we may affirm that men, in France, are four times as criminal as women. It must be observed, that the ratio 16 to 26 is nearly the same as that of the strength of the two sexes. However, it is proper to examine things more narrowly, and especially to take notice of individual crimes, at least of those which are committed in so great a number, that the inferences drawn from them may possess some degree of probability. For this purpose, in Table 2.11 I have collected the

---

* These conclusions only refer to the results of the four years before 1830. The numbers of the following years, which have been since added to the table, give almost the same ratios.

Table 2.10 Influence of Sex on Propensity to Crime, France, 1826–1831

Years	Crimes against Persons			Crimes against Property		
	Men	Women	Ratio	Men	Women	Ratio
1826	1639	268	0.16	4073	1008	0.25
1827	1637	274	0.17	4020	998	0.25
1828	1576	270	0.17	4396	1156	0.26
1829	1552	239	0.15	4379	1203	0.27
Averages	1601	263	0.16	4217	1091	0.26
1830	1412	254	0.18	4196	1100	0.26
1831	1813	233	0.13	4567	993	0.22
Averages	1612	243	0.15	4381	1046	0.24

Table 2.11 Nature of Crime by Sex, 1826–1829

Nature of Crimes	Men	Women	Women to 100 Men
Infanticide	30	426	1320
Miscarriage	15	39	260
Poisoning	77	73	91
House robbery (*vol domestique*)	2648	1602	60
Parricide	44	22	50
Incendiarism of buildings and other things	279	94	34
Robbery of churches	176	47	27
Wounding of parents (*blessures envers ascendans*)	292	63	22
Theft	10,677	2249	21
False evidence and suborning	307	51	17
Fraudulent bankruptcy	353	57	16
Assassination	947	111	12
False coining (*fausse monnaie*), counterfeit making, false affirmations in deeds, &c.	1669	177	11
Rebellion	612	60	10
Highway robbery	648	54	8
Wounds and blows	1447	78	5
Murder	1112	44	4
Violation and seduction	685	7	1
Violation on persons under 15 years of age	585	5	1

numbers relating to the four years before 1830, and calculated the different ratios; the crimes are classed according to the degree of magnitude of this ratio. I have also grouped crimes nearly of the same nature together, such as issuing false money, counterfeits, falsehoods in statements or in commercial transactions, &c.

As we have already observed, to the commission of crime the three following conditions are essential—the will, which depends on the person's morality, the opportunity, and the facility of effecting it. Now, the reason why females have less propensity to crime than males, is accounted for by their being more under the influence of sentiments of shame and modesty, as far as morals are concerned; their dependent state, and retired habits, as far as occasion or opportunity is concerned; and their physical weakness, so far as the facility of acting is concerned. I think we may attribute the differences observed in the degree of criminality to these three principal causes. Sometimes the whole three concur at the same time: we ought, on such occasions, to expect to find their influence very marked, as in rapes and seductions; thus, we have only 1 woman to 100 men in crimes of this nature. In poisoning, on the contrary, the number of accusations for either sex is nearly equal. When force becomes necessary for the destruction of a person, the number of women who are accused becomes much fewer; and their numbers diminish in proportion, according to the necessity of the greater publicity before the crime can be perpetrated: the following crimes also take place in the order in which they are stated—infanticide, miscarriage, parricide, wounding of parents, assassinations, wounds and blows, murder.

With respect to infanticide, woman has not only many more opportunities of committing it than man, but she is in some measure impelled to it, frequently by misery, and almost always from the desire of concealing a fault, and avoiding the shame or scorn of society, which, in such cases, thinks less unfavourably of man. Such is not the case with other crimes involving the destruction of an individual: it is not the degree of the crime which keeps a woman back, since, in the series which we have given, parricides and wounding of parents are more numerous than assassinations, which again are more frequent than murder, and wounds and blows generally; it is not simply weakness, for then the ratio for parricide and wounding of parents should be the same as for murder and wounding of strangers. These differences are more especially owing to the habits and sedentary life of females; they can only conceive and execute guilty projects on individuals with whom they are in the greatest intimacy: thus, compared with man, her assassinations are more often in her family than out of it; and in society she commits assassination rather than murder, which often takes place after excess of drink, and the quarrels to which women are less exposed.

If we now consider the different kinds of theft, we shall find that the ratios of the propensity to crime are arranged in a similar series: thus, we have successively house robbery, robbery in churches, robberies in general, and, lastly, highway robbery, for which strength and audacity are necessary. The less conspicuous propensity to cheating in general, and to fraudulent bankruptcy, again depend on the more secluded life of females, their separation from trade, and that, in some cases, they are less capable than men—for example, in coining false money and issuing counterfeits.

If we attempt to analyse facts, it seems to me that the difference of morality in man and woman is not so great as is generally supposed, excepting only as regards modesty; I do not speak of the timidity arising from this last sentiment, in like manner as it does from the physical weakness and seclusion of females, As to these habits themselves, I think we may form a tolerable estimate of their influence by the ratios which exist between the sexes in crimes of different kinds, where neither strength has to be taken into consideration, nor modesty—as in theft, false witnessing, fraudulent bankruptcy, &c.; these ratios are about 100 to 21 or 17, that is to say, about 5 or 6 to 1. As to other modes of cheating, the difference is a little greater, from the reasons already stated. If we try to give a numerical expression of the intensity of the causes by which women are influenced, as, for example, the influence of strength, we may estimate it as being in proportion to the degree of strength itself, or as 1 to 2 nearly; and this is the ratio of the number of parricides for each sex. For crimes where both physical weakness and the retired life of females must be taken into account, as in assassinations and highway robberies, following the same plan in our calculations, it will be necessary to multiply the ratio of power or strength 1/2 by the degree of dependence 1–5, which gives 1–10, a quantity which really falls between the values 12–100 and 8–100, the ratios given in the table. With respect to murder, and blows and wounds, these crimes depend not merely on strength and a more or less sedentary life, but still more on being in the habit of using strong drinks and quarrelling. The influence of this latter cause might almost be considered as 1 to 3 for the sexes. It may be thought that the estimates which I have here pointed out, cannot be of an exact nature, from the impossibility of assigning the share of influence which the greater modesty of woman, her physical weakness, her dependence, or rather her more retired life, and her feebler passions, which are also less frequently excited by liquors, may have respectively on any crime in particular. Yet, if such were the characters in which the sexes more particularly differ from each other, we might, by analyses like those now given, assign their respective influence with some probability of truth, especially if the observations were very numerous. I do not speak of modes of justice, of legislation in general, of the state of knowledge, of means of providing for physical wants, &c., which may powerfully contribute to increase or diminish the number of crimes, but whose influence is generally not very evident as regards the ratio of the accused of each sex.

Perhaps it may be said, that if it be true that the morality of woman is not greater than that of man, house robbery should be as frequent for the one as for the other. This observation would be just, if it were proved that the class of individuals by whom house robberies are committed, were equally composed of men and women; but there are no data on this subject. All that can be laid down is, that men and women who live in a domestic state, rather commit crimes against property than against persons, which very materially confirms the observations made above, on the influence of retired life and sedentary habits. The *Compte Général de l'Administration de la Justice* in 1829, for the first time, gives the professions of the accused; and in the article *Domestiques*, we find 318 men and 147 women employed as farm-servants; and 149 men and 175 women as personal domestics: the total number of men is greater than that of women. Now, of these numbers, there were 99 accused of crimes against persons, and 590 of crimes against property: the ratio of these numbers is 1 to 6 nearly, and it has preserved exactly the same value in the years 1830 and 1831. But we have had occasion to see that this ratio for the mass of society is 1 to 3, when particular circumstances are not taken into consideration; and it would be only as 263 to 1091, or 1 to 4 nearly, if society were composed of women alone: thus, in all the cases, I think it has been sufficiently shown that men and women, when in the state of servants, commit crimes against property in preference to others.

As to capital crimes, we may arrange them in the manner shown in Table 2.12.

Adultery, domestic quarrels, and jealousy, cause almost an equal number of poisonings in both sexes; but the number of assassinations, and especially of murders, of women by their husbands, is greater than that of husbands by their wives. The circumstances bearing on this subject have been stated already.

Of 903 murders which have taken place from hatred, revenge, and other motives, 446 have been committed in consequence of quarrels and contentions at taverns; thus, more than one-third of the total number of

Table 2.12　Count of Capital Crime Accusation by Apparent Motive, France, 1826–1829

Apparent Motives: 1826–1829 Inclusive	Accused for				
	Poisoning	Murder	Assassination	Incendiarism	Total
Cupidity, theft	20	39	237	66	362
Adultery	48	9	76	—	133
Domestic dissensions	48	120	131	31	333
Debauchery, jealousy	10	58	115	37	220
Hatred, revenge, & divers motives	23	903	460	229	1615
Total	149	1129	1019	366	2663

Table 2.13   Intellectual State of Accused by Sex, France, 1828–1829 and 1830–1831

Intellectual State	Men	Women	Ratio: 1828–1829	Men	Women	Ratio: 1830–1831
Unable to read or write	6537	2152	3.0	6877	2042	3.3
Able to read and write imperfectly	3308	497	6.6	3422	451	7.6
Could read and write well	1399	110	12.7	1373	82	16.7
Had received an excellent education to the 1st degree	283	5	56.6	314	5	62.8
Intellectual state not mentioned	374	104	3.6	2	—	—
Total	11,901	2868	4.2	11,988	2580	4.6

murders have taken place under circumstances in which women are not usually involved.

The four last volumes of the *Comptes Généraux*, contain some interesting details on the intellectual state of the accused of both sexes: they are shown in Table 2.13.

These numbers give us no information on the population, since we do not know what is the degree of knowledge diffused in France; but we see, at least, that there is a great difference in the sexes. I think we might explain these results by saying, that in the lower orders, where there is scarcely any education, the habits of the women approach those of the men; and the more we ascend in the classes of society, and consequently in the degrees of education, the life of woman becomes more and more private, and she has less opportunity of committing crime, all other things being equal. These ratios differ so much from each other, that we cannot but feel how much influence our habits and social position have on crime.

It is to be regretted that the documents of justice for the Low Countries do not contain any thing on the distinction of the sexes; we only see (according to the returns of the prisons and the houses of correction and detention, in the *Recueil Official*), that on the 1st of January 1827, the number of men was 5162, that of women 1193, which gives 100 women to 433 men. Making use of the documents which have been disclosed to me by M. le Baron de Keverberg, I found that in 1825 this ratio was 100 to 314.

According to the report of M. Duepétiaux, on the state of prisons in Belgium, we enumerated 2231 men and 550 women, as prisoners on the 1et of January 1833, which gives a ratio of 405 to 100: among these prisoners were found 1364 men and 326 women who could not read or write; so that the intellectual state of the prisoners of both sexes was nearly the same; the ratio of the whole population to those who could neither read nor write, was as 100 to 61 among the men, and 100 to 60 among the women. To the number of prisoners just mentioned, may be added 419 individuals confined in the central military prison, of whom 282 could neither read nor write; this gives a ratio of 67 in 100.*

If we examine the accounts of the correctional (or minor) tribunals of France, we find the ratio between the accused of both sexes to be 529,848 to 149,565, or 28 females to 100 males. Thus, with respect to less serious offences, which are judged by the correctional tribunals, the women have there been rather more numerous compared with the men than in the case of weightier crimes.

2.5 Of the Influence of Age on the Propensity to Crime

Of all the causes which influence the development of the propensity to crime, or which diminish that propensity, age is unquestionably the most energetic. Indeed, it is through age that the physical powers and passions of man are developed, and their energy afterwards decreases with age. Reason is developed with age, and continues to acquire power even when strength and passion have passed their greatest vigour. Considering only these three elements, strength, passion, and judgment† (or reason), we may almost say, *à priori*, what will be the degree of the propensity to crime at different ages. Indeed, the propensity must be almost nothing at the two extremes of life; since, on the one hand, strength and passion, two powerful instruments of crime, have scarcely begun to exist, and, on the other hand, their energy, nearly extinguished, is still further deadened by the influence of reason. On the contrary, the propensity to crime should be at its maximum at the age when strength and passion have attained their maximum, and when reason has not acquired sufficient power to govern their combined influence. Therefore, considering

---

* According to the statistical tables of France, of young persons inscribed for military service in 1827, we enumerate (Bulletin de M. Férussac, Nov. 1829, p. 271):

	Absolute No.	Relative No.
Young persons able to read	13,794	5
Young persons able to read and write	100,787	37
Young persons not able to read or write	157,510	58
	272,091	100

This ratio of 58 in 100 is a little less unfavourable than that of prisons, which is 60 in 100.

† I am not speaking of the intellectual state, of religious sentiments of fear, shame, punishment, &c., because these qualities depend more or less directly on reason.

Table 2.14 Ratios of Crimes Against Persons and Property by Age and Sex, France, 1826–1829

Individuals' Age	Crimes against Persons	Crimes against Property	Crimes against Property in 100	Population according to Age	Degrees of the Propensity to Crime
Less than 16 years	80	440	85	3304	161
16 to 21 years	904	3723	80	887	5217
21 to 25	1278	3329	72	673	6846
25 to 30	1575	3702	70	791	6671
30 to 35	1153	2883	71	732	5514
35 to 40	650	2076	76	672	4057
40 to 45	575	1724	75	612	3757
45 to 50	445	1275	74	549	3133
50 to 55	288	811	74	482	2280
55 to 60	168	500	75	410	1629
60 to 65	157	385	71	330	1642
65 to 70	91	184	70	247	1113
70 to 80	64	137	68	255	788
80 and upwards	5	14	74	53	345

only physical causes, the propensity to crime at different ages will be a property and sequence of the three quantities we have just named, and might be determined by them, if they were sufficiently known.* But since these elements are not yet determined, we must confine ourselves to seeking for the degrees of the propensity to crime in an experimental manner; we shall find the means of so doing in the *Comptes Généraux de la Justice*. Table 2.14 will show the number of crimes against persons and against property, which have been committed in France by each sex during the years 1826, 1827, 1828, and 1829, as well as the ratio of these numbers; the fourth column points out how a population of 10,000 souls is divided in France, according to age; and the last column gives the ratio of the total number of crimes to the corresponding number of the preceding column; thus there is no longer an inequality of number of the individuals of different ages.

Table 2.14 gives us results conformable to those which I have given in my *Recherches Statistique* for the years 1826 and 1827. Since the value obtained for 80 years of age and upwards is based on very small numbers, it is not entitled to much confidence. Moreover, we see that man begins to exercise his propensity to crimes against property at a period antecedent to his pursuit of other crimes. Between his 25th and 30th year, when his powers are

---

* Here we are more especially considering crimes against persons; for crimes against property, it will be necessary to take notice of the wants and privations of man.

developed, he inclines more to crimes against persons. It is near the age of 25 years that the propensity to crime reaches its maximum; but before passing to other considerations, let us examine what difference there is between the sexes. The latter columns of Table 2.15 show the degrees of propensity to crime* reference being had to population, and the greatest number of each column being taken as unity.

Women, compared to men, are rather later in entering on the career of crime, and also sooner come to the close of it. The maximum for men takes place about the 25th year, and about the 30th for women; the numbers on which our conclusions are founded are still very few; yet we see that the two lines which represent the relative value for each sex are almost parallel. The latter column contains results calculated by the following very simple formula:

$$y = (1 - \sin x)\frac{1}{1+m}, \text{ supposing } m = \frac{1}{2x-18}$$

In this manner the degree of the propensity to crime is expressed according to age (*en fonction de l'âge*) x. We must take, as we see, for the axis of the abscissae, one-fourth of the corrected circumference (*circonférence rectifiée*),

---

* To give a new proof of the almost identity of results of each year, I have thought proper to present here the numbers collected between 1830 and 1831; we may compare them with those of the preceding tables, which are nearly exactly double, because they refer to four years:

Individuals' Age	Crimes against Persons	Crimes against Property	Crimes against Property in 100 Crimes	Accused Men	Accused Women	Women to 100 Men
Under 16 years	27	214	88	211	30	14
16 to 21 years	394	1888	83	1911	371	19
21 to 25	643	1708	72	1913	438	23
25 to 30	758	1872	70	2185	445	20
30 to 35	662	1741	72	2004	399	20
35 to 40	376	1088	74	1167	297	26
40 to 45	279	725	72	800	204	25
45 to 50	200	643	76	692	151	21
50 to 55	161	426	73	487	100	21
55 to 60	91	245	73	270	60	24
60 to 65	55	147	73	162	40	25
65 to 70	31	100	77	113	18	16
70 to 80	29	58	68	67	20	30
80 and upwards	6	1	14	6	1	16
All ages	3712	10,856	74	11,988	2580	22

Table 2.15 Degrees of Propensity to Crime by Age and Sex

Individuals' Age	Accused		Women to 100 Men	Degrees of the Propensity to Crime			
	Men	Women		In General	Men	Women	Calculated
Under 16 years	438	82	187	0.02	0.02	0.02	0.02
16 to 21 years	3901	726	186	0.76	0.79	0.64	0.66
21 to 25	3762	845	225	1.00	1.00	0.98	1.00
25 to 30	4260	1017	239	0.97	0.96	1.00	0.92
30 to 35	3254	782	240	0.81	0.8	0.83	0.81
35 to 40	2105	621	295	0.59	0.56	0.75	0.71
40 to 45	1831	468	256	0.55	0.54	0.6	0.60
45 to 50	1357	363	267	0.46	0.44	0.51	0.51
50 to 55	896	203	227	0.33	0.33	0.33	0.42
55 to 60	555	113	204	0.24	0.24	0.22	0.34
60 to 65	445	97	218	0.24	0.24	0.23	0.27
65 to 70	230	45	196	0.16	0.17	0.14	0.21
70 to 80	163	38	233	0.12	0.12	0.42	0.12
80 and upwards	18	1	56	0.05	0.06	0.01	0.04
All ages	23,270	5416	233	0.41	—	—	—

and divided into decimal parts. The results of this formula generally agree better with the results obtained for women. I have endeavoured to render them sensible by the construction of a curve, the greater or less divergences of which from the axis AB (see Figure 2.3) indicates the degree of the propensity to crime. The equation becomes a sinusoide:

$$y = 1 - \sin x$$

for ages above 30 years, because m evidently is equal to unity. It is not to be expected that we should find mathematical precision, for several reasons, of which the principal are

1. The numbers obtained for four years are not so great that we may adopt their results with perfect confidence.
2. To calculate the propensity to crime, we must combine these numbers with those which the tables of population have furnished; and it is pretty generally agreed that the table of the *Annuaire* does not give the state of the population of France with sufficient accuracy.
3. The propensity to crime can only be calculated from the whole of the individuals who compose the population; and as those who

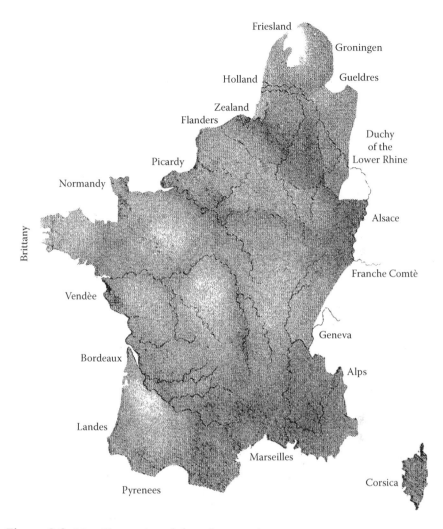

Figure 2.3 Map illustrative of the crimes against persons.

occupy the prisons are generally persons of more than 25 years of age, and who, from their state of captivity, cannot enter into the ratio for persons above 25 years of age, there must necessarily be a void (*lacune*). If, instead of taking crimes collectively, we examine each in particular in proportion to age, we shall have a new proof that the maximum of crimes of different kinds takes place between the 20th and 30th years, and that it is really about that period that the most vicious disposition is manifested. Only the period of maximum will be hastened or retarded some years for some crimes, according to the quicker or slower development of certain qualities of man which are proportioned to those crimes. These results are too curious to be omitted here; I have presented them in Table 2.16, according to the

Table 2.16 Breakdown of Selected Crimes by Age Levels

Nature of the Crimes	Under 16 years	16 to 21	21 to 25	25 to 30	30 to 35	35 to 40	40 to 45	45 to 50	50 to 55	55 to 60	60 to 65	65 to 70	70 to 80	80 and upwards
Violations on children under 15 years	4	120	71	96	73	39	34	45	22	18	26	17	21	2
House robbery	54	965	845	766	528	351	249	207	112	56	61	34	14	—
Other thefts	332	2479	2050	2292	1716	1249	1016	707	433	263	190	98	65	10
Violation and seduction	9	155	156	148	99	38	40	27	9	8	3	1	2	—
Parricide	6	13	12	13	6	3	2	1	4	2	—	—	—	—
Wounds and blows	6	180	300	359	219	129	101	95	55	35	23	10	7	1
Murder	15	139	198	275	172	103	84	49	48	30	25	17	9	—
Infanticide	1	40	99	134	76	44	30	8	7	1	8	4	2	—
Rebellion	5	67	129	156	115	51	51	35	29	16	16	5	5	—
Highway robbery	21	80	111	149	107	60	62	46	22	32	8	6	4	—
Assassination	10	90	144	203	183	100	104	89	53	32	24	13	15	1
Wounding parents	2	47	64	73	72	40	30	16	8	2	1	—	—	—
Poisoning	5	6	17	30	27	15	20	12	6	2	5	4	1	—
False witnessing and suborning	2	23	46	48	44	42	42	35	23	15	15	11	7	—
Various misdemeanours	8	86	202	276	312	244	207	185	129	78	75	28	28	2

documents of France, from 1826 to 1829 inclusively, classing them according to the periods of maxima, and taking into account the population of different ages. I have omitted the crimes which are committed in smallest number, because the results from that alone would have been very doubtful.

Thus the propensity to theft, one of the first to show itself; prevails in some measure throughout our whole existence; we might be led to believe it to be inherent to the weakness of man, who falls into it as if by instinct. It is first exercised by the indulgence of confidence which exists in the interior of families, then it manifests itself out of them, and finally on the public highway, where it terminates by having recourse to violence, when the man has then made the sad essay of the fullness of his strength by committing all the different kinds of homicide. This fatal propensity, however, is not so precocious as that which, near adolescence, arises with the fire of the passions and the disorders which accompany it, and which drives man to violation and seduction, seeking its first victims among beings whose weakness opposes the least resistance. To these first excesses of the passions, of cupidity, and of strength, is soon joined reflection, plotting crime; and man, become more self-possessed and hardened, chooses to destroy his victim by assassination or poisoning. Finally, his last stages in the career of crime are marked by address in deception, which in some measure supplies the place of strength. It is in his decline that the vicious man presents the most hideous spectacle; his cupidity, which nothing can extinguish, is rekindled with fresh ardour, and assumes the mask of swindling; if he still uses the little strength which nature has left to him, it is rather to strike his enemy in the shade; finally, if his depraved passions have not been deadened by age, he prefers to gratify them on feeble children. Thus, his first and his last stages in the career of crime have the same character in this last respect: but what a difference! That which was somewhat excusable in the young man, because of his inexperience, of the violence of his passions, and the similarity of ages, in the old man is the result of the deepest immorality and the most accumulated load of depravity.

From the data of the preceding tables, it is scarcely possible not to perceive the great influence which age exercises over the propensity to crime, since each of the individual results tend to prove it. I shall not hesitate to consider the scale of the different degrees of the propensity to crime, at different ages, deserving of as much confidence as those which I have given for the stature, weight, and strength of man, or, finally, those for mortality.

Account has also been taken of the ages of accused persons, who have appeared before the minor or correctional courts of France, but only preserving the three following heads, which refer but to the four years preceding 1830:

	Criminal Courts		Correctional Courts	
Ages	Men	Women	Men	Women
Under 16 years	2	2	5	6
From 16 to 21	17	13	14	16
More than 21	81	85	81	78
Total	100	100	100	100

Thus, the correctional cases are, in early age, all things being equal, more frequent than criminal cases; they are the first steps of crime, and consequently those most easily ascended. In Belgium, only four heads of ages have been made, and the results of correctional and criminal courts have been united, which renders our comparisons more difficult, since, as we have just seen, the numbers in each are not the same; it is also to be regretted that care has not been taken to distinguish the sexes. Be this as it may, by taking the total number of the accused and suspected (*prévenus*) as unity, we obtain the following results:

	Suspected (or Committed) and Accused				
Ages	1826	1827	1828	1829	Average Number
Under 16 years	4	5	5	5	5
From 16 to 21	13	11	12	11	12
From 21 to 70	81	82	81	82	81
Above 70 years	2	2	2	2	2
Total	100	100	100	100	100

These results are very similar to those of the correctional courts of France, and the latter elements ought certainly to predominate, when we make no distinction between the accused and those merely committed, since the latter are always more numerous than the accused. Yet it would seem that with us there are fewer offences between the ages of 16 and 21 than in France.

We do not find that the number of children brought annually before the courts of Belgium has diminished, either in an absolute sense, or compared with the numbers of other accused and committed persons. The same is nearly the case with France, as we see in Table 2.17, in which I have preferred giving the absolute numbers.

We must not, however, conclude from these results that education, which for some time has been diffused with such activity, has been of no effect in diminishing the number of crimes committed by young persons; several years more are necessary before its influence can become apparent, and before it can carry its effects into the bosom of families.

Table 2.17   Number of Children Appearing Before the Court, France, 1826–1831

Years	Under 16 Years	16 to 21	More than 21	Total
		Accused		
1826	124	1101	5763	6988
1827	136	1022	5771	6939
1828	143	1278	5975	7396
1829	117	1226	6030	7373
1830	114	1161	5687	6962
1831	127	1121	6358	7606
		Committed		
1826	5042	12,799	86,196	104,037
1827	5233	13,291	73,588	92,112
1828	5228	14,902	71,622	91,752
1829	5306	14,431	79,438	99,175
1830	2852	6452	47,812	57,116
1831	551	17,659	84,433	107,743

Note: Those committed for different kinds of offences are not included in these numbers.

It is a matter of regret, that as yet we possess so few accounts of the ages of criminals, calculated to render appreciable the influence of places and the customs of different nations. In general, we remark, that the number of children in prisons in England is much greater than with us; this would appear to be owing, especially in the metropolis, to children being trained in a manner to theft, while the really guilty act through their intermediation. In the penitentiary of Millbank, in the year 1827, 1250 individuals were registered as under 21 years of age out of a total number of 3020, which gives a ratio of 41 to 100, being more than double that of France and the Low Countries.*

The condemned persons in the jail of Philadelphia in 1822, 1823, and 1824, were proportioned as follows:†

Ages	1822	1823	1824	Totals
Under 21 years	52	72	58	182
From 21 to 30 years	151	143	122	416
From 30 to 40 years	72	67	79	218
Above 40 years	55	49	28	132

The total for the three years was 948. Taking the ratio of this sum to 1000, we find the following values, opposite to which I have placed those of France:

* Bulletin de M. de Férussac, May 1828.
† American Review, 1827, No. 12.

	Philadelphia	France
Under 21 years	19	19
From 21 to 30 years	44	35
From 30 to 40 years	23	23
Above 40 years	14	23
Total	100	100

Thus the prisons of Philadelphia present exactly the same number of criminals as those of France for individuals under 19 and for those between 30 and 40 years of age; they have fewer old men, but more men between 21 and 30, which may be owing to the nature of the population of the two countries.

France, Belgium, and Philadelphia agree then pretty nearly as to the number of criminals in proportion to the ages; but England differs very sensibly from the average values presented by these countries, and that is owing, no doubt, as I observed before, not so much to the character of the English people as to the modes of eluding the rigour of the laws which the malefactors make use of, acting through the inter-medium of children whom they have trained up as instruments of crime.

2.6 Conclusions

In making a summary of the principal observations contained in this chapter, we are led to the following conclusions:

1. Age (or the term of life) is undoubtedly the cause which operates with most energy in developing or subduing the propensity to crime.
2. This fatal propensity appears to be developed in proportion to the intensity of the physical power and passions of man: it attains its maximum about the age of 25 years, the period at which the physical development has almost ceased. The intellectual and moral development, which operates more slowly, subsequently weakens the propensity to crime, which, still later, diminishes from the feeble state of the physical powers and passions.
3. Although it is near the age of 25 that the maximum in number of crimes of different kinds takes place, yet this maximum advances or recedes some years for certain crimes, according to the quicker or slower development of certain qualities which have a bearing on those crimes. Thus, man, driven by the violence of his passions, at first commits violation and seduction; almost at the same time he enters on the career of theft, which he seems to follow as if by instinct till the end of life; the development of his strength subsequently leads

him to commit every act of violence—homicide, rebellion, highway robbery still later, reflection converts murder into assassination and poisoning. Lastly, man, advancing in the career of crime, substitutes a greater degree of cunning for violence, and becomes more of a forger than at any other period of life.

4. The *difference of sexes* has also a great influence on the propensity to crime: in general, there is only one woman before the courts to four men.

5. The propensity to crime increases and decreases nearly in the same degrees in each sex; yet the period of maximum takes place rather later in women, and is near the 30th year.

6. Woman, undoubtedly from her feeling of weakness, rather commits crimes against property than persons; and when she seeks to destroy her kind, she prefers poison. Moreover, when she commits homicide, she does not appear to be proportionally arrested by the enormity of crimes which, in point of frequency, take place in the following order: infanticide, miscarriage, parricide, wounding of parents, assassination, wounds and blows, murder; so that we may affirm that the number of the guilty diminishes in proportion as they have to seek their victim more openly. These differences are no doubt owing to the habits and sedentary life of woman; she can only conceive and execute guilty projects on individuals with whom she is in constant relation.

7. The *seasons*, in their course, exercise a very marked influence on crime: thus, during summer, the greatest number of crimes against persons are committed, and the fewest against property; the contrary takes place during winter.

8. It must be observed that age and the seasons have almost the same influence in increasing or diminishing the number of mental disorders and crimes against persons.

9. *Climate* appears to have some influence, especially on the propensity to crimes against persons: this observation is confirmed at least among the races of southern climates, such as the Pelasgian race, scattered over the shores of the Mediterranean and Corsica, on the one hand; and the Italians, mixed with Dalmatians and Tyrolese, on the other. We observe, also, that severe climates, which give rise to the greatest number of wants, also give rise to the greatest number of crimes against property.

10. The countries where frequent mixture of the people takes place; those in which industry and trade collect many persons and things together, and possess the greatest activity; finally, those where the inequality of fortune is most felt, all things being equal, are those which give rise to the greatest number of crimes.

11. Professions have great influence on the nature of crimes. Individuals of more independent professions are rather given to crimes against persons, and the labouring and domestic classes to crimes against property. Habits of dependence, sedentary life, and also physical weakness in women, produce the same results.

12. *Education* is far from having so much influence on the propensity to crime as is generally supposed. Moreover, moral instruction is very often confounded with instruction in reading and writing alone, and which is most frequently an accessory instrument to crime.

13. It is the same with *poverty*; several of the departments of France, considered to be the poorest, are at the same time the most moral. Man is not driven to crime because he is poor, but more generally because he passes rapidly from a state of comfort to one of misery, and an inadequacy to supply the artificial wants which he has created.

14. The higher we go in the ranks of society, and consequently in the degrees of education, we find a smaller and smaller proportion of guilty women to men; descending to the lowest orders, the habits of both sexes resemble each other more and more.

15. Of 1129 murders committed in France, during the space of four years, 446 have been in consequence of quarrels and contentions in taverns; which would tend to show the fatal influence of the use of *strong drinks*.

16. In France, as in the Low Countries, we enumerate annually 1 accused person to 4300 inhabitants nearly; but in the former country, 39 in 100 are acquitted, and in the second only 15; yet the same code was used in both countries, but in the Low Countries the judges performed the duty of the jury. Before correctional courts and simple police courts, where the committed were tried by judges only, the results were nearly the same for both countries.

17. In France, crimes against persons were about one-third of the number of crimes against property, but in the Low Countries they were about one-fourth only. It must be remarked, that the first kind of crimes lead to fewer condemnations than the second, perhaps because there is a greater repugnance to apply punishment as the punishment increases in severity.

I cannot conclude this chapter without again expressing my astonishment at the constancy observed in the results which the documents connected with the administration of justice present each year.

"Thus, as I have already had occasion to repeat several times, we pass from one year to another, with the sad perspective of seeing the same crimes reproduced in the same order, and bringing with them the same punishments in the same proportions." All observations tend likewise to confirm the truth of this proposition, which I long ago announced, that *every thing which pertains to the human species considered as a whole, belongs to the order of physical facts*: the greater the number of individuals, the more does the influence of individual will disappear, leaving predominance to a series of general facts, dependent on causes by which society exists and is preserved. These causes we now want to ascertain, and as soon as we are acquainted with them, we shall determine their influence on society, just in the same way as we determine effects by their causes in physical sciences.* It must be confessed, that, distressing as the truth at first appears, if we submit to a well followed out series of observations the physical world and the social system, it would be difficult to decide in respect to which of the two the acting causes produce their effects with most regularity. I am, however, far from concluding that man can do nothing for man's amelioration. I think, as I said at the commencement of this work, that he possesses a moral power capable of modifying the laws which affect him; but this power only acts in the slowest manner, so that the causes influencing the social system cannot undergo any sudden alteration; as they have acted for a series of years, so will they continue to act in time to come, until they can be modified. Also, I cannot repeat too often, to all men who sincerely desire the well-being and honour of their kind, and who would blush to consider a few francs more or less paid to the treasury as equivalent to a few heads more or less submitted to the axe of the executioner, that there is a budget which we pay with a frightful regularity—it is that of prisons, chains, and the scaffold: it is that which, above all, we ought to endeavour to abate.

---

* M. Guerry comes to the same conclusions from his researches on crimes, Essai sur la Statistique Morale, p. 69: "One of the most general conclusions we can make is, that they all concur to prove that the greater number of facts of a moral nature, considered in the mass, and not individually, are determined by regular causes, the variations of which take place within narrow limits, and which may be submitted, like those of a material nature, to direct and numerical observation." As this idea has continually presented itself to me in all my researches on man, and as I have exactly expressed it in the same terms as those of the text, in my conclusions on the Recherches sur le Penchant au Crime, a work which appeared a year before that of M. Guerry, I have thought it necessary to mention the point here, to prevent misunderstanding.

Localities of Crime in Suffolk (1856)

3

J. GLYDE

From Glyde, J. (1856). Localities of crime in Suffolk. *Journal of the Statistical Society of London*, 19, 102–106.

Suffolk, the county whose criminality we have carefully examined, is situated in the Eastern District of England, and is one of the largest of English shires. It must be classed as one of our best agricultural counties, although partly maritime, having nearly fifty miles of sea coast. In 1851 it had 69,282 inhabited houses, 71,451 separate occupiers, and 337,215 persons. It had 238 persons and 47 houses to a square mile, 28 acres to every 10 persons, and about 28 percent of its population was located in towns.

To trace the progress of crime is a matter of no slight difficulty. Statistical returns, comparing the number of prisoners at different periods, are open to many fallacies, and until we get a register of offences we must consider the criminal returns as a very uncertain test of the comparative morality at different periods. We shall, therefore, make no attempt in this article to indicate the progress of crime in Suffolk further than to state that at the commencement of the century this county stood in a favourable aspect, and that since 1801 crime has increased within its boundaries more rapidly than in the adjoining counties.

Leaving the nature, extent, and fluctuations of crime for more learned observers, we propose opening a new field of inquiry. By analysing the calendars for the five years ending 1853 we descend into particulars, and ascertain the localities in which the criminals have resided, and by tracing the prisoner to his home, the operation of the great producing causes of crime will be the more easily seen, and cause and effect, in many instances, be brought face to face.

Suffolk is divided into seventeen poor law unions, two only of which are town districts. As tables of crime for all England include counties of very various degrees of criminality, so does the average for the county of Suffolk include districts, towns, and villages of opposite moral tendencies as developed by their criminal aspects.

Table 3.1 exhibits the population of the Suffolk districts and the proportion of prisoners to population in each of the poor law unions, showing, at one view, how the respective unions stand in the order of criminality. The least criminal is placed at the top of the list, the others, increasing in crime, downwards.

**Table 3.1   Proportion of Prisoners to Populations for Poor
Law Unions in Suffolk, 1851**

Unions	Population in 1851	Ratio of Criminals to Population
Mutford	20,163	1 in 1,344
Mildenhall	10,354	1 in 1,207
Samford	12,493	1 in 1,086
Plomesgate	21,477	1 in 895
Risbridge	14,059	1 in 760
Blything	27,883	1 in 871
Thingoe	19,014	1 in 760
Woodbridge	23,776	1 in 820
Hoxne	15,900	1 in 781
Stow	21,110	1 in 752
Bosmere	17,219	1 in 688
Sudbury	23,406	1 in 680
Ipswich	32,759	1 in 643
Hartismere	19,028	1 in 620
Wangford	14,014	1 in 590
Cosford	18,107	1 in 464

There are striking differences exhibited in this table. Criminal tendencies are widely spread in some districts, and a glance at some of the previous
calendars proved to us that this tendency is not, by any means, confined to
the five years examined, but would, in some cases, be more strongly marked
by embracing a larger number of years. Our attention is immediately arrested
by the fact of some "unions" being far less criminal than others. Criminals
are nearly *three* times as numerous in Cosford as they are in Mutford, and
nearly twice as numerous in Hartismere as they are in Mildenhall.

It must not be supposed that every town and village in these "unions" is
equally favourable or unfavourable. The extremes are sometimes met with in
the same district. Mutford stands as the least criminal in the list of unions,
but its position will appear much more favourable if we subtract the criminals
furnished by the town of Lowestoft. In the five years ending 1853 Mutford
has furnished 75 prisoners, but 58 of these come from Lowestoft, thus leaving only 17 criminals in that period for the rest of the union, which, independent of the town named, contains 13,382 persons. Again, Wangford has
furnished 117 criminals, but of this number the towns of Beccles and Bungay
have sent 97, thus leaving 20 prisoners for all the villages in Wangford union.
But if we turn to the Cosford union, and deduct the population of the town
of Hadleigh, which is the *only* place in the union having a population of more
than 2,000 persons, we shall find that the deduction makes but little difference in the ratio of crime. Cosford furnished 196 prisoners, and of this
number the town of Hadleigh sent 46, leaving 150 for the rest of the union.

Table 3.2   **Proportions of Prisoners to Populations for Towns in Suffolk, 1851**

Towns	Population in 1851	Ratio of Criminals to Population
Southwold	2,109	1 in every 1,320
Framlingham	2,450	1 in every 1,020
Debenham	1,653	1 in every 555
Ipswich	32,914	1 in every 557
Lowestoft	6,580	1 in every 565
Sudbury	6,043	1 in every 475
Hadleigh	3,338	1 in every 405
Bungay	3,841	1 in every 370
Halesworth	2,529	1 in every 309

Leaving out the towns of Lowestoft, Beccles, Bungay, and Hadleigh, the ratio is in Mutford 1 criminal to every 3,977 persons, in Wangford 1 to every 1,443 persons, and in Cosford 1 to every 492 persons.

Towns, we all know, contain elements of moral progress nowhere else to be found; but as the great mass of offenders tried at assizes and quarter sessions are members of the labouring class, the highest ratio of offenders must be anticipated where labourers aggregate together. This at once points to towns as being, in all probability, more criminal than rural districts. In the towns of Suffolk there is as much difference in comparative criminality as we have shown to exist in entire poor law unions, as is shown in Table 3.2.

Great differences in small areas are here exhibited, and this table also shows that the aggregation in towns, is not, in all cases, a sure producer of crime. Stowmarket, the only town in the union which bears its name, was less criminal than the whole district to which it belongs. Framlingham was equally favourable. Southwold and Halesworth, towns nearly equal in population, and situated within a few miles of each other, stand singularly as the least; and most criminal in the county; there being four criminals in the latter to one in the former. Lowestoft is twice as criminal as Southwold, and they are both sea ports; and in proportion to population the criminals from Bungay are double those from Stowmarket, and those from Eye double those from Framlingham.

Are the towns as different for the *heinousness* as they are for the amount of their criminality? This question will naturally suggest itself to the reader, and we are glad to be able to show that a very large percentage of petty larcenies are committed by town residents, and that a less number of the gravest offences are committed by them than could fairly be anticipated. The percentage of larcenies in eight towns in the five years ending 1863 are shown in Table 3.3.

The small percentage of larcenies at Framlingham and Southwold is owing to the small number of offences, only 12 at the former and 8 at the

Table 3.3   Percentage of Larcenies in Eight Suffolk
Towns, 1859–1863

Towns	Percentage of Larcenies	Towns	Percentage of Larcenies
Southwold	50,000	Lowestoft	75,862
Framlingham	58,222	Halesworth	65,853
Debenham	60,000	Hadleigh	60,826
Ipswich	63,050	Bungay	61,538

latter in five years. Debenham appears to stand as bad as Hadleigh, but this also is attributable to the small number of criminals in one town compared with the other.

One of the most interesting fields of inquiry in connection with this subject is the comparative criminality of town and rural districts. The unions varied from 1 criminal in every 1,344 persons to 1 in every 464 persons. The towns likewise varied from 1 in every 1,820 persons to 1 in 309. Our analysis, however, convinced us that many villages in this county furnish a much larger proportion of prisoners than the towns. Compare the county town Ipswich with the village of Wickham Market, in the Plomesgate union. Ipswich contained 32,750 persons, and Wickham Market 1,697 persons. The great facilities that a large town naturally affords to a practised thief would lead any one to suppose that criminals would abound much more in the former than in the latter, but the examination proved the very reverse to be the fact. During the five years ending 1853 Ipswich had furnished 1 criminal to every 557 persons, whilst Wickham Market had sent 1 criminal to every 339 persons.

To test still further the accuracy of this comparison we took the fifteen towns in Suffolk and compared their criminal returns with fifteen villages from different poor law unions in the county, and the result is

- That fifteen *towns*, each with an average population of 5,000, furnished 1 criminal annually to every 593 persons.
- That fifteen *villages*, each with an average proportion of 820, furnished annually 1 criminal to every 317 persons.

Feeling that if we stopped here the comparison between the criminality of town and country would be very imperfectly exhibited, as the *character* of the offences committed by the respective populations would be entirely overlooked, we instituted a more minute and extended analysis for the purpose of showing whether the town or the country population have manifested the most serious phases of the criminal character. Having taken the residences of 228 prisoners, committed for trial for the gravest offences in the calendar, we felt that for this one county the number was amply sufficient to prove the

Table 3.4   Frequency Distribution of Selected Offences by
Town and Country Residential Status

Offences	Total Offenders	Town Residents	Country Residents
Murder	24	5	19
Maliciously cutting, &c.	12	3	9
Stabbing, shooting with intent, &c.	13	3	11
Highway robbery	4	2	2
Burglary and housebreaking	57	16	41
Arson	76	4	72
Rape	13	4	9
Assault, with intent	16	1	15
Unnatural offences	7	...	7
Sodomy	1	...	1
Bestiality	5	...	5
Total	228	38	190

point in question. Of the 228 prisoners 76 were committed for arson, 57 for burglary and housebreaking, 24 for murder, 12 for maliciously wounding, 14 for stabbing and shooting with intent, 12 for rape, 7 for unnatural offences, 1 for sodomy, 16 for assault with intent, 5 for bestiality, and 4 for highway robbery. These are offences which have their origin in malice, unbridled passions, and a lawless disregard of the rights of property; and a better index to the degree of criminal debasement in the town and country districts, than such a comparison will afford, could not well be offered. Of the 228 prisoners 38 only were residents in towns, and the remaining 190 belonged to the villages of Suffolk: 17 percent belonged to the former and 83 to the latter. It may be objected that the large proportion of cases of arson, which is essentially a rural offence, included in the above list of offences would materially influence the percentage of country offences. Admitting that there is some force in this objection, it is somewhat strange, considering the mass of agricultural labourers there are residing in the small towns of this county, that out of 76 offenders for the demoniacal crime of arson only 4 of the criminals were town residents. The details are shown in Table 3.4.

It must be admitted that this analysis is exceedingly favourable to the town residents, for although consisting of nearly 29 percent of the population, they have furnished only 17 percent of the serious crime of the county. In the class of crimes committed under the influence of sexual animalism only 5 offenders out of 42 belonged to towns.

We respectfully solicit the attention of statistical inquirers to the facts we have brought forward, and earnestly hope that some five or six gentlemen will make the experiment in mining, manufacturing, and agricultural counties, so as to ascertain whether the same differences in the ratio of criminals exist therein, and whether the town populations are, in all cases, so free from committing those grave offences that form the most serious blots on the moral character of the present age.

It must, however, be borne in mind by all who undertake similar inquiries that it is with the *residence* of criminals only, *not* with the place where the offence was committed, that the inquiry has to do.

Juvenile Delinquency in a Small City (1916)

4

E.W. BURGESS

From Burgess, E.W. (1916). Juvenile delinquency in a small city. *Journal of the American Institute of Criminal Law and Criminology*, 6, 724–728.

Numerous studies have been made of juvenile delinquency and dependency in the cities. The small city and the town have been overlooked. Yet the problems of child development are present in the smaller community, and are even more difficult of solution, because of the survival of the traditional point of view, and because of the absence of the trained social worker. The difficulty is increased rather than diminished by the fact that institutions, such as the juvenile court, which were developed to meet city needs, are transferred to the country unmodified with reference to a widely different situation.

The following study is a fragmentary one. Not enough cases are included to give it statistical value for the making of generalizations. But it does have a value as a pioneer attempt to indicate the main facts in the situation of child delinquency and dependency in a small city of 12,000 inhabitants in a rural state. With this end in view a study* was made of juvenile delinquents and dependents for a two-year period beginning May 1, 1912, and ending April 30, 1914. During this time fifty-two children were brought into the juvenile court.

The facts of age, sex, and race stood out at once. The majority of the children were in the age group from eleven to sixteen. There were only twelve children between the ages of five and ten, and but six boys and girls under five years. Thirty-two boys and but twenty girls were brought before the juvenile judge. The proportion of delinquency was higher among the colored than among the white children. A detailed analysis of the less obvious facts such as residence, nature of delinquency, and disposition of the cases will lead us closer to the underlying factors in the situation. A study of the residence of delinquent and dependent boys and girls brought out a striking difference in proportion of delinquents and dependents from the different wards. Table 4.1 gives us a classification of children by sex and race according to residence in the various wards.

The statistical method used here of computing the percentages of the delinquent juvenile groups upon the basis of the total population comprised

---

* Miss Eleanor Myers, a student in the Department of Sociology in the University of Kansas, gave valuable assistance in the collection and tabulation of the data presented here.

Table 4.1 Number of Children Appearing in the Juvenile Court, Classified by Ward, Sex, and Race; with Percentages of Delinquents and Dependents Based on Entire Juvenile Population

Ward	Boys White	Boys Colored	Girls White	Girls Colored	Total	Number in Age Group 5–16	Percent of Total No. Children in the City in Age Group 5–16
I.	11	2	2 (1)	2	17 (1)	16	2.82
II.	2	2	0	0	4	4	0.82
III.	3	1	4	0	8	88	1.55
IV.	7 (2)	1	5 (1)	3	16 (3)	13	8.36
V.	0	0	0	0	0	0	0.00
VI.	2	0	2 (1)	1 (1)	5 (2)	3	1.44
Transient	1		1		2	2	
Total	26 (2)	6	14 (3)	6 (1)	52 (6)	46	2.13

Note: Figures in parentheses indicate number of boys or girls in each group who were under five years of age.

in the juvenile group in question seemed to the writer to be the only fair method. By juvenile age group we mean the total number of children in the city of the ages from 5 to 16 years inclusive. By percentage number we denote the proportion of delinquents to the particular age group.

The groupings by sex and race show certain significant things. The colored boys lead in delinquency with a percentage number of 4.22, followed by the colored girls with a percentage number of 2.63, followed by the white boys with a percentage number of 2.59, with the white girls last with a percentage number of 1.24. As indicated here the difference between the sexes is somewhat more striking than the difference between the races. As to sex, the percentage numbers are 2.78 for the boys, both colored and white, and 1.48 for the colored and white girls. For race, we have a percentage number of 1.92 in the case of the white children as compared with a percentage number of 3.28 for the colored boys and girls. These ratios indicate the favorable position of the white girl: she is relatively one-half as likely to find her way into the juvenile court as her brother or her colored girl neighbor.

More significant than color or sex was the question of residence. In the fourth ward, for example, one out of every twelve children five years and over but under seventeen years old, appeared before the juvenile judge. If this proportion should be maintained throughout a twelve-year period (corresponding to the life of the child from 5 to 16 years in the juvenile age group), and if there were no "repeaters" during this time, one-half of all the children in the fourth ward would have appeared in the juvenile court. The fact that the proportion of juvenile delinquents from this ward is more than three times as large as that from any other ward gives us a clue to the causes of the situation. The race factor is not the chief one, because three-fourths of the juvenile delinquents from this ward are white. Besides, the proportion of juvenile delinquency is low in the fifth and sixth wards where the proportion of negroes to whites is the highest in the city. The fundamental cause is the low grade home environment which tends to the demoralization of the child. The bad housing conditions of the city are concentrated in the fourth ward. Poverty is present in the homes and finds expression in the stunted growth and undernourished bodies of the school children from this ward. This is the one ward within the city which has within its borders no church, nor school, nor playground. The report of the health supervision of school children showed that only one-eighth of the pupils in the school attended by the children from this ward were vaccinated. The business street which forms its western boundary has a distracting and quite demoralizing influence upon the children. A study of these facts demonstrates the necessity for conscious community action to save the child. Would the supervised playground here as in the city be the social prophylactic for juvenile delinquency?

A comparison of conditions in the fourth ward with wards five and six exhibits the influence of geography upon child development. The economic condition of the inhabitants of these wards differs but little from the ward studied above. Indeed, the proportion of negroes is greater here. Yet the fifth and sixth wards have an extremely low juvenile delinquency rate. Two geographical factors enter into this result.

The first one is the semirural character of the dwellings in these wards as compared with the housing in the fourth ward. The second geographical fact is the difference in proximity to the business street. In the rural settlement north of the river the life of the child is not distracted by the "call of the street." He is still responsive to the "call of the wild" in a situation where impulsive response does not lead to juvenile delinquency. The excess then of juvenile delinquency in the fourth ward appears to be due to the play impulse gone wrong because of the difference, not in the children, but in the geographical location.

A study of residence revealed the influence of the home, the neighborhood and the geographic environment. An analysis of the nature of the delinquency enables us to obtain a clear insight into the difficulties in the situation. Table 4.2 offers us this opportunity.

This table exhibits the influence of sex differences in the child's adaptation to the community. Dependency and neglect appear to account for the presence of two-thirds of the girls in the juvenile court. The remaining third of the girls, where the complaint is incorrigibility or immorality, constitute a more serious problem. But how different is the situation with the boys! Only one-fifth are dependent or neglected, while three-fourths of them are charged with undesirable motor activity, such as offenses against property and the like. This study shows the need of organized recreation to direct the activity of the boy. Otherwise the active life of the boy is likely to develop those vagrant

Table 4.2 Cause of Appearance in the Juvenile Court

	Boys	Girls
Dependent and neglected	6	13
Theft	11	0
Incorrigible and immoral	2	6
Disturbing the peace	6	1
Trespassing	4	0
Defacing property	2	0
Cigarette smoking	1	0
Total	32	20

and lawless tendencies which lead into the juvenile court, thence to the boys' industrial school and perhaps finally to the state reformatory and penitentiary. The small community needs a playground as much as a large city.

The work of the juvenile court as an institution, however, can be fairly studied only in the disposition of cases and the life history of its wards. The wisdom of the juvenile judge has been shown in the fact that only twelve of the fifty-two individuals have been sentenced to the state industrial school, and in the case of three of these sentence was suspended. Six children have been sent to the children's home and five have been adopted. The remainder have been put on probation. Experience has taught the judge of this court that the boy or girl should be sent to the state industrial schools only as a last resort.

In counties containing but small population, the juvenile court functions under grave limitations. The juvenile judge is elected as probate judge and the work of the juvenile court tends to become a by-activity with him both in office and when running for office. Then, too, the juvenile judge in the rural county faces conditions similar to those in the city, but without adequate means for meeting them. For example, in the small as well as the large community, a close correlation exists in a large proportion of the cases between feeble-mindedness and juvenile delinquency. But in the town and village there are no facilities for mental examination and no ungraded rooms in the public school for the mentally deficient. The compensation for the probation officer is so inadequate that only incompetent service is likely to be secured.

The problems of juvenile delinquency, then, in the town or small city appear to be as real and pressing as those of the large city. The agencies, transplanted from the large community, have, however, not as yet become adapted to the changed environment. The situation challenges the attention, interest and effort of the friends of the child. We need a constructive program for the promotion of the welfare of children in our smaller as well as in our larger communities.

Juvenile Delinquency and Urban Areas

A Study of Rates of Delinquency in Relation to Differential Characteristics of Local Communities in American Cities (1969)

5

C.R. SHAW
H.D. MCKAY

From Shaw, C.R., and McKay, H.D. (1969). *Juvenile Delinquency and Urban Areas: A Study of Rates of Delinquency in Relation to Differential Characteristics of Local Communities in American Cities* (pp. 140–169, 315–326). Chicago: University of Chicago Press.

Contents

5.1	Delinquency Rates and Community Characteristics	88
5.2	Indexes of Physical Status in Relation to Rates of Delinquents	90
	5.2.1 Population Increase or Decrease	90
5.3	Indexes of Economic Status in Relation to Rates of Delinquents	92
	5.3.1 Percentage of Families on Relief	92
	5.3.2 Median Rentals	92
	5.3.3 Home Ownership	95
5.4	Population Composition in Relation to Rates of Delinquents	98
	5.4.1 Percentage of Foreign-Born and Negro Heads of Families	98
5.5	Summary	108
	5.5.1 Variations in Community Characteristics by Zones	108
5.6	Conclusion	114
	5.6.1 Summary and Interpretation	114
	5.6.2 Implications for Prevention and Treatment	118
	5.6.3 A Program of Community Action	119

5.1 Delinquency Rates and Community Characteristics

The question has been asked many times: What is it, in modern city life, that produces delinquency? Why do relatively large numbers of boys from the inner urban areas appear in court with such striking regularity, year after year, regardless of changing population structure or the ups and downs of the business cycle? In preceding chapters different series of male juvenile delinquents were presented which closely parallel one another in geographical distribution although widely separated in time, and the close resemblance of all these series to the distribution of truants and of adult criminals was shown. Moreover, many other community characteristics—median rentals, families on relief, infant mortality rates, and so on—reveal similar patterns of variation throughout the city. The next step would be to determine, if possible, the extent to which these two sets of data are related. How consistently do they vary together, if at all, and how high is the degree of association?

Where high zero-order correlations are found to exist uniformly between two variables, with a small probable error, it is possible and valid to consider either series as an approximate index, or indicator, of the other. This holds true for any two variables which are known to be associated or to vary concomitantly. The relationship, of course, may be either direct or inverse. In neither case, however, is there justification in assuming, on this basis alone, that the observed association is of a cause-and-effect nature; it may be, rather, that both variables are similarly affected by some third factor. Further analysis is needed. Controlled experimentation is often useful in establishing the degree to which a change in one variable "causes" or brings about a corresponding change in the other. In the social field, however, experimentation is difficult. Instead, it is often necessary to rely upon refined statistical techniques, such as partial correlation, which for certain types of data, enable the investigator to measure the effects of one factor while holding others relatively constant. By the method of successive redistribution, also, the influence of one or more variables may be held constant. Thus, it is possible to study the relationship between rates of delinquents and economic status for a single nationality group throughout the city or for various nationality groups in the same area or class of areas. This process may be extended indefinitely, subject only to the limitations of the available data. In the analysis to be presented, both of the latter methods have been used in an attempt to determine how much weight should be given to various more or less influential factors.

Several practical considerations prevent the neat and precise statistical analysis which would be desirable. The characteristics studied represent only a sampling of the myriad forms in which community life and social relationships find expression. The rate of delinquents must itself be thought of as an imperfect enumeration of the delinquents and an index of the larger number of boys engaging in officially proscribed activities. Not only will there be chance fluctuations in the amount of alleged delinquency from year to year, but the policy of the local police officer in referring boys to the juvenile court, the focusing of the public eye upon conditions in an area, and numerous other matters may bring about a change in the index without any essential change in the underlying delinquency-producing influences in the community or in the behavior resulting therefrom. If the infant mortality rates or the rates of families on relief are looked upon as indexes of economic status or of the social organization of a community it is obvious that they can be considered only very crude indicators at best. The perturbing influence of other variables must always be considered.

Certain exceptional conditions are known to limit the value of other variables chosen as indicators of local community differentiation. Median rental has been used widely because of its popularity as an index of economic status, although in Chicago such an index is far from satisfactory, when applied to areas of colored population. The Negro is forced to pay considerably higher rents than the whites for comparable housing; thus his economic level is made to appear higher on the basis of rental than it actually is. Similarly, rates of increase or decrease of population are modified in Negro areas by restrictions on free movement placed upon the Negro population. Thus, in certain areas the population is increasing where it normally would be expected to decrease if there were no such barriers. Likewise, the percentage of families owning homes is not entirely satisfactory as an economic index in large urban centers, where many of the well-to-do rent expensive apartments. It is, however, an indication of the relative stability of population in an area.

Correlation of series of rates based on geographical areas is further complicated by the fact that magnitude of the coefficient is influenced by the size of the area selected. This tendency has been noted by several writers,* but no satisfactory solution of the problem has been offered. If it be borne in mind that a correlation of area data is an index of geographical association for a particular type of spatial division only, rather than a fixed measure of functional relationship, it will be apparent that a change in area size changes the meaning of the correlation. Thus, an r of .90 or above for two series of rates calculated by square-mile areas indicates a high degree of association between the magnitudes of the two rates in most of the square miles but does not tell us the exact degree of covariance for smaller or larger areas. With these limitations clearly in mind, a number of correlation coefficients and tables of covariance are presented. The statistical data characterizing and differentiating local urban areas may be grouped under three headings: (1) physical status, (2) economic status, and (3) population composition. These will be considered, in turn, in relation to rates of delinquents.

---

* See, e.g., Gehike and Biehl (1934).

5.2 Indexes of Physical Status in Relation to Rates of Delinquents

The location of major industrial and commercial developments, the distribution of buildings condemned for demolition or repair, and the percentage increase or decrease in population by square-mile areas were presented in chapter ii (pp. 17–42, in the original) as indications of the physical differentiation of areas within the city. Quantitative measures of the first two are not available, but inspection of the distribution maps shows clearly that the highest rates of delinquents are most frequently found in, or adjacent to, areas of heavy industry and commerce. These same neighborhoods have the largest number of condemned buildings. The only notable exception to this generalization, for Chicago, appears in some of the areas south of the central business district.

There is, of course, little reason to postulate a direct relationship between living in proximity to industrial developments and becoming delinquent. While railroads and industrial properties may offer a field for delinquent behavior, they can hardly be regarded as a cause of such activities. Industrial invasion and physical deterioration do, however, make an area less desirable for residential purposes. As a consequence, in time there is found a movement from this area of those people able to afford more attractive surroundings. Further, the decrease in the number of buildings available for residential purposes leads to a decrease in the population of the area.

5.2.1 Population Increase or Decrease

Increase or decrease of population and rates of delinquents, by square-mile areas, do not exhibit a linear relationship. A relatively slight difference in rate of decrease of population, or of rate of increase for areas where the increase is slight, is generally associated with a considerable change in rates of delinquents; while for large differences in rates of increase of population, where increase is great, there is little or no consistent difference in rates of delinquents. Thus, areas increasing more than 70 percent show no corresponding drop in rates of delinquents, although the relationship is clear up to this point. An adequate measure of the degree of association between rates of delinquents and rates of population change must take into account the curvilinearity of the relationship. Accordingly, the correlation ratio, η, has been used.* When the rates of delinquents in the 1927–1933 juvenile court series are thus correlated with the percentage increase or decrease of population

---

* In each instance the percentage increase or decrease of population will be taken as the independent, or X, variable; and the rate of delinquents as the dependent, or Y, variable. In other words, the regression of rates of delinquents (Y) on increase or decrease of population (X) will be considered. This will be indicated by the symbol η_{yx}.

between 1920 and 1930, by the 113 square-mile areas for which 1920 data are available, with rates of delinquents as the dependent variable, the correlation ratio, η_{yx}, is found to be .52. For the 1917–1923 series of delinquents and the percentage increase or decrease of population from 1910 to 1920, with rates of delinquents again the dependent variable, η_{yx} is .69. (In both these calculations all population increases above 200 percent were counted as 200.)

The sharp drop in the degree of association between the two series from one decade to the next is very largely due, no doubt, to the rapid increase during this period of the population in the colored district, where rates of delinquents were high. These were the only areas of significantly increasing population which also had high rates of delinquents. Conversely, some of the largest outlying areas, which show a marked growth in population, contain within them small areas near industrial developments where the population is decreasing and where a corresponding concentration of delinquents appears.

The general correspondence between rates of delinquents and population increase or decrease, by five classes of areas grouped according to population change, is presented in Table 5.1. The classes correspond to the five shadings

Table 5.1 Rates of Delinquents for Areas Grouped According to Percentage Increase or Decrease of Population: 1927–1933 and 1917–1923

Percentage Increase or Decrease of Population, 1920–1930		Rate of Delinquents, 1927–1933
Decreasing:		
20–39	(27.5)*	9.5
0–19	(7.9)*	6.3
Increasing:		
0–19	(9.2)*	4.1
20–39	(28.4)*	3.0
40 and over	(124.2)*	2.0
Percentage Increase or Decrease of Population, 1910–1920		Rate of Delinquents, 1917–1923
Decreasing:		
20–39	(32.5)*	9.7
0–19	(8.4)*	8.6
Increasing:		
0–19	(10.0)*	5.3
20–39	(29.9)*	4.0
40 and over	(87.5)*	3.4

* Percentage for class as a whole.

on Map 3 (p. 30 in the original). For comparison, rates of delinquents based on the 1917–1923 data are shown for five classes of areas grouped on the basis of population increase or decrease between 1910 and 1920.

It will be noted that in both these comparisons the highest rates of delinquents are in the classes of areas where the decrease in population is most rapid and that both indicate a consistent decrease in rates of delinquents with increasing population. The variation for the 1927–1933 juvenile court series is from 9.5 to 2.0 while for the 1917–1923 series it is from 9.7 to 3.4. These variations are presented graphically in Figure 5.1A and B.

These correlation ratios and tables establish the fact that there is a similarity between the pattern of distribution of delinquency and that of population growth or decline. The data do not establish a causal relationship between the two variables; however, the fact that the population of an area is decreasing does not impel a boy to become delinquent. It may be said, however, that decreasing population is usually related to industrial invasion of an area and contributes to the development of a general situation conducive to delinquency.

5.3 Indexes of Economic Status in Relation to Rates of Delinquents

5.3.1 Percentage of Families on Relief

When the rates of delinquents in the 1927–1933 series are correlated with percentages of families on relief in 1934, by 140 square-mile areas, the coefficient is 0.89 ± .01. The extent and nature of the correspondence between these two variables in Chicago are further indicated by the general comparison shown in Table 5.2 with rates of commitments added. Comparable data for the 1917–1923 series are presented for classes of areas grouped by 1921 dependency rates.*

The smooth variation in rates of delinquents with variation in the percentage of families on relief and rates of family dependency is presented graphically in Figure 5.1C and D.

5.3.2 Median Rentals

It is apparent from inspection, also, that there is a generally close association between equivalent monthly rentals and rates of delinquents. The areas of

---

* The rates of dependency are based upon a study made by Professor Erle Fiske Young and Faye B. Karpf, showing the total number of families receiving financial aide from the United Charities and the Jewish Charities.

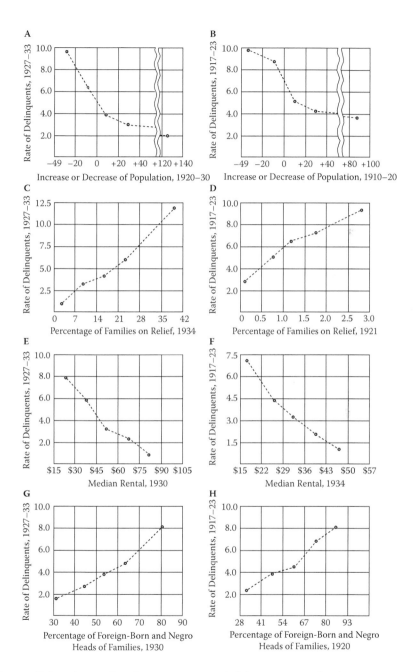

Figure 5.1 Relationship between rates of delinquents and other community characteristics.

Table 5.2 Rates of Delinquents and of Juvenile Court Commitments, for Areas Grouped by Percentage of Families on Relief or Dependent: 1927–1933 and 1917–1923 Series

Percentage of Families on Relief, 1934		Rate of Delinquents 1927–1933	Rate of Commitments 1927–1933
28.0 and over	(39.2)*	11.7	4.3
21.0–27.9	(23.8)*	6.1	1.9
14.0–20.9	(16.9)*	4.3	1.4
7.0–13.9	(9.8)*	2.9	0.7
0–6.9	(3.8)*	1.4	0.3
Rates of Dependency, 1921		Rate of Delinquents 1917–1923	Rate of Commitments 1917–1923
2.0 and over	(2.8)*	9.2	3.2
1.5–1.9	(1.7)*	7.1	2.5
1.0–1.4	(1.2)*	6.4	2.2
0.5–0.9	(0.7)*	5.1	1.5
0.0–0.4	(0.1)*	2.9	0.8

* Percentage for class as a whole.

lowest rentals as of 1930 correspond quite closely with those of high rates of delinquents, and vice versa, though the relationship is not entirely linear. The zero-order coefficient obtained when median rentals and rates of delinquents in the 140 square-mile areas are correlated is –.61 ± .04. The areas deviating most from the general trend are the South Side neighborhoods, where, as a result of special conditions, previously discussed, the relationship between income and rentals is not the same as for the rest of the city. It is interesting in this connection, however, that when the predominantly Negro areas are considered separately, the median rentals are seen to vary inversely with rates of delinquents, just as they do in the white areas. When logarithms of rates of delinquents are plotted against median rentals, the regression is nearly linear, the coefficient being –.71 ± .03 for the 140 areas.

The association between rentals and rates of delinquents is further indicated when rates of delinquents are calculated for the five classes of areas shown on Map 5 (chap. ii; p. 35, in the original). For comparison the same delinquency data were used to compute rates for classes of areas grouped according to median rentals, by communities instead of by square-mile areas/ from the Chicago census of 1934. The results are presented in Table 5.3.

The data of Table 5.3 indicate that the rate of delinquents in the lowest rental class is more than seven times as high as that in the highest rental class, when the 1930 data are used, and six times as high when the calculations are based on the 1934 census by larger community areas. These relationships are presented graphically in Figure 5.1E and F.

**Table 5.3 Rates of Delinquents and of Juvenile Court
Commitments for Areas Grouped by Median Rental (140 Square-
Mile Areas and 60 Communities), 1927–1933 Series**

Median Rentals, 1930 (140 Square-Mile Areas)		Rate of Delinquents 1927–1933	Rate of Commitments 1927–1933
$75.00 and over	($82.88)*	1.1	0.2
60.00–$74.99	(67.56)*	2.5	0.6
45.00–59.99	(52.72)*	3.4	1.2
30.00–44.99	(38.60)*	6.0	2.9
Under $30.00	(23.91)*	8.0	3.9
Median Rentals, 1934 (60 Community Areas)		Rate of Delinquents 1927–1933	Rate of Commitments 1927–1933
$43.00 and over	($47.49)*	1.2	0.3
36.00–$42.99	(40.13)*	2.2	0.6
29.00–35.99	(32.43)*	3.3	1.4
22.00–28.99	(26.77)*	4.5	2.3
Under $22.00	(17.31)*	7.2	3.5

* Rental for class as a whole.

5.3.3 Home Ownership

The relationship between families on relief and rates of delinquents, as has been shown, is positive and linear. Median rentals and home ownership, on the other hand are both inversely related to delinquency; but in the latter case, now to be considered, the relationship is not linear. The correlation ratio has therefore been used. When the 1927–1933 rates of delinquents are correlated with the percentage of families owning their homes in the 140 square-mile areas, as of 1930, the correlation ratio, η, is –.49. Similarly, when the 1917–1923 rates are correlated with the percentage of families owning homes in 1920, η is –.47. Both these correlations are naturally reduced by the low rates of home ownership in some apartment-house areas, where the rates of delinquents are also low. They are high enough, however, to indicate that, generally speaking, low rates of home ownership and high rates of delinquents tend to appear together throughout Chicago.

The general association of home ownership with rates of delinquents is clearly evident when the latter are calculated for classes of areas grouped on the basis of the rates of home ownership, as shown in Figure 5.2. Table 5.4 shows the rates of delinquents for these five classes of areas and for similar classes as of 1920.

As indicated previously, the association appears to be closer when rates of delinquents are compared with each of these variables for five general classes of areas than when the correlations are based on the 140 smaller areas into which the city has been divided for the purpose of this study. This is especially true

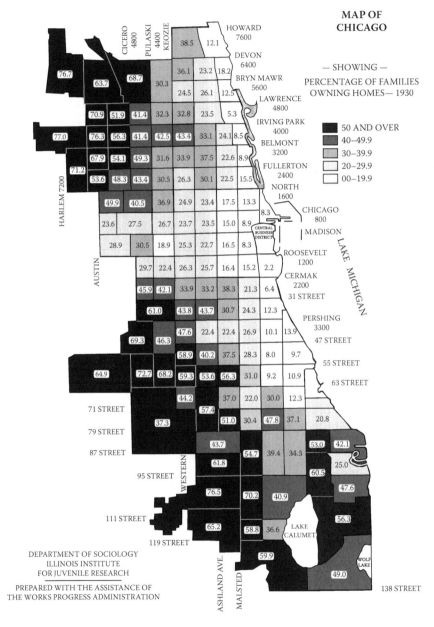

Figure 5.2 Home ownership, Chicago, 1930.

Table 5.4   Rates of Delinquents for Areas Grouped by Percentage of Families Owning Homes: 1927–1933 and 1917–1923 Series

Percentage of Families Owning Homes, 1930		Rate of Delinquents 1927–1933
Under 20	(12.0)*	7.6
20–29.9	(24.3)*	5.1
30–39.9	(33.8)*	3.0
40–49.9	(44.4)*	2.5
50 and over	(62.7)*	2.3

Percentage of Families Owning Homes, 1920		Rate of Delinquents 1917–1923
Under 15	(9.9)*	7.7
15.0–24.9	(20.0)*	6.6
25.0–34.9	(30.0)*	4.4
35.0–44.9	(38.8)*	3.2
45.0 and over	(56.2)*	3.8

* Percentage for class as a whole.

of the relation between rates of delinquents and percentages of home-owning families. The latter measure is no doubt, at the same time, an indication of economic level, of the desirability status of an area, and of mobility. When the correlation ratio is calculated for the 140 areas, the coefficient is reduced greatly by the fact that many apartment areas are characterized both by low rates of delinquents and by low rates of home ownership. It will be noted, however, that the inverse relationship between the two phenomena is almost perfect when the data are treated in the five general classes. In this case, it is the trend alone which is clear, since actual differences within the areas are obscured.

Before closing the discussion of economic characteristics in relation to delinquency, it is necessary to ask: What is the meaning of the facts assembled? In view of the marked degree of covariance throughout the city, it is easy to postulate a causal relationship between economic level and rates of juvenile delinquents. The correlation between rates of families on relief and rates of delinquents (indicated by an r of .89 ± .01) suggests that, where the percentage of dependent families is high, one may confidently expect also a high delinquency rate; yet the former is not in itself an *explanation* of the latter. There was little or no change in the rate of delinquents for the city as a whole from 1929 to 1934, when applications for assistance were mounting daily and the rates of families dependent on public and private relief increased more than tenfold. This would seem to indicate that the relief rate is not itself causally related to rate of delinquents. The patterns of distribution for both phenomena during these years, however, continued to correspond. Rentals, relief, and other measures of economic level fluctuate widely with the business cycle; but it is only as they serve to differentiate neighborhoods from one another that they seem related to the incidence of delinquency. It is when the rentals in an area are low, *relative to other areas in the city*, that this area selects the least-privileged population groups. On the other hand, rates of delinquents, of adult criminals, of infant deaths, and of tuberculosis, for any given area, remain relatively stable from year to year, showing but minor fluctuations with the business cycle. A rise or fall in one is usually accompanied by a corresponding change in the others, as shown in chapter iv (Distribution of Other Community Problems in Chicago, pp. 90–107, in the original), and apparently indicates a change in the relative status of the local area itself.

5.4 Population Composition in Relation to Rates of Delinquents

In Chicago, as in other northern industrial cities, as has been said, it is the most recent arrivals—persons of foreign birth and those who have migrated from other sections of this country—who find it necessary to make their homes in neighborhoods of low economic level. Thus, the newer European immigrants are found concentrated in certain areas, while Negroes from the rural South and Mexicans occupy others of comparable status. Neither of these population categories, considered separately, however, is suitable for correlation with rates of delinquents, since some areas of high rates have a predominantly immigrant population and others are entirely or largely Negro. Both categories, however, refer to groups of low economic status, making their adjustment to a complex urban environment. Foreign-born and Negro heads of families will therefore be considered together,* in order to study this segregation of the newer arrivals, on a city-wide scale.

5.4.1 Percentage of Foreign-Born and Negro Heads of Families

When the rates of delinquents in the 1927–1933 series are correlated with the percentage of foreign-born and Negro heads of families as of 1930, by 140 square-mile areas, the coefficient is found to be .60 ± .03. Similarly, when the 1917–1923 delinquency data are correlated with percentages of foreign-born and Negro heads of families for 1920, by the 113 areas into which the city was divided for that series, the coefficient is .58 ± .04.

---

* The categories "foreign born" and "Negro" are not comparable, since the former group is made up primarily of adults, while the latter includes all members of the race. The classification "heads of families" has been used, therefore, foreign-born and Negro family heads being entirely comparable groupings. The census classification "other races" has been included—a relatively small group, comprising Mexicans, Japanese, Chinese, Filipinos, etc.

When rates of delinquents are calculated for the classes of areas shown in Figure 5.3, wide variations are found between the rates in the classes where the percentage of foreign-born and Negro heads of families is high and in those where it is low. These data are presented in Table 5.5 and in Figure 5.1G and H. Since the number of foreign-born heads of families in the population decreased and the number of Negroes increased between 1920 and 1930, the total proportions of foreign-born and Negro heads of families in each class do not correspond. The variation with rates of delinquents, however, remains unchanged.

While it is apparent from these data that the foreign born and the Negroes are concentrated in the areas of high rates of delinquents, the meaning of this association is not easily determined. One might be led to assume that the relatively large number of boys brought into court is due to the presence of certain racial or national groups were it not for the fact that the population composition of many of these neighborhoods has changed completely, without appreciable change in their rank as to rates of delinquents. Clearly, one must beware of attaching causal significance to race or nativity. For, in the present social and economic system, it is the Negroes and the foreign born, or at least the newest immigrants, who have least access to the necessities of life and who are therefore least prepared for the competitive struggle. It is they who are forced to live in the worst slum areas and who are least able to organize against the effects of such living.

In Chicago three kinds of data are available for the study of nativity, nationality, and race in relation to rates of delinquents. These data concern (1) the succession of nationality groups in the high-rate areas over a period of years; (2) changes in the national and racial backgrounds of children appearing in the juvenile court; and (3) rates of delinquents for particular racial, nativity, or nationality groups in different types of areas at any given moment. In evaluating the significance of community characteristics found to be associated with high rates of delinquents, the relative weight of race, nativity, and nationality must be understood. Therefore, a few basic tables from a more extended forthcoming study will be presented, dealing, in order, with the three types of data referred to above.

Marked changes in population composition characterizing high-delinquency areas are indicated in Table 5.6, which shows for eight inner-city areas* the variation, within the total foreign-born population, of percentages born in each specified country, between 1884 and 1930.†

---

* These eight areas are 50, 52, 58, 66, 71, 79, 80, and 91.
† This tabulation includes most of the adult population, and consequently most of the parents of boys of juvenile court age. For example, in 1920, on the average, the fathers of 87 percent of all boys 10 to 16 years of age in these areas were foreign born. The percentage of delinquent boys in the eight areas in the same period whose fathers were foreign born was very nearly the same (83).

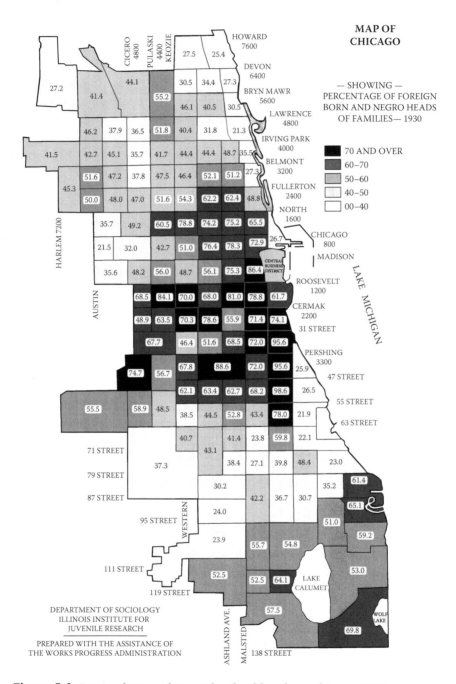

Figure 5.3 Foreign-born and Negro heads of families, Chicago, 1930.

Table 5.5 Rates of Delinquents for Areas Grouped by Percentage of Foreign-Born and Negro Heads of Families: 1930 and 1920

Percentage of Foreign-Born and Negro Heads of Families, 1930		Rate of Delinquents, 1927–1933
70.0 and over	(81.4)*	8.2
60.0–69.9	(64.5)*	4.8
50.0–59.9	(53.9)*	3.9
40.0–49.9	(45.5)*	2.8
Under 40.0	(30.0)*	1.7

Percentage of Foreign-Born and Negro Heads of Families, 1920		Rate of Delinquents, 1917–1923
80.0 and over	(85.3)*	8.4
67.0–79.9	(73.8)*	7.1
54.0–66.9	(60.2)*	4.6
41.0–53.9	(47.6)*	4.1
Under 41.0	(32.3)*	2.6

* Percentage for class as a whole.

Table 5.6 Distribution of Nationalities in the Foreign-Born Population at Intervals from 1884 to 1930, for Eight Chicago Areas Combined*

Country of Birth	Percentage in Total Foreign-Born Population for Eight Areas			
	1884[a]	1898	1920	1930
Germany	46.2	35.9	7.2	6.2
Ireland	22.2	18.7	2.8	2.3
England and Scotland	4.8	3.2	1.5	1.6
Scandinavia	16.9	19.8	2.4	2.0
Czechoslovakia	3.5	6.2	2.8	2.8
Italy	0.4	2.4	21.6	25.5
Poland	2.6	4.2	29.2	34.0
Slavic countries	0.1	2.2	19.6	14.0
All others	3.3	7.4	12.9	11.6
Total	100.0	100.0	100.0	100.0

* These have been areas of first immigrant settlement throughout the period studied.

[a] Area 91 is not included in computations for this column because in 1884 it was outside the boundaries of Chicago.

It is readily evident from the data in Table 5.6 that the proportions of Germans, Irish, English-Scotch, and Scandinavians in the foreign-born population in eight inner-city Chicago areas underwent, between 1884 and 1930, a decided decline (90.1 to 12.2 percent), while the proportions of Italians, Poles, and Slavs increased. As may be seen from a study of the rate maps representing the three juvenile court series, the eight areas maintained, throughout these decades, approximately the same rates of delinquents relative to other areas. Some increased slightly in rank, others dropped slightly; but no trend in either direction was apparent. This is indicated roughly by the fact that the mean percentile ranks for the eight areas, in the juvenile court series of 1927–1933, 1917–1923, and 1900–1906, were, respectively, 83, 85, and 85. It is significant, also, that when most families of a given nationality had moved out of these areas of first settlement, those who remained produced fewer delinquents than would be expected on the basis of their proportion in the population.

These eight areas are but samples of the high-rate areas where changes in the population occurred. A similar analysis of any one of the inner-city areas in Chicago would no doubt reveal great changes in the nationality composition of the population, without discernible effect on the comparative status of the area as to rates of delinquents.

The second type of data available pertaining to the movement of national groups out of the high-rate areas is seen in Table 5.7, which shows, over three decades, the changing proportion of delinquent boys whose fathers were born in each specified country.

Table 5.7   Percentage Distribution of Delinquent Boys by Country of Birth of Their Fathers, for Each Fifth Year Since 1900, Juvenile Court of Cook County

Country of Birth of Fathers	1900	1905	1910	1915	1920	1925	1930
United States							
White	16.0	19.0	16.5	16.5	23.0	21.7	19.5
Negro	4.7	5.1	5.5	6.2	9.9	17.1	21.7
Germany	20.4	19.5	15.5	11.0	6.3	3.5	1.9
Ireland	18.7	15.4	12.3	10.7	6.1	3.1	1.3
Italy	5.1	8.3	7.9	10.1	12.7	12.8	11.7
Poland	15.1	15.7	18.6	22.1	24.5	21.9	21.0
England and Scotland	3.4	3.0	2.5	2.6	0.9	0.7	0.6
Scandinavia	3.8	5.6	2.9	2.8	2.3	0.5	0.8
Austria	0.1	0.3	0.9	1.3	0.8	2.2	1.7
Lithuania	0.1	0.3	1.1	2.9	2.2	3.9	3.8
Czechoslovakia	4.6	4.3	5.5	3.0	2.2	2.8	4.2
All others	8.0	4.5	11.8	10.8	9.1	9.8	11.8
Total	100.0	100.0	100.0	100.0	100.0	100.0	100.0

Source: Shaw and McKay (1931: 95).

Following the shift out of the areas of first settlement on the part of each older immigrant nationality, the proportion of their children among the boys of foreign parentage appearing in the juvenile court underwent a notable decline. Just as they were being replaced in their old areas of residence by more recent immigrants, so their sons were replaced in the dockets of the court by the sons of new arrivals. Further, no evidence exists which would indicate that the children of the nationalities disappearing from the court records are reappearing as children of the native-born children of the native-born descendants of these newcomers. The rates of delinquents in areas populated by these descendants remain low, and in the juvenile court the proportion of boys born of native parents increases less rapidly than the proportion of native-parentage boys in the general population.

Further data dealing with the effect of nationality, nativity, and race on rates of delinquents are presented in Tables 5.8, 5.9, and 5.10. These indicate that the relatively higher rates found among the children of Negroes as compared with those of whites, the children of foreign-born as compared with those of native parents, and the children of recent immigrant nationalities as compared with those of older immigrants may be attributed to the different patterns of distribution of these population groups within the city at a given time rather than to differences in the capacity of their children for conventional behavior.

The data in Tables 5.8, 5.9, and 5.10 support three related propositions. First, comparisons indicate that the white as well as the Negro, the native as well as the foreign born, and the older immigrant nationalities as well as the recent arrivals range in their rates of delinquents from the very highest to the lowest. While each population group at a given moment shows a concentration on certain types of social areas, and hence a characteristic magnitude in rate of delinquents, adequate samples of each may be found also in areas which, for them, are at the time atypical. Thus, as indicated in Table 5.8, rates for children of the foreign born range from 0.53 to 15.45, and those for children of native whites from 0.48 to 14.94. Similarly, the rates for children of such diverse nationality groups as the Poles and the Italians, as well as for all other nationalities taken as a group, display a wide range. Racial comparisons present the same picture, although the variations are not so great. Data presented in Table 5.10 indicate that rates of delinquents among Negro children, as among whites, display wide variation. No racial, national, or nativity group exhibits a uniform, characteristic rate of delinquents in all parts of Chicago.

Second, within the same type of social area, the foreign born and the natives, recent immigrant nationalities, and older immigrants produce very similar rates of delinquents. Those among the foreign born and among the recent immigrants who from 1927 to 1933 lived in physically adequate residential areas of higher economic status displayed low rates of delinquents, while, conversely, those among the native born and among the older immigrants

Table 5.8 Number and Rates of Male Juvenile Delinquents, for Nativity Groups, by Classes of Areas Grouped by Rates of White Delinquents, 1927–1933

Area Rates of White Delinquents	Native White of Native Parentage (NWNP)			Native White of Foreign or Mixed Parentage (NWFP)			Percentage by which Rate for NWFP Exceeds Rate for NWNP
	Boys Aged 10–16	Juvenile Delinquents	Rate of Delinquents	Boys Aged 10–16	Juvenile Delinquents	Rate of Delinquents	
0.0–0.9	15,707	75	0.48	14,684	78	0.53	10.4
1.0–1.9	17,428	225	1.29	23,218	364	1.57	21.7
2.0–2.9	11,213	225	2.01	20,840	546	2.62	30.3
3.0–3.9	8,034	259	3.22	20,021	695	3.47	7.8
4.0–4.9	4,082	167	4.09	11,567	514	4.44	8.6
5.0–5.9	2,471	127	5.14	11,095	616	5.55	8.0
6.0–6.9	1,739	81	4.66	6,805	467	6.86	47.2
7.0–7.9	1,380	80	5.80	4,925	390	7.92	36.6
8.0–8.9	505	44	8.71	1,935	162	8.37	-3.9
9.0–9.9	747	80	10.71	3,029	276	9.11	-14.9
10.0–10.9	401	32	7.98	1,656	182	10.99	37.7
11.0–11.9	418	50	11.96	1,739	193	11.10	-7.2
12.0 and over	308	46	14.94	2,654	410	15.45	3.4
City	64,433	1,491	2.31	124,168	4,893	3.94	70.6
City (standardized)*	64,433	2,080	3.23	124,168	4,537	3.65	13.0

* In this redistribution the racial and national groups in each class of areas were adjusted to correspond with their proportion in the city as a whole, as of 1930. The classes used were based on rates of white delinquents. However, standardization by areas grouped according to median rentals or other index of economic status would no doubt give approximately the same result.

Table 5.9   Rates of Male Juvenile Delinquents for Nativity and Nationality Groups, by Classes of Areas Grouped by Rates of White Delinquents, 1927–1933

Area Rates of White Delinquents	White	Native White of Native Parentage	Native White of Foreign or Mixed Parentage	Polish Origin	Italian Origin	All Other Native White of Foreign or Mixed Parentage
			Rates of Delinquents			
0.0–0.9	0.50	0.48	0.53	0.53	0.89	0.52
1.0–1.9	1.45	1.29	1.57	1.98	2.18	1.35
2.0–2.9	2.41	2.01	2.62	2.97	4.08	2.24
3.0–3.9	3.40	3.22	3.47	3.97	3.73	3.13
4.0–4.9	4.35	4.09	4.44	5.22	5.36	3.75
5.0–5.9	5.48	5.14	5.55	6.11	5.55	4.95
6.0–6.9	6.41	4.66	6.86	7.34	7.95	5.77
7.0–7.9	7.45	5.80	7.92	7.16	9.25	7.66
8.0–8.9	8.44	8.71	8.37	9.43	8.30	7.87
9.0–9.9	9.43	10.71	9.11	9.46	7.37	9.46
10.0–10.9	10.40	7.98	10.99	12.50	11.46	10.08
11.0–11.9	11.27	11.96	11.10	14.48	10.78	9.20
12.0 and over	15.40	14.94	15.45	11.68	18.40	11.76
City	3.38	2.31	3.94	4.58	7.06	2.95
City (standardized)*	3.53	3.23	3.65	3.99	4.29	3.23

* In this redistribution the racial and national groups in each class of areas were adjusted to correspond with their proportion in the city as a whole, as of 1930. The classes used were based on rates of white delinquents. However, standardization by areas grouped according to median rentals or other index of economic status would no doubt give approximately the same result.

who in that period occupied physically deteriorated areas of low economic status displayed high rates of delinquents. Negroes living in the most deteriorated and disorganized portions of the Negro community possessed the highest Negro rate of delinquents, just as whites living in comparable white areas showed the highest white rates.

Third, certain population groups with high rates of delinquents now dwell in preponderant numbers in those deteriorated and disorganized inner-city industrial areas where long-standing traditions of delinquent behavior have survived successive invasions of peoples of diverse origin. By "standardizing" their distribution—that is, creating a hypothetical proportionate redistribution of each nativity, racial, and nationality group throughout the city—it is possible to see the effect of the actual disproportionate concentration of each group at present in the high-rate areas. Table 5.8 indicates that such

Table 5.10   Number and Rates of Male Juvenile Delinquents, for Racial Groups, by Classes of Areas Grouped According to Rate of White Delinquents, 1927–1933

Area Rates of Delinquents	White			Negro			Percentage by which Rate for Negroes Exceeds Rate for Whites
	Boys Aged 10–16	Juvenile Delinquents	Rate of Delinquents	Boys Aged 10–16	Juvenile Delinquents	Rate of Delinquents	
0.0–3.9	120,642	2,461	2.04	574	42	7.32	258.8
4.0–7.9	50,095	2,387	4.76	1,065	181	17.00	257.1
8.0 and over	17,864	1,536	8.60	7,600	1,482	19.50	126.7
City	188,601	6,384	3.38	9,239	1,705	18.45	445.9
City (standardized)*	188,601	6,786	3.60	9,239	1,054	11.41	216.9

* In this redistribution the racial and national groups in each class of areas were adjusted to correspond with their proportion in the city as a whole, as of 1930. The classes used were based on rates of white delinquents. However, standardization by areas grouped according to median rentals or other index of economic status would no doubt give approximately the same result.

standardization reduces the delinquency rate for white children of foreign or mixed parentage from 3.94 to 3.65, and raises the rate for those of native white parentage from 2.31 to 3.23. It is interesting to note that in the unstandardized data the rate for foreign-parentage children in the city as a whole was 70.6 percent greater than the city-wide rate for native-parentage children. Adjustment for disproportionate distribution of these two nativity groups reduced this excess to 13.0 percent. The difficulty of securing areas that are uniform with reference to their social characteristics, however, renders the statistical correction sought in the use of the standardizing procedure only an approximate one at best. It is not valid, for example, to assume that the children of the foreign born residing in areas of predominantly native population live in exactly the same life situation as do the children of native parents. Differences in status, values, and attitudes of associates are known to exist. If these differences could be statistically eliminated (an obvious impossibility), it is safe to assume that the difference in rate between these two nativity groups would approach zero.

Standardization with reference to parental nationality, as indicated in Table 5.9, lowers the Italian rate from 7.06 to 4.29 and the Polish rate from 4.58 to 3.99, while raising the rate of the "all others" group from 2.94 to 3.23. Similarly, Table 5.10 suggests the extent to which the Negro rate is a function of concentration in high-rate areas. Standardization here reduces the Negro rate from 18.45 to 11.41 and raises the white rate from 3.38 to 3.60.

It appears to be established, then, that each racial, nativity, and nationality group in Chicago displays widely varying rates of delinquents; that rates for immigrant groups in particular show a wide historical fluctuation; that diverse racial, nativity, and national groups possess relatively similar rates of delinquents in similar social areas; and that each of these groups displays the effect of disproportionate concentration in its respective areas at a given time. In the face of these facts it is difficult to sustain the contention that, by themselves, the factors of race, nativity, and nationality are vitally related to the problem of juvenile delinquency. It seems necessary to conclude, rather, that the significantly higher rates of delinquents found among the children of Negroes, the foreign born, and more recent immigrants are closely related to existing differences in their respective patterns of geographical distribution within the city. If these groups were found in the same proportion in all local areas, existing differences in the relative number of boys brought into court from the various groups might be expected to be greatly reduced or to disappear entirely.

It may be that the correlation between rates of delinquents and foreign-born and Negro heads of families is incidental to relationships between rates of delinquents and apparently more basic social and economic characteristics of local communities. Evidence that this is the case is seen in two partial correlation coefficients computed. Selecting the relief rate as a fair measure of economic level, the problem is to determine the relative weight of this and other factors. The partial correlation coefficient between rates of delinquents and percentage of families on relief, holding constant the percentage of foreign-born and Negro heads of families, in the 140 areas, is .76 ± .02. However, the coefficient for rates of delinquents and percentage of foreign-born and Negro heads of families, when percentage of families on relief is held constant, is only .26 ± .05. It is clear from these coefficients, therefore, that the percentage of families on relief is related to rates of delinquents in a more significant way than is the percentage of foreign-born and Negro heads of families.

It should be emphasized that the high degree of association between rates of delinquents and other community characteristics, as revealed in this chapter, does not mean that these characteristics must be regarded as causes of delinquency, or vice versa. Within certain types of areas differentiated in city growth, these phenomena appear together with such regularity that their rates are highly correlated. Yet the nature of the relationship between types of conduct and given physical, economic, or demographic characteristics is not revealed by the magnitude either of zero-order or partial correlation coefficients, or of other measures of association.

A high degree of association may lead to the uncritical assumption that certain factors are causally related, whereas further analysis shows the existing association to be entirely adventitious. This is apparently the case with the data on nativity, nationality, and race presented above. That, on the whole, the proportion of foreign-born and Negro population is higher in areas with high rates of delinquents there can be little doubt; but the facts furnish ample basis for the further conclusion that the boys brought into court are not delinquent *because* their parents are foreign born or Negro but rather because of other aspects of the total situation in which they live. In the same way, the relationship between rates of delinquents and each associated variable should be explored, either by further analysis, by experimentation, or by the study of negative cases.

5.5 Summary

5.5.1 Variations in Community Characteristics by Zones

All data presented in this chapter have been tabulated for the same zones used in analyzing the delinquency materials. Table 5.11 and Figure 5.4 bring together the phenomena associated with the 1927–1933 juvenile court series, and Table 5.12 and Figure 5.5 present similar comparisons for the 1917–1923 data.

Table 5.11   Rate of Delinquents, Increase or Decrease of Population, Economic Segregation, and Segregation by Race and Nativity, for 2-Mile Zones, 1927–1933 Juvenile Court Series

Community Characteristics	Zones				
	I	II	III	IV	V
Rate of delinquents	9.8	6.7	4.5	2.5	1.8
Percentage increase or decrease of population, 1920–1930	–21.3	–9.3	12.3	42.9	140.8
Economic Segregation					
Percentage of families on relief, 1934	27.9	24.0	14.8	8.6	5.9
Median rentals, 1930	$38.08	$36.51	$53.08	$65.38	$73.51
Median rentals, 1934	$21.45	$20.44	$29.42	$38.04	$42.52
Percentage of families owning homes, 1930	12.8	21.8	26.2	32.8	47.2
Percentage in domestic and personal services, 1930	14.0	9.1	7.7	7.1	4.7
Segregation by Race and Nativity					
Percentage of foreign-born and Negro heads of families, 1930	62.3	64.9	55.9	40.4	39.4
Percentage of Negroes and other races in total population, 1930	9.5	12.8	10.8	4.9	0.3
Percentage of foreign born in white population, 1930	33.2	33.1	28.7	23.5	20.7
Percentage of aliens in foreign-born population 21 and over, 1930	32.9	27.6	20.0	15.4	14.9
Percentage of aliens in white population 21 and over, 1930	15.0	14.2	8.7	5.0	4.5

It has been shown that, when rates of delinquents are calculated for classes of areas grouped according to rate of any one of a number of community characteristics studied, a distinct pattern appears—the two sets of rates in each case varying together. When values of these other community characteristics, in turn, are calculated for classes of areas grouped by rate of delinquents, the same consistent trends appear, as is seen in Table 5.13.

The data in this chapter indicate a high degree of association between rates of delinquents and other community characteristics when correlations are computed on the basis of values in square-mile areas or similar subdivisions, and a still closer general association by large zones or classes of areas. In the following chapters an attempt will be made to determine how the community conditions in question are related to delinquency—in short, to describe briefly the mechanisms and processes through which these conditions are translated into conduct.

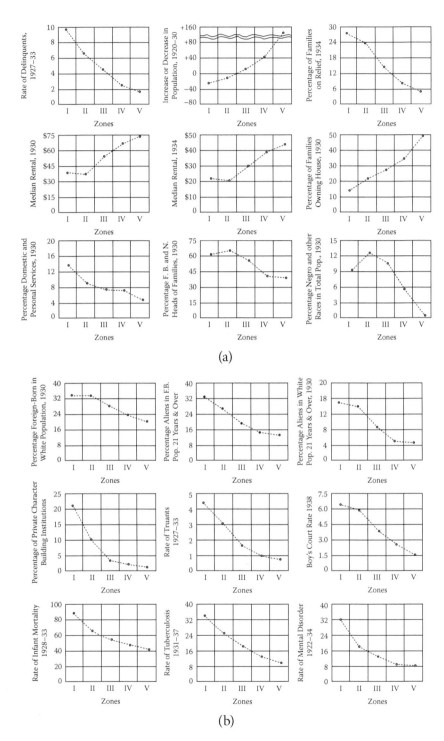

Figure 5.4 Variation in rates of community characteristics, by zones, 1927–1933.

Table 5.12   Rate of Delinquents, Percentage Increase or Decrease of Population, Economic Segregation, Segregation by Race and Nativity, and Employment by Type of Industry, for 2-Mile Zones, 1917–1923 Juvenile Court Series

Community Characteristics	Zones				
	I	II	III	IV	V
Rate of delinquents, 1917–1923	10.3	7.3	4.4	3.3	3.0
Percentage increase or decrease of population, 1910–1920	−22.8	−2.2	35.3	71.0	124.4
Economic Segregation					
Rate of family dependency, 1921	3.0	1.7	0.6	0.4	0.3
Juvenile court dependency cases, 1917–1923	1.7	1.2	0.7	0.5	0.4
Juvenile court mothers' pension cases, 1917–1923	1.7	1.2	0.7	0.4	0.3
Percentage of families owning homes, 1920	11.9	17.5	25.6	31.9	43.6
Segregation by Race and Nativity					
Percentage of foreign-born and Negro heads of families, 1920	72.3	69.7	55.1	42.6	40.6
Percentage of Negroes in total population, 1920	2.5	8.3	4.3	1.6	0.4
Percentage of foreign born in white population, 1920	41.0	37.5	30.1	23.6	22.6
Percentage of aliens in foreign-born population 21 and over, 1920	41.9	33.1	22.5	16.6	16.2
Percentage of aliens in white population 21 and over, 1920	24.0	19.0	9.9	5.7	5.6
Employment by Type of Industry, 1920					
Percentage manufacturing and mechanical	46.6	50.2	43.3	39.3	40.3
Percentage clerical	6.7	9.5	13.0	15.8	15.5
Percentage professional services	3.4	3.2	4.4	5.7	6.4
Percentage domestic and personal services	10.3	7.2	5.3	4.1	3.3

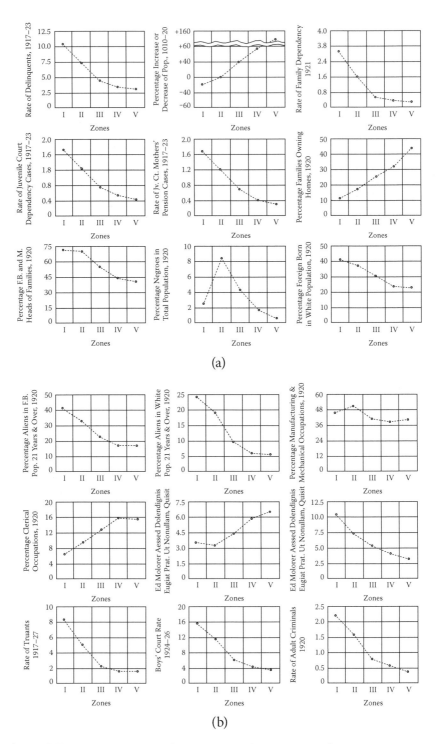

Figure 5.5 Variation in rates of community characteristics, by zones, 1917–1923.

Table 5.13 Community Characteristics, for Areas Grouped by Rate of Delinquents: 1927–1933 and 1917–1923 Series

Community Characteristics	Rates of Delinquents, 1927–1933				
	0.0–2.4 (1.5)*	2.5–4.9 (3.5)*	5.0–7.4 (5.8)*	7.5–9.9 (9.0)*	10.0 and Over (13.5)*
Percentage increase or decrease of population, 1920–1930[a]	59.7	28.6	−6.2	−14.0	−11.8
Median rental, 1930[b]	$67.96	$54.83	$38.19	$35.58	$36.41
Percentage of families on relief, 1934[b]	6.9	11.9	17.1	30.6	40.5
Percentage of families owning homes, 1930[b]	35.9	32.0	27.5	17.5	14.9
Percentage of foreign-born and Negro heads of families, 1930[b]	37.8	50.5	51.8	69.3	81.9
Rate of truants, 1927–1933[b]	0.7	1.5	2.8	3.9	5.4
Rate of young adult offenders, 1938[b]	1.7	3.0	4.6	6.9	11.5
Rate of infant mortality, 1928–1934[c]	41.8	55.1	72.0	72.9	78.3
Rate of mental disorder, 1922–1934[c]	9.4	12.5	19.0	26.9	23.6
Rate of tuberculosis, 1931–1937[d]	9.9	13.2	19.7	27.8	64.6

Community Characteristics[a]	Rates of Delinquents, 1917–1923				
	0.0–2.9 (2.0)*	3.0–5.9 (4.2)*	6.0–8.9 (7.1)*	9.0–11.9 (10.0)*	12.0 and Over (14.1)*
Percentage increase or decrease of population, 1910–1920	67.9	43.4	−0.4	−10.4	−19.2
Percentage of families owning homes, 1920	33.6	28.4	22.7	16.8	10.0
Percentage of foreign-born and Negro heads of families, 1920	43.9	52.4	68.4	75.5	77.6
Rate of truants, 1917–1927	0.9	2.0	5.1	7.6	9.8
Boys' court cases, 1924–1926	3.1	5.5	11.8	17.1	21.6
Juvenile court dependents, 1917–1923	0.3	0.7	1.1	1.6	2.4
Family dependency, 1921	0.2	0.6	1.7	2.1	2.6

* Rate for class as a whole.

[a] By 113 areas.

[b] By 140 areas.

[c] By 120 areas.

[d] By 60 areas.

5.6 Conclusion*

5.6.1 Summary and Interpretation

It is clear from the data included in this volume that there is a direct relationship between conditions existing in local communities of American cities and differential rates of delinquents and criminals. Communities with high rates have social and economic characteristics which differentiate them from communities with low rates. Delinquency—particularly group delinquency, which constitutes a preponderance of all officially recorded offenses committed by boys and young men—has its roots in the dynamic life of the community.

It is recognized that the data included in this volume may be interpreted from many different points of view. However, the high degree of consistency in the association between delinquency and other characteristics of the community not only sustains the conclusion that delinquent behavior is related dynamically to the community but also appears to establish that all community characteristics, including delinquency, are products of the operation of general processes more or less common to American cities. Moreover, the fact that in Chicago the rates of delinquents for many years have remained relatively constant in the areas adjacent to centers of commerce and heavy industry, despite successive changes in the nativity and nationality composition of the population, supports emphatically the conclusion that the delinquency-producing factors are inherent in the community.

From the data available it appears that local variations in the conduct of children, as revealed in differential rates of delinquents, reflect the differences in social values, norms, and attitudes to which the children are exposed. In some parts of the city attitudes that support and sanction delinquency are, it seems, sufficiently extensive and dynamic to become the controlling forces in the development of delinquent careers among a relatively large number of boys and young men. These are the low-income areas, where delinquency has developed in the form of a social tradition, inseparable from the life of the local community.

This tradition is manifested in many different ways. It becomes meaningful to the child through the conduct, speech, gestures, and attitudes of persons with whom he has contact. Of particular importance is the child's intimate association with predatory gangs or other forms of delinquent and criminal organization. Through his contacts with these groups and by virtue of his participation in their activities he learns the techniques of stealing, becomes involved in binding relationships with his companions in delinquency, and acquires the attitudes appropriate to his position as a member

---

* Editor's note: This forms the conclusion to the whole work, not only to sections included here.

of such groups. To use the words of Frank Tannenbaum: "It is the group that sets the pattern, provides the stimulus, gives the rewards in glory and companionship, offers the protection and loyalty, and, most of all, gives the criminal life its ethical content without which it cannot persist."*

In these communities many children encounter competing systems of values. Their community, which provides most of the social forms in terms of which their life will be organized, presents conflicting possibilities. A career in delinquency and crime is one alternative, which often becomes real and enticing to the boy because it offers the promise of economic gain, prestige, and companionship and because he becomes acquainted with it through relationships with persons whose esteem and approbation are vital to his security and to the achievement of satisfactory status. In this situation the delinquent group may become both the incentive and the mechanism for initiating the boy into a career of delinquency and crime and for sustaining him in such a career, once he has embarked upon it.

In cases of group delinquency it may be said, therefore, that from the point of view of the delinquent's immediate social world, he is not necessarily disorganized, maladjusted, or antisocial. Within the limits of his social world and in terms of its norms and expectations, he may be a highly organized and well-adjusted person.

The residential communities of higher economic status, where the proportion of persons dealt with as delinquents and criminals is relatively low, stand in sharp contrast to the situation described above. Here the norms and values of the child's social world are more or less uniformly and consistently conventional. Generally speaking, the boy who grows up in this situation is not faced with the problem of making a choice between conflicting systems of moral values. Throughout the range of his contacts in the community he encounters similar attitudes of approval or disapproval. Cases of delinquency are relatively few and sporadic. The system of conventional values in the community is sufficiently pervasive and powerful to control and organize effectively, with few exceptions, the lives of most children and young people.

In both these types of communities the dominant system of values is conventional. In the first, however, a powerful competing system of delinquency values exists; whereas in the second, such a system, if it exists at all, is not sufficiently extensive and powerful to exercise a strong influence in the lives of many children. Most of the communities of the city fall between these two extremes and represent gradations in the extent to which delinquency has become an established way of life.

It is important to ask what the forces are which give rise to these significant differences in the organized values in different communities. Under

---

* Tannenbaum (1938: 475).

what conditions do the conventional forces in the community become so weakened as to tolerate the development of a conflicting system of criminal values? Under what conditions is the conventional community capable of maintaining its integrity and exercising such control over the lives of its members as to check the development of the competing system? Obviously, any discussion of this question at present must be tentative. The data presented in this volume, however, afford a basis for consideration of certain points which may be significant.

It may be observed, in the first instance, that the variations in rates of officially recorded delinquents in communities of the city correspond very closely with variations in economic status. The communities with the highest rates of delinquents are occupied by those segments of the population whose position is most disadvantageous in relation to the distribution of economic, social, and cultural values. Of all the communities in the city, these have the fewest facilities for acquiring the economic goods indicative of status and success in our conventional culture. Residence in the community is in itself an indication of inferior status, from the standpoint of persons residing in the more prosperous areas. It is a handicap in securing employment and in making satisfactory advancement in industry and the professions. Fewer opportunities are provided for securing the training, education, and contacts which facilitate advancement in the fields of business, industry, and the professions.

The communities with the lowest rates of delinquents, on the other hand, occupy a relatively high position in relation to the economic and social hierarchy of the city. Here the residents are relatively much more secure; and adequate provision is offered to young people for securing the material possessions symbolic of success and the education, training, and personal contacts which facilitate their advancement in the conventional careers they may pursue.

Despite these marked differences in the relative position of people in different communities, children and young people in all areas, both rich and poor, are exposed to the luxury values and success patterns of our culture. In school and elsewhere they are also exposed to ideas of equality, freedom, and individual enterprise. Among children and young people residing in low-income areas, interests in acquiring material goods and enhancing personal status are developed which are often difficult to realize by legitimate means because of limited access to the necessary facilities and opportunities.

This disparity in the facilities available to people in different communities for achieving a satisfactory position of social security and prestige is particularly important in relation to delinquency and crime in the urban world. In the city, relationships are largely impersonal. Because of the anonymity in urban life, the individual is freed from much of the scrutiny and control which characterize life in primary-group situations in small towns and rural communities. Personal status and the status of one's community are, to a very great extent, determined by economic achievement. Superior status depends not so much on character as on the possession of those goods and values which symbolize success. Hence, the kind of clothes one wears, the automobile one drives, the type of building in which one lives, and the physical character of one's community become of great importance to the person. To a large degree these are the symbols of his position—the external evidences of the extent to which he has succeeded in the struggle for a living. The urban world, with its anonymity, its greater freedom, the more impersonal character of its relationships, and the varied assortment of economic, social, and cultural backgrounds in its communities, provides a general setting particularly conducive to the development of deviations in moral norms and behavior practices.

In the low-income areas, where there is the greatest deprivation and frustration, where, in the history of the city, immigrant and migrant groups have brought together the widest variety of divergent cultural traditions and institutions, and where there exists the greatest disparity between the social values to which the people aspire and the availability of facilities for acquiring these values in conventional ways, the development of crime as an organized way of life is most marked. Crime, in this situation, may be regarded as one of the means employed by people to acquire, or to attempt to acquire, the economic and social values generally idealized in our culture, which persons in other circumstances acquire by conventional means. While the origin of this tradition of crime is obscure, it can be said that its development in the history of the community has been facilitated by the fact that many persons have, as a result of their criminal activities, greatly improved their economic and social status. Their clothes, cars, and other possessions are unmistakable evidence of this fact. That many of these persons also acquire influence and power in politics and elsewhere is so well known that it does not need elaboration at this point. The power and affluence achieved, at least temporarily, by many persons involved in crime and illegal rackets are well known to the children and youth of the community and are important in determining the character of their ideals.

It may be said, therefore, that the existence of a powerful system of criminal values and relationships in low-income urban areas is the product of a cumulative process extending back into the history of the community and of the city. It is related both to the general character of the urban world and to the fact that the population in these communities has long occupied a disadvantageous position. It has developed in somewhat the same way as have all social traditions, that is, as a means of satisfying certain felt needs within the limits of a particular social and economic framework.

It should be observed that, while the tradition of delinquency and crime is thus a powerful force in certain communities, it is only a part of the community's system of values. As was pointed out previously, the dominant tradition in every community is conventional, even in those having the highest rates of delinquents. The traditionally conventional values are embodied in the family, the church, the school, and many other such institutions and organizations. Since the dominant tradition in the community is conventional, more persons pursue law-abiding careers than careers of delinquency and crime, as might be expected.

In communities occupied by Orientals, even those communities located in the most deteriorated sections of our large cities, the solidarity of Old World cultures and institutions has been preserved to such a marked extent that control of the child is still sufficiently effective to keep at a minimum delinquency and other forms of deviant behavior. As Professor Hayner has pointed out the close integration of the Oriental family, the feeling of group responsibility for the behavior of the child, and the desire of these groups to maintain a good reputation in American communities have all been important elements in preserving this cultural solidarity.*

It is the assumption of this volume that many factors are important in determining whether a particular child will become involved in delinquency, even in those communities in which a system of delinquent and criminal values exists. Individual and personality differences, as well as differences in family relationships and in contacts with other institutions and groups, no doubt influence greatly his acceptance or rejection of opportunities to engage in delinquent activities. It may be said, however, that if the delinquency tradition were not present and the boys were not thus exposed to it, a preponderance of those who become delinquent in low-income areas would find their satisfactions in activities other than delinquency.

In conclusion, it is not assumed that this theoretical proposition applies to all cases of officially proscribed behavior. It applies primarily to those delinquent activities that become embodied in groups and social organizations. For the most part, these are offenses against property, which comprise a very large proportion of all the cases of boys coming to the attention of the courts.

5.6.2 Implications for Prevention and Treatment

The theoretical formulation set forth in the preceding pages has certain definite implications with regard to the task of dealing with the problem of delinquency in large American cities. Some of the more important may be stated as follows:

1. Any great reduction in the volume of delinquency in large cities probably will not occur except as general changes take place which effect improvements in the economic and social conditions

---

* See Norman S. Hayner, "Five Cities of the Pacific Northwest," Chapter 16 in the original edition of Juvenile Delinquency and Urban Areas.

surrounding children in those areas in which the delinquency rates are relatively high.

2. Individualized methods of treatment probably will not be successful in a sufficiently large number of cases to result in any substantial diminution of the volume of delinquency and crime.

3. Treatment and preventive efforts, if they are to achieve general success, should increasingly take the form of broad programs which seek to utilize more effectively the constructive institutional and human resources available in every local community in the city. Tannenbaum states this point vividly: "The criminal is a product of the community, and his own criminal gang is part of the whole community, natural and logical to it; but it is only part of it. In that lies the hope that the rest of the community can do something with the gang as such."*

5.6.3 A Program of Community Action

It is suggested that one way in which current methods of dealing with the problem of delinquency in high-rate areas may be strengthened is through programs of community action, initiated and carried on by the concerted efforts of citizens and local residents interested in improvement of the community life in all its aspects. Such programs provide an opportunity to all residents to use their talents, energies, interests, and understanding in a common effort to strengthen, unify, and extend the constructive forces of the community. Through the leadership of local residents it is possible to effect a closer coordination of local institutions, groups, and agencies into a unified program for the area as a whole. By this means those private organizations maintained by persons residing outside of the community may take on more of the nature of instrumentalities through which the local residents seek to deal with their own problems.

It was for the purpose of assisting in the development of such programs of community action in low-income areas that in 1932 the Institute for Juvenile Research and the Behavior Research Fund initiated the work of what is now known as the Chicago Area Project, a private corporation with a board of directors made up of prominent citizens interested in delinquency prevention. Aid in the form of funds and personnel has been provided by foundations and a variety of city-wide public and private agencies, as well as by local residents, institutions, and agencies. The major features of the project are here set forth briefly, in order to indicate one way in which constructive forces in a neighborhood may be more effectively utilized.

---

* Tannenbaum (1938: 474).

The Neighborhood as the Unit of Operation. The local community area or neighborhood is the unit of operation in the Chicago Area Project. Thus far, activities have been developed in six small geographic areas, varying in size from approximately 1/2 square mile to 2 1/2 square miles, with populations ranging from 10,000 to 50,000. The work is developed upon a neighborhood basis because it is assumed that delinquency is a product chiefly of community forces and conditions and must be dealt with, therefore, as a community problem, even though it is recognized that the delinquency-producing communities themselves may be products of more general processes.

Planning and Management by Local Residents. In each area the activities are planned and carried on by a committee composed of representative local citizens. These committees include members of churches, societies, labor unions, trades and professions business groups, athletic clubs, and a miscellany of other groups and organizations. These committees function as boards of directors and assume full responsibility for sponsoring and managing all aspects of the community program.

This procedure of placing responsibility for the planning and managing of the program in the hands of local residents stands in sharp contrast to traditional procedures whereby many institutions and programs operating in low-income areas have been controlled and managed by boards of directors whose members live, for the most part, in outlying residential areas. Although the local residents may be partly dependent upon sources of financial support outside the community, they assume full leadership in the management of their welfare activities. They are participants in a creative enterprise in which their talents, capacities, and energies find opportunities for expression in socially significant affairs of the neighborhood. Instead of suffering the humiliations often entailed in receiving the services of philanthropy, they achieve a sense of self-reliance, preserve their self-respect, and enhance their status among their neighbors by contributing time and energy to the creation of better opportunities for children. The Area Project program is, therefore, a development by the people within a local community rather than a ready-made program or institution imposed from the outside. It seeks to build solidarity and unity of sentiments among the people by encouraging and aiding them to work together toward common objectives.

Employment of Local Workers. In so far as practicable, the staff in each neighborhood is recruited locally. Indigenous workers have intimate and significant relationships with local organizations, institutions, groups, and persons which are of great value in promoting programs of social action. Through institutes and training courses the local leaders are familiarized with the specialized knowledge and techniques necessary to their program work.

The emphasis placed upon local residents does not in any way minimize the value of the services of skilled, specially trained workers. By operating in conjunction with or through the committees of local residents, the professional worker in these communities has a chance to translate his special knowledge more effectively into the thinking, planning, and practices of the neighborhood people. While there is much that the lay resident can learn from the professional, it is equally true that the professional can learn from the lay resident.

Utilizing and Coordinating Community Resources. In developing the work in each area, the committee of local residents seeks the cooperation of churches, schools, recreation centers, labor unions, industries, societies, clubs, and other social groupings in a program of concerted action for the improvement of the neighborhood. The mothers and fathers participating in the citizens' committees, who understand the problems of their communities and have a vital interest in all local matters that bear upon the lives of their children and young people, thereby become instrumentalities through which the services of welfare agencies in the community are coordinated.

Activity Programs. Through the sponsorship of the committees of residents a great variety of activities is carried on. These include recreation, summer camping, scouting, handicraft, forums, and interest trips. Efforts have been made to improve housing, the physical appearance of the area, and sanitary conditions. Parent-teacher groups have been organized to effect a more satisfactory working relationship between school and community. To a limited extent, employment opportunities for young persons have been augmented. Especial attention has been directed to the task of providing for the needs of problem children and delinquents. In so far as possible, the committees concern themselves with all phases of community life, with special emphasis on those which bear upon the well-being of children.

Credit Given to Local Residents. It has been an established policy of the Chicago Area Project that all publicity concerning the program activities in the neighborhood shall be controlled by the local committees and that all credit for accomplishments in connection with the program shall be given to the local residents and the organizations and agencies cooperating with them. Actually the work of the project has been publicized primarily by reports released by the local committees. The board of directors and staff of the Chicago Area Project function as aids to these committees.

In this description of the Chicago Area Project no attempt has been made to give a detailed picture of the many activities and accomplishments of the program. Complete reports are being prepared by certain of the local neighborhood committees. At least two such reports will be ready for publication within the next year.

It may be said, however, that the achievements of the committees have been sufficiently outstanding to demonstrate the feasibility and desirability of programs of neighborhood action as a means of making more effective the welfare activities carried on in low-income areas of large cities. In each community where such programs have been undertaken, the residents have responded enthusiastically. They have demonstrated that they possess, contrary to widespread opinion, the talents and capabilities essential to effective participation in the planning and management of welfare institutions, agencies, and programs. As already suggested, they have planned, developed, and operated summer camps and community centers, planned and promoted health and sanitation programs, functioned effectively in relation to the improvement of their schools, contributed in a significant manner to the adjustment of juvenile and adult offenders, and in many other ways initiated activities designed to further the welfare of children and young people.

Altogether apart from what the achievements of the Area Project may be, the data in this volume provide a basis for the conclusion that programs for the prevention of delinquency in low-income areas of American cities are not likely to succeed unless they can effect certain basic changes in the conditions of life surrounding children. As long as the present condition exists, little change in the volume of delinquency should be expected.

Year after year, decade after decade, large cities—and especially certain areas in large cities—send to the courts an undiminished line of juvenile offenders. Year after year, decade after decade, likewise, society continues to organize or construct new agencies or institutions designed to reduce the number of these offenders and to rehabilitate those who have already offended against the law. Perhaps the unsatisfactory results of these treatment and prevention efforts have been due, in part at least, to the fact that our attention has been focused too much upon the individual delinquent and not enough upon the setting in which delinquency arises.

James S. Plant, on the basis of many years' experience in a psychiatric clinic, arrives at somewhat the same conclusion. He states:

> Society is, and has been, aroused over its misfits and the mass of human breakdown that is in the wake of its progress. It has erected every conceivable type of agency to study, salvage, or merely sweep up this debris. As the wreckage mounts, new agencies are demanded or "better standards of service" asked of those existing. The folly of believing that happiness and goodness can be fabricated by machinery (agencies) will be exposed only when we understand that the ills, corruptions, and hypocrisies of a cultural pattern flow into the child and man and "become a part of him for the day, for the year, or for stretching cycles of years." If it is true that the triumphs and tragedies of the street flow into and become a part of the child, then all programs of personality change must manage somehow to change the street.*

---

* Plant (1937: 18).

Whether or not we care to admit it, most delinquent boys reflect all too accurately what they have learned in the process of living in their own communities. If we wish to have fewer delinquents, or if we wish to modify the mode of life of those who already are delinquent, a way must be found to modify those aspects of the community life which provide the appropriate setting for delinquency careers and which give to these careers the sanction and approbation on which all social behavior depends.

Urban Ecological Aspects of Crime in Akron (1974)

6

G.F. PYLE
E.W. HANTEN
P.G. WILLIAMS
A.L. PEARSON II
J.G. DOYLE
K. KWOFIE

From Pyle, G.F., Hanten, E.W., Williams, P.G., Pearson, A. L. II, Doyle, J.G., and Kwofie, K. (1974). Urban ecological aspects of crime in Akron. In *The Spatial Dynamics of Crime* (pp. 103–141). Chicago: Department of Geography, University of Chicago.

Contents

6.1	Crime Numbers and Rates	126
6.2	A Canonical Approach to Multivariate Analysis of the Akron Area Crime Data	129
6.3	The Canonical Analysis of Summit County Data	132
	6.3.1 Factor I	134
	6.3.2 Factor II	138
	6.3.3 Factor III	138
	6.3.4 Factor IV	139
	6.3.5 Factor V	140
6.4	The Akron Canonical Analysis	140
	6.4.1 Factor I	141
	6.4.2 Factor II	143
	6.4.3 Factor III	144
	6.4.4 Factor IV	144
6.5	The Relative Value of the Canonical Analyses	145
	6.5.1 Crime-Distance Gradients	145
6.6	Additional Comments	154

The previous chapters serve as the building blocks for this chapter. It is possible to test some of the contentions revealed by the cartographic analysis (Chapter III, The Spatial and Temporal Distribution of Crime Index Offenses within Summit County, in the original) and to compare these results with those of the related studies described in Chapters II and IV. The approach is "urban ecological" in that crime data are compared to socioeconomic, demographic, and land use characteristics of census tracts in the study area. The analyses within this chapter are thus static in nature because they do not take into account the movements of criminal offenders within the study area and other aspects of criminal behavior. However, an interaction analysis follows in Chapter VI (An Exploration of Crime-Related Behavior within Akron, in the original). The statistical results are presented in full cognizance of the possible "ecological fallacies" which can result in such studies. In other words, certain statistical combinations of census tract characteristics and crime data are not taken as a blanket indictment of all persons dwelling within a particular area; however, the associations uncovered can tell us something about combinations of urban conditions which help "explain" the distribution of different kinds of crimes.

6.1 Crime Numbers and Rates

While it was useful within Chapter III to understand the specific locations of various crimes utilizing the actual amount of crime as a constant frame of reference, the more sophisticated statistical analysis developed here requires the use of some additional methods of scaling. For example, the discussion of the uniform application of rates derived by calculating the number of offenses of a specific crime in relation to census population of Chapter II indicates that several researchers in this area, for example, Lottier (1938), Boggs (1965), and Rengert (1972), have spelled out some of the possible pitfalls encountered by such application. In order that these problems be avoided here, some comparisons have been made as an aid in the selection of appropriate crime measures for the multivariate analysis which follows later in this chapter.

This comparison was accomplished in several steps. First, actual crime rates per 1000 persons for all nine crimes being studied were calculated. In addition, the rate of armed robberies per 1000 commercial structures and the rate of residential burglaries per 1000 dwelling units were determined. All of the rates mentioned above were then put to a pairwise correlation analysis which included the actual numbers of crimes as mapped in Chapter III. This procedure was carried out for the entire study area and for Akron with suburban areas removed. Table 6.1 includes the pairwise correlations for both sample sets of crime data. The correlations for Akron make up the lower triangle of the table, and those within the upper triangle are for the entire study area.

Table 6.1 Pairwise Correlations Comparing Rates and Numbers[1]

	1	2	3	4	5	6	7	8	9	10	11	12	13	14	15	16	17	18	19	20
1		.340	.273	.124	.307	.345	.136	-.023	.334	.854	.280	.103	.012	.209	.451	.066	-.071	.137	.214	.481
2	.319		.533	.373	.452	.443	.382	.079	.435	.313	.805	.302	.250	.304	.463	.208	.118	.257	.318	.457
3	.228	.504		.705	.532	.422	.497	.041	.718	.219	.507	.736	.596	.465	.456	.444	.288	.583	.526	.441
4	.067	.346	.707		.428	.155	.522	.153	.556	.101	.572	.808	.898	.505	.341	.583	.521	.600	.695	.350
5	.363	.484	.554	.405		.482	.345	.179	.492	.291	.327	.288	.224	.724	.509	.189	.144	.273	.454	.508
6	.339	.364	.319	.041	.478		.359	.178	.478	.158	.076	-.016	-.049	.061	.607	-.099	-.201	-.032	.295	.528
7	.194	.390	.575	.613	.324	.110		.487	.467	.160	.389	.479	.471	.321	.283	.521	.405	.366	.202	.294
8	.065	.372	.585	.541	.410	.553	.671		.116	-.103	.911	.638	.115	.001	-.112	.082	.424	-.004	-.064	-.114
9	.302	.362	.617	.502	.487	.360	.496	.678		.272	.431	.544	.404	.425	.540	.343	.251	.678	.512	.490
10	.880	.275	.115	.036	.255	.084	.190	-.055	.173		.414	.179	.042	.327	.505	.167	-.005	.234	.179	.518
11	.258	.790	.464	.553	.317	-.071	.454	.321	.323	.379		.587	.553	.463	.456	.479	.410	.543	.391	.438
12	.037	.240	.696	.809	.258	-.182	.570	.424	.474	.108	.542		.908	.609	.389	.816	.693	.873	.413	.349
13	-.036	.223	.600	.908	.205	-.148	.574	.463	.376	-.005	.539	.916		.455	.201	.725	.670	.677	.405	.214
14	.219	.290	.418	.493	.707	-.040	.395	.389	.360	.314	.444	.599	.446		.649	.660	.546	.667	.435	.559
15	.474	.373	.204	.217	.504	.355	.190	.076	.277	.488	.345	.248	.109	.665		.470	.248	.520	.541	.933
16	.032	.153	.381	.565	.150	-.251	.591	.352	.254	.125	.442	.806	.715	.665	.422		.843	.791	.215	.277
17	-.079	.140	.370	.589	.150	-.287	.479	.473	.314	.063	.474	.803	.737	.632	.314	.930		.701	.135	.149
18	.062	.167	.474	.562	.221	-.243	.416	.366	.595	.156	.480	.857	.670	.656	.380	.786	.834		.393	.445
19	.150	.254	.423	.653	.439	.794	.196	.184	.365	.090	.314	.329	.365	.396	.416	.134	.161	.270		.529
20	.512	.368	.229	.245	.500	.403	.221	.045	.254	.496	.333	.216	.137	.543	.098	.305	.181	.262	.412	

Note: Actual occurrences: 1: Homicide; 2: Rape; 3: Unarmed robbery; 4: Armed robbery; 5: Aggravated assault; 6: Residential burglary[2]; 7: Nonresidential burglary[2]; 8: Larceny[2]; 9: Automobile theft[2]. Rates per 1000 inhabitants: 10: Homicide rate[2]; 11: Rape rate[2]; 12: Unarmed robbery rate[2]; 13: Armed robbery rate; 14: Aggravated assault rate; 15: Residential burglary rate; 16: Nonresidential burglary rate; 17: Larceny rate; 18: Automobile theft rate. 19: Armed robberies per 1000 commercial buildings[2]; 20: Residential burglaries per 1000 dwelling units.

[1] The lower triangle is for Akron alone; the upper is for the entire study area.

[2] Actual variables selected for the canonical analyses.

Table 6.2   Violent Crime Correlations for Akron and Study Area

	Akron	Study Area
Rape	.790	.805
Unarmed robbery	.696	.736
Armed robbery	.908	.898
Aggravated assault	.707	.724

Table 6.3   Property Crime Correlations for Akron and Study Area

	Akron	Study Area
Residential burglary	.355	.507
Nonresidential burglary	.591	.521
Larceny	.473	.424
Automobile theft	.595	.678

Examination of Table 6.1 reveals that there are indeed some reasons to be wary of the uniform application of population rates to our data.* The problem is, in fact, more serious for property crimes than violent crimes, as would be expected. For example, when dealing with homicide, the pairwise correlation between rates and numbers for Akron is .880, and the same statistical associations for the entire study is .854. Table 6.2 shows correlations between rates and numbers for other violent crimes.

Conversely, different correlations showed up when comparing rates and numbers for property crimes, and these findings strongly influenced the final selection of variables used in multivariate analysis. Table 6.3 shows the pairwise correlations between population rates and numbers for property crimes.

The correlations for property crimes (Table 6.3) clearly indicate that it is inappropriate to uniformly apply population rates to all these crimes. However, as previously indicated, other kinds of rates should be tested for some of these crimes. The cartographic analysis accomplished in Chapter III, for example, showed that in 1971, high rates of residential burglary showed up for some areas made up predominantly of dwelling units. As indicated within Table 6.1, the correlations developed for residential burglaries per 1000 dwelling units against numbers and population rates for burglaries showed some interesting and useful comparisons. Within Akron, the correlation between the number of residential burglaries and the actual burglary rate per 1000 dwelling units was .403, and the same correlation for the entire

---

* When dealing with Chapter III comparisons of north central states and cities, it was necessary to reduce the crime data to rates in order to avoid the problem of numbers of crimes in relation to city size.

study area was .607. However, when utilizing population rates, the differences are only slight. The correlation between residential burglaries calculated on the basis of population and the dwelling unit method proved to be .908 for Akron and .933 for the study area as a whole. It could be argued by virtue of this association that it is statistically safe to use population rates in a multivariate analysis; however, the alternate rate was selected as a more direct measure.

However, when viewing violent crimes once more, the correlations for population rates and number for armed robbery were very high. These crimes are known to be concentrated within commercial areas, and for this reason, the measure selected for the multivariate analysis was armed robberies per 1000 commercial structures.

In general, Table 6.1 was used to make the following decisions with regard to the selection of variables for the canonical factor analysis developed in this chapter. Population rates were considered acceptable for the following violent crimes: homicide, rape, and aggravated assault. Actual numbers of crimes were used for unarmed robbery, nonresidential burglary, larceny, and auto theft. Rates used for armed robbery and residential burglary have already been indicated. Maps showing the rates as they pertain to Akron have been included here as Figures 6.1 to 6.5. Clearly, when the spatial distributions of rates are compared to numbers, the patterns for rape, homicide, armed robbery, and aggravated assault are similar (see Figures 10 to 12, pp. 64–67, in the original). These are the variables with the highest spatial correlations. Conversely, Figure 6.1, the map showing residential burglary per dwelling unit, is very different from Figure 15 (p. 71, in the original), the map showing actual numbers.

6.2 A Canonical Approach to Multivariate Analysis of the Akron Area Crime Data

Many earlier studies have indicated the strength of associations uncovered by simple pairwise correlations. The previous section confirms some of these earlier findings. Furthermore, the more elaborate modeling of particular combinations of dependent and independent variables for multiple regression has attempted to explain more complex interrelationships. However, the problems of collinearity and spurious relationships often cloud the findings of such studies. For example, variables such as percent Negro, percent of dwelling units vacant, unemployment, and percent of population below poverty level may all appear to combine to develop a high coefficient of determination in a multiple regression against some given crime variable. Close examination of the stepwise variance of the regression model may reveal that in fact only one of these variables is contributing most of the variance, and

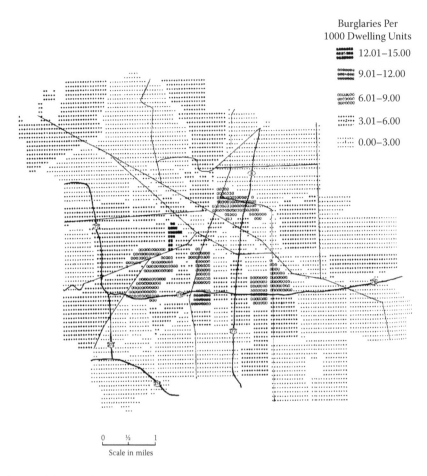

Burglaries Per
1000 Dwelling Units

    12.01–15.00

    9.01–12.00

    6.01–9.00

    3.01–6.00

    0.00–3.00

0   ½   1
Scale in miles

Figure 6.1 Residential burglary, 1971.

all are highly intercorrelated. Scholars using the more conventional forms of
orthogonally rotated factor analytic solutions have often created other problems. For example, when crime variables are combined with socioeconomic
and other indicator variables to arrive at independent dimensions in factor
analysis, there is the risk of having some dimensions entirely composed of
crime data while still other dimensions may contain no crime data. Still there
are certain aspects of both multiple regression and factor analysis which lend
these methods, or some combination of the two, to the analysis of urban
crime data.

Within the area of medical geography, for example, at least three successful applications of canonical analysis have been developed. In 1971,
Matulionis compared hospital-related morbidity (criterion) data to socioeconomic characteristics (predictors) of population groups in Buffalo to
find racial and ethnic health problem distinctions. In a less extensive study,

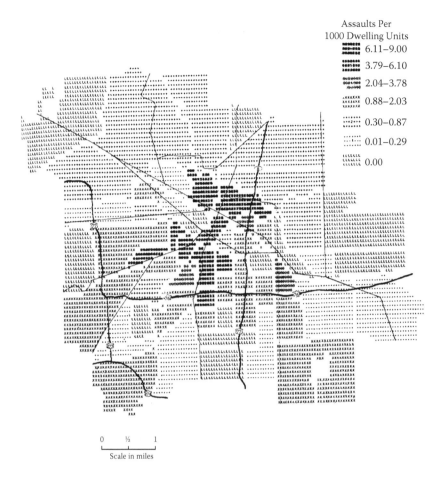

Figure 6.2 Aggravated assault, 1971.

Monmonier (1972) compared mortality rates and socioeconomic data for states of the United States and found strong age associations. Also, during 1972–73 a study was carried out by Lauer with the support of the Northeast Ohio Regional Medical Program using canonical analysis to examine mortality rates and population characteristics for Summit County, Ohio (Lauer 1973). Lauer showed the associations between poverty and disease to be so strong in Summit County that the first two dimensions in his canonical factor analysis related solely to high mortality rates and low income.

Canonical analysis has, therefore, demonstrated a high degree of success when used to compare sets of data similar to our Summit County information. Other methods had proved to be less successful in urban crime studies because of differences in reporting procedures; however, as indicated by Hotteling in his pioneer contributions, canonical analysis is particularly appropriate in various sampling situations (Hotteling 1936). It has already

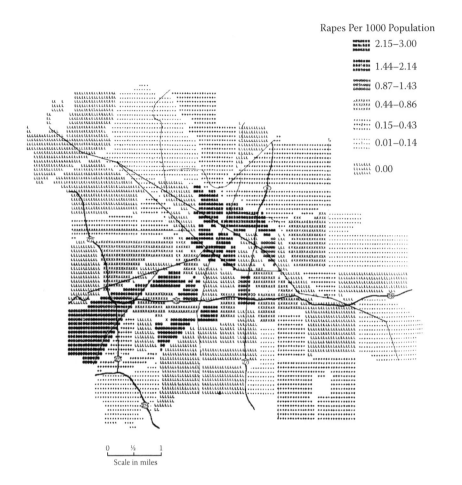

Rapes Per 1000 Population
- 2.15–3.00
- 1.44–2.14
- 0.87–1.43
- 0.44–0.86
- 0.15–0.43
- 0.01–0.14
- 0.00

0   ½   1
Scale in miles

Figure 6.3 Rape, 1971.

been indicated that reporting is a problem in analyses of crime data (Chapters II, III, and IV). Indeed, our discussions of the information system developed here have already indicated such a problem in Summit County. Given this reporting constraint, it would appear the canonical analysis is appropriate to our analysis for yet another reason.

6.3 The Canonical Analysis of Summit County Data

The first of two canonical factor analyses in this chapter considers the ninety-four census tracts comprising our Summit County study area. Initially, 49 variables were selected as the predictor set. Preliminary testing of pairwise correlations among the predictor set made it necessary to drop seven which were too highly intercorrelated with others, thus decreasing the possibility of

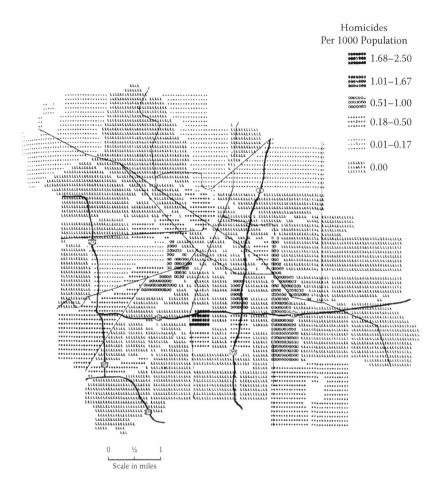

Homicides
Per 1000 Population

1.68–2.50

1.01–1.67

0.51–1.00

0.18–0.50

0.01–0.17

0.00

0   ½   1

Scale in miles

Figure 6.4 Homicide, 1971.

the occurrence of statistical collinearity. In addition, three predictor variables demonstrated nonsignificant correlations with the criterion (crime) variables. Table 6.4 thus contains the remaining thirty-nine variables comprising the final predictor set. As can be determined from the table, the predictor set includes static socioeconomic, land use, general demographic, and dynamic (change) variables.

The above predictor variables were combined with the crime variables in the form already mentioned within the Cooley–Lohnes canonical factor analysis. Five of the ten factors were considered significant in this analysis on the basis of the statistics shown in Table 6.5.

In general, both the redundancy and variance extracted showed a higher emphasis on the first factor of the criterion set than the predictor set. However, when the factor loadings shown within Table 6.5 are interpreted, the reader should be aware of the fact that with successive factors within the

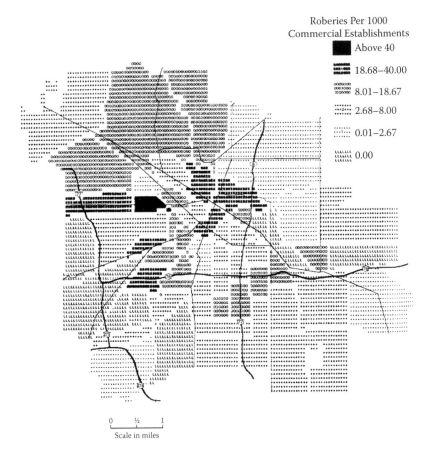

Roberies Per 1000
Commercial Establishments

Above 40

18.68–40.00

8.01–18.67

2.68–8.00

0.01–2.67

0.00

0   ½   1
Scale in miles

Figure 6.5 Armed robbery, 1971.

predictor set, numerically lower loadings become increasingly important. In other words, Factor IV shows a redundancy of .024 for the predictor set and .043 for the criterion set, thus making predictor variable loadings of .269 and .289 worthy of consideration. Conversely, the most important criterion loading is .538. Clearly, the first dimension is the most important, and it is useful to examine each of these factors separately (Table 6.6).

6.3.1 Factor I

Reference once more to Table 6.5 reveals that four crimes load highly on the first factor: unarmed robbery, automobile theft, homicide, and residential burglary. In turn, the most significant predictor set loadings are: percent of the tract area composed in expressways, streets, and alleys (.578), percent of male labor force unemployed (.664), percent of female labor force employed as blue collar workers (.608), percent of families with less than $5,000 annual

Table 6.4   Socioeconomic Variables

1	Population change, 1960–1970
2	Net residential density, 1970
3	Percent residential structures built before 1950
4	Percent units lacking some or all plumbing, 1970
5	Percent dwelling units vacant
6	Percent dwelling units owner occupied
7	Percent of tract in commercial land
8	Percent of tract in wholesale and manufacturing
9	Percent of tract in expressways, streets, and alleys
10	Percent same households as in 1965
11	Percent of school enrolled population in high school
12	Percent 16 to 21 not high school graduates and not enrolled
13	Median school years completed
14	Percent work force not commuting by auto
15	Percent male labor force over 16 unemployed
16	Percent female labor force over 16 unemployed
17	Percent males employed blue collar
18	Percent females employed blue collar
19	Percent families with annual income less than $5,000
20	Percent families with annual income $5,000 to $9,999
21	Percent families with annual income $10,000 to $14,999
22	Percent families with annual income $15,000 to $24,999
23	Percent families with annual incomes over $25,000
24	Percent families below poverty level
25	Median income
26	Percent population under 5 years old
27	Coefficient of change under 5 years, 1960–1970
28	Coefficient of change age 5 to 9 years, 1960–1970
29	Coefficient of change age 10 to 14, 1960–1970
30	Percent population 15 to 19 years of age
31	Coefficient of change age 15 to 19, 1960–1970
32	Coefficient of change age 20 to 24, 1960–1970
33	Percent population 45 to 64 years of age
34	Coefficient of change age 45 to 64, 1960–1970
35	Percent of population over 65 years of age
36	Coefficient of change age 65, 1960–1970
37	Percent Negro, 1970
38	Coefficient of change percent Negro, 1960–1970
39	Coefficient of change percent Negro, 1950–1970

Table 6.5   Summit County Canonical Factor Structure

		I	II	III	IV	V
	Criterion Set Factors					
1	Unarmed robbery	0.715	−0.488	0.329	0.081	0.300
2	Nonresidential burglary	0.297	−0.012	0.643	0.542	0.246
3	Larceny	0.089	0.003	0.423	0.210	−0.174
4	Automobile theft	0.696	−0.512	0.095	0.024	−0.001
5	Homicide	0.665	0.148	−0.075	0.351	−0.321
6	Rape	0.152	−0.169	−0.254	−0.015	0.538
7	Aggravated assault	0.227	−0.008	0.084	−0.395	0.184
8	Armed robbery	0.251	−0.163	−0.381	−0.025	0.263
9	Residential burglary	0.846	0.389	−0.107	−0.099	0.231
	Predictor Set Factors					
1	Population Change, 1960–1970	−0.539	0.060	−0.105	0.097	−0.254
2	Residential density, 1970	0.279	−0.373	0.277	0.084	0.598
3	Percent residential structures before 1950	0.299	−0.171	−0.117	−0.023	0.247
4	Percent units lacking plumbing, 1970	0.194	−0.249	0.389	0.289	0.378
5	Percent dwelling units vacant	0.436	−0.199	0.128	−0.000	0.332
6	Percent dwelling units owner occupied	−0.520	0.341	−0.122	0.066	−0.127
7	Percent of tract in commercial land	0.289	−0.394	0.346	−0.021	0.234
8	Percent of tract in wholesale and manufacturing	0.250	0.037	0.360	0.070	−0.144
9	Percent of tract streets	0.578	−0.065	0.004	−0.168	0.369
10	Percent same household as in 1965	−0.034	0.337	0.055	0.205	−0.031
11	Percent population in high school	−0.005	0.314	0.277	0.202	0.200
12	Percent 16 to 21 not high school graduates or enrolled	0.453	0.004	−0.074	0.100	0.196
13	Median school years completed	−0.615	−0.050	−0.157	0.004	−0.012
14	Percent work force not commuting by auto	0.239	−0.151	0.123	0.001	0.233
15	Percent male labor force over 16 unemployed	0.664	−0.102	0.193	0.020	0.282
16	Percent female labor force over 16 unemployed	0.501	0.204	−0.090	−0.123	0.082
17	Percent male employed blue collar workers	0.493	0.030	0.148	−0.056	0.110
18	Percent female employed blue collar workers	0.608	0.100	0.157	0.003	0.048
19	Percent families with annual income less than $5,000	0.732	−0.097	0.196	−0.029	0.205

Table 6.5   Summit County Canonical Factor Structure (*Continued*)

		I	II	III	IV	V
20	Percent families with annual income $5,000 to $9,999	0.289	−0.089	0.057	−0.179	0.232
21	Percent families with annual income $10,000 to $14,999	−0.546	0.173	−0.041	−0.007	−0.111
22	Percent families with annual income $15,000 to $24,999	−0.541	0.144	−0.077	0.060	−0.252
23	Percent families with annual incomes over $25,000	−0.227	−0.038	−0.149	0.082	−0.213
24	Percent families below poverty level	0.776	0.006	0.260	−0.051	0.133
25	Median income	−0.487	0.049	−0.239	0.045	−0.211
26	Percent population under 5 years old	0.399	0.472	−0.035	−0.172	0.213
27	Coefficient of change, under 5 years	−0.121	−0.004	−0.390	−0.269	−0.052
28	Coefficient of change, age 5 to 9	−0.101	0.093	0.158	0.108	−0.088
29	Coefficient of change, age 10 to 14	−0.134	0.089	0.141	0.141	−0.159
30	Percent population 15 to 19 years old	−0.075	0.087	0.169	0.101	−0.069
31	Coefficient of change, age 15 to 19	−0.449	−0.068	−0.182	0.010	−0.118
32	Coefficient of change, age 20 to 24	−0.118	0.079	0.149	0.074	−0.069
33	Percent population 45 to 64 years	−0.049	0.134	0.156	0.271	0.112
34	Coefficient of change, age 45 to 64	−0.518	0.208	0.013	0.099	−0.306
35	Percent of population over 65 years	0.363	−0.236	0.055	0.117	0.173
36	Coefficient of change, age 65	−0.116	0.062	0.094	0.362	−0.136
37	Percent Negro, 1970	0.881	0.139	0.045	−0.075	0.027
38	Coefficient of change percent Negro, 1960–1970	0.230	−0.114	−0.380	0.184	−0.078
39	Coefficient of change percent Negro, 1950–1970	0.240	−0.100	−0.386	0.042	0.011

Table 6.6   Summit County Canonical
Analysis Statistical Summary of Factors

Factor	R^2	X^2	Degree of Factor	Significance Level
1	0.929	627.77	351	0.001
2	0.808	444.11	304	0.005
3	0.703	329.55	259	0.015
4	0.554	245.16	216	0.05
5	0.526	189.09	175	0.25

income (.734), percent of families below poverty level (.776), and percent Negro (.881).

With the exception of the first of the predictor variables mentioned above, these are all indicators of the complex crime-poverty syndrome identified by previous researchers. The variable related to streets and expressways may, to some degree, imply greater accessibility on the part of the criminal offenders, but these data are for the entire study area. Many, but not all, of the poverty areas within Akron are characterized by a larger relative share of urban thoroughfares, and this loading may simply be a reflection of urban as opposed to suburban land use allocations. However, this variable takes on a more easily explainable loading in the results of the city of Akron canonical factor analysis.

6.3.2 Factor II

The second factor has been interpreted here, as is often the case with the results of a conventional factor analysis, to be a negative vector. Therefore, higher inverse loadings among both the criterion and predictor sets are considered to be associated. The highest crime variable loadings are for unarmed robbery (–.488) and automobile theft (–.512) and the most important predictor loadings are: percent of tract in commercial land (–.394), net residential density (–.373), and percent of population over 65 years of age (–.236). The variance extracted for these sets is, respectively, .081 and .034.

This interesting combination of variables is not unexpected for such associations had already been implied in our cartographic analysis (Chapter III). For example, the crime variables were two for which we had sufficient suburban data to map our entire study area meaningfully, the obvious implication being that these crimes tend to be more important in suburban locations than some of the crimes. Also, unarmed robbery, particularly in the form of mugging, is known to occur in more densely populated parts of Akron, and the victims are often the elderly. However, according to Table 6, p. 48 (in the original), only 4 percent of the actual victims of the above crime were over sixty-five years of age. This association is no doubt somewhat spurious, because an earlier study of crime in Summit County (G.F. Pyle 1971) showed a similar association when put to a stepwise regression analysis. The issue, in fact, becomes one of understanding the entire complex set of social and physical environmental circumstances underlying the known problem of crime victimization of the elderly poor literally trapped within aging and deteriorating neighborhoods.

6.3.3 Factor III

This dimension is characterized by a larger variance extracted for both sets, the criterion figure being .105 and predictor .040. The important loadings are accordingly higher. Again, the crime data combining within the criterion set here, larceny (.423), and nonresidential burglary (.643) are meaningful for suburban as well as central city analysis. The three most important predictor variables are: percent of dwelling units lacking some or all plumbing facilities (.389), an obvious sign of low-quality housing; percent of tract area in commercial land (.346); and percent of tract area in wholesale and manufacturing land uses (.360).

The cartographic analysis within Chapter III already has pointed out the problems inherent within the reporting system for larceny. However, this proportionately heavier suburban reporting has combined with known facts with regard to locations of both larceny (shopping centers) and nonresidential burglary to produce a combination of variables considered quite important. This factor supports the earlier findings of T. Morris (1957) in his comparison of department store thefts, and particularly those of Lottier (1938). Also the implications of this factor with regard to housing are similar to the findings of Rengert (1972). Conversely, the association uncovered in this study pertaining to manufacturing areas, is to our knowledge, one of the first of such findings. Few, if any, researchers in the area of urban crime have demonstrated close ties between urban crime and proximity to manufacturing land. There may be several reasons for this lack of finding, of which no small one is the bias toward anomie rather than opportunity structure. This association showed up in our analysis for at least two reasons. The first, and more obvious, reason is that our burglary data were subdivided into residential and nonresidential. The second reason is the actual use of canonical factor analysis as a method of identification of this association. It is suggested here that researchers in future studies consider these procedures in their endeavors.

6.3.4 Factor IV

Two crimes with high loadings on other factors combine as important criterion variables within this factor, nonresidential burglary (.542) and homicide (.351). However, some of the predictor variables are different. The variance extracted from the predictor set is only .018, thus making even lower loadings important. For example, significant predictors include units lacking sound plumbing (.289), an opportunity structure association also showing up within Factor III; change from 1960–1970 within the under five years of age cohort (.269), percent of population forty-five to sixty-five years of age (.271), and change from 1960–1970 with the over sixty-five years of age cohort (.362). For the first time in this analysis some importance can be attributed to static demographic and age change variables. Clearly, this finding is in keeping with some of the more classical ecological studies and the possible implications of anomie.

6.3.5 Factor V

This dimension includes unarmed robbery (.300), rape (.538), and armed robbery (.263) loading similarly with net residential density (.598), structures lacking plumbing (.378), percent of tract in expressways, streets and alleys (.369). This is obviously not the most significant factor. Unarmed robbery is clearly more important within the first two factors; however, the loading cannot be completely ignored. The housing variable, while important to two other factors (III and IV) is important particularly with regard to understanding patterns of rape. In part, the two robbery loadings can again be explained to the transportation variable, thus further supporting the earlier contention that urban access is a contributing element for this kind of crime.

The strongest association by far is that between rape and population density, and this finding is in agreement with many of the study results reviewed in Chapters II and IV of this study. Interestingly, while population density also was important to Factor II, the strongest loading for that variable row-wise is contained within the fifth factor. Thus, poor housing and density combine to best explain at least the actual reporting of this crime. It is also worthy of note that many studies of urban crime simply accept population density as an indicator for most crimes, and yet our study results for Summit County suggest that only a limited degree of crime can be attributed to density.

Two variables, aggravated assault and armed robbery, have not been explained well by this analysis. Only Factor V shows any moderate loading for armed robbery, while none of the factors (Table 6.5) contain an important loading for aggravated assault. It should be remembered that these crimes demonstrated almost no reporting at all from suburban locations during 1971, thus making a statistical comparison for the entire study area almost impossible. Fortunately, these crimes and some of the others can be more easily explained when viewing a canonical factor analysis for Akron without suburbs.

6.4 The Akron Canonical Analysis

More pronounced results are discernable when viewing the results of the canonical analysis for the fifty-nine Akron census tracts. However, obvious patterns of similarity with the Summit County canonical analysis do exist. More importantly, it is possible to derive a better explanation for all nine crime variables, and all thirty-nine predictor variables show some degree of importance in "explaining" one or more of the crimes. In this instance, a four- rather than five-factor solution proves to be significant.

The statistics shown in Table 6.7 also accompany the four leading factors.

**Table 6.7   Akron Canonical Analysis
Statistical Summary of Factors**

Factor	R^2	X^2	Degrees of Freedom	Significance Level
I	.981	482.38	351	.001
II	.917	346.91	304	.050
III	.868	263.69	259	.500
IV	.805	195.94	216	.200

The redundancy and variance extracted measures demonstrate a pattern of decreasing value with subsequent factors, similar to the Summit County analysis; however, for both of the Akron sets of data the amount of variance extracted is proportionately higher for both criterion and predictor sets when compared to the Summit County results. Table 6.8 contains the factor structure for the Akron analysis.

6.4.1   Factor I

More than half of the criterion variables have the highest loading on the first factor (variance extracted = .292). These crime variables are, with loadings:

Homicide (.565)
Rape (.498)
Aggravated assault (.715)
Armed robbery (.532)
Residential burglary (.949)

With the exception of the burglary variables, these measures all represent violent crimes, and it is again worthy of note that burglary clustered with violent crimes within the Chapter III factor analysis for the north central states. The most important predictor variables for this factor were:

Percent female blue collar workers (.717)
Percent male unemployed (.629)
Percent female unemployed (.645)
Percent below poverty level (.808)
Percent with annual incomes less than $5,000 (.719)
Percent Negro (.896)

Also of interest are high inverse loadings for median income and median education.

Table 6.8   Akron Canonical Factor Structure

		I	II	III	IV
	Criterion Set Factors				
1	Unarmed robbery	0.380	0.569	0.258	0.154
2	Nonresidential burglary	0.289	0.349	0.553	−0.101
3	Larceny	0.081	0.530	0.225	−0.087
4	Automobile theft	0.362	0.539	0.139	0.171
5	Homicide	0.565	0.204	0.079	0.460
6	Rape	0.498	0.395	−0.423	−0.042
7	Aggravated assault	0.715	0.480	0.083	−0.406
8	Armed robbery	0.532	0.087	−0.143	0.343
9	Residential burglary	0.949	−0.261	0.066	−0.020
	Predictor Set Factors				
1	Population change, 1960–1970	−0.553	−0.245	0.220	0.331
2	Residential density, 1970	0.169	0.389	−0.017	−0.153
3	Percent residential structures before 1950	0.065	0.090	−0.228	0.022
4	Percent units lacking plumbing, 1970	0.201	0.436	0.036	−0.095
5	Percent dwelling units vacant	0.336	0.400	−0.240	−0.142
6	Percent dwelling units owner occupied	−0.348	−0.583	0.190	0.192
7	Percent of tract in commercial land	0.122	0.485	0.188	−0.141
8	Percent of tract in wholesale and manufacturing	0.219	0.282	0.321	−0.156
9	Percent of tract streets	0.446	0.001	−0.024	−0.206
10	Percent same household as in 1965	−0.008	−0.395	0.311	0.171
11	Percent population in high school	0.192	−0.228	0.328	−0.093
12	Percent 16 to 21 not high school graduates or enrolled	0.476	0.171	−0.275	0.008
13	Median school years completed	−0.616	−0.267	0.006	0.085
14	Percent work force not commuting by auto	0.104	0.209	0.000	−0.163
15	Percent male labor force over 16 unemployed	0.629	0.196	0.104	−0.080
16	Percent female labor force over 16 unemployed	0.645	−0.003	−0.167	−0.132
17	Percent male employed blue collar workers	0.481	0.176	−0.059	−0.103
18	Percent female employed blue collar workers	0.717	0.240	−0.044	−0.079
19	Percent families with annual income less than $5,000	0.719	0.455	−0.118	−0.203
20	Percent families with annual income $5,000 to $9,999	0.124	0.151	−0.202	−0.263
21	Percent families with annual income $10,000 to $14,999	−0.571	−0.399	0.186	0.152
22	Percent families with annual income $15,000 to $24,999	−0.474	−0.387	0.240	0.165
23	Percent families with annual incomes over $25,000	−0.172	−0.104	0.061	0.083

Table 6.8   Akron Canonical Factor Structure (*Continued*)

		I	II	III	IV
24	Percent families below poverty level	0.808	0.385	−0.001	−0.230
25	Median income	−0.544	−0.410	0.160	0.201
26	Percent population under 5 years old	0.505	−0.412	0.176	−0.078
27	Coefficient of change, under 5 years	−0.276	−0.362	0.015	0.421
28	Coefficient of change, age 5 to 9	−0.171	−0.103	0.323	0.352
29	Coefficient of change, age 10 to 14	−0.136	−0.087	0.380	0.348
30	Percent population 15 to 19 years old	−0.064	0.021	0.285	0.225
31	Coefficient of change, age 15 to 19	−0.393	−0.005	−0.151	0.105
32	Coefficient of change, age 20 to 24	−0.507	−0.096	0.039	0.143
33	Percent population 45 to 64 years	−0.115	−0.166	−0.331	−0.070
34	Coefficient of change, age 45 to 64	−0.356	−0.296	0.383	0.197
35	Percent of population over 65 years	0.024	0.201	0.118	0.080
36	Coefficient of change, age 65	−0.348	−0.061	0.323	0.179
37	Percent Negro, 1970	0.896	0.135	−0.012	0.024
38	Coefficient of change percent Negro, 1960–1970	0.050	−0.128	−0.109	0.463
39	Coefficient of change percent Negro, 1950–1970	−0.006	−0.179	−0.149	0.355

Essentially, this factor contains all violent crimes except unarmed robbery in combination with residential burglary. Once again, the crime-poverty syndrome can be seen operating. In this instance, a clear-cut "inner city" association is manifested. Those parts of the city containing the poorest people, the least well educated, the most unemployed, and the highest number of families with women employed in unskilled occupations are most exposed to crimes of violence. Furthermore, the addition of the burglary element emphasized the aspect of the poor stealing from the poor, and this condition is further analyzed within Chapter VI.

6.4.2 Factor II

This particular factor (Table 6.8, column 2) contains high criterion set loadings for the following crime variables: unarmed robbery (.569), larceny (.530), and automobile theft (.539). There are also moderately high loadings for rape and aggravated assault, but these variables have their highest loadings within Factor I. The most important predictor variables (variance extracted = .169) are:

Population density (.389)
Percent of dwelling units without sound plumbing (.436)
Percent of dwelling units vacant (.400)

Percent of land in commercial use (.485)
Percent of families with annual income less than $5,000 (.455)

Once again, a dimension is uncovered related to a mix of land uses, deteriorating housing conditions, and general residential transition to other uses. This finding confirms some of the results of earlier studies placing emphasis on opportunity structure theories as well as social anomie. Also, this factor is similar to the second factor of the Summit County canonical solution; however, the previous solution does not include larceny with the other crimes. This is significant because of different methods used for the reporting of larceny in suburban locations. Thus, the data reflecting a uniform method of reporting places larceny more appropriately into the crime combination shown in the Chapter III factor analysis of thirty north central states cities. In general, this factor shows a combination of criterion and predictor variables known to coexist within many inner-city areas.

6.4.3 Factor III

The third factor demonstrates the highest loading (.553) on a single variable, nonresidential burglary. This factor is similar to the fourth factor in the Summit County analysis, but there are substantially more predictor variables with high loadings in this instance. For example, the most important predictor variables (variance extracted = .073) include:

Percent of land in wholesale use (.321)
Percent of families in the same household as in 1965 (.311)
Percent of population enrolled in high school (.328)
Percent of change in 5 to 9 year age cohort 1960–1970 (.323)
Percent of change in 10 to 14 year age cohort 1960–1970 (.380)
Percent of population 45 to 64 years of age 1970 (.331)
Percent of change in 45 to 64 age cohort 1960–1970 (.383)
Percent of change in over 65 years of age cohort 1960–1970 (.323)

The results of this combination indicate once more an association between wholesale-manufacturing related land use and nonresidential burglary, and the importance of this finding should not be under-estimated by law enforcement officials. Most of the remainder of the predictor variables tend to be other sorts of conditions of high nonresidential burglary areas, that is, conditions indicative of urban transition.

6.4.4 Factor IV

The fourth factor is manifested by a high loading on homicide (.460), but this crime also had a high loading within the first factor of the Akron solution.

However, this factor is still worthy of consideration because some different predictor variables show up as important. For example, three variables indicating demographic transition have high loadings: change within the under five year age cohort, 1960–1970 (.421), change within the five to nine year age cohort (.352), and change within the ten to fourteen year age cohort. In addition, and this combination did not show up at all within the Summit County solution, both variables reflecting racial change demonstrate high loadings.

The statistical association uncovered here can be interpreted as a reflection of high murder rates in areas of urban demographic transition. The changes in age structure go hand in hand with racial change. This combination is evidence of the known problem of the increased availability of handguns in "ghettoizing" parts of cities. In addition, the finding supports the documentation of other researchers in the area of either racial or juvenile aspects of crime (see Lentz 1956; Sutherland and Cressey 1966; Schulz 1969; Boggs 1965, Reckless 1967; and Allison 1972). Still, this factor can only be considered as a secondary explanation to homicide in Akron due to the higher loading of that crime on the first factor. The fact that it showed up in such a manner, however, indicates the many-faceted explanation of this crime.

6.5 The Relative Value of the Canonical Analyses

The two canonical analyses can be viewed as part of a static urban ecological approach to understanding crime in Akron and Summit County. As with the cartographic analysis within Chapter III, the contradicting definitions of crimes contained within the suburban reporting are rather obvious. On the other hand, many of the known urban ecological aspects of crime spelled out in earlier urban ecological analyses of other cities (Chapters II and IV) can be seen operating within the two canonical analyses. In addition, some interesting new contributions to the literature have been made, particularly with regard to understanding the opportunities structure method of interpretation and the added dimensionality of homicide within Akron. It is now also worthwhile to compare so-called "gradients" of crime within Akron as an added interpretation of the urban ecological analysis.

6.5.1 Crime-Distance Gradients

Generally, those researchers attempting to understand crime in relation to distance from some central portion of a city have either hypothesized a general decreasing "gradient" with increased distance away from the commercial core (Shaw 1929; Shaw and McKay 1942) by applying concentric zones a la Burgess (1925), hypothesized more property crimes taking place within the central business district (De Fleur 1967), have suggested that crime rates are higher for commercial areas (Lander 1954), or have implied that violent crimes are more dispersed than property crimes (Schmid 1960a, 1960b). Such an analysis is also accomplished for the city of Akron, but several constraints are applied due to the findings uncovered earlier in this study. In other words, the cartographic analysis indicated that some crimes appear to be centralized while others are more dispersed. The canonical analyses indicate that there are some associations that can be related to socioeconomic conditions, others can be tied to lack of social cohesion, others to opportunities, and still others to both demographic and physical environmental urban transition.

In order to account for all the above elements while still testing for distance-decay gradients, it is necessary to accomplish this without loss of the importance of the "predictor" variables. It would be easy enough to test through use of a conventional factorial ecology; however, we do have prior knowledge of the differential importance of thirty-nine crime-specific variables. The testing is therefore accomplished in several steps:

1. The thirty-nine variables used for the canonical factor analyses are put to Johnson's clustering algorithm (Harvey 1971; Pyle 1973) to determine six crime-specific ecological areas of Akron.
2. For each of the six areas crimes are divided into either property or violent groups, and the number of crimes within each census tract is compared to distance from the commercial core by crime groups. Therefore, there are two gradients for each of the six ecological areas.
3. Statistics are fit to each gradient to determine various slopes.

The resultant crime-specific ecological areas are shown within Figure 6.6, and these areas can be loosely defined as shown in Table 6.9. After the grouping solution was completed, a mean was determined for each variable as the data pertain to various census tracts comprising specific groups. The algorithm produced groups which in fact range in items of demographic characteristics and availability of resources. These are defined here as Groups I through VI, respectively. Groups I and II represent areas of the cities with less than average financial resources; Groups V and VI comprise areas containing more than the average amount of financial resources within Akron. The other two groups are transitional. If the cartographic pattern within Figure 6.6 resembles any of the more traditional "urban ecological" theories of spatial differentiation, it is that espoused by Hoyt (1933, 1939) in his classical high-income/low-income sector theory.

When the gradients developed for the various groups are analyzed, some strong regularities can be determined (Figures 6.7a to f). Some of these regularities are in agreement with those of the earlier studies mentioned above, but there are also some pronounced differences. Due to the differences in

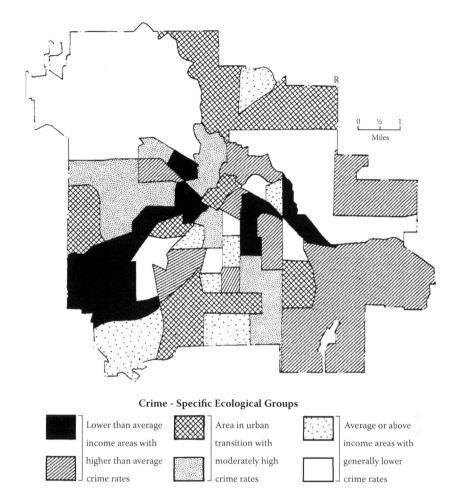

Crime - Specific Ecological Groups

■	Lower than average income areas with higher than average crime rates	▨	Area in urban transition with moderately high crime rates	⬚	Average or above income areas with generally lower crime rates

Figure 6.6 Clustering solution for crime-related variables.

sample sizes, only a simple linear regression fit was determined for purposes of comparison. Table 6.10 indicates the regression slopes that resulted.

As indicated by the regression slopes in Table 6.10 and Figures 6.7a to f, violent crimes for the most part displayed decreasing numbers with distance away from the commercial core. As already indicated, these slopes continue to drop once the suburbs are reached. One group (Group IV, Figure 6.6), however, displayed a very dispersed pattern of violent crimes with a slope of 0.18. While this pattern is in agreement with Schmid's findings, the areas are characterized by census tracts of an urban transitional nature, as well as racial change over the past two decades. In part, this finding supports that of Factor IV in the Akron canonical analysis.

The gradients for property crimes tell a different story. Those developed for the three lowest income groups consist of negative slopes, and this

Table 6.9 Crime-Specific Ecological Groups within Akron

	Variables	I	II	III	IV	V	VI	City
1	Population change, 1960–1970	0.856	0.953	0.857	0.798	0.877	0.980	0.902
2	Net residential density, 1970	30.936	30.833	26.100	26.550	26.143	23.540	27.380
3	Percent residential structures built before 1950	84.545	83.242	86.933	86.550	84.671	83.187	90.362
4	Percent units lacking some or all plumbing, 1970	4.400	4.467	10.150	3.075	3.543	3.293	4.436
5	Percent dwelling units vacant	12.945	5.533	5.400	5.287	7.457	4.913	6.939
6	Percent dwelling units owner occupied	45.082	53.642	59.600	52.487	61.114	60.340	55.085
7	Percent of tract in commercial land	8.627	4.000	6.100	4.612	4.686	3.460	5.103
8	Percent of tract in wholesale and manufacturing	9.673	8.933	7.683	5.362	4.843	5.880	7.198
9	Percent of tract in expressways, streets, and alleys	26.600	18.967	22.250	25.187	23.000	20.160	22.349
10	Percent same households as in 1965	48.336	50.333	56.250	52.850	58.486	56.520	53.444
11	Percent of school enrolled population in high school	22.036	20.742	27.367	24.537	25.657	24.413	23.688
12	Percent 16 to 21 not high school graduates and not enrolled	17.482	17.633	15.833	15.312	20.029	13.707	16.393
13	Median school years completed	10.655	10.925	11.300	11.087	10.914	10.520	11.644
14	Percent of work force not commuting by auto	19.545	21.792	19.850	14.312	13.329	19.807	18.652
15	Percent male labor force over 16 unemployed	14.618	5.333	7.250	4.287	5.314	4.660	6.944
16	Percent female labor force over 16 unemployed	6.400	5.767	6.350	7.662	5.343	7.273	6.534
17	Percent males employed blue collar workers	68.109	75.492	74.117	71.987	74.314	66.620	71.105
18	Percent females employed blue collar workers	44.664	44.883	39.467	42.762	42.243	36.347	41.520
19	Percent families annual income less than $5,000	22.845	22.908	26.383	23.837	22.143	19.407	22.395

20	Percent annual income $5,000 to $9,999	35.791	38.475	32.350	36.687	33.600	31.007	34.632
21	Percent annual income $10,000 to $14,999	28.118	26.825	28.350	26.850	29.871	28.253	27.949
22	Percent annual income $15,000 to $24,999	10.755	10.833	10.850	13.375	13.329	16.087	12.797
23	Percent annual income over $25,000	3.618	0.992	2.017	1.737	1.086	5.453	2.832
24	Percent families below poverty level	12.527	12.392	14.283	12.925	10.957	10.427	12.012
25	Median income	8426.633	8584.164	8788.644	8968.000	9356.285	10427.730	9187.945
26	Percent population under 5 years old	12.800	9.417	9.083	8.500	8.857	8.173	9.507
27	Coefficient of change under 5 years, 1960–1970	0.698	0.795	0.701	0.647	0.611	0.757	0.716
28	Coefficient of change age 5 to 9 years, 1960–1970	1.414	0.918	0.715	0.733	0.776	0.835	0.927
29	Coefficient of change age 10 to 14, 1960–1970	1.473	0.965	0.672	0.841	0.810	0.966	0.995
30	Percent population 15 to 19 years of age	9.236	12.483	8.767	8.825	11.700	9.393	10.125
31	Coefficient of change age 15 to 19, 1960–1970	1.258	1.635	1.285	1.183	1.309	1.401	1.370
32	Coefficient of change age 20 to 24, 1960–1970	1.499	1.527	1.344	1.267	1.416	1.850	1.537
33	Percent population 45 to 64 years of age	19.809	18.175	23.233	21.725	28.943	22.287	21.798
34	Coefficient of change age 45 to 64, 1960–1970	0.861	0.846	0.837	0.791	0.956	0.995	0.891
35	Percent of population over 65 years of age	13.145	10.450	12.677	12.837	15.357	13.213	12.786
36	Coefficient of change age 65, 1960–1970	1.059	1.218	0.852	0.997	1.215	1.376	1.161
37	Percent Negro—1970	25.536	16.208	27.217	30.387	11.000	18.960	21.071
38	Coefficient of change percent Negro, 1960–1970	18.062	12.626	2.179	8.596	2.623	2.925	8.377
39	Coefficient of change percent Negro, 1950–1970	19.383	21.550	19.247	25.283	5.341	6.730	15.727

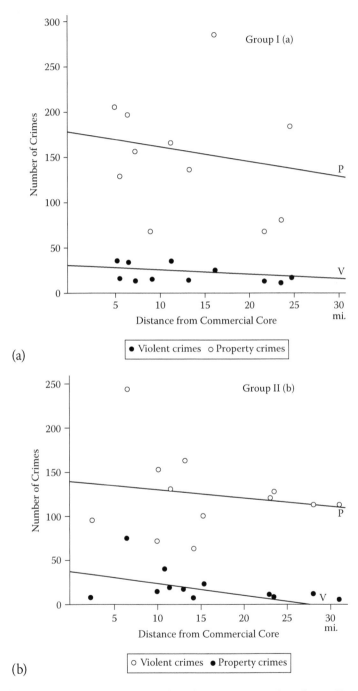

Figure 6.7 Akron City Groups I and II, by property and violent offenses and distances from Commercial Core.   *Continued*

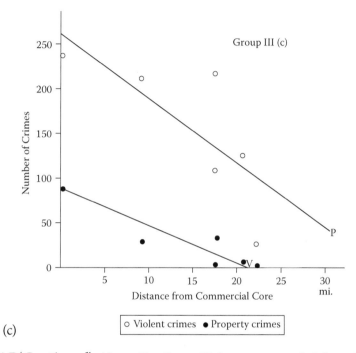

(c)

Figure 6.7 (*Continued*) Akron City Group III, by property and violent offenses and distances from Commercial Core.   *Continued*

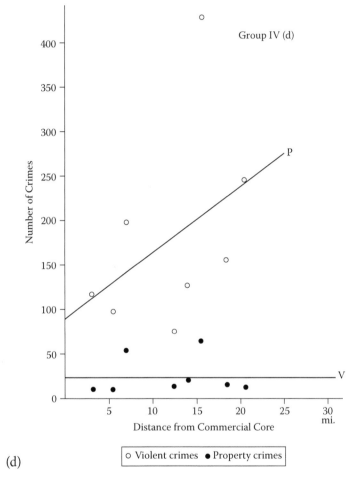

(d)

Figure 6.7 (Continued) Akron City Group IV, by property and violent offenses and distances from Commercial Core.   *Continued*

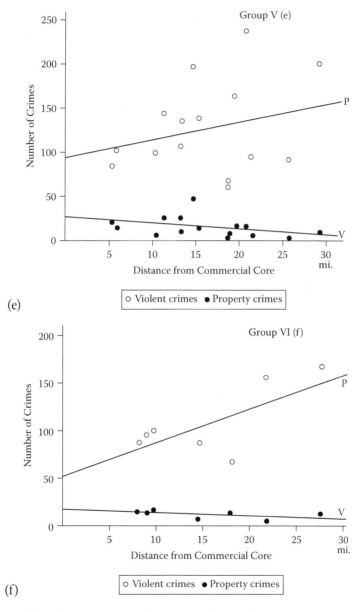

(e)

(f)

Figure 6.7 (Continued) Akron City Group V and VI, by property and violent offenses and distances from Commercial Core.

Table 6.10   Slopes of Regression for Violent and Property Crimes by Group

Group	Violent Crimes	Property Crimes
I	−0.74	−1.86
II	−0.89	−0.93
III	−3.67	−7.42
IV	0.18	7.60
V	−0.29	3.66
VI	−0.73	2.11

condition is in agreement with many of the findings of the traditional urban ecological theorists, that is, property crimes decrease with increased distance from the commercial core. However, the gradients developed for the medium to higher income groups show positive slopes, thus indicating an increase in property crimes with distance from the commercial core in areas with average to more than average financial resources. This pattern no doubt eventually tapers off with distance into the suburbs, but with lack of data from Fairlawn, Cuyahoga Falls, and Silver Lake, it is impossible to tell whether the gradient increases in those areas before tapering off.

In summary, the above findings indicate that violent crimes are either more central to the inner city or dispersed in areas of population transition. Property crimes tend to decrease with distance in lower income areas and increase with distance in higher income areas, again with the exception of transition areas (Group IV) where the most pronounced positive slope (7.60) shows up (Figure 6.7d). The more affluent areas then are the obvious targets of those involved with some crime against property, while violent crimes tend to victimize the less affluent.

6.6 Additional Comments

Generally, the findings in this chapter indicate some of the similarities and differences between the urban ecology of crime in Akron when comparisons are made with past studies of other cities. However, no analysis has been accomplished with regard to the residential location of the criminal offender. Our information system does contain such information, and Chapter VI is an attempt to better understand some crime-offender relationships within Akron.

Intraurban Crime Patterns (1974)

7

K.D. HARRIES

From Harries, K.D. (1974). *The Geography of Crime and Justice* (pp. 61–88). New York: McGraw-Hill.

Contents

7.1	Intraurban Crime Patterns	155
7.2	Macroenvironments	156
	7.2.1 Vignettes of Intraurban Crime	156
	7.2.1.1 Chicago	156
	7.2.1.2 London, England	158
	7.2.1.3 Birmingham, England	161
	7.2.1.4 Washington, D.C.	162
	7.2.1.5 Belgrade	166
	7.2.1.6 Seattle	170
	7.2.2 Generalizations	172
7.3	Microenvironments	173
	7.3.1 The Location of Crime	174
	7.3.2 Neighborhood Characteristics and Crime Control	178
7.4	Conclusions	180

7.1 Intraurban Crime Patterns

Studies of within-city crime patterns have been quite numerous, both in the United States and abroad. In this chapter, samples of the work that has been done are synthesized under two headings: macroenvironments and microenvironments. The former term encompasses vignettes of intraurban crime in six cities: Chicago, Seattle, and Washington, D.C., in the United States; London and Birmingham in England; and Belgrade, Yugoslavia. These vignettes suggest that cities usually possess distinctive high crime areas, which are often located in physically and economically blighted zones. A crime gradient is frequently observed, with the lowest rates in the suburbs and a peak at the center. Land use variations are in reality surrogate measures of opportunities for specific types of crime, as the discussion of Washington, D.C. illustrates. Each vignette tends to emphasize some facet of the geography of crime. For example, the role of immigrants in urban crime is discussed in relation to London, Birmingham, and Belgrade, while racial differentials in crime rates are illustrated particularly vividly for Seattle. In general the vignettes show that although some underlying crime distributions—such as central area concentration—are often replicated, each city does have a more or less unique arrangement of land uses, social groups, and economic conditions, as well as a unique cultural heritage. The interaction among these and other related factors produces a spatial distribution of crime that may or may not be typical of the pattern existing in the "average" city.

Following the vignettes, a discussion of microenvironments includes spatially detailed consideration of the location of criminal acts, and the relations of these acts to neighborhood characteristics. Macro- and microenvironments are not mutually exclusive; they merely reflect a broad dichotomy of scale for the convenience of organizing discussion.

7.2 Macroenvironments

7.2.1 Vignettes of Intraurban Crime

7.2.1.1 Chicago

No discussion of intraurban variations in crime could be adequate without consideration of the monumental works of Shaw and McKay. In his first analysis of juvenile delinquency in Chicago, Shaw (1929: 10) noted that

> the study of such a problem as juvenile delinquency necessarily begins with a study of its geographic location. This first step reveals the areas in which delinquency occurs most frequently, and therefore marks off the communities which should be studied intensively for factors related to delinquent behavior.

Delinquency rates were calculated on the basis of square-mile areas, rather than census tracts, since the tracts did not have large enough populations in some cases to permit the calculation of reliable delinquency rates. Several kinds of maps were produced: "spot maps" showed the locations of individuals; "rate maps" presented delinquency rates by square-mile areas; "radial maps" represented rates along rays or radials from the loop, following major thoroughfares; and "zone maps" were designed to emphasize delinquency rate gradients and expedite comparisons between various series of delinquency rate statistics (see Figure 7.1).

Six conclusions were reached in the 1929 study:

1. Truancy, juvenile delinquency, and adult criminality showed pronounced spatial variation, which included concentration around the central business district (CBD) and major industrial nuclei. This

Chicago Zone Maps for Three Juvenile Court Series

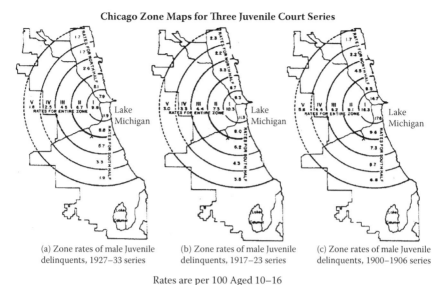

(a) Zone rates of male Juvenile   (b) Zone rates of male Juvenile   (c) Zone rates of male Juvenile
delinquents, 1927–33 series   delinquents, 1917–23 series   delinquents, 1900–1906 series

Rates are per 100 Aged 10–16

Figure 7.1 Chicago zone maps for three juvenile court series.

   variation could not be accounted for by geographical variations in
population size, crime reporting, or law enforcement.
2. Truancy, juvenile delinquency, and adult criminality rates were
   inversely related to distance from the city centers, though there were
   exceptions to this generality.
3. Patterns of truancy, juvenile delinquency, and adult crime were
   found to be highly intercorrelated.
4. Rates of the three forms of delinquency studied varied according to
   "community backgrounds." High delinquency rates were associated
   with physical dilapidation and diminishing populations.
5. Foci of high delinquency rates had been subject to high rates throughout the thirty-year period of the study, regardless of population
   composition.
6. Recidivism rates, like delinquency, were inversely related to distance
   from the city center (Shaw 1929: 198–204).

   High delinquency rate areas were found to be affected by transitional
land use in addition to being dilapidated and experiencing population decline
and disruption of local social and cultural cohesiveness. Attention was also
drawn to the cultural backgrounds of immigrant groups—often Europeans
or Southern blacks—who tended to experience a collapse of traditional social
and cultural controls in the new urban environment.
   Delinquent and criminal patterns arise and are transmitted socially
just as any other cultural and social pattern is transmitted. In time these

delinquent patterns may become dominant and shape the attitudes and behavior of persons living in the area. Thus the section becomes an area of delinquency (Shaw 1929: 206).

A later (1942) study (Shaw and McKay 1969) reinforced the earlier findings and emphasized the correspondence between low socioeconomic status and delinquency. Also made explicit was the suggestion that delinquency may constitute a rational response to social conditions, and not necessarily represent maladjustment (Shaw and McKay 1969: 316). Conclusions reached in the second study that added new insights to those reached earlier were as follows:

1. Suburban delinquency rates varied almost as much as those within the city.
2. Areas or locations did not produce delinquents, but social processes did.
3. Rapid population change was conducive to delinquency, owing to lack of preparedness of the incoming population for the new environment. In time, the situation tended to stabilize.
4. Racial or ethnic groups were not characterized by permanently high or low delinquency rates. Typically, new immigrants, regardless of race or ethnicity, generated high rates at first, which tended to decline later. The delinquency rate of an ethnic or racial group was perceived as "a function of the distribution of that group in different types of areas."
5. Black population delinquency rates were high in areas occupied by recently arrived blacks but low in established black communities where meaningful roles for youth had been developed. These communities had been high rate areas in the 1920s and 1930s (Shaw and McKay 1969: 383–386).

In addition to the detailed analysis of Chicago, Shaw and McKay presented data relating to cities which included Philadelphia, Boston, Cleveland, and Richmond. These revealed patterns quite similar to those of Chicago.*

7.2.1.2 *London, England*
The gradient of diminishing crime rates with distance from the city center, revealed by Shaw and McKay in Chicago, has been suggested by McClintock with respect to violent crime in London, although his maps represent frequencies rather than rates (McClintock 1963). (See Figure 7.2.) Those convicted of crimes of violence were predominantly male, and 70% were over age twenty-

---

* For a detailed review and critique of Shaw's work, see T. Morris (1957), Chapters IV and V.

one. However, specific offenses were strongly linked to age groupings; persons convicted of domestic violence tended to be aged over thirty while those aged under twenty-five were more likely to be involved in attacks in public places, attacks on police, and sexual violence. The importance of immigrants to the city, emphasized by Shaw and McKay, also appeared significant in London. In 1957, immigrants (mostly from the Irish Republic or the West Indies at that time) accounted for 30% of those convicted for crimes of violence. In the period 1950 to 1957, Irish immigrants contributed to most of the increase in convictions for violence, but from 1957 to 1962 West Indians experienced the largest increase. Related to the role of immigrants in violent crime was McClintock's finding that about one-third of the total offenders did not live at home (about half of the unmarried offenders). Furthermore, most offenders were classified occupationally as being "unskilled" or in "casual employment" (McClintock 1963: 133–136). Figure 7.2 illustrates the distribution of three types of violent crime: domestic and neighborhood altercations, fights related to pubs, cafes, etc. and other violence occurring in public places. Many of the areas shown to have a high incidence of violence in Figure 7.2 were described by McClintock as "depressed areas," often subject to urban renewal. High frequencies in some central areas related to major railroad terminals (e.g., Paddington and King's Cross), which were the foci of "poor-class" hotels and apartments. The distribution of some violence was attributed to intraurban migration caused by urban renewal (McClintock 1963: 198–199).

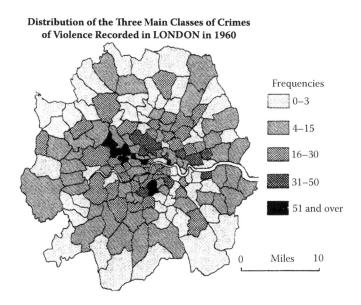

Figure 7.2 Distribution of the three main classes of crimes of violence recorded in London in 1960.

A study of juvenile delinquency in London by Wallis and Maliphant noted that maps of urban environmental phenomena correlated with patterns of delinquency. One interesting (non-causal!) relationship was observed between air pollution and delinquency. Pollution is simply a very obvious indicator of industrial activity, population density, and functionally obsolete dwellings with open fireplaces. The relationship between industrial land use and delinquency already noted in Chicago, occurred particularly strongly in older industrial areas: "the crime areas north and east of the city and south of the Thames fit fairly closely to the boundaries of the Victorian manufacturing belt" (Wallis and Maliphant 1967: 254). Positive correlations were computed between delinquency rates and several ecological measures, including persons per room (0.74), rented public housing (0.49), industrial land use (0.60), commercial land use (0.46), persons per acre (0.38), net increase of youthful population, 1951 to 1961 (0.49), rate of "colored"* immigration, 1951 to 1961 (0.58), rate of fertility (0.43), rate of "children" in county care (0.37), proportion of high-school dropouts (0.65), proportion of male workers in manual work (0.74), and proportion of male workers unemployed (0.55).† Wallis and Maliphant (1967: 282) suggested that the correlation between poor socioeconomic conditions and delinquency was less interesting than the *stability* that the relationships revealed when compared to earlier studies.

A major suburban London nucleus—the County Borough of Croydon—has been examined by Morris, who made some interesting observations on Shaw and McKay's findings in relation to his own. He found that the zonal approach to crime—the basis of much of the work in Chicago—was not appropriate in Croydon because the borough had not, through most of its history, developed in a zonal manner. Furthermore, land use was not particularly related to the locations of delinquents' homes, but was related to the offense pattern. Although Croydon is a large community (250,000 in 1951), its peripheral location in the London metropolitan area has contributed to a largely residential land use pattern; many workers commute to central London. Thus the heterogeneity of land use typical in a "central" city such as Chicago is not present, and the role of land use in the criminogenic process is different (T. Morris 1957: 111–116). Morris found crime concentrated in the CBD, mainly in the form of larcenies. Other shopping nuclei were also significant larceny centers. Offenders' homes were concentrated in various public housing projects ("council estates") and deteriorating slum areas. High offender location rates were found close to the CBD, but Morris disputed

---

* The term colored is the conventional British expression that includes Indian and Pakistani Caucasoids, for example, as well as West Indian Negroids. Colored is not necessarily a euphemism for "black," as it is in the United States.

† Wallis and Maliphant (1967), Table 1, p. 255; Table 2, p. 260; Table 3, p. 263; Table 4, p. 265; Table 6, p. 271; Table 7, p. 273; Table 8, p. 279.

the notion of implied causal relationship between physical deterioration and crime. The provision of public housing and its frequently concomitant crime problem indicated that planned areas of housing of standard quality could sustain high delinquency rates just like slum housing (T. Morris 1957: 122–130). Clearly, physical conditions could only provide a crude and indirect partial measure of social conditions in environments in which the housing market is modified by public policy.

7.2.1.3 Birmingham, England

This city has played host to a large number of colored immigrants from British Commonwealth or former Commonwealth areas. Wherever they have settled, these immigrants have been the butt of a high level of hostility from the indigenous population. The hostility has included inflammatory racist polemics from at least one nationally prominent politician, as well as the normal discrimination in housing, job opportunities, etc. There have also been "white" immigrants, primarily from the Irish Republic. Lambert studied crime in Birmingham, with particular emphasis on its racial aspects (Lambert 1970). The basis of his analysis was one of the divisional areas delineated by the Birmingham City Police (Division F in Figure 7.3). Zone I, the most central of the three zones of Division F, contained more than two-thirds of the colored immigrant population and more than half the Irish population in the Division. Most households lacked exclusive use of plumbing facilities, and overcrowded housing was twice the average for the

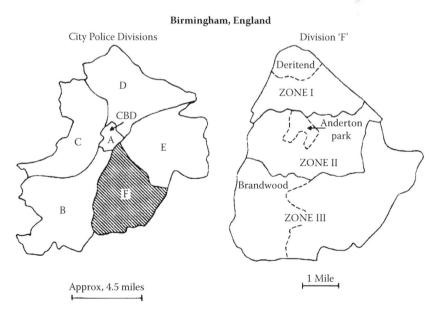

Figure 7.3 Birmingham, England.

Division. Sixty-four percent of the crime included in Lambert's analysis occurred in this zone. About a quarter of the Irish population and a fifth of the colored population were located in Zone II, the location of 21% of the crime surveyed. Zone III contained the homes of some 3,000 Irish (20% of the Division total) and 620 coloreds (less than 5%). Fifteen percent of the Division F crime was located in Zone III (Lambert 1970: 13–18). Considerable intrazonal variation in crime patterns was observed. In Zone I, for example, the Deritend district closest to the CBD had the highest rate of any subdivision of the zones. In Zone II, Anderton Park was dominant, and in Zone III, Brandwood's rate was highest. Offenders' addresses clustered particularly in areas of lodging houses and multifamily dwellings. With the exception of Deritend, the locations of offenders substantially correlated with locations of offenses. Lambert found that immigrant areas had the highest crime rates (excluding Deritend) and high criminal location rates. These immigrant areas were the most overcrowded and mobile. Significantly, it was concluded that "colored immigrants are very much less involved in the crime and disorder that surround them in the areas where they live than their white neighbors" (Lambert 1970: 124). Furthermore, even when the age and occupation structure of the Irish was taken into account, "it would seem that there is a greater propensity for crime among Irish immigrants than among other immigrants and than among the native English population" (Lambert 1970: 126).

7.2.1.4 Washington, D.C.

Crime in the national capital has been examined in some detail in the massive Report of the President's Commission on Crime in the District of Columbia (1966). The Washington SMSA had a population of 2.86 million to make it the seventh largest metropolitan area in the United States in 1970. The District of Columbia, however, contains only about one-fourth of the population of the Washington SMSA (U.S. Bureau of the Census 1971: 1–48, 1–178). Most of the District's population is black and residential segregation is pronounced. Rock Creek Park, which straddles the northern boundaries of Precincts 6 and 8 in Figure 7.4, is a racial divide, with most whites living west of the park. White newcomers to Washington tend to live in the suburbs, while black arrivals tend to locate in the District. The age structure of the black population has tended to become polarized, with increases in the youthful and aged populations and decreases among the middle aged. The black population is concentrated in several areas of the District. These areas are typified by low median family incomes and overcrowded housing. In the words of the President's Commission: "Tourists admiring the Capital's monuments and museums are seldom aware of the 262,000 people who live in the city at little more than a subsistence level, with incomes inadequate to provide them with decent housing, sufficient food and clothing, and other

District of Columbia:
Police Precincts and Selected Crime Rate Patterns, 1964
(Based on Rates per 1,000 Population)

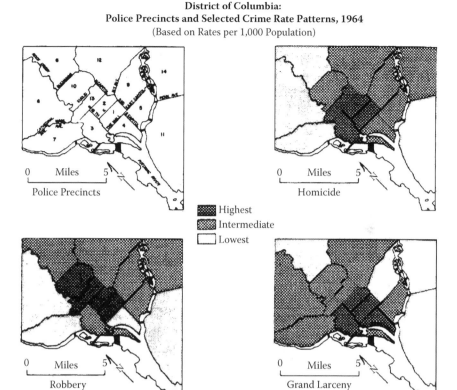

Figure 7.4 District of Columbia: police precincts and selected crime rate patterns, 1964.

necessities" (Report of the President's Commission on Crime in the District of Columbia 1966: 12). According to the Commission, the various social pathologies that it identified create an environment in which crime is likely to be produced.

The distribution of rates of several selected offenses is shown in Figure 7.4, and in more generalized form in Table 7.1. On a rate basis, Precincts 1, 2, 3, 4, 5, 10, and 13 exceeded the District value, while 6, 7, 8, 11, 12, and 14 were below the overall figure. Each of the offenses mapped in Figure 7.4 may be considered in more detail.

In terms of frequency, four precincts (2, 9, 10, and 13) accounted for 63% of all District murders in the period 1961 to 1965, while population-specific rates were highest in Precincts 1, 2, 3, and 13. The seasonal peak for murder was in July (with a nadir in November). Most murders occurred on Friday, Saturday, or Sunday, with more than a quarter on Saturday. About a quarter of all murders happened between midnight and 3:00 a.m. Most victims were aged between thirty and fifty. Seventy-eight percent of all victims were black

**Table 7.1   Washington, D.C.: Part I
Offenses by Precinct Rank and
Percent of Total**

Rank	Precinct	Percent of Offenses[a]
1	10	12.0
2	13	11.5
3	2	10.9
4	1	10.2
5	9	9.4
6	3	7.3
7	11	7.1
8	5	7.1
9	12	6.3
10	6	5.3
11	14	4.7
12	8	3.8
13	7	2.3
14	4	2.0

[a] Does not total 100.0 due to rounding.

*Source: Report of the President's Commission
on Crime in the District of Columbia,*
U.S. Government Printing Office,
Washington, D.C., 1966, p. 26.

in the period 1950 to 1965, and in the same period almost 70% of the victims were males. Most victims lived in Precincts 2, 9, 10, 11, and 13. Most were married, and 38% had previous arrest records. Eighty-six percent of offenders were black between 1950 and 1965, and over 80% of the offenders were males. Almost 80% of the victims were acquainted with offenders. Less than 7% of the murders analyzed were interracial. Murders were located overwhelmingly at the victim's home (51%). Other locations were streets (28%), offender's residences (4%), residences of third persons familiar to victims and/or offenders (8%), and other locations (9%). Most murders involved firearms, and alcohol was consumed prior to the event by 45% of the offenders and 47% of the victims.

Most robberies occurred in Precincts 2, 9, 10, and 13. Rates of robbery were highest in Precincts 1, 2, 10, and 13. Winter was the seasonal maximum. Friday and Saturday, between 6:00 p.m. and 12:00 a.m. were peak periods. Most victims were over 30 years of age, white, and male. Most offenders were black males under thirty. (Robbery is the only violent crime with more white victims than black.) About half of the ordinary robberies analyzed by the Commission were located on streets and alleys. Purse snatching and pocket picking, which also occur mainly in public places, made up 33%, and commercial robberies accounted for 11%.

Over 60% of all grand larcenies (property worth $100 or more) were con-
centrated in five precincts (1, 2, 3, 10, and 13). Rates were highest in Precincts
1, 2. 3, and 4. Seasonal variations in larceny were not pronounced. Friday
was the peak day, and the period from noon to 6:00 p.m. was the peak time.
About one-third of the grand larceny offenders were under twenty-one, and
80% of the offenders were black; most were males. Grand and petit larceny
offenses were broken down as follows: thefts from cars, 20.5%; bicycles,
14.7%; shoplifting, 13.4%; theft of car accessories, 12.9%; and "other," 38.5%
(Report of the President's Commission on Crime in the District of Columbia
1966: 32–97).

This sample of major offenses in the District of Columbia suggests a clear
geographical relationship of crime to the social pathologies of the Washington
black community. The Commission concluded that

> The adult offenders are predominantly Negro, male, poorly educated, youth-
> ful, products of broken homes and large families, unskilled and erratically
> employed. The juvenile offenders share many of these characteristics. Both
> groups consist largely of long-term District residents currently living in a few
> high-crime areas of the city. Ninety-two percent of the adults had previously
> been arrested at least once, over half had been arrested six or more times, and
> only 17% had never been convicted. Similarly, 61% of the juveniles had been
> referred to the Juvenile Court at least once before (Report of the President's
> Commission on Crime in the District of Columbia 1966: 140–141).

It is scarcely surprising that in 1968 Washington would be counted
among the cities with the most devastating riot damage, along with Chicago
and Baltimore.*

At a broader scale, Scarr has examined burglary in Washington, D.C.,
Fairfax County, Virginia, and Prince George's County, Maryland. The latter two counties are adjacent to the District of Columbia, Fairfax to the west
and Prince George's to the east. The three units together include about 65%
of the total population of the Washington SMSA in 1970 (U.S. Bureau of the
Census 1971: 1–48, 1–98, 1–109, 1–176). Fairfax County is the most affluent
of the three areas, has the lowest population density, the smallest proportion of black population, the lowest Index crime rate (including burglary
rate), and the lowest frequency of police officers per 1000 population. Prince
George's County is intermediate in rank for these indicators between Fairfax
County and the District of Columbia (Scarr 1973: 2–3). Scarr recognized that

---

* Civil disorders will not be discussed here, since another volume in this series has
  already reviewed the topic: Rose (1971: 84–101). See also Report of the National Advisory
  Commission on Civil Disorders (1968); Adams (1972); Spilerman (1970), pp. 637–639 deal
  specifically with "Geographic Contagion"; Wanderer (1969); Lieberson and Silverman
  (1965); Lupsha (1969).

burglary is an offense against property, and only indirectly against people. Thus he computed burglary rates in relation to the number of residential units available for burglary. These rates were then integrated with census data at the tract level in order to provide insights on the ecology of burglary. Analysis of residential burglary data for the years 1967–1969 indicated that Fairfax County experienced geographical instability in rates (related to rapid growth and change in the area). Maps suggested a tendency for rates to become higher in the east of the county (towards the District of Columbia). In Washington, rates were stable, and the city was divided spatially between the "high-risk southeastern section" and the "low-risk northwestern section," a finding replicating that of the President's Commission on Crime in the District of Columbia and constituting, according to Scarr, "confirmed folk knowledge"—at least to the folk in Washington. Prince George's County was intermediate in rate stability between Fairfax and the District, and the geography of burglary, based on the comparison of maps for the three successive years, suggested a development of concentration across the central part of the county, from Washington, D.C. to Bladensburg, Kent, and Marlboro. Correlations among four burglary indicators showed how differential land use patterns in the three areas affected burglary rates (Table 7.2). In Fairfax County, Table 7.2 shows that residential and nonresidential burglary frequencies were quite strongly related in 1968 and 1969. A similar relationship existed in Prince George's County (less marked in 1969), but not in Washington. Suburban shopping centers in Fairfax and Prince George's Counties meant that residential and nonresidential burglary potentials were spatially mixed and thus statistically correlated. In Washington, D.C., on the other hand, residential and nonresidential land uses are more segregated. The practical implication is that suburban police must be able to handle all types of burglaries, while urban police may be able to specialize in particular burglary types (Scarr 1973: 15). A detailed analysis of the highest and lowest rate residential burglary tracts revealed that social indicators discriminated poorly between high- and low-rate tracts in Fairfax County in 1967–1969, poorly in Prince George's County for 1967–1968, but well in 1969, and well in Washington in the two years for which data were available. Table 7.3 shows the results of tests of the hypothesis that high- and low-rate burglary tracts did not differ significantly with respect to the characteristics listed. Scarr suggested that Prince George's County "crossed the urban threshold" between 1968 and 1969 in such a way as to give it inner city characteristics that Fairfax County has not yet acquired (Scarr 1973: 17).

7.2.1.5 Belgrade

Juvenile delinquency rates for the city and an in-depth analysis of specific problem areas have been presented by Todorovich (1970). As areas for ecological analysis, he selected housing communities, a compromise between

Table 7.2   Intercorrelations among Burglary Indicators:* Fairfax County, Virginia, Washington, D.C., and Prince George's County, Maryland (1968 and 1969)

Burglary Indicators	1968			1969		
	RBF	NBF	BTF	RBF	NBF	BTF
Fairfax County, Virginia						
1. Residential Burglary Rate	0.41	−0.12	0.20	0.27	−0.17	0.09
2. Residential Burglary Frequency		0.66	0.93		0.63	0.93
3. Nonresidential Burglary Frequency			0.88			0.87
Washington, D.C.						
1. Residential Burglary Rate	0.55	0.30	0.56	0.51	0.22	0.54
2. Residential Burglary Frequency		0.19	0.80		0.10	0.91
3. Nonresidential Burglary Frequency			0.74			0.51
Prince George's County, Maryland						
1. Residential Burglary Rate	0.52	0.14	0.45	0.41	−0.07	0.32
2. Residential Burglary Frequency		0.60	0.97		0.34	0.95
3. Nonresidential Burglary Frequency			0.78			0.61

* RBF = residential burglary frequency; NBR = nonresidential burglary frequency; BTF = burglary total frequency.

Source: Harry A. Scarr, *Patterns of Burglary*, U.S. Department of Justice, Washington, D.C., 1973, Tables 32, 33, and 34, p. 52.

communes (too big) and census tracts or electoral districts (too small). In Yugoslavia, housing communities are neighborhood units, and their use enabled identification and surveillance of juvenile delinquency problems in the context of meaningful social areas. Figure 7.5 shows the pattern of rates of juvenile delinquents' home addresses in Belgrade, by housing communities. Todorovich suggested that rates of three or more per 1000 could be classified as "criminogenic" or "delinquency areas." Two high-rate delinquency areas in the Zemun commune—numbers 13 and 11—were selected for detailed study. Community 12, between 13 and 11 geographically as well as numerically, was a very low-rate area, and Todorovich was interested in determining why ultra-high-rate areas were juxtaposed with extremely low rates. Since statistical indicators for housing communities were not available, reliance was placed on data from social workers, plus some land use information pertaining to retail establishments attractive to juveniles, and to recreational spaces.

Housing community 13 was developed after 1945. Although some building was officially permitted, much was not. Some 2000 homes were built

Table 7.3　High vs. Low Residential Burglary Rate (RBR) Tract Comparisons: Washington, D.C.

Burglary and Social Indicators	1968			1969		
	High RBR Tracts Exceeding Median	Low RBR Tracts Exceeding Median	P†	High RBR Tracts Exceeding Median	Low RBR Tracts Exceeding Median	P
Residential burglary frequency	6/7*	2/10	0.05	8/8	1/10	0.01
Nonresidential burglary frequency	5/7	3/10	0.05	7/8	2/10	0.01
Burglary total frequency	7/7	1/10	0.01	8/8	1/10	0.01
Population	2/7	6/10	n.s.	3/8	6/10	n.s.
Percent white	1/7	7/10	0.10	0/8	9/10	0.01
Percent white aged 5–24	1/7	7/10	0.10	0/8	9/10	0.01
Percent husband-wife households	0/7	8/10	0.01	1/8	8/10	0.02
Percent aged 6–17	5/7	3/10	n.s.	7/8	2/10	0.02
Percent rooming houses	4/7	3/10	n.s.	5/8	3/10	n.s.
Percent overcrowded	7/7	1/10	0.01	8/8	1/10	0.01
Percent black overcrowded	5/7	3/10	n.s.	8/8	1/10	0.01
Percent black housing units	4/7	4/10	n.s.	7/8	1/10	0.01
Percent "lower" cost houses	6/7	2/10	0.05	8/8	1/10	0.01
Percent "lower" cost rentals	6/7	2/10	0.05	7/8	2/10	0.01
Percent owner occupied	0/7	8/10	0.10	3/8	5/10	0.01
Percent husband-wife households with children under 18	4/7	4/10	n.s.	7/8	2/10	0.01

* Indicates that six of seven tracts exceeded the median value for residential burglary frequency.
† Indicates the probability that the difference between high- and low-RBR tracts with respect to the various indicators could have arisen by chance. In column P, "n.s." means that the difference was "not significant." These probabilities were derived from the application of the Fisher Exact Probability Test. See Sydney Siegel, *Nonparametric Statistics*, McGraw-Hill Book Company, New York, 1956, pp. 96–104, for further explanation.
Source: Harry A. Scarr, *Patterns of Burglary*, U.S. Department of Justice, Washington, D.C., 1973, Table 41, p. 55.

Belgrade:
Distribution of Juvenile Delinquency, by Rate per Housing Community

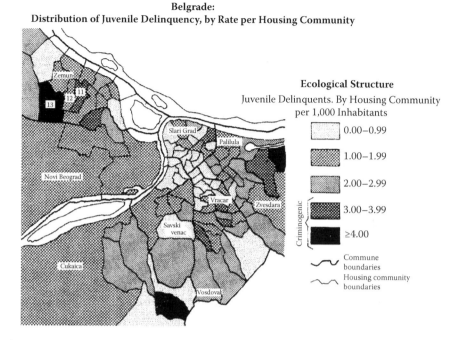

Figure 7.5 Belgrade: distribution of juvenile delinquency, by rate per housing community.

illegally in community 13, making it the major center of illegal construction in the Zemun commune. Unregulated building, "unregistered subtenants," and occupational heterogeneity were basic social elements in community 13. Several immigrant ethnic groups, typically with large families, occupied the area after 1945, including Serbs, Albanians, and Romanian gypsies. Social pathologies, such as prostitution, gambling, alcoholism, begging, fortune telling, quackery, and charlatanism were prevalent. No recreational open space existed in the community.

Housing community 11 had problems similar to those of 13, although illegal construction was not characteristic. Like 13, community 11 had a heterogeneous social structure and a predominantly immigrant population. Juvenile gangs were a particular problem, in addition to prostitution, alcoholism, etc. Again, no recreational open space was available.

Housing community 12 lacked "negative sociomorphological elements," particularly illegal construction. Most critical, perhaps, was the age structure of the population, which consisted mainly of retirees, although most were post-1945 immigrants, just as the inhabitants of communities 11 and 13 were. The pathologies of the other communities were absent or limited in extent in number 12. No recreational open space was present (Todorovich 1970: 68–71).

In a comparative sense, the most interesting aspects of Todorovich's findings are, first, that delinquency in Belgrade was not clustered around the central area and, second, that at least some of the high-rate delinquency areas were characterized by immigrant populations and ethnic diversity. Unfortunately, inadequate data were available to enable detailed intercommunity analyses of age structure and mobility, and no comments were made on the possible influence of elements of discrimination that may have been associated with ethnic status.

7.2.1.6 Seattle

This city has probably been the subject of more crime-oriented ecological analysis than any in the United States apart from Chicago. In the 1930s, Hayner (1933–1934) wrote on juvenile delinquency in Seattle (and Tacoma). Schmid (1960a, 1960b) published a detailed analysis in 1960, followed by a study of the State of Washington (containing much material on Seattle) by Schmid and Schmid in 1972, which was in part an extension and replication of the earlier study. Based on the period 1959–1961, two series of crime-related data—the locations of over 79,000 offenses in twenty-two categories) and of 30,000 offenders (in fourteen categories)—were combined with twenty-six socioeconomic indicators for the 115 census tracts of Seattle. Using a factor analysis approach comparable to that discussed for the inter-metropolitan analysis of U.S. cities in Chapter 3, the Schmids extracted nine factors, or generalized dimensions of the variation among the original sixty-two variables. Of these nine factors, the first three were of most interest, since they were associated most strongly with the offense and arrest data. Factor I was called "Low Social Cohesion–Low Family Status." Purse snatching, auto theft, and burglary were among the offense patterns associated with this factor. Arrest patterns included fraud, various kinds of theft, and assault. Socioeconomic indicators represented such phenomena as high rates of separation or divorce, lack of population growth and home ownership, low income levels, and multiunit housing structures. Factor II, named "Maleness–Crimes against Person," was strongly associated with unemployment and unmarried status among males, a typical Skid Row situation. Dominant arrest patterns included robbery, burglary, larceny, auto theft, and assault. This factor was described as being highly representative of "the urban crime dimension." Factor III, "Crimes against Property and Sex Offenses," was descriptive of offenses that tend to occur together spatially, such as shoplifting, check fraud, embezzlement, indecent exposure, and molesting women and children.

In general, crime in Seattle was concentrated in the central part of the city (Figure 7.6), with a small secondary nucleus to the west of the University of Washington, particularly for property and drug offenses. Crime focused on the center from the points of view of both locations of offenses and offenders (Schmid and Schmid 1972: 154–167).

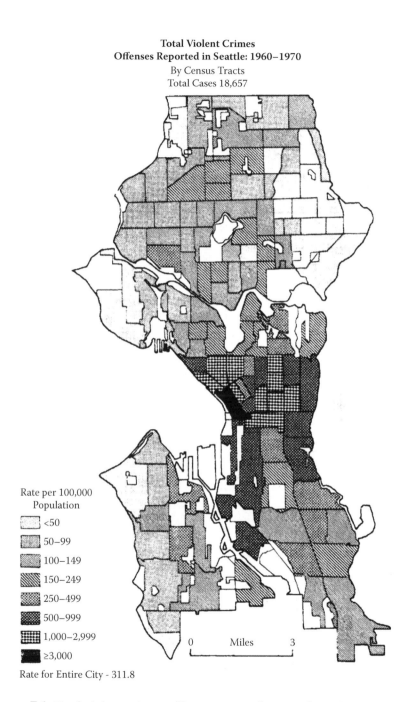

Total Violent Crimes
Offenses Reported in Seattle: 1960–1970
By Census Tracts
Total Cases 18,657

Rate per 100,000
Population

    <50
    50–99
    100–149
    150–249
    250–499
    500–999
    1,000–2,999
    ≥3,000

Rate for Entire City - 311.8

0   Miles   3

Figure 7.6 Total violent crimes: offenses reported in Seattle, 1960–1970.

Table 7.4   Comparative Values of Four Crime Indices* by Race, Based on Number of Male Arrestees per 100,000, Seattle: 1968–1970

Race	Index #1* Rate	Index #1* Score	Index #2* Rate	Index #2* Score	Index #3* Rate	Index #3* Score	Index #4* Rate	Index #4* Score
Indian	34,870	101.7	9,132	37.6	3,280	41.5	2,158	59.9
Negro	7,737	22.6	5,390	22.2	1,670	21.1	2,028	56.3
White	2,695	7.9	1,187	4.9	314	4.0	230	6.4
Filipino	1,306	3.8	861	3.5	168	2.1	307	8.5
Chinese	356	1.0	275	1.1	102	1.3	31	0.9
Japanese	343	1.0	243	1.0	79	1.0	36	1.0

* All four indices are mean crude rates for males per 100,000. (1) Index #1 is based on all male arrestees for all crime categories; (2) index #2 includes all crime categories except drunkenness, driving under the influence, and violation of liquor laws; (3) index #3 is based on male arrestees charged with one of the seven index crimes; (4) and index #4 represents six violent or aggressive crimes: (a) murder and nonnegligent manslaughter, (b) forcible rape, (c) robbery, (d) aggravated assault, (e) nonaggravated assault, and (f) possession of concealed weapons. In deriving score values, the rate for the Japanese for each index is taken as unity; accordingly, the respective scores for each racial group signify the number of times they are larger than those of the Japanese.

Source: Calvin F. Schmid and Stanton E. Schmid, *Crime in the State of Washington,* Law and Justice Planning Office, Washington State Planning and Community Affairs Agency, Olympia, 1972, p. 216.

The Schmids' study provided an informative insight in relation to race and crime. Six racial groups (Indian, Japanese, Chinese, Filipino, black, and white) were assigned four composite crime indices (Table 7.4). With the Japanese scores set at unity for each index, nineteen of the remaining twenty scores exceeded 1.0, and the Indian rate was consistently highest. When race was cross-tabulated with socioeconomic status and crime, an inverse relationship between the latter factors was apparent. The inconsistencies were that whites were more delinquent than their socioeconomic status would suggest, while Filipinos were less delinquent (Schmid and Schmid 1972: 213–219).

7.2.2   Generalizations

Intraurban ecological analyses of crime have been so numerous that no exhaustive review is possible here.* What generalities, or theoretical constructs, have emerged from the existing work? A common, but by no means universal, finding has been that crime rates tend to diminish outwards from the centers of cities. Certain social and physical conditions often associated with crime were commonly found in central areas, which tend to be the

---

* A short review is T. Morris (1962), from which this material was adapted.

oldest parts of cities physically and those which accommodate the poorest segment of the population. However, the assumption of central poverty and blight is based on the Burgess zonal hypothesis of city structure (Park and Burgess 1925), which may or may not be an adequate model in a given case. This empirical gradient construct is implicitly associated with several of the overlapping hypotheses advanced to explain criminal behavior.* The opportunity hypothesis suggests that the distribution of crime is primarily a function of opportunity; thus robbery will be most frequent where pedestrian counts are highest. The *drift* hypothesis focuses on the tendency for criminal types of persons to accumulate in certain areas of cities. A third hypothesis is associated with the concepts of *cultural transmission* and *differential association* and suggests that criminality will be high in areas where conventional values do not dominate. The *social alienation* hypothesis submits that criminals have been socially impersonalized, resulting in feelings of insecurity and hostility. One hypothesis is based on the *anomie* concept, which "implies a disturbance or disruption of the collective order, the external regulating force which defines norms and goals and governs behavior" (Schmid and Schmid 1972: 190). Cybriwsky (1972), for example, in a study of the social allocation of neighborhood space in Philadelphia, found that antisocial acts, including wall graffiti and muggings, were concentrated in "anomie locations," such as alleys and the end walls of row houses. A sixth hypothesis is eclectic, combining the anomie and differential association hypotheses with other ideas, including differentials in illegitimate means. Trends in the ecological analysis of crime suggest that one future focus will tend to be on individual conduct in urban areas, with less reliance on aggregate statistics for precincts or tracts.

7.3 Microenvironments

The finest scale of spatial resolution discussed here relates to specific locations of criminal acts—rooms or dwellings, stores and other interior locations, and various outside locations. It is shown that offenses have their own "ecologies of place"; neighborhood layout and design, as well as structural characteristics, may affect opportunity levels for particular types of crime. Population density, a factor usually accorded much attention as a causal element in crime, is reviewed and distinction is made between different measures of density and their capacities to provide explanations of crime rates. Discussion of microenvironmental factors demonstrates that offenses vary greatly in their amenability to control via manipulation of the physical

---

* This summary is based on a review in Schmid and Schmid (1972: 183–192).

environment. Intrafamily violence, for example, is unlikely to be affected by environmental considerations, while burglary and robbery may be relatively susceptible to control via urban and structural design.

7.3.1 The Location of Crime

Crime occurs in response to a complex interaction between social and physical conditions. Ultimately, however, an offender commits a crime in a precise location, the characteristics of which may be significantly related to the type of crime that is perpetrated. To some extent, this involves an obvious relationship between opportunity and occurrence: crimes against the person can only occur where there are people, automobile theft cannot occur where there are no automobiles, and so forth. It is instructive to look beyond the obvious at some of the more subtle links that exist between crime and place, starting with data descriptive of crime location at the micro level. Table 7.5 summarizes the spatial distribution of Index crimes against the person, other than homicide, for Chicago in a seven month period in 1965–1966. The table shows that males were most likely to be victimized on the street, but females were most frequently victimized at home. The patterns revealed in the table typify the spatial elements of the interpersonal relations system within which

Table 7.5 Victimization by Sex and Place of Occurrence for Major Crimes (Except Homicide) against the Person (%)

Place of Occurrence	Victims of Major Crimes against Person	
	Male	Female
School property	3.2	2.4
Residence	20.5	46.1
Transport property	1.4	0.4
Taxis and delivery trucks	2.6	—
Businesses	3.2	1.1
Taverns and liquor stores	5.7	2.8
Street	46.8	30.7
Parks	0.8	0.5
All other premises	16.0	16.0
	100.2[a]	100.0
N	(8,047)	(5,666)

[a] Error due to rounding

Source: President's Commission on Law Enforcement and Administration of Justice, *The Challenge of Crime in a Free Society*, Avon Books, New York, 1967e, Table 15, p. 141.

we operate. Males make more social contact away from home than women, which explains in part not only the high proportion of street locations for the victimization of men, but also the relatively high rank of taverns and liquor stores as places of conflict between men. What starts as a drunken brawl in a tavern may later become a street fight, for example. On the other hand, women are more commonly involved in violent confrontations in a domestic context (where they tend to spend most time) often with relatives or friends (President's Commission on Law Enforcement and Administration of Justice 1967e: 141–142). The geography of violence may be magnified further and extended in coverage to more cities (Table 7.6). The data show that homicide occurred about as frequently inside the home (34%) as outside (37%), with the balance (26%) consisting mainly of other inside locations (26%). The living room and bedroom, where personal contacts occur most frequently, were the principal home locations. Other indoor locations included bars or taverns (8%) and "miscellaneous" locations (14%). By far the largest proportion (25%) of outside killings occurred in the street, with male victims (Table 7.5) and male offenders. Young males often move from one diversion to another late at night, but a female out late is likely to be accompanied by a male, who eventually makes his way home, thus exposing himself to victimization. Married females tend to spend a lot of time at home, particularly during peak homicide periods. Intramarital conflict frequently occurs in the kitchen where deadly weapons are available.

Aggravated assault took place outside (52%) more often than in the home (26%) or in other inside locations. The living room was the most likely location for an assault in the home (16%). Outside assaults, like homicides were most commonly on the street (39%). Assault and homicide are similar acts and we would expect their spatial patterns to coincide. The most significant differences were lower proportions of assault in bedrooms bars and taverns. For both offenses, interactions in the primary social group were most likely inside, with other occurrences outside.

Appropriately, rape occurred most commonly in the bedroom (33%). Outside, "private transportation vehicles" (usually cars) were the commonest rape sites (11%). Alleys and streets accounted for the same proportion. Perhaps the most surprising element of the rape statistics is that about half the occurrences were in the home, suggesting a significant level of incest, in addition to interaction between friends or acquaintances.

Armed robbery was located outside in most cases (59%), and rarely in the home (6%). Commercial establishments other than service stations, chain stores, or banks dominated "other inside locations." The street was the commonest outside place (38%). As in the cases of homicide and assault females were victimized most often inside, and males outside, without regard to race. Unarmed robbery showed a somewhat different distribution. The home was more prominent (16%); other inside locations were less involved (9%

Table 7.6   The Place of Occurrence of Five Violent Crimes, 17 Cities, 1967 (%)

	Major Violent Crime Type				
Location	Willful Murder	Aggravated Assault	Forcible Rape	Armed Robbery	Unarmed Robbery
Bedroom	10.0	2.6	33.2	0.5	2.3
Kitchen	2.9	2.2	0.1	0.3	0.0
Living room, den, study	11.8	15.9	9.1	2.0	2.4
Hall, stair, elevator	7.0	5.4	3.9	3.4	10.1
Basement, garage	2.6	0.2	5.2	0.0	1.6
Total–Home	34.3	26.3	51.5	6.2	16.4
Service station	0.6	0.9	0.0	3.0	0.5
Chain store	0.0	0.4	0.0	1.7	0.0
Bank	0.0	0.0	0.0	3.0	0.0
Other commercial establishments	2.8	3.1	1.4	20.4	3.5
Bar, tavern taproom, lounge	7.6	2.8	0.6	2.4	0.1
Place of entertainment other than bar, etc.	0.9	0.9	0.6	0.0	0.0
Any other inside location	14.2	11.2	11.3	3.5	5.1
Total–Other Inside Location	26.2	19.3	13.9	34.0	9.2
Immediate area around residence	4.2	4.9	2.2	4.6	6.0
Street	24.9	39.1	4.8	37.6	48.8
Alley	1.0	1.2	6.1	2.1	1.9
Park	0.4	1.9	2.3	0.5	7.4
Lot	2.3	0.9	3.2	1.8	3.7
Private transport vehicle	2.1	1.1	11.0	3.5	3.6
Public transport vehicle	0.7	1.0	0.0	3.8	1.8
Any other outside location	1.3	2.0	4.3	5.4	1.1
Total–Outside Location	36.9	52.1	33.9	59.3	74.3
Unknown	2.5	2.5	0.7	0.4	0
Grand Total[a]	100.0	100.0	100.0	100.0	100.0
N	(668)	(1493)	(617)	(509)	(502)

[a] May not equal 100.0 due to rounding.

Source: Donald J. Mulvihill and Melvin M. Tumin, *Crimes of Violence*, Vol. 11. National Commission on the Causes and Prevention of Violence, Washington, D.C., 1969, Table 7, p. 221.

compared to 34%); and a larger proportion of events were outside (74% compared to 59%). Both armed and unarmed robbery usually involved individuals unrelated in a primary group (Mulvihill and Tumin 1969).

Property crimes are usually analyzed on the basis of point of entry or type of establishment victimized. Of 313 commercial burglaries surveyed by the President's Commission on Law Enforcement and the Administration of Justice, 7% involved entry through unlocked doors and 22% through unlocked windows. Thirty-five percent of the events involved forced entry by breaking windows, and locks were forced in 30% of the cases. One-third of the victimized establishments had burglar-resistant locks, but 62% of these were entered in some manner other than forcing the locks. Most of the burglarized commercial establishments were on the first floor (64%) (President's Commission on Law Enforcement and Administration of Justice 1967e: 132–145). Burglar alarms are apparently not very effective; a Small Business Administration field survey indicated that businesses with alarm systems experienced higher crime rates than those without (Joint Economic Committee, Subcommittee on Economy in Government 1970: 15). A detailed analysis of the environments surrounding commercial burglaries has shown that the "smash and grab" technique has become commoner in recent years. The criminal operates on the assumption that his intrusion time (Ti) will be short enough to ensure escape by the time police arrive (Luedtke and Associates 1970: 18a). The Ti factor and the Tap (time of arrival of police) are intercorrelated, and also closely related to the microenvironment. If Ti is long, Tap can be longer, too. If Ti is short, Tap must be short. In practice, Ti can be lengthened by various environmental design and security measures, providing limited law enforcement resources with more time to react.[*] A survey of seventy-three residential units (fifty-two single-family and twenty-one apartments) in Detroit indicated that about 77 of the burglaries involved side or rear entry. The "smash and grab" technique common in commercial burglaries is rising in significance in inner-city neighborhoods, since the Ti factor is small. Burglaries are commonest in or near corner residences, since detection is less likely (Luedtke and Associates 1970). Grand larceny occurs near victims' homes (29%) or in various other outdoor public places (25%), and the same locations dominate the distribution of vehicle theft (Ennis 1967: 39).

The data presented above suggest that each offense has its own "ecology of place." This microenvironment of crime is perceived by offenders and victims (or potential offenders and potential victims) and may result in various kinds of feedback affecting neighborhood quality and design.

---

[*] For a detailed cost/benefit model, see U.S. Senate, Select Committee on Small Business (1969: 219–223).

7.3.2 Neighborhood Characteristics and Crime Control

Perhaps the single most debated element of the urban microenvironment in the context of crime is population density. Intuitively, the idea of a positive relationship between density and crime is quite acceptable. We have noted already that crime rates are frequently highest in the central areas of cities, with a downward crime gradient towards the suburbs. This matches the typical gradient of population density, which is likewise highest in the inner city. It has been suggested by Newling (1966) that a *critical density* may be identified, about which social conditions (including crime) deteriorate, and population decline eventually occurs.* Opportunities for interpersonal conflict and for crimes against property are logically greatest where many people are located in a small area. The critical question is whether the opportunity element is magnified by an increased propensity to crime, due to high densities. Numerous observations of animal behavior have been made, with a view to learning about human behavior by analogy. Carstairs has reviewed such studies and listed some animal responses to high density, including enlarged adrenal glands, the breakdown of maternal behavior, asexual, hypersexual, or homosexual behavior, and various forms of aggressive conduct (Carstairs 1969). Although it has been shown that animals are adversely affected by high densities, different species react differently and it seems reasonable to assume that man's response pattern is also unique.

Just what is meant by *density*? Stokols has emphasized the importance of distinguishing between "density," which is a physical measurement of the number of people in an area, and "crowding," which is an individual's perception of too little space in relation to his needs (Stokols 1972). Galle, Gove, and McPherson (1972) have discriminated among several components of population density: persons per acre, structures per acre, housing units per structure, rooms per housing unit, and persons per room. These measures were related to five social pathologies, including the juvenile delinquency rate, for the seventy-five community areas of Chicago. For four of the five pathologies, including delinquency, *persons per room* was the most significant correlate, followed in importance by housing units per structure. It was concluded that a high number of persons per room would lead to "irritable, weary, harrassed, inefficient" parents, a repulsive environment for children, and a consequently high level of juvenile autonomy, which in turn contributes to the development of gangs of delinquents.

It would seem that conventional measures of population density (persons per acre or persons per acre of residential land) are quite inadequate as predictors of criminal environments. A "crowding index," such as persons

* For a detailed discussion of urban population densities, see Berry and Horton (1970), Chapter 9, pp. 276–305.

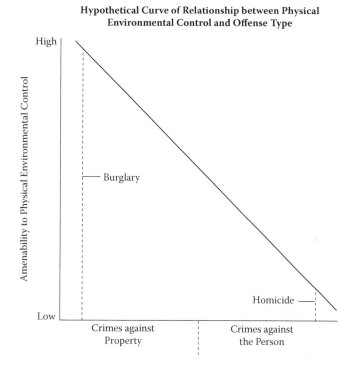

Figure 7.7 Hypothetical curve of relationship between physical environmental control and offense type.

per room, is apparently a much better measure since it approximates human reactions to space and is more likely to help us to predict areas of social pathology. If the locations of criminal areas can be predicted, can crime be controlled to some degree by the manipulation of various physical environmental elements? Figure 7.7 suggests that the amenability of crimes to physical environmental control varies considerably according to crime type. Thus, burglary is potentially amenable to control, since the security of structures can be increased (given unlimited expenditures) until they are virtually impregnable. At the other pole, we have already seen (Table 2.13, p. 32, in the original) that up to about 70% of homicides occur in situations in which the victim is a relative, friend, or acquaintance of the offender. Furthermore, 34% of homicides occur in the home and 61% in inside locations (Table 7.6). There is little scope for physical environmental control in these circumstances. Between burglary and homicide, there is overlap between property and personal crime in terms of potential for control. Property crimes such as fraud and embezzlement are less amenable, while personal offenses of the "stranger-to-stranger" type are more so.

A number of approaches to the modification of urban space have been suggested in order to improve crime control. Jane Jacobs (1961: 32–41) advocated mixed land uses in order to provide circulation on streets at all times. Angel identified *critical intensity zones*, areas in which possible victims attract possible offenders but where too few people are present to provide effective surveillance. Outside these zones, either too few people are available to provide victims, or there are too many to make the commission of crime safe. In either case, crime is greatly inhibited. It was proposed that areas suffering critical intensity (*e.g.*, pedestrian underground tunnels in Oakland, California) should have their pedestrian traffic adjusted. Among Angel's (1968: 16–28) suggested configurations for crime reduction were "evening squares," where nighttime activities would cluster with visible and accessible parking areas. Newman (1972: 27–33), in a study of crime in 100 housing projects in New York City in 1969, concluded that the crime rate was closely related to building height and, to a lesser extent, to project size. In projects with up to 1000 units and six stories, the mean number of crimes per 1000 was forty-seven, compared to sixty-seven in projects with more than 1000 units and higher than six stories. Furthermore, the spatial distribution of crime in projects differed in structures of different heights. In three-story structures, 17.2% of the crime occurred in interior public spaces; in buildings of thirteen stories or more, interior public space accounted for 54.8%. Within high-rise structures, elevators were the sites of 31% of all robberies. Newman (1972: 206) advanced the thesis that "it is possible through the provision of facilities in certain juxtapositions, to release potential behavioral attitudes and positive social relationships." Another approach to the manipulation of the urban physical environment has been the suggestion that water-based recreational facilities may have a role to play in crime control (Whitman, Davis, and Goldstone 1971).

7.4 Conclusions

Perceptions of crime in relation to our daily lives occur at both the macro- and microenvironmental levels. At the macro level we may wonder whether this city or that suburb is safe. At the micro level, the questions may be whether a block or neighborhood is safe, whether or not to open the door to a stranger, or whether the car, with its stereo tape deck, should be left unlocked. How are our perceptions of crime affecting the urban environment? Gold has identified several geographic elements of modern defensive cities, which constitute a model defensive environment:

1. The CBD would be protected by the presence of people during the day, but would be sealed off at night, with TV surveillance and improved microenvironmental security.

2. Inner-city affluent populations would live in expensively fortified "compounds."
3. Suburbs would be protected by distance from high-crime areas, and by racial and economic homogeneity.
4. Expressways would be "sanitized corridors" connecting safe areas. They would also be safe areas, due to the high-speed mode of transportation. Other types of transit would vary in their safety depending on location and time of day.
5. Other streets and residential areas in the central city would vary in their safety levels. In some areas, crime would be more or less uncontrollable, like parts of seventeenth-century Paris and eighteenth-century London (Gold, Murphy, and McGregor 1969; Gold 1970).

To arrive at this model, Gold has projected current trends into a pessimistic future. His assumption that central city crime has been a major element in suburbanization and the loss of white population from central cities has been questioned by Droettboom et al., who found that moves prompted by perceptions of crime were likely to lead to new domiciles in the central city, rather than in the suburbs. In essence, those most affected by crime—the poor and the black—have the lowest capacity to relocate (Droettboom et al. 1971). Other findings indicate that many people who want to move out of a neighborhood because they perceive it as being unsafe do not think that they will move soon (Kasi and Harburg 1972).

Central city crime is only one of many elements that have contributed to suburban growth. Much of this growth can be attributed to the physical necessity of accommodating an increasing population, combined with the attraction of new, functionally efficient housing. The expansion of minority communities through natural population increase and immigration, combined with the necessity of cheap housing, has inevitably led to the displacement of whites particularly when combined with the latter's overall negative perception of minority groups. A valid element of this negative stereotype is that crime rates are generally high in minority communities.

Classics in Environmental Criminology

The chapters selected for Part II: Classics in Environmental Criminology are the early theoretical and empirical pieces that define environmental criminology as a discipline. One of the most important aspects of these chapters is their change of analytical focus. Brantingham and Brantingham (1981a) refer to this change as shifting from a sociological imagination to a geographical imagination. Though at times the difference is subtle, it is profound.

In the early work on the ecology of crime, and much of the current ecological work as well, the focus is on the sociological aspects of neighborhoods that lead to criminal events. Consequently, it is the neighborhood with low socioeconomic status, high unemployment, high population turnover, and ethnic heterogeneity that has problems with crime. As such, the policy prescription for dealing with crime is to address the sociological "problems" within the respective neighborhoods. Similarly, it is argued that only with changes in these sociological variables will crime decrease.

Within environmental criminology, however, the focus is primarily on the individual. At times, particularly when testing these theories with census data, ecological units are the unit of analysis, but they are thought to represent the activities of the individuals that live within them. Of course, one must be careful not to commit the ecological fallacy when interpreting results.* This focus on the individual (for both offenders and victims) is central to all three main theoretical frameworks within environmental criminology. With a geographical imagination, environmental criminologists consider how an individual moves through the environment rather than how the individual is impacted by the sociological conditions of the neighborhood.

The first chapter, written by Lawrence Cohen and Marcus Felson, is the seminal article that introduces routine activity theory—Cohen and Felson prefer to use the term "approach" rather than "theory," but most authors use the term theory and we follow that practice here. In "Social Change and

---

* The ecological fallacy occurs if inference is made at the inappropriate scale: what is true of the whole is inferred to be true of all its parts. For example, a common relationship found in spatial criminology is that crime increases in neighborhoods with higher levels of unemployment; the ecological fallacy is committed if one infers that unemployed individuals within that neighborhood are more prone to crime.

Crime Rate Trends: A Routine Activity Approach" Cohen and Felson show why changes in the routine activities of individuals will impact the crime rate. Therefore, they are able to explain, theoretically and empirically, the rise in property and violent crime rates in the United States during the post–World War II period without invoking any change in the underlying sociological conditions. Because of changes in the frequency and ways we have come to move through our environment after the Second World War, we have simply created more opportunities for criminal victimization.

The empirical support Cohen and Felson find for their theory is at the national level for the United States. But if routine activity theory does represent reality, there must also be an effect at the individual level. In the next article, "Routine Activities and Crime: An Analysis of Victimization in Canada," Leslie Kennedy and David Forde found such an effect at the individual level for victimization in Canada. Though empirical verifications of routine activity theory had been published previously, Kennedy and Forde were the first to find empirical support for routine activity theory for both property and violent crimes. This advancement was possible because finer detail was available in the victimization data utilized by these authors.

The next three chapters are concerned with the geometric theory of crime. First comes "Notes on the Geometry of Crime." Based on the original work of Patricia Brantingham and Paul Brantingham, the geometric theory of crime (often simply referred to as "the geometry of crime") invokes concepts from the ways we move throughout our environment—paths, nodes, and edges—to explain the pattern of crime. Crime is just one of the many activities undertaken by (some) individuals and it follows the same principles of movement as noncriminal activities. Namely, we pursue our activities (criminal and noncriminal) in areas that are, more often than not, well known to us. As with routine activity theory, the focus in the geometric theory of crime is on the individual. Knowing *where* an individual spends most of his or her time will dictate *where* she or he offends or is victimized most of the time.

There are good tests of the geometric theory of crime, partially because the theory is, in essence, a truism. However, the first test of this theory, undertaken by George Rengert and John Wasilchick, in "The Use of Space in Burglary" largely confirms the predictions of the geometric theory of crime. Probably, the most compelling empirical investigation within the work of Rengert and Wasilchick is their study of directionality in (burglary) offending. They find that there is a strong directional component to where offenders find their targets: dominantly along the pathway between activity nodes (home, work, and recreation sites). Aside from a later edition of their own work, no other published work investigates the directionality of individuals involved in burglary.

These foundational works on the geometric theory of crime are followed by three chapters that cover the rational choice theory of offending. The first, written by Ronald Clarke and Derek Cornish, "Modeling Offenders' Decisions: A Framework for Research and Policy," and published in 1985, is the original article produced by these authors on the subject and it outlines the importance of offender decisions for theory, empirical work, and policy. Not only do Clarke and Cornish outline *why* rational choice theory is useful to the study of crime, but they also show *how* it could be implemented.

In a chapter from a book edited by Cornish and Clarke the following year, "Linking Criminal Choices, Routine Activities, Informal Control, and Criminal Outcomes," Marcus Felson shows the utility of a rational criminal choice theory when linking routine activity theory with social control theory. Felson demonstrates that routine activities and social controls are the context for criminal choices. Therefore, crime is a choice, just not a choice made within circumstances of our own choosing.

Though not a test of rational choice theory, the following chapter, "Understanding Crime Displacement: An Application of Rational Choice Theory," by Cornish and Clarke shows how a rational choice perspective can be used to understand crime displacement, or a lack thereof, by developing the concept of choice-structuring properties. In the past, critics of crime prevention efforts argued that crime is not "prevented" but simply displaced elsewhere. Cornish and Clarke argue that this is because crime has not been conceptualized as a choice, but as a release of pent-up energy charged by sociological conditions. Through the development of choice-structuring properties, Cornish and Clarke are able to provide a theoretical framework for explaining why crime displacement is not a necessary result of crime prevention efforts.

The last chapter on pattern theory is also written by Patricia and Paul Brantingham, "Environment, Routine, and Situation: Toward a Pattern Theory of Crime." Pattern theory is a first attempt at synthesizing the various perspectives within environmental criminology into a meta-theory. In this chapter, Brantingham and Brantingham show systematically the similarities (i.e., patterns) within and between the various theoretical frameworks presented in environmental criminology today. The ability to formulate such a meta-theory is critical because it forces one to see the patterns between the theories that define the discipline of environmental criminology, not just the patterns in crime that they individually predict.

Social Change and Crime Rate Trends

A Routine Activity Approach (1979)

L.E. COHEN
M. FELSON

From Cohen, L.E. and Felson, M. (1979). Social change and crime rate trends: A routine activity approach. *American Sociological Review*, 44, 588–608.

Contents

8.1	Abstract	188
8.2	Introduction	188
	8.2.1 The Structure of Criminal Activity	190
	8.2.2 Selected Concepts from Hawley's Human Ecological Theory	190
	8.2.3 The Minimal Elements of Direct-Contact Predatory Violations	191
	8.2.4 The Ecological Nature of Illegal Acts	191
8.3	Relation of the Routine Activity Approach to Extant Studies	193
	8.3.1 Descriptive Analyses	193
	8.3.2 Macrolevel Analyses of Crime Trends and Cycles	194
	8.3.3 Microlevel Assumptions of the Routine Activity Approach	196
8.4	Empirical Assessment	197
	8.4.1 Circumstances and Location of Offenses	197
	8.4.2 Target Suitability	199
	8.4.3 Family Activities and Crime Rates	200
8.5	Changing Trends in Routine Activity Structure and Parallel Trends in Crime Rates	204
	8.5.1 Trends in Human Activity Patterns	204
	8.5.2 Related Property Trends and Their Relation to Human Activity Patterns	206
	8.5.3 Related Trends in Business Establishments	206
	8.5.4 Composition of Crime Trends	207

8.6   The Relationship of the Household Activity Ratio to Five Annual
      Official Index Crime Rates in the United States, 1947–1974   208
      8.6.1   Findings   210
8.7   Discussion   214

8.1 Abstract

In this paper we present a "routine activity approach" for analyzing crime rate trends and cycles. Rather than emphasizing the characteristics of offenders, with this approach we concentrate upon the circumstances in which they carry out predatory criminal acts. Most criminal acts require convergence in space and time of likely offenders, suitable targets, and the absence of capable guardians against crime. Human ecological theory facilitates an investigation into the way in which social structure produces this convergence, hence allowing illegal activities to feed upon the legal activities of everyday life. In particular, we hypothesize that the dispersion of activities away from households and families increases the opportunity for crime and thus generates higher crime rates. A variety of data is presented in support of the hypothesis, which helps explain crime rate trends in the United States 1947 to 1974 as a byproduct of changes in such variables as labor force participation and single-adult households.

8.2 Introduction

In its summary report the National Commission on the Causes and Prevention of Violence (1969: xxxvii) presents an important sociological paradox: "Why, we must ask, have urban violent crime rates increased substantially during the past decade when the conditions that are supposed to cause violent crime have not worsened—have, indeed, generally improved?"

The Bureau of the Census, in its latest report on trends in social and economic conditions in metropolitan areas, states that most "indicators of well-being point toward progress in the cities since 1960." Thus, for example, the proportion of blacks in cities who completed high school rose from 43 percent in 1960 to 61 percent in 1968; unemployment rates dropped significantly between 1959 and 1967 and the median family income of blacks in cities increased from 61 percent to 68 percent of the median white family income during the same period. Also during the same period the number of persons living below the legally defined poverty level in cities declined from 11.3 million to 8.3 million.

Despite the general continuation of these trends in social and economic conditions in the United States, the *Uniform Crime Report* (FBI 1975: 49) indicates that between 1960 and 1975 reported rates of robbery, aggravated assault, forcible rape, and homicide increased by 263 percent, 164 percent, 174 percent, and 188 percent, respectively. Similar property crime rate increases reported during this same period* (e.g., 200 percent for burglary rate) suggest that the paradox noted by the Violence Commission applies to nonviolent offenses as well.

In this paper we consider these paradoxical trends in crime rates in terms of changes in the "routine activities" of everyday life. We believe the structure of such activities influences criminal opportunity and therefore affects trends in a class of crimes we refer to as *direct-contact predatory violations.* Predatory violations are defined here as illegal acts in which "someone definitely and intentionally takes or damages the person or property of another" (Glaser 1971: 4). Further, this analysis is confined to those predatory violations involving direct physical contact between at least one offender and at least one person or object which that offender attempts to take or damage.

We argue that structural changes in routine activity patterns can influence crime rates by affecting the convergence in space and time of the three minimal elements of direct-contact predatory violations: (1) motivated offenders, (2) suitable targets, and (3) the absence of capable guardians against a violation. We further argue that the lack of any one of these elements is sufficient to prevent the successful completion of a direct-contact predatory crime, and that the convergence in time and space of suitable targets and the absence of capable guardians may even lead to large increases in crime rates without necessarily requiring any increase in the structural conditions that motivate individuals to engage in crime. That is, if the proportion of motivated offenders or even suitable targets were to remain stable in a community, changes in routine activities could nonetheless alter the likelihood of their convergence in space and time, thereby creating more opportunities for crimes to occur. Control therefore becomes critical. If controls through routine activities were to decrease, illegal predatory activities could then be likely to increase. In the

---

* For their comments, we thank David J. Bordua, Ross M. Stolzenberg, Christopher S. Dunn, Kenneth C. Land, Robert Schoen, Amos Hawley, and an anonymous reviewer. Funding for this study was provided by these United States Government grants: National Institute for Mental Health 1-R01-MH31117-01; National Science Foundation, SOC-77-13261; and United States Army RI/DAHC 19-76-G-0016. The authors' name order is purely alphabetical.

Though official data severely underestimate crime, they at least provide a rough indicator of trends over time in the volume of several major felonies. The possibility that these data also reflect trends in rates at which offenses are reported to the police has motivated extensive victimology research (see Nettler 1974 and Hindelang 1976 for reviews). This work consistently finds that seriousness of offense is the strongest determinant of citizen reporting to law enforcement officials (Skogan 1976: 145; Hindelang 1976: 401). Hence the upward trend in official crime rates since 1960 in the United States may reflect increases in both the volume and seriousness of offenses. Though disaggregating these two components may not be feasible, one may wish to interpret observed trends as generated largely by both.

process of developing this explanation and evaluating its consistency with existing data, we relate our approach to classical human ecological concepts and to several earlier studies.

8.2.1 The Structure of Criminal Activity

Sociological knowledge of how community structure generates illegal acts has made little progress since Shaw and McKay and their colleagues (1929) published their path-breaking work, *Delinquency Areas*. Variations in crime rates over space long have been recognized (e.g., see Guerry 1833; Quetelet 1842), and current evidence indicates that the pattern of these relationships within metropolitan communities has persisted (Reiss 1976). Although most spatial research is quite useful for describing crime rate patterns and providing post hoc explanations, these works seldom consider—conceptually or empirically—the fundamental human ecological character of illegal acts as *events* which occur at specific locations in *space* and *time*, involving specific persons and/or objects. These and related concepts can help us to develop an extension of the human ecological analysis to the problem of explaining changes in crime rates over time. Unlike many criminological inquiries, we do not examine why individuals or groups are inclined criminally, but rather we take criminal inclination as given and examine the manner in which the spatiotemporal organization of social activities helps people to translate their criminal inclinations into action. Criminal violations are treated here as routine activities which share many attributes of, and are interdependent with, other routine activities.

This interdependence between the structure of illegal activities and the organization of everyday sustenance activities leads us to consider certain concepts from human ecological literature.

8.2.2 Selected Concepts from Hawley's Human Ecological Theory

While criminologists traditionally have concentrated on the *spatial* analysis of crime rates within metropolitan communities, they seldom have considered the *temporal* interdependence of these acts. In his classic theory of human ecology, Amos Hawley (1950) treats the community not simply as a unit of territory but rather as an organization of symbiotic and commensalistic relationships as human activities are performed over both space and time.

Hawley identified three important temporal components of community structure: (1) *rhythm*, the regular periodicity with which events occur, as with the rhythm of travel activity; (2) *tempo*, the number of events per unit of time, such as the number of criminal violations per day on a given street; and (3) *timing*, the coordination among different activities which are more or less interdependent, such as the coordination of an offender's rhythms with those of a victim (Hawley 1950: 289; the examples are ours). These components of temporal organization, often neglected in criminological research, prove useful in analyzing how illegal tasks are performed—a utility which becomes more apparent after noting the spatiotemporal requirements of illegal activities.

8.2.3 The Minimal Elements of Direct-Contact Predatory Violations

As we previously stated, despite their great diversity, direct-contact predatory violations share some important requirements which facilitate analysis of their structure. Each successfully completed violation minimally requires an *offender* with both criminal inclinations and the ability to carry out those inclinations, a person or object providing a *suitable target* for the offender, and *absence of guardians* capable of preventing violations. We emphasize that the lack of any one of these elements normally is sufficient to prevent such violations from occurring.* Though guardianship is implicit in everyday life, it usually is marked by the absence of violations; hence it is easy to overlook. While police action is analyzed widely, guardianship by ordinary citizens of one another and of property as they go about routine activities may be one of the most neglected elements in sociological research on crime, especially since it links seemingly unrelated social roles and relationships to the occurrence or absence of illegal acts.

The conjunction of these minimal elements can be used to assess how social structure may affect the tempo of each type of violation. That is, the probability that a violation will occur at any specific time and place might be taken as a function of the convergence of likely offenders and suitable targets in the absence of capable guardians. Through consideration of how trends and fluctuations in social conditions affect the frequency of this convergence of criminogenic circumstances, an explanation of temporal trends in crime rates can be constructed.

8.2.4 The Ecological Nature of Illegal Acts

This ecological analysis of direct-contact predatory violations is intended to be more than metaphorical. In the context of such violations, people, gaining and losing sustenance, struggle among themselves for property, safety, territorial hegemony, sexual outlet, physical control, and sometimes for survival itself.

---

* The analytical distinction between target and guardian is not important in those cases where a personal target engages in self-protection from direct-contact predatory violations. We leave open for the present the question of whether a guardian is effective or ineffective in all situations. We also allow that various guardians may primarily supervise offenders, targets, or both. These are questions for future examination.

The interdependence between offenders and victims can be viewed as a predatory relationship between functionally dissimilar individuals or groups. Since predatory violations fail to yield any net gain in sustenance for the larger community, they can only be sustained by feeding upon other activities. As offenders cooperate to increase their efficiency at predatory violations and as potential victims organize their resistance to these violations, both groups apply the symbiotic principle to improve their sustenance position. On the other hand, potential victims of predatory crime may take evasive actions which encourage offenders to pursue targets other than their own. Since illegal activities must feed upon other activities, the spatial and temporal structure of routine legal activities should play an important role in determining the location, type and quantity of illegal acts occurring in a given community or society. Moreover, one can analyze how the structure of community organization as well as the level of technology in a society provide the circumstances under which crime can thrive. For example, technology and organization affect the capacity of persons with criminal inclinations to overcome their targets, as well as affecting the ability of guardians to contend with potential offenders by using whatever protective tools, weapons, and skills they have at their disposal. Many technological advances designed for legitimate purposes—including the automobile, small power tools, hunting weapons, highways, telephones, etc.—may enable offenders to carry out their own work more effectively or may assist people in protecting their own or someone else's person or property.

Not only do routine legitimate activities often provide the wherewithal to commit offenses or to guard against others who do so, but they also provide offenders with suitable targets. Target suitability is likely to reflect such things as value (i.e., the material or symbolic desirability of a personal or property target for offenders), physical visibility, access, and the inertia of a target against illegal treatment by offenders (including the weight, size, and attached or locked features of property inhibiting its illegal removal and the physical capacity of personal victims to resist attackers with or without weapons). Routine production activities probably affect the suitability of consumer goods for illegal removal by determining their value and weight. Daily activities may affect the location of property and personal targets in visible and accessible places at particular times. These activities also may cause people to have on hand objects that can be used as weapons for criminal acts or self-protection or to be preoccupied with tasks which reduce their capacity to discourage or resist offenders.

While little is known about conditions that affect the convergence of potential offenders, targets, and guardians, this is a potentially rich source of propositions about crime rates. For example, daily work activities separate many people from those they trust and the property they value. Routine activities also bring together at various times of day or night persons of different background, sometimes in the presence of facilities, tools, or weapons which influence the commission or avoidance of illegal acts. Hence, the timing of work, schooling, and leisure may be of central importance for explaining crime rates.

The ideas presented so far are not new, but they frequently are overlooked in the theoretical literature on crime. Although an investigation of the literature uncovers significant examples of descriptive and practical data related to the routine activities upon which illegal behavior feeds, these data seldom are treated within an analytical framework. The next section reviews some of this literature.

8.3 Relation of the Routine Activity Approach to Extant Studies

A major advantage of the routine activity approach presented here is that it helps assemble some diverse and previously unconnected criminological analyses into a single substantive framework. This framework also serves to link illegal and legal activities, as illustrated by a few examples of descriptive accounts of criminal activity.

8.3.1 Descriptive Analyses

There are several descriptive analyses of criminal acts in the criminological literature. For example, Thomas Reppetto's (1974) study, *Residential Crime*, considers how residents supervise their neighborhoods and streets and limit access of possible offenders. He also considers how distance of households from the central city reduces risks of criminal victimization. Reppetto's evidence—consisting of criminal justice records, observations of comparative features of geographic areas, victimization survey data, and offender interviews—indicates that offenders are very likely to use burglary tools and to have at least minimal technical skills, that physical characteristics of dwellings affect their victimization rates, that the rhythms of residential crime rate patterns are marked (often related to travel and work patterns of residents), and that visibility of potential sites of crime affects the risk that crimes will occur there. Similar findings are reported by Pope's (1977a; 1977b) study of burglary in California and by Scarr's (1973) study of burglary in and around the District of Columbia. In addition, many studies report that architectural and environmental design as well as community crime programs serve to decrease target suitability and increase capable guardianship (see, for example, Newman 1972; Jeffery 1971; Washnis 1976), while many biographical or autobiographical descriptions of illegal activities note that lawbreakers take into account the nature of property and/or the structure of human activities as they go about their illegal work (see, e.g., Chambliss 1972; Klockars 1974; Sutherland 1937a; Letkemann 1973; Jackson 1969; Martin 1952; Maurer 1964; Cameron 1964; Williamson 1968).

Evidence that the spatiotemporal organization of society affects patterns of crime can be found in several sources. Strong variations in specific predatory crime rates from hour to hour, day to day, and month to month are reported often (e.g., Wolfgang 1958; Amir 1971; Reppetto 1974; Scarr 1973; FBI 1975, 1976), and these variations appear to correspond to the various tempos of the related legitimate activities upon which they feed. Also at a microsociological level, Short and Strodtbeck (1965: Chapters 5 and 11) describe opportunities for violent confrontations of gang boys and other community residents which arise in the context of community leisure patterns, such as "quarter parties" in black communities, and the importance, in the calculus of decision making employed by participants in such episodes, of low probabilities of legal intervention. In addition, a wealth of empirical evidence indicates strong spatial variations over community areas in crime and delinquency rates* (for an excellent discussion and review of the literature on ecological studies of crimes, see Wilks 1967). Albert Reiss (1976) has argued convincingly that these spatial variations (despite some claims to the contrary) have been supported consistently by both official and unofficial sources of data. Reiss further cites victimization studies which indicate that offenders are very likely to select targets not far from their own residence (see USDJ 1974a, 1974b, 1974c).

8.3.2 Macrolevel Analyses of Crime Trends and Cycles

Although details about how crime occurs are intrinsically interesting, the important analytical task is to learn from these details how illegal activities carve their niche within the larger system of activities. This task is not an easy one. For example, attempts by Bonger (1916), Durkheim (1951, 1966), Henry and Short (1954), and Fleisher (1966) to link the rate of illegal activities to the economic condition of a society have not been completely successful. Empirical tests of the relationships postulated in the above studies have produced inconsistent results which some observers view as an indication that the level of crime is not related systematically to the economic conditions of a society (Mansfield, Gould, and Namenwirth 1974: 463; Cohen and Felson 1979b).

---

* One such ecological study by Sarah Boggs (1965) presents some similar ideas in distinguishing familiarity of offenders with their targets and profitability of targets as two elements of crime occurrence. Boggs's work stands apart from much research on the ecology of crime in its consideration of crime occurrence rates separately from offender rates. The former consist of the number of offenses committed in a given area per number of suitable targets within that area (as estimated by various indicators). The latter considers the residence of offenders in computing the number of offenders per unit of population. Boggs examines the correlations between crime occurrence rates and offender rates for several offenses in St. Louis and shows that the two are often independent. It appears from her analysis that both target and offender characteristics play a central role in the location of illegal activity.

It is possible that the wrong economic and social factors have been employed in these macro studies of crime. Other researchers have provided stimulating alternative descriptions of how social change affects the criminal opportunity structure, thereby influencing crime rates in particular societies. For example, at the beginning of the nineteenth century, Patrick Colquhoun (1800) presented a detailed, lucid description and analysis of crime in the London metropolitan area and suggestions for its control. He assembled substantial evidence that London was experiencing a massive crime wave attributable to a great increment in the assemblage and movement of valuable goods through its ports and terminals.

A similar examination of crime in the period of the English industrial expansion was carried out by a modern historian, J.J. Tobias (1967), whose work on the history of crime in nineteenth century England is perhaps the most comprehensive effort to isolate those elements of social change affecting crime in an expanding industrial nation. Tobias details how far-reaching changes in transportation, currency, technology, commerce, merchandising, poverty, housing, and the like had tremendous repercussions on the amount and type of illegal activities committed in the nineteenth century. His thesis is that structural transformations either facilitated or impeded the opportunities to engage in illegal activities. In one of the few empirical studies of how recent social change affects the opportunity structure for crime in the United States, Leroy Gould (1969) demonstrated that the increase in the circulation of money and the availability of automobiles between 1921 and 1965 apparently led to an increase in the rate of bank robberies and auto thefts, respectively. Gould's data suggest that these relationships are due more to the abundance of opportunities to perpetrate the crimes than to short-term fluctuations in economic activities.

Although the sociological and historical studies cited in this section have provided some useful *empirical* generalizations and important insights into the incidence of crime, it is fair to say that they have not articulated systematically the *theoretical* linkages between routine legal activities and illegal endeavors. Thus, these studies cannot explain how changes in the larger social structure generate changes in the opportunity to engage in predatory crime and hence account for crime rate trends.* To do so requires a con-

---

* The concept of the opportunity for crime contained in the above research and in this study differs considerably from the traditional sociological usage of the differential opportunity concept. For example, Cloward and Ohlin (1960) employed this term in discussing how legitimate and illegitimate opportunities affect the resolution of adjustment problems leading to gang delinquency. From their viewpoint, this resolution depends upon the kind of social support for one or another type of illegitimate activity that is given at different points in the social structure (Cloward and Ohlin 1960: 151). Rather than circumstantial determinants of crime, they use differential opportunity to emphasize structural features which motivate offenders to perpetrate certain types of crimes. Cloward and Ohlin are largely silent on the interaction of this motivation with target suitability and guardianship as this interaction influences crime rates.

ceptual framework such as that sketched in the preceding section. Before attempting to demonstrate the feasibility of this approach with macrolevel data, we examine available microlevel data for its consistency with the major assumptions of this approach.

8.3.3 Microlevel Assumptions of the Routine Activity Approach

The theoretical approach taken here specifies that crime rate trends in the post-World War II United States are related to patterns of what we have called routine activities. We define these as any recurrent and prevalent activities that provide for basic population and individual needs, whatever their biological or cultural origins. Thus routine activities would include formalized work, as well as the provision of standard food, shelter, sexual outlet, leisure, social interaction, learning, and child rearing. These activities may go well beyond the minimal levels needed to prevent a population's extinction, so long as their prevalence and recurrence makes them a part of everyday life.

Routine activities may occur (1) at home, (2) in jobs away from home, and (3) in other activities away from home. The latter may involve primarily household members or others. We shall argue that, since World War II, the United States has experienced a major shift of routine activities away from the first category into the remaining ones, especially those nonhousehold activities involving nonhousehold members. In particular, we shall argue that this shift in the structure of routine activities increases the probability that motivated offenders will converge in space and time with suitable targets in the absence of capable guardians, hence contributing to significant increases in the direct-contact predatory crime rates over these years.

If the routine activity approach is valid, then we should expect to find evidence for a number of empirical relationships regarding the nature and distribution of predatory violations. For example, we would expect routine activities performed within or near the home and among family or other primary groups to entail lower risk of criminal victimization because they enhance guardianship capabilities. We should also expect that routine daily activities affect the location of property and personal targets in visible and accessible places at particular times, thereby influencing their risk of victimization. Furthermore, by determining their size and weight and in some cases their value, routine production activities should affect the suitability of consumer goods for illegal removal. Finally, if the routine activity approach is useful for explaining the paradox presented earlier, we should find that the circulation of people and property, the size and weight of consumer items, etc., will parallel changes in crime rate trends for the post-World War II United States.

The veracity of the routine activity approach can be assessed by analyses of both microlevel and macrolevel interdependencies of human activities. While consistency at the former level may appear noncontroversial, or even obvious, one nonetheless needs to show that the approach does not contradict existing data before proceeding to investigate the latter level.

8.4 Empirical Assessment

8.4.1 Circumstances and Location of Offenses

The routine activity approach specifies that household and family activities entail lower risk of criminal victimization than nonhousehold-nonfamily activities, despite the problems in measuring the former.*

National estimates from large-scale government victimization surveys in 1973 and 1974 support this generalization (see methodological information in Hindelang et al. 1976: Appendix 6). Table 8.1 presents several incident-victimization rates per 100,000 population ages 12 and older. Clearly, the rates in Panels A and B are far lower at or near home than elsewhere and far lower among relatives than others. The data indicate that risk of victimization varies directly with social distance between offender and victim. Panel C of this table indicates, furthermore, that risk of lone victimization far exceeds the risk of victimization for groups. These relationships are strengthened by considering time budget evidence that, on the average, Americans spend 16.26 hours per day at home, 1.38 hours on streets, in parks, etc., and 6.36 hours in other places (Szalai 1972: 795). Panel D of Table 8.1 presents our

---

* Recent research indicates the existence of substantial quantities of family violence which remains outside of the Uniform Crime Report (UCR) data (see annotated bibliography of family violence in Lystad 1974). While we cannot rule out the likelihood that much family violence is concealed from victimization surveys, the latter capture information absent from police data and still indicate that nonfamily members are usually much more dangerous than family members are to each other (see text). Also, when family violence leads to death, its suppression becomes quite difficult. The murder circumstances data indicate that about two-thirds of killings involve nonrelatives. Without denying the evidence that the level of family violence is far greater than police reports would indicate, available data also suggest that time spent in family activities within households incurs less risk of victimization than many alternative activities in other places. In addition, many of the most common offenses (such as robbery and burglary) always have been recognized as usually involving nonfamily members.

Table 8.1   Incident-Specific Risk Rates for Rape, Robbery, Assault, and Personal Larceny with Contact, United States, 1974

	Rape	Robbery	Assault	Personal Larceny with Contact	Total
A.* Place of Residence					
In or near home	63	129	572	75	839
Elsewhere	119	584	1,897	1,010	3,610
B.* Victim-Offender Relationship					
(Lone offender)					
Relative	7	13	158	5	183
Well known	23	30	333	30	416
Casual acquaintance	11	26	308	25	370
Don't know/sight only	106	227	888	616	1,837
(Multiple offender)					
Any known	10***	68	252	43	373
All strangers	25***	349	530	366	1,270
C.* Number of Victims					
One	179	647	2,116	1,062	4,004
Two	3	47	257	19	326
Three	0	13	53	3	90
Four plus	0	6	43	1	50
D.** Location and Relationship (Sole Offender Only)					
Home, stranger	61	147	345	103	654
Home, nonstranger	45	74	620	22	761
Street, stranger	1,370	7,743	15,684	7,802	32,460
Street, nonstranger	179	735	5,777	496	7,167
Elsewhere, stranger	129	513	1,934	2,455	4,988
Elsewhere, nonstranger	47	155	1,544	99	1,874

*   Calculated from Hindelang et al., 1977: Tables 3.16, 3.18, 3.27, 3.28. Rates are per 100,000 persons ages 12 and over.

**   See fn. 6 for source. Rates are per billion person-hours in stated locations.

***   Based on white data only due to lack of suitable sample size for nonwhites as victims of rape with multiple offenders.

estimates of victimization per billion person-hours spent in such locations.*
For example, personal larceny rates (with contact) are 350 times higher at
the hands of strangers in streets than at the hands of nonstrangers at home.
Separate computations from 1973 victimization data (USDJ 1976: Table 48)
indicate that there were two motor vehicle thefts per million vehicle-hours
parked at or near home, 55 per million vehicle-hours in streets, parks, play-
grounds, school grounds, or parking lots, and 12 per million vehicle-hours
elsewhere. While the direction of these relationships is not surprising, their
magnitudes should be noted. It appears that risk of criminal victimization
varies dramatically among the circumstances and locations in which people
place themselves and their property.

8.4.2 Target Suitability

Another assumption of the routine activity approach is that target suitability influences the occurrence of direct-contact predatory violations. Though
we lack data to disaggregate all major components of target suitability (i.e.,
value, visibility, accessibility, and inertia), together they imply that expensive
and movable durables, such as vehicles and electronic appliances, have the
highest risk of illegal removal.

As a specific case in point, we compared the 1975 composition of stolen
property reported in the Uniform Crime Report (FBI 1976: Tables 26 and
27) with national data on personal consumer expenditures for goods (CEA
1976: Tables 13 to 16) and to appliance industry estimates of the value of
shipments the same year (*Merchandising Week* 1976). We calculated that
$26.44 in motor vehicles and parts were stolen for each $100 of these goods
consumed in 1975, while $6.82 worth of electronic appliances were stolen
per $100 consumed. Though these estimates are subject to error in citizen
and police estimation, what is important here is their size relative to other
rates. For example, only 8 cents worth of nondurables and 12 cents worth of
furniture and nonelectronic household durables were stolen per $100 of each

---

* Billion person-hours can easily be conceptualized as 1,000,000 persons spending 1,000
hours each (or about 42 days) in a given location (Szalai 1972: 795). Fox obtained these
data from a 1966 time budget study in 44 American cities. The study was carried out by
the Survey Research Center, the University of Michigan. We combined four subsamples
in computing our figures. We combined activities into three locations, as follows: (1) at
or just outside home; (2) at another's home, restaurants or bars, or indoor leisure; (3) in
streets, parks, or outdoor leisure. Our computing formula was

$$Q = [(R \div 15^5) \div (A \cdot 365)] \cdot 10^9$$

where Q is the risk per billion person-hours: R is the victimization rate, reported per 10^5
persons in Hindelang et al. (1976: Table 318); A is the hours spent per location calculated
from Szalai (1972: 795): 365 is the multiplier to cover a year's exposure to risk; and 10^9
converts risk per person-hour to billion person-hours.

category consumed, the motor vehicle risk being, respectively, 330 and 220 times as great. Though we lack data on the "stocks" of goods subject to risk, these "flow" data clearly support our assumption that vehicles and electronic appliances are greatly overrepresented in thefts.

The 1976 Buying Guide issue of *Consumer Reports* (1975) indicates why electronic appliances are an excellent retail value for a thief. For example, a Panasonic car tape player is worth $30 per lb., and a Phillips phonograph cartridge is valued at over $5,000 per lb., while large appliances such as refrigerators and washing machines are only worth $1 to $3 per lb. Not surprisingly, burglary data for the District of Columbia in 1969 (Scarr 1973: Table 9) indicate that home entertainment items alone constituted nearly four times as many stolen items as clothing, food, drugs, liquor, and tobacco combined and nearly eight times as many stolen items as office supplies and equipment. In addition, 69 percent of national thefts classified in 1975 (FBI 1976: Tables 1 and 26) involve automobiles, their parts or accessories, and thefts from automobiles or thefts of bicycles. Yet radio and television sets plus electronic components and accessories totaled only 0.10 percent of the total truckload tonnage terminated in 1973 by intercity motor carriers, while passenger cars, motor vehicle parts and accessories, motorcycles, bicycles, and their parts, totaled only 5.5 percent of the 410 million truckload tons terminated (ICC 1974). Clearly, portable and movable durables are reported stolen in great disproportion to their share of the value and weight of goods circulating in the United States.

8.4.3 Family Activities and Crime Rates

One would expect that persons living in single-adult households and those employed outside the home are less obligated to confine their time to family activities within households. From a routine activity perspective, these persons and their households should have higher rates of predatory criminal victimization. We also expect that adolescents and young adults who are perhaps more likely to engage in peer group activities rather than family activities will have higher rates of criminal victimization. Finally, married persons should have lower rates than others. Tables 8.2 and 8.3 largely confirm these expectations (with the exception of personal larceny with contact). Examining these tables, we note that victimization rates appear to be related inversely to age and are lower for persons in "less active" statuses (e.g., keeping house, unable to work, retired) and persons in intact marriages. A notable exception is indicated in Table 8.2, where persons unable to work appear more likely to be victimized by rape, robbery, and personal larceny with contact than are other "inactive persons." Unemployed persons also have unusually high rates of victimization. However, these rates are consistent with the routine activity approach offered here: the high rates of victimization suffered by the

Table 8.2 Selected Status-Specific Personal Victimization Rates for the United States (per 100,000 Persons in Each Category)

Variables and Sources	Victim Category	Rape	Robbery	Assault	Personal Larceny with Contact	Personal Larceny without Contact
A. Age (Source: Hindelang et al., 1977: Table 310, 1974 rates)	12–15	147	1,267	3,848	311	16,355
	16–19	248	1,127	5,411	370	15,606
	20–24	209	1,072	4,829	337	14,295
	25–34	135	703	3,023	263	10,354
	35–49	21	547	1,515	256	7,667
	50–64	33	411	731	347	4,588
	65+	20	388	492	344	1,845
B. Major activity of victim (Source: Hindelang et al., 1977: Table 313, 1974 rates)	(Male 16+)					
	Armed forces	—	1,388	4,153	118	16,274
	Employed	—	807	3,285	252	10,318
	Unemployed	—	2,179	7,984	594	15,905
	Keep house	—	0	2,475	463	3,998
	In school	—	1,362	5,984	493	17,133
	Unable to work	—	1,520	2,556	623	3,648
	Retired	—	578	662	205	2,080
	(Female 16+)					
	Keep house	116	271	978	285	4,433
	Employed	156	529	1,576	355	9,419
	Unemployed	798	772	5,065	461	12,338
	In school	417	430	2,035	298	12,810
	Unable to work	287	842	741	326	1,003
	Retired	120	172	438	831	1,571

Continued

Table 8.2 (*Continued*)　Selected Status-Specific Personal Victimization Rates for the United States (per 100,000 Persons in Each Category)

Variables and Sources	Victim Category	Rape	Robbery	Assault	Personal Larceny with Contact	Personal Larceny without Contact
C. Marital status (Source: USDJ: 1977, Table 5, 1973 rates)	(Male 12+)					
	Never married	—	1,800	5,870	450	16,450
	Married	—	550	2,170	170	7,660
	Separated/divorced	—	2,270	5,640	1,040	12,960
	Widowed	—	1,150	1,500	—	4,120
	(Female 12+)					
	Never married	360	580	2,560	400	12,880
	Married	70	270	910	220	6,570
	Separated/divorced	540	1,090	4,560	640	9,130
	Widowed	—	450	590	480	2,460

Note:　— indicates too few offenses for accurate estimates of rate. However, rates in these cells are usually small.

Table 8.3 Robbery-Burglary Victimization Rates by Ages and Number of Adults in Household, 1974 and 1976 General Social Survey

Age	Number of Adults in Household		Ratio
	1	2 or more	
18–35	0.200 (140)	0.095 (985)	2.11
36–55	0.161 (112)	0.079 (826)	2.04
56 and over	0.107 (262)	0.061 (640)	1.76
All ages	0.144 (514)	0.081 (2451)	1.78

Note: Numbers in parentheses are the base for computing risk rates.

Source: Calculated for 1974 and 1976 General Social Survey, National Opinion Research Center, University of Chicago.

unemployed may reflect their residential proximity to high concentrations of potential offenders as well as their age and racial composition, while handicapped persons have high risk of personal victimization because they are less able to resist motivated offenders. Nonetheless, persons who keep house have noticeably lower rates of victimization than those who are employed, unemployed, in school, or in the armed forces.

As Table 8.3 indicates, burglary and robbery victimization rates are about twice as high for persons living in single-adult households as for other persons in each age group examined. Other victimization data (USDJ 1976: Table 21) indicate that, while household victimization rates tend to vary directly with household size, larger households have lower rates per person. For example, the total household victimization rates (including burglary, household larceny, and motor vehicle theft) per 1,000 households were 168 for single-person households and 326 for households containing six or more persons. Hence, six people distributed over six single-person households experience an average of 1,008 household victimizations, more than three times as many as one six-person household. Moreover, age of household head has a strong relationship to a household's victimization rate for these crimes. For households headed by persons under 20, the motor vehicle theft rate is nine times as high, and the burglary and household larceny rates four times as high as those for households headed by persons 65 and over (USDJ 1976: Table 9).

Although the data presented in this section were not collected originally for the purpose of testing the routine activity approach, our efforts to rework them for these purposes have proven fruitful. The routine activity approach is consistent with the data examined and, in addition, helps to accommodate within a rather simple and coherent analytical framework certain findings which, though not necessarily new, might otherwise be attributed "descriptive" significance. In the next section, we examine macrosocial trends as they relate to trends in crime rates.

8.5 Changing Trends in Routine Activity Structure and Parallel Trends in Crime Rates

The main thesis presented here is that the dramatic increase in the reported crime rates in the United States since 1960 is linked to changes in the routine activity structure of American society and to a corresponding increase in target suitability and decrease in guardian presence. If such a thesis has validity, then we should be able to identify these social trends and show how they relate to predatory criminal victimization rates.

8.5.1 Trends in Human Activity Patterns

The decade 1960 to 1970 shows noteworthy trends in the activities of the American population. For example, the percent of the population consisting of female college students increased 118 percent (USBC 1975: Table 225). Married female labor force participant rates increased 31 percent (USBC 1975: Table 563), while the percent of the population living as primary individuals increased by 34 percent (USBC 1975: Table 51; see also Kobrin 1976). We gain some further insight into changing routine activity patterns by comparing hourly data for 1960 and 1971 on households *unattended* by persons ages 14 or over when U.S. census interviewers first called (see Table 8.4). These data suggest that the proportion of households unattended at 8:00 a.m. increased by almost half between 1960 and 1971. One also finds increases in rates of out-of-town travel, which provides greater opportunity for both daytime and nighttime burglary of residences. Between 1960 and 1970, there was a 72 percent increase in state and national park visits per capita (USBC 1975), a 144 percent increase in the percent of plant workers eligible for three weeks' vacation (BLS 1975: Table 1 16), and a 184 percent increase in overseas travelers per 100,000 population (USBC 1975: Table 366). The National Travel Survey, conducted as part of the U.S. Census Bureau's Census of Transportation, confirms the general trends, tallying an 81 percent increase in the number of vacations taken by Americans from 1967 to 1972, a five-year period (USBC 1973a: Introduction).

The dispersion of activities away from households appears to be a major recent social change. Although this decade also showed an important 31 percent increase in the percent of the population ages 15 to 24,

Table 8.4 Unattended Households

Time of Day	1960 Census (%)	November, 1971 Current Population Survey	Percent Change
8:00–8:59 a.m.	29	43	+48.9
9:00–9:59 a.m.	29	44	+58
10:00–10:59 a.m.	31	42	+36
11:00–11:59 a.m.	32	41	+28
12:00–12:59 p.m.	32	41	+28
1:00–1:59 p.m.	31	43	+39
2:00–2:59 p.m.	33	43	+30
3:00–3:59 p.m.	30	33	+10
4:00–4:59 p.m.	28	30	+7
5:00–5:59 p.m.	22	26	+18
6:00–6:59 p.m.	22	25	+14
7:00–7:59 p.m.	20	29	+45
8:00–8:59 p.m.	24	22	−8

age structure change was only one of many social trends occurring during the period, especially trends in the circulation of people and property in American society.*

The importance of the changing activity structure is underscored by taking a brief look at demographic changes between the years 1970 and 1975, a period of continuing crime rate increments. Most of the recent changes in age structure relevant to crime rates already had occurred by 1970; indeed, the proportion of the population ages 15 to 24 increased by only 6 percent between 1970 and 1975, compared with a 15 percent increase during the five years 1965 to 1970. On the other hand, major changes in the structure of routine activities continued during these years. For example, in only five years, the estimated proportion of the population consisting of husband-present, married women in the labor force households increased by 11 percent, while the estimated number of non-husband–wife households per 100,000 population increased from 9,150 to 11,420, a 25 percent increase (USBC 1976: Tables 50, 276; USBC 1970–1975). At the same time, the percent of population enrolled in higher education increased 16 percent between 1970 and 1975.

---

* While the more sophisticated treatments of the topic have varied somewhat in their findings, most recent studies attempting to link crime rate increases to the changing age structure of the American population have found that the latter account for a relatively limited proportion of the general crime trend (see, for example, Sagi and Wellford 1968; Ferdinand 1970; and Wellford 1973).

8.5.2 Related Property Trends and Their Relation to Human Activity Patterns

Many of the activity trends mentioned above normally involve significant investments in durable goods. For example, the dispersion of population across relatively more households (especially non-husband–wife households) enlarges the market for durable goods such as television sets and automobiles. Women participating in the labor force and both men and women enrolled in college provide a market for automobiles. Both work and travel often involve the purchase of major movable or portable durables and their use away from home.

Considerable data are available which indicate that sales of consumer goods changed dramatically between 1960 and 1970 (as did their size and weight), hence providing more suitable property available for theft. For example, during this decade, constant-dollar personal consumer expenditures in the United States for motor vehicles and parts increased by 71 percent, while constant-dollar expenditures for other durables increased by 105 percent (calculated from CEA 1976: Table B-16). In addition, electronic household appliances and small houseware shipments increased from 56.2 to 119.7 million units (*Electrical Merchandising Week*, 1964; *Merchandising Week* 1973). During the same decade, appliance imports increased in value by 681 percent (USBC 1975: Table 1368).

This same period appears to have spawned a revolution in small durable product design which further feeds the opportunity for crime to occur. Relevant data from the 1960 and 1970 Sears catalogs on the weight of many consumer durable goods were examined. Sears is the nation's largest retailer and its policy of purchasing and relabeling standard manufactured goods makes its catalogs a good source of data on widely merchandised consumer goods. The lightest television listed for sale in 1960 weighed 38 lbs., compared with 15 lbs. for 1970. Thus, the lightest televisions were 2½ times as heavy in 1960 as 1970. Similar trends are observed for dozens of other goods listed in the Sears catalog. Data from *Consumer Reports Buying Guide*, published in December of 1959 and 1969, show similar changes for radios, record players, slide projectors, tape recorders, televisions, toasters and many other goods. Hence, major declines in weight between 1960 and 1970 were quite significant for these and other goods, which suggests that the consumer goods market may be producing many more targets suitable for theft. In general, one finds rapid growth in property suitable for illegal removal and in household and individual exposure to attack during the years 1960 to 1975.

8.5.3 Related Trends in Business Establishments

Of course, as households and individuals increased their ownership of small durables, businesses also increased the value of the merchandise which they transport and sell as well as the money involved in these transactions. Yet the Census of Business conducted in 1958, 1963, 1967, and 1972 indicate that the number of wholesale, retail, service, and public warehouse establishments (including establishments owned by large organizations) was a nearly constant ratio of one for every 16 persons in the United States. Since more goods and money were distributed over a relatively fixed number of business establishments, the tempo of business activity per establishment apparently was increasing. At the same time, the percent of the population employed as sales clerks or salesmen in retail trade declined from 1.48 percent to 1.27 percent between 1960 and 1970, a 14.7 percent decline (USBC 1975: Table 589).

Though both business and personal property increased, the changing pace of activities appears to have exposed the latter to greater relative risk of attack, whether at home or elsewhere, due to the dispersion of goods among many more households, while concentrating goods in business establishments. However, merchandise in retail establishments with heavy volume and few employees to guard it probably is exposed to major increments in risk of illegal removal than is most other business property.

8.5.4 Composition of Crime Trends

If these changes in the circulation of people and property are in fact related to crime trends, the composition of the latter should reflect this. We expect relatively greater increases in personal and household victimization as compared with most business victimizations, while shoplifting should increase more rapidly than other types of thefts from businesses. We expect personal offenses at the hands of strangers to manifest greater increases than such offenses at the hands of nonstrangers. Finally, residential burglary rates should increase more in daytime than nighttime.

The available time series on the composition of offenses confirm these expectations. For example, Table 8.5 shows that commercial burglaries declined from 60 percent to 36 percent of the total, while daytime residential burglaries increased from 16 percent to 33 percent. Unlike the other crimes against business, shoplifting increased its share. Though we lack trend data on the circumstances of other violent offenses, murder data confirm our expectations. Between 1963 and 1975, felon-type murders increased from 17 percent to 32 percent of the total. Compared with a 47 percent increase in the rate of relative killings in this period, we calculated a 294 percent increase in the murder rate at the hands of known or suspected felon types.

Thus, the trends in the composition of recorded crime rates appear to be highly consistent with the activity structure trends noted earlier. In the next section we apply the routine activity approach in order to model crime rate trends and social change in the post-World War II United States.

Table 8.5   Offense Analysis Trend for Robbery, Burglary, Larceny and Murder, United States, 1960–1975

A. Robberies[a]	1960	1965	1970	
Highway robbery	52.6	57.0	59.8	
Residential robbery	8.0	10.1	13.1	
Commercial robbery	39.4	32.9	27.1	
Totals	100.0	100.0	100.0	
B. Burglaries	**1960**	**1965**	**1970**	**1975**
Residential	15.6	24.5	31.7	33.2
Residential nighttime	24.4	25.2	25.8	30.5
Commercial	60.0	50.2	42.5	36.3
Totals	100.0	99.9	100.0	100.0
C. Larcenies	**1960**	**1965**	**1970**	**1975**
Shoplifting	6.0	7.8	9.2	11.3
Other	94.0	92.2	90.8	88.7
Totals	100.0	100.0	100.0	100.0
D. Murders	**1960**	**1965**	**1970**	**1975**
Relative killings	31.0	31.0	23.3	22.4
Romance, arguments[b]	51.0	48.0	47.9	45.2
Felon types[c]	17.0	21.0	28.8	32.4
Totals	100.0	100.0	100.0	100.0

[a] Excluding miscellaneous robberies. The 1975 distribution omitted due to apparent instability of post-1970 data.

[b] Includes romantic triangles, lovers' quarrels, and arguments.

[c] Includes both known and suspected felon types.

Source: Offense analysis from UCR, various years.

8.6 The Relationship of the Household Activity Ratio to Five Annual Official Index Crime Rates in the United States, 1947–1974

In this section, we test the hypothesis that aggregate official crime rate trends in the United States vary directly over time with the dispersion of activities away from family and household. The limitations of annual time series data do not allow construction of direct measures of changes in hourly activity patterns, or quantities, qualities, and movements of exact stocks of household durable goods, but the Current Population Survey does provide related time series on labor force and household structure. From these data, we calculate annually (beginning in 1947) a household activity ratio by adding the number of married, husband-present female labor force participants (source:

BLS 1975: Table 5) to the number of non-husband–wife households (source: USBC 1947–1976), dividing this sum by the total number of households in the United States (source: USBC 1947–1976). This calculation provides an estimate of the proportion of American households in year t expected to be most highly exposed to risk of personal and property victimization due to the dispersion of their activities away from family and household and/or their likelihood of owning extra sets of durables subject to high risk of attack. Hence, the household activity ratio should vary directly with official index crime rates.

Our empirical goal in this section is to test this relationship, with controls for those variables that other researchers have linked empirically to crime rate trends in the United States. Since various researchers have found such trends to increase with the proportion of the population in teen and young adult years (Fox 1976; Land and Felson 1976; Sagi and Wellford 1968; Wellford 1973), we include the population ages 15 to 24 per 100,000 resident population in year t as our first control variable (source: USBC various years). Others (e.g., Brenner 1976a, 1976b) have found unemployment rates to vary directly with official crime rates over time, although this relationship elsewhere has been shown to be empirically questionable (see Mansfield, Gould, and Namenwirth 1974: 463; Cohen and Felson 1979b). Thus, as our second, control variable, we take the standard annual unemployment rate (per 100 persons ages 16 and over) as a measure of the business cycle (source: BLS 1975).

Four of the five crime rates that we utilize here (forcible rape, aggravated assault, robbery, and burglary) are taken from FBI estimates of offenses per 100,000 U.S. population (as revised and reported in OMB 1973). We exclude larceny-theft due to a major definitional change in 1960 and auto theft due to excessive multicollinearity in the analysis.* For our homicide indicator we employ the homicide mortality rate taken from the vital statistics data collected by the Bureau of the Census (various years). The latter rate has the advantage of being collected separately from the standard crime reporting system and is thought to contain less measurement error (see Bowers and Pierce 1975). Hence, this analysis of official index crime rates includes three violent offenses (homicide, forcible rape, and aggravated assault), one property offense (burglary), and one offense which involves both the removal of property and the threat of violence (robbery). The analysis thus includes one offense thought to have relatively low reporting reliability (forcible rape), one thought to have relatively high

---

* The auto theft rate lagged one year correlated quite strongly with the predictor variables. This multicollinearity impaired our difference equation analysis, although we again found consistently positive coefficients for the household activity ratio. We were able to remove autocorrelation by logging all variables and including the unemployment as a control, but do not report these equations.

reliability (homicide), and three others having relatively intermediate levels of reporting quality (Ennis 1967).

Since official crime rates in year t are likely to reflect some accumulation of criminal opportunity and inclinations over several years, one should not expect these rates to respond solely to the level of the independent variables for year t. A useful model of cumulative social change in circumstances such as this is the difference equation, which can be estimated in two forms (see Goldberg 1958). One form takes the first difference $(y_t - y_{t-1})$ as the dependent variable—in this case, the change in the official crime rate per 100,000 population between year $t - 1$ and year t. Alternatively, one can estimate the difference equation in autoregressive form by taking the official crime rate in year t as a function of the exogenous predictors plus the official crime rate in year $t - 1$ on the right-hand side of the equation. (See Land 1978 for a review of these and other methods and for references to related literature.) Both forms are estimable with ordinary least squares methods, which we employ for the years 1947 through 1974. The N is 28 years for all but the homicide rate, for which publication lags reduce our N to 26.

Even if a positive relationship between the household activity ratio and the official crime rates is observed, with controls for age and unemployment, we are open to the charge that this may be a spurious consequence of autocorrelation of disturbances; that is, the possibility that residuals are systematically related for nearby time points. While spurious relationships are a risk one also takes in cross-sectional regression analysis, time-series analysts have devised a variety of methods for monitoring and adjusting for spuriousness due to this autocorrelation, including the Durbin and Watson (1951) statistic, Durbin's h statistic (Durbin 1970), the Griliches (1967) criterion, as well as Cochrane and Orcutt (1949) corrections. We employ (but do not report in detail) these methods to check for the likelihood that the observed relationship is spurious. (See Land 1978 for a review of such tests and the related literature on their applicability and robustness; see Theil 1971 for a methodological review.)

8.6.1 Findings

Our time-series analysis for the years 1947 to 1974 consistently revealed positive and statistically significant relationships between the household activity ratio and each official crime rate change. Whichever official crime rate is employed, this finding occurs—whether we take the first difference for each crime rate as exogenous or estimate the equation in autoregressive form (with the lagged dependent variable on the right-hand side of the equation); whether we include or exclude the unemployment variable; whether we take the current scales of variables or convert them to natural log values; whether we employ the age structure variable as described or alter the ages examined (e.g., 14–24, 15–19, etc.). In short, the relationship is positive and significant in each case.

Before calculating the difference equations, we regressed each crime rate in year t on the three independent variables for year t. This ordinary structural equation also produced consistent positive and significant coefficients for the routine activity coefficient, the total variance explained ranges from 84 percent to 97 percent. However, the Durbin–Watson statistics for these equations indicated high risk of autocorrelation, which is hardly surprising since they ignore lagged effects. Reestimated equations taking first differences as endogenous reduced the risk of autocorrelation significantly (and also reduced variance explained to between 35 percent and 77 percent). These equations also consistently produce significant positive coefficients for the household activity variable. When unemployment is included in these equations, its coefficients are all negative and near zero.

The top panel of Table 8.6 presents regression estimates of first differences for five official crime rates, with the age structure and household activity variables in year t as the only predictors. Again, the household activity coefficients are consistently positive, with t ratios always significant with a one-tailed test. Except for the aggravated assault equation, the household activity variable has a t ratio and standardized coefficient greater than that of the age structure variable. The standardized coefficients for the household activity variable range from .42 to .72, while the age structure coefficients are consistently positive. In general, the household activity variable is a stronger predictor of official crime rate trends than the age structure.

The equations in the top panel of Table 8.6 generally have lower variance explained but also lower risk of autocorrelation of disturbances than those reported above. For all five equations, the Durbin–Watson statistic allows acceptance of the null hypothesis that autocorrelation is absent at the 1 percent level. A 5 percent level (which increases the likelihood of proving the statistic nonzero) allows us neither to accept nor reject the null hypothesis that autocorrelation is absent in the homicide and robbery equations.

Though autocorrelation has not been proven to exist in these five equations, its risk may be sufficient in two to motivate further efforts at equation estimation (see the bottom panel of Table 8.6). We estimated the equations in autoregressive form to see if the risk abates. Since the Durbin–Watson statistic was not designed for evaluating autocorrelation in these equations, we calculated Durbin's h, a statistic specifically designed for equations estimated with a lagged dependent variable (Durbin 1970), and recently found to be robust for small samples (Maddala and Rao 1973). This statistic allows acceptance of the null hypothesis (at both 1 percent and 5 percent levels) that autocorrelation is absent for all five equations. Application of the Griliches (1967) criterion further allows acceptance of each equation as manifesting distributing

Table 8.6 Regression Equations for First Differences in Five Index Crime Rates and Sensitivity Analyses, the United States, 1947–1974

	(1) Nonnegligent Homicide	(2) Forcible Rape	(3) Aggravated Assault	(4) Robbery	(5) Burglary
	First Difference Form				
Constant	-2.3632	-4.8591	-32.0507	-43.8838	-221.2303
t ratio	.3502	5.3679	7.6567	3.4497	3.7229
Proportion 15–24 (t)					
Standardized	.1667	.1425	.4941	.2320	.1952
Unstandardized	3.2190	6.4685	132.1072	116.7742	486.0806
t ratio	1.0695	.7505	3.3147	.9642	.8591
Household activity ratio (t)					
Standardized	.7162	.6713	.4377	.4242	.5106
Unstandardized	4.0676	8.9743	34.4658	62.8834	374.4746
t ratio	4.5959	3.5356	2.9364	1.7629	2.2474
Multiple R^2 adjusted	.6791	.5850	.7442	.3335	.4058
Degrees of freedom	23	25	25	25	25

Durbin–Watson value	2.5455	2.3388	2.3446	1.4548	1.7641
1% test	Accept	Accept	Accept	Accept	Accept
5% test	Uncertain	Accept	Accept	Uncertain	Accept
	Autoregressive Form				
Multiple R^2 adjusted	.9823	.9888	.9961	.9768	.9859
Durbin's h	−1.3751	−.7487	.9709	1.5490	1.1445
−1% test	Accept	Accept	Accept	Accept	Accept
−5% test	Accept	Accept	Accept	Accept	Accept
Griliches criterion	Accept	Accept	Accept	Accept	Accept
Cochrane–Orcutt correction, effect upon household activity	Minimal	Minimal	Minimal	Minimal	Minimal
Unemployment rate as control, effect upon household activity	Minimal	Minimal	Minimal	Minimal	Minimal

lags rather than serial correlation. We also employed the Cochrane–Orcutt (1949) iterative procedure to calculate a correction estimate for any autocorrelation present. The resulting correction for the household activity coefficient proves minimal in all five cases. Finally, we calculated each of the above equations for natural log values of the relevant variables, finding again that the household activity coefficient was consistently positive and statistically significant and the risk of autocorrelation reduced still further.

The positive and significant relationship between the household activity variable and the official crime rates is robust and appears to hold for both macro- and microlevel data; it explains five crime rate trends, as well as the changing composition of official crime rates reported in Table 8.5. These results suggest that routine activities may indeed provide the opportunity for many illegal activities to occur.

8.7 Discussion

In our judgment many conventional theories of crime (the adequacy of which usually is evaluated by cross-sectional data, or no data at all) have difficulty accounting for the annual changes in crime rate trends in the post-World War II United States. These theories may prove useful in explaining crime trends during other periods, within specific communities, or in particular subgroups of the population. Longitudinal aggregate data for the United States, however, indicate that the trends for many of the presumed causal variables in these theoretical structures are in a direction opposite to those hypothesized to be the causes of crime. For example, during the decade 1960–1970, the percent of the population below the low-income level declined 44 percent and the unemployment rate declined 186 percent. Central city population as a share of the whole population declined slightly, while the percent of foreign stock declined 0.196, etc. (see USBC 1975: 654, 19, 39).

On the other hand, the convergence in time and space of three elements (motivated offenders, suitable targets, and the absence of capable guardians) appears useful for understanding crime rate trends. The lack of any of these elements is sufficient to prevent the occurrence of a successful direct-contact predatory crime. The convergence in time and space of suitable targets and the absence of capable guardians can lead to large increases in crime rates without any increase or change in the structural conditions that motivate individuals to engage in crime. Presumably, had the social indicators of the variables hypothesized to be the causes of crime in conventional theories changed in the direction of favoring increased crime in the post-World War II United States, the increases in crime rates likely would have been even more staggering than those which were observed. In any event, it is our belief that criminologists have underemphasized the importance of the convergence of suitable targets and the absence of capable guardians in explaining recent increases in the crime rate. Furthermore, the effects of the convergence in time and space of these elements may be multiplicative rather than additive. That is, their convergence by a fixed percentage may produce increases in crime rates far greater than that fixed percentage, demonstrating how some relatively modest social trends can contribute to some relatively large changes in crime rate trends. The fact that logged variables improved our equations (moving Durbin–Watson values closer to "ideal" levels) lends support to the argument that such an interaction occurs.

Those few investigations of cross-sectional data which include household indicators produce results similar to ours. For example, Roncek (1975) and Choldin and Roncek (1976) report on block-level data for San Diego, Cleveland and Peoria and indicate that the proportion of a block's households that are primary individual households consistently offers the best or nearly the best predictor of a block's crime rate. This relationship persisted after they controlled for numerous social variables, including race, density, age and poverty. Thus the association between household structure and risk of criminal victimization has been observed in individual-level and block-level cross-sectional data, as well as aggregate national time-series data.

Without denying the importance of factors motivating offenders to engage in crime, we have focused specific attention upon violations themselves and the prerequisites for their occurrence. However, the routine activity approach might in the future be applied to the analysis of offenders and their inclinations as well. For example, the structure of primary group activity may affect the likelihood that cultural transmission or social control of criminal inclinations will occur, while the structure of the community may affect the tempo of criminogenic peer group activity. We also may expect that circumstances favorable for carrying out violations contribute to criminal inclinations in the long run by rewarding these inclinations.

We further suggest that the routine activity framework may prove useful in explaining why the criminal justice system, the community, and the family have appeared so ineffective in exerting social control since 1960. Substantial increases in the opportunity to carry out predatory violations may have undermined society's mechanisms for social control. For example, it may be difficult for institutions seeking to increase the certainty, celerity, and severity of punishment to compete with structural changes resulting in vast increases in the certainty, celerity, and value of rewards to be gained from illegal predatory acts.

It is ironic that the very factors that increase the opportunity to enjoy the benefits of life also may increase the opportunity for predatory violations. For example, automobiles provide freedom of movement to offenders as well as average citizens and offer vulnerable targets for theft. College enrollment, female labor force participation, urbanization, suburbanization, vacations, and new electronic durables provide various opportunities to escape the confines of the household while they increase the risk of predatory victimization. Indeed, the opportunity for predatory crime appears to be enmeshed in the opportunity structure for legitimate activities to such an extent that it might be very difficult to root out substantial amounts of crime without modifying much of our way of life. Rather than assuming that predatory crime is simply an indicator of social breakdown, one might take it as a byproduct of freedom and prosperity as they manifest themselves in the routine activities of everyday life.

Routine Activities and Crime
An Analysis of Victimization in Canada (1990)

9

L.W. KENNEDY
D.R. FORDE

From Kennedy, L.W., and Forde, D.R. (1990). Routine activities and crime: An analysis of victimization in Canada. *Criminology*, 28, 137–152.

Contents

9.1	Abstract	217
9.2	Introduction	218
9.3	Review of Literature	218
9.4	The Study	220
9.5	Measures of Crime	220
9.6	Individual Characteristics	221
9.7	Group Characteristics	222
9.8	Findings	222
	9.8.1 Impact of Individual-Level Characteristics and Routine Activities on Victimization	222
	9.8.2 Impact of Urban Structure on Routine Activities and Victimization	225
9.9	Discussion and Conclusions	229

9.1 Abstract

Miethe, Stafford, and Long (1987) have suggested that there are strong interaction effects between demographic characteristics of victims and certain routine activities that occur at night and away from home, but only for victims of property crime. This same pattern does not appear for victims of violent crime, they maintain, because unlike property crime, violent crime often involves interpersonal conflict and disagreement and is therefore spontaneous. Using data from the Canadian Urban Victimization Survey, which contains detailed measures of routine activities not available in the

U.S. study by Miethe and colleagues, this study finds contrary evidence that suggests that personal crime is contingent on the exposure that comes from following certain lifestyles. This is particularly true for certain demographic groups, particularly young males. The findings are considered in the light of the literature focusing on the interaction between situation and personality and the importance of the resulting conflict styles in promoting or reducing the opportunity for crime in certain settings and under certain conditions.

9.2 Introduction

There is a considerable interest in the research literature about the effect that crime has on the ways in which people adapt to their environments. Much has been made about the influence that being alone in one's neighborhood at night has on the fear levels that people express in victimization surveys (see Kennedy and Silverman 1984–85; Skogan and Maxfield 1981). Implicit in this work is the belief that fear will reduce the pursuit of day and night-time activities that raise one's exposure and vulnerability to crime. Using a perspective that draws from the work of the routine activities theorists, we examine how the social context of urban environments may influence the relationship between activities and certain types of criminal victimization. The importance of this research rests with the attempts that have been made to educate the public about how to deal with fear while maintaining normal routines and with the attempts by police to address the need to reduce public exposure to criminal victimization while keeping people from taking risks that raise their vulnerability to crime.

9.3 Review of Literature

Based loosely on the works of Shaw and McKay (1942) and Hawley (1950), routine activities theory uses regularities in behavior to predict criminal victimization. According to Cohen and M. Felson (1979a), much behavior is both repetitive and predictable. With the convergence in space and time of motivated offenders, suitable targets, and the absence of capable guardians, the probability of being a victim increases. Routine daily activities affect the likelihood that property and personal targets will be both visible and accessible to illegitimate activities. Routine activities will also determine whether personal and property targets have high visibility and accessibility at particular times. The timing of the criminal acts will be based on what the offender thinks he or she knows about the activities of the target.

Most of the research directly related to routine activities has involved macro-level analysis (Cohen and M. Felson 1979a; M. Felson and Cohen

1980) that examines the effects of urban structure, including measures of community size and density, on crime rates. In this research, routine activities have good predictive capability in explaining general patterns of urban criminality. The results of micro-level analysis, however, have not been completely consistent with routine activities predictions. Miethe, Stafford, and Long (1987), using data from the U.S. National Crime Survey, examined lifestyles based on day and nighttime activities both in and away from the home. They found strong interaction effects between demographic characteristics of victims and nighttime activities away from home, but only for victims of property crime. The same pattern does not appear for victims of violent crime. They speculate that, unlike property crime, from which the offender may materially benefit, violent crime often involves interpersonal conflict or disagreement. Miethe and colleagues suggest that because much violent crime is spontaneous, it defies the assumption of routine activities theory that criminals are rationally motivated and are able to calculate the risks of their crime. Also, exposure to high-risk situations is necessary but does not suffice as an explanation of criminal violence.

Sampson and Wooldredge (1987) make use of data from the British Crime Survey to examine specifically the link between micro- and macro-level phenomena in explaining the effect of routine activities on criminal victimization. They conclude that demographic and structural aspects have the largest impact on victimization. Routine activities that do not vary by these characteristics are less important in predicting crime. Sampson and Wooldredge argue that while certain lifestyles do lead to a greater vulnerability to crime than others, those variations are less important than the variations in offending rates by demographic and structural characteristics, such as age, sex, and urbanization. They propose that the only way to understand criminal victimization is to take into account the lifestyle, structural constraints, and demographic contexts of the urban environments in which criminal victimizations occur.

In this paper we focus on two major issues in the research literature on routine activities and criminal victimization. First, Miethe and colleagues report that routine evening activities will differentially affect criminal victimization, that is, that property crime but not personal crime is affected by routine behaviors. This is put into further perspective by the findings of J.P. Lynch (1987) that specific effects of victimization may be dependent on the context in which routine activity takes place, such as work or leisure. Second, Sampson and Wooldredge highlight the problem of examining routine activities outside the context of the structural and demographic factors that operate in the community to increase the probability that people who engage in certain high-risk routine activities will be met by high-risk offenders.

We examine data from a national study, the Canadian Urban Victimization Survey (CUVS), to test whether there are differential effects on personal versus property victimization depending on the nature of the activities that people routinely follow. Second, we examine the effects of structural differences that exist in the environments in which people live in order to evaluate the influence of different routine activities on victimization. This approach enables us to account for the adjustment that individuals make in dealing with their assessment of risk in their environment, adjustments that establish a threshold for activities that reduce their exposure while enabling them to continue following their preferred routines.

The Canadian study provides an opportunity to examine the different activities that people undertake in greater detail than was possible in the study by Miethe et al., which was based on composite measures of routine activities. In addition, the breakdowns of criminal victimization provided in the Canadian data set are more detailed than those reported in U.S. studies. With these better measures, can we find the same patterns as those discussed in the U.S. studies?

9.4 The Study

This research examines the data from the Canadian Urban Victimization Study (1984) conducted by the Solicitor General of Canada in 1982. The data set includes criminal victimizations between January 1 and December 31, 1981, in seven major urban centers in Canada: Greater Vancouver, Edmonton, Winnipeg, Toronto, Montreal, Halifax-Dartmouth, and St. John's. Statistics Canada pretested and helped conduct the telephone survey. A random sample of telephone numbers in each urban area, excluding commercial and institutional numbers, was used to select respondents. No stratification procedure was employed (Hoffman and Catlin 1985). Within each household a single respondent 16 years or older was randomly selected. Sample sizes ranged from 6,910 to 9,563 and contact was made with approximately 1 in 68 households of the residential population in each urban area. Statistics Canada used estimated weighting variables with the data set that were matched to census population characteristics for individuals and households within each urban area. We use the unweighted data in this analysis because we do not estimate victimization for the total population. We examine the unweighted incident-based information gathered from 74,463 respondents about their experience with specific crimes.

9.5 Measures of Crime

The Canadian Urban Victimization Survey reports the primary crime classification for each incident of victimization. Multiple incidents were rarely reported by survey respondents (Canadian Urban Victimization Survey 1988); thus, we had to use a single category of victimization (dichotomized as yes = 1 and no = 0). The use of single- rather than multiple-incident counts leads to some missing data but since the occurrence of multiple victimization is rare, this should not greatly affect the analysis. We use logistic regression analyses to estimate the structural parameters for victimization of breaking and entering, vehicle theft, robbery, and assault.* We analyze the data based on collapsed cases rather than through case-by-case form. Reduced degrees of freedom reflect the use of collapsed data.† We evaluate the overall fit of the models through the use of a pseudo R^2.‡ We use a criterion that the ratio of coefficient to standard error is greater in magnitude than 2.0 to compare the relative significance of variables contributing to the model (Aldrich and Nelson 1984).

9.6 Individual Characteristics

Previous research on the relation between routine activities and crime has included socio-demographic characteristics and nighttime and daytime activities as independent variables (Cohen and Felson 1979a). The socio-demographic variables that we examine are sex (1 = male, 0 = female), marital status (1 = married, 0 = other), age group as transformed to approximate a normal distribution (1 = 16–17, 2 = 18–20, 3 = 21–24, 4 = 25–29, 5 = 30–39, 6 = 40–49, 7 = 50–59, 8 = 60+), and family income as given in the CUVS (1 = <$9,000, 2 = $9,000–$14,999, 3 = $15,000–$19,999, 4 = $20,000–$24,999, 5 = $25,000–$29,999, 6 = $30,000–$39,999, and 7 = $40,000+). We use several nighttime activities rather than a general measure of nighttime activity to determine if these activities have differential effects on crime. The nighttime activity variables are coded as number of times per month for the following: sports, bar or pub; movie, theater, or restaurant; meetings or bingo; work or class; visit friends; and walk or drive. We examine the effect of daytime activity by including a dummy variable for the main occupation of respondents, full-time worker or student, versus others to replicate the measures used in previous studies (Miethe, Stafford, and Long 1987; Sampson and Wooldredge 1987).

---

* The data for attempted and actual sexual assault have not been publicly released by Statistics Canada. The total counts of unweighted actual or attempted cases are 679 robberies, 4,046 assaults, 5,408 breaking and entering, and 1,045 vehicle thefts.
† This procedure is explained in SPSS (1988: 811-812).
‡ This is calculated using the formula $x^*/(N + x2)$ (see Aldrich and Nelson 1984: 57).

9.7 Group Characteristics

We explore the influence of social context on victimization using economic and cultural measures of social disorganization. The units of analysis are census metropolitan areas (CMAs).* The Canada Census (1981) is the source of group-level data. The independent variables are measured as the percentage of one-person households, single, detached units, one-parent households, unemployment, divorce, low-income families, and population density per square mile for a CMA. Finally, to consider regional geographic variations in crime, we include dummy variables to distinguish Atlantic, central, and western Canadian cities.

9.8 Findings

9.8.1 Impact of Individual-Level Characteristics and Routine Activities on Victimization

We consider property crimes first and then personal crimes. For breaking and entering, the effects of routine activities are as they appear in the U.S. studies. In an analysis of demographic variables alone, all demographic variables have significant effects but the model fits the data poorly. Table 9.1 shows that the pseudo R^2s, estimates of the fit of the model, are significantly improved with the addition of routine activities variables. Looking at the demographic variables in Table 9.1, family income is not a factor, whereas being unmarried and young are strong predictors of victimization. Victimization also very likely coincides with activities that take people away from their home, including attending sports events, frequenting bars, going to movies and restaurants, going to work, and being out of the house walking or driving around. These findings support the view that people are vulnerable to property crime because of the absence of guardians from the homes of the targets of this crime.

The results for vehicle theft are similar; victimization relates significantly with age, sex, and income. However, a demographic model fits poorly with the data. With the inclusion of the routine activities variables, the pseudo R^2s improve, but the model has only a weak fit to the data. These results suggest that those who are likely to go to bars or out to work or class in the evening are more likely to be victims of vehicle theft (Table 9.2). The victimization is similar to that experienced with property crime at home. The absence of

---

* Although urban environments do not contain homogeneous structures that would affect all households equally, the comparison across the Canadian CMAs, which range in size from 100,000 people to over 2 million, enables us to explore variations in the effect of urban structural variables on victimization (see Sampson and Wooldredge 1987).

Table 9.1   Logistic Regression Predicting Breaking and Entering by Respondent Characteristics and Routine Activities

Independent Variable	Regression Coefficient	Coefficient/S.E.
Family income	−.001	.16
Sex	.005	.16
Married	−.095*	−2.65
Age group	−.027*	−2.93
Shopping	−.029	−.74
Sports	.075*	2.11
Bar	.084*	2.31
Movie	.139*	3.19
Bingo	.029	.85
Work/class	.168*	4.93
Friends	.005	.11
Walk/drive	.124*	3.74
Major occupation	.102*	2.28
Intercept	−2.59	97.59

* 2.0 times S.E.
  Model χ^2 = 17770.3, d.f. = 17777, p = .513.
  Pseudo R^2 (demographic) = .31.
  Pseudo R^2 (overall) = .50.

Table 9.2   Logistic Regression Predicting Vehicle Theft by Respondent Characteristics and Routine Activities

Independent Variable	Regression Coefficient	Coefficient/S.E.
Family income	.066*	3.36
Sex	.336*	4.48
Married	.122	1.57
Age group	−.140*	−7.33
Shopping	−.162	1.82
Sports	.096	1.22
Bar	.156	1.99
Movie	−.120	−1.27
Bingo	−.081	−1.05
Work/class	.159*	2.17
Friends	−.014	−.14
Walk/drive	.119	1.64
Major occupation	−.063	−.62
Intercept	−3.862	37.50

* 2.0 times S.E.
  Model χ^2 = 17569.9, d.f. = 17257, p = .05.
  Pseudo R^2 (demographic) = .38.
  Pseudo R^2 (overall) = .50.

Table 9.3   Logistic Regression Predicting Assault by Respondent Characteristics and Routine Activities

Independent Variable	Regression Coefficient	Coefficient/S.E.
Family income	−.050*	−4.94
Sex	.528*	13.44
Married	−.469*	−10.89
Age groups	−.203*	−19.70
Shopping	−.030	−.66
Sports	.072	1.71
Bar	.449*	10.84
Movie	.121*	2.21
Bingo	.058	1.43
Work/class	.245*	6.47
Friends	.020	.37
Walk/drive	.197*	5.19
Major occupation	.019	.34
Intercept	−2.379	90.45

* 2.0 times S.E.
   Model χ^2 = 17404.0, d.f. = 18045, p = 1.0.
   Pseudo R^2 (demographic) = .25.
   Pseudo R^2 (overall) = .51.

guardianship over the vehicle in conjunction with increased exposure to risk is likely to lead to a higher probability of theft.

The findings about personal crime are quite different from those reported by Miethe, Stafford, and Long (1979) and are consistent with the predictions of routine activities theory (see M. Felson and Cohen 1980). Looking at assault, all demographic variables significantly predict victimization, but there is a poor fit to the data. With the addition of the routine activities variables (Table 9.3), there is an improved fit to the data. The most vulnerable groups are young, unmarried males who frequent bars, go to movies, go out to work, or spend time out of the house walking or driving around.* It appears that it is this public lifestyle that creates exposure to risk and, although it may be the case that violent crime is spontaneous, the targets of violent crime are more likely to be people who are in places where conflict flares up. This does not explain motivation, but it does explain exposure to crime and identifies those groups that are most likely to experience this exposure.

A similar pattern appears for robberies (Table 9.4). Young, unmarried males who frequent bars and who are out walking or driving around are

---

* Victimization surveys may underreport domestic assault of women. The CUVS was not specifically designed to study domestic violence, although it did question respondents about assaultive behavior with their spouse over the previous year. Excluded from this were relationships other than spousal (see Kennedy and Dutton 1989).

Table 9.4 Logistic Regression Predicting Robbery by Respondent Characteristics and Routine Activities

Independent Variable	Regression Coefficient	Coefficient/S.E.
Family income	−.098*	−4.02
Sex	.496*	5.35
Married	−.702*	−6.60
Age groups	−.127*	−5.40
Shopping	−.039	−.36
Sports	.116	1.15
Bar	.487*	4.86
Movie	−.190	−1.60
Bingo	−.015	−.15
Work/class	−.101	−1.10
Friends	−.075	.61
Walk/drive	.307*	3.37
Major occupation	−.035	.27
Intercept	−3.862	32.60

* 2.0 times S.E.
Model χ^2 = 16321.9, d.f. = 18100, p = 1.00.
Pseudo R^2 (demographic) = .44.
Pseudo R^2 (overall) = .53.

likely to be victims of this crime. This evidence is contrary to the prediction made by Miethe and colleagues that violent crimes are poorly predicted by routine activities. Again, however, this does not address the issue of how these crimes evolve, only the groups that are most vulnerable to them. The routine activities theory suggests that for crimes to occur, there must be opportunity, motivated offenders, and an absence of capable guardians. The lifestyles that lead one to frequent bars and to be on the street clearly lead to situations in which these factors coincide in presenting offenders with opportunities to commit crime. The suggestion that capable guardians are not available in these environments is difficult to confirm using these data. Also, much information is missing in the CUVS about offenders. Analysis of victim and offender relationship would require a detailed breakdown of data, which takes us away from the focus of the research reported here.

9.8.2 Impact of Urban Structure on Routine Activities and Victimization

We again consider property crimes first and then personal crimes. To begin the analysis, we trimmed the individual-level models, retaining the significant demographic and routine activities variables, because of limitations in the number of variables that can be included using the SPSS-X (Version 3.0)

Table 9.5   Reduced Form Logistic Regression Predicting Breaking and Entering by Respondent Characteristics, Routine Activities, and Structural Variables

Independent Variable	Regression Coefficient	Coefficient/S.E.
Married	−.044	−1.43
Age groups	−.022*	−2.72
Sports	.104*	3.23
Bar	.115*	3.49
Work/class	.174*	5.62
Walk/drive	.100*	3.36
Major occupation	.112*	2.98
Percent one-parent families	.017	.43
Percent one-person households	.009	.91
Percent single, detached units	−.004*	−2.14
Percent unemployment	−.039*	−2.24
Percent divorced	.294*	5.07
Percent low-income families	.106*	4.00
Intercept	−5.068	12.37

* 2.0 times S.E.
  Model $\chi^2 = 6390.4$, d.f. = 5224, p = .001.
  Pseudo R^2 (overall) = .45.

statistical package. We considered the effect of urban structure by including the group-level variables.

Table 9.5 shows how urban structure affects significantly the explanation of breaking and entering victimizations. Where there are more low-income families and more divorced persons there is a greater likelihood of being a victim of breaking and entering. Also where there are fewer single, detached housing units and where there is a lower level of unemployment there is a higher likelihood of victimization. We dropped regional location and the city's population density from the analysis because they did not influence victimization significantly.

Are there consistencies in the types of variables for individual- and group-level analysis? The economic variables are clearly important for explaining breaking and entering at the individual and group levels. Factors such as the percentage divorced and the individual-level dummy variable for marriage, however, are not consistent at the individual and group levels. The dummy variable for married suggests a compatible direction for the parameter estimate, but the result is only a marginally significant predictor of victimization. These results suggest that demographic and structural aspects will affect individual victimization, and they underline the importance of both micro and macro features in the development of a routine activities theory.

Table 9.6 Reduced Form Logistic Regression Predicting Vehicle Theft by Respondent Characteristics, Routine Activities, and Structural Variables

Independent Variable	Regression Coefficient	Coefficient/S.E.
Family income	.083*	4.71
Sex	.343*	4.82
Age groups	−.138*	−7.45
Bar	.146*	2.00
Work/class	.143*	2.00
Percent one-parent families	−.084	−.89
Percent one-person households	−.002	−.09
Percent single, detached units	.004	.92
Percent unemployment	.052	1.28
Percent divorced	.600*	3.93
Percent low-income families	.170*	2.59
Intercept	−7.648	2.20

* 2.0 times S.E.
  Model χ^2 = 3255.5, d.f. = 3035, p = .003.
  Pseudo R^2 (overall) = .48.

Moving to vehicle theft (Table 9.6), the pseudo R^2 shows that the inclusion of structural variables provides about the same overall fit as the individual-level variables in Table 9.2. Higher levels of divorce and greater percentages of low-income families are more likely to be associated with motor vehicle theft. We dropped population density and regional location from the analysis because they did not influence victimization significantly. The results show, however, that age, family income, and sex are the most significant variables for the estimation of victimization for vehicle theft.

Overall, for property crimes these findings suggest that individual- and group-level economic variables are significant predictors of property crime. This is consistent with Sampson and Wooldredge's (1987) finding that demographic and community variables have an impact on victimization.

Looking at personal crimes, the findings suggest that urban structure has a significant impact on assault (Table 9.7). Residents in areas where there are higher levels of unemployment, more one-person households, fewer one-parent families, and fewer low-income families are more likely to be victims of assault. Individual-level variables, however, are more important for the estimation of victimization. Victimizations were most likely for younger, unmarried males with lower incomes. Also, it is necessary to consider the nighttime activities of residents. The routine activities variables suggest that residents who go to bars, work or go to class, or go for a walk or drive at night are likely to be victims.

Table 9.7   Reduced Form Logistic Regression Predicting Assault by Respondent Characteristics, Routine Activities, and Structural Variables

Independent Variable	Regression Coefficient	Coefficient/S.E.
Family income	−.058*	−5.73
Sex	.541*	13.82
Married	−.431*	−9.98
Age groups	−.223*	−20.93
Bar	.450*	10.99
Movie	.102	1.93
Work/class	.251*	6.61
Walk/drive	.203*	5.41
Major occupation	−.006	−.11
Percent one-parent families	−.122*	−2.56
Percent one-person households	.053*	4.61
Percent single, detached units	−.006*	−2.40
Percent unemployment	.125*	6.06
Percent divorced	−.043	−.58
Percent low-income families	−.172*	−5.27
Intercept	−.034	19.72

* 2.0 times S.E.

Model χ^2 = 15270.6, d.f. = 15280, p = .520.

Pseudo R^2 (overall) = .52.

As for contextual variables, economic variables are significant and consistent in predicting more victimization in locations with greater unemployment and for those with lower family incomes. Family disruption variables, on the other hand, are inconsistent predictors, as shown by the significance of percentage of unmarried persons and the insignificance of divorce rates for predicting victimization.

Similar findings are evident for robbery. The results suggest that the percentages of low-income and one-parent families affect victimization (Table 9.8). The inclusion of structural variables in the model causes a slightly weaker fit to the data. It appears that individual-level demographic variables are the most important for estimating victimization. It is still necessary, however, to take routine activities variables into account. Residents who go out at night to a bar or out for a walk or drive are more likely to be victims.

This study finds that routine activities variables contribute significantly to the explanation of personal victimizations. This result is consistent with previous studies using macro- and multilevel units of analysis (see, respectively, Messner and Blau 1987; and Sampson and Wooldredge 1987).

Table 9.8 Reduced Form Logistic Regression Predicting Robbery by Respondent Characteristics, Routine Activities, and Structural Variables

Independent Variable	Regression Coefficient	Coefficient/S.E.
Family income	−.102*	−4.40
Sex	.520*	5.76
Married	−.687*	−6.50
Age groups	−.132*	−5.62
Bar	.423*	4.47
Walk/drive	.282*	3.21
Percent one-parent families	.281*	2.65
Percent one-person households	.032	1.11
Percent single, detached units	−.003	−.61
Percent unemployment	.113*	2.21
Percent divorced	−.046	−.26
Percent low-income families	−.202*	−2.67
Intercept	−4.042	3.32

* 2.0 times S.E.

Model χ^2 = 5264.4, d.f. = 5304, p = .648.

Pseudo R^2 (overall) = .50.

9.9 Discussion and Conclusions

Miethe, Stafford, and Long (1987) suggest that routine activity theory is not applicable to victims of violent crime because violent crime involves interpersonal conflict and disagreement and is therefore spontaneous. While we agree with this characterization of violent crime (see Kennedy 1990), we present data that suggest that this is still contingent on the exposure that comes from following certain lifestyles.

It is not surprising that those most directly affected by routine activities that expose them to conflict situations, the young males, are least likely to be able to avoid the consequences of this exposure, as reflected in the findings reported above for assaults and robberies. It would appear, however, that property crimes occur less because of conflict and more because of opportunity afforded through routine activities that remove victims from their place of residence.

Our findings related to property and personal crime require that we include in our explanation of victimization the degree of exposure that individuals experience by following certain lifestyle patterns. Those patterns, or routines, may actually promote certain conflict styles (see Hocker and Wilmot 1985). The situation, and the third parties who interact with victims, combine to create opportunities for crime. Further research is needed on ways to resolve these problems beyond the simple solution of avoiding high-risk circumstances (Kennedy 1988). The need for greater attention to conflict-resolution tactics in handling potentially violent situations has been promoted in dealing with problems encountered by children in schools (Maynard 1985), neighborhood conflicts (Merry 1982; Snyder 1978), and other situations in which people find it difficult to stop the escalation of disputes (R.B. Felson and Steadman 1983). Further work on routine activities should examine how conflict resolution would mediate the impact of exposure to high-risk situations, thereby reducing victimization.

Notes on the Geometry of Crime (1981)

10

P.L. BRANTINGHAM
P.J. BRANTINGHAM

From Brantingham, P.J. and Brantingham, P.L. (Eds.), *Environmental Criminology* (pp. 27–53). Beverly Hills, CA: Sage Publications.

Contents

10.1	Case 1: Basic Search Area for Individual Offender	234
10.2	Case 2: Basic Search Area for a Cluster of Criminals	236
10.3	Case 3: Complex Search Area for One Individual Offender	237
10.4	Case 4: Complex Search Area for Multiple Offenders	241
10.5	Case 5: Selective Search Area for Multiple Offenders	242
10.6	Case 6: Selective Search Area for a Single Offender	243
10.7	Case 7: Selective Search Area for Multiple Offenders	246
10.8	Case 8: Dynamic Search Area for a Single Offender	246
10.9	Case 9: Dynamic Search Area for Multiple Offenders	248
10.10	Summary	249
10.11	Consequences	250
10.12	Conclusion	255

Spatial patterning of crime has long been observed. Guerry (1833) noted conviction rate differences between the departments of France early in the nineteenth century. Tobias (1972: 122-147) has lately described fine differences in the distribution of criminal residences and crimes in Victorian London and Manchester. Burt (1925), Shaw and McKay (1969), and many other criminal ecologists (see Voss and Petersen 1971) reported the spatial patterning of criminal residence, while Brearley (1932), Reckless (1933), Schmid (1960a, 1960b), Shannon (1954), Harries (1971), and others reported the spatial patterning of criminal events.

Though observations of patterning abound, explanations have, until recently, tended to the simplistic. Most explanations have centered on areal correlations between crime phenomena and other social phenomena (Plint 1851; Shaw and McKay 1969; Bagley 1965; Turner 1969b) in an attempt to describe variations in motivations to commit crime. Implicit in most such attempts at explanation is the assumption that variations in motivation lead directly to variations in spatial patterning. Under such an assumption, the spatial pattern itself is merely derivative and of little scientific interest. Wolfgang (1958: 120), for instance, in his classic study of homicide in Philadelphia, argued that the spatial pattern of offenses was of no importance, and was of local interest only to police; and the *Journal of Criminal Law and Criminology* has declined to print crime occurrence maps in the interest of saving space (see, for example, Bullock 1955: 567).

Within the last ten years, the discipline of criminology has begun to attract scholars of diverse background. Environmental psychologists, geographers, and urban planners have joined sociologists, lawyers, and clinical psychologists in studying crime. With an increase in the diversity of research orientations has come a renaissance of interest in the spatial patterning of crime. With growing interest in the patterning of crime has come an interest in how the distribution of opportunities for criminal acts influences the actual commission of crimes (Jeffery 1977; P. Mayhew et al. 1976; Brantingham and Brantingham, 1975, 1977).

Much current work on crime patterning assumes (explicitly or implicitly) an opportunity/motivation interaction rubric for explaining observed crime (see Jeffery 1977; Baldwin and Bottoms 1976; Brantingham and Brantingham 1978; Carter and Hill 1980; Mayhew et al. 1976). This chapter will build on the current trend and propose a theoretical model for looking at crime as it occurs in urban space. The model will use concepts of *opportunity* and *motivation* and will tie these together with concepts of *mobility* and *perception.**

We have previously proposed a model for crime site selection which can be described by the following propositions (Brantingham and Brantingham 1978):

1. Individuals exist who are motivated to commit specific offenses.
   a. The sources of motivation are diverse. Different etiological models or theories may appropriately be invoked to explain the motivation of different individuals or groups.
   b. The strength of such motivation varies.
   c. The character of such motivation varies from affective to instrumental.
2. Given the motivation of an individual to commit an offense, the actual commission of an offense is the end result of a multistaged decision process which seeks out and identifies, within the general environment, a target or victim positioned in time and space.

---

* The term perception is used here to include cognition or structuring of visual images. Geographers and planners generally use the term perception to mean cognition. Psychologists usually separate the two terms. This chapter uses the terminology of geographers and planners.

    a. In the case of high affect motivation, the decision process will probably involve a minimal number of stages.

    b. In the case of high instrumental motivation, the decision process locating a target or victim may include many stages and much careful searching.

3. The environment emits many signals, or cues, about its physical, spatial, cultural, legal, and psychological characteristics.

    a. These cues can vary from generalized to detailed.

4. An individual who is motivated to commit a crime uses cues (either learned through experience or learned through social transmission) from the environment to locate and identify targets or victims.

5. As experiential knowledge grows, an individual who is motivated to commit a crime learns which individual cues, clusters of cues, and sequences of cues are associated with "good" victims or targets. These cues, cue clusters, and cue sequences can be considered a template which is used in victim or target selection. Potential victims or targets are compared to the template and either rejected or accepted depending on the congruence.

    a. The process of template construction and the search process may be consciously conducted, or these processes may occur in an unconscious, cybernetic fashion so that the individual cannot articulate how they are done.

6. Once the template is established, it becomes relatively fixed and influences future search behavior, thereby becoming self-reinforcing.

7. Because of the multiplicity of targets and victims, many potential crime selection templates could be constructed. But because the spatial and temporal distribution of offenders, targets, and victims is not regular, but clustered or patterned, and because human environmental perception has some universal properties, individual templates have similarities which can be identified.

These propositions are not spatially specific. They posit that criminals engage in a search behavior which may vary in intensity, and that criminals use previous knowledge to evaluate and select targets. The propositions do not describe the spatial characteristics of the search patterns or the selection patterns. The model presented in this chapter will attempt to articulate these general propositions *spatially*.

In presenting the spatial model, simple cases will be presented first. These initial cases, with simple initial conditions or simplifying assumptions, will be transformed into more realistic situations in stepwise fashion. The cases will describe the search areas of criminals under varying spatial distributions of criminals and victims or targets within varying hypothetical urban forms. The theoretical cases will be built up using what, empirically, is known about the spatial distribution of crime, what is known about criminal and noncriminal spatial behavior, and inductive relationships.

10.1 Case 1: Basic Search Area for Individual Offender

Initial Conditions:

1. Single, individual criminal
2. Uniform distribution of potential targets
3. The criminal based in a single home location

Empirical work in criminology has repeatedly demonstrated that most offenders commit a large number of their offenses "close" to home. What is "close" varies by offense and city, but in all offenses which have been studied, it has been found that crimes usually occur only a short distance from the home of the offender, or, put slightly differently, the average crime trip is short. Bullock (1955: 571) showed that 40 percent of all Houston homicides in 1945–1949 occurred within one city block of the offender's residence and 74 percent occurred within two miles. Pokorny (1965) found similar patterns in homicides in Houston in 1958–1961. Capone and Nichols (1976) report such a pattern for robberies in Dade County, Florida, in 1971. Amir (1971) found such a pattern for rape in Philadelphia. Baldwin and Bottoms (1976: 78–98) found this pattern for larceny, breaking offenses, and taking and driving away offenses in Sheffield. The pattern varies somewhat by offense. Crimes against the person such as homicide, assault, and rape occur "closer" to home, with fewer long journeys to a crime site, while property crimes such as larceny and burglary occur further from offenders' homes, with more long crime trips (White 1932; Reiss 1967; Pyle et al. 1974; Baldwin and Bottoms 1976). But, overall, there is a decrease in crime as distance increases.

Such a phenomenon, the reduction of activity or interaction as distance increases, has been repeatedly observed in spatial behavior of all types and can be generically referred to as "distance decay." Shopping patterns, personal social interactions, telephone calls, migration, and even criminal behavior appear to cluster around home or base locations (see Lowe and Moryadas 1975; Haggett 1965). Capone and Nichols (1976) fit robbery to a distance decay function. Smith (1976) fits crime trips in Rochester, New York, to a gravity potential function.

A rationale for such a pattern is easy to construct. It takes time, money, and effort to overcome distance. If any of these factors is constrained, then close locations have inherent advantages over distant locations. In addition, in any movement in space away from a home base, the close locations will be seen more frequently. Consequently, more information will be available

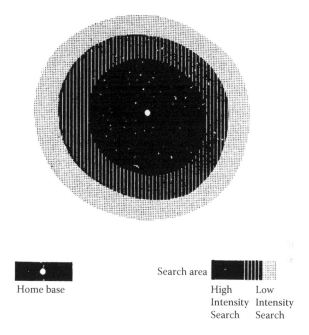

Figure 10.1 Search area for individual offender.

about locations close to the home base than about locations far away. As criminals search for targets, they are likely to be able to find an area that emits cues associated with a "good" target when the "good" crime area is close to the home base. Information flows should bias search behavior toward previously known areas.

In the hypothetical case presented here, it is assumed that there is only one criminal, based at one home location, and that potential targets are distributed evenly in space. In such an idealized situation, the expected target area would be a circular field and the probability of any particular potential target becoming an actual target would decrease as the distance from the home base increased (see Figure 10.1). In fact, the decline away from home might be stepwise, dependent on a number of distance thresholds.

Before considering more realistic initial conditions, this most basic case must be modified slightly. In their search behavior criminals are looking for "good" victims or targets. Part of what makes a victim or target "good" or "bad" is availability, potential payoff, and the risk of apprehension or confrontation associated with it (Reppetto 1974: 14–17, 28–29; Letkemann 1973: 137–157; Waller and Okihiro 1978). Information about potential victims and targets is probably spatially biased toward the home base, but information is also spatially biased for the other people who live close to the criminal's home base. While criminals know more of the area close to home and are more likely to locate a target easily, they are also more likely to *be* known

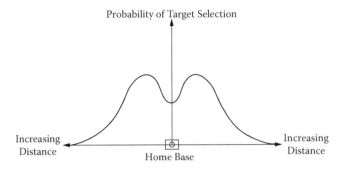

Figure 10.2 Modified search area for individual offender (cross-section view).

and increase their risks close to home. One would expect that there would be an area right around the home base where offenses would become less likely (see Figure 10.2). This small zone of relatively decreased activity was reported by Turner (1969a) in his study of Philadelphia delinquents. In that study, a distance decay model developed from a peak about a city block distant from home with a zone of very little delinquent activity within a city block of home. (Homicide might be expected to be an exception to this case 1 variant: it is an explosive crime which occurs in the home or its immediate vicinity with little or no victim search behavior by the killer. Note, however, that homicide differs from other crimes in that it has a high discovery and clearance rate—a pattern consistent with the risk inherent in criminal activity too close to home.)

10.2 Case 2: Basic Search Area for a Cluster of Criminals

Initial Conditions:

1. Cluster of offenders
2. Uniform distribution of targets
3. Offenders working from home location

One recurring spatial fact in criminology is that criminals, both adult and juvenile, are often spatially clustered. Petrovich (1971: 243–244) describes the spatial clustering of criminal residences in Paris in the last half of the eighteenth century. Inciardi (1978: 32–37) describes the development of criminal districts in New York City during the colonial period and then during the first half of the nineteenth century. Tobias (1972: 130–135, 142–144) describes the criminal "rookeries" of London and Manchester in the middle of the nineteenth century. Shaw and McKay (1969) describe the criminal areas of Chicago and other major American cities during the 1920s

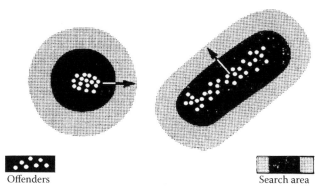

Offenders   Search area

Figure 10.3 Search area for clustered offenders.

and 1930s. T. Morris (1957) describes the delinquency areas of Croydon, an industrial suburb of London, in the 1950s. Baldwin and Bottoms (1976) describe the offender areas of Sheffield in the 1960s. In all cases, it is clear the criminal residences cluster together. In fact, much research in criminological motivation has really involved correlating criminal residence with sociodemographic areal characteristics (Voss and Petersen 1971).

The clustering of criminals is just a special case of clusterings of human groups in space. Urban areas can be viewed as a mosaic of clusters of people—clusters that are measurably, internally homogeneous on social, economic, and demographic characteristics (Timms 1971). Criminals have also been shown to be disproportionately represented in certain subpopulations which can be identified along sociodemographic dimensions such as wealth, age, sex, and ethnicity. Consequently, criminal residences usually cluster within certain restricted urban areas.

When the search area of a single criminal is generalized to a search area for a cluster of criminals, new criminal search patterns emerge (see Figure 10.3). The specifics of the search pattern will depend on how potential offenders cluster.

10.3 Case 3: Complex Search Area for One Individual Offender

Initial Conditions:

1. One individual offender
2. Uniform distribution of potential targets
3. Offender is no longer tied solely to a home base, but works, or goes to school, and shops in other parts of the urban area

One of the striking things about criminals, often forgotten, is that most of them behave as ordinary people most of the time. Most offenders are not tied exclusively to some home base, but, like other people, are mobile. They move about the city. They develop information about other parts of an urban area through working (even sporadically), traveling to school, shopping or seeking out entertainment and recreation. Criminals will develop an action space* based on both their criminal *and* their innocent activities. Their actions help form an "awareness space," the parts of the city they have some knowledge about. Information about the urban area will be distorted by movement patterns.† Criminals can thus be said to possess a nonuniform information base defined by their awareness space.

Given a uniform distribution of targets, and a nonuniform information base, criminals will probably commit most of their offenses close to home, work, shopping, their usual entertainment areas, or along paths between home, shopping, work, and entertainment areas: in general, offenses should occur within the criminal's awareness space. It seems unlikely that they will stray into unknown areas of a city.

In fact, research into specific crimes has demonstrated that most property offenders ply their trade in lower and working class areas which are probably not far from home or other well-known nodes. Reppetto's (1974) sample of Boston burglars operated in neighborhoods they knew despite the fact that they identified other types of areas as having better targets. Rengert (1975) found that Philadelphia burglars committed most offenses close to home or in the central business district and speculated that differences in the spatial clustering of male and female burglaries might be explained by action space differentials produced by socially defined differences in mobility patterns. A West German study has shown that many out-of-town burglars commit their offenses on or very near the major arterial highways, while locally resident burglars commit their offenses throughout the town (Fink 1969). Clinard and Abbott (1973: 37) examined a sample of property offenders in Kampala and found offense patterns consistent with an awareness space model: 23 percent of the offenders had stolen from employers, 26 percent had stolen from friends or neighbors, 28 percent from strangers, 4 percent had stolen from stores, only 2 percent had stolen from relatives.

Direct evidence for the patterning of crime around the nodes and the paths between them that form offenders' action spaces is found in two more recent studies. Porteous's study (1977: 253) of the Burnside gang in Saanich, British Columbia, found that the activity space defined by home, school,

---

* For a general description of action spaces, see Horton and Reynolds (1971).
† For discussion of information spaces, see, generally, Appleyard (1969), Klein (1967), Saarinen (1969), or Porteous (1977).

work, shopping and recreation areas contained most of the gang's delinquent acts. Rengert and Wasilchick's (1980) research with burglars in Delaware County, Pennsylvania (a suburb of Philadelphia) showed a very strong relationship between crime location and principal pathways from home to work and from home to recreation locations.

The type of awareness space, and, consequently, action space, that a criminal develops is likely to be slightly different in general characteristics from the awareness space of most other urban residents. In common with other people, the criminal's awareness space is likely to be dominated by major nodes in his field of mobility: home, shopping areas, school or workplace, entertainment centers. But, since a criminal, particularly a property offender, is often actively engaged in a target search process, we might expect that his awareness space would expand from the nodes themselves (and the paths between them) to include, at least, the fringes of residential and commercial areas found along the paths and close to the nodes. Studies of burglary and robbery in Detroit (Luedtke and Associates 1970: 30) and of robbery in Oakland (Angel 1968; Wilcox 1973) have described such a diffusion effect reaching outward about two blocks into residential areas from major shopping centers, commercial strips along major highways, major industrial and other employment and entertainment centers.

The awareness space and action space of offenders should vary with age just as the awareness and action spaces of most urban residents vary by age. Chapin and Brent (1969) surveyed people in 43 metropolitan areas. The old, those with young children, women, and those who were unemployed had more limited action spaces and spent more time at home. Young, unattached people spent the most time away from home. Similarly, cognitive maps of urban areas seem to vary by age, sex, and race (Everitt and Cadwallader 1972; Orleans and Schmidt 1972). Women who are tied to the home and the very young and the old have more limited cognitive maps than men and working aged people. It was also found that cognitive maps varied by socioeconomic status (Orleans 1973). Inhabitants of poorer areas of the city had more limited cognitive maps of the larger urban area than people from affluent areas.

Criminological findings consistent with these deductions on age have been reported by Baldwin and Bottoms (1976) for offenders in Sheffield and by Reppetto (1974) for burglars in Boston. Rengert (1975) reports differentials in male and female burglar behavior in Philadelphia that are consistent with expectations. Reppetto's findings are consistent with expectations on racial differences, but Baldwin and Bottom's findings are only partially consistent with respect to socioeconomic status expectations.

Finally, the awareness space of the offender, and his cognitive map, probably varies with the actual urban form of the city. It has been proposed that awareness spaces are primarily based on nodes centered at home, work or school, shopping locations, recreational areas, and the paths connecting these. In an urban area where shopping, recreation, and work locations are dispersed, awareness spaces should tend to be larger. In urban areas where these activities are concentrated, awareness spaces should be spatially restricted. For all people, even criminals, much of any city is really unknown territory which either does not exist (cognitively) at all, or is populated with the terrors of the unfamiliar.

Since awareness spaces are dominated by regular activities and movement between these activities, it seems reasonable to assume that the form of movement between activities will influence the level of awareness. In an urban area dominated by fixed rail mass transit, awareness spaces should, primarily, be nodal with less cognitive emphasis on path elements. We might expect criminal activity to be greater near major nodes in the transportation network. In urban areas that are serviced by bus transit or automobiles, we might expect criminal activity to be more linear, stretched out along the major transportation paths between nodes. This pattern should be especially strong in urban areas that have a few major transportation arteries which could be expected to be a part of many criminals' awareness spaces.

The crime pattern expected from the search activities of a single criminal operating within a normal awareness space, assuming a uniform distribution of targets or victims, is shown by Figure 10.4.

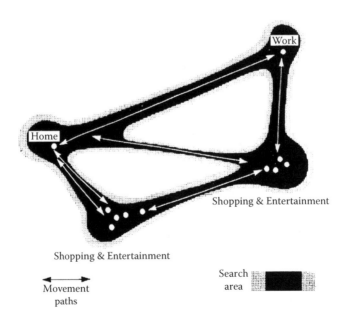

Figure 10.4 Complex search area for individual offender.

10.4 Case 4: Complex Search Area for Multiple Offenders

Initial Conditions:

1. Multiple offenders
2. Uniform distribution of targets
3. Home, work or school, shopping, and entertainment bases

The pattern described in the third case can be generalized to a cluster of offenders by overlaying, conceptually, the individual patterns. Home locations are likely to be spatially clustered (see Shaw and McKay 1969; Voss and Petersen 1971). Work, shopping, and entertainment locations may be more dispersed depending on the structure of individual urban areas. The crime patterns should relate to shopping and entertainment centers used by the crime-prone population, not the total shopping and entertainment complex of the urban area (see Figure 10.5). In addition, since much criminal activity, especially among juveniles, is group based, there should be some communality in the overlaying.

The traces of this hypothesized composite search pattern can be seen in much empirical criminology. Probably the best example is by Porteous (1977), who studied the Burnside gang in Saanich, a suburb of Victoria, British Columbia. He found that the home residences, schools, and meeting places (entertainment locations) of the gang members formed the core area (some 1.5 miles in diameter) for the gang's activities and that 80 percent of the gang's delinquent acts occurred within this core area. T. Morris (1957) found that juveniles in Croyden, England, committed the largest proportion

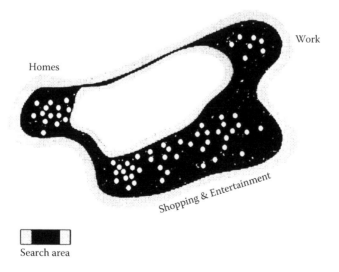

Figure 10.5 Complex search area for cluster of offenders.

of their offenses in the shopping areas they normally frequented. Wilcox's (1973) study of robbery in Oakland might also fit the pattern, as she found that the overwhelming majority of offenses occurred in or near low-cost entertainment areas.

10.5 Case 5: Selective Search Area for Multiple Offenders

Initial Conditions:

1. Multiple offenders distributed uniformly in the urban area
2. Nonuniform distribution of potential targets
3. Offender based in a single location

The first four cases assumed that there was a uniform distribution of targets. This obviously is not the condition of the real world. Targets or potential victims are very unevenly distributed across space and time. For example, street robbery requires the presence of victims on the street. Certain parts of cities (at certain times of day) have many pedestrians. In other parts of cities and at other times of day, the streets may be deserted.

Robbery targets are spatially and temporally clustered. As another example, auto theft obviously requires that the offender locate an automobile in time and space. Clearly automobiles are unevenly distributed in space and the distribution of them changes radically between working and nonworking hours. As Sarah Boggs (1965) has demonstrated, and subsequent studies in opportunity have reaffirmed (for example, Mayhew et al. 1976), the gross availability of targets influences the pattern of crime occurrence.

Consider then, the simplest situation with a nonuniform distribution of targets, but with a uniform distribution of offenders. In this situation we would expect that offenses would vary with the concentration of targets (see Figure 10.6).

Linking this nonuniform distribution of targets with what is known about distance decay spatial behavior and the bias in spatial knowledge to places close to home, work, or recreation areas, we would expect that potential offenders living far away from the clustering of targets would be less likely to actually commit offenses.

This pattern is consistently reported in the criminological literature. Ernest W. Burgess (1916) reported it in the delinquency patterns of Lawrence, Kansas, before World War I. He found "geographical ... proximity to the business street" to be the critical determinant of why the children of one ward had very high delinquency rates while the children of other wards, similar on sociodemographic and economic measures, had low delinquency rates. Thrasher (1963 [1927]), in the largest study of juvenile gangs ever undertaken,

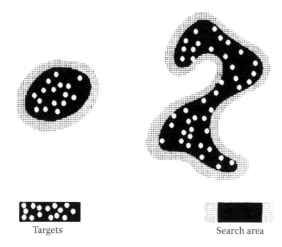

Targets   Search area

Figure 10.6 Search area with nonuniform distribution of targets and uniform distribution of offenders.

argued that the physical environment and especially the residential proximity to opportunities for theft were major determinants of a gang's criminal activity. Shaw (1929) and Shaw and McKay (1931, 1969) reported proximity to criminal opportunities as critical determinants of areal delinquency rates in a series of studies covering some six decades of data in Chicago. In their report to the National Commission of Law Observance, for instance, Shaw and McKay (1931: 68) argued that "in general, proximity to industry and commerce is an index of the areas of Chicago in which high rates of delinquents are found."* Lander (1954) found high delinquency residence rates related to commercial land use concentrations, but not to industrial concentrations. Most graphic, perhaps, is Tobias's (1972) mapping of Mayhew's nineteenth century reports on London rookeries. All of the rookeries were strategically located on the boundary of the City of London, in proximity to several sets of criminal opportunity.

10.6 Case 6: Selective Search Area for a Single Offender

Initial Conditions:

1. Single offender
2. Nonuniform distribution of potential targets
3. Home, work or school, shopping, and recreational bases

---

* Editor's note: Peculiarly, they denied that this consistently observed fact could have any analytic importance. This refusal to treat empirical findings as having direct value is considered by Brantingham and Jeffery in the Afterword of the original.

As was pointed out in Case 2, offenders are not uniformly distributed in urban space. Part of the variation may be the result of an apparent higher motivation to commit crimes within selected socioeconomic groups (see Hindelang 1978).

Part of the variation may be the result of knowledge of and access to potentially "good" targets or victims. The commission of a crime requires that a motivated individual come in contact with a potential target or victim. Using the terminology developed in the preceding descriptive cases, the criminal's "awareness space" must include targets which he considers "good."

Those parts of the urban area that the offender knows fairly well and is likely to travel through represent a "potential" space for criminal activity. A criminal's search for targets is likely to be biased toward his habitual awareness space, particularly, as is described in the propositions at the beginning of the chapter, toward those subareas within the awareness space that are perceived as "good" target areas. One characteristic of a good target area is the availability of targets. Thus, a criminal will probably be spatially biased toward seeking targets in the subarea of his action space which contains a clustering of targets, a choice of criminal opportunities (see Figure 10.7).

Another aspect of a good target area is low perceived risk. Except in the highest affect crimes, such as murder, the potential criminal searches for

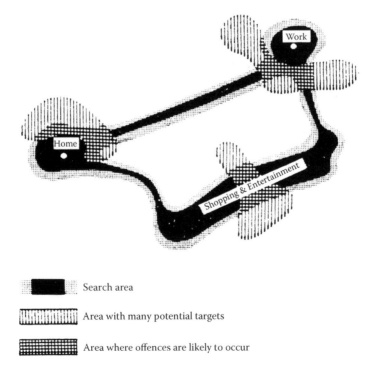

    Search area

    Area with many potential targets

    Area where offences are likely to occur

Figure 10.7 Selective complex search area for individual offender.

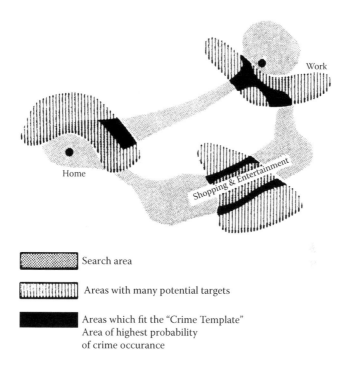

Search area

Areas with many potential targets

Areas which fit the "Crime Template"
Area of highest probability
of crime occurance

Figure 10.8 Selective crime occurrence area for individual offender.

targets in situations where he feels "safe." The actual area of criminal activity is likely to be a subset of the intersection of the criminal's awareness space with the areas containing targets or victims. These will be the areas that fit the template of a good target area (see Figure 10.8).

Several recent studies in the crime prevention through environmental design (CPTED) literature and in the spatial analysis of crime have reported results consistent with the idea that crimes are more likely to occur in sub-parts of a criminal's traditional awareness space which are perceived to be "safe" and which have ample targets. For example, the surge of branch bank robberies near major highways could be considered consistent with this pattern. The highways are likely to be pathways in the criminal's usual awareness space; and the banks are vulnerable. The criminal can escape quickly on the highway.

Similarly, the growth in convenience store robberies is also consistent with this pattern. As Duffala (1976) reported in his study of such robberies in Tallahassee, Florida, the stores that were near major roads and which had no surrounding evening business activity were most vulnerable. The nearness to the major roads placed the stores within the awareness spaces of many urban residents (the obvious marketing reason for their location). The stores also became part of the action spaces of robbers. If robbers are looking for low risk, it seems likely that stores near but not on main roads will have lower risks than stores directly on main roads and will be more likely to be victimized. Those stores near the main road will be quieter, surrounded by fewer potential witnesses, have fewer people around who might intervene in the robbery.

Generally, remote, inaccessible locations or people in remote locations are not victimized. Such remoteness can be measured in various metrics. Bevis and Nutter (1977), for instance, have shown that differential accessibility produced by differences in the permeability of the street network affects the burglary rates of neighborhoods in Minneapolis. Neighborhoods rendered inaccessible by the complexity of the street system had lower rates than those that were easily accessible. Crime occurs near areas of activity, along transportation paths, or in residential areas close to where criminals live.

10.7 Case 7: Selective Search Area for Multiple Offenders

Initial Conditions:

1. Multiple offenders
2. Nonuniform distribution of potential targets
3. Home, work or school, shopping and recreation bases

Case 6 represented the hypothetical pattern for a single offender. The pattern for all offenders can be constructed by simultaneously considering the individual patterns. Those areas within the general urban space that are part of the most individual selective crime occurrence areas will have the most numerous crimes (see Figure 10.9).

Evidence for Case 7 is found in Rengert's (1972) study of the distribution of arson and vandalism in Philadelphia. Considering a model that took into account areal opportunities, areal risks (in terms of relative police efficiency), relative aggregate familiarity with areas, and accessibility of the police districts of Philadelphia, he was able to explain 73 percent of the observed variance in the spatial distribution of these crimes.

10.8 Case 8: Dynamic Search Area for a Single Offender

Initial Conditions:

1. Single offender
2. Nonuniform distribution of potential offenders
3. Home, work or school, shopping and recreation bases

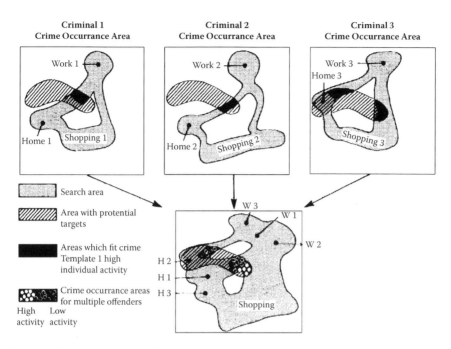

Figure 10.9 Selective 50/50 core crime occurence areas.

The previous two cases identified subareas within a criminal's awareness space where crimes are more likely to take place. It was assumed, implicitly, that the awareness spaces of individuals in general, and criminals in particular, are fixed over time. A more reasonable assumption would be that the awareness space is dynamic and can change over time. In terms of the general propositions presented at the beginning of this chapter, a "new" or "novice" criminal begins with an awareness space developed through noncriminal activities. When the novice criminal begins to search out victims or targets, he probably uses cues learned from friends who may have committed crimes (Letkemann 1973: 117–136; Mack 1964: 51), cues learned from the media (note the imitative crimes that have followed "caper" dramas on American television), and generalizations from previously learned feelings of security. The novice probably looks for targets within his awareness space and may even search fringe areas. He is unlikely to penetrate into totally foreign areas where he will feel uncomfortable or stand out as different or not belonging (Brantingham and Brantingham 1975; Reppetto 1974; Newman 1972; compare, Sacks 1972). Over time, if the novice continues to commit offenses, his awareness space is likely to accumulate more detailed information about the areas in which he has searched and found good targets. Over time, the criminal is also likely to expand his awareness space to include areas that were adjacent to his previous awareness space (see Figure 10.10).

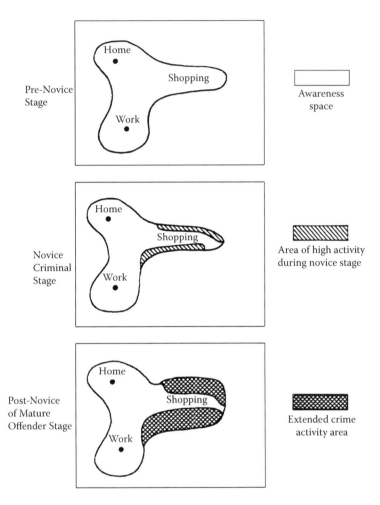

Figure 10.10 Maturation of crime search area.

10.9 Case 9: Dynamic Search Area for Multiple Offenders

Initial Conditions:

1. Multiple offenders
2. Nonuniform distribution of targets or victims
3. Home, work or school, shopping and recreation bases

As in the other generalizations from individual patterns to patterns for multiple offenders, the individual patterns can be overlaid. In discussing dynamic search areas, it should be mentioned that it is likely that information will flow between offenders and that an individual's awareness space is

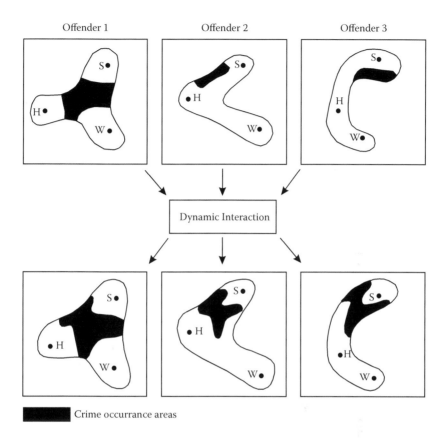

Crime occurrance areas

Figure 10.11 Dynamic changes in crime occurrence area.

likely to be modified by what he learns from other offenders. The interaction by communication of knowledge between offenders has been discussed in the learning of criminal behavior and skills which is supposed to occur in prison (Letkemann 1973; Mack 1964). It seems likely that information about "good" target areas diffuses within criminal social networks (Shover 1972; Mack 1964). Over time, the awareness spaces of criminals who have common social contacts are likely to converge, at least the subpart of the awareness spaces that identifies good target areas (see Figure 10.11). This convergence should result in more clustered crime patterns.

10.10 Summary

The hypothetical cases presented above were an attempt to articulate, spatially, the target selection behavior of criminals. Basically, it has been argued that the spatial patterning of crime in a particular urban area depends on:

1. The spatial distribution of potential offenders
2. The spatial distribution of potential targets
3. The general awareness spaces of potential offenders
4. Whether the awareness space includes potentially "good" targets in perceived "good" crime areas
5. The dynamic interchange of information between potential offenders which may modify their awareness spaces

It has been argued that the patterning of crime, and even the volume of crime, depends on motivation and opportunity, and mobility and perception. Crime occurrence is not the direct, unmediated result of motivation. Crime is a dependent phenomenon modified by urban form and general patterns of perception or cognition.

10.11 Consequences

Using the hypothetical cases as a starting platform, it is possible, deductively, to arrive at some general statements about crime patterns and to explain certain empirically reported patterns which previously had been unexplained.

(1) Older cities with a generally concentric zonal form, and with a dense core, will have a crime pattern which clusters toward the core. There should be a relatively steep crime gradient.

In a city with a concentric zone form there is a central business district surrounded by a zone-in-transition which is, in turn, surrounded by residential areas of increasing cost. In such a city, the socioeconomic groups with the highest incidence of criminal behavior are likely to live in or near the zone-in-transition. Entertainment and work opportunities are likely to be close to the homes of potential offenders. Commercial and industrial targets will be close to the residences of potential criminals. There is also likely to be foot traffic in the core areas. All of these conditions provide targets for crime. Employing concepts of "distance decay," crime should be highest toward the core and around the zone-in-transition, and decrease away from the zone-in-transition. This, of course, is the classic pattern reported by the Chicago School ecologists.

(2) Newer cities with a mosaic urban form will have a more dispersed crime pattern, with less concentration of crime than in older, denser cities.

With a mosaic urban form, concentrations of potential criminals will be dispersed in clusters throughout the urban area. Entertainment centers and work locations are likely to be separated from the residential areas where many potential criminals live. The potential offenders of a mosaic city are likely to have larger awareness spaces than potential offenders in a concentric zone city because they must move more extensively in order to reach work, shopping, and entertainment locations. With larger awareness spaces, the potential offenders of a mosaic city will have a broader target search area and will be likely to find targets in more places, producing a dispersed crime pattern. This is the pattern reported in post-World War II studies in cities affected by dispersed public housing policies or by rapid development keyed to the transport potentials of the automobile.

(3) New cities with dispersed shopping and much strip commercial development have a higher potential for property crime.

Looking back to the hypothetical cases describing the distribution of targets, dispersed shopping and strip development put retail and commercial business into the awareness spaces of more individuals and within close reach of more people. Such easier access, which is the obvious marketing rationale for dispersing commercial activity, should make property offenses more frequent. An individual who is weakly motivated to commit a commercial property offense might be deterred if he had to walk two miles to find a target, but might not be deterred if he only had to walk two blocks.

The relative desirability of various combinations of travel mode and travel time is, of course, open to empirical investigation. Reppetto's (1974) Boston burglars expressed specific time-trouble-distance limits to their journeys to crime. But for illustrative purposes, consider a clustered commercial shopping area which is roughly circular, with a radius of one-half mile. Suppose that the average juvenile will travel about one-half mile to commit a property offense such as theft or burglary (Figure 10.12). The donut-shaped area one-half mile wide is the feeder area providing potential offenders to the central

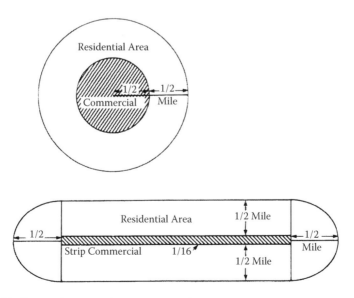

Figure 10.12 Feeder areas for commercial activities.

commercial area. This feeder area is 2.35 square miles. If the same amount of commercial activity were converted into strip development one-sixteenth of a mile wide, it would produce a strip 12.56 miles long (Figure 10.12). Using the same basic idea that a juvenile will travel up to one-half mile to commit a property offense, the strip commercial area will have a feeder area 13.4 square miles in area. This strip feeder area is 5.7 times larger than the feeder area for the cluster development. Assuming that the two feeder areas are similar demographically, and have similar densities, the stores in the hypothetical strip development will suffer exposure to a far larger number of potential offenders and will be at much greater risk of becoming a target.

(4) Development of major transportation arteries leads to a concentration of criminal events close to the highways, particularly near major intersections.

Major transportation arteries are likely to become part of the awareness space of many urban residents, including potential criminals. To use Kevin Lynch's terminology (1960), the transportation arteries become paths. Major intersections are likely to become nodal points. We have argued in this chapter that a criminal's search area begins within his awareness space. Paths and nodes become reasonable starting points in such a search.

Areas close to major paths and intersections have other attractions for instrumental type offenses such as robbery or burglary. Robbers and burglars look for targets within "safe" crime areas. Major transportation arteries, if the criminal has a car, offer easy escape.

Because of easy access and availability to customers, stores and services locate along the traffic arteries and at nodes. Such stores and services are potential targets.

The areas adjacent to major transportation arteries are likely to have a disproportionate number of potential targets, be perceived as relatively "safe" crime search areas, and be part of many offenders' awareness spaces. All this should lead to higher crime rates near major arteries, particularly near nodal points on arteries (see Fink 1969; Wilcox 1973; Luedtke and Associates 1970).

(5) Areas with grid networks, in general, have higher potential crime rates than areas with organic street layouts.

In order for a crime to occur, the criminal has to locate a target or victim in his awareness space. A criminal's awareness space will change with new information and as the result of searching. The expansion of an awareness space will most probably occur in a connected fashion; the borders or edges of currently known areas will be explored first. In exploring new areas, the potential offender will find it easier to penetrate areas with predictable road networks. Areas with grid street layouts are more predictable than areas with winding roads, cul-de-sacs, or dead ends.

Criminal behavior in searching new areas is *spatially* similar to other urban residents. Since residential areas with more organic street layouts and cul-de-sacs and dead ends are more difficult to use as through paths, these residential areas are less likely to experience much through traffic. Nonresidents are less likely to be found in these areas, therefore they are more likely to be identified by residents when present. Because nonresidents are more easily identifiable, and because they may become lost or disoriented, offenders are less likely to expand their search areas very far into nongrid residential areas (see Bevis and Nutter 1977).

(6) Older cities with dispersed low income housing and public transit are likely to have a concentration of crime around the core, and nodes of higher crime around the low income housing areas.

This statement about crime patterns is really just a corollary to the first statement which described crime gradients in the "zonal" city. Because of public policy in many countries, particularly Britain, subsidized low income housing has been dispersed in many older cities. Given that, historically, more criminals have been found in low income groups (a point reaffirmed by Hindelang's 1978 cross-analysis of arrest, victimization, and self-report data), this dispersal will have an obvious impact on crime patterns. In older cities with a dominant core, the awareness spaces of criminals living in the low income housing areas will include their home area and the core area. Their search for targets will be biased towards these areas. Such a pattern of crime was found by T. Morris (1957) in Croyden, and Baldwin and Bottoms in Sheffield (1976), and was reported by McKay in the post-World War II data for Chicago in the revised edition of the Shaw and McKay classic, *Juvenile Delinquency and Urban Areas* (1969).

(7) The shifting of work areas out of core areas into fringe areas of a city will tend to increase crime in suburban areas.

In many growing urban areas industrial and wholesale trade operations are increasing in urban fringe areas, or in the outer ring of urban areas, and decreasing in the urban core. The shift away from the core is partly the result of the industrial move to one-floor plants which obviously require the larger blocks of land which are available at lower cost in fringe areas and partly the result of improved urban highway systems which decrease the accessibility advantage of central core locations.

Whatever the reasons for the shift, the movement of work locations to the urban fringe should influence crime patterns. Because journey-to-work patterns will change, awareness spaces will change for those criminals who work (regularly or occasionally). Those fringe and suburban work locations and suburban residential and commercial areas along the paths to and from work areas will become part of the awareness spaces of employed criminals and may even become part of the awareness spaces of nonworking criminals who communicate with workers.

In addition, the movement of industrial and wholesale trade changes the opportunity structure, putting more targets within the reach of those people who live in suburban areas and may be motivated to commit property offenses.

(8) Major entertainment complexes such as sports arenas are likely to produce localized associated increases in crime. If these complexes are near residential areas with many potential offenders, the associated crime should increase disproportionately.

Major entertainment complexes are likely to become part of the awareness space of most urban residents. These complexes also produce temporally concentrated clusters of victims and targets when activities are going on. Thus, a concentration of targets is likely to occur within the awareness space of many criminals.

If, in addition, the entertainment complexes are located near residential areas with many people who are motivated to commit crimes, the easy accessibility and the strength of the awareness space of residents should increase associated crime even more.

(9) Cities with a core "red light district" are likely to have concentrations of crime in those areas. However, dispersing the activities which cluster in a "red light district" will not necessarily decrease the total amount of crime, though the spatial patterning of crime should change.

Historically, cities have always had red light districts, areas where prostitution, gambling, and bars concentrate. These areas attract potential victims and potential offenders. In fact, in these areas the offender and victim distinction can become blurred. In the case of murder and assault, the victim precipitation literature shows how easily the victim might have been the offender (Vetter and Silverman 1978: 76). In street robbery, the victim may become an offender on another day.

City administrators try to control such areas through traditional means such as enforcing criminal code violations, passing municipal ordinances controlling businesses, and increasing police presence. In some cities the activities in the district are broken up, often to appear in a more dispersed pattern in other parts of the city. Reckless (1933) documented such a dispersal of the Chicago red light district in 1912 and noted the migration of the vice area from the urban core to the suburban fringe.

The dispersal of the red light activities may increase or decrease the amount of crime. Whether crime increases or decreases depends on the distribution of targets after the dispersal and how the awareness spaces of potential criminals change. If the breakup of a red light district results in a total decrease in red light activities and the remaining activities become part of the awareness spaces of fewer potential criminals (or patrons in general), then the total amount of crime may decrease. However, the breaking up a red light district may backfire on city administrators. New areas may pick up the red light businesses, the awareness spaces of the former patrons and criminals who "worked" the old red light district will change. For some, new areas with increased red light activities will be incorporated into their awareness spaces. Potential criminals will be attracted into previously unknown parts of the city. If these previously unknown parts of the city have many good targets or victims, then crime may increase. Reckless (1933) recorded an increase in crime in the Chicago suburbs, together with an overall decrease in metropolitan levels of crime as some red light businesses were driven outside Chicago proper, while others folded after the 1912 clean-up. More recently, Harries (1976: 384) has reported that urban renewal in Lawton, Oklahoma, destroyed the city's compact vice area and dispersed the businesses throughout the suburbs, creating a tough law enforcement problem and an incredibly high crime rate.

10.12 Conclusion

In conclusion, it has been argued in this chapter that crime occurrence is not the direct result of motivation, but is mediated by perceived opportunity. This, in turn, is influenced by the actual distribution of opportunities, urban form, and mobility. It has been argued that criminals are not random in their behavior and that by exploring urban structure and how people interact with the urban spatial structure, it should be possible to predict the spatial distribution of crime and explain some of the variation in volume of crime between urban areas and between cities.

The Use of Space in Burglary (1985)

11

G.F. RENGERT
J. WASILCHICK

From Rengert, G.F., and Wasilchick, J. (1985). The use of space in burglary. In *Suburban Burglary: A Time and a Place for Everything* (53–75). Springfield, IL: Charles C. Thomas.

Contents

11.1 Introduction   257
11.2 Important Terms and Concepts   258
11.3 The Burglar's Awareness of Space   261
11.4 The Burglars' Evaluation of Space   262
11.5 Learning about Space   264
11.6 Relationship of Crime to Noncriminal Spatial Activity   267
    11.6.1 Orientation of Crime Sites to Workplaces   268
    11.6.2 Orientation of Crime Sites to Recreation Places   269
    11.6.3 Orientation through Secondary Information Sources 269
11.7 Summary and Conclusions   271

11.1 Introduction

Suburban residential burglary, unlike many urban crimes, requires several prior decisions. Many urban burglaries are spontaneous reactions to opportunities that present themselves during the course of daily activity. These spontaneous crimes are called situational crimes and occur while the burglar is working, or on his way to and from another activity. The only real decision is to seize the opportunity at hand.

Criminals in the suburbs face different conditions. They are not likely to just happen upon an unlocked door or other spontaneous opportunity. Suburban burglars usually need an automobile to reach the target area, and the decision to commit a burglary is usually made before they ever leave their homes. Suburban burglars must search for their opportunities.

11.2 Important Terms and Concepts

Suburban residential burglars must make at least two interrelated decisions to be in business (Rengert 1980). The first is the basic decision to commit the crime. The second involves a decision about how and where to commit the crime. The decision about whether or not to commit a burglary has received the most research attention by criminologists. Their interest is in what makes a person want to commit any crime, including burglary. The primary reason stated by the burglars we interviewed for deciding to commit a burglary was simply to obtain money. Without describing family background, demographic characteristics and socio-economic standing in detail, we can state that the need for money did not result from a struggle to feed and clothe a family. Many of these individuals were middle class or lower middle class, and many had employable skills. The need for money rose out of psychologically defined needs, not subsistence needs. These psychologically defined needs are things like a faster lifestyle, drugs, and gambling. These activities demand more money than these people can earn legitimately. The decision to commit burglaries was a purposeful, rational decision in almost every case.

Our main concern here is the second question posed: Where is the burglary to be committed? We seek insight into how burglars choose a crime site. We want to know why they choose one area over the others available. The choice of a specific house rather than its neighbor will not be discussed here. This is a very idiosyncratic choice that will be touched on in the next chapter. Here, we are trying to understand the decisions made by burglars when they evaluate their environment. Environment in this sense includes the physical, social, and economic infrastructure that the individual interacts with. Think of the environment as a stage on which the individual is an actor, and acts out his life without a predetermined script. The physical, economic, and social factors are like the props and setting of the play.

This analogy makes it clear that the individual does not consider or perhaps even know about the environment beyond the stage where his life is acted out. In other words, people do not know all places equally well. People cannot evaluate places they have never visited or have no knowledge of. Proximity does not always equal familiarity.

Let us consider the relationship between spatial perception and the criminal use of space. The conceptual model of this relationship often used by geographers is useful to illustrate how space is perceived and used in different ways (Wolpert 1964; Brantingham and Brantingham 1984, Chapter 12). Consider a large region, such as a metropolitan area or county as an example. Property criminals that are residential burglars cannot commit a crime unless they are aware of a location that provides an opportunity for burglary. This location is contained within the criminal's "awareness space" according to our model. The awareness space is the set of all places about which the criminal has some knowledge. Stated another way, it is a subset of the total regional environment.

The awareness space of a burglar contains places of varying utility for criminal exploitation. It is assumed that the criminal actively chooses among the available places within this awareness space. Not all places are considered. Only those places that are above a threshold or "breakeven" level of expectation for profitability and probability of success are considered. Several burglars laughed at even the suggestion of traveling to the city of Chester to perform a burglary. This is because of Chester's reputation as an economically distressed ghetto. One burglar even remarked, "You could get robbed in Chester."

Several black burglars flatly stated that the wealthy areas of Marple and Radnor were off limits for them. The risk for a black man in a "lily white" community was too great. Their presence alone would be noticed. Another burglar, also black, was not afraid of those areas. He went to great lengths to present himself in a context where he would not stand out. "You gotta dress for the occasion" as he put it. Dressed as a mover or workman driving a van or truck, he felt he had a high probability of success in areas of white wealth. The threshold varies and each burglar has his own rationale for evaluating the utility of an area.

The places that are above the threshold of profitability and safety form the criminal's "search space." The search space is a further subset of the criminal's awareness space. At each step, the field of potential areas for burglary becomes smaller.

Finally, within the criminal's search space is an area considered best or most comfortable for criminal activity. This chosen area is termed the "criminal activity space." It is the area actually exploited by the criminal. The criminal will continue to operate in this area until he judges it no longer profitable, or too dangerous. Danger in this sense can come from fear of recognition, a change in policing patterns, or an intuitive feeling that luck is running out.

This model provides a useful way to sort out areas that have burglary potential. Areas that have the same potential in an objective way may be judged by the burglar to have widely varying utility. This is because of the subjective nature of this process.

The model assumes that the criminal is actively engaged in the criminal evaluation and use of space (Figure 11.1). Because of this, the model will not be useful in evaluating the special cases of situational crimes and criminal opportunities discovered through secondary sources such as fences or friends.

Let's turn our attention to a real-world application of this conceptual model. It suggests a few questions, and as far as we can tell, criminals have never before been asked questions like these.

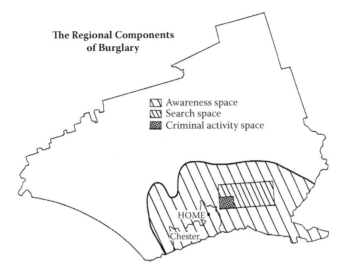

Figure 11.1 The use of space in crime.

1. How much territory are criminals actually aware of?
2. How do criminals evaluate this territory for criminal purposes?
3. How does the subjective spatial behavior of the criminals orient and direct the search for crime sites?

We mentioned previously* that Delaware County is well suited from a spatial perspective for this kind of analysis. It is a diverse area with a wide range of neighborhood and community types. Many socio-economic groups are represented (Figure 11.2). Add to this the compact and accessible nature of the county. Major transportation arteries fan out over the county so that all areas are well served and easily reached. One can drive from one end of the county to the other in any direction in less than thirty minutes.

Almost all the burglars interviewed lived in one of two areas. The first cluster of burglars' residences is found in the southeastern corner of the county not far from the Philadelphia line. The second clustering is in the area in and around the city of Chester. Given the range of affluence and knowing where the burglars lived, it makes sense that there is strong economic incentive for these residential burglars to travel north in their search for a profitable burglary target. This situation is an almost ideal environmental laboratory to test ideas about the awareness and use of territory by residential burglars.

* Editor's note: In an earlier chapter introduction of *Suburban Burglary*.

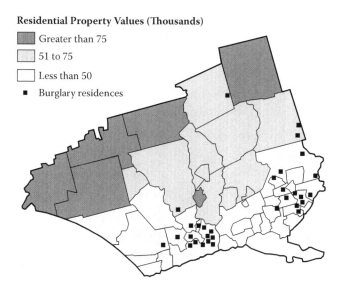

Residential Property Values (Thousands)

Greater than 75
51 to 75
Less than 50
■ Burglary residences

Figure 11.2 Residential property values (thousands).

11.3 The Burglar's Awareness of Space

We can see that Delaware County offers a wide range of opportunities to a burglar, but what does the burglar see? The first step in our analysis is to determine how much of Delaware County our group of residential burglars is familiar with.

We measured the burglar's familiarity with different Delaware County locations through the use of a semantic differential scale. Each person interviewed was asked to rank each municipality and town in the county according to how well they knew the place on a scale of zero to ten. Interviewees were asked to rank their home area as ten, and places they had no knowledge of as zero. Every other area was then ranked with respect to these two reference points. The respondents were moderately familiar with about fifty percent of the places in the county, although there was considerable spatial clustering of known places in the southern part of the county. Generally, burglars were most familiar with areas close to their home, and these were clustered in the southern and southeastern parts of the county. The only exceptions were Media and Thornbury Township for obvious reason. Media is the county seat and location of Common Pleas court, and Thornbury Township is the location of the prison. There was a clear decline in familiarity as these burglars were asked about other places in the north of Delaware County.

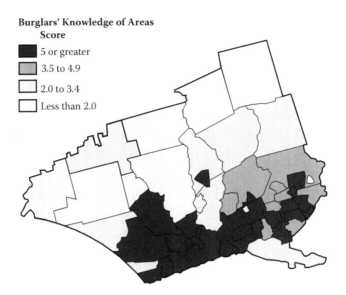

Figure 11.3 Burglars' knowledge of areas.

11.4 The Burglars' Evaluation of Space

The next step in our analysis is to examine how burglars evaluated the places they had knowledge of as potential burglary sites. In this analysis, we asked the burglar to evaluate only those areas that he was familiar with, using a rating scale. Ten on the scale was assigned to the location felt to be the best in the county for residential burglary, and one was given to the worst place. Zero was assigned to places they had no knowledge of and was excluded from the scaling analysis. All other places were rated between one and ten (Figure 11.3).

Again, we see distances from the southern part of the county as important. The southernmost part of the county was rated low as a potential area for burglary. We expected this, based on low property values. The highest ranked areas surprisingly are not the most affluent areas. The highest ranking went to areas in the tier of mid-priced housing just outside the home area of the burglars. An exception is well known, affluent Radnor Township located in the northernmost part of the county. Radnor was rated very high by those burglars who had heard of it, but the burglars we interviewed had rarely committed a burglary there. The high ranked areas close to home, though not as rich as Radnor, were far more popular as burglary sites. These areas were those most often burglarized by the interviewees during their burglary careers (Figure 11.4). It seems that distance and familiarity are as important as economic consideration in the criminal evaluation of places (Reppetto 1974; Scarr 1973; Cohen and Cantor 1981).

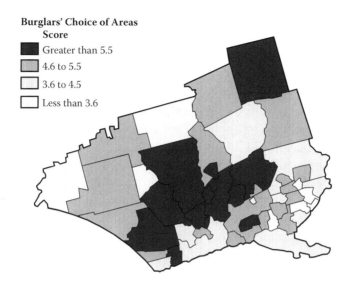

Figure 11.4 Burglars' choice of areas.

Cultural perceptions also play an important role in the criminal evaluation of areas (Morrill 1965). "You'll get shot if you're caught there" was a common response of blacks with respect to white housing areas, and whites with respect to black housing areas. Everyone was cautious toward Marcus Hook and Trainer. These areas were heavily populated by motorcycle gangs in the recent past. The burglars were especially afraid of the "Pagans," the local motorcycle gang. Several burglars described graphically what they thought would happen to them if the house they happened to break into was occupied by a "Pagan." A local gang can provide protection to a community from criminals living outside their residential area (Ley 1974).

As described in the introduction,* a cultural barrier to spatial movement in physical form seems to be West Chester Pike, Route 3. Although the highway can be crossed easily, it seems to act as a perceptual dividing line between northern and southern parts of the county. There seems to be relatively little social interaction between residents living north and south of the highway. For instance, until recently most of the high schools south of Route 3 did not play high schools north of Route 3 in sports. The affluent areas north of the highway resemble the adjoining areas of Chester and Montgomery Counties much more than areas closer, but south of Route 3. The wealth, style, and attitudes of the Main Line flow north and west. Areas south of Route 3 are middle class in every way and are more oriented to Philadelphia as a social and work center. Farther south and nearer the Delaware River are the

---

* Editor's note: The introduction to *Suburban Burglary*.

distinctive blue collar industrial communities. In short, Route 3, although easily crossed, seems to divide the county culturally into a northern and southern part. Using Lynch's terminology these are two different "districts" and Route 3 is the "edge" (Lynch 1960).

This led us to question what really attracts criminals to specific search areas. We began to consider the burglars' possible sources of information, and how they learned about space to better understand this decision.

11.5 Learning about Space

Spatial perception is the awareness of two-dimensional extended space in the form of the world around us. Spatial awareness is the result of a learning process encompassing a variety of information sources (Golledge 1981). This learning process may be either active or passive depending upon the information source. Passive spatial learning occurs as spatial knowledge is accrued through day-to-day activities. The purpose of these activities can be anything in our daily lives except exploring new areas to gain spatial knowledge. In everyday activities such as traveling to work, shopping or a social occasion, we passively assimilate spatial information. We learn quickly about new road construction when it affects our regular route to work, although we don't travel the route specifically to determine road conditions.

Passive learning journeys are characterized by habit (Pipkin 1981). These are journeys that are traveled regularly and by force of habit. Studies show that when an individual changes jobs or moves, he seldom tries more than three alternatives before he settles on a specific route that becomes routine (Hensher 1976). Changes to this travel pattern are resisted after this habitual route has been decided. Notice how quickly many people become irritated on their way to work if they are forced off a familiar route by road construction or some other barrier. We tend to avoid the unfamiliar in our journeys through space.

Relatively little additional spatial knowledge is gained after the initial exploration to find the best route. Any spatial knowledge gained is gained passively while completing the journey. We tend to ignore spatial information around us unless something unusual gets in the way. One might wonder how passive journeys are important to criminal activity. The habitual spatial paths of passive journeys tend to directionally orient criminal activity. As we will demonstrate, this occurs even when information from these spatial journeys is not directly used in criminal activity.

When starting on a journey, we tend to be directionally oriented by familiar paths even when we set out to explore unfamiliar areas. For example, many of us have had the experience of starting out on a Sunday drive and, without noticing, found ourselves halfway to our work place. Another

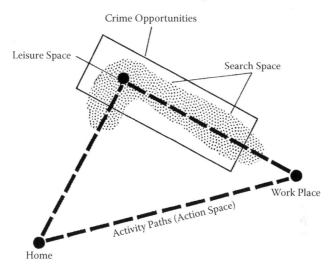

Action and Search Spaces

Figure 11.5 Action and search spaces.

example commonly occurs when we are driving to a destination in the same direction as our work place, and we forget to turn toward our destination. Again, we wind up most of the way to a place we had no intention of going. The automobile seems single-minded. In short, familiar habitual journeys tend to direct even unfamiliar journeys in familiar directions.

This brings us to the second way individuals obtain spatial knowledge—through the active evaluation and exploration of space (Figure 11.5). The whole purpose of spatial activity in the active learning process is to obtain information for later use. The environment is actively examined or cased and evaluated for its usefulness. This may entail entering unfamiliar areas. In this case, the process is termed "spatial exploration."

Unfamiliar territory is entered either by extending a known activity path into unfamiliar territory or by traveling in a different direction that leads to new places at shorter distances. In either case, the environment is actively evaluated for its utility for the purpose in mind, whether criminal or non-criminal. This evaluation process is the same for criminal activity as it would be for determining the best location for a fast food restaurant. We will show that for criminal activity individuals tend to extend familiar habitual paths, rather than travel in an unfamiliar direction.

Secondary sources of information are a special case. Individuals obtain spatial information from secondary sources such as friends, the media, working partners or fences. These information sources do not depend on the past spatial knowledge of the individual to orient the direction of spatial activity. The knowledge of the new location is a "chance location" from the perspective of the spatial actor. Previous spatial behavior of the individual gives us few clues as to the probable location of the new spatial knowledge. There is no identifiable probability of the direction or distance of the spatial location from the individual. The new location is almost a shot in the dark compared to the order and structure of our learned spatial knowledge.

This model of behavior puts criminal spatial activity into perspective for those cases where the criminal is actively engaged in the criminal evaluation and use of space. It is less useful in interpreting situational crimes. These crimes are opportunities that present themselves to the criminal in the course of everyday events, and are just too good to pass up. Situational crimes are not actively sought out, and there is usually no planning involved. These crimes are located well within the individual's daily activity space in most cases.

A recent incident provides a good example. Joey Coyle had not set out to commit a crime or even considered the possibility when he happened upon a cash bag from an armored car lying in the middle of the intersection of Wolf and Swanson in south Philadelphia. The bag contained 1.2 million dollars in unmarked one hundred dollar bills. The money had just fallen from the back of an armored car, unnoticed by the guards. As the armored car drove away, Coyle could not resist. The opportunity was just too great. He scooped up the sack of money and disappeared.

The Philadelphia police followed every anonymous tip, and even used a hypnotist to elicit information from bystanders in the area at the time. Every bar bill paid with a one hundred dollar bill was considered a lead. A big break came when Coyle entered the wrong house in New Jersey, boasting in a loud voice about his new wealth. When Coyle discovered his mistake, he apologized and gave the amazed residents of the home several hundred dollars on his way out. This led to a thorough description of Coyle. Finally, after a lengthy investigation, Coyle was apprehended at Kennedy International Airport in New York. He was waiting to board a flight for Mexico. He had over $100,000 in one hundred dollar bills stuffed in his boots.

His plea at trial was that the sight of all that money made him temporarily insane. As an aside, Mr. Coyle was found not guilty, and over $100,000 of the money was never found. Although the incident took place along one of his familiar activity paths, the crime did not depend on his spatial knowledge. The crime was a chance occurrence. Ironically, the clue that led to his apprehension was an equally chance occurrence, and a very unfortunate mistake in space use for Mr. Coyle (Larson 1981).

A final consideration is the style of the very best burglars. These criminals rely heavily on research rather than spatial search (Cohen and Cantor 1981). Individuals or wealthy neighborhoods are selected, and the individual's behavior studied. The burglar strikes when the resident is away and the conditions are right. The methods used are those appropriate to the site, and not the burglar's routine method. Site, timing and method are all chosen as a result of analysis of the target. As we mentioned earlier,* one of Philadelphia's sports teams was the target for such a burglar. These burglars are extremely analytical and thorough in their work. They are almost impossible to stop, if you are their target. Fortunately for us all, burglars of this brilliance are rare.

Clearly, we need to understand the nature of the information source used by the criminal to locate a criminal activity site if we hope to make sense of the spatial pattern of crime occurrences. Consider the distance from the criminal's home to the crime site. We can conceptualize the probable location of the crime. Closest to home will be situational crimes happened upon during the criminal's daily activities. Next are crime opportunities located through the criminal's evaluation of places he knows about. Finally, the farthest are crime opportunities located through spatial exploration. Randomly distributed among and along this continuum are criminal opportunities identified by fences or friends.

These are some of the relationships between spatial learning and criminal behavior suggested by the information we gathered from active burglars. We have already established the amount of space the burglars are aware of, and how they evaluate its crime potential through the use of ratings. Next, we would like to break down some of this information by the burglar's source of information. This comparison of crime site, spatial knowledge, and information source will illustrate clearly how active and passive information sources shape the spatial form of criminal activity. Emphasis will fall on the journey to work because of its influence in determining the likely direction of criminal activity from the burglar's residence. As stated by Pipkin (1981: 148), "The work-trip is numerically the most important trip for most adults."

11.6 Relationship of Crime to Noncriminal Spatial Activity

When we began this chapter, we suggested that the noncriminal use of space would affect the criminal evaluation and use of space. In other words, it is daily activities like traveling to work or school that orients criminals toward crime sites and helps them choose those with the best potential. In order to test this notion, we needed information on the daily use of space for both criminal and noncriminal activities. We gathered this information from the daily diaries, mentioned in the previous chapter,† that we asked the burglars to construct. Each individual traced a typical day starting with

---

* Editor's note: In the previous chapter of *Suburban Burglary.*
† In the previous chapter of *Suburban Burglary* [editor's note].

the time they awoke in the morning through to the time they went to bed at night. They described hour by hour the typical activities that they habitually completed during the day. Almost every prisoner enjoyed recalling better times. We were often struck by the sharp contrast between the freedom they described and the austere discipline of the prison. For several individuals, we were saddened by the emptiness of their lives. Reconstructing their lives outside the prison was not a difficult task because daily life is habit forming. Most prisoners seemed to genuinely enjoy describing their life outside the prison.

This information allowed us to identify work places and habitual travel paths to work for those who had held jobs during the year prior to their conviction. We were also able to identify weekend recreation areas and routes traveled to these locations. Work places are easy to identify because in most cases they do not vary from day to day. Recreation sites vary, but in almost all cases, the immediate response was something like, "On Saturday, I usually go to the park and drink a few beers with my buddies," or an equally explicit response. We accepted this response as typical and representative of the individual's leisure activities. We used these responses to locate each individual's leisure activities.

11.6.1 Orientation of Crime Sites to Workplaces

Now we know where the burglar lived, worked, and spent his leisure time. We also know the location of each burglar's crime sites. We took the latter information from the district attorney's records. The first question pursued with this information was the spatial relationship between the workplaces and the burglary sites. To test this spatial relationship for each burglar interviewed, burglary sites were plotted on a map along with the home of the burglar. To measure the distance and directional orientation of the crime sites, a protractor was placed on the map with the zero axis set on the home–workplace direction. The direction of the burglary sites can then be measured with respect to this axis. One hundred and eighty degrees would be a crime site located in the opposite direction from the workplace and ninety degrees would be at right angles to the home–workplace axis. The distance of the workplace of each employed interviewee is measured along the zero axis and the distance to each burglary site is scaled in the direction it occurred with respect to the home–work axis (Adams 1969).

There is a marked orientation of the crime sites in the direction of the workplace (Figure 11.6). Visually, this is very clear. Thirty-one of the forty burglary sites of fourteen burglars who had worked within a year of their conviction are located in the quartile between zero and forty-five degrees. This directional bias implies that the search behavior of the burglars is oriented, if not constrained, by the habitual, familiar journey to work. Many of

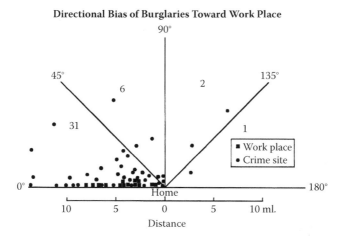

Figure 11.6 Directional bias of burglaries toward workplace.

the crime sites were just beyond the workplace. Many were located just off the familiar path from home to work. We feel this implies that the burglar's search may extend the familiar path to work, or veer off it at some point along the way. In either case, the burglar is strongly influenced by the direction of his workplace in his search for a crime site.

11.6.2 Orientation of Crime Sites to Recreation Places

We can use the same information to examine the influence of recreation places. Recreation places are plotted for the thirteen burglars who were not employed within a year of their conviction, but actively searched for crime locations. We noticed that routes to recreation sites tend to be longer on the average than routes to work for our group of suburban burglars. This is opposite to the relationship found by Chapin in Washington, D.C. (1974).

Again we notice a directional bias of burglary sites compared to the journey to recreation places (Figure 11.7); but there is less clustering of burglary sites in the home–recreation axis than in the home–work axis. Twenty of thirty-five burglary sites were located between zero and forty-five degrees of this axis. It seems that both work and recreation travel tend to orient the direction of the burglar's search behavior. However, the direction of the workplace seems more important than the direction of the recreation place.

11.6.3 Orientation through Secondary Information Sources

Finally, we can compare these spatial patterns with a natural control group: individuals who did not use their own spatial knowledge because they used secondary sources to identify crime sites. In other words, a fence, the media,

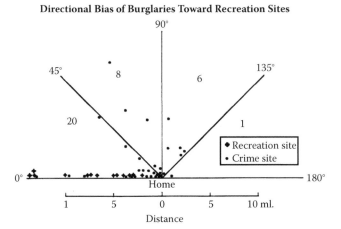

Figure 11.7 Directional bias of burglaries toward recreation sites.

a friend or some other source told them about a site, and the burglar's own search never even began. Second-hand spatial information results in a much more randomly distributed spatial pattern of burglary sites than a first-hand search (Figure 11.8). The average distance from home is also somewhat longer. There are fewer places clustered near the home of the burglar.

When secondary information sources are used, crime sites are located in all directions and at greater distances from the burglar's home. Comparing the spatial patterns of active search and secondary information sources for locating crime sites confirms for us the idea that habitual travel influences nonhabitual travel. People tend to start off in familiar directions even if they are going into unfamiliar territory. And they tend to minimize the distance necessary to locate their objective. In this case, intervening opportunities are

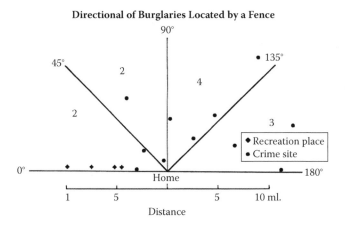

Figure 11.8 Direction of burglaries located by a fence.

utilized. In other words, when these burglars have a choice, they use closer rather than more distant crime sites.

There is always the possibility in an analysis of this type that the results will be misleading. This is a concern here because of the number of people interviewed and the ideal nature of Delaware County as a setting. We felt more comfortable about the home–work result after working on the home–recreation information. After reviewing the home–secondary source site axis, we are confident that all the results are genuine. We look forward to replicating the test with a larger sample in another area.

11.7 Summary and Conclusions

It seems clear from this analysis that many of the assumptions used in aggregate models do not hold for our group of residential burglars. For example, these people are not familiar with all the area around them. They do not give equal consideration to all the area they are aware of in their criminal evaluation of space. They are guided by past travel habits. Finally, a large group of property criminals have their criminal spatial decisions made for them by fences and others. Their situation, spatially, may be relatively trivial in predicting the probable location of their crime sites.

It's interesting to note that some burglars did not always use the information they had. Those burglars from the southernmost areas of the county who knew about places like Radnor still preferred the closer tier of mid-priced housing to the wealthier part of the county. One impression we were left with is that these burglars are comfortable burglarizing people one social class up from themselves. Those in blue collar areas burglarized middle class neighborhoods. The only burglars we interviewed who operated on the wealthy Main Line were themselves from middle class and upper middle class areas like Haverford and Newtown Townships.

Work and recreation places seem to orient the direction of the search for burglars actively searching for crime locations. Recent trends in metropolitan transportation will bring about change and possibly increase the suburban crime rate by increasing everyone's awareness space. The suburbanization of industry has brought many blue collar employees who traditionally live in inner city areas out to the industrial parks of the suburbs (Muller 1981). These are people who may have had no prior knowledge of the suburbs and will expand their awareness space dramatically. The suburban shopping mall attracts customers from a wide area and draws them to a local suburban area. This again expands the awareness space of those who learn a new travel path. Property crime rates can be expected to rise in localities that have attractions such as these. Further, little known suburban areas that are relatively crime free can be expected to experience more crime as a greater number of people become familiar with these outlying areas.

These considerations highlight the ethical considerations of identifying and strengthening barriers to criminal spatial mobility. When crime is displaced from one area to another, rates rise and fall. Politicians and policy makers often confuse displacing crime with attacking the problem of what causes the decision to engage in criminal activity in the first place.

When crime is displaced into a relatively low income area that is economically less capable of combating crime, there is a temptation to "write off" the area and the problem. For example, inner-city criminals sometimes get more lenient sentences than suburban criminals for the same crime (Epstein 1978). This can be interpreted as the judicial system "writing off" the inner city while protecting suburban or more affluent areas. Inner-city areas suffer a higher crime rate than suburban areas partly through the false economy of spending less for imprisonment and rehabilitation than the suburban areas. The attitude of many suburban residents is that the higher urban crime rate is somehow "natural" and to be expected. This deflects concern away from the victims of inner-city crimes and focuses it on how to keep crime from *spreading* to the suburbs. Obviously, victims of crime should receive consideration equally, without regard to where they live. Ironically, continued concern for how to stop the spread of crime, rather than how to alleviate criminogenic situations, almost insures that crime will diffuse out into previously safe areas.

During the course of interviewing, a baseball story came to mind because it so aptly described the search behavior of burglars. "Hit 'em where they ain't" is how Wee Willie Keeler described successful batting in baseball. It is a comment that describes well a burglar's intuitive consideration of both time and space.

Nodes, Paths, and Edges
Considerations on the Complexity of Crime and the Physical Environment (1993)

12

P.L. BRANTINGHAM
P.J. BRANTINGHAM

From Brantingham, P.L., and Brantingham, P.J. (1993). Nodes, paths and edges: Considerations on the complexity of crime and the physical environment. *Journal of Environmental Psychology*, 13, 3–28.

Contents

12.1 Abstract	274
12.2 Overview	274
12.3 Background	274
12.4 Framework	277
12.5 Complex Etiology	279
12.6 Individual Criminal Behavior: The Influence of the Physical Environment	285
12.6.1 Routine Activities/Travel Paths/Nodes	286
12.6.2 Target Choice	290
12.6.3 Crime Template	291
12.7 Aggregate Crime Patterns: The Influence of the Physical Environment	296
12.7.1 The Urban Mosaic and Crime	296
12.7.2 Activity Nodes	298
12.7.3 Pathways	300
12.7.4 Edge Effects	301
12.7.5 Territoriality: Residential Areas	302
12.7.5.1 Outsiders	304
12.7.5.2 Insiders	306
12.7.6 Aggregate Patterns Summary	307
12.8 Conclusions	308

12.1 Abstract

Crime has long been thought to be intimately associated with the physical environment in which it occurs. Theoretical and empirical developments over the past 20 years demonstrate that this relationship is complex and varies substantially at different levels of spatial and temporal resolution. Research on the distribution of property crimes in time and space resonates with research on the target selection processes of offenders to suggest that crime is strongly related to aggregate elements of the perceived physical environment: nodes, paths, edges, and an environmental backcloth. The relationship between crime and the physical environment is mediated through individual awareness and action spaces. This implies a series of research issues and crime control policies for future exploration.

12.2 Overview

Trying to understand patterns in crime poses fascinating and long-standing questions. Why do some people commit crimes and not others? Why do some criminals commit one type of crime, such as robbery, and not another, such as burglary? Why do some people and places suffer a lot of crime and others almost none? The answers to these questions, if they can be found at all, must be complex. A long tradition of failed searches for simple answers and uncomplicated unicausal models—Bentham's model of rational calculation (1789), Lombroso's theory of biological atavism (1911), Sutherland's theory of differential association (1947), for instance—has established the point. Since the 1970s theoreticians and researchers have added more questions: how do criminals choose their targets? What in the surrounding environment influences whether someone decides to commit a crime? Do criminals see their surroundings in a fashion similar to the way they are seen by noncriminals? This article attempts to give an overview of what has been found in trying to answer these questions, while putting emphasis on how the physical environment appears to influence criminal decision making and shape criminals' views of their surrounding environments. While emphasizing research on the physical environment, this article does not and cannot ignore what the authors believe is the transactional nature of crime. Crime is an inclusive event.

12.3 Background

The idea that the physical environment influences criminal behavior is hardly new, though research on the issue is relatively new. High walls are built to keep criminals out, locks are meant to keep people from entering unless they have a key, guard dogs are kept to raise alarms and attack intruders. In fact, until quite recently people in general seem to have held extreme physical determinist views. Pictures of classical and medieval cities mostly show walled cities with a few controlled entry gates (Gold 1970). In his Statute of Winchester of 1285, the great reforming medieval English king, Edward I, tried to control highway robbery by forcing property owners to clear the verges of highways (i.e. cut down the trees and bushes along the sides of highways) so that robbers would have no place near the road to hide in ambush. Property owners who failed to do so were held legally liable for any robberies occurring along their uncleared verges (Plucknett 1960: 90).

Modifications of the physical environment formed a major component of crime control efforts in the eighteenth and nineteenth centuries. Both London and Paris introduced street lighting in the eighteenth century to increase safety and reduce crime on their streets at night. Street robberies were so frequent in the great cities spawned by the industrial revolution that people who could afford to avoid streets did not walk outside at night. Only the poor remained on the streets after dark. Lights were introduced with the intention of providing visibility and thereby making those persons walking on the street "safe" because they could see other people approaching them and because they could be seen by people who might come to their aid (Lowman 1983).

The great nineteenth-century European and North American cities featured poor and criminal neighborhoods ecologically located near the clusters of criminal opportunities, such as Oxford Street or the Strand in London, or on the edges of differentials in law enforcement authority and potential, such as the border between the City of London and the Metropolitan Police District at Temple Bar (Brantingham and Brantingham 1984: 298–304) or behind the barricades like St. Antoine in Paris (Vidler 1986).* (See further, Petrovich 1971, for Paris; Tobias 1972, for London and Liverpool; Inciardi 1978, for New York). Called "rookeries" in England, these criminal neighborhoods were generally believed to have been physically adapted over the years to support crime and criminal lifestyles. The social journalist Henry Mayhew described the notorious St. Giles rookery in London as a cluster of streets and buildings forming "an almost endless intricacy of courts and yards crossing each other, [which] rendered the place like a rabbit warren." He described Jones Court, at the heart of the St. Giles rookery, as composed of houses that "were connected by roof, yard, and cellar with those in [adjacent streets],

---

* The barricades in Paris were "edges" for major government/Parisian battles. Governmental "attacks" on poverty in the worst quarters of the city were also "attacks" on the neighborhoods that were seen to have been adapted to and supported criminals and the Parisian street warriors. Major boulevards were built to separate residential areas and, among other things, to give police ready access to the heart of criminal neighborhoods. See Vidler (1986).

and with each other in such a manner that the apprehension of an inmate or refugee in one of them was almost a task of impossibility to a stranger, and difficult to those well acquainted with the interior of the dwellings" (Mayhew 1861–1862: 299–300).

Criminals could reside in a rookery in relative safety from police, venture forth to commit crimes in nearby target areas, and disappear safely back into the rookery's physical maze when police gave chase. Much nineteenth-century urban renewal in England had, as a major objective, the physical destruction of rookeries and the dispersal of their residents. The construction of New Oxford Street, for instance, was largely driven by a desire to destroy the St. Giles rookery (Dyos 1957; Lowman 1983). While social ideals were considered, much of the reconstruction in Paris was aimed at control of criminal and dangerous neighborhoods (Vidler 1986).

Enrico Ferri, the great Italian positive school criminologist, perhaps summed up much of this belief in simple causal connections between the physical environment and crime in 1896 when he argued that: "High roads, railways, and tramways dispersed predatory bands in rural districts, just as wide streets and large and airy dwellings with public lighting and the destruction of slums prevent robbery with violence, concealment of stolen foods, and indecent assaults" (Ferri 1896: 123).

While much of the general public and many criminologists (e.g. Coleman 1985, 1989) still seem to believe in simple physical determinism, most current researchers and theoreticians have moved beyond Ferri and are now beginning to view crime occurrence as the result of an individual's perception of and knowledge about the surrounding environment, and are paying particular attention to how this perception and knowledge is shaped by underlying states of criminal motivation and the actual presence of criminal opportunities (e.g. Carter and Hill 1979; Wilson and Hernstein 1985; Cornish and Clarke 1986a; Felson 1987; Barlow 1990; Gottfredson and Hirschi 1990; Brantingham and Brantingham 1991). That is, many different types of behavior are defined as crimes. Individuals commit crimes for many reasons, ranging from affective motivations such as rage or thrill seeking to highly instrumental motivations such as greed. Crimes occur in diverse situations under highly varied circumstances. In fact, some researchers are beginning to see motivation and the perception of criminal opportunities as functioning interactively. Variations in perceived criminal opportunities influence motivation; motivation influences both the definition of and the search for criminal opportunities.

A growing amount of research in environmental criminology is action oriented. When a discernible aggregate pattern of criminal behavior is found, governments may change laws and create "new" crime reduction strategies (Poyner 1983; Clarke 1992). For example, steering wheel locks were first introduced by mandatory legislation during the 1970s to make theft of automobiles for "joyriding" difficult for casual thieves. Research in both Germany and Britain has shown that the locks reduced joyriding as intended, but had less effect on professional car theft (Webb and Laycock 1992). More recently, in jurisdictions such as Canada which have not defined minimum engineering standards for such locks, some manufacturers have begun installing steering wheel locks that are easily broken and joyriding appears to be increasing rapidly again. Planners also pursue action research on the relation between crime and the physical environment. Both Appleyard (1981) and the Institute for Architecture and Urban Studies (IAUS; 1986) included investigations of "crime" related issues in their detailed studies of how streets ought to be designed. Both studies seemed to equate "crime" with robbery or fear of robbery, and to recommend action strategies accordingly. The IAUS project team in particular seemed to loop backward in time to eighteenth-century strategies, recommending that Binghampton, New York, provide additional street lighting as a way to increase safety from crime.* The pressure for action research focused on finding environmental designs that reduce crime is increasingly driven, particularly in the United States, by civil law suits in which crime victims sue landlords for negligence in failing to provide protectively designed and securely maintained premises (e.g. Jeffery and White 1985).

In addition to this natural desire to find design techniques for reducing crime, there is a growing awareness that, because of the high variability in what is called a crime, in the people who commit crimes and in the sites and situations in which criminal events occur, solutions to crime problems will often have to be focused and specialized.

Consistent with this understanding, for example, British Columbia police are given a specialized training course in environmental criminology and use this training in both long-range interventions such as reviewing site design applications to municipal planning boards and short-term efforts to analyze and reduce existing crime problems through situational interventions (Brantingham and Brantingham 1988).

12.4 Framework

In order to describe a broad range of studies, this article uses a theoretical framework describing: (1) the complex etiology of crime; (2) the crime

---

* Recent English research seems to demonstrate that the introduction of street lighting into "black spot" problem areas where there was none can have beneficial effects on fear of crime and possibly on the incidence of crime in those areas, but that incremental lighting increases in areas that already have some street lights, however dim, have no impact on crime at all (Atkins, Husain, and Storey 1991; Ramsey 1991).

patterns of individuals, with particular attention to how the physical environment influences their behavior; (3) aggregate crime patterns, with particular attention to how the physical environment influences them.

Crime must be thought of as a broad range of actual behaviors, which, while sometimes appearing similar, may be the result of many different incentives or etiological processes. The individual criminal event takes place in a setting sought by the offender, a place where that person feels "comfortable" or "sure of what will happen." This is usually a place that emits cues fitting a learned template of the characteristics of a "good" crime site. An offender searches for a "suitable target," whether some object or some person, positioned in time and space in a "good" crime site and situation.

The search process used to find a suitable target is not random, but seems to involve looking for targets near the criminal's usual travel paths between major routine activity nodes: home, work or school, shopping venues, and favored leisure locations such as bars, fast food restaurants, or recreation centers. The elements of a standard mental template defining a "good" crime site and a "suitable target" have been extensively researched for burglary. The type of neighborhood, the site's location within a neighborhood, the site's position on the street network, the position of the building on the site, and a variety of site wealth indicators all appear to be positive attractors. The potential or actual surveillance of the area adjacent to a possible site seems to be a recurrently found detractor for criminals (M. Maguire 1982; Bennett and Wright 1984c; Rengert and Wasilchick 1985; Cromwell et al. 1991). The crime template (Brantingham and Brantingham 1978a, 1991; Macdonald and Gifford 1989) is under-researched for crimes other than burglary, yet research on both shoplifting (Walsh 1978; Carroll and Weaver 1986) and robbery (Feeney 1986; Gabor et al. 1987) seems to point to environmental elements that give the offender the feeling that he (or she) belongs to the setting and does not stand out as ecologically incongruent (Sacks 1972) and is consequently unlikely to be noticed by anyone who might intervene. Some research begins to explore the potential influence of territoriality in reducing some types of crime (Suttles 1968; Newman 1972, 1979; R. Taylor, Gottfredson, and Brower 1984; R. Taylor and Gottfredson 1987). Other research explores territorial conflict as a trigger for crime (Poyner 1983, 1988; Czarnowski 1986; Fowler 1987). The field is new and more research is clearly needed.

At a more aggregate level, criminal behavior is highly patterned and frequently localized. Some parts of cities never seem to experience much crime; others persistently experience high volumes of crime. The aggregate distribution of crime seems to be substantially related to the socioeconomic and demographic mosaic of cities, as well as the location of major population attractors. Major urban planning decisions, from zoning to design review to transportation planning, help shape crime (Brantingham and Brantingham 1984, 1991; Fowler 1987; Brantingham et al. 1990).

12.5 Complex Etiology

Overall, there is a growing awareness that to understand crime we must understand the complexity of crime as a type of behavior. Crime is, for analytic purposes, similar to a backache. Backaches will never be attributable to any single cause; neither will criminal acts. Such events can be the result of a variety of causes. Many different types of spinal or muscular difficulties might produce back pain; when a heavy object is lifted improperly, even healthy backs can experience pain. Many socioeconomic and psychological conditions may result in someone engaging in theft. Shoplifters might steal for economic gain, for thrills, for revenge, or out of self-indulgence (Turner and Cashdan 1988). No single factor or etiology is likely to explain all similar criminal events.

The complex etiology of crime is further varied by the dynamically changing lives of both victims and offenders as well as a constantly changing environment. A teenager may wish to steal some new sports shoes, but is at school, in history class, an inappropriate behavior setting for such activity (Barker and Wright 1955; Barker 1968; Kaminski 1989)? As the day passes and that teenager moves to a physical education class, or to a shopping mall after school, the desire to steal such shoes may well intersect with an opportunity to do so, in an appropriate behavior setting. Similarly, a house may be an attractive break-in target for an intending thief, but the owners may clearly be home, making the house temporarily unattractive. At a later time, the house may be empty: whether it then becomes victimized will be a function of the continuing attention and desire of the intending thief. Someone whose motivation for doing burglaries is a need for money with which to support a drug habit may break into the house even when it is occupied, converting the burglary into a confrontation and robbery, even though most burglars shy away from occupant confrontation. What is seen as an attractive and acceptable criminal target varies depending on the expectations of the potential offender in conjunction with the site and situation of the moment.

Over the past two decades criminologists have begun to accept the idea that a crime must be viewed as an event that occurs at a specific site and in a specific situation (e.g. Brantingham and Brantingham 1978a, 1981c, 1991; Felson 1987; Barlow 1990; Gottfredson and Hirschi 1990) and that the individual who commits the offence is influenced by and influences both the site and situation. Criminal events become transactional in the sense defined by Altman and Rogoff (1987). There are "no separate elements or sets of discrete relationships into which the system [in this case, the criminal event] is divisible. Instead, the whole is composed of inseparable aspects that simultaneously and cojointly define the whole" (Altman and Rogoff 1987: 24).

While no separate or distinct elements or sets of discrete relations or relationships may ultimately be defined, we must create theoretical frameworks or models, ways of viewing what we "see" in order to understand.* Potentially, the most productive model in environmental criminology is one that places both the actual criminal events at a specific site, situation, and time and the individual committing the crime while in a specific motivational state on (or in) an environmental backcloth, that may itself be mostly stable, regular and predictable or may instead be irregular, rapidly changing, and unpredictable.

The term "environmental backcloth" is used within environmental criminology to attach a label to the uncountable elements that surround and are part of an individual and that may be influenced by or influence his or her criminal behavior. Environmental psychology has always debated and had to address the issue of what influences behavior, perception, cognition, expectations, judgments, and schemata. When looking at crime and criminal events, it is essential to see them, to the extent possible, in narrow focus. But it is also important to see them within a broader focus as well. We need to see both the tree and the forest. Research conducted in either a narrow or broad focus must explore how potential criminals "see" and react to what surrounds them; how they know cognitively what is where; and how they utilize that knowledge (and process for learning what surrounds them) to develop the decision process by which crime choices are made.†

Underneath what is seen, known, and used in decision making is a physical dimension of the backcloth, that is, objects, characteristics of objects, characteristics of areas, and quanta of interconnectedness between them. What might be called objects or characteristics of the backcloth are more than infinite, they are actually uncountable.‡

What is explored in looking at the physical characteristics that influence criminal behavior is really exploring how different individuals and categories of individuals seem to react to or "see" the surrounding physical environment and what they do with what they "see" or what is done by others who "see" them. What stands out and why? For an individual, the backcloth is a bit like the surrounds that emit cues that are interpreted (Brunswick 1956). The individual is, however, part of the backcloth and may hunt for or produce cues that make a crime more or less likely to occur. A vagrant in an

---

* See A.I. Miller (1987) for an interesting linking of Einstein's mode of thinking to gestalt psychology.
† The idea of an environmental backcloth is not just relevant to criminological research, but in some ways may be understood better when the event—a crime—is clear.
‡ When conceptually exploring a physical (or cognitive) environment, the objects and their characteristics are uncountable, not just infinite. As an analogy, in numbers, fractions are infinite {1/2, 1/3, 1/4, 1/5 ... 2/2, 2/3, 2/4, 2/5 ...; ... 1/n, 2/n, 3/n, 4/n ...} but countable. That is, a method exists for enumerating all fractions. Real numbers are uncountable as well as infinite. For two real numbers, 0.123 and 0.124, for example, there are an uncountable number of intervening real numbers. As with real numbers, you cannot "look" at an object and identify all its characteristics. You may identify a set of characteristics you wish to study; but these will never be all of them.

expensive part of the city is unlikely to ever break into a house—he or she is "seen" and emits warning cues to others; or, more probably, the vagrant will expect reactions from others and avoid rich neighborhoods. The same vagrant could break into rooms in a poor, transient neighborhood where he or she forms part of the unrecognized, always changing, but visually similar set of expected people and cues.*

The backcloth is neither rigid nor unchangeable. It varies moment to moment, area to area, place to place, object to object, focus to focus. With uncountable dimensions and uncountable foci, it might appear that research is useless. Yet, to use an analogy that is close to the source of the term back-cloth, you can discover (or create) understandable patterns from this unlimited complexity. You can see clear differences between the state of a piece of cloth hanging from a clothesline in a blowing wind and the state of the same piece of cloth when there is no wind. You can tell which way the wind is blowing and make judgments about the force of the wind, independently of the color of the cloth. You would, however, see varying patterns of vibration in different types of material. Heavy canvas and light silk move differently in the wind. The ripples and billows in the cloth would also vary with the strength and direction of the wind. The spatial location of any point on the surface of the cloth would vary from moment to moment as it moved in the wind.

Regardless of the type of cloth attached to the clothesline, your view of its movement would change as you approached it from a distance. Your understanding of what was happening would change even more radically if it were possible from your viewpoint to approach the cloth closely enough to merge with it and become part of it. Depending on where you joined the cloth you might observe only relative stasis near the clothesline or you might observe vast and rapid movements out near the free edge. Even further, you could jump up and down (even if visually jumping parallel to the ground) and vibrate the cloth, creating the motion equivalent to that produced by a light breeze. More mathematically, when you become part of the cloth, you lose the multidimensionality necessary to "see" the cloth moving in the wind, and in a two-dimensional world you would see no movement.

The backcloth must, necessarily, be conceptually divided when studying concrete events, including criminal events. Though the use of the term "dimensions" imposes an arbitrary ordering on the uncountable elements of the backcloth and runs the danger of obscuring its interconnectedness, the limitations of our current mathematical tools make it necessary to define

---

* This example could be expanded. Within a transient, poor section of a city there will be places that have some regularity and repetitive appearances of particular individuals. In these places an "outsider," a true vagrant, might be identified by the regulars. This "outsider" might be the victim of a robbery or might steal something. Microanalysis of what happens to the insider or the outsider is an unresearched area of environmental criminology.

some working backcloth for analytic purposes. At a minimum, the working backcloth for studying criminal events should have social, cultural, legal, spatial and temporal dimensions. This working backcloth would also explicitly include the physical infrastructure of buildings, roads, transit systems, land uses, design and architecture, as well as the people located within that physical infrastructure.

Research using the idea of the backcloth is a different way of thinking about problems. The physical infrastructure is, like the rest of the backcloth, constantly created, changed and interpreted by people. Someone who wants to commit some specific crime will search for a place that he (or she) interprets as "ideal" for that crime, a place that fits a target template, a mental image of the right place and the right victim for the crime. Such a person might look for a particular type of residence for a burglary or wait in an "ideal" place for a particular type of person to rob; he might even break a streetlight to create the right place for a particular crime. Research using the idea of the backcloth has to be process oriented, sensitive to decision processes and the ways in which people perceive the environment and how people remember information for use in future decisions.

Understanding crime as the backcloth varies is not easy. We frequently are tripped up by the ecological fallacy or by adherence to such levels of detail that general patterns become invisible, or by the imposition of views on data that force them into a preferred pattern. For example, it is believed and asserted by many that unemployment causes crime. Yet the relationship between unemployment and crime depends on what period of history is being studied, what definition of crime is being used, what culture is being studied, and what level of analysis—macro, meso or micro—is being used (Kennedy, Silverman, and Forde 1991).

In preindustrial societies and in underdeveloped countries many crimes seem to be tied to true physical survival needs: people steal to fend off starvation during hard economic times (Brantingham and Brantingham 1984). In the modern, industrialized world, poverty and crime have a more complex relationship. Internationally, property crime rates are higher in prosperous countries. In fact, the property crime rate appears to be a measure of the strength of an economy. This, of course, makes obvious sense: property crimes are, to a significant extent, a function of the existence of something to steal. In Canada, crime rates are highest in the provinces with the lowest unemployment rates and the most prosperous economies. (These differences are great. In Newfoundland, a province with a high unemployment rate of 15.8% and a low labor force participation rate of only 55.7% in 1989, the property crime rate was 2665 offences per 100,000 population. In British Columbia, with a much lower unemployment rate of 9.1% and a much higher labor force participation rate of 66.8% in 1989, the property crime rate was 8096 offences over 100,000 population.)

From this perspective, it would seem that high unemployment rates and a poor economy would reduce property crimes by reducing opportunities even when many would have an apparent "need" to steal. More individuals would spend more time at home, possibly reducing the risk of household related property crimes. Fewer individuals would be able to go out, reducing both their likelihood of committing property offences such as shoplifting and their risk of being victimized by offences such as theft or assault. At the same time, their stay-at-home pattern would increase the protection of their homes at night. The unemployed would become the guardians of their own property (Cohen and Felson 1979a; Felson 1987). This speculation is supported by the consistent finding of victimization surveys that criminal victimization, both of the individual person and of the individual's household property, is strongly, inversely related to the number of evenings per week respondents go out (Kennedy and Forde 1990; van Dijk, Mayhew, and Killias 1990).*

To add more complexity to the issue, recent research has found that in the aggregate, juvenile offenders were more likely to have had jobs than were juvenile nonoffenders and that most persistent offenders are employed at the time they are arrested (Holzman 1983). Even among those offenders who are unemployed at arrest, research has demonstrated that many had quit their jobs to make it easier to take advantages of the "best" times during the day to commit offences (Rengert and Wasilchick 1985; Cromwell, Olson, and Avary 1991).†

Yet within a city there are concentrations, or "hot spots" (Illinois Criminal Justice Information Authority 1989; Sherman, Gartin, and Buerger 1989; C.R. Block 1990) of property crimes, frequently, but not always, associated with areas of a city where employment rates are high (Shaw and McKay 1942; Brantingham and Brantingham 1984; Shannon 1988; Wikstrom 1991). Moreover, criminal and delinquent behavior and susceptibility to criminal victimization are strongly associated with lower socioeconomic status (Wolfgang, Figlio, and Sellin 1972; Wolfgang, Thornberry, and Figlio 1987; Fattah 1991: 122, 319).

The difficulty in finding a replicable pattern over varying levels of resolution, as is seen in the poverty-crime relationships, is, we believe, tied to the failure of much research to place the criminal event on (or in) a backcloth and

---

* The relationship is even stronger when patterns of multiple victimization are taken into account. In a study of British Crime Survey data, Lasley and Rosenbaum (1988) found that those who go out two or more nights a week are the most frequent repeat victims. They also found that others with substantial amounts of free time, students and the unemployed, were also frequent repeat victims.
† The definition of "need" is clearly different in preindustrial societies and post-industrial societies with differing social welfare bases. In post-industrial societies with some welfare base, need may be better understood as relative deprivation (Wilson and Herrnstein 1985: 57; Brantingham and Brantingham 1984: 288-290), not an absolute need to survive.

to consider the changes in the backcloth over time, space, place, and the level of resolution.* Micro-level results are not necessarily similar to meso, nor meso to macro. What becomes an unexplained and assumed random variation at one level of analysis becomes the center of explanation at another.

Building a working backcloth may well require imagination and methodological innovation. Traditional parametric statistical techniques are unlikely to work. Such techniques require the use of Euclidean distance measures in all calculations as well as permitting only a limited number of variables. The potential features on a backcloth are uncountable. Environmental psychology and the growing cognitive philosophy of science (Churchland 1989) begin to point the way. More qualitative analysis similar to Lynch and Rivkin's (1959) "A Walk around the Block"; Appleyard, Lynch, and Meyer's (1964) The View from the Road; or Cromwell, Olson, and Avary's (1991) work with what burglars "see" when they "walk around the block" is necessary. For obvious ethical reasons, a researcher certainly does not want to identify the location of "good" targets for criminals, so this line of research seems likely to develop through the use of simulations of the environment, with all the associated limitations (Kaplan 1985; M. Taylor and Nee 1988; Whyte 1988; Macdonald and Gifford 1989). Techniques are likely to range from the use of photograph sets to the creation of moving images in video simulation labs such as those at the University of California at Berkeley or at the University of Victoria in Wellington, New Zealand. Architectural computer-aided design (CAD) with "walk through" capabilities offers new possibilities for this type of research.†

In addition to qualitative analysis and simulation research, mathematical modeling of the backcloth using point-set topology, algebraic topology and fractals (Brantingham and Brantingham 1978b; Arlinghaus and Nystuen 1990; Barnsley 1988; Massey 1989; Fotheringham 1990; Batty 1991; DeCola

---

* The problem is sometimes tentatively addressed by criminologists who argue about needing to situate analyses in context. The backcloth idea is massively nonrecursive, however, while context arguments are typically static models based on the uses of census tract data as control variables in statistical analyses.

† Much research needs to be done in this area. What level of detail is needed to actually simulate the environment? Architectural physical models and "blue prints" may create a good cognitive image of the building for architects but do not necessarily create a reliable image for most "users" of the building. The new CAD systems through which a person may simulate a journey through the building may improve the type of image created. If CAD systems are used in studies of potential offenders' perceptual searching techniques or procedures for determining crime templates, they may well make it possible to move from a limited number of changes in photographs or drawings (Brown and Altman 1991; Brower, Dockett, and Taylor 1983; Macdonald and Gifford 1989) to mathematical continuous functional changes. Using such mathematical changes it may well prove easier to define the boundaries or edges of change that are recognized. There are bound to be "fuzzy" regions. Traditional perceptual research may begin to merge with non-laboratory perceptual research.

1991) should make it possible to begin to develop mathematical backcloths where patterns, designs, edges "stand out" in attempts at representations of the uncountable complexity of the never static backcloth. Analysis of crime patterns against such mathematical backcloths may make it possible for us to "see" in research what we "see" in living.

Within whatever backcloth model is created, individual criminal behavior and associated decisions should be recognizable and understandable, for while each criminal act is unique there is some similarity between criminal acts and some commonality in how people who commit crimes perceive and learn that which surrounds them and that which they surround.

12.6 Individual Criminal Behavior: The Influence of the Physical Environment

Crime is an event that occurs when a person with some readiness to commit a crime comes across a target judged suitable in a situation sufficient to activate a "readiness potential" (Brantingham and Brantingham 1993). Readiness is a state, a willingness to commit a crime. All that is needed is a triggering event. But while readiness is a state, it is not static and is derivative from a complex etiology.

Readiness is not sufficient to produce the event. The person ready to commit a crime must decide whether a potential target falls into a class of persons or things that might be considered suitable and whether to commit the criminal act. Suitability depends on the individual and the crime. A suitable target for robbery is obviously not the same as a suitable target, as appraised or determined by the one who wishes to commit the crime, for an auto theft. A target suitable for a young teenage offender is different from a "good" target for an older, professional criminal.

A triggering situation also depends on the individual and what he or she is after. People seem to commit crimes for different reasons such as to get goods or money, or for the thrill of it, or for vengeance, or to show domination of other people, or for power (Cusson 1983). What constitutes risk and reward for one crime or criminal may be different from what constitutes risk and reward for another. Fortunately, but not unexpectedly, similarity in definition of risk and reward does occur, but varies by type of crime. Generally, most crime appears to fall into patterns of "normal" criminal behavior in which the person committing the offence seems to follow decision patterns that others should appraise as reasonable (Clarke and Cornish 1985; M. Taylor and Nee 1988; Cromwell, Olson, and Avary 1991). In some ways most criminal behavior is very much like Barker's (1968) description of expected behavior in specific behavior settings. There are criminal behavior settings and normal expectations of criminal behavior in such behavior settings. Even victims and nonoffenders have expectations about the types of criminal behavior that can be accepted as normal and the types that should be considered abnormal in particular criminal behavior settings. Theft from an automobile parked in a public parking garage is normal. When the theft involves vandalism and destruction of the vehicle without any apparent reason, the crime becomes abnormal for that setting.

A criminal follows some decision process (whether consciously or unconsciously) in locating suitable targets and "good" crime situations. In a bar fight, a spilled beer might trigger an angry response in which the man whose beer was spilled reaches for a bottle to hit the person who spilled "his" beer. The search is minimal and the decision quick.* A burglary is quite different from an assault. For a household burglar, the target search might involve several areas of a city but be restricted to mid-afternoon when most residences are vacant (Pettiway 1982; Rengert and Wasilchick 1985).†

12.6.1 Routine Activities/Travel Paths/Nodes

In both of the examples just given, and for most crimes, people who commit crimes spend most of their time in noncriminal activities. The people who commit crimes know a city largely from legitimate, routine activities and seem to restrict most of their criminal behavior to these legitimately known areas (e.g. Reppetto 1974; Carter and Hill 1979; Maguire 1982; Pettiway 1982; Rengert and Wasilchick 1985). It appears that people may "search" for a crime site and situation in a manner similar to the way we "search" for a gasoline station. We may see one immediately when the warning light goes on in the car or we may know the station we want: it is "on the way home." We know how to find gasoline stations in unknown towns: find a major street and look for gas stations at busy intersections. Or, when we have no luck at first, look for the gas station at the front edge of a small shopping mall. Offenders seem to use similar strategies in finding criminal targets: look where you are, look in areas you know well or at a specific site you know, or look in the areas that are understandable and predictable.

Individual offenders' property crime target choices generally fall near the nodal points in their daily activity patterns or along their normal travel paths (Rengert and Wasilchick 1985). Personal crimes primarily occur at home or where people go to drink (Bullock 1955; Engstad 1975; Baldwin and Bottoms 1976; Rand 1986; Roncek and Pravatiner 1989; Fattah 1991; Wikstrom 1991).

---

* Some municipalities in British Columbia, Canada, eliminate the sale of beer in bottles and require sale of canned beer during special events to reduce the likelihood of concussions, cuttings, and possible deaths when assaults occur.

† Burglary, which was once a night-time activity, has become a daytime activity since residences are more likely to be vacant during the day than at night because of changed family work patterns (Cohen and Felson 1979a).

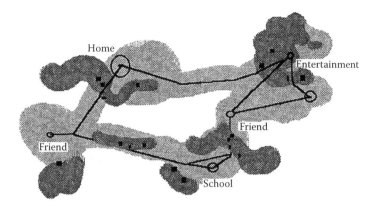

Figure 12.1 Target choice behavior.

Property crimes occur at or near major personal attractors such as home, known shopping centers, work or school, or well-known sports areas, parks or recreation centers, or along major routes connecting these nodes (e.g. Wilcox 1973; Engstad 1975; Duffala 1976; Roncek and Lobosco 1983). Research generally finds that crime is highly patterned by daily behavior.

Figure 12.1 presents a general model. Crimes tend to occur in known places or near limited travel knowledge spaces. For example, in some of the earliest research in point, Porteous (1977) found that a juvenile gang in Victoria, British Columbia, picked most of its targets near the homes of the members or near a common hang-out center or within the limited space contained within the connecting pathways for these places. More recently, Rengert and Wasilchick (1985) found that convicted Philadelphia area burglars usually picked their targets within a limited distance of their normal travel paths, primarily along the axis of their usual home-to-work travel path. Rengert has also found that burglaries committed to get cash to buy drugs cluster around "crack" houses. The clusters of burglaries move as the crack houses do. The criminal activity spaces and awareness spaces of drug users change as the crack houses are forced out of one area into another. Cromwell, Olson, and Avary (1991) found a similar pattern when studying uncaught burglars in Texas: burglary targets were principally located in the offenders' usual, noncriminal, action spaces. Feeney (1986) and Gabor et al. (1987) found that individual choice of robbery locations was oriented or directed towards personally well-known locations.

People in general, including those who commit crimes, develop routine activity spaces. Some areas within these routine spaces become better known than others; areas outside their routine space may be vaguely known, but will typically lack detail (Orleans 1973; Brantingham and Brantingham 1981c, 1991; Ley 1983). All people, including those who commit crimes, develop an awareness space that builds upon the activity space and its associated places. Criminal targets are usually picked from within this awareness space. Exploration of the unknown is not part of the target search process for most individuals.

The awareness space varies by age and by socioeconomic status. The poor and the young know less about the world around them (see Ley 1983, for a general review of the cognitive maps of people by their background). For the poor and the young, the criminal target selection space is limited spatially and temporally. It expands as children age and jumps sharply when they begin to drive (lawfully or unlawfully). When new mass transit systems are introduced into a city, opening up previously "untouchable" or unknown areas to many people, their criminal awareness spaces also expand (Brantingham and Brantingham 1981c, 1991; Brantingham, Brantingham, and Wong 1991).

Many crimes, in fact, appear to be highly opportunistic and involve little or no conscious searching (Maguire 1982; Barlow 1990; Cromwell, Olson, and Avary 1991). As an example, a boy may walk to school every day cutting through the yard of some family living about six or seven blocks from his home. One day the family leaves a new mountain bike outside. The boy "knows" the family is not home. They are always gone by the time he gets there or he would not cut through their yard. He takes the bike for the day, but is afraid to take the bike home in the evening. His parents will know it is not his bike, so he drops it at a shopping mall close to his home. This example, while hypothetical, fits the pattern of many property offences.

What becomes of major interest is how people learn pathways, how cognitive maps or representations are formed and what constitutes cognitive representations.* The relationship between perception, cognition, and behavior is essential but under-researched in environmental criminology. Studies by Letkemann (1973), Wise and Stoks (1981), Beavon (1984), Rengert and Wasilchick (1985) and by Gabor et al. (1987) find strong links between usual daily activities (and their associated travel paths) and the identification of targets. Both Letkemann and Gabor et al. report these links on the basis of descriptions given by offenders in interviews. For Rengert and Wasilchick, the link was established as a pattern developed from materials obtained in interviews. Beavon found the relation between travel paths and crime site choice by analyzing the locations of crimes reported to the police. While it represents only one community, Beavon found that for all types of reported crimes except bicycle theft†, crime dropped off rapidly as potential targets were

---

* See Gärling and Golledge (1989) for a general review of the approaches to cognitive imaging, and distancing. See also Evans and Pezdek (1980); Gärling, Book, and Lindberg (1984); Golledge (1987); Gärling (1989); Aitken and Prosser (1990).

† The exception for bicycle theft is not all surprising. Major paths for children are not necessarily roads. Beavon (1984) found a concentration of the thefts in the areas close to schools and parks.

located further from highly accessible main roads. Wise and Stoks used both field observations and officially reported problems to establish these links.

Studying which paths are learned and why they are learned has great impact in the action research and legal changes that sometimes flow out of research about crime. Criminals tend to commit their crimes near their major paths, but will explore around them. The exploration appears to be limited and tied to known or easily knowable spaces or places. Crime, like the rat-racing of cars during a rush hour, seems to be tied to the complexity of the road network. A person on foot may be willing to explore one or two blocks off a known path. People who commit property crimes usually avoid risk. They want to see their potential escape route. In a grid system, exploration is easy. The cognitive maps are straightforward for the rat-racing commuter and the exploring burglar alike. In a complex road network, exploration is more difficult.

Bevis and Nutter (1977) performed perhaps the most interesting study of crime and road network complexity to date. They found that for Minneapolis as a whole, crime rates were not related to street network complexity. But when they restricted their analysis to areas with some crime (many parts of most cities experience little or no crime) strong associations between road network complexity and crime emerged. When an area is not generally attractive to criminals, then the complexity of the road network makes no difference. Within the areas that are attractive to criminals, residences on grid streets experienced the highest rate of burglary. The proportion of corner houses increases in grid street networks. M. Taylor and Nee's (1988) recent work shows that burglars express consistent preference for corner houses. As the road network complexity of criminally attractive areas increased, Bevis and Nutter found, burglary rates dropped. Cul-de-sacs and dead-end streets experienced the lowest burglary rates in criminally attractive areas.

An informal study done by the police in Delta, British Columbia, a suburb of Vancouver, found that studies of path networks should not be limited to road networks. Like many suburbs, Delta has been building subdivisions with complicated road networks, including many cul-de-sacs or dead-ends that connect to local roads that are only indirectly attached to the primary collector streets. In many of these subdivisions the roads are not intended for use by children going to school, visiting friends, or going to the local mall on foot. Instead, the cul-de-sacs are interconnected by pedestrian pathways designed for the children. When the road network and pathway system are considered jointly from the perspective of the movement patterns of children, the travel network becomes less complex and more like a grid system. The police found that household burglaries were higher on the cul-de-sacs with walkways and much lower on the dead-ends and cul-de-sacs excluded from the pathway system. In one subdivision several walkways were closed to reduce the flow of children. The burglaries on these streets stopped (Sheard 1991).

12.6.2 Target Choice

Not all potential targets on paths or at high activity nodes known and used by potential offenders experience a similar chance of being victimized by property crime. Targets must be seen as "suitable" by offenders before they are victimized (Cohen and Felson 1979a; Felson 1987). But what is seen as "suitable" probably varies by crime, by offender, by site, by situation and with variations in the backcloth. From a physical landscape perspective, for instance, what is suitable for burglary in the daytime in a suburban residential area is not necessarily similar to what is suitable in a dense urban apartment cluster late at night (Reppetto 1974; Waller and Okihiro 1978; Bennett and Wright 1984c). What is suitable for theft is not necessarily suitable for robbery (Duffala 1976; Carroll and Weaver 1986; Gabor et al. 1987). What is suitable for a resident in an area is not necessarily suitable for an outsider.

A comparison of juvenile crime in Toledo, Ohio, and Rosario, Argentina, conducted by David and Scott (1973) illustrates this point nicely. Although the cities were similar in climate, population, and economy, their physical structures differed sharply: Toledo exhibited the classic zonal structure made familiar by the researches of the Chicago school sociologists (e.g. Reckless 1933; Faris and Dunham 1939; Shaw and McKay 1942), with an impoverished zone-in-transition of slums and undesirable land uses surrounding the central business core. Rosario exhibited classic South American urban form with its slums and least desirable land uses clustered outside city limits on the urban periphery. Although the socio-demographic profiles of the juveniles who committed crimes in the two cities were similar, the patterns of those crimes were different. The local characters of the environmental backcloth against which criminal motivation could be acted out were quite different. Toledo's routine activities and daily rhythms were largely organized around an abundance of goods available through widely dispersed self-service shops accessed by private automobile while Rosario's routine activities and daily rhythms were structured around a more limited supply of consumer goods sold through service intensive shops accessed by foot or public transit by a population owning few private automobiles. Toledo's juvenile crime was dominated by shoplifting, car theft, burglary, and other crimes that hinged on access to opportunities in the absence of a guardian or personal victim. Rosario's juvenile crime was much more strongly biased toward personal contact crimes: purse snatching and other forms of robbery, and assault. Burglary patterns were strikingly different in the two cities: Toledo's pattern was tied both to the daily exposure of residential suburbs that emptied as adults went to work and children to school, and to the extensive use of unprotected glass display windows in business and shopping precincts that emptied after dark. Rosario's pattern was tied to its limited separation of commercial and residential uses, and to the customary use of protective steel shutters by businesses after hours. Clearly, the crime patterns in these cities were tied to their physical differences, no matter what level of resolution is used. Choice of crime and target were not random, but were shaped by the physical layouts of the cities, their transport modes, and the daily activity rhythms dictated by the physical environment.

12.6.3 Crime Template

Target choice is a decision, and like all decisions depends on many factors: the characteristics of the individual offender, the characteristics of the potential crime site, the characteristics of the immediate situation at potential sites, and the characteristics of the backcloth against which the decision is made (e.g. Brantingham and Brantingham 1978a; Cornish and Clarke 1986a; Cromwell, Olson, and Avary 1991). One approach used in the past to help identify which factors influence target selection is to describe a crime template (Brantingham and Brantingham 1978a, 1984, 1991). The environment around us gives off cues, sequences of cues, and clusters of cues about its immediate characteristics and about the local shape of the backcloth. People tend, through experience, to form these cues into an overall template, a mental model that helps identify and label a particular kind of object, place, or situation. Subsequently, people use a template as a mental shortcut in appraising places and situations. Criminals construct templates of sites and situations that are suitable for commission of particular sorts of crime and use these crime templates in selecting targets or victims and in deciding to commit the crime at a particular place and time (see, e.g. Macdonald and Gifford 1989; Cromwell, Olson, and Avary 1991 for burglary; Gabor et al. 1987: 57–58, for robbery; Carroll and Weaver 1986, for shoplifting). The templates are not a simple list of easily identifiable and measurable characteristics, but more a holistic image with a complex interaction of pasts and relationships seen from varying perspectives.

As mentioned at the beginning of this article, the potential criminal offender is also part of the criminal event. Crime templates may well reflect how the offender expects others to react. This may take on very different forms depending on the type of crime and the motivation of the criminal. For example, many who engage in joy-riding auto theft appear to look for recognition from police and actually try to stimulate a car chase (Cusson 1983; Webb and Laycock 1992). They may pull in front of a police car repeatedly, apparently hoping to have the car identified as stolen and so start a chase. People who break into single family houses may be trying to avoid any contact with others, providing themselves as much anonymity as possible. Fear of contact may be strong. This is particularly evident from the studies that have asked burglars where they would like to break into homes, where they actually do break into homes, and why they choose the places they do invade (Reppetto 1974; Waller and Okihiro 1978; Maguire 1982; Pettiway 1982; Bennett and Wright 1984; Messner and South 1986; Sampson 1987; Cromwell, Olson, and Avary 1991). Most say they would like to break into expensive houses, but choose places near where they live, where they feel comfortable and do not stand out. Along a similar line, some professional burglars do go to expensive areas (the burglary rates are still generally the lowest in expensive housing areas), but do so in disguise. They dress as handymen, delivery persons or other "acceptable" outsiders. They then may move freely in the area. Much more information is needed about crime templates, both those created by criminal offenders and those created by people who see themselves as potential victims.

Oscar Newman is perhaps the best known developer of what might be called a defensive areal template that was supposed to deter potential criminals. Newman (1972), inventor of the term "defensible space," tried to define a strategy for use by architects and planners that would reduce crime by building in barriers and territorial markers that would increase private and semiprivate space while decreasing semipublic and public space. His original approach was supposed to engender defensive mutualism among the residents within these "defensible space" buildings. In his initial book, Defensible Space (1972), and some related government reports (1976), he advanced definite guidelines on how to design urban housing developments to reduce all types of crimes. Newman made no distinction between types of crime or between the characteristics or motivations of those committing crime. Nor did he treat in any serious way the backcloth against which criminal events occur. He focused instead on site characteristics in a highly deterministic way: over seven stories is bad, double stairways in apartments are bad, low visibility in entry hallways of apartments is risky, low rise apartments with limited families per entrance are good, and symbolic barriers are good. He identified ways he believed all types of crime could be prevented or reduced by diverting people from attacking a set of homes and their residents.*

Newman's 1972 work triggered much interest on the part of urban planners and architects, but has been attacked academically because of its conceptual limitations (e.g. Bottoms 1974; Mawby 1977; R. Taylor 1988; Macdonald

---

* Newman also explored the image and milieu of a public housing project's "distinctiveness resulting from interruption of urban circulation patterns"; "distinctiveness of building height, project size, materials and amenities"; "distinctiveness of interior finish and furnishings"; and the "juxtaposition of the housing project to other land uses" (1972: 103–117).

and Gifford 1989) and lack of empirical support* (e.g. Mayhew 1979; R. Taylor 1988; Macdonald and Gifford 1989). Newman was looking at selected low-income residential complexes only. His statistical analysis did not support his arguments. He appeared to have assumed that crimes were committed by outsiders and appeared not to have considered whether offences were being committed by people who themselves lived within the complexes. Symbolic barriers may or may not serve as effective barrier edges to outsiders,† and they may or may not help stimulate mutual defense against outsiders‡ on the part of insiders, but they are unlikely to have any effect whatsoever if the wrong-doers are already insiders. In fact they may give the insiders more attractive places to defend themselves and places from which they may begin the search for targets. Newman's defensible space appears to be more closely linked to feelings of safety on the part of residents, that is, what is frequently called reductions in fear of crime (R. Taylor 1988), than it is to the control of crime.

Newman himself recanted much of his work from the early 1970s. In some ways it could be argued that his early work was really an attack against modern architecture and a desire to return to what he found to be more "liv-able" surroundings, early steps towards the reduced scale of many postmodern residential buildings. It also can be argued that he was perceiving minor variations in architectural and landscape design that might not be visible or understood by nonarchitects. Experts in a field develop a communication mode, but that mode may not be understandable to nonexperts. This is obviously possible with architects trying to convey a "meaning," but using a subtlety not recognizable or "readable" by others. If semiotics is accepted, it may well be the "early" Newman did not identify meaningful codes. (See Jencks and Baird 1969, for an introduction to the semotic analysis of architecture; see Jencks 1987, for an example of the architectural meaning of post-modernism.) Somewhat similarly, architects may be imposing their own views of what an "attractive" housing area should look like. In 1969, around

---

* The appendices to his original work provided no real statistical support for his position. His analyses were based solely on offences reported to the New York Housing Authority Police. Many serious crimes were probably reported directly to the New York City Police rather than to the housing police while many minor crimes were probably not reported to anyone. In the appendices Newman accepted the complexity of the issues he addresses and pulled back from many of the assertions in the main text.

† Newman's suggested symbolic barriers appear intuitively appropriate to many trained architects and planners, but research on target selection with burglars, at least, suggests that these types of criminals do not even notice these types of barriers. See especially, Cromwell, Olson, and Avary (1991); Rengert and Wasilchick (1985); Bennett and Wright (1984).

‡ Gifford (1987: 144–145) begins to make the distinction between insider and outsider in an analysis of the research by Brower, Dockett, and Taylor (1983) into the reactions of residents of high and low crime areas to drawings with and without symbolic barriers, and with and without a person in the front yard and someone walking. Reactions differed depending on background crime levels.

the time of Newman's early work, Lansing and Marans found that planners' views of what good neighborhood designs looked like did not match those preferred by residents of Detroit. One of the biggest differences was residents' preferences for open, not spatially enclosed, cluster housing. Only those respondents with a university education seemed to like what Newman likes. In any case, a number of studies with burglars have found that they seem generally not to even notice most of the key territorial markers the early Newman considered important.

While Newman has seen a need to consider the varying views, feelings and life styles of the people who may live in particular physical settings, his early, strongly physically deterministic views have recently been revived in a slightly different form in Great Britain by Alice Coleman (1985, 1989). Her work has been subjected to criticism both conceptually and for its rather strange use of statistics and various non-statistics (Poyner 1988; van de Voordt 1986). Although Coleman examines many forms of social incivility such as vandalism or the distribution of piles of excrement in public parts of residential areas, she has at least taken one step beyond Newman and accepts that many crimes are probably committed by juveniles (and others) near where they live. Unfortunately, like the early Newman, she focuses on a series of fixed architectural design characteristics she believes are associated with all of the different types of problems she considers and prescribes a series of architectural fixes for problem housing: buildings should never be more than three stories tall; no more than 12 families should ever share a common entrance; connecting elevated walkways should be eliminated; ground floor parkades should be eliminated; and so forth.

Several short case studies by Barry Poyner (1988) have demonstrated that Coleman's specific analyses and prescriptions are too sweeping. Removal of overhead walkways connecting high rise residences in one housing estate appeared to reduce crime, but closer analysis showed that the crime reduction had been effected before the removal of the walkways, by simply locking the various buildings' doors so that the walkways became more difficult to use as major pathways. Introduction of entry controls at another large housing estate reduced the incidence of graffiti and vandalism, but had little effect on serious crime. The criminals were insiders, legitimate residents of the buildings against whom physical entry controls were useless. They had keys. Poyner found a similar pattern in a third housing estate that introduced a reception service, staff who greet people from kiosks built into the entries of large residences. Again, the serious criminals appeared to be insiders. Physical entry barriers and human entry guardians were ineffective. It is very likely that Coleman's advocacy of the creation of some physical barriers and the removal of some design problems in order to deter or otherwise prevent a broad range of undesirable behavior will prove as difficult to support in practice as Newman's early formulations. Crimes are highly varied and crime reduction principles unlikely to work when crimes are treated as a homogeneous group.

Basically, both the early Newman and Coleman looked at a limited number of environmental cues that might influence criminal behavior as if they always acted upon a fixed and limited set of situations and sites and upon a static backcloth. Recent studies by Macdonald and Gifford (1989) and Cromwell, Olson, and Avary (1991) show the complexity of the cues, cue sequences and cue clusters that may influence criminal decision making in varied settings and against quite different forms of the environmental back-cloth. Macdonald and Gifford were able to show photographs to both juve-nile and adult burglars. Fixed defensible space cues of the sort identified by Newman, that is, actual and symbolic barriers, proved to be poor predictors of how convicted burglars rated photographs for target "attractiveness." They found that when they defined Brown and Altman's categories (1983) for rat-ers and let the raters use their own cognitive abilities to weigh and combine cues seen in the photographs, the raters' scores produced the best predictors of vulnerability ratings given by the burglars. These results support the theo-retical model of crime site selection first presented in 1978 by Brantingham and Brantingham (1978a).

Surveillability, that is, the possibility of surveillance by someone whom the offender believes might interfere, is found by many researchers (e.g. Bennett and Wright 1984a; Bennett 1989; Cromwell, Olson, and Avary 1991; Pease 1992; Poyner 1992a, 1992b; Poyner and Webb 1992) to have a stronger effect on criminal decision making than territorial markers do. Detectability by those who might successfully intervene is perhaps a good indicator of what might deter many offenders from many types of crimes (see Brown and Altman 1991, for a description of detectability). But who might intervene depends on the type of crime and its site and situation. Both the actual pros-pect of someone intervening in the commission of a crime and the belief on the part of a potential offender that an intervenor is likely to appear are likely to be different when the crime is a burglary in a residential area or a robbery in a park. Crowds or groups of people may deter a robber or purse snatcher in a residential area, but may make the crime much easier in a public place (Poyner 1983; Poyner and Webb 1992). What constitutes surveillability and detectabil-ity varies with type of crime and the characteristics of the criminal.

Much additional work is needed to determine what makes up the common crime templates for a broad range of crimes that have been little researched. There are many questions that need answering: does the rare or infrequent offender make decisions in ways that are substantially different from the deci-sion processes of more persistent criminals? Do appraisal methods change with age? If so, how? What really is the perceived risk in different types of crimes committed for different reasons? Since thrill crimes may very well be increasing, how does the thrill motivation influence the template? How do crime templates develop as criminal experience grows? Do they begin with vagueness or with specificity learned from others? How do crime patterns change when a person moves often? Do such people become the real explorers? Since many juveniles who commit crimes have part-time jobs and those jobs frequently involve delivery, how does the increased knowledge of the road networks learned from such jobs effect their target choices? While some work has been done by Cromwell, Olson, and Avary (1991), more needs to be learned about the influence of drugs and alcohol on the crime template and the target search process. The questions are endless; the field is new.

The findings of research on how people learn about a city, how they develop cognitive maps or cognitive representations, how knowledge changes by age and socioeconomic or cultural background and how cognitive images influence behavior and spatial choices is highly relevant to environmental criminology. The work of Lynch (1960, 1976, 1981), Orleans (1973), Downs (1981), Evans and Pezdek (1980), Gärling, Book, and Lindberg (1984), Golledge (1987), Gärling (1989), and Aitken and Prosser (1990) all suggest interesting research on criminal behavior and decisions made when committing a crime. Work has begun, but much more is needed.

12.7 Aggregate Crime Patterns: The Influence of the Physical Environment

The offender does not exist in isolation. He or she may make decisions, appraise situations, apply templates and succeed or fail, then adjust templates, try again or wait awhile, or stop. Individuals work within their own cognitive knowledge bases about a city, but rarely work in isolation and without communicating with others. Many children commit their first crime by the time they are age 14. In the aggregate, criminal behavior peaks at around 17 years of age, yet not all children commit crimes and most who do actually commit only minor offences. There is, in addition, a small proportion of individuals who start committing crime when young and continue over most of their lives.

12.7.1 The Urban Mosaic and Crime

The types and forms of crime that are committed seem to vary by socioeconomic background, with the more serious crimes being committed more frequently by those from lower socioeconomic backgrounds (Wolfgang, Figlio, and Sellin 1972; Wolfgang, Thornberry, and Figlio 1987; Elliott et al. 1983). The type of crime may well be tied to relative desire for goods and limited means of obtaining them; a desire for a thrill or excitement but limited legal opportunities; anger or a need for domination. Whatever the underlying factors, cities are really urban mosaics with clusters of individuals of similar economic, racial, ethnic background or age living in separate, distinct areas. As cities grow and change, the areas age, the population may change, a poor area may be gentrified, a middle-class area may become a poorer area. New areas are created. Old areas are destroyed. Even as cities change, the urban mosaic remains.

The mosaic structure of most cities has important implications for our understanding of the relation between crime and the physical environment. Neighborhoods are strongly affected by the architectural and planning fashions of the times in which they are constructed. Alleys and lane ways open a neighborhood to exploration and massively increase the surface area of residences and commercial establishments exposed to criminal risk. Some neighborhoods have them, because they were in fashion at the time of construction, others do not. So the city is a mosaic of differential exposures to target searches. In the same way, the different building styles fashionable when different neighborhoods were built may provide easy or difficult entry for burglars. Suburbs with patios and sliding glass doors (Molumby 1976) are vulnerable in ways quite different from city centers with their high rise apartment buildings (Butcher, 1991). Easy ground floor entry is what is liked. The average size of living quarters varies in different neighborhoods. Large quarters allow residents to focus their activities within their homes; small quarters force more activities onto the street, into neighborhood bars, and into other public venues. The consequences are different backcloths, both in terms of exposure to risk of victimization (Kennedy and Forde 1990) and exposure of criminal activities to the scrutiny of police and other intervenors. Similar observations could be made about the impact of zoning and licensing decisions on the distribution and concentration of shops, restaurants, bars, industrial plants, and other targets and population attractors in different neighborhoods in the urban mosaic. The best known effect this physical mosaic has on crime, of course, is the concentration of criminal neighborhoods and enterprises in the zone in transition from old residential to new commercial use identified in the work of the Chicago School sociologists (e.g. Shaw and McKay 1942).

The result of the mosaic, the slow or fast change in an area and the underlying infrastructure of roads, bridges, highways, and public transit routes, is that groups of people seem to develop similar knowledge of a city or an urban area.* The knowledge may be limited or extensive (Ley 1983; Gifford 1987: 34–39). Embedded within the groups are individuals who are ready to commit crimes. With common or similar cognitive knowledge comes the high likelihood that crimes committed by persons living in the same sub-part of

---

* Though the knowledge varies with work/school locations and areas where friends live where they like to spend time.

the mosaic and working or going to school in the same area will follow a similar pattern.

12.7.2 Activity Nodes

Probably the strongest physical characteristic of crime is that the sites where crimes occur are concentrated. Regardless of whether the crime under consideration is murder, or rape, or assault, or theft, or burglary, or vandalism, a limited number of sites and situations constitute the loci for the vast majority of offences (Wilcox 1973; S. Wilson 1981; Wise and Stoks 1981; Brantingham and Brantingham 1984; Rengert and Wasilchick 1985; Sherman, Gartin, and Buerger 1989; Wikstrom 1991). For example, in Vancouver one-sixth of all the homicides that occurred over the seven-year period 1980 through 1986 happened within a two block radius of a single street intersection (Coburn 1988: 107). The single census tract containing that intersection accounted for 23 percent of Vancouver's homicides and had a homicide rate of 168 per 100,000 population (Coburn 1988: 94).* The same holds true in other cities and for less serious crimes (Bullock 1955; Brantingham and Brantingham 1984). Costanzo, Halperin, and Gale (1986) analyzed the journey to crime and demonstrated offenders living near to one another tend to travel in the same direction to crime sites, but that high crime nodes tend to attract criminals from many different directions.

Target searches are not conducted in any simple Euclidean distance decay fashion (Brantingham and Brantingham 1981d, 1991),† a result that might be expected on the basis of general research on development of cognitive images and on distance and direction learning (see Gärling and Golledge 1989) if it were assumed that criminals were normal people in this respect. Aggregate robbery target choice locations are shown by the research literature to cluster near centers of high activity (Wilcox 1973; Gabor et al. 1987). These nodal high activity spots are sometimes called "crime generators" (Brantingham and Brantingham 1981c, 1991) or "hot spots" (Sherman, Gartin, and Buerger 1989; Block 1990). Nodal concentrations of crime appear both in research using objective, Euclidean measures (Capone and Nichols 1976; Sherman, Gartin, and Buerger 1989); and in research using cognitive images or non-Euclidean measures (Carter and Hill 1979; Brantingham and Brantingham 1981d).

Only a small proportion of crimes are resolved by the arrest and conviction of an offender. Because of this, research with the convicted may

---

* This compares with a homicide rate of about 5 per 100,000 in Vancouver as a whole and about 2.5 per 100,000 in Canada as a whole over this period. It is comparable to the reported homicide rates of Lesotho and the Philippines during the mid-1980s (Brantingham 1991).
† But compare Capone and Nichols (1976).

Table 12.1   **Cognitive Activity Nodes and Burglary**

Fast Food		Bars		Restaurants	
Node	Burglary Rate	Node	Burglary Rate	Node	Burglary Rate
FF1	8.9	B1	13.1	R1	11.0
FF2	8.9	B2	8.8	R2	10.0
		B3	9.7	R3	9.0

Note: City-wide commercial burglary rate: 4.8 per 10 stores.

produce unrepresentative results based on the behavior and perceptions of a restricted population. To offset this possibility, research must also be conducted by comparing general aggregate behavior patterns and general cognitive images or representations or noncriminal environmental assessments with observed aggregate crime patterns. It has to be assumed that measures derived from observed aggregate crime patterns and general perception and cognition reflect, at least to some degree, the patterns of the full set of active criminals.* A study conducted in New Westminster, British Columbia, using this approach compared nodal activity points identified in general cognitive maps of the city with the distribution of commercial burglary in the city (Brantingham and Brantingham 1981d). Residents were sampled from across the city and asked to identify the three fast food restaurants, three bars, and three restaurants they knew best. From this information, the businesses were rank ordered by category in order to identify cognitive activity nodes. The commercial burglary rates for the two blocks around each of the nodes are shown in Table 12.1.

Burglary rates expressed as break and enter per 10 buildings were calculated for a three-year period bracketing the nodal point survey. The nodal areas around each high activity establishment were identified as those blocks within two turnings of the nodal point: that is, either two blocks linearly along the street on either side of the nodal point, or the block containing the nodal point together with one block in either direction (a 90° turn in this city's grid road network) at the next intersections. This is a non-Euclidean but connective topological measure. The commercial burglary rates of the nodal areas were compared with the general commercial burglary rates within the city. As can be seen in Table 12.1, the nodal areas generally have substantially higher commercial burglary rates than commercial blocks in general.

Variability in area commercial burglary rates probably reflect some of the uniqueness of all potential sites and situations, the potential differences between the general knowledge and activity patterns of the residents sampled

---

* This type of research may be better when the "noncriminal" studies use people who are similar to those committing offences or have experience observing actual crime sites. The police may be a good source of subjects for site assessment or symbolic appraisal of "suitable" targets.

and those committing the burglaries, and the variation in the clustering of different types of commercial establishments that may be attractive to those committing the commercial burglaries. Physical clusters of particular types of land use shape the movement and concentration of people, the awareness spaces of potential offenders, and the distributions of crime. In the New Westminster study, the two highest rated fast food stores were clustered on the same block and two of the three best known bars were clustered on adjacent blocks.

Since young persons commit most offences (Wilson and Hernstein 1985; Gottfredson and Hirschi 1990; Brantingham 1991), identification of attractors and nodes popular with this age group also helps identify where crimes occur. Research such as that done by Cotterell (1991) on where and why adolescents "like" to congregate or by Van Vliet (1983) looking at the home range of city and suburban teenagers, while not directed towards criminal behavior, is highly relevant to environmental criminology. Local land use policies that physically cluster or disperse particular types of attractors can be analyzed in conjunction with this type of research for predicting where the most common forms of crime are most likely to occur and for explaining why it came high in one part of a city and low in another.

12.7.3 Pathways

The pathways between high activity nodes are also the sites of many offences. Violent offences tend to occur at the "end points" of paths, especially at home, at favored drinking establishments or at the homes of persons known by the victim or the offender. Property crimes occur near high activity nodes, but are also strung out along the paths between nodes. When viewed from an aggregate level, many property crimes occur on or near the main roads that carry lots of traffic or major public transit stops and therefore fall into the awareness spaces of a large number of people, including potential offenders (Wilcox 1973; Duffala 1976; Brantingham and Brantingham 1984).

When an area is well known to offenders, "nearness" covers a much broader area away from the main road. When the area is less well known, crime sites cluster closer to the main travel path. The physical structure of the road network itself seems to influence how far crime spreads from major pathways. Limited access highways seem to concentrate crimes near highway exits (Fink 1969; Maguire 1982). Complicated road networks are beyond the short-term learning curve of the outsider looking for a target, tending to keep the offender closer to the main roads (Bevis and Nutter 1977; Beavon 1984). When a person lives in an area, more of the road and pedestrian pathways are well known as a result of normal daily activities in the area. This increases the size of the insider's criminal search area and probably contributes to a less clustered distribution of offences. Even so, insider crimes tend to concentrate along insider pathways.

12.7.4 Edge Effects

The urban mosaic is full of perceptual edges, places where there is enough distinctiveness from one part to another that the change is noticeable. At an extreme, the land bordering on a river is an edge; the houses behind a commercial strip development and the businesses on the strip form a perceptual edge. Parks have edges. Residential areas have edges. Commercial areas have edges. Land use zoning and transportation planning frequently work in tandem, with the result that major roads follow perceptual edges between different types of areas. The major roads themselves can produce an edge.

Edges can be characterized in a variety of ways. They can be considered in terms of physical barriers; or of the strong cognitive images of paths with diverse land uses on either side of a road (Lynch 1960); or the limits of perceptual comfort on the part of outsiders (Sacks 1972; Reppetto 1974; Carter and Hill 1979; Rengert and Wasilchick 1985; Cromwell, Olson, and Avary 1991); or the spatial limits of mutual territorial functioning (R. Taylor 1988) among a group of people; or as areas of potential territorial conflict between different groups or land uses (Shaw and McKay 1942; Suttles 1968).

However they are characterized, it appears that edges constitute areas that experience high crime rates (Shaw and McKay 1942; Suttles 1968; Brantingham and Brantingham 1975, 1978b; Brantingham, Brantingham, and Molumby 1977; Herbert and Hyde 1985; Walsh 1986). This pattern might be attributed to a variety of mechanisms. The edges may create areas where strangers are more easily accepted because they are frequently and legitimately present, while the interiors of neighborhoods may constitute territories where strangers are uncomfortable and subject to challenge. Alternatively or additionally, edges may contain mixes of land uses and physical features that concentrate criminal opportunities. This seems particularly likely on edges formed by major roads.

A micro-level study of burglary in Tallahassee, Florida (Brantingham and Brantingham 1975), found that burglary rates decreased rapidly towards the core of homogeneous residential areas and were high on the edges defined by parks, roads, changes in land use, and even sharp changes in the cost of housing. Using point set topological techniques, varying degrees of homogeneous neighborhoods were constructed from over 1000 blocks using 1970 census block level information (Brantingham and Brantingham 1975, 1978b). The borders or edges of these homogeneous neighborhoods were mathematically identified. Some borders formed sharp edges, that is, dividing points between neighborhoods at many levels of variation from many variables. Other edges were less pronounced, representing gradual changes between neighborhoods. Edges ranged in strength, metaphorically, from cliffs to hills to stair steps. The burglary rate for residential blocks located on sharp edges (strong borders or conceptual cliffs) between neighborhoods was 36 per 100 dwelling units. The burglary rates for residences located on blocks in the interiors of neighborhoods was 8.2 per 1000 dwelling units (p < 0.0001).

Some further confirmation of the edge effect in the distribution of burglary, though methodologically non-topological, has been provided by Walsh's (1986) work on burglars' spatial preferences in target selection; by Herbert and Hyde's (1985) studies of the spatial distribution of crime in Wales; by Brantingham and Brantingham's (1977) analysis of burglary in relation to gradual or sharp transitions between housing forms and densities; and, somewhat more softly, by traditional criminological studies showing heavy concentrations of crime in "transitional" areas (e.g. Shaw and McKay 1942; Rhodes and Conly 1991).

Of particular importance is the edge effect of crowds and high activity areas. Many of the crimes that occur at high activity locations such as sporting arenas or commercial centers, or that occur at high activity times such as store closing or bar closing, in fact occur at the edges of the high activity location or high activity time. Crimes cluster on the street near the subway station or bus stop, at the edge of the normal waiting area (Shellow, Romualdi, and Bartel 1974; Levine and Wachs 1985; Brantingham, Brantingham, and Wong 1991). Crimes often cluster in the alley behind a strip of shops (Wilcox 1973). Robberies in Oakland, California, have been shown to cluster on the fringe of parking lots and in the temporal edge half an hour after closing time in the commercial areas (Wilcox 1973). Angel (1968) has also conducted an interesting analysis of crime clustered on activity and temporal edges in Oakland.

While edges sometimes identify an open access space, they may also identify territorial limits of boundaries that separate areas of high and low crime rates. Ley and Cybriwsky (1974a) and R. Taylor (1988) have shown how graffiti serve as territorial markers for groups of urban teenagers, defining the limits of their normal activity spaces. Suttles (1968) showed how complex territorial cues at neighborhood edges can sometimes form buffer zones between neighborhoods that reduce social conflict and crime for those areas. In Peanut Park, Suttles found that Mexican-American, Greek-American, Afro-American and Italian-American males defined their own separate spaces and avoided conflict by avoiding each other's territory. The territorial edges were effective social cliffs that separated them.

12.7.5 Territoriality: Residential Areas

Crime clusters at high activity nodes, along major paths, and along edges. The clustering of crime in some residential areas, housing projects and subdivisions has drawn much research interest. This was touched upon in our earlier discussion of Oscar Newman's work (1972, 1976), but has been studied sufficiently to warrant more attention. Some of the residential clustering may be property crimes such as burglary or theft, theft from autos, theft of autos, or personal robbery. Personal violence clusters in and around drinking establishments or in residential areas. Crimes are higher around the areas where juveniles live and spend their time.

The residential patterns seem clear when a city is viewed ecologically as an urban mosaic while considering that many types of crime are themselves clustered in different socioeconomic groups, cultural groups, and with younger people. Mapping those parts of a city where persons with the highest likelihood of engaging in criminal behavior usually live or work or go to school normally identifies the actual clusters of crime.

Yet even within a residential area with high crime rates there are some spots that experience few if any crimes. For example, though a simple study based on access, Butcher (1991) found that in a 48-block area in the residential core of downtown Vancouver* residential burglaries occurred most frequently in ground floor units. A wide variety of territorial screens and markers were considered: bushes, trees, and street lights. They had no measurable effect on which ground floor apartments were victimized. Second floor† units had the next highest burglary rates. Top floor units had the third highest rates. In high rise apartments, mid-level floors had extremely low burglary rates, so that high rise apartment structures as a whole had low burglary rates, while smaller three or fewer story buildings had much higher burglary rates. Yet not all small apartment buildings experienced burglaries: a few buildings experienced many burglaries while most experienced few or none over the study's five-year reference period.

The factors that may be influencing the clustering, compression of crime sites or their expansion, are probably related in part to the daily activities of those who live and work there and their associated interrelationships. Perhaps the best way to begin to look at residential areas and the crime patterns within is to make a distinction between the crime patterns produced by people who live or work in an area and those produced by outsiders. The insider/outsider distinction may be essential to avoid falling into the trap that caught the early Newman (1972). Knowing whether crimes are being

---

* The area is economically mixed, ranging from rooming houses to luxury condominiums. Mostly, it is upper middle-class, attracting many retired people, many families with two workers, and many persons working and living on their own. Fear of crime is relatively low. Neighborhood satisfaction is relatively high. There is little evidence of neighboring or territorial functioning among the residents (Brantingham, Brantingham, and Butcher 1986).

† As identified in North America. In Britain, this floor would normally be referred to as the first floor, to denote the first story of the building above ground level.

committed by insiders or outsiders greatly influences our understanding of the "crime templates" of offenders and therefore our ability to interpret crime patterns.*

12.7.5.1 Outsiders

Reaction to outsiders depends on some sense of territoriality. While there is no real agreement on the specifics of a comprehensive definition of territoriality, there seems to be some agreement on the idea that, at some level, people feel some sense of "owning" or having proprietorship over objects or places. Given the existence of such feelings, there is agreement that people sometimes take proactive or reactive actions to protect what they "own" from outsiders. Outsiders are defined by the "owner" and the definition of outsider may vary from object to object and from place to place. Altman and Chemers (1980) define territoriality as being either primary (a person wants complete control for an indefinite time span) or temporary (a person wants only temporary control). In some places there is no real sense of control. Someone's property (ownership) can be invaded or violated. That person usually reacts. For crime, the reaction is most frequently a call to the police.

For some people, territoriality is restricted to part of a room or an apartment or to the inside of a house. Others extend themselves outside. Newman (1972) was trying to get people to extend themselves outside their homes, but extension depends on many factors. Friendship networks may make extension geographically noncontiguous. For others, their territory could cover large areas. Street traffic may make it impossible to have local networks (Appleyard 1969). Some people and cultures want separation (Brantingham, Brantingham, and Butcher 1986); some want and show higher levels of contact (R. Taylor, Gottfredson, and Browser 1984). What makes up what the person considers "his or her territory" varies.

Taylor describes mutual territorial functioning of residents at a block level, but is concerned specifically with personal crime. His research is of particular interest in this article because of this general interest in crime. (See R. Taylor 1988: 259, for a general model of the relationship between territorial functioning and crime.)† Signs of care in an area, such as recently painted houses, neat yards or streets that give the appearance that there are

---

* The distinction is being made between insiders and outsiders in residential areas. This distinction is also important when exploring occupational crime. There are insiders and outsiders at work. The characteristics of the crime template identifying suitable targets vary for these two groups. Workers know about and have access to different crime opportunities than the clients or users of services. See Pretto (1991) for an in-depth exploration of the templates in four major types of occupational crime.

† For Taylor territorial functioning is place specific and group specific. He, in fact, uses person-to-person contact as a fundamental component.

natural guardians (Cohen and Felson 1979a; Felson 1987) who would intervene or, in a Jane Jacobs's "eyes on the street" approach (1961), the actual
presence of people who might interfere might reduce the attractiveness of an
area for certain types of offenders and crimes (R. Taylor 1988). Mutual territoriality seems more closely tied to reducing fear of crime and the sense of
personal risk (R. Taylor 1988) than to reducing crime as such, though it may
reduce personal property crimes at the street block level if the possibility of
potential "watchers" makes the area feel risky to criminal outsiders (Brower,
Dockett, and Taylor 1983).

Measuring and testing the impact of mutual feelings of territoriality on
crime at any level of geographical aggregation is not simple. Mutual feelings
of territoriality seem easiest to establish and husband in stable, homogeneous,
higher socioeconomic status residential areas of the type that characteristically experience little crime. These are the areas where Neighborhood Watch
can be easily established, but where it tends to die out since there is nothing
really to "watch" (Skogan 1988a: 45). While Taylor works at the block level,
his ideas might be expanded to limited multiblock areas with some functional link such as a common elementary school. Conversely, there may be
many areas with little or no sense of mutual territoriality, but which have low
crime rates because they are in parts of the urban mosaic that are unknown
or unapproachable to outsiders who commit crimes.

Mutual territoriality may also be tied to perceived or actual similarity
between residents; or to basic street and building design where it is difficult for residents to be unaware of what their neighbors do, that is, to have
a functional lack of privacy. Property offenders do not want to stand out, be
distinctive and noticeable. Consequently, for example, most young offenders
will tend to stay away from residential areas that have few children or young
persons resident.

Within a more mixed residential area, with highly transient populations,
a sense of belonging or "owning" is more difficult to develop. Crime prevention programs such as Neighborhood Watch rarely work in such areas (Skogan
1988a), although it is worth noting that a new version of Neighborhood Watch
has been made to work in such areas by focusing on an induced form of very
small area territoriality called "cocooning" (Forrester, Chatterton, and Pease
1988; Pease 1992). Once burgled, victimized residences and their immediate
neighbors have a much higher chance of repeat victimization than unburgled
residences and areas even a short distance away. In the Kirkholt project in
England, neighbors surrounding a victimized residence were informed of the
burglary and recruited into active roles as "watchers" for a specified period
following the crime. They were encouraged to form small, mutually vigilant
and protective groups and to branch into a variety of other crime prevention activities ranging from property marking to activities with the police,
in addition to the watching. The approach was apparently successful, both in

terms of inducing mutual territoriality and in terms of reducing repeat bur-glaries, though the key appeared to be the small size of the "cocoon."

12.7.5.2 *Insiders*

Much residential crime is committed by insiders, that is, many people com-mit offences in areas they know well, to which they have legitimate access and to which they belong in a social and cultural sense. What deters insiders is not necessarily what deters outsiders. Since insiders belong in the settings they victimize, they cannot necessarily be identified as ecologically incon-gruent (Sacks 1972). Some insiders, of course, may be considered to be poten-tial problems by their neighbors and may well be carefully watched (a natural or controlled application of cocooning). Several studies had local offenders indicate they were aware of where residents who might intervene lived and avoided these spots within the residential area or complex when the watchers were around although not necessarily when these residents were away.*

Insiders have a better awareness of the area, of the routine daily activi-ties of individuals and families and of who is actually home than outsiders are ever likely to develop. Territorial markers and signs of occupancy may have one meaning for insiders, and totally different meanings for outsiders. It has been reported in some studies that outsiders will actually ignore ter-ritorial markers and occupancy traces and knock on the door to determine whether residents are home, asking for directions to a bogus address if some-one answers.

Ethnic clustering and housing segregation patterns may have strong implications for whether crime patterns are principally attributable to insiders or outsiders. In his study of Milwaukee, where there is a well-bounded black community, Pettiway (1982) found that 65 percent of the offender population in what was labeled a "black ghetto" committed their crimes within that area. Resident offenders committed 74 percent of their burglaries and 58 percent of their robberies as insiders, within the ghetto. Pettiway sees the difference in these percentages as a reflection of the opportunistic side of burglary.

Insiders may produce other problems as well. Many neighborhood insid-ers focus their sense of territory, of mutual functioning, on small subgroups within the area rather than the local community as a whole. The possibilities for micro-level conflicts between different groups of territorial insiders over the use of park benches or pathways for instance, or over noise and other nuisances are implicit in many communities. Recent work by Levy-Leboyer and Naturel (1991) on varying reactions to noise begins to touch the poten-tial problems in many residential areas. The potential for problems among insiders seems to go up as areas become less homogeneous, particularly if the

---

* See R. Taylor (1988: 260) for a general review of some studies reporting the possibility of micro-displacement of property crimes in residential areas.

insiders include people with very different lifestyles, the rich and the poor or the young and the old, or if the insider mix is multicultural with different signs for "this is mine" and different expectations for public behavior.

12.7.6 Aggregate Patterns Summary

Territoriality and crime are interrelated in a complex way. Knowledge of the territory and actions of residents can shape a template (go where it is safe). Lack of knowledge can shape another template (stay where you are safe) or may shape highly opportunistic crime. Highly opportunistic crimes can be reduced when residents have some feeling of mutual territoriality and someone is home, or when a potential offender thinks or knows someone is watching.

Interiors of residential areas, off main paths, with either few children or a parent at home are unlikely to experience much crime and have at least some proportion of the population who feel a need to protect the territory of neighbors. Areas near high schools and main roads, with many apartments, a mixed, heterogeneous residential population with most adults away during the day will experience a lot of property crime, particularly the corner buildings and houses or apartments on grid streets or by "cut-through" paths. Persons with strong feelings of territorial defense may well get into conflicts with teenagers who also feel they "own" the area. As well, persons are probably attracted to places where they can interact at a level they enjoy. For example, someone who enjoys personal privacy, anonymity and isolation from neighbors (Appleyard 1969; Brantingham, Brantingham, and Butcher 1986) that can be realized in urban settings will not be attracted to or necessarily enjoy the "natural" interaction with neighbors on a suburban cul-de-sac. Mobility and housing choice is not "open" to all or at all points in a person's life, but different preferences do exist. But how do preferences influence mutual territorial functioning that might control residential criminal behavior?

Aggregate crime patterns are, when viewed from the perspective of environmental criminology, in need of much more research. Our environment shapes us, but we shape what is around us. More needs to be known about the behavior settings for crime. More needs to be known about behavior in public space, though research has begun on vandalism and graffiti (Wilson 1981; Levy-Leboyer 1984; Scott 1989; Sloan-Howitt and Kelling 1990). In both of these minor crimes, people seem to be showing off and to be declaring territory.

Much more research is needed on the relationship between fear of crime and actual risk of victimization. Those with low risk usually have the highest fear levels (Fattah 1991) or have fear tied to disorder and incivility such as trash, broken windows, or the "unknown" on the street. Research is needed into how changes in transportation systems and other public systems change the behavior of potential offenders and victims and consequently change the patterns of crime. For example, much needs to be done in looking at the urban planning fixation with the construction of green spaces. These green spaces may become crime or fear generators as they open new access paths through the city and create new nodal gathering points for people.

Of particular interest are shopping malls, especially those attracting heterogeneous clientele. Malls are becoming the centers for huge shares of all of our activities, both legal and illegal. Shoplifting at malls is now common across all socioeconomic groups. Drug sales have followed crowds of juveniles into the malls.

Learning more about the reactions of victims to the settings of their victimizations is important. Brown and Harris (1989) and Schepple and Bart (1983) have begun to show the relationship between being victimized in areas in which you feel safe: recovery is slower than when the victimization occurred in an area that seemed unsafe in the first place.

12.8 Conclusions

Environmental criminology is a growing interest in criminology that has generated many unanswered questions. The interests in environmental criminology are similar in many ways to those in environmental psychology and can use what is being learned. Hopefully it can also trigger interest to get more researchers and theoreticians interested in crime.

Crime is an event, a behavior. It is not a simple event, but highly varied and complex. Shoplifting and robbery are different. Vandalism and burglary are different. Yet there are similarities across crimes, similarities that seem to be related to how people "see" what is around them; how they learn what to consider as a suitable target or site or situation for a crime; how they develop, maintain and use crime templates; and how they locate targets.

For highly opportunistic crimes such as theft from work, shoplifting, or theft from an automobile, the crime process may be seen as almost incidental. Normal daily activities influence the patterns of these events. This is particularly important because many people engage in occasional opportunistic crimes. Normal daily activities also appear to be critical in shaping where and when vaguely, as opposed to carefully, planned criminal events and crimes of emotion occur. These crimes concentrate around routine activities, normal activity nodes, and routine travel paths.

Looking at it from the opposite direction, the individual offender's readiness to commit a crime must be triggered before the criminal event can occur. The triggering usually flows out of routine activities and, if routine activities do not include many potential triggering events, then crime is less likely. The person committing the crime must make decisions (even if they are almost instantaneous in some types of crime) but exists within his or her own environment. For example, many juveniles walking to and from school steal goods from residences. If their normal travel path does not take them by empty houses or apartments, they are unlikely to steal. Conversely, juveniles spend hours in malls. There the opportunities for theft are endless. The desire for thrill is great. Shoplifting is not an unexpected behavior.

The actual decision to commit an offence does involve an appraisal of the situation and site or a search for a target. In all cases, a crime template is used. Determining the characteristics of the template has been at the center of much of the research to date, but is still really just beginning. Template construction and use is now reasonably well understood for burglary, and has been explored in tentative ways for shoplifting and for robbery, but is otherwise largely unexplored. Surveillance, detectability, perceived risk, and perceived rewards all must influence criminal decisions somehow and all relate to the physical environment that forms the settings in which crimes must occur. Some transactional view of events and surroundings is the appropriate approach. Events transpire in an immediate site and situation that rests on or in a backcloth composed of uncountable relations between the physical, social, legal, cultural, economic, and temporal environments* functioning cojointly and holistically. Research will be challenging and will have to focus on the multiple ways of "seeing" what surrounds us. The cognitive physical and spatial environment does not exist independently of the cognitive social, cultural, economic, legal, and temporal environments. Our hope is that research can be done that can look at and be part of the environmental backcloth at the same time.

As we move into a challenging area of research and theory construction, we feel confident in saying:

1. Cognitive maps, knowledge of spatial relations influences crime location.
2. The cognitive representations reflect high activity nodes and the paths between them and through those representations shape the location of crime.
3. The type of crimes are varied, but some are highly opportunistic and highly dependent on daily activities and the physical availability of suitable targets and suitable crime situations, frequently including lack of surveillance or a feeling of anonymity.

---

* Obviously, given our conceptualization of the backcloth, any enumeration of this sort is inadequate and is provided merely as a rhetorical convenience.

4. Those who commit crimes have their own behavior settings, influenced by social surrounds but also by simpler characteristics such as safe access.*

5. Within a major urban area the city planners and other decision makers use zoning, transportation planning, and site review to shape travel paths, store locations, school locations, parks, and special activity centers and consequently create crime generator locations and produce some of the actual pattern of crime.

Crime is a part of our way of living. It is tied to the physical distribution of people and objects, to the routine activity patterns of daily life, and to the ways in which people perceive and use information about the environment. Although we can say some things with confidence about how these things relate to and shape the patterns of a few crimes, notably burglary, the research agenda that lies ahead is vast.

---

* Pretto (1991) found that armored car personnel charged with delivering payrolls and putting money into automated teller machines left the payrolls alone, but stole from ATM supplies because a routine three-day delay between servicings left the banks unable to determine whether missing money should be attributed to theft or to ATM malfunction.

Modeling Offenders' Decisions

A Framework for Research and Policy (1985)

13

R.V.G. CLARKE
D.B. CORNISH

From Clarke, R.V., and Cornish, D.B. (1985). Modeling offenders' decisions: A framework for research and policy. *Crime and Justice: A Review of Research*, 6, 147–185.

Contents

13.1 Abstract 312
13.2 Introduction 312
13.3 Relevant Concepts 314
    13.3.1 Sociology of Deviance 314
    13.3.2 Criminology 316
    13.3.3 Economics 319
    13.3.4 Cognitive Psychology 322
13.4 Models of Criminal Decision Making 325
    13.4.1 Modeling Criminal Involvement and Criminal Events 327
    13.4.2 The Need for Models to Be Crime Specific 328
    13.4.3 The Example of Residential Burglary 329
    13.4.4 Initial Involvement 330
    13.4.5 The Criminal Event 331
    13.4.6 Continuance 332
    13.4.7 Desistance 335
    13.4.8 Some General Observations 335
13.5 Conclusions 336
    13.5.1 Policy 336
    13.5.2 Research 338
    13.5.3 Final Remarks 339

13.1 Abstract

Developments in a number of academic disciplines—the sociology of deviance, criminology, economics, psychology—suggest that it is useful to see criminal behavior not as the result of psychologically and socially determined dispositions to offend, but as the outcome of the offender's broadly rational choices and decisions. This perspective provides a basis for devising models of criminal behavior that (1) offer frameworks within which to locate existing research, (2) suggest directions for new research, (3) facilitate analysis of existing policy, and (4) help to identify potentially fruitful policy initiatives. Such models need not offer comprehensive explanations; they may be limited and incomplete, yet still be "good enough" to achieve these important policy and research purposes. To meet this criterion they need to be specific to particular forms of crime, and they need separately to describe both the processes of involvement in crime and the decisions surrounding the commission of the offense itself. Developing models that are crime specific and that take due account of rationality will also demand more knowledge about the ways in which offenders process and evaluate relevant information. Such a decision perspective appears to have most immediate payoff for crime control efforts aimed at reducing criminal opportunity.

13.2 Introduction

Most theories about criminal behavior have tended to ignore the offender's decision making—the conscious thought processes that give purpose to and justify conduct, and the underlying cognitive mechanisms by which information about the world is selected, attended to, and processed. The source of this neglect is the apparent conflict between decision-making concepts and the prevailing determinism of most criminological theories. Whether framed in terms of social or psychological factors, these theories have traditionally been concerned to explain the criminal dispositions of particular individuals or groups. More recently, faced with the need to explain not just the genesis of people's involvement in crime but also the occurrence of particular criminal acts, greater attention has been paid by theory to the immediate environmental context of offending. But the resulting accounts of criminal behavior have still tended to suggest deterministic models in which the criminal appears as a relatively passive figure; thus he or she is seen either as prey to internal or external forces outside personal control, or as the battlefield upon which these forces resolve their struggle for the control of behavioral outcomes.

A number of developments, however, have combined to question the adequacy of explanations or models of offending that do not take account of the offender's perceptions and thought processes. Interest in the criminal's view of his world—characteristic of the "Chicago School" of sociology—revived during the early 1960s within the sociology of deviance that was beginning to stress the importance of developing an understanding of the offender's perspective. In mainstream criminology a similar revival of interest was also fueled by the apparent failure of the rehabilitative ideal—and hence, many argued, of deterministic approaches to criminological explanation. Disenchantment with treatment also shifted attention and resources to other means of crime control, such as incapacitation, deterrence, and environmental approaches to crime prevention; and it became apparent that offenders' perceptions might be salient to the success of these alternatives. As a result, interest grew in the 1970s in ecological studies of criminal activity, in criminal life histories, in cohort studies of criminal careers, and in offenders' accounts of how they went about their activities. At the same time, other academic disciplines such as economics and psychology were exploring, and in some cases applying to criminological problems, concepts and models of information processing and decision making.

Despite the vigor with which these diverse developments have been pursued, little serious attempt has been made to synthesize them; in particular, no concerted attempt has been made to draw out their implications for thinking about crime control policies. This may not be surprising given that most sociologists of deviance—whose theoretical concerns most directly corresponded to those of criminologists—had repudiated criminology's crime control goals (see Sparks 1980). And the antideterministic rhetoric that accompanied the explorations of deviancy sociologists, to say nothing of the ideological climate within which their studies tended to be conducted, further limited the impact both of methodologies and findings on mainstream criminology.

This essay reviews these developments primarily from the standpoint of their possible contribution to crime control policies. This might seem unnecessarily and even harmfully restrictive, but a narrowing of focus can sometimes be an advantage in policy-relevant research. When describing the long-term development of the Home Office Research Unit's program of crime control research, we have argued (Clarke and Cornish 1983) that simple and parsimonious accounts of criminal behavior—such as those provided by dispositional or situational theories—can have considerable heuristic value. They do not have to be "complete" explanations of criminal conduct, but only ones "good enough" to accommodate existing research and to suggest new directions for empirical enquiry or crime control policy. As soon as they no longer serve these ends they should be modified or discarded. We illustrated our argument by tracing the successive development of (1) dispositional theories "good enough" to guide research into treatment effectiveness; (2) "environmental/learning" theories that accounted for the principal findings of the treatment research (that under the powerful influence of the contemporary environment the effects of intervention tend to dissipate rapidly); (3) "situational" accounts that were developed from the environmental/learning perspective in order to guide the direction of research into crime prevention; and (4) rudimentary "choice" theories that were developed to provide a means of understanding crime displacement (which is often the result of situational crime prevention measures).

It is with the enhancement and refinement of rational choice models of crime, made necessary by the recent growth of research interest documented below, that this essay is concerned. Section 13.2 documents the convergence of interest among a variety of academic disciplines—the sociology of deviance, criminology, economics, and cognitive psychology—upon a conception of crime as the outcome of rational choices and decisions. A brief and selective review is undertaken of each discipline's major contributions to the notion of crime as the outcome of rational choices—the intention being to provide a flavor of each approach and a summary of what seem to be its main limitations. Section 13.3 outlines the main requirements of decision models, temporarily "good enough" to explain the processes of criminal involvement (initial involvement, continuance, and desistance) and the occurrence of criminal events. In essence, these models are flowchart diagrams that identify the main decision points and set out the groups of factors bearing upon the decisions made. For reasons that we discuss, decision models need to be specific to particular kinds of crime, and we have chosen to illustrate the construction of such models with the example of residential burglary. In conclusion, Section 13.4 discusses the implications of the decision models for ways of thinking about crime control policies and associated research efforts.

13.3 Relevant Concepts

The following discussion of research relevant to the rationality of offending is couched in the form of brief reviews—and even briefer critiques—of the contributions made by each of the disciplines concerned. The reviews are intended to illustrate the confluence of interest in rationality and to provide the material for the synthesis of concepts and findings attempted in Section 13.3.

13.3.1 Sociology of Deviance

In contrast to most earlier sociological formulations, the "deviancy theories" that were developed in the 1960s explicitly emphasized the cultural relativity of definitions of delinquency, the relationship between social control and the distribution of political and economic power in society, and the need to appreciate the meaning of deviance from the actor's perspective. Of greater relevance for our purposes, these theories also explicitly rejected deterministic and pathological explanations of crime in favor of those emphasizing its purposive, rational, and mundane aspects (see Taylor, Walton, and Young 1973; Box 1981)—concerns also shared by much previous oral history research (Bennett 1981). For example, Taylor et al. asserted that "a social theory must have reference to men's teleology—their purposes, their beliefs and the context in which they act out these purposes and beliefs .... Thus men rob banks because they believe they may enrich themselves, not because something biologically propels them through the door" (p. 61).

A substantial body of ethnographic work illustrates and supports many of the tenets of deviancy sociology. The following examples relate to the rational, largely nonpathological, and commonplace nature of much crime and illustrate how it is accommodated in the individual's day-to-day life:

1. Howard Becker's (1963) observation—based on his studies of marijuana use among jazz musicians in the 1950s—that deviants frequently see their conduct as a rational and obvious response to the pressures and opportunities of their particular circumstances. They may come to this position in a series of rationalizing "private conversations" in which they reconcile public and private morality. To justify their conduct, they may make use of "techniques of neutralization" (Matza 1964; Sheley 1980) such as: "everyone else does it"; "I am only borrowing it"; "he shouldn't have started it"; and so on.

2. Evidence from the life histories of individual offenders that criminal involvement is frequently initiated by relatives, friends, or acquaintances, and hence that the drift into crime is seen as unremarkable and almost natural (Samuel 1981); that legal and illegal ways of earning a living are not necessarily in conflict and may even be complementary (Klockars 1974; Prus and Irini 1980; Maguire 1982); that offenders frequently develop an increasingly more sophisticated and businesslike approach to crime (Shover 1972); and that certain forms of crime, such as bank robbery or truck hijacking, provide both the excitement and the large sums of money that are requirements of "life in the fast lane" (Gibbs and Shelly 1982).

3. Documentation from participant-observation research that in many (if not most) occupational groups, such as waiters (S. Henry 1978), bread roundsmen (Ditton 1977), and dockworkers (Mars 1974), pilfering and cheating are commonplace and are largely accepted by managers and workers alike as legitimate perquisites. Indeed, as Denzin (1977) suggests in his case study of the American liquor industry, illegal activity may be routine, institutionalized, and essential to the satisfactory performance of the industry.

4. Evidence that offenders may decide that the risks of continued criminal behavior are not justified by the rewards: among Parker's (1974)
group of adolescents many gave up shoplifting and opportunistic
theft of car radios when, as a consequence of increased police activity, some of their number were apprehended and placed in custody.
West's (1978) study of the careers of young thieves provides similar
evidence of the rational nature of decisions to desist.

5. Matza's (1964) observation that much delinquency is "episodic"—that
individuals choose to engage in delinquency at certain times but not
at others; that "manufacture of excitement" provides the reason for
much adolescent delinquency; and that much offending is of a petty,
everyday, even "mundane" character. Similarly, Humphreys' (1970)
findings showed that even behavior commonly viewed as pathological—casual homosexual encounters in public lavatories—often
represents clearly encapsulated episodes within essentially normal
heterosexual and "respectable" lifestyles.

6. The observation made by S. Cohen (1972) in his study of clashes
between groups of "mods" and "rockers" and by Marsh, Rosser, and
Harre (1978) in their studies of football hooliganism, that much of
the "uncontrollable" violence between rival gangs of youths is highly
ritualized; it rarely causes serious injury and is calculated to produce
maximum effect upon onlookers.

7. Evidence from interviews with offenders convicted of serious violence (Athens 1980; Felson and Steadman 1983) that many apparently unpremeditated or impulsive acts of violence are in fact the
result of intentions formed during a sequence of confrontations
between offender and victim immediately prior to the incident or
sometimes even days or weeks beforehand.

While deviancy theory has generated a mass of suggestive data on the
perspectives, attitudes, and lifestyles of offenders, its limitations in terms of
the crime control orientation of this discussion stem from three of its fundamental premises—the deliberate eschewal of the test of immediate practical
or policy relevance, the belief that individuals are in a position to provide
comprehensive and valid accounts of the reasons for their behavior, and the
rejection of more quantitative and controlled methods of data collection. The
end result is that although the ideas produced may provide valuable insights
and hypotheses, their validity and generalizability are frequently suspect.

13.3.2 Criminology

The past two decades have seen a great expansion of criminological research—
largely the result of direct funding by governments—and a marked change

in the topics investigated. General disillusion with the rehabilitative ideal and criticisms of the determinism of mainstream criminology, especially in Britain, meant that credence was once more given to "classical" views about crime that emphasized the offender's own responsibility for his conduct. This has been reflected in the reaffirmation of the importance of such sentencing principles as just desert and due process for juvenile offenders, as well as an increased interest in deterrent sentencing and incapacitation. And in response to the same disappointment with rehabilitation, criminologists began to explore methods of prevention focused not upon the offender's inner personality but on the immediate circumstances surrounding the offense. Improved understanding was sought about the rewards of crime, the relationship between criminal opportunities and crime, and the ways in which crime becomes part of the offender's everyday life. Some of the themes of these new lines of research can be grouped together as follows:

1. The findings of *longitudinal cohort studies* (e.g., Wolfgang, Figlio, and Sellin 1972; Petersilia 1980; D.J. West 1982) that, while large proportions of boys in any age group may commit acts of delinquency, most even of the more persistent offenders appear to desist from crime as they reach their late teens or twenties. This may be because they decide that continued criminality is incompatible with the demands of holding a full-time job or settling down to marriage and a family (see Greenberg 1977; Trasler 1979)—or for some it may represent a shift from "street crime" to occupational deviance.

2. Recent research in the *ecological* tradition that has inferred from the distribution of particular crimes that offenders make rational choices. For example, on the basis of findings that it is the homes on the border lines of affluent districts that are at most risk of burglary, Brantingham and Brantingham (1975) suggested that burglars preying on such districts will select the nearest of the suitable targets because escape may be easier and because they prefer to operate where they feel least conspicuous. Similar considerations of reducing risk and effort, minimizing inconvenience, and trading on familiarity explain other findings about the ecology of crime, such as that juvenile offenders seldom stray far from their immediate neighborhoods (e.g., Downes 1966); that crimes tend to be committed en route between an offender's place of residence and his habitual place of work or leisure (Rengert and Wasilchick 1980); that offenses tend to cluster along main roads (Fink 1969; Luedtke and Associates 1970; Wilcox 1973); that neighborhoods with easily understandable "grid" layouts tend to have higher rates of victimization than those with more "organic" street layouts, that is, with winding avenues, culs-de-sac, or crescents (Bevis and Nutter 1977); and that offenders' "images

of the city"—their familiarity with its different parts or their perception of the differential ease or rewards of offending—correspond
with observed crime patterns (Carter and Hill 1979).

3. *Crime-specific* studies of burglary (Scarr 1973; Reppetto 1974;
   Waller and Okihiro 1978; Walsh 1980; Maguire 1982; Winchester
   and Jackson 1982), vandalism (Ley and Cybriwsky 1974a; Clarke
   1978), and shoplifting (Walsh 1978), which have shown that the
   vulnerability of particular targets can be explained largely on the
   basis of factors such as ease of opportunity, low risk, and high gain.
   For example, Winchester and Jackson (1982) found in their study
   of burglary in Southeast England that the most important factors
   determining victimization were the apparent rewards, the chances
   that the house was occupied, and the siting of the building, which
   either facilitated or restricted access. Thus, they found that houses
   standing in their own grounds were much more likely to be burglarized than ones in the middle of a terrace. Waller and Okihiro (1978)
   and Reppetto (1974) found that apartment blocks given protection
   by a doorman had particularly low levels of burglary. Shoplifters are
   more likely to operate in large self-service stores where it is easy to
   steal, and which provide a more impersonal target (Walsh 1978). As
   for vandalism, the targets are more likely to be public property such
   as telephone kiosks or bus shelters (Sturman 1978) or private property that has been abandoned or left in a state of disrepair (Ley and
   Cybriwsky 1974). In other words, vandals appear to choose targets
   that are afforded less protection or (perhaps) where repair will not
   cause individual owners too much hardship.

4. These findings from crime-specific studies about target vulnerability
   are complemented by information obtained from offenders themselves. For example, interviews with convicted burglars by Reppetto
   (1974), Waller and Okihiro (1978), Walsh (1980), Maguire (1982), and
   Bennett and Wright (1983, 1984c) confirm that, the decision having
   been made about the locality in which to commit burglary, the choice
   of the particular house is made on judgments of the likelihood of
   its being occupied and the difficulty of entering without being seen.
   And interviews with muggers (Lejeune 1977) have shown that victims are chosen as being unlikely to resist while yielding an acceptable payoff.

5. Studies of the opportunity structure for crime have shown that fluctuations in levels of offending reflect the supply of available opportunities. This has been demonstrated for auto crime by Wilkins (1964),
   Gould (1969), and Mansfield, Gould, and Namenwirth (1974) and for
   residential burglary by Cohen and Felson (1979a). The latter mounted
   a persuasive case for regarding increases in burglary as the outcome

of the increased portability of electronic goods and of an increase in numbers of unoccupied houses as more women go out to work.

6. *Crime prevention experiments* have shown for a wide variety of offenses (including vandalism, car theft, football hooliganism, aircraft hijacking, and theft or robbery on public transport) that reducing opportunities or increasing risks through environmental management and design can achieve reductions in the incidence of crime (see Clarke 1983). In many cases offenders appear to decide that the risks and effort of offending are no longer worthwhile. For example, few of the motorists prevented from using illegal "slugs" in a particular district of New York by the installation of redesigned meters are likely to have parked their cars in some other more distant place so as to save a few pennies (Decker 1972). In other cases, reduction of opportunities has simply displaced the attention of offenders to some other time, place, or target of crime (see Reppetto 1976). For instance, the introduction of steering-column locks on all new cars from 1971 onward did not produce the expected immediate reduction of car thefts in England and Wales—because most car theft is for temporary use, offenders simply turned their attention to unprotected pre-1971 models (Mayhew et al. 1976).

These various strands of research provide much useful information about offenders' decision making, but they have been pursued too much in isolation from each other and without the benefit of a coherent theoretical perspective. The decision-making concepts employed have been derived from common sense or culled from the unsystematic accounts of offenders. In consequence the relevance of the research for policy is limited. For example, the concept of displacement—of central importance for policy making—has not been disassociated from its theoretical origins as the outcome of powerful internal drives toward criminality. This has meant that much, perhaps undue, skepticism has been expressed about the value of situational crime prevention. But it is not difficult to see how displacement could be accommodated within a decision-making framework (i.e., as the outcome of choices and decisions made by the offender in the face of changed circumstances) and how this might give a better basis for advocating the reduction of criminal opportunities.

13.3.3 Economics

As with recent work in the sociology of deviance and criminology, developments in the economic analysis of criminal behavior have tended to revive some of the concerns of classical criminology. Located in the utilitarian tradition of Beccaria and Bentham, these approaches argue that individuals, whether criminal or not, share in common the properties of being active, rational decision makers who respond to incentives and deterrents. In Gary Becker's words, "a useful theory of criminal behavior can dispense with special theories of anomie, psychological inadequacies, or inheritance of special traits and simply extend the economist's usual analysis of choice" (1968, p. 170).

In contrast to classical economic and criminological theories, however, the new economic formulations take account of the existence and influence of a restricted number of potential individual differences (see Ehrlich's [1979] discussion of the role of "preferences" and Cook's [1980] discussion of subjective evaluation). The economists' emphasis on the importance of the concepts of rewards and costs and their associated probabilities has much in common with the accounts of behavioral psychology. Where economic models depart radically from behavioral ones is in their stress on the importance of the concept of choice.

To chart the various economic models of criminal behavior and the econometric studies to which these models have given rise is outside the purpose of this brief review (but see Palmer 1977; Orsagh and Witte 1981; Freeman 1983; Orsagh 1983; D.J. Pyle 1983), as is the extension of economists' interests into the fields of resource allocation by law enforcement agencies (D.J. Pyle 1983) or the development of complex mathematical models to study criminal justice decision making (Garber, Klepper, and Nagin 1983; Klepper, Nagin, and Tierney 1983). The relevance of economic models of rational choice to the present discussion may be summarized as follows:

1. Whatever their current limitations, economic models of criminal decision making effectively demystify and routinize criminal activity. Crime is assumed a priori to involve rational calculation and is viewed essentially as an economic transaction or a question of occupational choice—a view compatible with many of the recent sociological and criminological studies of crime as work (e.g., Letkemann 1973; Inciardi 1975; Åkerström 1983; Waldo 1983). In the same way, phenomena such as displacement or recidivism can be provided with economic rationales as alternatives to explanations that emphasize offender pathology (see, e.g., Furlong and Mehay's [1981] econometric study of crime spillover).

2. Such economic models are currently extending their analysis beyond crimes motivated predominantly by financial gain. Thus, attempts are being made to find room for nonpecuniary gains as a component of expected utilities (through their translation into monetary equivalents) and to suggest models for so-called expressive crimes— such as those involving violence to the person (Ehrlich 1979)—which emphasize their responsiveness to incentives and deterrents.

3. Economic models suggest that law enforcement agencies are justified in proceeding on the basis that criminals are deterrable; thus they

both provide some grounds for optimism and suggest a range of factors (beyond traditional deterrence theory's preoccupation with certainty and severity of punishment) which might be manipulated in the interests of crime control. These include, for example, the potential rewards of crime and the degree of effort required. Similarly, exploration of the relationship between unemployment and crime (Orsagh and Witte 1981; Freeman 1983) also provides some economic rationale for rehabilitative programs designed to improve offenders' prospects of legitimate work.

Despite the welcome rigor these contributions have brought to criminological theorizing and to the evaluation of policy, there are a number of problems that for the purposes of the current discussion limit the usefulness of existing economic models of criminal decision making. A variety of economic models have recently been proposed (e.g., Heineke 1978; Orsagh and Witte 1981), which recognize the need to include individual differences, but they have generated little empirically based micro analysis of individual criminal behavior. Some attempts to study such models using individual-level data have recently been made (e.g., Witte 1980; Ghali 1982). But it remains the case that, as Manski (1978) pointed out, economic modelers seem largely unaware of the growing empirical data on criminal behavior from other disciplines; they continue to produce theoretical accounts of individual choice behavior which "are too idealized and abstract from too much of the criminal decision problem to serve as useful bases for empirical work" (p. 90). Where empirical investigations are undertaken they tend to be macro analyses using aggregated crime data; and the interaction between micro analysis (uninformed by empirical data) and macro analysis (using imperfect and inadequate data, and uninformed by relevant information about the bases of individual criminal decision making) may be impoverishing both efforts.

These criticisms suggest that current economic models have yet to achieve satisfactory accounts of the bases upon which individual criminals actually make choices, and that they may also underplay individual differences in information-processing capacities and strategies (Cook 1980). The question whether the increasingly sophisticated empirical research on deterrence using aggregated data provides a valid means of monitoring the effectiveness of criminal justice policy lies outside this discussion (but see D.J. Pyle 1983). So far as the development and evaluation of more specific crime prevention and control policies in relation to particular offenders and offenses is concerned, however, it may be that this requires the investigation of actual decision processes rather than the further elaboration, in isolation, of a priori models. In this connection it is interesting to note that, as a result of their review of empirical economic studies using aggregate and individual-level data, Orsagh and Witte (1981) remarked that the relationship between economic viability and crime might vary with the type of crime and the individual involved. Such comments indicate the pressing need for further empirical data, such as those provided by Holzman's (1983) study of labor force participation among robbers and burglars, to clarify these issues and to encourage the construction of narrow-band empirically informed models.

13.3.4 Cognitive Psychology

With the few exceptions noted below, a considerable body of recent psychological research on information processing and decision making has passed largely unnoticed by criminologists. The impetus for this work, which itself contributed to criminological theory, should be briefly mentioned. During the 1960s, many psychologists were becoming disenchanted with the concepts of personality traits and predispositions as determinants of behavior; more attractive was the suggestion of radical behaviorism that the most important influences in relation to criminal behavior (reinforcements and punishments) lay outside the organism. This approach, which has some similarity to economic theories of crime, emphasized the importance not only of incentives and deterrents but also of current situational cues and opportunities. This latter emphasis became a primary influence on British studies of situational crime prevention (Mayhew et al. 1976), the further development of which drew attention to the need for a fuller understanding of criminal decisions (see Clarke and Cornish 1983).

Within academic psychology, the reaction during the last decade against the environmental determinism of radical behaviorism has led to an increasing recognition of the important role played by cognitive processes. This can be seen in the development of more sophisticated "social learning" theories (Bandura 1969, 1977) that stressed additional mechanisms of learning, such as imitation (which required the assumption of symbolic mediational cognitive processes), and reintroduced person variables in the guise of cognitive competencies and capacities (Mischel 1973, 1979). Several attempts to apply selected social learning concepts to an analysis of criminal behavior have been made (e.g., Akers 1977; Feldman 1977; Conger 1978).

It is not in respect of social learning theory alone, however, that developments of direct relevance to an understanding of criminal decision making have occurred. Studies of the professional judgments of clinicians and similar personnel concerning risky decision making, and of information-processing strategies in decision making, provide their relevant insights and analogies. The contributions itemized below relate as much to the methods and concepts as to substantive findings in this area:

1. Psychological studies of professional judgments made in clinical and similar settings have for a long while suggested that even experts

often handle information in less than perfectly rational or efficient ways (Meehl 1954; Wilkins and Chandler 1965; Wiggins 1973).

2. These findings received further support from early studies of risky decision making (see Kozielecki [1982] for a review) which suggested that people did not always behave in accordance with economic models of the rational, efficient decision maker—they frequently failed to make decisions that were objectively the "best" (Cornish 1978). An attempt to apply one such model (the subjective expected utility model) to an experimental study of the factors involved in juveniles' decisions about committing hypothetical crimes is reported by Cimler and Beach (1981).

3. Some of the reasons for the failure of a priori models to explain decision making were identified by Slovic and Lichtenstein (1968). They suggested that real-life decision makers might be led to pay selective attention to certain risk dimensions over others by reason of their "importance-beliefs"—notions derived from past experience, logical analysis of the decision task, or even quite irrational fears and prejudices.

4. These conclusions led naturally to an increased emphasis upon information-processing models and strategies in relation to real-life decision making (see Cornish [1978] on gambling; Carroll [1982] on criminal behavior). "Process tracing"—a technique for studying decision making as it actually occurs in natural settings by asking subjects to think aloud about the decision task (Kleinmuntz 1968)— has recently been applied to the investigation of offending decisions by Carroll and Herz (1981) and Bennett and Wright (1983).

5. Payne (1980) has suggested that more attention should be paid to the characteristics of the decision maker as information processor and their effect on the handling of choice problems. Warr and Knapper's (1968) model for person perception emphasizes the effects on information processing of the perceiver's stable personal characteristics, of ephemeral moods, previous experiences, and expectations, and of the decision rules employed by the decision maker's "processing center." Crucial to the operations involved might be Slovic and Lichtenstein's (1968) "importance-beliefs," Cook's (1980) "standing decisions," and the wider concept of "knowledge structures" used by Nisbett and Ross (1980).

6. An emphasis on decision rules suggested that inferential "rules-of-thumb" are universally employed in order to enable decision making to proceed rapidly and effectively. Some of these judgmental heuristics (Tversky and Kahneman 1974; Kahneman, Slovic, and Tversky 1982) can lead to error: for example, too much attention may be paid to information that is readily available or recently presented, and

inductive rules may be too quickly formulated on the basis of unrepresentative data.

7. Finally, it appears that the riskiness of an individual's decisions may vary according to whether the decision is made alone, or as a group member. Early studies had suggested that group decision making tended to be more "risky"; hence the phenomenon was termed "risky-shift" (Pruitt 1971). Recent reviews (Myers and Lamm 1976), however, suggest a more complex picture in which group decisions may also become more cautious under certain conditions.

The facts that people do not always make the most "rational" decisions, that they may pay undue attention to less important information, that they employ shortcuts in the processing of information, and that group decisions may be different from individual ones are all clearly relevant to an understanding of criminal decision making. But cognitive psychology is still at an early stage in its development and the topics studied so far are not necessarily those that best illuminate criminal decision making. For example, there has been perhaps too much concentration upon bias and error in information processing (see Nisbett and Ross 1980), whereas, in fact, the judgmental heuristics involved usually enable individuals to cope economically and swiftly with very complex tasks (Bruner, Goodnow, and Austin 1956)—a process Simon (1983) has termed "bounded rationality." And there are some other basic issues, perhaps of particular relevance to crime control policies, which have scarcely been addressed by the discipline. These include the extent to which cognitive strategies are produced consciously or unconsciously, the degree to which they are under the individual's own control, whether they indicate a predisposition to process information in a certain manner or merely a preference for doing so, and the extent to which individuals differ in their information-processing capacities and competencies.

Finally, of special relevance to the present discussion, the question has not properly been considered whether those individuals who habitually make criminal decisions think in different ways from other people. This, in fact, is the claim made by Yochelson and Samenow (1976) on the basis of detailed clinical interviews with 240 criminals, most of whom had been detained in hospital as a result of being found guilty by reason of insanity. Yochelson and Samenow believe that criminals choose specific thinking patterns—of which they identify fifty-two characteristic modes, including suspiciousness, self-seeking, manipulativeness, impulsiveness, concrete and compartmentalized thinking, and excitement or sensation seeking—which inevitably lead to crime. Such thought patterns, while internally logical, consistent, and hence "rational" to the offender, may be regarded as both irresponsible and irrational by the noncriminal.

Many methodological criticisms have been made of Yochelson and Samenow's work (e.g., Burchard 1977; Jacoby 1977; Nietzel 1979; Sarbin 1979; Void 1979), but it remains true that the thinking patterns identified have much in common with many of the concepts reviewed above, that is, with individual information-processing styles and strategies and with motivational and cognitive biases. Moreover, they reflect themes commonly encountered in criminal life histories (Hampson 1982) such as the offender's preoccupation with maintaining "machismo" and with "techniques of neutralization." This further reinforces the point that a full (and policy-relevant) understanding of the processes of criminal decision making will not be gained through studies of "normal" decision making alone.

13.4 Models of Criminal Decision Making

Even allowing for some selective perception on our part, we believe that the material in Section 13.2 demonstrates that during the past decade there has been a notable confluence of interest in the rational choice, nondeterministic view of crime. This is a natural perspective for law and economics, but it has also achieved wide currency in criminology's other parent disciplines—sociology and psychology—as well as within the different schools of criminology itself. That the shift is part of a broader intellectual movement is suggested by the increasing popularity of economic and rational choice analyses of behaviors other than crime. Why there should be this movement at the present time and what social forces and events might be implicated is difficult to say, but cross-fertilization of ideas between different groups of people working on similar problems always occurs, and certain individuals have deliberately applied the same theoretical perspective to a variety of different problems. For instance, Gary Becker (1968) pioneered his economic analyses of crime when dealing with the economics of discrimination and has since extended his method to choice of marriage partner (Becker 1973, 1974).

Despite the shift of interest described above, there has been little attempt to construct a synthesis—within a rational choice framework—of the concepts and findings provided by the various approaches. As an illustration of the value of such a synthesis, it is worth making brief reference to the approach adopted by one of us in a review of the research on the determinants of gambling behavior (Cornish 1978). While not adopting so explicit a decision-making orientation, the review made similar use of concepts from sociology, psychology, and economics as a basis for analyzing existing control measures and for suggesting future directions for policy and research. It recognized, first, the importance of rational though not exclusively economic considerations when explaining a behavior commonly regarded as being pathologically motivated; second, the need to treat gambling, not as a unitary form of behavior, but as a collection of disparate behaviors each with their own distinctive features; third, and as a corollary, the need to pay close attention to situational factors relating to the gambling "event"; fourth, the need to develop explanations of gambling behavior which would make specific reference to factors determining, respectively, likelihood and degree of involvement; fifth, the role of learning in the development of heavy involvement in certain forms of gambling; and last, the scope for both exploiting and controlling gambling behavior through manipulation of people's information-processing activities.

The models of crime presented below also offer a way of synthesizing a diverse range of concepts and findings for the purpose of guiding policy and research, but they are developed within the context of much more explicit decision making. They are not models in which relationships are expressed either in mathematical terms (as in, e.g., economic models) or in the form of testable propositions (see, e.g., Brantingham and Brantingham's [1978] model of target selection). Nor are they even "decision trees" that attempt to model the successive steps in a complex decision process (see Walsh [1980] for an example relating to burglary). Rather, they are schematic representations of the key decision points in criminal behavior and of the various social, psychological, and environmental factors bearing on the decisions reached. Our models resemble most closely the kind of flow diagrams frequently employed to represent complex social processes—for example, the explanatory models for fear of crime developed by Skogan and Maxfield (1981) and for victimization proneness by Hindelang, Gottfredson, and Garofalo (1978).

The models, which need to be separately developed for each specific form of crime, are not theories in themselves but rather the blueprints for theory. They owe much to early attempts to model aspects of criminal decision making by Brantingham and Brantingham (1978), Brown and Altman (1981), and Walsh (1978, 1980). But these earlier models were largely confined to just one of the criminal decision processes—target selection—and they also depended upon a commonsense explication of the likely decision steps taken by the "rational" criminal. Our models are concerned not just with the decision to commit a particular crime, but also with decisions relating to criminal "readiness" or involvement in crime; and they also take some account of the recent psychological research on cognitive processing.

This research is still at a relatively early stage, and as yet there is only a comparatively small body of criminological data relevant to decision making upon which to draw. Any attempt to develop decision models of crime must at this stage be tentative. Thus our aim is only to provide models that are at present "good enough" to accommodate existing knowledge and to guide research and policy initiatives. Even such "good enough" models, however, have to meet the criticism that they assume too much rationality on the part of the offender. But as the review in Section 13.2 has indicated, rationality must be conceived of in broad terms. For instance, even if the choices made or the decision processes themselves are not optimal ones, they may make sense to the offender and represent his best efforts at optimizing outcomes. Moreover, expressive as well as economic goals can, of course, be characterized as rational. And lastly, even where the motivation appears to have a pathological component, many of the subsequent planning and decision-making activities (such as choice of victims or targets) may be rational.

13.4.1 Modeling Criminal Involvement and Criminal Events

There is a fundamental distinction to be made between explaining the involvement of particular individuals in crime and explaining the occurrence of criminal events. Most criminological theorists have been preoccupied with the former problem and have neglected the latter. They have sought to elucidate the social and psychological variables underlying criminal dispositions, on the apparent assumption that this is all that is needed to explain the commission of crime itself. But the existence of a suitably motivated individual goes only part of the way to explaining the occurrence of a criminal event—a host of immediately precipitating, situational factors must also be taken into account. And a further distinction that must be recognized by theorists concerns the various stages of criminal involvement—initial involvement, continuance, and desistance. That these separate stages of involvement may require different explanatory theories, employing a range of different variables, has been made clear by the findings of recent research into criminal careers (see Farrington 1979; Petersilia 1980).

The distinctions between event and involvement have to be maintained when translating traditional perspectives into decision terms. It may be that the concepts of choice or decision are more readily translatable and more fruitful in relation to continuance and desistance than to initial involvement, but to some extent this may depend on the particular offense under consideration. For some offenses, such as shoplifting or certain acts of vandalism, it might be easier to regard the first offense as determined by the multiplicity of factors identified in existing criminological theory and as committed more or less unthinkingly, that is, without a close knowledge or consideration of the implications. But however much people may be propelled by predisposing factors to the point where crime becomes a realistic course of action, it may still be legitimate (or, at least, useful) to see them as having a choice about whether to become involved. Once the offense is committed, however, the individual acquires direct knowledge about the consequences and implications of that behavior; and this knowledge becomes much more salient to future decisions about continuance or desistance. It may also provide the background of experience to render initial involvement in another crime a considered choice (see Walsh's [1980] discussion of burglary as a training ground for other crimes).

13.4.2 The Need for Models to Be Crime Specific

The discussion above has anticipated another important requirement of decision models of crime: whether of involvement or of event, these must be specific to particular kinds of crime. Recent preoccupation with offender pathology and the desire to construct general statements about crime, deviancy, and rule breaking have consistently diverted attention from the important differences between types of crime—the people committing them, the nature of the motivations involved, and the behaviors required. Whatever the purposes and merits of academic generalization, it is essential for policy goals that these important distinctions be maintained. And, moreover, it will usually be necessary to make even finer distinctions between crimes than those provided by legal categories. For instance, it will not usually be sufficient to develop models for a broad legal category such as burglary (Reppetto 1976). Rather it will be necessary to differentiate at least between commercial and residential burglary (as has already been done in a number of studies) and perhaps even between different kinds of residential and commercial burglaries. For example, burglary in public housing projects will be a quite different problem from burglary in affluent commuter areas, or from burglary in multioccupancy inner-city dwellings. And the same is obviously true of many other crimes, such as vandalism, robbery, rape, and fraud. The degree of specificity required will usually demand close attention to situational factors, especially in event models.

The emphasis on specificity, however, should not be taken as contradicting the fact, established in research on criminal careers, that particular individuals may be involved in a variety of criminal activities. But their involvement in separate activities does not necessarily derive from the same sources, though *in practice* the separate processes of involvement in different crimes may be interrelated. This means that in explaining a particular individual's pattern of criminal activity it may be necessary to draw upon a variety of specific models and perhaps to describe the links between them. However, this is a matter for those interested in the etiology of individual criminality and in related policies—such as rehabilitation and incapacitation—focused upon the individual offender. Whether they are specialists or generalists, our own interest in offenders is primarily restricted to occasions when they are involved in the offense under consideration. This is because each form of crime is likely to require specific remedies and, by shifting the focus from offender to offense, a range of neglected options is likely to be brought into the policy arena. All our models reflect this focus of interest and our purpose below is to lay out their formal requirements.

13.4.3 The Example of Residential Burglary

We have chosen below to illustrate the construction of decision models of crime through the example of residential burglary in a middle-class suburb. Although it might have made more interesting reading to have selected a less obviously instrumental offense, our choice in the end was made for reasons of convenience: knowledge about this offense is relatively well advanced and we have been involved in some of the recently completed research (Clarke and Hope 1984). This work suggests that the offenders involved are generally rather older and more experienced than those operating in public housing estates, but less sophisticated than those preying on much wealthier residences. Since decision models are for us primarily intended to make criminological theorizing of greater relevance to crime control policies, we believe that practical considerations should play a large part in determining the specificity of the model: the offense modeled should be as specific as current knowledge allows, while at the same time sufficiently common or serious to justify the development of special preventive policies.

In the following pages we will present four models—one concerned with the criminal event and the others with the three stages of criminal involvement—since the decision processes for each model are quite different. It may not always be necessary for policy purposes to model all four processes; indeed, as said above, decisions about which models to develop, and at what level of detail, ought to be governed by policy goals. Our present aim is primarily didactic: first, to set out the models in order to identify the links between them; second, to locate and to give some hint of the ways in which existing criminological data might be interpreted within a decision framework; and third, to illustrate how, through development and examination of the models, the most fruitful points of intervention in the criminal decision process might be identified. As our purpose is not to develop fully elaborated decision models of residential burglary, but only to demonstrate their feasibility, we shall not usually indicate where they draw upon empirical findings (which in any case have been mentioned above) and where they rely upon our own armchair theorizing.

One obvious implication of the need for specificity is that the configuration of the models may vary significantly among different kinds of crime. For instance, models involving offenses that appear to depend primarily upon "presented" opportunities (e.g., shoplifting; Carroll and Herz [1981]) will probably be simpler than those (such as residential burglary) involving opportunities that must be "sought" (see Maguire 1980). And these in turn will be simpler than those involving offenses where the opportunities are created or planned (e.g., bank robberies).

13.4.4 Initial Involvement

Figure 13.1 represents the process of initial involvement in residential burglary in a middle-class suburb. There are two important decision points: the first (box 7) is the individual's recognition of his "readiness" to commit this particular offense in order to satisfy certain of his needs for money, goods, or excitement. Readiness involves rather more than receptiveness: it

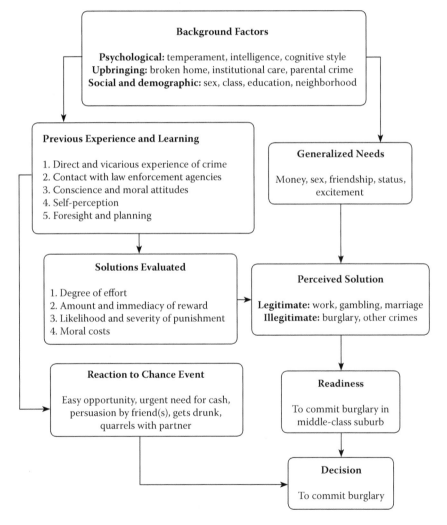

Figure 13.1 Initial involvement model (example: burglary in a middle-class suburb).

implies that the individual has actually contemplated this form of crime as a solution to his needs and has decided that under the right circumstances he would commit the offense. In reaching this decision he will have evaluated other ways of satisfying his needs and this evaluation will naturally be heavily influenced by his previous learning and experience—his moral code, his view of the kind of person he is, his personal and vicarious experiences of crime, and the degree to which he can plan and exercise foresight. These variables in turn are related to various historical and contemporaneous background factors—psychological, familial, and sociodemographic (box 1). It is with the influence of these background factors that traditional criminology has been preoccupied; they have been seen to determine the values, attitudes, and personality traits that dispose the individual to crime. In a decision-making context, however, these background influences are less directly criminogenic; instead they have an orienting function—exposing people to particular problems and particular opportunities and leading them to perceive and evaluate these in particular (criminal) ways. Moreover, the contribution of background factors to the final decision to commit crime would be much moderated by situational and transitory influences; and for certain sorts of crime (e.g., computer fraud) the individual's background might be of much less relevance than his immediate situation.

The second decision (box 8), actually to commit a burglary, is precipitated by some chance event. The individual may suddenly need money, he may have been drinking with associates who suggest committing a burglary (for many offenses, especially those committed by juveniles, immediate pressure from the peer group is important), or he may perceive an easy opportunity for the offense during the course of his routine activities. In real life, of course, the two decision points may occur almost simultaneously and the chance event may not only precipitate the decision to burgle, but may also play a part in the perception and evaluation of solutions to generalized needs.

13.4.5 The Criminal Event

Figure 13.2 depicts the further sequence of decision making that leads to the burglar selecting a particular house. As mentioned above, for some other crimes the sequence will be much lengthier; and the less specific the offense being modeled, the more numerous the alternative choices. For example, should a more general model of burglary be required, a wider range of areas and housing types would have to be included (see Brantingham and Brantingham 1978). In the present case, however, there may be little choice of area in which to work, and in time this decision (and perhaps elements of later decisions) may become routine.

This is, of course, an idealized picture of the burglar's decision making. Where the formal complexity of the decision task is laid out in detail, as in

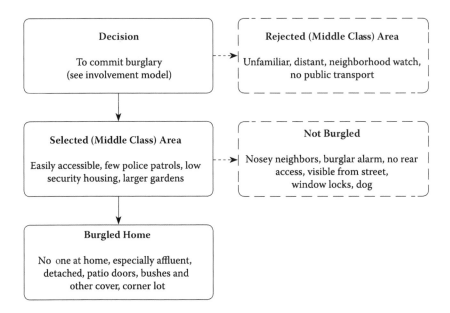

Figure 13.2 Event model (example: burglary in a middle-class suburb).

Walsh's (1978, 1980) work, there may be a temptation to assume that it entails equally complex decision making. In real life, however, only patchy and inaccurate information will be available. Under these uncertain circumstances the offender's perceptions, his previous experience, his fund of criminal lore, and the characteristic features of his information processing become crucial to the decision reached. Moreover, the external situation itself may alter during the time span of the decision sequence. The result is that the decision process may be telescoped, planning may be rudimentary, and there may be last-minute (and perhaps ill-judged) changes of mind. Even this account may overemphasize the deliberative element, since alcohol may cloud judgment. Only research into these aspects of criminal decision making will provide event models sufficiently detailed and accurate to assist policy making.

13.4.6 Continuance

Interviews with burglars have shown that in many cases they may commit hundreds of offenses (see, e.g., Maguire 1982); the process of continuing involvement in burglary is represented in Figure 13.3. It is assumed here that, as a result of generally positive reinforcement, the frequency of offending increases until it reaches (or subsequently reduces to) some optimum level. But it is possible to conceive of more or less intermittent patterns of involvement for some individuals; and intermittent patterns may be more common for other types of offenses (e.g., those for which ready opportunities occur less frequently). It is unlikely that each time the offender sets out to commit an

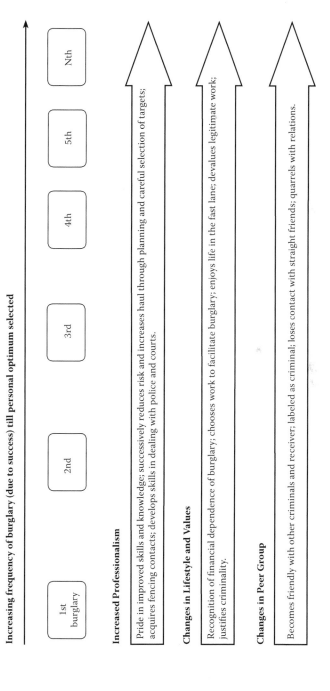

Figure 13.3 Continuing involvement model (example: burglary in a middle-class suburb).

offense he will actively consider the alternatives, though this will sometimes be necessary as a result of a change in his circumstances or in the conditions under which his burglaries have to be committed. (These possibilities are discussed in more detail in regard to the "desistance" model of Figure 13.4.)

More important to represent in the continuing involvement model are the gradually changing conditions and personal circumstances that confirm the offender in his readiness to commit burglary. The diagram summarizes three categories of relevant variables. The first concerns an increase in

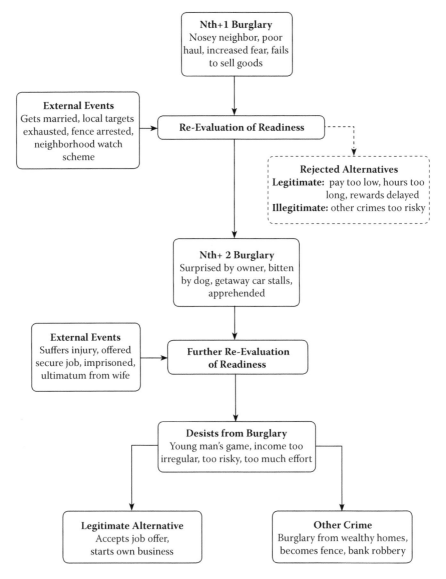

Figure 13.4 Desistance model (example: burglary in a middle-class suburb).

professionalism: pride in improved skills and knowledge; successive reductions of risk and an improvement in haul through planning and careful selection of targets; and the acquisition of reliable fencing contacts. The second reflects some concomitant changes in lifestyle: a recognition of increased financial dependence on burglary, a choice of legitimate work to facilitate burglary, enjoyment of "life in the fast lane," the devaluation of ordinary work, and the development of excuses and justifications for criminal behavior. Third, there will be changes in the offender's network of peers and associates and his relationship to the "straight" world. These trends may be accelerated by criminal convictions as opportunities to obtain legitimate work decrease and as ties to family and relations are weakened.

This picture is premised upon a more open criminal self-identification. There will be, however, many other offenses (e.g., certain sexual crimes) that are more encapsulated and hidden by the offender from everyone he knows.

13.4.7 Desistance

It is in respect of the subject of Figure 13.4 in particular—desistance from burglary—that paucity of relevant criminological information is especially evident. While the work of, for example, Parker (1974), Greenberg (1977), W.G. West (1978), Trasler (1979), Maguire (1982), and D.J. West (1982) provides some understanding of the process of desistance, empirical data, whether relating to groups or individuals and in respect of particular sorts of crime, are very scanty. Nevertheless, there is sufficient information to provide in Figure 13.4 an illustration of the offender's decision processes as he begins a renewed evaluation of alternatives to burglary. This follows aversive experiences during the course of offending and changes in his personal circumstances (age, marital status, financial requirements) and the neighborhood and community context in which he operates (changes of policing, depletion of potential targets). These result in his abandoning burglary in favor of some alternative solution either legitimate or criminal. While desistance may imply the cessation of all criminal activity, in other cases it may simply represent displacement to some other target (commercial premises rather than houses) or to another form of crime. Desistance is, in any case, not necessarily permanent and may simply be part of a continuing process of lulls in the offending of persistent criminals (D.J. West 1963) or even, perhaps, of a more casual drifting in and out of particular crimes.

13.4.8 Some General Observations

The decision models illustrated above should be seen as temporary, incomplete, and subject to continual revision as fresh research becomes available. Even now they could probably be improved by the explicit specification of linkages within and between models. Moreover, accepting the "good enough" criterion governing their development, they are still open to two general criticisms. On the one hand, it might be argued that the benefits of a decision approach have been oversold by selecting a crime such as burglary, which has clear instrumental goals and requires planning and foresight. However, the decision elements in many other forms of crime—such as fraud or traffic offenses (see I.D. Brown [1981] for the latter)—may be even more salient. And, as our earlier review suggests, a decision approach is applicable to all forms of crime, even apparently impulsive or irrational ones. On the other hand, considering the aptness of residential burglary for treatment in decision terms, one might have expected the resulting models to be better articulated and less dependent upon anecdotal evidence. Moreover, given the amount of further empirical data required to make even the burglary models adequate, can it be realistic to suggest that such models have to be developed for all the different kinds of crime? The answer must be that since the models are intended to assist policy making, pragmatic considerations should be preeminent: the harm caused by the particular crime under consideration must be considered sufficient to justify the investment in research.

13.5 Conclusions

During the course of this discussion a number of deficiencies in current criminological theorizing have been identified. Many of these flow from two underlying assumptions: that offenders are different from other people and that crime is a unitary phenomenon. Hence, the preoccupation with the issue of initial involvement in crime and the failure to develop explanations for specific kinds of offending. Moreover, explanatory theories have characteristically been confined to a limited selection of variables derived from one or another of criminology's contributory disciplines; and none of the dominant theories has taken adequate account of situational variables. A decision-making approach, however, stresses the rational elements in criminal behavior and requires explanations to be specific to particular forms of crime. It also demands that attention be paid to the crucial distinction between criminal involvement (at its various stages) and criminal events. By doing so it provides a framework that can accommodate the full range of potentially relevant variables (including situational ones) and the various competing but partial theories.

13.5.1 Policy

These advantages for explanation also hold for analysis of policy. Instead of defining the search for effective policy in terms of coping with broad problems such as juvenile delinquency or the rise in crime, the decision models encourage a policy focus upon the specific crimes, such as school vandalism, joy riding, rape by strangers, and pub violence, which may be giving rise to the broader concerns. Breaking down larger problems into more clearly defined constituent parts usually affords a greater prospect of effective action. But the distinctions between crimes need to be finer, not only than those of existing theory (e.g., between instrumental and expressive offenses, or between predatory and violent offenses) but also than those provided by legal categories. In addition, the more comprehensive view of the determinants of crime provided by the interlocking decision models of involvement and event identifies a broader range of both policy options and possible points for intervention. Options can then be prioritized in relation to the specific offense under consideration in terms of practicality, immediacy of effect, and cost effectiveness. For example, the appropriate involvement and event models for joy riding (theft of vehicles for personal use) might suggest a variety of measures, including increased leisure provision for juveniles at risk, community service for convicted offenders, "lock-your-car" campaigns, and the provision of better public transport. The most cost-effective method might turn out to be the improvement of vehicle security, since the assumption of rationality underlying the decision perspective supports measures that either increase (or seem to the offender to increase) the costs and effort of offending or decrease the rewards. The costs of this improved security would need to be carefully assessed; they should be weighed against the costs of the offense—these latter being broadly defined to include personal inconvenience and waste of police time—and any possible costs incurred by displacement.

Both the crime-specific focus for policy and the decision perspective are likely to favor more narrowly defined situational or deterrent measures by, for example, enabling the limits of displacement to be more clearly specified. While there is much unrealized potential for such measures (see Clarke 1983), there are dangers in going too far down this road. For example, different crime problems are sometimes concentrated together in the same localities and this may suggest coordinated action. It may also be the case that the best chance of apprehending individuals involved in certain particularly vicious criminal behavior—multiple rapes, for instance—lies in crackdowns on certain other offenses such as "curb crawling" or "cruising" by men in automobiles looking for prostitutes.

This latter point relates directly to the issue how far offenders are generalists rather than specialists, which is at the heart of questions about the policy value of the decision models. There is certainly evidence from the criminal careers research cited above that many of the most recidivist offenders are generalists. But it is not entirely clear to what extent they may specialize in certain forms of crime at particular times. It seems likely that the more closely offenses are defined, the more they will be found to be committed by characteristic offender types. Thus children involved in vandalism of schools may be different from those who assault teachers or, indeed, who vandalize other targets. To the extent that their special characteristics, in particular the motives and reasons underlying their conduct, can be identified and described, it may be possible to suggest more carefully tailored forms of intervention. Catch-all interventions for loosely defined offender groups are unlikely to achieve their objectives.

There are other ways in which the decision approach helps to account for the limited effectiveness of current treatment efforts. Programs tend to pay too much attention to modifying the influence of "disposing" variables and in doing so take too little account of the posttreatment environment, including the offender's current social and economic situation, the role of chance events, and the specific opportunities open to him for crime. To be successful, treatment must take more account of these contemporaneous influences. Where the pressures and inducements are primarily economic, the measures needed are ones likely to increase the attractions and possibilities of conformity, such as programs that give the offender new skills or ways of earning a living. These programs must be based not only on a more careful analysis of the particular needs and circumstances of the target group, but also of the market for labor: it may be, for example, that work programs are of limited effectiveness for those already in work or for those able to earn considerably more money by illegitimate means.

As for incapacitation, the relevance of decision models lies in the fact that they demand a detailed understanding of continuance and desistance. In particular more needs to be known about offenders' reasons for switching crimes or for engaging in a variety of different crimes at a particular time. Knowledge of this kind will help to determine the feasibility of identifying suitable target groups for containment.

13.5.2 Research

The decision approach suggests three important directions for research: the mounting of further crime-specific studies, the devotion of more attention to the offender's perspective when criminal careers are studied, and the elucidation of decision processes at the point of offending. Some notable examples of crime-specific research have been quoted in this essay. But there is much more scope for work of this kind, particularly if, as our analysis seems to require, finer distinctions between crimes are adopted. As for offenders' perspectives on their careers, examples of the sorts of information needed have already been given. A question of central importance concerns the part played in desistance by changes in personal circumstances as compared with being arrested and sentenced. For example, an understanding of the impact of law enforcement and criminal justice systems will require study of the offenders' sources of information and the way in which the information is evaluated. It cannot be assumed that offenders' views of the system and its measures bear a close relation to those of policymakers. It will be important to ask, for example, whether the official information is reaching its targets, whether the message is consistent, and whether it is believed. The need to understand the processing of information is also salient to modeling decision processes at the point of offending. More knowledge is needed, in particular, about the heuristic devices employed in assessing costs and payoffs, about how anxieties concerning the morality of the act and the risk of apprehension are dealt with (e.g., through shutoff mechanisms and techniques of neutralization) and about the effect of alcohol (see Bennett and Wright 1984a), of anger, or, indeed, of other emotions.

Getting the questions right will help to determine the appropriate methodologies, and our preceding discussion has illustrated the wealth of available techniques to acquire the necessary information—participant observation, retrospective interviews, experimental studies of decision making, ecological mapping, crime site surveys, and "process tracing" in vivo or by using films and photographs. For some offenses, such as residential burglary, there may already be enough data to attempt a detailed simulation of the decision process.

Each of these methods makes certain theoretical assumptions and has its characteristic limitations. For example, the use of interviews and introspection to investigate criminal decision making may reveal more about people's post hoc commonsense or self-serving explanations for their behavior than about either the processes involved or the factors actually taken into account (Nisbett and Wilson 1977). Again, it should not be assumed that decision making in the real world can be easily simulated in the laboratory (see Ebbesen and Konecni 1980). Given the complexities of the issues and the dearth of information, triangulation of methods is essential, though any technique that enables criminal choices to be studied as they occur in naturalistic settings (see Payne's [1980] advocacy of process tracing) may be especially valuable.

The separation in the discussion above among theoretical formulations, policy, and research is, of course, artificial. In successful policy-relevant programs of research, there must be a dynamic interplay among theories, empirical studies, and policy implications. In particular, ongoing research should have a powerful feedback effect upon the construction of models. And the impact of decision modeling on the structure of research is every bit as important as the policy applications discussed above.

13.5.3 Final Remarks

In conclusion, two general points seem worth emphasizing. First, the models have been developed primarily for the limited purposes of improving crime control policies and developing policy-relevant research. Such models have only to be "good enough"; they may not necessarily be the most appropriate or satisfactory for more comprehensive explanations of criminal behavior—though it seems likely that a decision approach might provide a useful starting point even for academic purposes. For example, Box (1981) has developed a sophisticated initial involvement model, based on control theory, which contains decision elements; while Glaser's (1979) more general "differential anticipation" theory incorporates elements of a decision approach within a hybrid involvement-event framework.

Second, decision models of crime might appear to imply the sort of "soft" determinism or modified classicism advocated by Matza (1964), namely, that while choices may be constrained, some leeway to choose still exists. And a criminology that makes use of such voluntaristic concepts might seem to have forsaken its traditional determinism.

A fuller discussion of this issue is beyond the scope of this essay (but see Glaser 1976; Schafer 1976). It is possible, however, to take a more pragmatic stance: while it is true that the concept of choice is likely to prove useful for generating and providing a framework for decision-making data, the resulting information supplies as many clues about determinants of behavior as it does about reasons and motives. This, in turn, enables both voluntaristic and deterministic models of offending to be elaborated further; it may be too soon, for example, to discount the sophisticated noncognitive accounts suggested by radical behaviorism (Skinner 1964, 1978). Perhaps, as Glaser (1976) implies, voluntaristic and deterministic assumptions are always best regarded as alternative heuristic devices for generating and organizing data. Under such circumstances it would not be surprising if the usefulness of their respective contributions to the task in hand—the more effective control of crime—appeared to vary from time to time. We believe, then, that decision-making concepts can be used for the purposes of constructing "good enough" theories without necessarily being firmly committed to a particular position in the free will/determinism debate—or to any consequential implications for crime control (Cressey 1979) or criminal justice (Norrie 1983). Indeed, the resulting policies remain, as before, the outcome of an uneasy blend of deterministic and neoclassical assumptions.

Linking Criminal Choices, Routine Activities, Informal Control, and Criminal Outcomes (1986)

14

M. FELSON*

From Felson, M. (1986). In D.B. Cornish and R.V. Clarke (Eds.), *The Reasoning Criminal: Rational Choice Perspectives On Offending* (pp. 119–128). New York: Springer-Verlag.

People make choices, but they cannot choose the choices available to them. Nor can they be sure what chain of events will follow from their choices, including choices made by others. People blunder and fail, just as they often get what they want. This chapter seeks to place rational choice theories of crime into a broader context. This context considers how the larger structure of opportunities sets the stage for criminogenic choices as well as influences whether these choices result in successes or failures for those who make them. This approach takes into account regularities in how choices become available or remote to those with criminal inclinations or to those who might, by choice or happenstance, contribute to the informal social control of criminal behavior. The focus here is upon exploitative crimes in which a victim is clearly distinguished from an offender.

---

* Marcus Felson's chapter is an ingenious attempt to link two currently influential theories in criminology: his own routine activity theory, which explains the supply of criminal opportunities but takes the supply of offenders as given, and Travis Hirschi's control theory, which does precisely the opposite. Felson's key linking concepts are those of the "handled offender," the individual susceptible to informal social control by virtue of his or her (perhaps idiosyncratic) bonds to society, and the "intimate handler," someone with sufficient knowledge of the potential offender to grasp the "handle" and exert control. The routine activities of everyday life set the scene for the web of interaction between these people and between the crime target and any guardians. Felson's chapter also attempts to link these two themes with a rational choice perspective, arguing that, together, routine activity theory and control theory provide the context within which choices are made. This aspect of his synthesis would seem to need further elaboration; at first glance it seems to us to neglect some of the social, psychological, and perhaps even constitutional influences on decision making. Nevertheless the chapter as a whole represents an important pioneering effort to provide a synthesis of theories.

This chapter takes certain human inclinations as given. It is assumed that some people are inclined to break laws, that others are inclined to protect their own person and property, that others are inclined to keep their children out of trouble. These inclinations may vary, but that variation is not the topic of concern here. Rather, this chapter considers how the structure of social life makes it easy or difficult for people to carry out these inclinations.

The hallmark of this analysis is that, although people may have lots of desires and inclinations, they cannot always carry them out. The opportunity structure of society places a limit on human ability to act, including acting on inclinations to commit crimes, to avoid victimization, or to control one's offspring. Moreover, changes in community life can indeed produce more crime without requiring any change in motivations of the population of likely offenders.

Economists might call this a supply question, but most economic theory is based on markets, where supply is allocated to demand via price. I want to buy nails, you want to sell them, and the price is influenced by supply and demand.

Exploitative crime is fundamentally different. If bashing heads is your business, I do not want you to bash mine. We have no meeting of the minds in this matter, and hence no market. If you catch me, it is not by my choice but rather my misfortune. Your mother probably disapproves of your behavior, as well. To attack other people or their property, you usually need to gain direct physical access to them. You have to find or stumble upon them, or they may stumble upon you. This suggests a fundamental principle for understanding the rational order of exploitative crime: The criminal event is a systematic result of the convergence of people and things over space and time. It has a rational order in the sense that we can study it systematically, like the movements of electrons or the responsiveness of price to supply and demand. This does not mean, however, that every party to the event chooses or prefers it or knows the facts leading up to it. It is a convergence without a concurrence, a product of uncoordinated, asymmetric choices.

Indeed, each event requires that one party fail to get what it wants. If a crime occurs, the victim failed to get what he or she wanted. If a crime does not occur, the potential victim succeeded but not the offender. The rational order of how many of the one and how many of the other occur goes beyond the preferences of one actor. Moreover, its dependence upon the physical structure of social phenomena—where people are when and what they are doing—renders crime analysis a special case of the ecology of daily life. Routine activity patterns provide choices to individuals, including criminals, and set the stage for subsequent events determining the success of the offender in carrying out the crime, or of the potential victim in avoiding victimization, however unwittingly (see Felson 1983). This boils down to a simple theory of crime production: Changes in the daily life of the community alter the amount of criminal opportunity in society, hence altering crime rates.

This chapter considers the rational structure of crime from the viewpoint of the analyst, not of the offender. The rational crime theory must explain not only the offender's successes but also the offender's failures, as well as the successes and failures of the potential victim.

Let us assume that criminals think and forget, plan and blunder, work and idle, choose and stumble, reason and react, all with some order and predictability. Let us assume also that most victims think or fail to think about their risks, are informed or misinformed, move about or stay put according to certain regularities. Furthermore, let us consider that parents interact predictably with their children, informally controlling them or failing to do so. Finally, let us assume that daily life systematically brings together or disperses offender and victim, parent and child, person and property, and so on.

The basic elements of crime and its control as suggested in this chapter include something old, something borrowed, and something new. To repeat (Cohen and Felson 1979a), a criminal act has three minimal elements: a likely offender, a suitable target, and the absence of capable guardians against crime. The capable guardian is seldom a policeman, more likely a housewife, brother, friend, or passerby. These three elements must converge in time and space for a direct-contact, predatory violation to occur.

Now, let us borrow from Travis Hirschi (1969) the fundamentals of control theory. Hirschi's four elements in the informal social control of delinquency are commitments, attachments, involvements, and beliefs. He reviews these in another chapter of this volume, but I am going to summarize them with one word: handle. Society gains a handle on individuals to prevent rule breaking by forming the social bond. People have something to lose if others dislike their behavior, if their future is impaired, if their friends and families are upset with them, if they are occupied with conventional activities, or if their beliefs can be situationally invoked to make them feel bad every time they break a rule.

The handle is a necessary condition for informal social control to occur. Lacking commitment to the future, attachments to others, or conventional involvements and beliefs in the rules, an individual has no handle that can be grasped, and informal social control is impossible. The social bond is the handle. This chapter does not consider how handles are affixed as people grow up. Just assume that almost everyone has a handle, and consider how others may grasp that handle to impose informal social control.

In some cases, handles may be sufficiently graspable that they work without names. An older stranger scolds a child, who walks away shamed, informal sanctions having succeeded anonymously. A young adolescent is humiliated by being told that he will never amount to anything, and he does not stop to think that the humiliator does not know his name, address, or parents.

In time, children learn to go in groups, cheering one another up after scoldings by adults and inoculating one another against future scoldings. On reaching this stage, anonymous scolding loses its force, and handles cannot be grasped by just anyone.

Some youths scoff at parents and the future, but most seem to have specific handles, even if they are not readily controlled by sheer respect for adults in general. If Fred wants to hide his misbehavior from anybody at all, if he pursues any long-term goal, or if his mind contains any belief by which he can be shamed, then a handle remains. Such handles are personal and specific. To grasp the handle you have to know it. Information about Fred's actions last Friday may reach somebody who knows Fred's handle and can grasp it. This information makes Fred subject to informal social control, and its absence makes Fred immune from such control. Effective informal social control over Fred is possible, using his strong social bonds. Yet this potential informal control may be difficult to put into practice. This difficulty stems from poor channels of communication and interaction that prevent existing handles from being grasped by persons who might know how to keep Fred in line.

Combining the old and the borrowed, here is something slightly new. Figure 14.1 presents the "web of informal control" as it applies to exploitative offenses. Four minimal elements are considered: (1) a handled offender, that is, someone who can both offend and be handled; (2) an intimate handler, that is, someone close enough to grasp the handle; (3) a suitable target of crime; and (4) a capable guardian against such a violation. (In the special case where a potential offender is unhandled—that is, lacking in commitments, attachments, involvements, and beliefs—the intimate handler does not exist. In this case, the four minimal elements are reduced to three: offender, target, and guardian.)

To assess the importance of the four elements and the web linking them, let us start with the situation of tightest informal social control and work toward the situation in which such control is most lax. Informal control is tightest when all four elements are in direct physical contact and when relevant people know one another very well. Imagine a duplex with a boy and

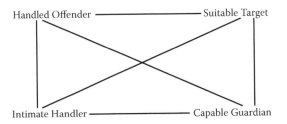

Figure 14.1 The web of informal crime control.

his mother living on the left and a nice television set and its owner living on the right. The boy has some criminal inclination and is tempted by the TV set, but he is close to his mother, who would never allow him to steal it. She is also a significant mother in crime-control terms because she is at home, knows the neighbor, and recognizes the neighbor's TV set. (She may even function partly in the role of guardian for the neighbor's TV, but we will neglect this point to keep the discussion tidy.) In such a situation, theft is highly unlikely. Even if mother is out and her son can easily monitor the guardian next door, he may be reluctant to risk mom's return at an inopportune moment. Household items and scents may also serve to remind him of his social bonds and to discourage him from committing delinquent acts.

It is likely that this youth will look for or stumble upon criminal opportunities further from home, where he can escape his mother's watchful eye as well as reminders of her bond. However, if he goes a block away, he is endangered by an important intermediary omitted from Figure 14.1: the informant. Someone who knows him and his mother might tell her she saw him over there after dark. Someone who recognizes the television set might ask what he is doing with it. Someone else may function as a guardian.

A tight community—where people know people, property, and their linkages—offers little opportunity for common exploitative crime. The Israeli kibbutz, where crime rates are low because there is not much to steal and nowhere to go with it, is a case in point (David Bordua, personal communications 1973, 1982). The dispersion of kinship and friendship over a wider metropolitan space and the automobilization of the population make more difficult the kind of informal control discussed earlier.

Nonetheless, carrying out an ordinary violation requires that minimal conditions be met, even in a modern metropolis. The handled offender must not have the intimate handler near and must get to a target with the guardian away. As daily activity patterns disperse people away from family and household situations (Felson and Gottfredson 1984; Cohen and Felson 1979a), it is more likely that criminogenic conditions will apply. Not only will offenders find targets with guardians absent, but they will be able to get away from their handlers and be fairly sure that their handlers will not recognize the loot or compare notes with the guardians. It is not that urbanites lack friends or family ties, or that they are unhandled, but merely that their handlers are scattered and segregated from the suitable targets and capable guardians. Informants are less and less likely to link the handler to the evidence that Fred has been bad.

Even if Fred is apprehended in a theft situation, the guardian will not be able to invoke informal control easily, not knowing Fred's name or his family. The choices available are to invoke the law of the jungle or the criminal justice system, but not informal social control. It does not take Fred long to learn that "I'll call your mama" is an empty threat from a total stranger, who probably will not notice his lawbreaking anyway.

Some technological and genetic factors assist informal control. Telephones may allow informants to call around quickly and try to find out who the freckle-faced boy belongs to and which one is missing from school at the moment. Adults can compare notes and solve the puzzle. Genetic inheritance of appearance makes it so that, without knowing your name, I might be able to ask, "Is that red-haired kid one of the Johnson boys? He was hanging around when your TV was taken. Maybe I'll have a talk with his dad." The modern, multinucleated family, with stepparents and half-brothers, makes this genetic branding less dependable and reduces the clear link between the intimate handler and the handled delinquent.

The single-parent household gives the community only one parent to know and hence reduces the potential linkages that can be evoked for informal social control. Lower fertility has the same effect. In large families, there is a greater chance I will know one of the brothers and have a good guess that this is the O'Reilly kid. In smaller families, this is less likely, and knowing the particular Smith becomes necessary. High geographic mobility rates make it harder to maintain recognition of one family versus another and to piece together the relationships needed for evoking informal social control. The automobile makes it simpler for youths to evade the risk that this will happen in the first place.

In the event that informants do figure out who an offender is and talk to his or her parents, if they are complete strangers there is greater likelihood that the parents will dismiss the stranger's accusation rather than blame their own flesh and blood. In a tight community, however, where one parent knows another, they may accept the unpleasant truth that their freckled, angel-faced boy broke the law, and then impose informal social control.

Application of technology to personal appearance further clouds responsibilities for informal social control. If the Jones family all have curly, red hair and light complexions, identifying Jones Jr.'s transgressions is simpler. If each Jones selects a different wave and tint, informal social control is complicated. Adolescent adornment patterns may impair informal social control without the need of a subculture simply by impeding identification. Increases in within-family variance and decreases in between-family variance in appearance may be a long-term social trend detracting from informal social control. Similarly, mass production of goods makes them difficult to identify with a particular owner.

That conventional activities serve to control delinquency was well explained by Hirschi (1969). In his treatment of the issue, involvements in conventional activities can reduce delinquency by keeping youths occupied. Other possibilities can also be imagined. Conventional activities might reduce delinquency if they occur near handlers or their informants, or if they produce new handlers. Also, involvement in desirable activities provides handlers with something they can withdraw as a punishment for delinquency, and hence with an extra handle. When conventional activities have a routine time, place, and list of participants, informants have some facts to check if delinquency is suspected at nearby times and places or if someone is suspiciously absent from conventional activities. The location and timing of conventional activities can be important, for these can be proximate or distant from criminal opportunities. Conventional activities can tie down potential delinquents, but they can also hamstring potential handlers and guardians. Sometimes they bring offender and target together, assemble accomplices, or facilitate transgressions at proximate times and places, after the adults have gone home (see M.W. Klein 1971). Clearly, conventional involvements are a mixed bag. Indeed, Cohen and Felson (1979a) argued that increases in certain conventional activities fostered rising crime rates.

None of this discussion hinges on normlessness or changing standards. Indeed, crime can increase even when social bonds persist, parents care deeply, and offender motivation stands pat. All one needs for a crime wave is a decline in the ability of handlers to handle or guardians to guard. What varies is the pattern of daily life and the structure of households, work, school, and transport, as these make it more or less possible for conventional parents to carry out their inclinations and keep their kids out of trouble. Indeed, criminal opportunity can increase greatly if the changing physical structure of communities obstructs the watchful eye of parents (see Felson and Gottfredson 1984). When people choose to drive a car, to let their children drive the family car or have their own, to live several miles from work and relatives, to have smaller families, to divorce and remarry, to send their children away to college, to purchase lightweight durable goods, to enjoy alcoholic beverages, or to go out at night, these choices set the stage for criminal events. The latter occur as the result of combinations of choices by different actors, moving about but not consulting one another. They are happenstances resulting from prior decisions. Highly predictable on an actuarial basis, with systematic consequences for crime rates, they yet occur without a meeting of the minds. Handled offenders, intimate handlers, capable guardians, and victims converge and diverge without consultation.

Let me add one more triplet of simple concepts: space, time, and relationships. Here we have some basics of human ecology and social control. People and things stay put and move over space and time and are tied into relationships while doing so. Things belong to people who belong to each other, but these ties are not always reinforced by proximity. When those so tied move together, guardianship and handling are simple. When they diverge, guardianship and handling are impaired. One might envision daily life as an ebb and flow of routine activities, setting the stage for informal social control to succeed much of the time, but not always.

Social change alters the stage, alters the probability that a handled offender and a suitable target will converge without handler or guardian near. The technology of the automobile disperses people over space and time, away from their property, guardians, and handlers. The organization of daily life in the modern metropolis assembles or disperses people for work, school, shopping, and leisure in a fashion that invites crime. Modern metropolitan life disperses people away from family and household settings, drawing strangers together, assembling adolescents without parents or other adults who know them, and otherwise putting informal social control at a disadvantage. The rational order of modern metropolitan life is one in which likely offenders have a greater supply of choices and less room for blunder and are more likely to get what they want, whereas potential victims are less likely to get what they want with regard to evading crime. Moreover, freedom and prosperity, enticing people with social life or stereo components, systematically expose them to the risk of victimization.

Human choice enters at many steps in this process. The choice to move to a new neighborhood is as important as the choice to steal a car. The decision to buy a new car is, in the most basic sense, criminogenic. The decision to buy your son a car may be even more criminogenic. The decision to select a residence on a cul-de-sac or to move to the countryside may be criminocclusive. Different stages of choice affecting the genesis or occlusion of criminal opportunity have been considered by different scholars. Cusson (1983) considers strategic analysis from the offender's viewpoint, taking into account not only property gain but also power and excitement. Brantingham and Brantingham (1984) cataloged the spatial, temporal, and activity features of criminal choice. Rengert and Wasilchik (1980) explored geographic impingements on offender awareness and choice. Hindelang, Gottfredson, and Garafolo (1978) showed that decisions about lifestyles greatly influence risk of victimization. Mayhew et al. (1976) demonstrated that public system planning has consequences for crime rates. Each of these studies have added an important piece to the puzzle, demonstrating that the rational structure of crime rates has more to it than an all-seeing, all-knowing offender. Indeed, the criminally inclined population, too, is subject to the irreducible and stubborn facts of the larger environment.

Criminal decision analysis must therefore consider many choices made by many actors at many stages in social and economic life, nor can these decisions be considered in isolation from the physical world. The convergences and divergences of people and things needed for normal crime to occur and the possibility that decisions will go sour make rational analysis of crime more complex. Let me specify another triplet: decisions, situations, and outcomes. To understand criminal opportunity, we need to know not only some of the decisions made by offenders, human targets, guardians, and handlers, but also the situations of their physical convergence as a result of these decisions, regardless of whether the decision makers know what we, as analysts, know. And we have to know the outcome. Was the offender wrong, missing a golden opportunity or committing a silly blunder? Did the getaway car stall or did the selected target trap him? Did the victim succeed by going through the day safe from crime, regardless of whether he or she thought about it? What choices on the part of a citizen produce an unplanned victimization and impair or assist guardianship of targets and handling of offenders? Indeed, a criminal situation is made possible by various decisions by those who set the stage for the convergence of the four minimal elements, however inadvertently. Any set of decisions that assembles a handled offender and a suitable target, in the absence of a capable guardian and intimate handler, will tend to be criminogenic. Conversely, any decision that prevents this convergence will impair criminal acts. Even though an offender may prefer to violate the law, his or her preference can be thwarted by the structure of decisions made by others, regardless of whether they know they are preventing a crime from occurring. In short, we cannot understand the rational structure of criminal behavior by considering the reasoning of only one actor in the system.

These ideas lead to practical advice for the crime researcher and theorist: Count television sets, monitor their portability, check their location. Examine travel patterns away from home; numbers of persons moving about with family, friends, or strangers; adolescent activities with peers and parents; automobilization of youth; shopping patterns, parking patterns, and so forth. Check household composition, housing types, and patterns of occupancy of buildings and of ties among occupants. Examine when crime fails and when it succeeds, as well as its control. Look at hourly patterns of activity and where people are on the map. Check parental position vis-à-vis their own children and patterns of recognition among neighbors. Like physics and physiology, criminogenesis derives from a movement of physically bounded and identifiable entities about the physical world—movements that can be tracked according to map, clock, and calendar, and that from time to time assemble or disperse the four minimal elements in the web of informal crime control.

A good start can be made by studying just three populations of entities: adolescents, parents, and television sets. Find out the size, location, movements, and convergence of these three populations of entities and you will go a long way in understanding crime rates and their variance over space and time.

Although any event may surprise, the larger population of events is systematized by daily life: the volume of people and goods, their location, and their movements over space and time (see Felson 1980).To understand the rational order of crime, one must study the volume and composition of people and property, their relationships, and their movements according to map, clock, and calendar.

Understanding Crime Displacement
An Application of Rational Choice Theory (1987)

15

D.B. CORNISH

R.V.G. CLARKE

From Cornish, D.B., and Clarke, R.V.G. (1987). Understanding crime displacement: An application of rational choice theory. *Criminology*, 25, 933–947.

Contents

15.1 Abstract	351
15.2 Introduction	351
15.3 A Rational Choice Perspective on Crime Displacement	352
15.4 The Concept of Choice-Structuring Properties	353
15.5 Choice-Structuring Properties of Crimes	357
15.6 Choice-Structuring Properties and Offender Perceptions	360
15.7 Rational Choice Theory and Crime-Control Policy	363

15.1 Abstract

It has been claimed that the rational choice perspective, which sees criminal behavior as the outcome of decisions and choices made by the offender, can provide a useful framework for analyzing crime control policies. By developing the concept of "choice-structuring properties," which refers to the constellation of opportunities, costs, and benefits attaching to particular kinds of crime, this paper attempts to develop rational choice theory in order to improve analysis of crime displacement—a concept frequently invoked by the critics of opportunity-reducing measures of crime prevention.

15.2 Introduction

The model of the offender as a decision maker underlies much criminological work recently undertaken by psychologists, economists, and sociologists of deviance (Clarke and Cornish 1985; Cornish and Clarke 1986a). This "rational choice" perspective on crime assumes that offenders seek to benefit themselves by their criminal behavior; that this involves the making of decisions and choices, however rudimentary on occasions these choices might be; and that these processes, constrained as they are by time, the offender's cognitive abilities, and by the availability of relevant information, exhibit limited rather than normative rationality. Our own formulation of rational choice theory was founded on the additional premise that the decision processes and the factors taken into account are likely to vary greatly at the different stages of decision making and among different crimes. For this reason, we drew attention to the needs both to be crime-specific when analyzing criminal choices and to treat decisions relating to the various stages of criminal involvement in particular crimes (initial involvement, continuation, desistance) separately from those, such as target selection, relating to the criminal event itself (Clarke and Cornish 1985; Cornish and Clarke 1986a).

15.3 A Rational Choice Perspective on Crime Displacement

Our intention in developing an emphasis upon criminal decision making was to provide a general framework for thinking about the prevention and deterrence of crime, but our particular interest in rational choice theory arose out of work on "situational" crime prevention—a range of preventive measures, including defensible space architecture, target-hardening, and neighborhood watch, designed to reduce the opportunities for, and increase the risks of, committing specific kinds of crime (Clarke 1983). Despite evidence of its utility, critics have seized upon one apparent weakness of the approach: that preventive measures that increase the difficulties of a particular crime will merely result in criminal activity being "displaced"—for example, to other targets, times, places, or types of crime (Reppetto 1976; Gabor 1981). Crucial to this objection is the belief that, to the offender, many if not most crimes are functionally equivalent—a view that derives from the traditional hydraulic view of offending as the product of enduring criminal drives or dispositions (Cornish and Clarke 1986b).

Crucial to the viability of situational approaches, on the other hand, is the contrasting view that displacement is far from inevitable and occurs only under particular conditions. Rational choice theory assumes that offenders respond selectively to characteristics of particular offenses—in particular, to their opportunities, costs, and benefits—in deciding whether or not to displace their attentions elsewhere. Indeed, since the existence of criminal dispositions is questioned, so too is the corresponding notion of criminal "energies" which have to be displaced into alternative actions. If frustrated from committing a particular crime, the offender is not compelled to seek out another crime nor even a noncriminal solution. He may simply desist from any further action at all, rationalizing his loss of income (for example) in various ways: "It was good while it lasted"; "I would have ended up getting caught"; and so on. Such an analysis is consistent with the available empirical research, which is indicative of the contingent nature of displacement. For example, the fitting of steering column locks to *all* cars in West Germany in 1960 brought about a 60 percent reduction in car thefts, whereas their introduction only to new cars in Great Britain displaced theft to the older, unprotected vehicles (Mayhew et al. 1976). Again, while a variety of security measures dramatically reduced airliner hijackings in the early 1970s (Wilkinson 1977), a police "crackdown" on subway robberies in New York City displaced robberies to the street (Chaiken, Lawless, and Stevenson 1974).

Research of this kind, however, which merely analyzes crime patterns, is likely to yield only limited information about displacement. This is because, just as reductions in target crimes brought about by situational measures may be modest and difficult to detect, especially when crime as a whole is rising, so, too, evidence of displacement may lie concealed within the same overall crime statistics. Moreover, such research on its own fails to provide an adequate explanation for the occurrence or absence of displacement, although reasons may sometimes be inferred. Given these problems, additional ways of investigating displacement are needed and, in particular, studies which focus upon the offender's own explanations for his decisions and choices.

15.4 The Concept of Choice-Structuring Properties

A more promising approach to the study of displacement is suggested by rational choice theory's emphasis upon the need to adopt a crime-specific focus when attempting to explain or prevent criminal behavior. Rather than assuming that potential offenders are fueled by a general disposition to offend which makes them relatively indifferent to the nature of the offense they commit, the rational choice perspective asserts that specific crimes are chosen and committed for specific reasons. Decisions to offend, in other words, are influenced by the characteristics of both offenses and offenders, and are the product of interactions between the two. Thus, the final decision to become involved in a particular crime is the outcome of an appraisal process which (however cursory) evaluates the relative merits of a range of potential courses of action, comprising all those thought likely in the offender's view to achieve his or her current objective (for example, for money, sex, or excitement).

It follows that an understanding of the factors which the offender takes into account when performing this rudimentary cost-benefit analysis is necessary. These factors relate both to offense and offender characteristics but, for the present, can be usefully viewed as those properties of offenses (such as type and amount of payoff, perceived risk, skills needed, and so on) which are perceived by the offender as being especially salient to his or her goals, motives, experience, abilities, expertise, and preferences. Such properties provide a basis for selecting among alternative courses of action and, hence, effectively structure the offender's choice. The characteristics of offenses which render them differentially attractive to particular individuals or subgroups (or to the same individuals and groups at different times) have therefore been termed choice-structuring properties. It follows that the readiness with which the offender will be prepared to substitute one offense for another will depend upon the extent to which alternative offenses share characteristics which the offender considers salient to his or her goals and abilities. A recognition of the contingent, crime-specific nature of criminal decision making therefore has important implications for an understanding of displacement.

In the absence of information from offenders, some a priori selection of properties thought likely to be salient to offender decision making has to be made. For illustrative purposes, this is attempted later in the paper in relation to two broad groups of offenses—those of theft involving cash and of illegal substance abuse (Table 15.1). The concept of choice-structuring properties was first employed, however, in the attempt to clarify policy issues relating to gambling and suicide (Cornish and Clarke 1989).

In the case of gambling (and following the work of Weinstein and Deitch 1974), choice-structuring properties such as number and location of gambling outlets, frequency of events on which bets can be made, time elapsing before payment of winnings, range of odds and stakes, degree of personal involvement, skills needed or perceived, and "nerve" required, were employed to identify forms of gambling more or less designed to encourage high degrees of involvement and to attract the participation of particularly susceptible individuals (Cornish 1978). In Britain, the widespread provision of "betting shops" in prime urban locations enables off-course gambling to take place throughout the afternoon. These premises offer a vast range of simple and complex betting strategies, a feeling of personal involvement and challenge fostered by the exercise of handicapping skills, and an atmosphere of "action" encouraged by the rapidity of events and payouts, presence of other gamblers laying bets and collecting winnings, and the use of live television commentary from the course—a combination of properties which provides an environment designed to encourage continuous gambling. The contrast with the choice-structuring properties of lotteries is significant: lotteries are held relatively infrequently, involve lengthy periods between staking and payout, offer the minimum of personal involvement, little scope for social interaction or the exercise of skill (real or perceived), a limited range of odds and bets, and very long odds against winning. The prime attraction to their adherents, therefore, is the possibility they offer of a big "windfall" for very little initial outlay. "Numbers," on the other hand, while ostensibly rather similar to the

Table 15.1   Choice-Structuring Properties of Two Offense Groupings

Theft Involving Cash

Availability (numbers of targets; accessibility)

Awareness of method (e.g., pickpocketing vs. insurance fraud)

Likely cash yield per crime

Expertise needed

Planning necessary (pickpocketing vs. bank robbery)

Resources required (transport; equipment)

Solo vs. associates required

Time required to commit

Cool nerves required (bank robbery vs. computer fraud)

Risks of apprehension

Severity of punishment

Physical danger

Instrumental violence required

Confrontation with victim (mugging vs. burglary)

Identifiable victim

Social cachet (safecracking vs. mugging)

"Fencing" necessary

Moral evaluation

Illegal Substance Abuse

Availability (glue from hardware stores vs. prescription drug)

Awareness (special knowledge of doctors or pharmacists)

Social cachet (cocaine vs. heroin)

Solitary vs. social

Knowledge/skills required to administer (heroin vs. marijuana)

Technical equipment required (heroin)

Dangerousness of substance (crack vs. marijuana)

Primary method of administration (injecting vs. smoking)

Different forms substance can take

Nature of psychological effects

Number, type, and severity of side effects

Dependency

Length/intensity of "high" per dose

Financial costs

Legal penalties

Detectability

Interference with everyday tasks

Moral evaluation

lottery, offers a wider variety of staking levels and odds, a larger number of events and swifter turnaround, greater perceived scope for the invocation of personal luck, and more social interaction—features which go some way to explaining why attempts to promote lotteries as legal alternatives to the numbers racket have proved unsuccessful (L. Kaplan and Maher 1970).

It is in examples like these, where activities are examined in some detail, that the value of choice-structuring properties in clarifying the unique constellations of motives, opportunities, rewards, and costs offered by different forms of gambling becomes evident. Attention to these parameters also suggests a means of controlling participation in potentially dangerous forms of gambling through regulation of these properties. Indeed, this strategy appears to guide the efforts of regulatory bodies and legislators when monitoring and controlling certain forms of gambling such as betting and gaming, and those of promoters when trying to increase rates of participation and encourage escalation of involvement into more profitable forms. Manipulation of the choice-structuring properties of bingo, for example, in order to shorten the duration of individual games, the development of "linked bingo" to enable larger prizes to be offered, and the introduction, as "interval games," of gaming machines—whose choice-structuring properties, especially when deliberately manipulated by casino promotors (Hess and Diller 1969), tend to encourage continuous gambling—all provide graphic examples of these strategies (Cornish 1978).

In the case of suicide, properties of the various methods such as the degree of prior planning necessary, the courage required, likely pain, distastefulness of method, extent of disfigurement, time taken to die when conscious, scope for second thoughts, and chances of intervention, were used to explain why, when deprived of more acceptable methods, people do not always turn to other means of killing themselves. Domestic gas, for example, used to have particular advantages as a method of suicide: it was painless, very widely available, required little preparation, was highly lethal (death could take place in less than half an hour), was not bloody, and did not disfigure. These features help to explain how the detoxification of domestic gas—a method that had formerly accounted for over 50 percent of all suicides (Kreitman 1976; Kreitman and Platt 1984; Clarke and Mayhew 1988)—brought about a 35 percent decline in the national rate of suicide in Britain during the 1960s. Some population subgroups such as the elderly and the less mobile may have found these advantages particularly compelling; there is evidence, for example, that suicidal women are more attracted by self-poisoning and more repulsed by violent and bloody methods (Marks 1977). Since the needs and circumstances of particular subgroups may make certain methods uniquely attractive, then, it seems likely that reducing opportunities to use particular methods need not simply result in displacement to others, but can bring about genuine gains in the prevention of suicide deaths. Thus, an apparently obvious alternative to gassing, such as overdosing, which might appear to offer many of the same advantages, may nevertheless be subject to disadvantages which limit its viability as a substitute; for example, access to the most lethal drugs may require the cooperation of a doctor, or long-term planning and the faking of relevant symptoms, in order to build up sufficient quantities, while the range of more accessible nonprescription drugs may be either less lethal or, in the case of other alternatives such as domestic poisons, more painful to ingest (Clarke and Mayhew 1988).

15.5 Choice-Structuring Properties of Crimes

Identifying an activity's unique blend of choice-structuring properties emphasizes its distinctive features and this, in turn, facilitates the making of comparisons between different activities. But, because crimes are such a heterogeneous group of behaviors, it is not immediately clear on what basis to group crimes for comparison. One possible criterion is suggested by the aim of the exercise, which is to enable the conditions under which displacement is more or less likely to occur to be specified. Since few would expect displacement across behaviors engaged in for widely differing purposes, the goals of offending could provide the primary criterion for selecting the crimes to be compared. Thus, crimes whose main purpose appears to be to obtain money might be analyzed together, while those whose goal is sexual outlet would need to be separately analyzed. Some a priori determination—later refined by empirical research—of the purposes being served by particular offenses will therefore need to be made before they are grouped together in order to analyze their choice-structuring properties. Although it may be the case that many crimes serve a mixture of goals, one of these will usually be dominant. This will provide the appropriate criterion for analysis, the remaining subsidiary purposes taking on the role of further choice-structuring properties for the particular offenses being compared.

For the sake of simplicity, it has so far been assumed that the individual chooses only from among criminal alternatives when seeking to achieve his goals. Given the wide range of noncriminal alternatives also available to the offender, however, confining comparisons of choice-structuring properties to those among *criminal* means alone may seem unduly restrictive. A crime such as drunken driving, for example, whose purpose is very specific and temporary (that is, the need to get home after drinking) and in relation to which alternative crimes are few or none, illustrates the point that for some crimes most, if not all, of the alternative means being compared will be noncriminal. In addition, displacement will usually be directed in such cases to legal behaviors: more likely alternatives to drunken driving may be to call a cab, use public transportation, or walk, rather than to persuade an equally drunk companion to drive the car instead. Notwithstanding this example, it seems intuitively more likely that criminal behavior will usually be contemplated only after legitimate means have been foreclosed or rejected. Drunken driving, it could be argued, is a special case since one of the effects of alcohol may be to short-circuit this usual sequence. Under these circumstances, the capacity of the otherwise law-abiding citizen to consider the long-range consequences of his actions may be temporarily impaired, and this may lead him to entertain criminal actions much sooner (Campbell and Gibbs 1986: 126, 177). If criminal means are usually only considered at a later stage, this may suggest that they do in fact have something in common with each other and that these features provide some justification for limiting comparisons to crimes alone. But, while this meets the above objections, it also opens the door again to the very dispositional explanations of offending that the rational choice perspective was designed to challenge, since it suggests explanations in terms of offender characteristics, such as the tendency to select means which offer immediate gratification of needs, regardless of the consequences for others. Consequently, the preference at this stage is to defend confining comparison to crimes alone, not because criminal behavior is inherently different from other behaviors, but on pragmatic grounds alone: it is the possibility of displacement to other crimes which constitutes the major problem for crime control policy.

Before embarking on a more detailed discussion of their application to the problem of crime displacement, it may be useful to provide hypothetical lists of the choice-structuring properties of two quite different offense groupings: those designed to yield cash (for example, burglary, theft with or without contact, shoplifting, mugging, bank robbery, fraud, tax evasion, and auto theft); and those concerned with the ingestion of illegal substances (such as marijuana, opiates, LSD, cocaine, "crack," amphetamines, barbiturates, and volatile substances).

As can be seen from Table 15.1, while specifying the dominant purpose and confining comparisons to criminal means takes one some way toward the goal of drawing up lists of choice-structuring properties, the resulting groupings of offenses will usually be rather broad. While it may be tempting to try for somewhat narrower arrays of offenses, such as those sharing a common modus operandi, this may be unhelpful when estimating the likelihood of displacement since it may result in the omission of important choice-structuring properties. In turn, their omission may make it difficult to explain, for example, why burglars who prey on distant affluent suburbs would never consider breaking into apartments in their neighborhood; why the shoplifter might be reluctant to contemplate mugging; or why the computer fraudster might give up crime entirely if it became too difficult to continue his frauds. In the course of his investigation of robbers' decision making, for example, Feeney (1986) notes the surprising fact that many of them thought burglary too unpredictable and risky.

Similar considerations apply to offenses of illegal substance abuse. An analysis of their choice-structuring properties indicates that different substances provide different experiences, and this—together with considerations of availability, cost, risk, expertise required, and social context of usage suggests that displacement and escalation among substances may be more limited than is usually thought. Information from opiate abusers, for example, suggests that a desire to join a specific drug culture of users may be an important determinant of initial involvement (Bennett 1986); an alternative culture such as that represented by teenage glue sniffing may be seen to offer rather different, and less attractive, experiences in terms of social cachet, excitement, and alternative lifestyle. In addition, the specific psychological effects of the drugs themselves may restrict substitutability: today's energetic, acquisitive "yuppie" cocaine user may typically be of similar social background to the 1960s cannabis-using hippie, but the effects of cocaine may be more in tune with modern lifestyles and aspirations than those produced by cannabis.

Choice-structuring properties may also highlight similarities between apparently different behaviors. For example, crimes such as burglary in a public housing project, in a middle-class suburb, or in a wealthy enclave may, *for some offenders,* have fewer attractive properties in common than apparently different offenses, such as burglary or mugging, committed in their own neighborhoods. While the latter offenses may involve different skills or risks, these may be counterbalanced by the advantages of offending within familiar territory. For these reasons, again, the most appropriate level of analysis for choice-structuring properties would seem to be at the most general level consistent with the likelihood of displacement.

Since the lists in Table 15.1 derive from a rational choice perspective on offending, they both concentrate upon the opportunities, costs, and benefits of the various alternatives being compared. Though no particular attempt has been made to reconcile differences between the two lists, some categories of choice-structuring properties (especially the more generally applicable ones such as "availability") are common to both, while others inevitably reflect unique features of each offense grouping. The properties listed are not necessarily those taken into account by the offender, who may not be fully aware either of the range of properties involved or of the part they play in his decisions. Rather, the properties listed have been selected on a priori grounds as being of most relevance to the task of comparing offenses and, hence, of establishing the likely limits of displacement within each offense grouping. Thus, there is likely to be more displacement between particular theft offenses where they share similar profiles of choice-structuring properties—for example, where the likely cash yield per crime is comparable, where similar skills and resources are required, and where the physical risks are the same. In contrast, where the profiles differ, this may clarify why displacement is unlikely to occur. Lastly, some choice-structuring properties may have a more pivotal role to play in decisions concerning displacement. It is generally accepted, for example, that some offenders will not contemplate crimes that involve the use of violence.

Little is known at present about offender decision making, and because of this the above lists may need modifying in the light of empirical research. But even at this stage such lists should provide a useful tool for those involved in crime prevention. By directing attention to those features of crimes that make them attractive to particular groups of offenders, such an approach will make it easier for policy makers to anticipate the direction and amount of any displacement to other forms of crime. In the past, for example, uncritical and often hidden assumptions that illegal substances are equivalent in their attractiveness and effects may have had damaging effects upon policy formation through their tendency to encourage preoccupation with the inevitability of displacement and escalation. Careful attention to choice-structuring properties of different activities, however, will enable the accuracy of assessments to be improved about the likely costs and benefits of undertaking new crime prevention initiatives in relation to specific forms of crimes. The lists will also alert policy makers to action that needs to be taken in order to forestall criminal displacement or even to facilitate displacement to noncriminal alternatives. Finally, lists of choice-structuring properties should assist in the evaluation of crime prevention initiatives by helping to orient the search for displacement.

15.6 Choice-Structuring Properties and Offender Perceptions

The choice-structuring properties in Table 15.1 attempt to provide a comprehensive list of the salient ways in which crimes with similar goals differ from each other. Although policy makers require such comprehensive information in order to think constructively about displacement, it should not be assumed that offenders will utilize the data in a similar way. As mentioned above, they may lack information about the full range of offenses that could satisfy their goals, they may be unaware of the extent to which available opportunities have structured their choices, they may be ignorant of all the costs and benefits of the different offenses, and they may assign particular importance to certain choice-structuring properties (such as eschewing the use of violence, or restricting selection of victims to those of particular socioeconomic or ethnic groups), which then come to exert a disproportionate influence upon involvement and displacement decisions. Moreover, in practice, offenders may not always take account of the full range of properties. For example, the choice-structuring properties listed in Table 15.1 are mainly relevant to an individual's initial decision whether or not to get involved in a particular crime. They may have rather less application to more immediate decisions relating to the commission of a particular offense (or what may be termed the criminal "event"), although a similar comparison process—albeit using a different and more restricted range of properties— undoubtedly takes place when potential targets or victims are being compared. The present lists would become more salient again when, having committed the offense, the offender had to decide whether to continue with a particular form of crime or to desist. Last, as a result of the experience of committing the offense in question, further choice-structuring properties may become apparent to the offender and existing ones may assume a different value. Thus, the degree of steady nerves required may only become apparent once a mugging has been attempted.

As well as exemplifying one of the major premises of the rational choice perspective—that the offender's decision-making processes will tend to display limited rather than normative rationality—the above points also illustrate the dynamic nature of criminal decision making. Thus far it might well appear that a rather passive role has been assigned to choice-structuring properties in that it has been implied that offenders' needs lead them to search out suitable criminal opportunities in their environments. But, as the term implies, choice-structuring properties may often play a more active role in generating offending. Some of the opportunities may offer a constellation of properties sufficiently attractive to provide a temptation to crime, as is often argued to be the case with petty offenses such as shoplifting. These points underline the threefold distinction made by Maguire (1980) and by Bennett and Wright (1984c) among offenders who seize, search for, or create opportunities. It is also clear that, as well as specifying features of behaviors (kinds of gambling, methods of suicide, types of crime), choice-structuring properties implicitly specify salient characteristics of the actor, such as his or her needs, preferences, personal characteristics, and perceptions. In other words, the term "choice-structuring property" is a relational concept designed to provide an analytic tool for increasing an understanding of the interaction between person variables and arrays of behaviors—in the case of crime, to specify more closely offenders as well as the offenses they commit. Thus, where crime displacement occurs, a knowledge of the choice-structuring properties which the offenses share may permit more accurate identification of the subgroups of offenders involved; and this may well prove a more fruitful way of investigating the interface between offense and offender—and, in particular, issues relating to specialization and generalization (Cornish and Clarke 1989)—than the more static and rigid offender typologies of traditional criminology.

Greater knowledge about all these matters would undoubtedly improve policy makers' ability to predict the likelihood and direction of displacement. But, as well as requiring more information about the way offenders perceive and utilize the choice-structuring properties of crimes, more needs to be known about the criminal opportunity structure within which the offender operates if a complete picture of the determinants of displacement is to be given (Cook 1986b). First, at a macro level, more ecological research is required in order to explore the changes in opportunities and, hence, in crime rates, brought about by changes in routine activities, lifestyles, and commercial practices. As has been indicated above, the detoxification of domestic gas in Britain brought about a substantial decline in the national suicide rate during the 1960s. In the same way, participation in gambling rises whenever new facilities are created (Cornish 1978). In relation to crime, Wilkins (1964) showed how rises in the rates of auto theft in Britain parallel the increased rates of new car registrations, and Cohen and Felson (1979a) showed how increases in burglary in the United States reflected the rise in "stealable" property and in numbers of women working outside the home. More recently, Tremblay's (1986) research on credit card bank frauds has indicated how the introduction of new commercial marketing strategies may also sometimes have unforeseen consequences. Thus, a move by certain Canadian banks to extend facilities for check cashing to nonregular customers able to guarantee the transaction by means of a credit card, offered existing credit card thieves a novel and lucrative way of preying directly upon the banking system itself instead of upon retailers alone.

The processes through which these changes in opportunities at the macro level take place also require elucidation. The escalation in deaths from car exhaust fumes in Britain from the beginning of the 1970s, for example, suggests that learning may have an important role to play in determining changes in suicide rates over time, as people gradually come to identify a novel and attractive method of suicide (Clarke and Lester 1987). At the micro level, Tremblay's work provides some hints about the circumstances under which, for one particular form of crime, such diffusion of innovation might come about. Previous experience in committing similar forms of crime may sensitize offenders to new variations on their favorite themes; membership of criminal knowledge networks may speed up the diffusion of information among specialists, while the media may spread such information more widely among the noncriminal population. The more dramatic the event—such as hijacking, bank robbery, rape, murder, or suicide—the more vivid, detailed, and widespread the coverage, and the more often, at the time of the event and subsequently at committal and trial, the details are repeated. Under these circumstances, the likelihood of "copycat" offenses may be further enhanced.

15.7 Rational Choice Theory and Crime-Control Policy

The rational choice perspective was originally developed to provide policy makers with a useful framework to guide thinking about crime prevention and control. In line with this objective, the present paper has attempted to develop certain aspects of the theory in the interests of answering critics of situational crime prevention who have implicitly assumed that the outcome of such efforts is simply (and, seemingly, inevitably) to displace offending. A similar analysis, making use of the concept of choice-structuring properties, has also been attempted elsewhere to clarify aspects of the long-standing debate over whether offenders are generalists or specialists (Cornish and Clarke 1989). Rational choice approaches have also proved useful in suggesting reasons for the limited effectiveness of rehabilitative efforts (Cornish 1987) in emphasizing the need of deterrent policies to pay greater attention to offenders' perceptions of opportunities, risks, costs, and benefits (Bennett and Wright 1984), and in identifying potentially adverse side effects of policies such as selective incapacitation (Cook 1986a).

More generally, a rational choice perspective on offending can suggest, if not explanations, lines of enquiry to account for stability and change in criminal behavior. The importance of this for directing crime prevention policy and practice should not be underestimated. Taking Tremblay's study as an example once again, it is instructive to note that, even under the most apparently favorable of circumstances, displacement was by no means inevitable: only 10 percent of Tremblay's "checkmen" actually switched their attentions to credit card bank frauds. Before dismissing this discrepancy as a crude exemplification of Zipf's (1949) principle of least effort, it should be recognized that this low take-up may well have resulted from the logistics of the situation—the limited period for which this particular "window of vulnerability" was left open by the banks and the fact that, even as knowledge grew about this novel form of crime, so were the risks and effort involved in its commission rapidly escalating. Critics of situational crime prevention might well take pause for thought from this example. For, whatever the value of longer-term social prevention strategies that attack the "root" causes of crime, the constant innovation in criminal methods in response to the changing criminal opportunity structure demands similar vigilance and continued investment of time and effort on the part of those engaged in crime control. It is hoped that the rational choice perspective can offer some assistance in this enterprise.

Environment, Routine, and Situation
Toward a Pattern Theory of Crime (1993)

16

P.L. BRANTINGHAM
P.J BRANTINGHAM

From Brantingham, P.L., and Brantingham, P.J. (1993). Environment, routine and situation: Toward a pattern theory of crime. *Advances in Criminological Theory*, 5, 259–294.

Contents

16.1 Introduction	365
16.2 Pattern Theory	371
16.2.1 Event Process	373
16.2.2 Template/Activity Backcloth	374
16.2.3 Readiness/Willingness	379
16.3 Application of Pattern Theory	382
16.3.1 Pilfering of Office Supplies	383
16.3.2 Household Burglary	384
16.3.3 Serial Rape	387
16.4 Conclusions	388

16.1 Introduction

As a discipline, criminology tries to understand and explain crime and criminal behavior. This poses fascinating and long-standing questions: Why do some people commit crimes while others do not? Why are some people frequently victimized while others suffer only rarely? Why do some places experience a lot of crime while other places experience almost none? The answers to these questions seem, to us, to reside in understanding the patterns formed by the rich complexities of criminal events. Each criminal event is an opportune cross-product of law, offender motivation, and target characteristic arrayed on an environmental backcloth at a particular point in space-time. Each element in the criminal event has some historical trajectory shaped by past experience and future intention, by the routine activities and rhythms of life, and by the constraints of the environment.* Patterns within these complexities, considered over many criminal events, should point us toward understandings of crime as a whole.

Unfortunately, despite the inherent complexity in criminal events, most attempts at explanation have been restricted to simple, unicausal models of criminality, for example, Bentham's (1789) hedonistic psychology, Lombroso's (1911) biological predisposition, Sutherland's (1937a) learned attitudes, Lemert's (1951) secondary deviation, Cloward and Ohlin's (1960) blocked social opportunity, and Taylor, Walton, and Young's (1973) capitalist socioeconomic structure. Such classic criminological theories have been far too limited, focusing primarily on conceptually constrained origins of the desire or willingness to commit crimes rather than on the complex patterns in crimes. The primary weakness in most criminological theory is a tendency to equate criminality with crime when criminality is but one of the elements contributing to a criminal event. This confusion has frequently been compounded by an insistence that a theory of criminality must lie completely within the domain of a single academic discipline. Thus for instance, although Sutherland (1937a), Taylor, Walton, and Young (1973), and Gottfredson and Hirschi (1990) might have agreed about little else, they all insisted that the explanation of criminality must be fundamentally sociological. Moreover, occasional attempts to construct multidisciplinary explanations of criminality have seemed to attract large volumes of criticism from all directions (e.g., Wolfgang and Ferracuti 1967; Wilson and Herrnstein 1985; Jeffery 1990).

Since the early 1970s, an alternative theoretical movement has focused on criminal events. Aimed explicitly at development of conceptual frameworks for explaining crimes and criminal behavior that cross disciplinary boundaries, this theoretical movement has accepted the need to explain crimes as etiologically complex patterns of behavior. The movement has assumed that crimes can be no more easily explained than headaches or backaches. Such classes of events will never be attributable to any single cause or understood through any single explanation. Understandable, interpretable patterns of events may, however, be derived from a diversity of causes. Many different types of spine and muscle difficulties can produce back pain for people who must lift heavy objects. But even perfectly healthy backs can be injured and produce prodigious quantities of pain if improper lifting techniques are used. Many different socioeconomic situations and psychological conditions can result in particular persons engaging in shoplifting, but no single factor will explain all, or even most, shoplifting. No single, simple model explains

---

* The term environment used in this article includes all that surrounds: the sociocultural environment, the economic and legal environment, and the institutional and physical structure of the area. The environment may be considered and analyzed at a micro-, meso-, or macrolevel, or at all levels simultaneously.

either back pain or crime. But patterns in events can point toward different etiologies or clusters or etiologies under different conditions.

The set of ideas encompassed by this alternative theoretical movement have developed under a variety of names: rational choice theory (Clarke and Cornish 1985; Cornish and Clarke 1986a; Carter and Hill 1979; Walsh 1978; Brantingham and Brantingham 1978); routine activities theory (Felson 1987; Cohen and Felson 1979a; Sherman, Gartin, and Buerger 1989); environmental criminology (Brantingham and Brantingham 1991, 1984, 1981c; Herbert and Hyde 1985; Cromwell, Olson and Avary 1991); strategic analysis (Cusson 1983); or lifestyle theory (Hindelang, Gottfredson, and Garofalo 1978). Research, application, and expansion of these theoretical ideas appear under such names as crime prevention through environmental design (Jeffery 1971); situational crime prevention (Clarke 1980); hot spot analysis (Block 1990; Illinois Criminal Justice Information Authority 1989); or opportunity theory (Barlow 1990; Carroll and Weaver 1986). These new theoretical research and practical approaches to the study of crime vary in content and specific focus, they do have several things in common:

- Criminal events are best viewed as the end points in a decision process or sequence of decision steps. This decision process may not always involve conscious and explicit sequential decision making, but does result, in almost all cases, in rationally predictable actions. For example, cars seem to "drive themselves to work" many mornings, but the route "they" follow and the decisions "they" make on the way are the product of conscious decisions that have been made in the past in establishing the pathways routinely used for trips to work. On such mornings, of course, people are really driving without needing to pay much conscious attention to routine decisions. Sometimes, of course, the driving process is fully conscious because the trip is not routine: an accident changes traffic flows, the driver has a meeting at a client's office he or she has not visited before, and so forth. The decisions that take an offender to a particular criminal event may similarly be conscious or subconscious or some mixture, but they are neither random nor unpredictable and they are reconstructable (Clarke and Cornish 1985; Cusson 1983; Brantingham and Brantingham 1978; Walsh 1978; Willmer 1970).*
- The decision process leading to the commission of any particular crime begins with someone who is in a state of readiness for crime (Clarke and Cornish 1985), that is, someone who has sufficient current criminal motivation and knowledge both to perceive and act upon

---

* While focus tends to fall on the offender, similar decision processes are assumed to lead the victim or the target, witnesses, and intervenors to the criminal event as well.

some available criminal opportunity when it is discovered within known activity areas and associated awareness spaces (Brantingham and Brantingham 1984, 1981c). Opportunities may be discovered either in the course of ordinary noncriminal activities or through a specific search for criminal targets. Someone who is ready to commit a bank robbery may see a "good" bank serendipitously while eating lunch with a friend (Letkemann 1973) or may find one after careful search and surveillance (Gabor et al. 1987: 57–60). Burglars tend to look for targets within familiar areas, starting from a few key activity nodes such as home, a work site, a favorite pub, or a shopping center where they spend a good deal of time (Brantingham and Brantingham 1981c; M. Maguire 1982; Rengert and Wasilchick 1985; Cromwell, Olson, and Avary 1991).

- Particular criminal motivation levels or states of readiness to commit crime come from diverse, but quite understandable, sources. Motivation or readiness may be seen as tied to goals. These goals involve a desire for action or a search for thrills or self-defined fun, or a wish to acquire some object or make a profit, or an inclination toward aggression or highly emotional behavior in defense or in vengeance, or a wish to dominate (Cusson 1983; D.J. West 1982).

- Whether a general state of readiness is reflected in criminal acts depends in part on psychological, social, and cultural background states of the individual, the economic environment, a history of past activities, and, to a large extent, the opportunities available.* For example, a group of teenagers' desire for "action" may involve a noisy walk down a business street after closing hours when no one is around or it may involve a confrontation with awakened residents of a street in a suburban neighborhood. The confrontation may lead to the teenagers' departure or to more noise or it may result in the teenagers vandalizing fences or stealing bicycles to "get even."

- The number and sequence of decision points in the process that leads to a criminal event vary with the type and quality of crime (Brantingham and Brantingham 1978). Traditional divisions of crimes into violent and property categories are insufficient to address these variations. Some violent crimes, such as serial rape, may involve long decision sequences, while others such as bar assaults may involve very short decision sequences. Some property crimes, such as antique burglary (M. Maguire 1982: 90–121) or store robbery (Gabor et al. 1987: 59) may involve long decision sequences, but oth-

---

* The critical character of location, setting, situation, and opportunity to delinquency patterns was identified more than 75 years ago by Ernest W. Burgess (1916).

ers, such as teenage burglary, shoplifting, or vandalism may involve very short decision sequences.

- Criminal readiness levels are not constant in any individual but vary over time and place given both the individual's background behavior and site-specific situations. For example, burglary is sometimes the product of changes in mood and perception brought on by drugs or alcohol, but is sometimes undertaken to get money with which to buy drugs (Cromwell, Olson, and Avary 1991; Chaiken and Chaiken 1990; Rengert and Wasilchick 1985; M. Maguire 1982). Readiness clearly is also related to age (Brantingham 1991; Gottfredson and Hirschi 1990). Criminal activity, in the aggregate, is dominated by the young.
- Neither motivated offenders nor opportunities for crime are uniformly distributed in space and time. Specific types of crime tend to be closely tied to the locations of targets and the regular travel patterns of potential offenders. The locations of targets and of potential offenders usually vary with the time of the day, the characteristics of specific targets, and the site and situation surrounding the targets. Shoplifting is obviously tied to hours the stores are open and places where stores are located. Spousal (or partner) assault is usually an evening or weekend crime occurring at home or in a bar. Car thefts are tied to the locations of unguarded cars, and follow a rhythm associated with commuting patterns during the week and with leisure activities on weekends. Routine activities develop the framework of opportunities for crime (Felson 1987; Cohen and Felson 1979a).

Target suitability is tied both to the characteristics of the target and to the characteristics of the target's surroundings. The declining weight of portable television sets over the course of the 1950s and 1960s serves as a good predictor of increasing theft over time (Felson and Cohen 1981). Portable computers may be attractive objects but they are not suitable targets for theft when they are in use.* The same object found unsuitable as a target at one time of day may become a suitable target at a different time of day, when it is not in use, and no one is around. Cars may have been attractive targets early in the century, when they were rare and extremely valuable, and when registration procedures were primitive and uncertain; they became less suitable during the mid-century period when they became commonplace and when registration procedures became more rigorous (Gould 1969; but see Mayhew

---

* While research has not yet been done, we have heard anecdotal information from schools and recreation centers that theft of personal computers has soared as they have started to buy fully portable machines. Even clumsy multicomponent personal computers were being stolen at a high rate before the switch to portables.

1990). A convenience store may be a good robbery target when only a single clerk is present, but may be an unsuitable target when customers or multiple clerks are present (Hunter and Jeffery 1992; Duffala 1976).

The identification of what makes a good or suitable target is itself a multistaged decision process contained within some general environment. The process may involve just a few stages or many. This process, first described in 1978 (Brantingham and Brantingham 1978; Walsh 1978) and well supported by subsequent research (e.g. Walsh 1986; Cromwell, Olson, and Avary 1991), involves several levels tied to actual perception and learning about the surrounding environment.

Individuals develop "images" of what surrounds them. Not all environmental details are recognized in these images; some stand out. The image that is formed depends on the underlying characteristics of the surrounds, but also on what a person is doing. A person engaged in the process of committing a crime will be looking for details, conditions, a "feeling" of correctness that are related to that specific form of crime.

These images, representing a process-based perception of objects within a complex environment, are frequently called *templates*[*] (Brantingham and Brantingham 1978). A template is an aggregate holistic image that is not always easily analyzed or understood by fragmenting it into discrete parts (Brantingham and Brantingham 1978; Macdonald and Gifford 1989; Cromwell, Olson, and Avary 1991). It is generally formed by developing an array of cues, cue sequences, and cue clusters that identify what should be considered a "good" target in specific sites and situations.[†]

Templates vary by specific crimes, offenders, and the general context for the crime. What makes a "good" target and crime situation for a robber in central Houston is different from what makes up a "good" target and crime situation for a first-time shoplifter in a suburban mall, yet the templates are understandable. For some they involve evaluating risk and benefits; for others, excitement; for others, showing "importance." Yet there is enough similarity in how people engage in crime, how they perceive or grow to have a cognitive

---

[*] The terms prototype and place schemata are also sometimes used in the literature.
[†] Templates are not just created to identify "good" targets or "good" sites or situations for crimes. Individuals develop templates for identifying where they want to eat, to live, to shop. General functioning within the infinitely complex cue-emitting environment involves the development of cognitive images and cognitive maps and the use of these images. See Gärling and Golledge (1989) for a general review of theory and research in cognitive images and their use. See Garling et al. (1986) and Genereux, Ward, and Russell (1983) for basic location, orientation, and movement models that are highly relevant to crime pattern analysis.

image of an environment, that general templates can be "constructed" to help explain specific crime patterns.*

Overall, this newer approach to criminology sees crimes as complex, but even assuming high degrees of complexity, finds discernible patterns both for crimes and for criminals at both detailed and general levels of analysis. *Pattern* is a term used to describe recognizable interconnectiveness of objects, processes, or ideas. This interconnectiveness may be physical or conceptual, but recognizing the interconnectiveness involves the cognitive process of "seeing" similarity, of discerning prototypes or exemplars of interconnections within cases distorted by local conditions (Churchland 1989). A pattern is sometimes obvious, but sometimes is discernible only through an initial insight, particularly an insight that is embedded within the environment as a whole.† Crimes are patterned; decisions to commit crimes are patterned; and the process of committing a crime is patterned. These patterns are nontrivial, though opaque, when crime is being explained by some unicausal model, but become clear when crimes are viewed as etiologically complex and as occurring within and as a result of a complex surrounding environment.

16.2 Pattern Theory

The complementary work being done in this new movement fits together into what could be called pattern theory. Crimes do not occur randomly or uniformly in time or space or society. Crimes do not occur randomly or uniformly across neighborhoods, or social groups, or during an individual's daily activities, or during an individual's lifetime. In fact, arguing a uniformity seems indefensible. Why would 5 percent or 40 percent of all Europeans or females or teenage males or residents of Chicago commit a robbery or a theft or an assault every day at 4:00 p.m. or every week on Friday? Neither is an argument for the complete randomness of behavior plausible. Bar fights do occur with greater frequency on Friday nights than on Tuesday afternoons; shoplifting does occur during a restricted set of hours in the day; income tax evasions do cluster around payment due dates; some neighborhoods do have a lot more crime than others. Yet while

---

* Unfortunately, many research techniques used in studying what forms the template takes must, of necessity, identify one or two characteristics and only study those. In some situations, a crime is straightforward enough that one or two characteristics of targets dominate the template and are accessible through straightforward research. In other situations, the crime itself may be complex, involving many nonrecursive or holistic decisions beyond the capacity of most currently used statistical techniques to address.
† The environment forms patterns. Ultimately understanding crime, or any behavior, involves understanding patterns within patterns.

we accept nonuniformity and the nonrandomness of crime, most theoretical approaches to crime define concepts that point toward uniformity and assume randomness for the impact of all concepts not included in the theory. They fail to provide concepts or models that can be used to account for the patterned nonuniformity and nonrandomness that characterizes real criminal events.

The limitations of most criminological theories come from many sources. We want conceptually limited models. All sciences, social or natural, want understandable theories. In the natural sciences, such as physics or chemistry, theories are developed within a well-defined, closed intellectual environment.[*] The social sciences cannot exist in a closed or limited environment. The concepts in social sciences may never be conceived or viewed, except as a game, without considering how they interact with a highly variable, never static environmental backcloth, that is, an ever-changing set of sociocultural, economic, legal, structural, and physical surroundings that include, among other things, the activities of individuals, of groups, and of organizations. No firm boundary can be placed around particular elements within a theory that can separate them from the backcloth.[†]

Elements of the backcloth are interconnected and never static. Change is a constant condition of the backcloth, but the types of changes, degrees of change, and rates of change among the elements vary. Change is sometimes slow and minimal; sometimes rapid, massive, and dramatic. For example, the general backcloth for theft in Chicago in 1910 and 1990 might not be considered very different if we were to consider only the street network, but when changes in the character of goods (Felson and Cohen 1981), in the composition of the work force (Cohen and Felson 1979a), and in the modes of travel are considered, it is clear why Chic Conwell's description of the good places and situations in which to pick pockets (Sutherland 1937b) no longer holds.

A theory of crime must be flexible, able to explain criminal events against diverse variations in the backcloth. To be of much value, a theory must make it possible to recognize and understand both individual and aggregate patterns of behavior at many levels of resolution. Recognizing patterns, however, is not easy when criminologists focus on fixed theoretical concepts that cannot vary as the backcloth varies. An explanation of how criminal behavior changes as the backcloth varies will produce clear patterns, but such an explanation requires a focus on process, that is, on change itself. Crime is an

---

[*] This is not to say that the concepts in the natural sciences are simple, only that, at a theoretical level the ideas can be developed with fixed initial conditions. The applied sciences may be seen as undertaking the integration of the basic ideas with actual, varying conditions.

[†] Praxis and theory are not separable in criminology.

event that is best viewed as an action that occurs within a situation at a site on a nonstatic backcloth. Crime is the product of varying initial conditions under which the decision processes leading to criminal events unfold. The likelihood of a criminal even transpiring depends on the backcloth, the site, the situation, an individual's criminal readiness, routine activity patterns, and the distribution of targets. None of these elements can, independently, be expected to explain criminal events. They must be considered cojointly with special emphasis on how they shape choices.

Crime is an event that occurs when an individual with some criminal readiness level encounters a suitable target in a situation sufficient to activate that readiness potential. This essentially simple model becomes remarkably complex in real applications because all of its elements are variables. Readiness to commit a crime is not constant: it varies from person to person and it varies for each individual person across time and space as the backcloth varies. It also varies as the awareness of opportunities to commit a crime varies. Targets are not constant. The types of objects and the categories of people that constitute good targets vary in time and space as the backcloth changes. The distributions of targets vary in time and space. The situation required to activate criminal behavior also varies with the backcloth and the distribution of targets and the level of a given individual's readiness to commit a crime. Motivation influences the commission of crimes; the characteristics of targets and decisions about the quality of a given opportunity to commit a crime influence motivation.

To understand more about criminal behavior and crimes, it is perhaps useful to consider (1) the actual process of committing a crime, (2) the general crime templates and activities of offenders at the moment of crime commission, (3) offenders' readiness or willingness to commit a crime, and (4) the interaction of process, template, activity, and readiness as they are arrayed on the environmental backcloth.

16.2.1 Event Process

Figure 16.1 shows a simplified view of the process followed in the commission of a crime by an individual. A person is engaging in some behavior. An event occurs that "triggers" the desire or willingness to commit a crime. The person, depending on the type of criminal behavior, may see a situation and site making the crime possible (immediately) or may engage in search behavior to find a good site and situation (or "place") for the crime. A person could be drinking with friends and someone comes by saying there is a chance to break into the electronics store down the block. This chance may trigger the person into going along to the store and, assuming no problems are encountered, breaking into the store. Or a man could be drinking with friends when someone he does not like walks by and accidentally spills beer

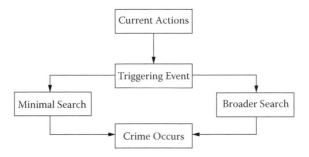

Figure 16.1 Process.

on him. The spilled beer could trigger an angry exchange—vicious words or gestures—leading to a fight.*

The process shown in Figure 16.1 may be broken down into many steps and considered in detail. The detailed process for shoplifting (Walsh 1978) is different from the detailed process for robbery (Gabor et al. 1987; Feeney 1986). The process for shoplifting in a market (Poyner 1983; Poyner and Webb 1992) is different from the process for shoplifting in a department store (Carroll and Weaver 1986). The process for street robbery is different from the process for store robbery or bank robbery (Gabor et al. 1987; Feeney and Weir 1973; Clarke, Field, and McGrath 1991; Ekblom 1992). Yet, there are common elements in the processes involved in all of these crimes, common elements that produce discernible patterns for each type of crime: decisions or choices occur in the process of committing all crimes. Choices are made and actions follow the choices. The process of decision making and the resulting patterns of decisions must be understood as a prelude to understanding crime (Clarke and Cornish 1985, Cornish and Clarke 1986a; Cusson and Pinsonneault 1986).

16.2.2 Template/Activity Backcloth

While forming patterns in the foreground, the event process rests on a general backcloth† formed by routine activities (including repeat or routine criminal activities) and on a template that helps identify what a "great" chance is or what a "good" opportunity would be or how to search for chances and

---

* This sounds banally simple, but legislation has been adopted to address just such triggering events in bars. In British Columbia, for example, people in bars and pubs may not walk around carrying a drink. Bar fights are common and were seen by the Provincial Legislative Assembly to be often caused by just such spilled drinks. To drink, you must be seated.

† Backcloth is a term used for the variable, ever-changing context that surrounds the daily lives of individuals. While the backcloth changes, it is comprehensible and it forms patterns.

opportunities. Almost everyone develops activity routines, a set of repetitive processes that organize most of life's actions. People who commit crimes spend most of their time engaged in noncriminal behavior. These activity routines form a patterned backcloth on which criminal events are played out and against which crime may be studied. As with all patterned behavior, routine activities can be viewed at many levels of analysis or aggregation. At a microlevel, descriptions would involve a minute by minute log of activities and actions. At a mesolevel descriptions would involve the general timing and sequencing of activities in broad categories such as sleep hours, travel time, work hours. Macro-descriptions might look at annual or seasonal patterns of behavior.

Individual patterns at any level of analysis may be aggregated into group patterns spanning many individuals. The aggregate pattern may be viewed temporally or spatially or both. As an extreme example, there are points in any city that are always congested at rush hour, others that are empty during work hours. Both individuals and aggregates display routine activity patterns (see Chapin 1974; Cohen and Felson 1979a; Rengert and Wasilchick 1985; Felson 1987). At all levels of aggregation, actual current activities describing what is happening in a particular instance can be compared to routine activity patterns. Ordinarily, current actions are very strongly related to recent routine activity patterns. Past actions and activities do help "drive" current actions, just as a car might "drive itself" to work or to the supermarket, but unusual events can shape current actions or alter routine activity patterns for a short time.

Routine activities shape an activity space (both in time and in physical space) and, from that activity space, people develop an awareness space (Brantingham and Brantingham 1984). The awareness space is limited, both physically and temporally. Residents do not know their entire city or town. Workers know only a limited space around their workplace. This awareness space is formed by past activities and shapes the time and location of future activities. Routine activity space places people in situations, both physically and temporally, where crime triggering events are more or less likely to occur. If a criminal event is triggered, the awareness space shapes the search area in which targets or victims are sought. For example, routine activities define target search patterns by burglars (Brantingham and Brantingham 1975; Carter and Hill 1979; M. Maguire 1982; Rengert and Wasilchick 1985; Cromwell, Olson, and Avary 1991) and high activity bars identify centers of violence (Bullock 1955; Engstad 1975; Brantingham and Brantingham 1981c; Roncek and Pravatiner 1989; Roncek and Maier 1991).

Routine activities of potential offenders generally define both the areas where and the times when they are likely to commit a crime. The routine activities of potential victims also shape the patterns of crimes (Fattah 1991; Kennedy and Forde 1990; Lasley 1989; Maume 1989). For example, the routine activities in residential areas (many homes are empty during the workday) and of residents (regularly away from home during the workday) and the routine commercial display activities of department stores create the base pattern of opportunities from which potential property offenders who know about the area select sites and targets.* The routine activity and awareness spaces of repeat offenders change as a result of their prior crimes. They also change as modes and means of transit change. Suburbanization, mass transit, and new highways alter movement patterns, routine activities, and awareness spaces. Residents' knowledge of areas grows. Exploration in known areas may increase as knowledge grows. At the opposite extreme, burglars from "out of town" rarely seem to pick targets far from the main roads traversing a community (M. Maguire 1982; Fink 1969). Their local awareness space is limited.†

Target selection also depends on mental templates used to shape searches for targets or victims and to predefine the characteristics of a suitable target or suitable place for finding targets. The templates, that is, the sets of cues, cue sequences, or holistic cue clusters used to find and identify suitable targets, vary by crime, by site and situation, and by the offender and his or her reason for the crime. For example, Eck and Spelman (1992) identify the differences in the templates used by a group of white offenders and a group of black offenders who are both stealing from cars parked in the same massive parking lot. Similarly, but using a much more formal procedure for understanding template construction, Macdonald and Gifford (1989) identify cues used by adult and juvenile burglars. They find support for the idea that offenders construct and use holistic templates in identifying suitable targets, but also find that holistic judgment is related to specific crimes and situations in very understandable ways.

Figure 16.2 shows the relationship between the crime process and the backcloth formed by past activity. Routine activities, activity space, awareness space, and crime template may vary by individual, but probably form aggregate patterns for different categories of people and specific types of crimes. While these patterns do vary, they are frequently structured by age, sex, income, home location, friends' locations, work or school locations, the locations of places such as shops, bars, or restaurants that attract visitors, and the sociogeographic and physical structure of an area such as bus routes or highways.

Understanding crime patterns requires an understanding of these activity patterns. For example, the routine activities of juveniles form the base for higher volume crimes. Juveniles frequently hang out around a 24-hour convenience store or a fast-food restaurant. The store becomes a node in

---

* See Clarke (1992) for a broad range of examples.
† While not developed for crime analysis, Gärling et al. (1986) have developed a model of factors influencing spatial navigation consistent with the results of Fink's (1969) analysis and the "edge effect" in target choice (Brantingham and Brantingham 1975; 1978).

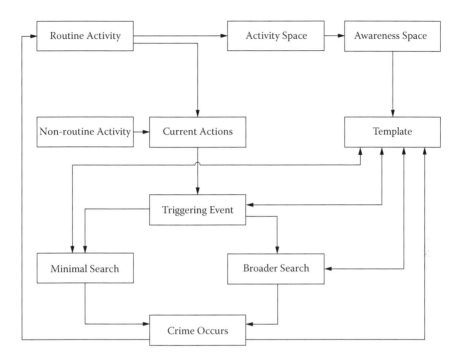

Figure 16.2 Process and activities.

their routines and thereby becomes a node in their activity and awareness spaces. Casual, adventitious exploration around the convenience store makes surrounding streets and buildings a better known part of their awareness spaces. Vandalism, thefts from cars, common theft, and burglary are all likely to be higher in these awareness spaces. If it happens that the hangout location is not surrounded by "good" targets, then juvenile goals of excitement will probably be expressed in other ways—noise, on-site vandalism, fighting—rather than through property crime. As another example, search patterns and associated awareness spaces and templates vary with experience. First offenders begin within a normal awareness space generated by noncriminal behavior (Brantingham and Brantingham 1984). Little Sidney Blotzman's career as a juvenile delinquent started with a theft of fruit from the corner store and expanded to shoplifting in the big department stores in the Loop as he and his friends gained more mobility by riding public transit (Shaw and Moore 1931). This implies that first offenders have imperfect templates and are at greater risk of error in picking targets and situations than are more experienced offenders. This also implies that beginners run greater risks of getting caught than experienced offenders, a possibility hinted at in the Cambridge cohort study (D.J. West 1982: 23).

Generally, individuals create templates used to identify "good" or "bad" or questionable targets. Felson (1987) uses the term suitable target to describe targets identified as "good." Whether the offender is a shoplifter or a serial rapist, the potential target or victim and the site and situation surrounding help define what is considered "suitable." As Felson's work makes clear, the presence of a guardian for the target can be a critical situational variable. A shoplifter will not ordinarily try to steal something when a clerk or security guard is standing next to it. A serial rapist does not normally commit the rapes in public. Robbers do commit their robberies in public, but usually do not try to rob armed police officers. The presence of a guardian is not always dispositive, however. A fighting drunk may well try to hit a police officer who intervenes in an effort to break up a fight.

Different crimes occur in different behavior settings (Barker 1968) and unfold in different patterns of actions. What is suitable for one crime or crime site or situation is not necessarily suitable for another. Patterned behavior sets appear that define the usual or expected or "normal" actions associated with particular types of crimes and also define abnormal or unexpected actions for that type of crime in that behavior setting. Of course, behaviors that would be abnormal for one offense type would not necessarily be abnormal for another. Overall, it appears that identification of target suitability, that is, judgment of conformance with a template, is a gestalt-like process (Brantingham and Brantingham 1978; Macdonald and Gifford 1989; Cromwell, Olson, and Avary 1991) that is not dependent on some limited number of fixed characteristics, but rather on an overall decision or sequence of decisions at a summary level. Viewed from the opposite direction, however, individual characteristics of the potential target site or situation may make some specific crimes unattractive. Consider Felson's concept of guardianship. A person sitting in a car may make that car and the cars surrounding it safe from theft; but the absence of someone in the car may not be enough to make an otherwise unappealing target criminally attractive. It might, like a rusted-out Yugo, be a generally undesirable make or model, even to car thieves.

Templates, awareness spaces, and routine activities are all interrelated and influence crime patterns and victimization (Cusson 1989). This is not a unidirectional influence. For first offenders, routine activities and general views may form a crime template that limits possible targets. Crime becomes a routine activity for repeat offenders who reinforce and change their initial crime templates, that is, build more stable images of target search and target selection processes. The changes in the process are shown with the directional arrows in Figure 16.2. The large number of directional arrows represents the process of decision making when a crime is committed by an individual whether for the first time or the nth time. The feedback loops may have less importance for the analysis of aggregate crime patterns, but they are very important for understanding what happens during the commission of the initial crimes by both those who will be repeat offenders and those who will be "scared" off crime by the experience.

Process decisions, site and situation factors, the routine behavior of both the offenders and the potential victims, and availability of targets all help form the patterns of criminal events. There are triggers that actually touch off individual criminal events. These triggers and the consequences of criminal acts are sometimes, though not always, predictable but can be understood retrospectively. This lack of predictability comes in part from nonroutine, unusual, or extraordinary events. Nonroutine events, as noted in Figure 16.2, may influence actions and, consequently, affect crime. At the extreme, natural disasters such as hurricanes, earthquakes or floods, or administrative disasters such as police strikes or electric power blackouts may open areas to looting. Large crowds at special events such as soccer matches, rock concerts, movie openings, and civic festivals may push people from boisterousness into riot.* In most of these situations, the nonroutine event has no long-lasting impact, but has a strong influence on criminal behavior in the short run.

16.2.3 Readiness/Willingness

A particular criminal event depends on an individual being triggered. The triggers are generated or experienced during an activity, an action process. The triggers occur in a nonstatic, though mostly routine, situation. They are shaped by the surrounding environment, past experience, and the crime template. Generally, the commission of a crime is a decision process occurring within a limited activity environment and associated with bounded knowledge of the broader surroundings, but a process that is understandable when explored with event and environmental detail.

The criminal event is not independent of the existence of individuals with a readiness or willingness to commit a crime. As described earlier, much traditional criminology has been devoted to finding some unicausal source of motivation. All research and all well-reasoned arguments point, in our view, toward a complex etiology of the sort depicted in Figure 16.3. The origin of the complex etiology seems clear when criminal events are explored within the pattern theory described in this article. There is no single force or single goal behind all crime. Individuals seem clearly tied to a multiplicity of identifiable goals. Cusson (1983) defines a taxonomy for goals of criminal behavior: action, appropriation, aggression, and domination.† For example, some may be bored

---

* When the problems at events become regular, they are no longer nonroutine and become predictable. With the predictability comes the possibility of reducing or eliminating the problems (Clarke 1992: 14; see Bell and Burke 1992, for cruising).

† Cusson's Why Delinquency? constructs a well-supported taxonomy of the goals of delinquent behavior. Delinquency research has repeatedly found reasonable, understandable goals behind behavior that help explain the variety of crimes that occur. He also provides a firm basis for identifying the logical and empirically identified flaws in most unicausal theories of criminality.

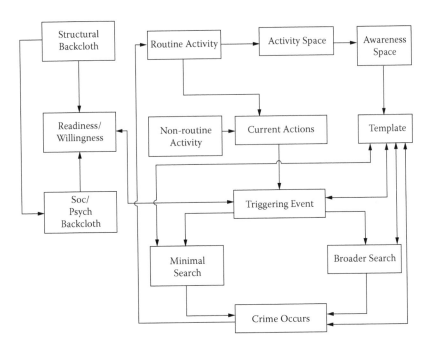

Figure 16.3 Process, activities, and motivation.

and want excitement; others may be after a specific object; still others may want vengeance or want to gain prestige with their peers. Some may have multiple goals or have their goals change over time. In particular, the action/thrill goal making burglary attractive to young teenagers may change to the goal of appropriating money as the teenager gets older. The act, burglary, stays the same, but the purpose for it changes. The goal is tied or linked to a readiness or willingness to commit a crime (or readiness or willingness to engage in other behavior that satisfies the goal). The link depends on the routine activities of individuals, the range of potential triggering events and their template of what represents a good target to satisfy their goal. Goals are also tied to the social/psychological and situational backcloth in and upon which a person lives.

It is the interactive nature of the link that is of primary importance. A goal of possession of an object, such as a portable computer, or for a particular type of action/excitement, like theft of a car, is tied to the availability of the object (computer or car) and its accessibility (seen as a suitable target).* The transformation

---

* Research into various types of service delivery find that actual usage of a service is tied to three factors: the availability of the service, its accessibility within reasonable limits of effort, and a willingness on the part of the prospective clients to use the service. All three are necessary elements in service utilization. See Brantingham and Brantingham (1984) for a discussion of legal aid utilization. This body of research may prove useful in understanding the way that the elements of a criminal event must come together in the presence of a trigger for the event to actually occur.

of goals into readiness and willingness is tied to routine activities that help identify availability within someone's awareness space and the development of a template that identifies suitable targets. Readiness and willingness associated with goals do have varying levels. Action/excitement may mean a desire for a short thrill; it may mean a desire for a long-lasting thrill. The readiness to steal is also tied to readiness to take risks of being caught. The risks people will accept vary, but probably not in an inexplicable pattern.

Crime type variation in readiness. The level of readiness or willingness necessary to commit a crime varies by type of crime. Stated another way, for certain types of offenses, such as petty thefts, it does not take much readiness for a situation to present a triggering event. For other types of crime, such as a residential break-in or a convenience store robbery, the state of readiness must be much higher before a criminal event can be triggered. Readiness for many crimes may be tied to actual risk. Some risk may lead to excitement; too much risk may lead to deterrent fear.

Feedback effects. Willingness or readiness to commit a crime is unlikely to be independent of the site and situation of a potential crime or of past criminal events or of the triggering event. A person might steal cash off a table in a restaurant if it was a substantial amount and no one was around the empty table. A juvenile might be afraid and reluctant on his* first burglary, but be more comfortable the second time around, when his template identifying good targets has been better defined. A burglar might be forced into contact with the owner of a store he has entered and make a better haul as a result. Robbery might start to look easier. A serial rapist might encounter resistance and use excessive force for the first time. Excessive force might become part of the rape pattern thereafter (Hazelwood, Reboussin, and Warren 1989). That is, the relationship between readiness and site and situation are mutually nonrecursive over time, with site and situation experiences feeding back into readiness as amplification or suppression loops, and reinforced or suppressed readiness feeding back into the crime template and the assessment of site and situation (Wilkins 1964; Clarke and Cornish 1985; Jeffery 1990; Cromwell, Olson, and Avary 1991).

Temporal variation. Readiness/willingness is unlikely to stay fixed over long periods of time. The base readiness/willingness of the entire population whether measured by criminal justice system statistics (Brantingham 1991) or through self-reports (Flanagan and Jamieson 1988: 294–318) is known to vary with age, rising sharply in the later teens and into young adulthood, then dropping sharply in the later 20s and early 30s. Despite some small criminal subgroups shown by longitudinal studies to have higher rates of offending regardless of age (Farrington 1986), this general effect appears to be related

---

* The gender pattern in burglary is clear. While not exclusively masculine, burglary is predominantly committed by males. Masculine pronouns and adjectives are used in burglary examples to reflect this fact.

to changes in both the prevalence of offending and the incidence of offending at different ages (Loeber and Snyder 1990). Moreover, this base variation is mirrored in victimization rates, which vary with age in a pattern similar to that found in offender data (Gottfredson 1986).

In a more proximate arena, the readiness of any given individual will vary with changes in that person's social, economic, and emotional situation. Few burglars work steadily at doing burglaries. A successful and profitable run of crimes will lead to a reduced interest in doing more burglaries, while the money holds out. Few burglars will commit offenses while under obvious police scrutiny. At such times, readiness drops and obvious opportunities will be bypassed unless they form an ideal fit with the individual's crime template. When police scrutiny stops, or the money begins to run out, or simple boredom with life sets in, readiness rises, opportunities are considered more positively, and the offender can be triggered into doing a burglary more easily. At such periods of heightened readiness, the burglar enters a satisficing mode (Cromwell, Olson, and Avary 1991), and settles for crude fits between an opportunity and the crime template. (See, generally, M. Maguire 1982; Rengert and Wasilchick 1985; Cromwell, Olson, and Avary 1991.) A burglar's readiness and use of a crime template also appears to vary with drug use, rising and allowing riskier behavior with the use of alcohol or cocaine; falling and limiting risky behavior with the use of marijuana and opiates (Cromwell, Olson, and Avary 1991).

16.3 Application of Pattern Theory

Pattern theory may appear complex when crime, criminality, and criminal motivation are viewed as fixed objects. Criminologists frequently treat concepts as fixed and nonvarying. Crime, criminality, and criminal motivation are indeed complex if they are seen as invariant and unresponsive to what surrounds them. The elements shown in Figure 16.3 are not all equally important in every crime or in every type of crime or to every group of potential offenders, but even when they have relatively less importance in a particular crime they do not disappear. Crime and criminal readiness are better understood as processes, that is, mathematically as functions. When considered as mathematically functional relationships the variation in the links between different elements and how they interact becomes apparent.* Several examples will illustrate some of these functional relationships.

---

* Conceptually, this is different from using multivariate statistical techniques to show interrelations. The elements shown in Figure 11.3 are not independent of crime. They influence crime, but crime influences them. (Similar statements apply for criminality and criminal motivation.) Different elements within the figure can become the focus of a particular crime. Changes in the routine behaviors of criminals may be the focus or triggering events that result in minimal searches; or, they may be the product of past criminal behavior. Pattern theory is not rigid.

16.3.1 Pilfering of Office Supplies

For example, at one extreme consider the pattern of office supply theft (pens, pencils, pads of paper in small numbers) from the workplace. Pilfering is a common crime, one committed at some time or other by almost everyone who has ever worked within an environment that maintains accessible office supplies.* For this type of crime, the basic conditions are:

Readiness/willingness.—Almost everyone is willing to take small office supplies home. The goal is the possession of minor goods.

Structural backcloth.—All administrative offices maintain inventories of office supplies such as pens, pencils, paper, and envelopes. Businesses are clustered into a few parts of town by zoning rules and economic considerations.

Activity backcloth.—A broad socioeconomic range of people work in offices as cleaners, clerks, officers, administrators, managers, and executives. Small office supplies are everywhere. Rarely are there any restrictions on supplies. There are rarely any situational factors that make this crime risky.

Event process.—An office worker's children need some extra school supplies. The worker sees a bunch of pens on his or her desk, remembers the "need" at home, puts some of the pens in his or her briefcase, and takes them home to the children.

Expected crime pattern.—Spatially, crimes will be clustered in areas with offices. The volume of theft may just reflect the size of offices and, given a commonly accepted view that the mother is responsible for the children's school needs, the concentration of female jobs. Temporally, office supplies will be pilfered at the highest rate in the fall, as school begins, although they will disappear at some minimal rate all the time. The Christmas season increases the pilfering of cellophane tape for sealing presents.†

Relationship of elements.—Figure 16.4 shows the relationship between the elements that probably dominate formation of the pattern of a simple crime like pencil theft. The structural backcloth of the town,

---

* Other occupational crimes follow more complex patterns, in particular the interaction between perceived need of goods and identification of opportunities. Pretto (1991) explored several occupational crimes and found varying feedbacks between motivation and opportunity. In particular, he explored the theft of bill payments through banks by tellers when they, themselves, get in "over their heads" in debt. Goals, readiness, triggering events, routine activities, and a template for safe targets are all clearly important.

† Parenthetically, we have been told by constables in a number of different police forces that it is difficult to find operational flashlights, radios, or tape recorders around their offices during the Christmas season. The batteries disappear into toys.

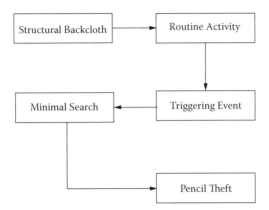

Figure 16.4 Office theft.

the routine activities inherent in an office job held by the potential thief, easy access to office supplies, a perceived "need" as a trigger, and the minimal search required to find the wanted supplies in a situation in which they can be taken all play roles in forming this fairly uncomplicated pattern.

The relationships between elements in Figure 16.4 are presented in a format that tries to maintain their relative location within the larger mode shown in Figure 16.3. While all of the elements shown in Figure 16.3 are present in every crime, only a subset of these elements are likely to dominate the formation of a pattern for any particular crime and therefore to be critical to understanding that crime. The other elements are part of the backcloth and shape the appearance of the crime pattern as it presents to researchers, practitioners, and the public at large.

16.3.2 Household Burglary

Readiness/willingness. Household burglaries are committed for many reasons, but thrill seeking and appropriation of goods appear to be the dominant goals behind most burglaries (Bennett and Wright 1984c; Rengert and Wasilchick 1985; Cromwell, Olson, and Avary 1991). The level of readiness to commit a crime and willingness to run risks is substantially higher in residential burglaries than in pilfering of office supplies from work. Many who are after thrills or who are after goods are at their peak level of willingness to take risks when they commit a burglary. Such persons might be ready to commit a crime requiring some lesser risk, such as shoplifting, but might be unwilling to commit a robbery. Other burglars, however, who have aggressive or dominance goals might be ready to commit more confrontational offenses, such as robbery, but be bored by simple theft.

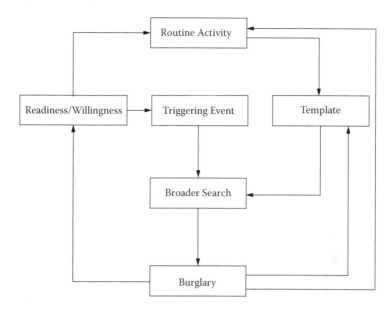

Figure 16.5 Burglary.

Structural backcloth. Residential areas are not located across the entire city or town. There are, instead, urban mosaics formed by many different land uses. Routine activities create different windows of opportunity in different residential areas. Those with sufficient readiness for household burglary are often clustered in limited parts of town and have limited access to transport (e.g., Baldwin and Bottoms 1976; Shannon 1988).*

Activity backcloth. Household burglaries are committed by different types of people who have different routine activities. Yet, the activity and awareness spaces in which they act are frequently limited and, given an urban mosaic as a base, identifiable. From within these limited activity spaces, templates of suitable targets are constructed. What is considered suitable will vary with the individual but should show clear patterns by clustering of some similar offenders. Fifteen year olds living in a suburb of single-family dwellings will develop templates that differ from those developed by young adults living in poor apartment areas located near the center of a city (Reppetto 1974; Waller and Okihiro 1978; Carter and Hill 1979; M. Maguire 1982; Bennett and Wright 1984; Rengert and Wasilchick 1985; Cromwell, Olson, and Avary 1991). The robber who also does burglaries will develop a crime template that is different from that developed by a house burglar who is never willing to do a planned robbery.

---

* Changing the structural transportation backcloth should produce a "sprawl" of residential burglary (Brantingham and Brantingham 1981c; Brantingham et al. 1991; Burgess 1925).

Event process. What triggers the crime will vary with the type of individual committing the offense. For some, the crime will be immediately opportunistic, triggered by noticing an attractive possibility or by the urgings of friends. For others, the crime is more firmly directed at getting money. For the more opportunistic group, the crime may involve a brief search but is critically dependent on quick discovery of a target that closely conforms to an idealized crime template. For the individuals with a higher level of readiness and a more focused goal of appropriation, the search may be longer and more complex, and a suitable target may require fewer points of congruence with the idealized crime template. But in common with search behavior conducted in noncriminal pursuits, the search patterns in these types of burglaries will be fairly predictable (Brantingham and Brantingham 1991; Rengert and Wasilchick 1985; Cromwell, Olson, and Avary 1991; Capone and Nicols 1976; Costanzo, Halperin, and Gale 1986). Those with higher states of readiness may give up for the time being and try later if they fail to find targets that conform in some reasonable way with their crime templates within reasonable time periods, but they are not likely to give up completely. Many of these very ready burglars report giving up for the time being, but going back out on subsequent occasions (M. Maguire 1982).

Expected crime patterns. Spatially, the burglaries should cluster within restricted activity spaces. At an aggregate level, high activity nodes for teenagers and young adults from certain areas of a city should identify areas where the crimes will occur. When the nodes change the crime patterns change. Shannon (1988) documents the changing spatial distributions of crime in Racine as principal recreation nodes moved from the city center to the periphery in response to increasing automobile use. Rengert and Wasilchick (1990) document the movement of burglary distributions in relation to changes in the location of crack houses in the Philadelphia area. The details of what happens once inside the dwelling, whether mere theft or theft coupled with extensive vandalism, relates back to the goal underlying the crime, but probably does not relate back to the location of the crime.

Temporally, burglaries are, for those for whom burglary is the highest level of acceptable crime, aimed at times when the residence is empty and at residences that are most frequently empty. The emptiness may be based on personal knowledge (the McKinneys are on vacation), on the general observation that mid-afternoons are generally empty times (kids are in school, parents are at work or shopping), or on assumptions derived from routine activities (apartments are empty in mid-morning when everyone is at work). The crimes may, instead, become nighttime crimes for those willing to risk encountering residents or seeking more thrills or excitement. Someone willing to commit nighttime burglaries probably has a readiness for more confrontational and serious offenses such as robbery or rape than someone

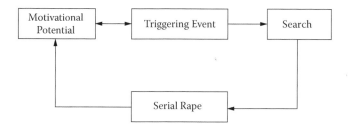

Figure 16.6 Serial rape.

who commits only daytime breaking and enterings in clearly empty homes (Linedecker 1991; Clarke and Weisburd 1990).

Relationship between elements. In this type of crime the feedback loops between the criminal events and the potential offender's readiness/willingness, routine activities patterns, and, indirectly, triggering events become more important as the criminal behavior pattern develops and should vary in weight or importance as the offenders change from a subgroup of teenagers who break into houses to long-term, repeat burglars.*

16.3.3 Serial Rape

Readiness/willingness. Serial rape was chosen as the last example. It is both a nonproperty offense and a rare type of crime. There are few serial rapists. Their goals, in addition to sexual gratification, appear to involve shows of aggression or acts of domination. Serial rapists may repeat their offense behaviors over and over, changing only the particular victim, or they may escalate in frequency and violence as their readiness and willingness is raised to higher levels by the reinforcement of repeated success (Hazelwood, Reboussin, and Warren 1989; LeBeau 1985, 1987).

Structural backcloth. Since serial rape is a rare criminal behavior pattern, each offender tends to be tied uniquely to the structural backcloth of his own locale. Some underlying commonalities in transportation networks and in the distribution of women and girls in time and space, at schools or shopping malls for instance, may be part of a general backcloth common to many Western or industrialized societies that can be applied to an understanding of the individualized structural backcloths of particular serial rapists.

Activity backcloth. The reported rapes tied to serial offenders do tend to show an activity bias linked to each offender's routine activities and the nodal locations where the offender spends substantial amounts of time (LeBeau 1985, 1987; Maume 1989). The crime template is tied to the special

---

* Cusson (1983) reproduces results of research done by Fréchette and LeBlanc (1978) showing how the goal behind offending may change as teenagers age. Action/excitement as a goal seems to change into appropriation as a goal as repeat offenders age.

characteristics of the offender's modus operandi and to the character of the triggering events that can touch off a new offense. Yet even with repetitive events, analysis of individual serial rapists' activity patterns has to be tied to analysis of individual routine activities and awareness spaces. Aggregate analysis is only possible on a transformed space representing generic routine activities and awareness spaces.* Offense patterns are also tied to the routine activities of potential victims.

Event process. Each actual crime is tied to readiness level, to the triggering event—which could be a fantasy or seeing someone who fits a victim template within a fantasy—and to an individual search process involving a broader, more careful search to find the right target.

Expected crime patterns. Spatially, the patterns may only be analyzed at an individual offender's level. Serial rapists are rare. There is no aggregate cluster pattern, but from an individual perspective there may be a general pattern. Attacks away from main roads or near high activity centers may well mean the area is well known to the offender, part of his current or past routine daily activities. Attacks near main roads or at high activity nodes such as large shopping malls may well mean that the rapist is being drawn to target concentrations, out of areas he knows well. Temporally, the rapes may well follow a clear pattern: always on the weekend or always near a holiday. The pattern is shaped in some way by the routine rhythms of daily life. It is also most likely influenced by prior "success" and whatever is the driving force behind the rapes. The time period between successive offenses may well decrease as the offender's behavior is reinforced.

Relationship between elements. This type of crime is under-researched although LeBeau (1985, 1987) and Hazelwood, Reboussin, and Warren (1989) have done some work.† It appears with this type of crime that process dominates and that no elements are completely static except, perhaps, what is defined by the offender as a suitable target or target situation. The dominant relationships may well be between readiness, triggering event, and search using a clearly defined template.

16.4 Conclusions

Pattern theory is derived from the multidisciplinary approaches to understanding crime and criminality found in rational choice theory, routine

---

* See Rengert and Wasilchick (1985) for a technique for just such analysis applied to burglar activity patterns.
† A two-year study of the geographic patterns in serial rape is currently being conducted at the FBI Academy by Roland Reboussin, Robert R. Hazelwood, and Janet I. Warren under National Institute of Justice auspices.

activities theory, environmental criminology, strategic analysis, lifestyle theory, crime prevention through environmental design, situational crime prevention, hot spot analysis, and opportunity theory. It explores patterns of crime and criminal behavior. Not all people commit crimes; not all areas experience crimes. The patterns in crime are potentially explicable when the decision process that is crucial to its commission is viewed in conjunction with the actual activity backcloth of offenders and victims, together with general variations in criminal motivation that are themselves not independent of the opportunity backcloth. In some types of offenses triggering events dominate crime patterning. For other types of crimes, past behavioral history, the actual availability of suitable targets, the creation of a decision template, and the current activities of potential offenders drive the pattern.

While the theory is general, it is specifically developed to make it easier to understand patterns of crime and, more specifically, the diversity in patterns of crime. What we "see" is understandable when we look at the specific criminal event, the site, the situation, the activity backcloth, the probable crime templates, the triggering events, and the general factors influencing the readiness or willingness of individuals to commit crimes. Aggregate patterns are understandable because they contain some similarity or commonality when viewed from the perspective of the processes in activities and criminal decision making: the use of goals for actions, the construction and use of templates in search behavior, the development of a state of readiness awaiting a triggering event, the process of the triggering event itself. Patterns are based on a more complex view of both crime and criminality than is used by many in the field.

Research strongly supports this approach to looking at crime. Patterns of crime are discernible and understandable. Future research, however, will have to begin to explore alternative analytic techniques. The elements of the decision process, the activity backcloth, the variation in criminal readiness, and the environmental backcloth are interrelated in feedback and iterative loops of a sort to which most of our current analytic tools are poorly suited at best. Future advancements in this field of research may require more reliance on alternative analytic tools such as point-set or algebraic topology, or nonlinear systems models and fractal constructs, as well as a continual expansion into alternative methodologies to gain a better understanding of crime occurrence within a cognitive as well as a more objectively defined environment.*

Even using current qualitative and quantitative techniques, the elements and interrelationships shown in Figure 16.3 may be researched from many

---

* Future research may best be placed in cognitive philosophy of science. We do not reason in simple linear ways, or by abduction, but more by prototypes leading to what are called "activation vectors" (Churchland 1989).

perspectives. Table 16.1 contains a short list of possible research questions, some of which have already been mentioned in this article.

Much research has already been conducted in this new criminology. Perhaps most importantly, it already has a strong applied or action research arm. Crime reduction is possible when crime is viewed from a detailed microperspective (Clarke 1992; Jeffery 1990). Breaking away from the idea that "crime" is generated by some simple, single factor or constitutes some single, simple class of behaviors frees criminology to focus on specific types of crime occurring in specific types of situations enfolded in a specific configuration of the environmental backcloth. Looked at in this way, specifically defined problems make it easy to devise focused intervention tactics to deal with concrete criminal situations (see Clarke 1992). Solutions to specific problems can be found* by looking at who probably commits the crime, the probable goals behind the crime, whether crimes are related to controllable triggering events, why certain targets or victims, sites and situations are selected, and how formal changes to the site, situation, or backcloth might alter the "who," the "why," and the "where" of crimes in ways that would reduce their overall prevalence and incidence.

---

* Or determined to be insoluble because the solution is politically unpalatable. Some crime prevention tactics might force unacceptable changes in noncriminal lifestyles. Some crime prevention tactics might be prohibitively expensive. Some tactics would be unacceptably repressive. Some tactics would be immoral.

Table 16.1 Research Topics

Templates
How do templates vary by past criminal experience?
Can people who commit crimes be "clustered" by what defines a "good" target? Is this a better way to categorize offenders than using legally defined categories?
Do templates vary with culture? Are they highly dependent on which country is being studied? If so, is the difference based on varying activity patterns or varying sociocultural patterns?
Triggering Events/Readiness
How "strong" do triggering events have to be?
Does their required strength vary by the site and situation or current activity? Are triggers only functional in certain environments or, stated another way, are they nonfunctional in some situations but not in others?
Does the trigger change as goals change?
How do responses to the trigger influence aggravating and mitigating circumstances in sentencing?
Activity Space
Are activity spaces like ecological niches? Do people feel highly constrained to remain within usual activity spaces?
Does routine location in or near a perceived high risk alter people's activities leading them to avoid specific places, or indulge in reactive aggression or retreat in the face of specific situations?
What are the expected crime patterns and downstream costs of policing associated with major changes in the structural backcloth (roads, trains, bridges, etc.) of a locale?
Are we heading, economically, for more exposure to highly opportunistic crimes?
Readiness
Do media increase readiness by providing examples?
Does readiness/willingness stay vague and poorly defined before witnessing or being part of a crime?
Why are most minor property crime opportunities ignored? Is readiness/willingness strongly tied to goals and associated crime preferences or to goods and easy/frequent activities likely to include triggering events?
Conversely, since opportunities are so vast, are minor property crimes low because goals like excitement and thrills can be obtained in many other ways?

Environmental Criminology and Crime Prevention

In its origins, environmental criminology was concerned with the prevention of crime. This is most apparent in the title of the seminal book written by C. Ray Jeffery, *Crime Prevention through Environmental Design*. In this last part of the anthology, we include five of the key articles for understanding crime prevention through the lens of an environmental criminologist.

The first chapter, "A Conceptual Model of Crime Prevention," was written by Paul Brantingham and Frederic Faust and is concerned with conceptualizing crime prevention. Until Brantingham and Faust published this article in 1976, the term *crime prevention* was used to describe a number of overlapping and confusing activities. The framework that is provided by Brantingham and Faust clarifies different forms of crime prevention based on the timeframe within which they operate. This allows for environmental criminologists, and anyone else concerned with the prevention of crime, to see how their activities fit into the broad perspective of crime prevention and if their activities are operating along the timeframe desired.

The next two chapters, "Crime Prevention and Control through Environmental Engineering" and "Criminal Behavior and the Physical Environment: A Perspective," are written by C. Ray Jeffery. The first of these chapters is the first known work that explicitly deals with alterations to the environment for the purposes of preventing crime before it occurs. This seminal contribution of Jeffery is most often cited by reference to his book *Crime Prevention through Environmental Design*, but the 1969 article summarizes his book very well. The following article by Jeffery summarizes the second edition of his book, including the theoretical foundation Jeffery uses in his second edition—theories rooted in the psychology of the brain. The distinction between the two editions is important because Jeffery incorporated learning into his model for crime prevention. Though many of the theoretical foundations for Jeffery's work are no longer *en vogue*, it is important to recognize that Jeffery's model for crime prevention is based on theory, just different theory than emerged from, or is related to, his work—his theoretical base was the operant conditioning form of learning theory.

The original article that explicitly discussed the role of situational factors in crime prevention follows the chapters by Jeffery and is written by Ronald

Clarke, "Situational Crime Prevention: Theory and Practice." In this article, Clarke questions the conventional thinking of what crime prevention ought to be, that is, this thinking should be based on an understanding of the root causes of crime. Though this must force us to ask what those root causes are, conventional wisdom at the time considered sociological changes to be paramount. Clarke argued for a simpler approach: reducing opportunities and increasing risk for criminal activities. Many criminologists at the time viewed criminal behavior as reflexive or involuntary—an unreasoned action determined by the offender's upbringing and socioeconomic position in society. Clarke reintroduced the idea of personal agency; he argued that offenders make choices between alternative courses of conduct when they commit offences. Changing the opportunity structure would, he argued, cause many potential offenders to choose noncriminal behavioral options. At the time, focusing on the prevention of crime, rather than the development of criminal personalities or criminal motives, was a radical shift in focus. Also, Clarke's work on situational crime prevention can be seen more generally as a prelude to his work on the rational choice model for crime.

This anthology concludes with an article by Marcus Felson, "Routine Activities and Crime Prevention in the Developing Metropolis," which considers the impact of routine activities on crime prevention initiatives. Through the use of a number of examples, Felson discusses how changes in the nature of our society change our routine activities; this change in our routine activities, in turn, changes the nature of crime, and must change the way we try to prevent it. Therefore, this last chapter clearly outlines the idea that we adapt to our environment, changing our behavior when our environment changes. Because our environment is dynamic, so must be our crime prevention activities. We end our collection as a whole with a look by J. Bryan Kinney at where we have gone, coupled with a short investigation of what the future of environmental criminology may entail.

A Conceptual Model of Crime Prevention (1976) 17

P.J. BRANTINGHAM
F.L. FAUST

From Brantingham, P.J., and Faust, F.L. (1976). A conceptual model of crime-prevention. *Crime and Delinquency*, 22, 284–296.

Contents

17.1 Abstract   395
17.2 Introduction   395
17.3 Punishment, Treatment, and Crime Prevention   396
17.4 A Paradigm for Analysis of Crime Prevention   399
17.5 Application of the Model   400
17.6 Directions for Crime Prevention   404

17.1 Abstract

Crime prevention is the professed mission of every agency found within the American criminal justice system. In practice, the term "prevention" seems to be applied confusingly to a wide array of contradictory activities. This confusion can be avoided through the use of a conceptual model that defines three levels of prevention: (1) primary prevention, directed at modification of criminogenic conditions in the physical and social environment at large; (2) secondary prevention, directed at early identification and intervention in the lives of individuals or groups in criminogenic circumstances; and (3) tertiary prevention, directed at prevention of recidivism. The use of such a conceptual model helps to clarify current crime prevention efforts, suggests fruitful directions for future research by identifying current lacunae in practice and in the research literature, and may ultimately prove helpful in addressing the seemingly endless debate between advocates of "punishment" and advocates of "treatment."

17.2 Introduction

Prevention, probably the most overworked and least understood concept in contemporary criminology, might be defined simply as any activity, by an individual or a group, public or private, that precludes the incidence of one or more criminal acts. But caution is warranted here, for the simplicity is deceptive. Can crime prevention be logically conceived to encompass such divergent actions as long-term incarceration and pretrial diversion from the justice system? Solitary confinement and remedial reading instruction? The improvement of automotive antitheft devices and the development of neighborhood recreation centers? Or psychosurgery and the levying of fines? Considering the goal definition of crime prevention, the answer might well be "yes." But where means are concerned, the matter is heavily clouded by definitional ambiguity and theoretical contradiction.

The purpose of the following discussion, then, is threefold: (1) to examine briefly the philosophical roots and related definitional issues of crime prevention; (2) to outline a conceptual framework that will provide a more useful understanding of crime prevention; and (3) to specify the most fruitful direction for the development of theory, research, and programming in crime prevention. Considering the present state of competing and contradictory views on the prevention of criminal behavior, we judge this to be a timely endeavor.

17.3 Punishment, Treatment, and Crime Prevention

Punishment is a persistent problem for social theorists: its definition is elusive and its justification is debatable.* Nevertheless, a definition of the standard case of punishment, roughly acceptable to utilitarians, seems to have evolved from the work of Antony Flew (1954).† Under this definition, punishment is (1) a painful or unpleasant consequence (2) intentionally imposed by other persons (3) upon an offender (4) for his offense against legal rules (5) under authority of the legal system against which the offense was committed.‡ The paramount utilitarian justification for the imposition of punishment has been that it will prevent crime (Beccaria 1963; Bentham 1948; Packer 1968: 31).

Recent scholarship has shown, however, that the ethical issues involved in the application of painful or unpleasant consequences to individual men by agents of legal systems cannot properly be circumscribed by the concept of punishment. Troublesome children, retarded people, madmen, and drug

---

* Recent collections that probe the debate between utilitarians and retributionists include Murphy (1973), Gerber and McAnany (1972), Grupp (1971).

† Those who have adopted Flew's position include Hart (1968) and Packer (1968).

‡ Packer (1968: 31) attempted to make the definition workable for both utilitarians and retributionists by adding a sixth condition to the standard case adduced by Flew: "That it be imposed for the dominant purpose of preventing offenses against legal rules or of exacting retribution from offenders, or both."

abusers are all currently subject to treatment through legal process at the hands of what Kittrie (1971) has called the "therapeutic state." The actual consequences accruing to people being treated differ very little from the consequences accruing to people being punished.

Herbert Packer (1968: 25–30) has observed that punishment and treatment can be distinguished primarily by the *purpose* for which the consequence is imposed: crime prevention or retribution, or both, in the case of punishment; social protection or individual betterment, or both, in the case of treatment. But that distinction blurs when social protection is equated with prevention of social harms (including crimes) in the more aggressive literature of deterministic criminology (Wootton 1963; Ancel 1966; Menninger 1968). This blurring of a weak distinction increases in many legislative formulations. "Prevention of harm to self or others," for instance, is the seventh most frequently mandated ground for exercise of juvenile court jurisdiction in American juvenile court legislation.* The British Mental Health Act of 1959 provides for compulsory hospital commitment of the retarded, psychopathic, or mentally ill person in the interest of his health or safety, or for the protection of others.†

Though punishment and treatment are generally regarded as closely related concepts, one common conceptual tie has not been developed. Both the general justification of punishment and treatment and the specific justification of particular forms of punishment and treatment, as well as hybrid penotherapeutic practices such as probation and halfway house confinement, are considered to be crime prevention. We suggest that analysis of this common conceptual goal—crime prevention—may be the key to a better understanding of the definitional and ethical distinctions between punishment and treatment.

One of the more striking features of the Anglo-American system of criminal justice is a divergence between systemic activity and systemic ideology. The system‡ in action deals in *post hoc* assessment, of culpability and assignment of punishment.

Police arrest offenders after the offense occurs; courts adjudicate offenders after the offense occurs; prisons punish offenders after the offense occurs.§ Yet

---

* From a list of thirty-four such grounds compiled in Sussman and Baum (1968: 12).
† Mental Health Act 1959 § 26; cf. §§ 60, 61, permitting commitment of retarded, psychopathic, or mentally ill convicts to the same mental hospitals in lieu of sentence.
‡ It is a "system" in the formal sense—a set of elements that interact in some significant way. We do not imply that the interaction is necessarily smooth or efficient. The criminal justice system is amazingly inefficient.
§ The juvenile justice system, compulsory narcotics addict commitment schemes, eugenic sterilization laws, and sexual psychopath laws have all tried to deal with potential offenders before any offense has been committed. All have been under serious attack of late as distributively unjust.

each major element of the criminal justice system professes a special calling to prevent crime. Thus, says the American Bar Association, "Police administrators ... characterize prevention as their primary goal."* The President's Commission on Law Enforcement and Administration of Justice (1967c: 13) pointed out that "It is generally assumed that police have a preventive ... role as well." And the recent report by the National Advisory Commission on Criminal Justice Standards and Goals (1973: 103–105) defined the primary goal of police as crime prevention.

According to the American Law Institute, the prime purpose of a penal code is "to forbid and prevent" crimes, and the principal purpose of sentencing and treatment of offenders is "to prevent the commission of offenses."† Since courts necessarily make contact with suspected actual offenders and convicted offenders rather than potential offenders, prevention takes two forms: general deterrence through exemplary sentencing and special deterrence through selective sentencing involving combinations of punishment and treatment. The goal of sentencing courts is crime prevention (R.M. Jackson 1971: 311–330).

The preventive purpose of correctional agencies is less directly expressed than that of police or courts but appears strongly in the American Correctional Association's (1966: 6–12) equation of modern penology with "rehabilitation"—the reform or control of offenders so that they will not commit new crimes when released from custody or supervision.‡ Of course, the historical penitentiary was designed to serve general and special deterrence purposes. The goal of the correctional subsystem, then, is to prevent recidivism.

Outside of the criminal justice system, many community organizations and agencies engage in activities of which crime prevention is at least one of the major purposes. These include such diverse programs as parent education, mental health services, recreational activities, vocational education and employment counseling, drug abuse treatment services, remedial academic classes, public information programs on protection of self and property, crisis intervention telephone services, school programs on youth and the law,

---

* American Bar Association Project on Standards for Criminal Justice, Standards Relating to the Urban Police Function, approved draft (Chicago: American Bar Association, 1973), p. 56. The standards also point out that the first commissioner of the London Metropolitan Police set crime prevention as the first priority for the new police—ahead of apprehension and prosecution of offenders (Ibid., pp. 55–56). The standards themselves, however, reverse that order, giving apprehension first priority and prevention second priority out of a ranked list of eleven priorities (Ibid., § 2.2).

† American Law Institute, Model Penal Code, Proposed Official Draft (Philadelphia: American Law Institute), §§ 1.02, pp. 2–3.

‡ See also the ACA's statement on objectives of the correctional system: "Simply stated, the basic goal of a correctional system is to provide public protection by aiding in the prevention of crime" (American Correctional Association 1966: 1).

and so forth. Every public reference to crime prevention is coupled with a proposal for some form of further community involvement in reducing the opportunity for, deterring, or treating criminality.

Clearly, with each of the major criminal justice subsystems as well as several noncriminal justice systems being committed to crime prevention, the concept must have wide temporal and behavioral scope—so wide, in fact, that it is of dubious value without definitional refinement.

17.4 A Paradigm for Analysis of Crime Prevention

A legitimate argument may be made that each of the subsystems referred to above poaches on the crime prevention functions of the others—business organizations engage in security and law enforcement activities, community agencies provide services to probationers and parolees, police engage in adjudication and correctional activities through informal probation and cautioning schemes, prosecutors and probation officers become involved in detective work, and correctional officers investigate and adjudicate rule violations by in-custody offenders. Most of the time, however, the preventive activities of noncriminal justice programs, police, courts, and correction are substantially different. The points of distinction may be identified most clearly by the level or stage in the development of criminal behavior at which intervening activity is implemented. Since it is similarly conceived as intervention at different developmental levels, the public heath model of disease prevention is analogous and useful.*

The public health model posits three levels of activity (Leavell and Clark 1965: 19–28).† *Primary* prevention identifies disease-creating general conditions of the environment and seeks to abate those conditions (e.g., sewage treatment, mosquito extermination, small-pox vaccination, job-safety engineering, personal hygiene education). *Secondary* prevention identifies groups or individuals who have a high risk of developing disease or who have incipient cases of disease and intervenes in their lives with special treatments designed to prevent the risk from materializing or the incipient case from growing worse (e.g., chest x-rays in poor neighborhoods, special diets for overweight executives, rubella vaccinations for prospective but not-yet-expectant mothers, dental examinations). *Tertiary* prevention identifies individuals with advanced

---

* We recognize the risk inherent in borrowing a conceptual model from medicine. Criminology is only just beginning to recover from the damage done by the Positivist School's use of the medical analogy of crime as disease. In borrowing from public health concepts here, we have modified the public health model to fit the criminological situation rather than vice versa.

† We are indebted to Jack Wright, of the Florida Department of Health and Rehabilitative Services, for bringing the public health paradigm to our attention.

cases of disease and intervenes with treatment to prevent death or permanent disability (e.g., stomach pumping for poisoning, open-heart surgery for defective heart valves, radiation therapy for some forms of cancer), provides rehabilitation services for those persons who must live under the constraints of permanent disability (e.g., Braille training for the blind, prosthetic limbs for amputees), and provides a measure of relief from pain and suffering for individuals with incurable diseases (e.g., opiate therapy for terminal cancer patients, leper colonies).* Tertiary prevention, then, aims at three forms of prevention: (1) prevention of death or disability; (2) prevention of a decline to a less adequate level of social, economic, and physical activity; (3) prevention of more physical and social pain than necessary in an inevitable demise.

Crime prevention can be conceptualized as operating at these same three levels.† (See Table 17.1) *Primary* crime prevention identifies conditions of the physical and social environment that provide opportunities for or precipitate criminal acts. Here the objective of intervention is to alter those conditions so that crimes cannot occur. *Secondary* crime prevention engages in early identification of potential offenders and seeks to intervene in their lives in such a way that they never commit criminal violation. *Tertiary* crime prevention deals with actual offenders and involves intervention in their lives in such a fashion that they will not commit further offenses. With this classification in view, let us examine the relationship of these levels of crime prevention to contemporary issues in criminal justice. For the purpose of analysis, we will consider the three levels of crime prevention in reverse order.

17.5 Application of the Model

The correctional subsystem within the criminal justice system is charged with tertiary prevention. The optimistic—perhaps heroic—assumption is

---

* We have modified the groups of activity within the primary, secondary, and tertiary classifications described above to facilitate their use for criminological purposes. See Leavell and Clark (1965: 20–21). For an argument that an unmodified public health model is not useful to criminological thinking, even in the drug abuse area, see Brotman and Suffet (1975: 55–56).

† Lejins (1967) has developed a tripartite classification of crime prevention which cuts orthogonally across our model. Thus, he describes (1) punitive prevention (a primary and tertiary form), (2) corrective prevention (a primary and secondary form), and (3) mechanical prevention (a primary and tertiary form). Wolfgang's (1970) tripartite categorization of prevention appears to be a breakdown of secondary and tertiary forms of prevention. The Florida State Bureau of Criminal Justice Planning has developed a typology of crime prevention programs which also cuts across our model. It defines programs of prevention aimed at (1) the initiating conditions of crime (primary prevention) and (2) the sustaining conditions of crime (secondary prevention) (Florida Bureau of Criminal Justice Planning and Assistance, The Florida Annual Action Plan for 1974 [Tallahassee, Fla., 1974], pp. 1–21).

Table 17.1 Models of Prevention

Public Health Paradigm

Primary		Secondary		Tertiary
Health Promotion	Specific Protection	Early Diagnosis	Disability Limitation	Rehabilitation
Health education	Personal hygiene	Case finding	Treatment for advanced disease	Retraining
General social and physical well-being programs	Specific immunizations	Screening		Community placement and support
Nutrition	Job safety engineering	Selective examinations		
Genetics	Environmental sanitation			
Periodic examinations				

Criminological Paradigm

Primary	Secondary	Tertiary		
		Reform	Rehabilitation	Incapacitation
Environmental design	Early identification	Community treatment	Training	Institutional custody
General social and physical well-being programs	Pre-delinquent screening	Institutional treatment	Support	
Crime prevention education	Individual intervention	Punishment	Surveillance	
	Neighborhood programs			

made that, through effective intervention, the offender will be fully restored to a permanent, functional level of socially acceptable behavior. For those offenders whose behavior is not amenable to modification through known forms of punishment or treatment, tertiary prevention aims to provide such control of the offender's behavior as is necessary to protect society and elicit the highest and most sustained level of conforming behavior possible.* The preventive aspect of intervention at this level may be found in the notion that such intervention keeps society from being placed at increased risk, keeps the offender from being placed at greater risk for his own harmful behavior and from the excessive retaliation of others (Canadian Committee on Correction 1969), and keeps conditions from occurring which offer no opportunity and encouragement for whatever higher level of conforming behavior the offender might be capable of achieving at some future time.

For offenders whose criminal behavior is not amenable to correction through known forms of punishment and treatment and who are seen as potentially dangerous to society, the traditional societal reaction has been incapacitation—the imposition of lifetime or long-term confinement in a secure setting. This confinement has been justified as societal protection.† Theoretically, it is assumed that the behavior of offenders in this category might improve to some degree but not sufficiently to warrant their release from custody in the near future. But still, any behavioral improvement is desirable. Toward this end, the President's Commission on Law Enforcement and Administration of Justice (1967a: 58) recommended that offenders of this type be transferred to special institutions that would "encourage the development of more imaginative programs for long-term prisoners—special industries, perhaps greater independence and self-sufficiency within the confines of a secure institution." For those offenders who are not seen as potentially serious threats to society, the correctional system combines rehabilitation and reform to elicit more conforming behavior. The hope is that the behavioral improvements for these prisoners will be sufficient to inhibit further illegal activities.

Effective tertiary prevention is the primary goal of the correctional subsystem. It is also one of the goals of the courts and the probation and parole

---

* Capital punishment does not fall within this conceptual model without straining the analogy considerably since the legal and ethical tenets of public health medicine do not include the intentional infliction of death, regardless of the patient's medical threat to the health of others. If we do strain the analogy, however, the death penalty might be viewed as the most extreme form of tertiary prevention, with general deterrence feedback to the primary prevention level.

† Capital punishment is excluded from consideration here and is not treated seriously within the general model of crime prevention, since the principal justification for imposition of the death penalty is retribution rather than any utilitarian judgment that the offender is not amenable to reform or rehabilitation and is too dangerous for less final methods of incapacitation.

service as these subsystems interact and interlink with correction. Effective tertiary prevention is, and always has been, more ideal than actual. But the justification of particular forms of both punishment and treatment is grounded on their efficacy in achieving this level of prevention. As a result, corporal punishment has been generally abolished because it fails to prevent recidivism rather than because it is inhumane, even though a case can be made for it on retributive grounds. Other forms of punishment such as imprisonment and other forms of treatment such as castration of sexual offenders are currently under attack because they fail to reduce recidivism below the levels attained by cheaper and less drastic methods. On the other hand, forms of punishment such as fines and forms of treatment such as psychosurgery, which promise improved tertiary prevention, are currently fashionable even though retributive and humanitarian problems are raised.*

Secondary prevention is the level at which crime prevention is most fervently pursued in research and program funding. Courts, probation and parole services, general social services, educational institutions, planners, private citizens, and police all engage in secondary prevention. It is argued that poverty, low educational level, lack of vocational skills, minority status, and poor physical and mental health are all associated with criminal activity. The assumption is that these social and physical problems are causally related to crime, although most current research rejects the causal link.

Without question, the great bulk of intervention activities labeled "crime prevention" must be categorized as secondary prevention—i.e., early identification of potential offenders, followed by action designed to reduce the risk of future involvement in more serious forms of antisocial behavior, particularly criminal behavior. For example, during the 1960s, massive federal, state, and local programs were mounted to identify and deal with problems of school drop-outs, vocationally untrained and economically disadvantaged youth, physically and mentally handicapped individuals, minority group members, etc., with the assumption that such intervention would curb and reverse the increasing crime rates (Marris and Rein 1973; Moynihan 1968). While these endeavors have been launched toward laudable objectives, they have frequently rested on the false assumption that they were striking at the root "cause" of crime and delinquency when, instead, they were dealing only with observable symptoms (Jeffery 1971).

Primary prevention—identification of those conditions of the physical and social environment that provide opportunities for or precipitate criminal

---

* See generally, Mabe (1975), for a group of articles probing state-of-the-art issues in behavioral control. Note that the ethical and legal issues surrounding such modes of behavioral control make them politically vulnerable as secondary and tertiary prevention techniques. See, e.g., "Clockwork Orange Projects Banned," Crime & Delinquency, July 1974, pp. 314–315.

behavior and the alteration of those conditions so that no crimes occur—is clearly the ideal objective. In fact this is the objective that is posited as the justification for most secondary prevention activities, but obviously the identification of incipient cases implies that the opportunity for primary prevention (in those instances at least) has already passed. With a few notable exceptions, there has been little systematic study of primary prevention of criminal behavior (Jeffery 1971; Newman 1972). The work accomplished at this level has been largely pursued along one of three lines: (1) psychological immunization from certain types of behavioral tendencies, (2) preclusion of criminal activity by redesign of the physical environment, and (3) general "deterrence" of criminal activity by exemplary sentences and the presence of correctional facilities. The first two directions of inquiry have raised serious ethical and legal questions, to say nothing of the problem of resource allocation for implementation on a scale large enough to affect crime rates significantly.

17.6 Directions for Crime Prevention

Using the three-part model we can classify criminal justice system activities and noncriminal justice system activities designed to prevent crime. As can be seen by examining Tables 17.2 and 17.3, most crime prevention activity has occurred in secondary and tertiary prevention. Less effort has been spent on primary prevention.

Tertiary prevention, currently, consists mostly of efforts to "treat" offenders, but this "treatment" is given in the absence of knowledge and competence to permanently "reform" tendencies toward illegal behavior. Most of what is done in the name of "treatment" is, in reality, little more than an effort to help offenders cope and to control them through externally imposed pressures. If this fact were more widely recognized in contemporary correction and the widespread myth of available effective treatment were dispelled until human behavior is more fully understood, then resources could be more appropriately allocated between control activities and much needed behavioral research. For example, probation and parole officers recognize that their job has dimensions of both control and treatment—i.e., on the one hand, surveillance and serving as a source of information and, on the other, some type of therapeutic counseling. The type of training that probation and parole personnel generally receive, however, places great emphasis on the treatment function and virtually ignores control technology. As a result, these persons frequently spend the largest share of their time and effort attempting to accomplish an unrealistic therapeutic task and resist the performance of less interesting and often routine control activities which could produce more effective results. Further, the control relationship between correctional personnel generally and offenders and their families might be considerably

Table 17.2   Prevention Activities of the Criminal Justice System

	Primary	Secondary	Tertiary
Police	General deterrence (through "presence") Citizen education programs	Intelligence operations Social service operations (athletic programs, family crisis units, sensitivity training) Patrol peace-keeping actions ("move-along" orders, stop-and-frisk contacts) Intervention and diversion (drunk detoxification, juvenile supervision)	Arrest and prosecution Misdemeanor correctional institutions
Courts	General deterrence (through "exemplary" sentences)	Pre-adjudication diversion	Post-adjudication diversion, reform, rehabilitation, and incapacitation (through sentence)
Correction	General deterrence (through existence)	Operation of diversion programs	Reform (through punishment, community treatment, institutional treatment) Rehabilitation (through aftercare support, training, and surveillance) Incapacitation (through custody)

strengthened if the delusion of effective treatment, and the subsequent disillusionment of failure, were removed.

This leads to the conclusion, then, that the rhetoric of effective treatment should be dropped, except for those few activities where the consequences of therapeutic intervention have been rigorously tested and the outcome can be predicted with confidence (e.g., the controlled use of chemotherapy in certain cases of aggressive behavior, or brain surgery where tumors are determined to be the cause of acts of violence). Such a narrowing of the operational definition of treatment is quite consistent with legal arguments and recent court decisions relating to the "right to treatment" and would help to put the justification for coerced loss of liberty into proper perspective (Kittrie 1971; Toomey, Simonsen, and Allen 1975). Clearly differentiating between rehabilitative control and treatment in tertiary prevention may spare many offenders imprisonment for nonexistent therapy, in favor of more humane

Table 17.3   Prevention Activities outside the Criminal Justice System

	Primary	Secondary	Tertiary
Private citizens	Household and business security precautions General charity	Big brother programs Delinquency specific social activities	Correctional volunteers
Schools	General education	Pre-delinquent screening Educational intervention programs	Prosecution of truants and delinquents Institutional education programs
Business	Security provisions	Employee screening	Prosecution of offenders Hiring of ex-offenders
Planners	Modification of physical environment to reduce criminal opportunity Modification of social environment to reduce impulsions towards criminal behavior	Crime location analysis for neighbourhood education and modification programs Criminal residence study for neighbourhood social work	Institutional design
Religious and social agencies	Moral training Family education General social work	Welfare services: child protection, programs for disadvantaged & pre-delinquent youth, crisis intervention	Aftercare services

and economical rehabilitative programming. Research is also needed in the other forms of tertiary prevention; e.g., special deterrence, postadjudicative diversion, and the deterrent effect of arrest and prosecution.

At the level of secondary prevention, there is certainly a need for continued research that will lead to the development of more accurate diagnostic instruments for the early identification of potential offenders and more effective intervention approaches. At present, however, the inadequate state of knowledge precludes such diagnosis and intervention, except in rather rare instances, and suggests that premature and inappropriate assignment of the "potential offender" label contributes to the crime problem (Faust 1973). Thus, as with tertiary prevention, effective intervention at the secondary level will have to await the scientific achievement of a more complete understanding of human behavior in general and criminal behavior in particular and careful evaluation of existing secondary prevention schemes.

On the basis of the foregoing discussion, it should come as no surprise that primary prevention is viewed as the most fruitful direction for the future development of theory, research, and programming insofar as preventing criminal behavior is concerned. Perhaps the most cogent argument in support of this position is that presented by C. Ray Jeffery (1971) in his *Crime Prevention through Environmental Design*. The logic that crime can most effectively be curbed by altering conditions that precipitate or provide opportunities for criminal behavior can hardly be challenged. The problems of implementation, however, are staggering—not just problems of required resources and legal and ethical considerations (these have always been major challenges to the advancement of science), but more significantly the necessary shift in public policy from almost total commitment to crisis intervention to an equally strong commitment to long-range behavioral research.

Such a shift is by no means impossible, but under the most advantageous conditions it would be ponderously slow in taking place and the question of how to deal with the crime problem in the interim is legitimately raised.

The answer, of course, is that we cannot turn our backs on the problem while we work to influence public policy toward basic behavioral research and wait for the products of that research. Rather, we can place greater emphasis on more effective rehabilitative control, on the one hand, and basic research in primary prevention (involving limited pilot and demonstration projects), on the other, using a significant share of the resources currently being expended on ineffective secondary and tertiary prevention programs. We entertain no illusions about the problems to be confronted in this endeavor. It is certainly an ambitious goal, but it holds promise for ultimately preventing much, if not most, criminal behavior before rather than after it has occurred.

Crime Prevention and Control through Environmental Engineering (1969) 18

C.R. JEFFERY

From Jeffery, C.R. (1969). Crime prevention and control through environmental engineering. *Criminologica*, 7, 35–58.

Contents

18.1 The Existing Model: The Individual Offender   409
    18.1.1 Schools of Criminology   409
    18.1.2 Studies of Individual Offenders   411
    18.1.3 Behavior and Environment   412
    18.1.4 Rehabilitation as an Ideal   413
    18.1.5 Role of Punishment in Criminology   414
    18.1.6 Therapeutic Approaches to Rehabilitation   415
    18.1.7 The Criminal Justice System   417
    18.1.8 Reasons for the Failure of Correctional Programs   421
    18.1.9 Community Action Programs   422
18.2 A New Model: Environmental Control of Criminal Behavior   424
    18.2.1 Science and Technology   424
    18.2.2 Urban Planning and Design   425
    18.2.3 Behavioral Science and Research   426
    18.2.4 Training of Criminologists   428
18.3 Conclusions   428

18.1 The Existing Model: The Individual Offender

18.1.1 Schools of Criminology

Two schools of criminology have been identified in the history of criminology: the classical school (Bentham, Beccaria) and the positive school (Lombroso, Garofalo, Ferri; Radzinowicz 1966; Mannheim 1960; Hall 1945).

The classical school was a reaction to the harsh and arbitrary use of capital punishment during the Middle Ages. The eighteenth-century liberals advocated strict and precise legal definitions of crimes and punishment, set penalties which were certain and proportionate in severity to the infraction, and deterrence of crime before rather than after it occurred.

The positivists of the nineteenth century followed the new scientific movement of their time in advocating focusing on *criminals,* not *crimes, reforming* criminals and protecting society, and replacing legal concepts of crime with social concepts. The positive school questioned the ability of criminal law to deter or reform criminals through punishment.

Whereas the classical school advocated punishment via legal means to ensure protection of civil liberties, the positivist emphasized studying the individual offender after the offense in order to rehabilitate him. The following basic assumptions of positivism form a theoretical structure for criminological thinking:

1. Criminology studies characteristics of the *individual offender,* not characteristics of the environment in which crimes occur.
2. Rehabilitation of the individual offender is a major concern of American correctional practices.
3. Individual offenders can be rehabilitated through the use of psychiatric, psychological, and sociological concepts.
4. Punishment is not a successful means of changing human behavior.
5. The causes of crime can be found in the *past* experiences and heredity of criminals.
6. Criminal behavior can be controlled through the manipulation of noncriminal behavior, that is, by indirect means.
7. Criminology deals with individual criminal acts after they have occurred, not before.
8. By training people in services rather than scientific research we can control crime.

In contrast to the above assumptions, the writer will argue in this paper that:

1. Crime cannot be controlled through measures designed for individual offenders, but can be controlled through manipulation of the environment in which crimes occur.
2. Prevention and not rehabilitation must be the major concern of criminologists.
3. Given our present state of scientific knowledge, we do not know how to rehabilitate offenders.
4. Punishment is a powerful means for controlling behavior.
5. The causes of crime are to be found in the responses of individuals to *present* environmental conditions and *future* consequences of such behavior.

6. Criminal behavior can best be controlled through *direct* means which influence the criminal behavior itself.
7. Crime control programs must focus on crime before it occurs, not after it has occurred.
8. Criminology must shift from a *service* orientation to a scientifically based *research* orientation.

18.1.2 Studies of Individual Offenders

Theories of criminal behavior are based on studies of individual offenders, following the positivistic tradition in criminology. "All contemporary scientific criminology is positivistic in method and in basic formulations" (Vold 1958: 39).* Studies of criminals have been made from biological, psychological, and sociological perspectives. The biological school emphasized genetic and constitutional types, theories that did not withstand careful scrutiny. Psychological studies drew distinctions between criminals and noncriminals in terms of intelligence and personality structure. The Freudian theory of personality was especially prominent in the history of criminology as a framework for explaining criminal behavior. Inner needs, drives, and motivations are viewed as critical variables in this approach to criminality (Cavan 1962: 702ff; Sutherland and Cressey 1966: 161ff; Reckless 1967: 388ff; Vold 1958: 109ff). Sutherland and Cressey (1966: 180) conclude that "no trait of personality has been found to be very closely associated with criminal behavior."

Sociological analysis, starting with Quetelet and Guerry, placed emphasis upon ecological and social variables such as age, sex, residence, social disorganization, and race. The theoretical system used by sociologists to explain criminality is best summed up in Sutherland's theory of differential association which states that criminal behavior is learned in association with those who maintain criminal attitudes and values, that is, "a person becomes delinquent because of an excess of definitions favorable to violation of law over definitions unfavorable to violation of law" (Sutherland and Cressey 1966: 81). This statement is in itself one of individual behavior, as seen in the authors' subsequent comment that "the preceding explanation of criminal behavior purports to explain the criminal and noncriminal behavior of individual persons" (Sutherland and Cressey 1966: 83). Several modifications and criticisms of Sutherland's theory have appeared in print (Sutherland and Cressey 1966: 83ff), with some critics noting the absence of empirical work to support the Sutherland statement. Though Professor Donald Cressey has been an outstanding and capable advocate of the theory, from his own study of embezzlers he concluded that differential association could not be shown

---

* See also Hall (1945: 346ff), Radzinowicz (1966: 56ff), Matza (1964: 3ff), and Jeffery (1956: 658ff).

to apply to financial trust violations or even other kinds of criminal behavior (Sutherland and Cressey 1966: 93). Cressey states that differential association may not explain individual behavior, though it can explain the epidemiology of crime or differential crime rates (Sutherland and Cressey 1966: 93). This is an admission of the failure of differential association to do what it was intended to do (explain individual behavior), while it has been used to explain the statistical distribution of crime rates. In his most recent book Cressey (1969: 290ff) advocates attacking the problem of organized crime as a problem in organizational theory, not as a problem of individual acts, though he states that individual crimes must be dealt with by individual means.

More recent sociological writings have carried on the Sutherland tradition with emphasis on group processes, subcultural systems, and differential opportunity structure. Such theories attach importance to group norms and anomie, but such concepts are still derived from the study of individual offenders and are used to explain individual criminality. Studies of the individual offender have not revealed any scientific propositions of a causal nature (Wootton 1959; Hirschi and Selvin 1967), and as Lady Wootton has observed, such studies have focused on an individualistic approach rather than an environmental approach to social problems (Wootton 1959: 329ff). The exception to this is ecological studies of crime rates, such as is seen in the Sarah Boggs study quoted later in this paper. The issue is whether we study the individual offender or the environment in which crimes are committed and in which opportunities to commit crimes are present.

18.1.3 Behavior and Environment

In recent years more emphasis has been placed upon the scientific study of the physical aspects of behavior, and less emphasis given to mental states, introspection, and other nonphysical interpretations of behavior. Natural science methodology has been introduced into the behavioral sciences, and have resulted in behaviorism, environmentalism, systems analysis, and decision theory (Handy and Kurtz 1964; de Grazia et al 1968; Kretch, Crutchfield, and Livson 1969: 288ff; Charlesworth 1967). Behavior is regarded as an adaptation of an organism or system to an environment, this system being capable of receiving messages from and responding to environmental conditions. An input-output or open system model is used (Buckley 1968: 6ff).

Recent experiments have shown that brain growth and development is directly a function of environmental stimulation. Children who live on a low-protein diet will have fewer brain cells than those with a protein-rich diet. Other experiments have shown that experiences are carried in the chemistry of the neuron, in changes in the RNA structure of the cells, thus learning can be related to chemical changes in the neuron (Kretch, Crutchfield, and Livson 1969: 468–471).

Criminologists have insisted upon explaining criminal behavior in terms other than the criminal behavior itself. If a man steals a car it is because of a lack of love, hatred of his mother, a broken home, poverty, poor intelligence, delinquent associations, or blocked legitimate opportunities. Such an approach assumes that the causes of behavior lie in the past experiences and heredity of the individual offender. A more contemporary view of behavior, as found in behaviorism, decision theory, and game theory states that behavior is a response to present environmental conditions and future consequences of such behavior. Criminal behavior is a direct and immediate response to an environmental situation, based on the potential gain or loss from the criminal act. In other words, criminal behavior can be explained directly at the level of the behavior itself, and not in terms of other intervening variables.

18.1.4 Rehabilitation as an Ideal

The hallmark of the positivist is the belief that the control of crime must be through the criminal, not through the environment; in other words, rehabilitate the offender through individualized treatment.

Peter Lejins distinguishes three types of crime prevention programs: punitive, corrective, and mechanical. He writes, "when a person with a social science orientation speaks about prevention of crime today, he is usually thinking in terms of corrective prevention. ... Corrective prevention is clearly on the ascendency and dominates interest and practical innovation, especially in the United States. ... The emphasis is on conceptualizing, theory-building, and structuring in the field of corrective prevention" (Lejins 1967: 4–7).

Francis Allen has noted that the rehabilitative ideal has so dominated American criminology that other theories have been slighted or ignored (Allen 1959: 226–232; Wootton 1959: 336). As a result individual liberties and rights have been overlooked in the name of treatment, e.g., alcoholism and addiction are to be treated as mental illnesses, not crimes. If we classify a person as ill, we can then justify any type of treatment, including incarceration for life in an institution called a hospital which may resemble a prison (Lewis 1953: 224ff; Szasz 1963, 1965). The theory of rehabilitation has led to such innovations as probation, parole, sexual offender laws, and the juvenile court movement, all designed to remove the offender from a punitive situation while placing him within a therapeutic or treatment setting. The rejection of the theory of deterrence has had some rather unfortunate consequences for criminology, as has been noted by Hall, Allen, Wootton, Radzinowicz, and others. It is of interest to note that the above-named individuals are lawyers who have had some exposure to the legal tradition expressed in the classical school of criminology. In recent years Norval Morris and his associates at the University of Chicago Law School have undertaken a detailed study of the place of deterrence in the criminal justice system. To quote them, "Our dedication to corrections must not lead us to repudiate deterrence. Our criminal law system has deterrence as its primary and essential postulate" (Morris and Zimring 1969).

18.1.5 Role of Punishment in Criminology

Professor Ball (1955) has written that "American criminologists have frequently dismissed the deterrent principle as unjustifiable. Indeed, some penal reformers appear to regard deterrence and all forms of punishment as stigmata of barbarism." The most recent attack on punishment has been by Dr. Karl Menninger, a psychiatrist, who in his book *The Crime of Punishment* views punishment as our (the punisher's) secret need for crime, and our need to displace our guilt feelings by punishing criminals (Menninger 1968).

The rejection of punishment is a reaction to the frequent use of punishment during the Middle Ages and its failure to control criminal behavior. Both the classical and positive schools were reactions to extreme and cruel use of punishment, and as a consequence legal reforms occurred which limited its use to a few select cases. During the late eighteenth and early nineteenth centuries debates between William Paley and Sir Samuel Romilly occurred as to the proper place of capital punishment in the criminal justice system. Paley favored capital punishment for many offenses but implemented in only a few instances as examples to the public. Romilly argued that capital punishment should be reserved for a few cases but should be used in every case for which it was prescribed. According to Romilly, following the classical school, certainty was more crucial than severity. "So evident is the truth of that maxim, that if it were possible that punishment could be reduced to absolute certainty a very slight penalty would be sufficient to prevent almost every species of crime" (Michael and Wechsler 1940: 250ff).

Dr. Azrin, an experimental psychologist who has done outstanding work on the influence of punishment on behavior, defines punishment as a procedure that reduces the future probability of the punished response. To be effective punishment must be delivered immediately after the response to be controlled, must be delivered with certainty, and must be unavoidable (Honig 1966: 380ff).

Punishment can be a most effective way to control behavior, though it has several aspects which make it undesirable or ineffective within the legal context.

1. Punishment creates an anxiety reaction which can interfere with other desired behaviors.
2. Punishment creates avoidance and escape responses, which means the individual avoids or escapes from a punishing situation. A criminal can avoid detection or capture, or he can escape from prison. The

criminal law thus shapes avoidance behavior rather than law-abiding behavior.

3. Few criminal acts are ever punished. The arrest rate is low, the conviction rate is low, and these facts run counter to the statement that "certainty, not severity" is the important element in punishment.

4. The time gap between the criminal act and the punishment is too long. To be effective, punishment must be an immediate consequence of behavior.

5. The criminal act pairs a reinforced consequence with punishment. The immediate consequence of criminal behavior is positive—money, a car, sexual gratification. The possibility of punishment is remote and in the future. The stimulus most immediate to the response controls the behavior.

6. Punishment, as we use it in the criminal law, is positive, an aversive consequence such as imprisonment or execution. Much more effective is negative punishment, the removal of a desired object or condition. A child can be more easily controlled by taking away something he wants, such as a movie or ice cream cone, than by a spanking.

18.1.6 Therapeutic Approaches to Rehabilitation

Psychiatry and social work have approached criminal behavior from a Freudian framework, and the treatment for criminality was therapy either of an individual or group nature. The therapy dealt with the individual offender after the offense was committed. Psychiatry views criminal behavior as a product of inner conflicts between id, ego, and superego which resulted in criminal behavior, and the purpose of therapy is to bring to the surface and deal with these inner needs and conflicts.

Therapy is a matter of catharsis, insight, transference, and free association, carried on through the verbal interaction of patient and therapist. Because of the verbal quality of psychotherapy, it has often been labeled "talking therapy," or as two psychologists phrase it "a condition where two people sit privately in an office and talk about the thoughts and feelings of one of them" (Munn, Fernald, and Fernald 1969: 562).

The effectiveness of psychotherapy in altering human behavior is subject to great dispute. Berelson and Steiner (1964: 287) concluded that "there is no conclusive evidence that psychotherapy is more effective than general medical counseling or advice in treating neurosis or psychosis. Strictly speaking, it cannot even be considered established that psychotherapy improves a patient's chances of recovery beyond what they would be without any formal therapy whatsoever." H.J. Eysenck (1961: 712–713) summarized studies of psychotherapy by stating that "they show that roughly two-thirds of a group of neurotic patients will recover or improve to a marked extent whether they are treated by means of psychotherapy or not." Halmos (1966) has argued that psychiatry is a matter of faith in the healing power of love and empathy. Ehrenwald (1966) states that therapy is based as much on myth as on scientific method.

Psychotherapy has not had a very successful role in criminal rehabilitation. The Gluecks surveyed the Judge Baker Guidance Center in the 1930s and found an 88 percent rate of recidivism. The clinic director, Dr. William Haley, concluded that the experiment was "the close of another chapter in criminology." "It is impossible for child guidance clinics, through their work with individual cases, to be playing any very important part in the prevention of delinquent and criminal careers" (Witmer and Tufts 1964: 37–39).

The Cambridge–Somerville project attempted to provide guidance and social services for 300 predelinquent boys. Evaluations of the project found it to be a failure since the treatment group had a higher delinquency rate than the control group (Powers and Witmer 1951).

A study of social work intervention in treating female delinquency found that social casework was ineffective in the treatment of delinquency (Meyer, Borgota, and Jones 1966).

The failure of traditional therapy has resulted in the development of guided group interaction and self-help models wherein delinquents act as nonprofessional aides in changing criminal behavior, both their own and others. The President's Commission on Law Enforcement (1967a: 38–39) found no clear evidence of success or failure for guided group interaction as used at Highfields and Pinehill. In a review of the Highfields Program, Arthur Pearl found some inadequacies that did not allow the program to prepare the delinquent for reintroduction into society (Riessman, Cohen, and Pearl 1964: 481ff).

The use of excriminals to rehabilitate criminals has been advocated by Cressey, Grant, and others. The Joint Commission on Correctional Manpower and Training (1968) has published a seminar report on the use of offenders as a correctional manpower source, but these papers failed to evaluate the effectiveness of such programs.

The observation that nonprofessionals can "cure" whereas the professional cannot has been reinforced by such self-help groups as Alcoholics Anonymous and Synanon. Glaser (1964: 141ff) concluded from his study of the federal correctional system that worker supervisors had the greatest influence while prison psychologists had the least influence on releases from federal institutions. A study at the University of California at Berkeley revealed that nonprofessional therapists had success with young boys (Kretch, Crutchfield, and Livson 1969: 790–791).

The use of group pressures to change behavior is effective insofar as the group attaches positive and negative consequences to the behavior of its members. Synanon uses the "encounter" or verbal abuse in handling its members, as well as the threat of expulsion from the group.

Some of the most promising work going on is in behavior theory, wherein the consequences of behavior are closely regulated by the therapist-conditioner in order to recondition response patterns of a neurotic or psychotic nature. Ayllon has used behavioral techniques in working with mental patients in a hospital setting, and he uses nurses as agents for behavioral change (Munn, Fernald, and Fernald 1969: 560; Ulrich, Stachnik, and Mabry 1966). A major difference between clinical therapy and behavioral therapy is that in clinical therapy the therapist regards the behavior as symptomatic of an underlying problem, whereas the behaviorist regards the behavior as the problem which must be dealt with. Another difference is that the clinician deals with the *individual patient* whereas the behaviorist manipulates the *environment* of the patient.

Reality therapy, as practiced by Dr. William Glasser, contains some elements very similar to behavior therapy, though Glasser himself does not identify it as behavior therapy. Reality therapy is a set of procedures for establishing realistic responses and responsibility in the patient. The patient must realize the consequences of his behavior, and he must realize there are better alternative behaviors he can engage in to gain what he needs or wants (W. Glasser 1965). "In Reality Therapy we are much more concerned with behavior than with attitudes. Once we are involved with the patient, we begin to point out to him the unrealistic aspects of his irresponsible behavior" (Glasser 1965: 27–28). The story of Helen Keller and Annie Sullivan is a classical example of behavior or reality therapy (Glasser 1965: 26).

Therapy based on controlling the environment rather than the individual will probably be more systematically developed in future years. However, we are still dealing with the individual offender, and the influence of the therapist, individual, or group is still limited and only controls criminal behavior in a very weak and indirect manner. Therapy does not alter the environment in which criminal behavior occurs, and if it is true that behavior is responsive to the environment, then the environment, not the individual offender, must be changed. The theoretical structure of criminology states that criminality is something people carry around inside themselves, either as biological traits, psychological traits, or as sociological traits produced by differential association and subcultural groups.

18.1.7 The Criminal Justice System

The criminal justice system—police, courts, and corrections—works on the model of detecting, convicting, and punishing and/or rehabilitating the individual offender. The model starts with the commission of a crime, as seen in

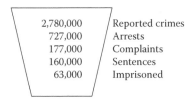

2,780,000	Reported crimes
727,000	Arrests
177,000	Complaints
160,000	Sentences
63,000	Imprisoned

Figure 18.1 Counts through criminal justice system stages.

the models presented by the President's Commission on Law Enforcement (1967b) and the New York State Intelligence and Information System:

$$\text{Crime} \rightarrow \text{Police} \rightarrow \text{Prosecution} \rightarrow \text{Courts} \rightarrow \text{Corrections}$$

The President's Commission (1967c) stated that 22 percent of all property offenses are cleared by arrest (42). Figure 18.1 illustrates the effectiveness of the criminal justice system (President's Commission on Law Enforcement and Administration of Justice 1967c: 61).

The law enforcement system has been variously characterized as crime control versus due process (Packer 1966: 238ff), law versus order (Skolnick 1966), enforcement of criminal laws versus maintenance of order (J.Q. Wilson 1968a, 1968b), and law enforcement versus services (H. Goldstein 1968). The policeman has no well-defined role. He spends over 60 percent of his time in noncriminal matters. J.Q. Wilson (1968a) estimates that 10 percent of the calls to police involve law enforcement issues. We must ask whether we are weakening our police system by asking the police to maintain order, provide social services, and enforce the criminal law.

The police are asked to enforce unenforceable laws, those involving "crimes without victims" as seen in addiction, alcoholism, and sex offenses (Schur 1965; Kadish 1967). The police are given great discretionary power in making arrests, which power is never visible or made a part of general policy (Goldstein 1960; Kadish 1962; La Fave 1967). Recent United States Supreme Court decisions have limited police action in areas such as search and seizure, confessions, right to counsel, and wiretapping.* Though such court decisions have had an impact on police behavior, it is too early to determine whether or not the Supreme Court has handcuffed the police. It can be noted that Supreme Court decisions have reduced the certainty of punishment and have extended the time between the criminal act and punishment, and therefore the overall effectiveness of punishment has been reduced to some as yet unmeasured degree by the legal process.

---

* Mapp. v. Ohio, 367 U.S. 643 (1961); Rochin v. California, 342 U.S. 165 (1952); McNabb v. U.S., 318 U.S. 332 (1943); Mallory v. U.S., 354 U.S. 449 (1957); Escobedo v. Illinois, 378 U.S. 478 (1964); Miranda v. Arizona, 384 U.S. 436 (1966).

The police can act as a deterrent only if they apprehend criminals, and at present they lack the technological and organizational means to do so at a rate that is meaningful. New emphasis in police organization must be given to the prevention of crime before it occurs, and the police can play a major role in this regard. New technology must be developed which will increase the efficiency of the police. New training procedures must be developed for preparing the police for duty in the twentieth-century urban slum environment.

The courts are severely limited by (1) the efficiency of the police in arresting offenders and (2) the efficiency of the behavioral sciences in rehabilitating offenders. The courts are no better than the input-output capabilities of the remainder of the system. Within the judicial process guilt is determined and sentence passed. Since the judicial process is geared to positivism, it places emphasis upon the rehabilitation of offenders through imprisonment, probation, and parole. We engage in elaborate legal procedures to determine if a man is guilty or innocent (as witnessed in the insanity plea, for example), and then we send the convicted offender to an institution that does not rehabilitate the offender. The courts lack the behavioral means to implement its policies. Because of reduced pleas, dismissed cases, and other legal technicalities, the uncertainty of the legal process is compounded, all of which diminish the effectiveness of the system.

The courts have in recent years rendered decisions that support the rehabilitative ideal. In *Durham v. U.S.* (mental illness),* *Driver v. Hinnant* (alcoholism),† *California v. Robinson* (drug addiction),‡ *Easter v. District of Columbia* (alcoholism),§ the courts held that certain behaviors were illnesses to be treated, not crimes to be punished.

Several other decisions have found, however, that the rehabilitative ideal has failed. In *Kent v. U.S.*¶ the court held that "there may be grounds for concern that the child receives the worst of both worlds: that he gets neither the protections accorded to adults nor the solicitous care and regenerative treatment postulated for children." In *The Matter of Gault*, Justice Fortas wrote: "Certainly these figures and the high crime rates among juveniles could not lead to the conclusion that ... the juvenile system is effective to reduce crime or rehabilitate offenders."**

In *Rouse v. Cameron*†† the court held that persons committed to a mental hospital by reason of insanity under the Durham rule had a right to

* Durham v. U.S., 214 F. 2d 862 (1954).
† Driver v. Hinnant, 356 F. 2d 761 (1966).
‡ California v. Robinson, 370 U.S. 660 (1962).
§ Easter v. District of Columbia, 361 F. 2d 50 (1966). See also Powell v. Texas, 392 U.S. 514 (1968), for a reversal of earlier decisions on alcoholism.
¶ Kent v. U.S., 383 U.S. 556 (1966).
** In the Matter of Gault, 87 S. Ct. 1428 (1966).
†† Rouse v. Cameron, 373 F. 2d 451 (1967).

treatment, and if treatment is not forthcoming the patient must be released from custody. We thus arrive at a position in legal history where an offender cannot be placed in prison because the law states he should be rehabilitated, not punished, and he cannot be retained in a mental hospital because such institutions do not afford adequate or proper treatment.

The court, by accepting the rehabilitative model, has weakened whatever deterrent potential the criminal law might possess, while at the same time not coming forth with successful treatment alternatives.

Suggested reform measures, such as more facilities and personnel to reduce court congestion, better administrative procedures, preventive detention of suspects, and so forth, might in some cases increase the efficiency of the courts, but such measures would increase, not decrease, the crime rate since they would allow for the processing of more cases.

The failure of the correctional system is well documented in penology. Studies have shown a 60 to 70 percent recidivism rate for prison inmates (Sutherland and Cressey 1966: 665; Caldwell 1965: 502). The FBI careers in crime project indicated that 60 to 90 percent of those arrested for federal offenses were rearrested within four years (FBI 1967: 37).

John Conrad (1965: 64–65), from a survey of international corrections, concluded that "Correctional research consistently finds that social restoration depends largely on attention to the social system from which the client came and to which he returns." In this survey he found a 75 percent recidivism rate in Scandinavia, which led him to write, "if good intentions and community support of humane objectives will reassociate offenders, then the outcome of Scandinavian corrections should be impressively reasonable. ... There is a limit to what kindness can accomplish in correctional practice" (pp. 135–136).

Bailey (1966), from a survey of 100 reports on correctional treatment, concluded that "evidence supporting the efficacy of correctional treatment is slight, inconsistent, and of questionable reliability." McKay found that institutions for delinquents did not rehabilitate or resocialize delinquent offenders (President's Commission on Law Enforcement and Administration of Justice 1967d).

The results of probation and parole are better than those of imprisonment. Sutherland and Cressey find the success rate to be 75 percent for probation and parole, though the Gluecks on the basis of a study of 500 offenders put the success rate at 21 percent (Sutherland and Cressey 1966: 495ff, 652ff). The FBI study showed that 52 percent of those on probation and 59 percent on parole were rearrested within four years (FBI 1967: 37).

Glaser (1964) has challenged the 66 percent recidivism rate as being too high, and he concluded from his study that 33 percent was a more realistic recidivism figure. However, other figures in the Glaser study seriously challenge the effectiveness of prison programs. He found that prison behavior is a poor indicator of postrelease success. Only 10 percent of the prisoners released showed benefit from job training, and only 20 percent benefited from the prison's educational program (Glaser 1964: 294, 251, 271). Glaser (1964: 191) found no significant relationship between group counseling and parole outcome. He did find that the critical factors in parole success were the environmental factors to which the inmate is exposed after release, such as employment, financial resources, and so forth (Glaser 1964: 311ff).

Wheeler, Cottrell, and Romasco, in a summary of the report on juvenile delinquency by the President's Commission, concluded that "there are no demonstrable proven methods for reducing the incidence of serious delinquent acts through prevention or rehabilitative procedures" (President's Commission on Law Enforcement and Administration of Justice 1967d: 410).

A recent issue of the *Annals* devoted to "The Future of Corrections" noted the failure of prisons as a means for behavioral change. One California study revealed that the longer a man was in prison, the greater the recidivism rate (Conrad 1965). The general consensus of opinion was that substitutes for imprisonment were needed, such as training programs and community-based programs. And yet one author wrote that "Despite the general enthusiasm with which the National Crime Commission applauded the establishment of new community-based programs and encouraged their extension, there is little hard evidence that any of the programs have achieved the objectives which they have sought" (Conrad 1965: 86).

18.1.8 Reasons for the Failure of Correctional Programs

Several of the many reasons that could be given for the failure of corrections will be discussed herein.

1. Correctional programs operate on the model of indirect controls over behavior via remedial education, job training, and/or therapy. The assumption is made that a man who is educated or employed will not commit a crime, though the empirical evidence does not support such statements.
2. Prisoners adjust to the environment of the prison, and the behavior shaped is that appropriate to the environment. Imprisonment does not change the environment in which crimes are committed.
3. The deterrent effect of punishment depends on the apprehension and conviction rate. The avoidance of punishment by many criminals makes the future contingency of punishment somewhat remote when the criminal act is committed.
4. To be effective punishment must be paired with an alternative response. A punished response will be extinguished if an alternative response is available to the individual. Our legal system is based on

punishment; we do not as yet reward the lawful behavior we desire in an effective manner. Glaser (1965: 486) notes that "it is well established in psychology that punishment does not change behavior patterns as effectively as rewarding alternative behavior." Conrad (1965: 303) writes: "The problem, as expounded by Skinner and Homans, is to extinguish criminal behavior by seeing to it that it goes unrewarded, and to reinforce some more acceptable form of behavior."

18.1.9 Community Action Programs

Since the time of Bonger, the thesis that poverty causes crime has been a popular one in criminology. Vold (1958: 169) summarized the studies made of economic cycles and crime by stating that "from the earlier studies to the present, the conclusion has usually been taken for granted that poverty and unemployment are major factors producing criminality." "It would be more logical to conclude that neither poverty nor wealth ... is a major determining influence in crime and delinquency" (Vold 1958: 172).

In recent years poverty and criminality have been reemphasized by the Cloward–Ohlin thesis of differential opportunity structure. The federal government, through the Office of Juvenile Delinquency, used the opportunity theory as the core of its delinquency prevention program (Marris and Rein 1967). Mobilization for Youth in New York City was based on the Cloward–Ohlin thesis. "A year after the project had entered its action phase, reducing poverty was given first priority in order to prevent and control delinquency" (Brager and Purcell 1967: 88–89).

Commenting on this theory, the British criminologist Radzinowicz noted, "When Cloward and Ohlin speak of criminal opportunities they are thinking primarily of the chance to learn criminal attitudes and techniques. It seems to me, however, that in trying to account for crime in an affluent society we cannot ignore criminal opportunities in another sense—the sheer frequency with which situations present themselves which make crime both tempting and easy" (Radzinowicz 1966: 98). Speaking of the heavy investment the Ford Foundation made in action programs, Radzinowicz (1965: 30–31) stated that "these schemes are primarily concerned with social policy, social welfare, and social services and it is essential to emphasize that ... they should not be identified too closely in the public mind with programs of crime prevention. ... If these grants are intended to help reduce crime, a much larger portion of them should be devoted to objectives more specifically connected with combating it."

Marshall Clinard also rejects the idea that poverty causes crime. He questions the validity of the Cloward–Ohlin thesis, and he finds it without any empirical evidence (Clinard 1968: 157ff, 238ff).

From 1954 to 1957, a total community action project was undertaken in Boston, involving the community, the family, and the gang. Walter Miller (1962: 181) concluded that the Boston project had a negligible impact on delinquency, since major offenses for males increased by 11.2 percent. Miller (1962: 169, footnote 1) points out that a model that was a failure in Boston was used in the total community attack on delinquency undertaken in the United States in the 1960s.

Marris and Rein (1967: 89) made a comprehensive survey of community action projects and concluded that "while projects could claim many individual successes, and may well have increased somewhat the range of opportunities, they did so at great cost and without benefit to perhaps two-thirds of those who sought their help." Marris and Rein (1967: 132, 195) found that the poverty program was never primarily concerned with delinquency and crime, since the assumption made was that *if* poverty were reduced, *then* ipso facto crime and delinquency would be reduced.

Daniel P. Moynihan, a department of labor assistant secretary during the Kennedy–Johnson years and presently assistant to the president for Urban Affairs, has published a book most critical of the poverty program, especially the Mobilization for Youth project and the role of social scientists in the poverty program (Moynihan 1968: 46ff, 102ff). Moynihan (1968: 188ff) argues that social scientists did not have the knowledge to alleviate poverty and delinquency, and they thus became advocates of social reform rather than scientific evaluators of results.

The President's Commission (1967d: 41ff, 222ff) placed great emphasis on job training and education as a means of combating delinquency. The high correlation between delinquency, undereducation, and unemployment has often been cited in the literature. However, as Daniel Schreiber (1963: 18) noted from his study of school dropouts, "it is imperative to be extremely precise in their interpretation, since with the increase of concern about the dropout problem, there is developing a tendency to equate the dropout with the delinquent. They state—nothing more than this—that the sentenced delinquent is much more likely to be a dropout, than an in-school student or a graduate. Beyond this, it would probably be impossible to establish any strictly causal relationship between the phenomena, e.g., that a youngster is delinquent because he was a dropout, or a dropout because he was delinquent."

Attempts at remedial education have been discouraging. The Coleman Report (1966) on Educational Opportunities found that school facilities, faculties, equipment, special programs, and counseling made little or no difference in the performance of students. What did make a difference was the family and community background of the students.

The United States Commission on Civil Rights (1967) concluded that compensatory educational programs are not successful with racially separated populations, and the Commission recommended desegregation as the answer. Coleman (1967) has argued that integration should not be confused with providing opportunities for educational performance.

Dentler and Warshauer (1965: 64) found no significant relationship between dropouts and illiteracy on the one hand and the quality of school and welfare programs on the other.

The Model School Project in Washington, D.C., was a failure, as was a similar project in Brooklyn set up by New York University (Model School Division 1966). Many other such projects could be discussed if space permitted.

One project that did work with delinquents–dropouts used programmed teaching machines to improve the educational level of the subjects; however, the delinquency rate of the subjects was not reduced via the educational program (Jeffery and Jeffery 1969).

The failure of such programs can be related to (1) the failure of current educational techniques to improve academic behavior to a point significant in the life career of the delinquent, and (2) the failure of education to control delinquent behavior.

Education is an *indirect* control over delinquent behavior, and there is no psychological reason why one set of responses should control another set of responses. If criminality is a response to the environment, then the response will continue even though other behaviors of the individual are altered.

18.2 A New Model: Environmental Control of Criminal Behavior

18.2.1 Science and Technology

The model of crime prevention discussed up to this point has been one of rehabilitating the individual *offender after* the offense; the model herein proposed is one of *environmental* engineering *before* the offense is committed. This model has never been developed, and what the writer suggests is of an exploratory and experimental nature, and is not to be viewed as anything more than a rough blueprint for serious future research and development.

Science and technology must play a crucial role in such a program. Behavioral science must be developed and applied to criminal behavior. Biological, physiological, and experimental psychology and more scientific aspects of sociology can contribute heavily to a better understanding of human behavior. A scientific view of behavior must replace a clinical view now in vogue in much thinking about criminality. Behavioral therapy (including reality therapy) must be developed beyond the present usage to include major environmental changes. "Environment and behavior" will be the major focus.*

---

* See the new journal Environment and Behavior, published, starting in 1969, by Sage Publications, Beverly Hills. California. See also Barker (1968).

New crime prevention technology must be developed, as is discussed by Congressman James Scheuer (1969) in his recent book. The use of computers to process records concerning wanted persons, stolen property, stolen vehicles, fingerprints, and so forth is an information collection and storage system, *not* a crime prevention system. Computerized systems may increase the apprehension rate, but this will only result in more congestion in the courts and prisons.

A better model is one that makes the commission of a crime impossible. Better response times for processing police calls will increase the apprehension rate and will increase police effectiveness. Surveillance and alarm systems will harden the targets and make the commission of crimes more difficult. Many homes and buildings that are burglarized are inadequately protected even by existing means, such as locks and alarm systems (President's Commission on Crime in the District of Columbia 1966: 86ff).

The police can play a more effective role in crime prevention through emphasis on prevention and control through the environment rather than apprehension of individual criminals after the fact.

Since von Hentig's (1949) book appeared, it has been recognized that many crimes are victim-precipitated. Potential victims must be educated in prevention techniques, and by changing the behavior of potential victims we can change the behavior of criminals.

A science of crime prevention has yet to be developed, and it would be senseless to state here what might be involved as a final product, but it can go beyond locks and alarms as they now exist. The President's Commission (1967b) spent only three pages in the entire report discussing the topic of reducing the opportunities for crimes, and they discussed only automobile thefts and street lighting. We must go beyond this level of analysis if we hope to control crime.

18.2.2 Urban Planning and Design

Though environmental planning as regards air and water pollution, noise, sanitation, transportation, and housing has taken place, we are not yet planning our cities for personal and property securities. Jane Jacobs (1961: 29ff) is one of the few writers who has taken note of the relationship between urban planning and crime. She observed that streets and parks that are isolated, unused, and nonfunctional are unsafe, whereas streets and parks with mixed usage are safe. It is well known that certain streets and parks are not safe because of their environmental location and design.

Building design, with unprotected elevators, stairwells, basements, and passageways, likewise contributes to criminal opportunities.

Urban planning can also contribute to social cohesion. As Alexander has observed, urban design can be used to reestablish human contact in the city.

Anomie, alienation, and loneliness have characterized certain urban areas, with high correlates of mental illness, suicide, alcoholism, drug addiction, and other behavioral disorders. Alexander argues that we cannot create artificial primary groups via guided group interaction or T group training; rather, we must design houses and streets in such a manner that personal intimate interaction occurs between members of the community (Ewald 1967: 69).

Potential criminal environments, such as bus terminals, parks, streets, and buildings must be made part of urban planning which includes behavioral reactions to environmental planning as well as the more traditional aspects of such planning.

One study that did focus on the environmental opportunities specific to each crime was made by Sarah Boggs (1965). She devised a crime occurrence rate based on environmental opportunities to commit crimes, as found in the ecological distribution of crime targets—safes, cash registers, people, cars, and so forth. Since crime occurrence rates differ from criminal offender rates (where criminals live) "the crime occurrence rate cannot be explained by the same factors that account for the prevalence of offenders" (Boggs 1965: 900).

Boggs discovered through factor analysis that there is an association between crime rates and criminal residential area rates in the case of crimes involving residential targets—homicide, assault, and residential burglary. However, in the case of crimes against business targets—business robbery, nonresidential burglary, and larceny—the criminals do not live in the area where the crimes are committed. She explains the former as due to familiarity of the offender with the victim or with the target of the crime. The latter she explains in terms of the location of profitable targets for criminal acts (Boggs 1965: 903–907).

The Boggs study demonstrates the value of an analysis of the characteristics of the environment in which crimes occur as compared to an analysis of the characteristics of the individual offender. A great deal can be learned about crime from a study of the relationship between crime and the environment which is not revealed by a study of those who commit the crimes.

18.2.3 Behavioral Science and Research

Michael and Adler (1932) concluded from a survey of criminology that criminology would not be a science until we have first developed a science of behavior. In 1967 the President's Crime Commission (1967d: 8) found that "delinquency is a behavior, and until the science of human behavior matures far beyond its present confines, an understanding of delinquency is not likely to be forthcoming."

Approximately 15 percent of the Defense Department's annual budget is allocated to research. While different fields call for different levels of research, it is worth noting that research commands only a small fraction of 1 percent of the total expenditure for crime control. There is probably no subject of comparable concern to which the nation is devoting so many resources and so much effort with so little knowledge of what it is doing. Many kinds of knowledge about crime must await better understanding of social behavior (President's Commission on Law Enforcement and Administration of Justice 1967e: 273).

Disciplines related to criminology have historically devoted themselves to human services, not research. Social work, clinical psychology, psychiatry, sociology, and law all have had a strong humanistic/social action orientation. Service to mankind is not to be questioned, but the means by which behavioral change is secured is not above examination. We pass laws and hire workers to combat poverty, delinquency, addiction, and racial segregation, and yet the social problems associated with urban America are greater today than ever before.

Our social programs, exemplified by social welfare, are to a very large extent based upon providing services to those in need, rather than programs designed to discover and alleviate the causes of such conditions. We treat symptoms, not causes, when it comes to behavioral disorders.

Although we spend millions each year on crime, we do not have adequate research facilities for criminological research, and most such research is carried on as part of action or demonstration projects (Radzinowicz 1965). A service or social action program that is not based on scientific knowledge concerning human behavior has not yet succeeded, as Moynihan concluded from his analysis of the poverty program.

We must use a systems approach to the control of crime. Systems analysis would force criminologists to focus on the interrelationship of parts of the criminal justice system, the consequences of certain policy decisions on future events, and the effectiveness of the system in reaching general goals or ends. Systems analysis, as developed in management, engineering, and organizational theory, can do a great deal to clarify the issues and solutions involved in crime control. Systems analysis looks to the future outcome or consequences of present decisions. It is scientific in its view of behavior, and is interested in what will occur if one does so and so under such and such conditions.

Decision theory, and related topics of game theory, strategy theory, and simulation studies, attempts to build a model of the way in which human decisions are (or ought to be) made (Charlesworth 1967: 175–211). Maximization of gain and minimization of loss are key elements in decision theory, with certain obvious usages in crime prevention. The whole point of crime control is to maximize gain (reduction in crime) while minimizing loss (costs, ineffective programs, loss of civil liberties). A game strategy is present in crime when the police and community on the one hand resort to strategies to reduce crime, whereas the criminal on the other hand resorts to strategies to maximize his gain from crime. Public policy as concerns crime could make liberal use of decision theory and systems analysis.

18.2.4 Training of Criminologists

A recently published survey by the Office of Juvenile Delinquency and Youth Crime revealed that the major focus for training probation and parole officers was social work, whereas for correctional workers the preferred training was in corrections. Social work schools provide no specialized training in criminology or corrections. Law schools are the only professional schools that prepare their graduates for work in criminal justice, but most law school deans oppose interdisciplinary work above and beyond legal training for their students (Piven and Alcabes 1969: Vol. 1, 11–42, Vol. 2, 13ff).

The major sources of treatment personnel for correctional institutions are social work, psychiatry, and clinical psychology, with only psychiatry devoting any effort to specialized training in criminology or criminal justice (Piven and Alcabes 1969: Vol. 2, 26ff).

The government study reveals some basic glaring defects in our criminological instructional system. The almost complete absence of behavioral science (criminology, sociology, behavioral psychology) from training programs is perhaps the most notable fact (Piven and Alcabes 1969: Vol. 2, 35), not to mention the complete absence from such programs of work in urban planning and design, systems analysis, computer technology, game theory, and environmental psychology. The emphasis is placed squarely on training in service-oriented, not research-oriented, disciplines—social work, psychiatry, clinical psychology, and law. We train people to provide legal, social, and psychiatric casework for our criminals, not to do scientific research on the causes of crime.

18.3 Conclusions

Sutherland and Cressey state that crime prevention is needed since reformation and punishment have failed to reduce crime rates. "The policy of prevention must be emphasized if the crime rate is to be reduced significantly. ... It is futile to take individual after individual out of the situations which produce criminals and permit the situations to remain as they were" (Sutherland and Cressey 1966: 682ff). They list as possible prevention programs community organization, organized recreation, casework, group work, coordinating councils, and institutional reorganization.

The President's Crime Commission (1967e: 12–15) related crime control to resources (manpower, equipment, facilities), public involvement and support, and a willingness to change.

Neither the Sutherland and Cressey statement nor the Commission statement breaks away from the individualistic, positivistic, "reform the criminal" orientation that has dominated American criminology for 100 years.

The two major theoretical positions now in vogue are (1) poverty and opportunity theory, and (2) differential association, group processes, and the use of offenders to change offenders. Neither of these positions goes beyond changing the criminal or the group to which the criminal belongs.

The future of crime control might well be a matter of urban planning, surveillance technology, decision theory, game theory, and systems analysis. We have examined the individual criminal in terms of his biological, psychological, and sociological properties. Criminal behavior is a biological–psychological–sociological response to an environmental situation that makes crimes profitable. From the perspective of behavioral psychology, criminal behavior is a product of differential reinforcement, the difference between the reward or gain from the crime compared to the chances of apprehension and punishment. Decision theory maintains that we weigh alternatives and make decisions on the basis of the probable outcome of our behavior. If we engineer the environment in such a way as to make the cost factor in the commission of a crime greater than the potential gain, the behavior will not occur.

We have two models of crime control available to us: (1) reform or punish the criminal after he has committed a criminal act, or (2) alter the physical environment within which crimes occur before they occur. We can resort to *indirect controls* over criminal behavior via therapy, self-help groups, education, job training, or casework, or we can resort to *direct controls* via changing the environment in which crimes are committed.

The classical school placed emphasis upon deterrence, a position rejected by many contemporary criminologists. What is here suggested is prevention not geared to punishment of offenders, as was the classical school, but one based on a concept of prevention geared to environmental engineering which removes the reinforcement from the criminal act.

Criminal Behavior and the Physical Environment

A Perspective

19

C.R. JEFFERY

From Jeffery, C.R. (1976). Criminal behavior and the physical environment: A perspective. *American Behavioral Scientist*, 20, 149–174.

Contents

19.1 Models of Behavior   432
19.2 The Environment in Sociology   436
19.3 Environmental Psychology   437
19.4 Interaction of Organism and Environment   440
19.5 Criminology: The Individual and the Environment   442
19.6 Methodological Issues   443
19.7 Criminal Behavior and the Physical Environment   445
19.8 Conclusions   447

Recent years have witnessed a revival of interest in environmental approaches to criminal behavior. In criminology we can trace three different sources of interest in criminal behavior and the physical environment. From the academic community we have a book on crime prevention and environmental design (Jeffery 1971), a book on the geography of crime (Harries 1974), and a book on the spatial analysis of crime (Pyle et al. 1974). Harries and Pyle are geographers, not criminologists.

Another source of interest in crime and the physical environment came from Britain and the police. Since the early 1950s the British police (Koepsell-Girard and Associates 1975) have been involved in crime prevention through the manipulation of the physical environment. These practices came to the United States in the early 1960s through the efforts of John Klotter at the University of Louisville where the National Crime Prevention Institute was established to train police in crime prevention methods.

The third source of interest and research comes from the architects, especially work carried out for the Law Enforcement Assistance Administration by Newman (1972), Reppetto (1974), and Sagalyn (1973).

It should be mentioned that at this time the prevention and control of crime through environmental design has had at best a marginal impact on professional criminology. It has had a much more visible impact on architecture, urban planning, and police practices. As Reppetto states in his article in this series [*American Behaviorial Scientist*, Volume 20, Issue 2], the Newman book has not been reviewed in any professional criminological journals. I might add that my book was not found worthy of review by sociologists as well. This lack of interest is seen in the fact that crime prevention and environmental design are not mentioned in the *Crime and Justice Annual* (Messinger et al. 1973; Halleck 1974), or in the ninth edition of *Criminology* (Sutherland and Cressey 1974), or in an article by Empey (1974) on crime prevention in the *Handbook of Criminology*.

The Sutherland and Cressey text discusses crime prevention in terms of local community organization, organized recreation, casework, and institutional reorganization. Empey discusses prevention in terms of labeling theory, normative systems, socializing institutions, illegitimate traditions, agencies of social control, and diversionary tactics. He concludes that crime prevention involves "means by which a person acquires a legitimate identity and a stake of conformity" (Empey 1974: 1095–1118).

19.1 Models of Behavior

Why is it that criminal behavior has not been studied in the context of the physical environment? The criminologist has had a model of behavior that does not allow for a physical environment. Kuhn (1962) has reminded us that scientific revolutions occur not because of the accumulation of knowledge and facts, but because of social psychological variables related to the acceptance or rejection of a view of nature held by the controlling interest in a given academic discipline. Major paradigms emerge in science based on assumptions made as to what questions should be asked and how they should be answered. What is popular in science depends on the political forces controlling publications. This is nowhere better illustrated than in the area of Skinnerian operant conditioning when investigators began to challenge the antibiological and antigenetic assumptions of the model. An article by Garcia which reported on the biological limitations of learning was greeted by a review that "these findings are no more likely than bird ... in a cuckoo clock" (Seligman and Hager 1972: 15).

If we assume that crime rates are a reflection of the physical environment, then we assume that behavior is related to the physical environment, and this involves a man–environment model of interaction. Three critical terms are involved: behavior, organism, and environment. The basic thesis of this paper is that the basic paradigm or paradigms pursued in criminology are such as to make the understanding and control of criminal behavior an

Table 19.1   Model I: Introspective Sociology and Psychology

Environment	→	Organism	→	Environment
Social norms		Mind–body dualism		Social norms
Values		Introspection		Values
Institutions		Psychic determinism		Institutions
Subjective meanings		Social determinism		Meanings

impossibility. It is the basic assumption in criminology that a nonphysical organism is interacting with a nonphysical environment. We wish to explore several models of behavior and to suggest that a biosocial learning theory model is now available for understanding the man–environment interactional process.

According to Ritzer (1975), sociology uses three different paradigms: (1) social factism, or the reality of social facts, norms, roles, institutions, change, and conflict; (2) social definitionism, or introspection, symbolic interactionism, and phenomenology; and (3) social behaviorism, or Skinnerian psychology applied to sociology. Ritzer hints that a new paradigm of biological sociology is emerging in the midst of political turmoil, but he does not pursue this issue in his theory book.

In psychology it is usual to differentiate a biogenic model, a psychogenic model, and a learning theory model (Franks and Wilson 1975: 375; Davidson and Neale 1974: 34–41). We will diagram three models of behavior based on these basic paradigms.

Model I (shown in Table 19.1) combines the social factist model of social reality as social norms and values, the social definitionist model of symbolic interactionism and phenomenology, and the psychogenic properties of introspective psychology. For the psychologist the environment might be real, but it is altered through perception, feeling, cognition, and thought to mental states. For the sociologist the environment is nonphysical. Thus, the problem of how does a nonphysical mental state interact with a physical environment? We either assume the alteration of physical states into mental states or we assume a nonphysical organism interacting with a nonphysical environment.

The following domain assumptions are held by sociologists and by sociological criminologists. These assumptions are derived from Model I, or from the social factist and social definitionist paradigms of sociology:

1. Man is a social animal; therefore, he cannot be biological or psychological.
2. Behavior is learned, and the learning process precludes biological and psychological processes.
3. Individual differences as found in behavioral genetics are not important in explaining behavior.

Table 19.2   Model II: Behaviorism and Environmentalism

Environment	→	Organism	→	Environment
Physical stimuli		Empty organism		Operant changes in environment

4. The environment to which people adapt is social, not physical.
5. The organism adapting to the environment is nonphysical, that is, introspective and symbolic.

Model II (Table 19.2) is the psychology of Skinner and Watson, an S-R model of learning without a physiological framework or base. There is nothing between the stimulus and the response, thus the term "empty organism" psychology. This is a pure environmentalism approach to behavior, with a complete denial of genetics and brain function (McClearn and DeFries 1973: 31; Thiessen 1972: 4–7; Brunswik 1956: 48–72). The early learning theorists were environmentalists, placing all the emphasis on nurture and not nature (Brunswik 1962: 49). The environmentalism of psychology was part of a general political move to glorify the environment at the expense of heredity (Eysenck 1973). The rejection of genetics in Russia under the name of Lysenko is the culmination of environmentalism as political dogma (Joravsky 1970).

Skinnerian psychology has had little impact on sociology and criminology, though Ritzer does discuss it as the third major paradigm of sociology.

The third model of behavior (Table 19.3) is one that has emerged in the past twenty years from behavioral genetics and psychology. It places a genetic system within psychology, and it regards the stimulus-response system as mediated by a brain and central nervous system. The organism consists of a sensory-motor process. The brain has the capacity to receive, code, store, retrieve, and make use of past experiences or information as a basis for future behavior. Functions usually delegated to cognition and introspection are now understood as brain functions. Emotions, for example, can be located in the limbic system. Higher thought processes are cortex functions. Motivation is related to the pleasure and pain centers of the brain (Thompson 1975).

Learning theory today is moving in the direction of psychobiology. The old distinctions between classical and operant conditioning are disappearing, and in their place learning theorists are involved in the biological bases of learning and in auto-shaping and sign-tracking (Hearst and Jenkins

Table 19.3   Model III: Biosocial Learning Theory

Environment	→	Organism	→	Environment
Physical		Biological		Physical
		Genetic		
		Brain–central nervous system		

1974, Pribram 1969: Hinde and Stevenson-Hinde 1973; Schneiderman 1973; Seligman and Hager 1972). We started out with behavioral models that separated the mind from the brain, the biological organism from the psychic organism, and the organism from the environment. Today we are no longer viewing behavior in terms of dualistic models. The mental-physical dualism is now a psychobiological model, learning theories are not separated from genetic and brain studies, and the organism is not separated from the environment.

> Human behavior is always the product of brain–environment interaction. Neither of these two influences can solely determine behavior, but many sociologists and some neurologists talk and act as if this were so. Brain scientists have largely discredited the mind–body dualism, but the brain–environment dualist lives in the minds and actions of many social scientists. (Mark and Ervin 1970: 138)

Past models of behavior have either had a nonphysical organism interacting with a nonphysical environment, a nonphysical organism interacting with a physical environment, or all S-R relationship without an organism. As Barker stated, the crucial problem in ecological psychology is "How can psychology hope to cope with nonpsychological inputs?" However, Barker notes in this connection that brain lesions, muscle contractions, and hormone concentrations are not psychological (Barker 1968: 6–7). If brain function is not psychological, then we can never solve the problem of a nonphysical organism interacting with a physical environment. Our model of the organism must be one that can receive, code, and respond to physical stimuli. The reason we react to environmental information is that sound waves and light waves are changed through transduction to chemical systems and nerve impulses. We only sense what our genetic system has "prewired" us to receive. The problem of nonpsychological inputs can be handled by a psychological system congruent with it. We are not arguing for a naive reductionism, but we are arguing that the genetic and biological bases of behavior must fit the models we use for explaining human learning and human behavior.

The biosocial approach to learning is now appearing in a number of places. Millon and Millon (1974: viii) state that

> in contrast to colleagues who de-emphasize man's physiological tendencies, ours is a biosocial-learning model, reflecting the belief that people differ significantly in their basic biological equipment. Biological tendencies increase the likelihood that certain life events will be experienced as positively or negatively reinforcing, therefore influencing the forms of behavior which are ultimately learned.

Handy and Harwood (1973: 11) write:

Behavior is used here as a name covering all the adjustmental processes of organism-in-environment. This differs from those who restrict behavior either to muscular and glandular activities *within the organism, or to those who* restrict behavior to so-called gross overt activities as contrasted with inner or mental activities. Man is viewed here as a biosocial organism, that is, as a biological organism operating in-and-by-means-of a social environment.

E. Wilson (1975: 5) presents the following diagram of these relationships:

Integrative	Ethology and Physiological	Sociobiology
		Behavioral
Neurophysiology	Psychology	Ecology

Wilson argues that

the transition from a purely phenomenological to fundamental theory in sociology must await a full, neuronal explanation of the human brain. … Skinner's dream of a culture predesigned for happiness will surely have to wait for a new neurobiology. The second contribution of evolutionary sociobiology will be to monitor the genetic basis of social behavior. (E. Wilson 1975: 575)

19.2 The Environment in Sociology

In sociology during the 1920s there was a shift from human ecology to social ecology, or from biological-ecological systems to social systems. Michelson argues that the social ecologist left behind in the dust the physical environment, and he cites Duncan's statement that "one searches the literature in vain for more than superficial reference to the brute facts that men live in a physical environment" (Michelson, 1976: 8). He writes that human ecologists fixate on human aggregates, that is, group data rather than individual data, whereas the relationship between man and his physical environment is much more microscopic than is revealed by aggregate data. Also, disciplinary barriers determine what is studied, and sociologists have deemed it advisable to stay at the social level rather than looking at the interdependence of biological, psychological, and social variables (Michelson 1976: 19–20).

Recently there was formed a section of the American Sociological Association called environmental sociology. In a statement on the differences between environmental sociology and human ecology Catton noted the separation of human ecology from bio-ecology. Wolf (1975: 17) quotes him: "the sociological dread of reductionism and the aversion to biological analogies, together with the sociological axiom that social phenomena are *sui generis*, would continue to insulate human ecology from ecology." He then quotes Klausner to the effect that "belief in an evolutionary discontinuity between man the symbolizer and other biological creatures came to be the preponderant, though not the unanimous, opinion of contemporary sociologists" (Wolf 1975: 17).

Zeisel (1975), in a monograph on environmental sociology, states that the classical figures in sociology ignored or underplayed the role of the physical environment in human behavior. He states that a man–environment model must be developed, but he does not spell out in detail the psychological dimensions of such a model.

The point to be made is that there has been no attempt to develop a man–environment model in sociology based on the physical environment. It is in itself amazing that a group of sociologists would have to form an "environmental sociology" section since this act suggests that there is nonenvironmental sociology, which leaves one wondering where human social activities take place. It reminds one of Homans' (1964) presidential address to the American Sociological Association where he argued that we should "bring men back in" to sociology; again, the implication is that sociology does not deal with organisms any more than it deals with the physical environment.

Homans wants to bring man back into sociology. Van den Berghe recently suggested sociology "bring the beast back in" (van den Berghe 1974, 1975), by which he meant the biological aspects of human social behavior. Mazur and Robertson (1972) have also suggested a biosocial system. *Sociobiology* (E. Wilson 1975) is a classic in the field and will mark the way for bio-sociology, and if we bring man back in, and if we bring the beast back in, then the nature of sociology will be somewhat changed. It is not the intent of this paper to either outline or discuss the possible changes in sociology which such a physical-environment/physical-organism model will evoke; however, to use Ritzer's three-paradigm model of sociology, we would say a fourth or perhaps a fifth paradigm would have to be developed. This will not occur without all of the political furor associated with scientific revolutions noted by Kuhn and Ritzer.

19.3 Environmental Psychology

If we are to build a man–environment model, or an environment–organism–environment model, we must have a psychological model of behavior that will allow the organism to receive information from the environment and to respond to the information through an operant act which operates on or changes the environment. If our model includes a physical environment, then we must have a model of a physical organism capable of interacting with the environment. As we indicated above, one model involves a nonphysical organism interacting with a nonphysical environment; the other involves a stimulus-response situation with an empty organism. The third model involves physical-organism–physical-environment interaction.

Environmental psychology ought to be of help in developing a model of behavior, since this brand of psychology is most interested in man–environment relations. Environmental psychology has borrowed heavily from Gestalt psychology, from the works of Kohler, Koffka, and Lewin (Ittelson et al. 1974: 67–70). The major emphasis here is on perception and the explanation of holistic configurations and cognitive processes. This is contrasted to a behavioral S-R approach where each stimulus-response system is analyzed as a separate behavioral transaction. It is difficult to deal with perception as defined in the classical Gestalt system. As Goldiamond demonstrated in a 1962 article (Bachrach 1962), perception cannot be approached within the introspective psychological system found in Gestalt psychology, and he suggests that perception can better be analyzed in terms of learning theory. Goldiamond argues that classical perception studies such intervening experiential states as seeing, hearing, or touching and the perceptual response is a verbal response or *verbal behavior* which is learned behavior and which follows the laws of operant conditioning. He quotes Boring to the effect that "introspection is doing its business under various aliases, of which verbal report is one" (Bachrach 1962: 309). Perception is defined in these terms:

$$\text{Stimulus} \quad \rightarrow \quad \text{Perception} \quad \rightarrow \quad \text{Response}$$
$$\text{System} \qquad\qquad \text{System} \qquad\qquad \text{System}$$

Perceptual psychology makes use of inferential mental states and it is of limited value in developing a model of man–environment interaction. What is suggested here is that *learning processes* replace perceptual processes as the core conceptual system in a man–environmental model.

Brunswik has developed a representation of the several schools of psychology in terms of their assumptions about the environment–organism–environment arc (Brunswik 1956: 51). This chart has been used by Barker (1968: 138) as a basis for his development of an ecological psychology (see Figure 19.1).

From this representation we can note that molar behaviorism satisfies all the requirements of a man–environment model. As Brunswik notes, molar behaviorism includes distal stimulus objects as well as distal achievement results, and such a model deals with central reference, either of a physiological nature or of an inferential nature. As he notes, Tolman's purposive behaviorism was inferential; however, he leaves room for a behaviorism that replaces inferential mental states with central brain and central nervous system processes (Brunswik 1956: 67-70).

Neither Brunswik nor Barker develops a physiological psychology to place between the stimulus and response. They do hint, however, that it is

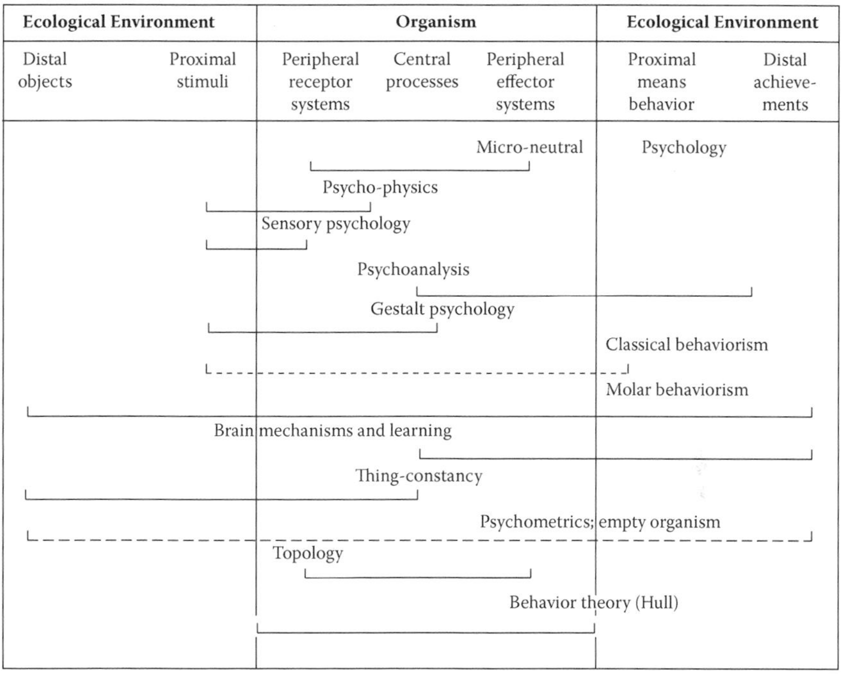

Ecological Environment		Organism			Ecological Environment	
Distal objects	Proximal stimuli	Peripheral receptor systems	Central processes	Peripheral effector systems	Proximal means behavior	Distal achieve-ments

Micro-neutral — Psychology

Psycho-physics

Sensory psychology

Psychoanalysis

Gestalt psychology

Classical behaviorism

Molar behaviorism

Brain mechanisms and learning

Thing-constancy

Psychometrics; empty organism

Topology

Behavior theory (Hull)

Figure 19.1 Schools of psychology, assumptions about environment–organism–environment. (All phenomena considered (——), single line; only initial and terminal phenomena considered (----), e.g., stimulis and response dotted line.)

one possible model. Ittelson et al. (1974) describe themselves as Gestalt psychologists and not behaviorists, but they do state that perception involves physiological processes:

The reader will find that a fairly complete and comprehensive picture of perception as a psychological process, that is, as activity of the nervous system of a particular individual, is emerging from current work. He will find what are perhaps unfamiliar terms such as sensory register, short-term memory, long-term memory, control processes, coding strategies, and information processing (Ittelson et al. 1974: 103).

Morgan and King (1971: 254–283) discuss perception as a process involving sensory systems and the brain, and the organization of sensation which the Gestalt psychologist wished to study must be studied as a complex function of brain structure.

Hubel and Wisel (P.G. Zimbardo and Ruch 1975: 247) have studied in detail the neural elements involved in visual perception, and they have established definite relationships between perception and brain functioning. Model III, a biosocial learning theory, is a molar behavioral model that makes use of the brain and central nervous system in place of inferential mental states and mental mapping. Neurological processes replace mental processes, and learning theory replaces perception. Learning becomes the major way in which the organism adapts to the environment; we do not need one psychology for perception and another for learning. As Michaels (1974) observed in his article on ecology and behaviorism, "human ecology has been discussed in relation to the *cognitive* branch of social psychology. The relation between human ecology and the *behavioral* branch of social psychology has apparently not been considered." He notes that a man–environment model of interaction dominates both ecology and learning theory, by which he means Skinnerian operant conditioning theory, and he suggests that ecological psychology should be behavioristic, ignoring internal mental states and concentrating on external environmental conditions related to behavior.

All behavioral scientists agree that behavior is *learned*. This would include biologists, psychologists, and sociologists. Criminologists start with Sutherland's theory of differential association, which is a learning theory of sorts. If we agree that behavior is learned, then we can start to examine the latest trends in learning theory which state simply that behavioral genetics and psychobiology are relevant and important to learning theory. We need not assume, as do many sociologists, that if behavior is learned it is not biological or psychological.

19.4 Interaction of Organism and Environment

There are four types of interaction between organism and environment that can be delineated:

1. The interaction of genotype and environment to produce the phenotype. The genetic basis of behavior is found in this interaction and is expressed in the pathway mechanisms: the brain, central nervous system, and endocrine system (McClearn and De Fries 1973; Rosenthal 1970; Thiessen 1972; Manosevits, Lindzey, and Thiessen 1969). Not only does the organism alter the environment, but the environment alters the organism. This is seen most dramatically in the impact of environmental input on brain growth and development. A lack of protein and stimulation from the environment can result in a defective and abnormal brain (Rosenzweig, Bennett, and Diamond 1972; Lewin 1975). We have attempted for years to alter criminal and delinquent behavior through poverty programs, all at a social level. If we take seriously the evidence that by the age of two a child reared in poverty has a defective brain due to a lack of protein and sensory stimulation, then we must ask how much intervention into human behavior is possible through social programs that ignore

the brain. Programs to feed school children a breakfast are now popular; however, this occurs at the age of six or older after the damage has occurred. Compensatory education at the age of six or sixteen is of limited or no value.

2. The second level of interaction of organism and environment occurs when the phenotype and environment interact, that is, when sensory experience or information from the environment enters the organism. This information is stored and coded in the brain through biochemical processes, and these processes we commonly refer to as memory and learning. All learning involves biochemical changes in the brain. Past experiences affect present behavior only if they are contained in the present, that is, are a part of the organism's psychobiological system. We usually ignore this problem with such terms as personality, attitudes, cognition, and so forth. We state that people act at the age of twenty on the basis of experiences at the age of five, but what kind of magic is this? It is magic if we assume a nonphysical entity that remembers and acts upon past experiences. It is not magic if we view memory and learning as permanent changes in brain chemistry.

3. The third level of interaction of organism and environment is at the present moment when behavior occurs. The present state of the organism, the present state of the environment, the genetic makeup, and the past experiences intersect at the moment when a response occurs.

4. The fourth level of interaction is contained in the process of the future blending with the present. The environment affords a setting whereby behavioral responses occur and have a consequence. This is what Brunswik and Barker call the distal achievements. In Skinnerian terms the organism "operates" on the environment so as to alter the environmental stimulation related to pleasure and pain. When a rat presses a lever for food the act combines genetic makeup, past experiences, present conditions, and future contingencies associated with the lever response. For Tolman this is the purposive nature of behavior.

The interaction of environment and organism is dynamic; that is, the organism changes the environment, the environment changes the organism. This is a dynamic equilibrium, constantly changing throughout the process of organism–environment interaction. Environmental input changes the structure of the brain, which in turn alters future responses to environmental contingencies. Philosophical problems of free will and control over one's future destiny are not problems within the context of this dynamic interaction of organism and environment.

19.5 Criminology: The Individual and the Environment

Early criminology was organized around biological and genetic concepts, to be replaced by Freudian psychology in the 1910–1920 period. In 1924 Sutherland published his textbook *Criminology*, which based criminology on sociology—on a brand of sociology founded at Chicago with W.I. Thomas. This is symbolic interaction, or Model I, which we discussed above. Sutherland's statement that criminal behavior is due to attitudes and values is the same as Thomas's statement that behavior is caused by definitions of the situation (Nettler 1974: 192–201).

Sutherland gave Shaw and McKay credit for his theory of differential association (Cohen 1956: 15). This is not surprising, since Sutherland used the Shaw and McKay materials as a basis for his theory. An important and critical turning point in human ecology and criminology occurred with the works of Sutherland, Shaw, and McKay. Earlier studies of ecology and crime had focused on crime and ecological areas (T. Morris 1957; Harries 1974; Pyle et al. 1974). Shaw and McKay turned the study of ecology into the study of *individual offenders*. They studied the addresses of delinquents, not crime occurrence sites. Offenders, not offenses, came to be the object of study (T. Morris 1957: 20). Shaw and McKay completely removed the crime from its physical surroundings, and the environment became one of social disorganization and cultural conflict. Shaw and McKay used a symbolic interactionist model of behavior and located the cause of behavior in conflicting norms of behavior. "Areas where the rates of delinquency are high are characterized by wide diversity in norms and standards of behavior. ... Within the same community theft may be defined as right and proper in some groups and as immoral, improper, and undesirable in others" (Shaw and McKay 1969: 171). This statement is in essence Thomas's definition of the situation and Sutherland's theory of differential association.

Sutherland, Shaw, and McKay turned sociological criminology into a symbolic interactionist framework or paradigm, to use Ritzer's terminology. This is the nonphysical organism interacting with the nonphysical environment. I commented above how in the past ten years several radical sociologists have suggested bringing man back into sociology, bringing the beast back into sociology, and now bringing the physical environment back into sociology. The basic theme of this series of papers on criminal behavior [*American Behaviorial Scientist*, Volume 20, Issue 2] involves a biosocial organism interacting with the physical environment. This model goes beyond the social factist model or the social definitionist model of behavior; it goes beyond behaviorism to a learning model based on genetics and psychobiology.

Morris has observed that the Shaw and McKay data suggest that crimes are committed where the opportunity structure exists rather than where specific attitudes of community members exist (T. Morris 1957: 94). Boggs (1965) found in her study of St. Louis that opportunity structures for crime differ from residential patterns of criminals. Baldwin (1974), a British social ecologist, has suggested that social area analysis as used by Shevsky and Bell is a poor ecological tool and is misleading when used to study crime rates. Social area analysis makes use of census tract data grouped according to economic status, family background, and ethnic and racial characteristics of the population. The assumption made is that one can correlate social variables with crime rates and tell something about why individuals commit crimes. Such statements appear in the works of sociological criminologists such as Polk, Schmid, Willie, and Quinney (Baldwin 1974; Baldwin and Bottoms 1976: 19–24). Such statements appear in spite of the fact that in 1950 Robinson spoke of the "ecological fallacy" by which demographic data are used to make statements about an individual phenomenon (Ittelson et al. 1974: 240). In their book on the urban criminal Baldwin and Bottoms (1976) show that *offense* areas are not the same as *offender* areas, and they argue for the analysis of offense areas and the study of crime from an ecological point of view. They find, for example, that the distance travelled by offenders is a critical variable, a finding duplicated in this country by Pyle, Capone, and Nichols, whose papers appear in this series [*American Behaviorial Scientist*, Volume 20, Issue 2].

Two serious assumptions/mistakes are found in the ecological analysis of crime. One, that one studies the individual offender and not the crime, and two, that one studies social area correlations and not the physical environment. The physical environment is totally ignored in ecological studies in criminology, as it is in sociology, as was discussed above.

19.6 Methodological Issues

Several methodological issues have been raised in the course of this discussion of environment and behavior. For one, the nature of the organism and its learning capabilities is crucial. This means that individual differences must be recognized; each individual is unique. As Lindzey has noted (Manosevitz, Lindzey, and Thiessen 1969: 6–7), individual genetic differences must be taken into account in any theory of behavior, since each individual is unique genetically. No sociological or criminological study is sound in this regard, for such studies use group data and lump unlike individuals together and treat them as the same for genetic and biological purposes. Studies that make use of social group data, such as studies of offenders by socioeconomic class or racial background, confound social and biological variables, and they fail to take into account the interaction of social and biological variables. We cannot make causal statements on the basis of a study of two thousand criminals studied for their social characteristics. The ecological fallacy noted by Robinson is but one form of this mistake of explaining individual behavior on the basis of group data. This is the difference between a case study method as found in medicine and a statistical study as found in sociology or criminology. A study of cancer involves one case around forty or fifty variables, not two thousand cases around one or two variables. The study of cancer involves genetics, virology, epidemiology, cytology, and many other academic specialties. One case is examined in terms of as many variables as is possible, with particular attention to the possible interaction of variables.

Another issue raised in the environment and behavior area is that of level of analysis. Ittelson and his associates (Ittelson et al. 1974: 249) have suggested that we need more than socioeconomic indicators, we need a microscope and not a telescope. We need a finer grain of resolution in our pictures of man and his environment. I remember a recent television program that started with a camera shot of a girl on a swing in her backyard. Over a period of several minutes the camera moved from the girl to her block, to the city, the state, the nation, and so forth until finally the view was that of earth taken from the moon. The process was then reversed and the camera moved closer and closer to earth until finally one saw a backyard with a girl on a swing. The analysis of crime has always been by square miles (Shaw and McKay) or by census tract data. Regional, state, city, and census tract data have been used for this purpose. One gets an entirely different feel for crime rates if one looks at national, regional, or state data, compared to block data or even individual crime site data. Bullock (1955) discovered that murders in Houston occurred along four streets. Feeney and Weir (1973) discovered that 25 percent of the robberies occurred in 4 percent of the city; in the case of commercial robbery all occurred within 12 percent of the city. An analysis of crime by census tracts, state, regional, or national units reveal certain interesting things about crime rates, but they mask the relationship of crime to the physical environment. If one bar has all the murders and 5 percent of the robberies, we want to study that one bar, not the murder rate for the city of Los Angeles or the state of California. The Brantinghams have included some maps of burglary and murder in this series of papers, moving from the national to the state, local, and block levels. Their analysis shows quite clearly that a finer grade of resolution reveals things about crime not seen at a more macroscopic level. The analyses of convenience store robberies by Duffala and of crimes in a married student housing project by Molumby, included in this series, show how individualized crime targets are. It is not every apartment or every convenience store that is burglarized or robbed, and crime targets are clearly a product of the physical environment and environmental design.

19.7 Criminal Behavior and the Physical Environment

The present series of papers represents an interdisciplinary effort to understand crime in relation to the physical environment. Several of the papers represent the efforts of urban geographers (Pyle, Capone, and Nichols) to become involved in the study of crime. Earlier works by Pyle et al. (1974) and Harries (1974) involve geographers in the spatial analysis of crime. Thus for the first time in a long time we have geographers, or urban ecologists if they prefer, entering the fields of crime analysis and research. Paul Brantingham is a lawyer and a criminologist, while his wife Patricia is a mathematician and urban planner. In the past urban planners have almost totally neglected crime as a problem for urban planning, as seen for example in the one slight reference to Newman's work in the Ittelson book. At this time in history it appears that urban planning will become more and more involved in crime prevention and control.

Reppetto is a former police officer turned academician who has been involved in crime prevention studies and research for a number of years. Reppetto reviews some general issues in crime and the physical environment as they have emerged in the experience of the United States. The British have a most active crime prevention unit, but we were unable to secure a paper from them. However, they have recently published studies on automobile thefts and bus vandalism in which they found that auto thefts in England and Germany have declined considerably since automatic locking devices appeared, and bus vandalism is very much related to the structure of the bus, the location of the conductor, the seating arrangement, and the door arrangement (Mayhew et al. 1976). This reminds me of my first paper on crime prevention, presented at the AAAS [American Association for the Advancement of Science] meeting in Denver in 1961, in which I was literally hooted from the room for suggesting that mechanical devices be used in place of prison terms or probation to reduce auto theft.

Duffala and Molumby are graduate students at Florida State University who have analyzed robberies of convenience stores and crimes in a student housing project on the basis of the physical environment. This research shows the impact of the environment on the distribution of crime rates.

Allen is a sociologist who participated in an interdisciplinary research effort on sociopathy and its treatment. His paper is entirely different from the others; it looks at the internal neurological functioning of sociopaths, not at the external environment. I have argued that a man–environment model involves an organism with a capacity to learn and to interact with the environment. Some psychologists have known for years that sociopaths do not condition to anxiety or the threat of punishment as do normal subjects (Eysenck 1964; Trasler 1973; Schachter and Latane 1964; Hare 1970; Goldman et al. 1974). This research shows a basic neurological difference between normal persons and sociopaths, due to a state of brain chemistry that produces under-arousal, which in turn makes avoidance conditioning to the threat of punishment and anxiety impossible. Such persons, who make up a large part of our prison population, are easily treated with a stimulant such as imipramine, which increases the state of arousal of the autonomic nervous system. In spite of this success, the project has been involved in excessive and needless political interference and is not being actively pursued at this moment. We are in the middle of a major controversy concerning a return to punishment and the use of prisons for our criminals. Some of our leading criminologists, lawyers, and political scientists are urging us to use more punishment and more prisons and to give up on treatment and rehabilitation (N. Morris 1974; J.Q. Wilson 1975). At the same time lawyers are arguing that behavior treatment techniques are cruel and unusual punishment (Jeffery and Jeffery 1975). Our ethic is such that we can execute a man or send him to prison for a long period of time, but we cannot treat him with the latest techniques available from psychobiology, psychiatry, and psychology.

Neurological intervention is especially critical in the area of personal crimes, e.g., murder, assault, and rape. So far the discussion of physical design and crime has been limited to street crimes, usually burglary and robbery. Environmental design has not touched murder and rape. If we hope to understand and control violence and aggression, we must be aware of the brain and its role in such behaviors. This is not to suggest that robbery is not a psychobiological response, it only suggests that intervention methods must differ. For stranger-to-stranger murder and rape environmental design works. It does not work if one is murdered or raped by a friend or relative.

The Supreme Court held in June of 1976 that capital punishment is neither cruel nor unusual punishment. This argument is based on an assumption that punishment is a deterrent to criminal behavior. A recent study by an economist concluded that capital punishment was a deterrent (Ehrlich 1975). The Ehrlich study used a statistical approach looking at such variables as probability of arrest, probability of conviction, probability of execution, age of population, unemployment, income, and time. From these variables Ehrlich concluded that criminals should be executed. Another statistical analysis of the data revealed no such relationship between executions and murder rates (Passell 1975). Past studies of deterrence (Tittle and Logan 1973; Zimring and Hawkins 1973) have revealed no conclusive results on this issue. Such studies have looked at probability of execution, severity and certainty of sanctioning processes, nature of the offense, length of the sentence, and so forth. And yet all of these studies of deterrence are worthless for most purposes since none of them addresses the issue of genetic and biological differences in conditionability to punishment. The death penalty works on the basis of the conditionability of the autonomic nervous system, and if there are individual genetic differences which make it impossible to condition a class of individuals (sociopaths) to the fear of pain, then the use of punishment is ineffective for that class of individuals. Deterrence does not work for psychobiological reasons which Supreme Court decisions and legal opinions do not change. We must alter the psychobiological structure of the sociopath, not execute more criminals for senseless reasons.

19.8 Conclusions

The implication of these papers is clear. We must assume the following: Behavior is learned. Criminal behavior is learned. Learning involves genetic and neurological processes. Learning involves a physical environment. The organism involved in crime is physical. The environment involved in crime is physical. The old model of nonphysical organism and a nonphysical environment must be replaced if we are to control crime. We must pay attention to the psychobiological nature of the criminal and the physical environment of the crime in interaction. We have started to develop an environmental psychology and a psychobiological psychology. We have not yet joined psychobiology and environmental psychology, nor have we joined these with criminology in an environmental criminology. The papers in this series will help in the development of an interdisciplinary criminology.

From these papers it is obvious that social area analysis of crime, which looks at social variables, must be replaced with a bio-ecological analysis. No longer can we afford to go from Shaw and McKay to Sutherland to differential opportunity structure to poverty programs to failure.

The future of crime prevention and control is now at stake. We can develop crime prevention programs based on a new model of man and his environment or we can retreat to the position taken by our politicians and the Supreme Court and hold that capital punishment is not cruel and unusual. We can follow this line of retribution or we can put as much effort into the prevention of crime as into the execution of criminals. If the political climate of the United States does not allow for the use of new knowledge to prevent crime, then perhaps we can use our new-found knowledge of physical design and criminal behavior to redesign hangman's knots and electric chairs. Our knowledge should not be wasted.

Situational Crime Prevention
Theory and Practice

20

R.V.G CLARKE

From Clarke, R.V.G. (1980). Situational crime prevention: Theory and practice. *British Journal of Criminology*, 20, 136–147.

Contents

20.1 "Dispositional" Theories and Their Preventive Implications   450
20.2 Preventive Implications of a "Choice" Model   452
20.3 Reducing Physical Opportunities for Crime and the Problem of Displacement   453
20.4 Increasing the Risks of Being Caught   456
20.5 Some Objections   457
20.6 Summary   459

Conventional wisdom holds that crime prevention needs to be based on a thorough understanding of the causes of crime. Though it may be conceded that preventive measures (such as humps in the road to stop speeding) can sometimes be found without invoking sophisticated causal theory, "physical" measures that reduce opportunities for crime are often thought to be of limited value. They are said merely to suppress the impulse to offend which will then manifest itself on some other occasion and perhaps in even more harmful form. Much more effective are seen to be "social" measures (such as the revitalisation of communities, the creation of job opportunities for unemployed youth, and the provision of sports and leisure facilities), since these attempt to remove the root motivational causes of offending. These ideas about prevention are not necessarily shared by the man-in-the-street or even by policemen and magistrates, but they have prevailed among academics, administrators and others who contribute to the formulation of criminal policy. They are also consistent with a preoccupation of criminological theory with criminal "dispositions" (cf. Ohlin 1970; Gibbons 1971; Jeffery 1971) and the purpose of this paper is to argue that an alternative theoretical emphasis on choices and decisions made by the offender leads to a broader and perhaps more realistic approach to crime prevention.

20.1 "Dispositional" Theories and Their Preventive Implications

With some exceptions noted below, criminological theories have been little concerned with the situational determinants of crime. Instead, the main object of these theories (whether biological, psychological, or sociological in orientation) has been to show how some people are born with, or come to acquire, a "disposition" to behave in a consistently criminal manner. This "dispositional" bias of theory has been identified as a defining characteristic of "positivist" criminology, but it is also to be found in "interactionist" or deviancy theories of crime developed in response to the perceived inadequacies of positivism. Perhaps the best known tenet of at least the early interactionist theories, which arises out of a concern with the social definition of deviancy and the role of law enforcement agencies, is that people who are "labeled" as criminal are thereby prone to continue in delinquent conduct (see especially H.S. Becker 1963). In fact, as Tizard (1976) and Ross (1977) have pointed out, a dispositional bias is prevalent throughout the social sciences.

The more extreme forms of dispositional theory have moulded thought about crime prevention in two unfortunate ways. First, they have paid little attention to the phenomenological differences between crimes of different kinds, which has meant that preventive measures have been insufficiently tailored to different kinds of offence and of offender; second they have tended to reinforce the view of crime as being largely the work of a small number of criminally disposed individuals. But many criminologists are now increasingly agreed that a "theory of crime" would be almost as crude as a general "theory of disease." Many now also believe, on the evidence of self-report studies (see Hood and Sparks 1970), that the bulk of crime—vandalism, auto-crime, shoplifting, theft by employees—is committed by people who would not ordinarily be thought of as criminal at all.

Nevertheless, the dispositional bias remains and renders criminological theory unproductive in terms of the preventive measures that it generates. People are led to propose methods of preventive intervention precisely where it is most difficult to achieve any effects, that is, in relation to the psychological events or the social and economic conditions that are supposed to generate criminal dispositions. As James Q. Wilson (1975) has argued, there seem to be no acceptable ways of modifying temperament and other biological variables, and it is difficult to know what can be done to make parents more inclined to love their children or exercise consistent discipline. Eradicating poverty may be no real solution either, in that crime rates have continued to rise since the war despite great improvements in economic conditions. And even if it were possible to provide people with the kinds of jobs and leisure facilities they might want, there is still no guarantee that crime would drop; few crimes require much time or effort, and work and leisure in themselves provide a whole range of criminal opportunities. As for violent crime, there would have to be a much clearer link between this and media portrayals of violence before those who cater to popular taste would be persuaded to change their material. Finally, given public attitudes to offending which, judging by some opinion surveys, can be quite punitive, there may not be a great deal of additional scope for policies of diversion and decriminalization which are favoured by those who fear the consequences of "labeling."

These difficulties are primarily practical, but they also reflect the uncertainties and inconsistencies of treating distant psychological events and social processes as the "causes" of crime. Given that each event is in turn caused by others, at what point in the infinitely regressive chain should one stop in the search for effective points of intervention? This is an especially pertinent question in that it is invariably found that the majority of individuals exposed to this or that criminogenic influence do not develop into persistent criminals. Moreover, "dispositions" change so that most "official" delinquents cease to come to the attention of the police in their late teens or early twenties (presumably because their lives change in ways incompatible with their earlier pursuits, cf. Trasler 1979). Finally, it is worth pointing out that even the most persistently criminal people are probably law abiding for most of their potentially available time, and this behaviour, too, must equally have been "caused" by the events and experiences of their past. Some of the above theoretical difficulties could be avoided by conceiving of crime not in dispositional terms, but as being the outcome of immediate choices and decisions made by the offender. This would also have the effect of throwing a different light on preventive options.

An obvious problem is that some impulsive offences and those committed under the influence of alcohol or strong emotion may not easily be seen as the result of choices or decisions. Another difficulty is that the notion of "choice" seems to fit uncomfortably with the fact that criminal behaviour is to some extent predictable from knowledge of a person's history. This difficulty is not properly resolved by the "soft" determinism of Matza (1964) under which people retain some freedom of action albeit within a range of options constrained by their history and environment. A better formulation would seem to be that recently expounded by Glaser (1977): "both free will and determinism are socially derived linguistic representations of reality" brought into play for different explanatory purposes at different levels of analysis and they may usefully coexist in the scientific enterprise.

Whatever the resolution of these difficulties—and this is not the place to discuss them more fully—commonsense as well as the evidence of ethnographic studies of delinquency (e.g. Parker 1974) strongly suggest that people are usually aware of consciously choosing to commit offences. This does not mean that they are fully aware of all the reasons for their behaviour nor that their own account would necessarily satisfy a criminologically sophisticated observer, who might require information at least about (1) the offender's motives; (2) his mood; (3) his moral judgments concerning the act in question and the "techniques of moral neutralization" open to him (cf. Matza 1964); (4) the extent of his criminal knowledge and his perception of criminal opportunities; (5) his assessment of the risks of being caught as well as the likely consequences; and finally, as well as of a different order, (6) whether he has been drinking. These separate components of subjective state and thought processes that play a part in the decision to commit a crime will be influenced by immediate situational variables and by highly specific features of the individual's history and present life circumstances in ways that are so varied and countervailing as to render unproductive the notion of a generalised behavioural disposition to offend. Moreover, as will be argued below, the specificity of the influences upon different criminal behaviours gives much less credence to the "displacement: hypothesis; the idea that reducing opportunities merely results in crime being displaced to some other time or place has been the major argument against situational crime prevention.

In so far as an individual's social and physical environments remain relatively constant and his decisions are much influenced by past experience, this scheme gives ample scope to account not only for occasional offending but also for recidivism; people acquire a repertoire of different responses to meet particular situations and if the circumstances are right they are likely to repeat those responses that have previously been rewarding. The scheme also provides a much richer source of hypotheses than "dispositional" views of crime for the sex differences in rates of offending: for example, shoplifting may be a "female" crime simply because women are greater users of shops (Mayhew 1977). In view of the complexity of the behaviours in question, a further advantage (Atkinson 1974) is that the scheme gives some accommodation to the variables thought to be important in most existing theories of crime, including those centred on dispositions. It is perhaps closest to a social learning theory of behaviour (Mischel 1968; Bandura 1973) though it owes something to the sociological model of crime proposed by the "new criminologists" (I. Taylor, Walton, and Young 1973). There are three features, however, that are particularly worth drawing out for the sake of the ensuing discussion about crime prevention: first, explanation is focused more directly on the criminal event; second, the need to develop explanations for separate categories of crime is made explicit; and, third, the individual's current circumstances and the immediate features of the setting are given considerably more explanatory significance than in "dispositional" theories.

20.2 Preventive Implications of a "Choice" Model

In fact, just as an understanding of past influences on behaviour may have little preventive pay-off, so too there may be limited benefits in according greater explanatory importance to the individual's current life circumstances. For example, the instrumental attractions of delinquency may always be greater for certain groups of individuals such as young males living in inner-city areas. And nothing can be done about a vast range of misfortunes which continually befall people and which may raise the probability of their behaving criminally while depressed or angry.

Some practicable options for prevention do arise, however, from the greater emphasis upon situational features, especially from the direct and immediate relationship between these and criminal behaviour. By studying the spatial and temporal distribution of specific offences and relating these to measurable aspects of the situation, criminologists have recently begun to concern themselves much more closely with the possibilities of manipulating criminogenic situations in the interests of prevention. To date studies have been undertaken of residential burglary (Scarr 1973; Reppetto 1974; Brantingham and Brantingham 1975; Waller and Okihiro 1978), shoplifting (Walsh 1978), and some forms of vandalism (Ley and Cybrinwsky 1974b; Clarke 1978) and it is easy to foresee an expansion of research along these lines. Since offenders' perceptions of the risks and rewards attaching to different forms of crime cannot safely be inferred from studies of the distribution of offences, there might be additional preventive benefits if research of this kind were more frequently complemented by interviews with offenders (cf. Tuck 1979; Walker 1979).

The suggestions for prevention arising out of the "situational" research that has been done can be conveniently divided into measures that (1) reduce the physical opportunities for offending or (2) increase the chances of an offender being caught. These categories are discussed separately below though there is some overlap between them; for example, better locks that take longer to overcome also increase the risks of being caught. The division also leaves out some other "situational" crime prevention measures such as housing allocation policies that avoid high concentrations of children in certain estates or that place families in accommodation that makes it easier for parents to supervise their children's play and leisure activities. Both these measures make it less likely that children will become involved in vandalism and other offences (cf. Wilson 1978).

20.3 Reducing Physical Opportunities for Crime and the Problem of Displacement

Variations in physical opportunities for crime have sometimes been invoked to explain differences in crime rates within particular cities (e.g. Boggs 1965; Baldwin and Bottoms 1975) or temporal variations in crime; for example, Wilkins (1964) and Gould and his associates (Gould 1969; Mansfield, Gould, and Namenwirth 1974) have related levels of car theft to variations in the number of vehicles on the road. But these studies have not generally provided practicable preventive ideas—for example, the number of cars on the road cannot be reduced simply to prevent their theft—and it is only recently that there has been a concerted effort on the part of criminologists to find viable ways of blocking the opportunities for particular crimes.

The potential for controlling behaviour by manipulating opportunities is illustrated vividly by a study of suicide in Birmingham (Hassal and Trethowan 1972). This showed that a marked drop in the rates of suicide between 1962 and 1970 was the result of a reduction in the poisonous content of the gas supplied to householders for cooking and heating, so that it became much more difficult for people to kill themselves by turning on the gas taps. Like many kinds of crime, suicide is generally regarded as being dictated by strong internal motivation and the fact that its incidence was greatly reduced by a simple (though unintentional) reduction in the opportunities to commit it suggests that it may be possible to achieve similar reductions in crime by "physical" means. Though suicide by other methods did not increase in Birmingham, the study also leads to direct consideration of the fundamental theoretical problem of "displacement" which, as Reppetto (1976) has pointed out, can occur in four different ways: time, place, method, and type of offence. In other words, does reducing opportunities or increasing the risks result merely in the offender choosing his moment more carefully or in seeking some other, perhaps more harmful method of gaining his ends? Or, alternatively, will he shift his attention to a similar but unprotected target, for example, another house, car, or shop? Or, finally, will he turn instead to some other form of crime?

For those who see crime as the outcome of criminal disposition, the answers to these questions would tend to be in the affirmative ("bad will out") but under the alternative view of crime represented above matters are less straightforward. Answers would depend on the nature of the crime, the offender's strength of motivation, knowledge of alternatives, willingness to entertain them, and so forth. In the case of opportunistic crimes (i.e. ones apparently elicited by their very ease of accomplishment such as some forms of shoplifting or vandalism) it would seem that the probability of offending could be reduced markedly by making it more difficult to act. For crimes such as bank robbery, however, which often seem to be the province of those who make a living from crime, reducing opportunities may be less effective. (This may be less true of increasing the risks of being caught except that for many offences the risks may be so low at present that any increase would have to be very marked.) Providing effective protection for a particular bank would almost certainly displace the attention of potential robbers to others, and if all banks were given increased protection many robbers would no doubt consider alternative means of gaining their ends. It is by no means implausible, however, that others—for example, those who do not have the ability to develop more sophisticated methods or who may not be willing to use more violence—may accept their reduced circumstances and may even take legitimate employment.

It is the bulk of offences, however, which are neither "opportunistic" nor "professional" that pose the greatest theoretical dilemmas. These offences include many burglaries and instances of auto-crime where the offender, who may merely supplement his normal income through the proceeds of crime, has gone out with the deliberate intention of committing the offence and has sought out the opportunity to do so. The difficulty posed for measures that reduce opportunity is one of the vast number of potential targets combined with the generally low overall level of security. Within easy reach of every house with a burglar alarm, or car with an antitheft device, are many others without such protection.

In some cases, however, it may be possible to protect a whole class of property, as the Post Office did when they virtually eliminated theft from telephone kiosks by replacing the vulnerable aluminium coin-boxes with much stronger steel ones (cf. Mayhew et al. 1976). A further example is provided by the recent law in this country which requires all motor-cyclists to wear crash helmets. This measure was introduced to save lives, but it has also had the unintended effect of reducing thefts of motor-cycles (Mayhew et al. 1976). This is because people are unlikely to take someone else's motorbike on the spur of the moment unless they happen to have a crash helmet with them—otherwise they could easily be spotted by the police. But perhaps the best example comes from West Germany where, in 1963, steering column locks were made compulsory on *all* cars, old and new, with a consequent reduction of more than 60 percent, in levels of taking and driving away (Mayhew et al. 1976). (When steering column locks were introduced in this country in 1971 it was only to new cars and, although these are now at much less risk of being taken, overall levels of car taking have not yet diminished because the risk to older cars had increased as a result of displacement.)

Instances where criminal opportunities can be reduced for a whole class of property are comparatively few, but this need not always be a fatal difficulty. There must be geographical and temporal limits to displacement so that a town or city may be able to protect itself from some crime without displacing it elsewhere. The less determined the offender, the easier this will be; a simple example is provided by Decker's (1972) evidence that the use of slugs in parking meters in a New York district was greatly reduced by replacing the meters with ones that incorporated a slug-rejector device and in which the last coin inserted was visible in a plastic window. For most drivers there would be little advantage in parking their cars in some other district just because they could continue to use slugs there.

The question of whether, when stopped from committing a particular offence, people would turn instead to some other quite different form of crime is much more difficult to settle empirically, but many of the same points about motivation, knowledge of alternatives, and so forth still apply. Commonsense also suggests, for example, that few of those Germans prevented by steering column locks from taking cars to get home at night are likely to have turned instead to hijacking taxis or to mugging passers-by for the money to get home. More likely, they may have decided that next time they would make sure of catching the last bus home or that it was time to save up for their own car.

20.4 Increasing the Risks of Being Caught

In practice, increasing the chances of being caught usually means attempting to raise the chances of an offender being seen by someone who is likely to take action. The police are the most obvious group likely to intervene effectively, but studies of the effectiveness of this aspect of their deterrent role are not especially encouraging (Kelling et al. 1974; Manning 1977; Clarke and Hough 1980). The reason seems to be that, when set against the vast number of opportunities for offending represented by the activities of a huge population of citizens for the 24 hours of the day, crime is a relatively rare event. The police cannot be everywhere at once and, moreover, much crime takes place in private. Nor is much to be expected from the general public (Mayhew et al. 1979). People in their daily round rarely see crime in progress; if they do they are likely to place some innocent interpretation on what they see; they may be afraid to intervene or they may feel the victims would resent interference; and they may encounter practical difficulties in summoning the police or other help in time. They are much more likely to take effective action to protect their own homes or immediate neighbourhood, but they are often away from these for substantial periods of the day and, moreover, the risks of crime in residential settings, at least in many areas of this country, are not so great as to encourage much vigilance. For instance, assuming that about 50 percent of burglaries are reported to the police (cf. Home Office 1979), a house in this country will on average be burgled once every 30 years. Even so, there is evidence (Department of the Environment 1977; Wilson 1978) that "defensible space" designs on housing estates confer some protection from vandalism, if not as much as might have been expected from the results of Newman's (1973) research into crime on public housing projects in the United States (cf. Clarke 1979; Mayhew 1979).

A recent Home Office Research report (Mayhew et al. 1979) has argued, however, that there is probably a good deal of unrealized potential for making more deliberate use of the surveillance role of employees who come into regular and frequent contact with the public in a semiofficial capacity. Research in the United States (Newman 1973; Reppetto 1974) and Canada (Waller and Okihiro 1978) has shown that apartment blocks with doormen are less vulnerable to burglary, while research in this country has shown that vandalism is much less of a problem on buses with conductors (Mayhew et al. 1976) and on estates with resident caretakers (Department of the Environment 1977). There is also evidence (in Post Office records) that public telephones in places such as pubs or launderettes, which are given some supervision by staff, suffer almost no vandalism in comparison with those in kiosks; that car parks with attendants in control have lower rates of auto-crime (*Sunday Times* April 9, 1978); that football hooliganism on trains has been reduced by a variety of measures including permission for club stewards to travel free of charge; and that shoplifting is discouraged by the presence of assistants who are there to serve the customers (Walsh 1978). Not everybody employed in a service capacity would be suited or willing to take on additional security duties, but much of their deterrent role may result simply from their being around. Employing more of them, for greater parts of the day, may therefore be all that is needed in most cases. In other cases, it may be necessary to employ people more suited to a surveillance role, train them better to carry it out, or even provide them with surveillance aids. Providing the staff at four London Underground stations with closed circuit television has been shown in a recent Home Office Research Unit study (Mayhew et al. 1979) to have substantially reduced theft and robbery offences at those stations.

20.5 Some Objections

Apart from the theoretical and practical difficulties of the approach advocated in this paper, it is in apparent conflict with the "nothing works" school of criminological thought as given recent expression by Wolfgang (1977): "the weight of empirical evidence indicates that no current preventative, deterrent, or rehabilitative intervention scheme has the desired effect of reducing crime." But perhaps a panacea is being sought when all it may be possible to achieve is a reduction in particular forms of crime as a result of specific and sometimes localised measures. Examples of such reductions are given above and, while most of these relate to rather commonplace offences of theft and vandalism, there is no reason why similar measures cannot be successfully applied to other quite different forms of crime. It has been argued by many people (Rhodes 1977, provides a recent example) that reducing the availability of hand guns through gun-control legislation would reduce crimes of violence in the United States and elsewhere. Speeding and drunken driving could probably be reduced by fitting motor vehicles with devices that are now at an experimental stage (Ekblom 1979). And there is no doubt (Wilkinson 1977) that the rigorous passenger and baggage screening measures introduced at airports, particularly in the United States, have greatly reduced the incidence of airline hijackings. There are many crimes, however, when the offender is either so determined or so emotionally aroused that they seem to be beyond the scope of this approach. A further constraint will be costs: many shops, for example, which could reduce shoplifting by giving up self-service methods and employing more assistants or even store detectives, have calculated that this would not be worth the expense either in direct costs or in a reduction of turnover. Morally dubious as this policy might at first sight appear, these shops may simply have learned a lesson of more general application, that is, a certain level of crime may be the inevitable consequence of practices and institutions that we cherish or find convenient and the "cost" of reducing crime below this level may be unacceptable.

The gradualist approach to crime prevention advocated here might also attract criticism from some social reformers, as well as some deviancy theorists, for being unduly conservative. The former group, imbued with dispositional theory, would see the only effective way of dealing with crime as being to attack its roots through the reduction of inequalities of wealth, class, and education—a solution that, as indicated above, has numerous practical and theoretical difficulties. The latter group would criticise the approach, not for its lack of effectiveness but—on the grounds that there is insufficient consensus in society about what behaviour should be treated as crime—for helping to preserve an undesirable status quo. Incremental change, however, may be the most realistic way of achieving consensus as well as a more equitable society. Most criminologists would probably also agree that it would be better for the burden of crime reduction to be gradually shifted away from the criminal justice system, which may be inherently selective and punitive in its operation, to preventive measures whose social costs may be more equitably distributed among all members of society. The danger to be guarded against would be that the attention of offenders might be displaced away from those who can afford to purchase protection to those who cannot. This probably happens already to some extent and perhaps the best way of dealing with the problem would be through codes of security that would be binding on car manufacturers, builders, local transport operators, and so forth. Another danger is that those who have purchased protection might become less willing to see additional public expenditure on the law enforcement and criminal justice services—and this is a problem that might only be dealt with through political leadership and public education.

Many members of the general public might also find it objectionable that crime was being stopped, not by punishing wrongdoers, but by inconveniencing the law abiding. The fact that opportunity-reducing and risk-increasing measures are too readily identified with their more unattractive aspects (barbed wire, heavy padlocks, guard dogs, and private security forces) adds fuel to the fire. And in some of their more sophisticated forms (closed circuit television surveillance and electronic intruder alarms) they provoke fears, on the one hand, of "big brother" forms of state control and, on the other, of a "fortress society" in which citizens in perpetual fear of their fellows scuttle from one fortified environment to another.

Expressing these anxieties has a value in checking potential abuses of power, and questioning the means of dealing with crime can also help to keep the problem of crime in perspective. But it should also be said that the kind of measures discussed above need not always be obtrusive (except where it is important to maximise their deterrent effects) and need not in any material way infringe individual liberties or the quality of life. Steel cash compartments in telephone kiosks are indistinguishable from aluminium ones, and vandal-resistant polycarbonate looks just like glass. Steering column locks are automatically brought into operation on removing the ignition key, and many people are quite unaware that their cars are fitted with them. "Defensible space" designs in housing estates have the additional advantage of promoting feelings of neighbourliness and safety, though perhaps too little attention has been paid to some of their less desirable effects such as possible encroachments on privacy as a result of overlooking. And having more bus conductors, housing estate caretakers, swimming bath attendants, and shop assistants means that people benefit from improved services—even if they have to pay for them either directly or through the rates.

Finally, the idea that crime might be most effectively prevented by reducing opportunities and increasing the risks is seen by many as, at best, representing an over-simplified mechanistic view of human behaviour and, at worst, a "slur on human nature" (cf. Radzinowicz and King 1977). (When the contents of *Crime as Opportunity* [Mayhew et al. 1976] were reported in the press in advance of publication an irate psychiatrist wrote to the Home Secretary demanding that he should suppress the publication of such manifest nonsense.) As shown above, however, it is entirely compatible with a view of criminal behaviour as predominantly rational and autonomous and as being capable of adjusting and responding to adverse consequences, anticipated or experienced. And as for being a pessimistic view of human behaviour, it might indeed be better if greater compliance with the law could come about simply as a result of people's free moral choice. But apart from being perilously close to the rather unhelpful dispositional view of crime, it is difficult to see this happening. We may therefore be left for the present with the approach advocated in this paper, time consuming, laborious, and limited as it may be.

20.6 Summary

It is argued that the "dispositional" bias of most current criminological theory has resulted in "social" crime prevention measures being given undue prominence and "situational" measures being devalued. An alternative theoretical emphasis on decisions and choices made by the offender (which in turn allows more weight to the circumstances of offending) results in more support for a situational approach to prevention. Examples of the effectiveness of such an approach are provided and some of the criticisms that have been made of it on social and ethical grounds are discussed.

Routine Activities and Crime Prevention in the Developing Metropolis (1987)*

21

M. FELSON

From Felson, M. (1987). Routine activities and crime prevention in the developing metropolis, *Criminology*, 25, 911–931.

Contents

21.1 Abstract   461
21.2 Introduction   462
21.3 Crime Types and Requirements   463
21.4 Offender Routines   463
21.5 Systematic Accident   464
21.6 Urban Physical Structures   465
21.7 Metroreef to Metroquilt: The Role of Facilities   468
21.8 Imbalanced Crime Production and Occurrence   471
21.9 A New Role for Facilities   476

21.1 Abstract

Routine activities deliver easy crime opportunities to the offender. Astute planners and managers can interfere with this delivery, diverting flows of likely offenders (such as adolescents) away from streams of suitable targets (such as television sets). They can engineer traffic to provide "natural surveillance." Past trends encouraged crime rate increases, but the developing metropolitan facility could reverse this, privatizing substantial portions of metropolitan turf.

---

* For sharing ideas, I owe a debt of gratitude to Ron Clarke, Travis Hirschi, Michael Gottfredson, Maurice Cusson, and James Wise. In addition, the wives and families of the first four had to put up with hours of meandering discussion while they wined and dined me.

21.2 Introduction

Pan was the humble Greco–Roman god of the woods, fields, and flocks. Originally a local deity who wandered the earth making love to the Dryads, Pan became the personification of nature and god of earthy realities. Following "Pan's criterion," criminologists can pay close attention to tangible terrestrial processes.

The "routine activity approach to crime rate analysis" (Cohen and Felson 1979a) does just that. (1) It specifies three earthy elements of crime: a likely offender, a suitable target, and the absence of a capable guardian against crime. (2) It considers how everyday life assembles these three elements in space and time. (3) It shows that a proliferation of lightweight durable goods and a dispersion of activities away from family and household could account quite well for the crime wave in the United States in the 1960s and 1970s, without fancier explanations. Indeed, modern society invites high crime rates by offering a multitude of illegal opportunities.

Despite recent declines in the proportion of the population in prime-crime ages (due to the aging of the baby boom), and despite increasing strictness of the criminal justice system, official crime rates have gone back up recently in the United States. These increments have a suspicious correspondence to the widespread marketing of light and valuable video cassette recorders. Moreover, evidence continues to indicate that, at least for recent decades, an improved economy tends to increase crime rates by providing more things to steal and more activities exposing person and property to illegal attack (Felson and Cohen 1981). The routine activity approach offers the best explanation for the otherwise unforeseen upsurge, giving criminologists reason to keep tabs on metropolitan change. This paper discusses some important metropolitan trends that offer new opportunities to prevent crime.

In the years since the routine activity approach was presented, criminologists have discovered or rediscovered many humble but stubborn facts about crime and its prevention. Some researchers have detailed how crime prevention can be accomplished through situational and environmental design (see reviews in Clarke 1983; Brantingham and Brantingham 1984; Poyner 1983). Others have explored how offenders move about in urban space and how they think about and respond to illegal opportunities (Cornish and Clarke 1986a; Brantingham and Brantingham 1981c). The early work on defensible space (Newman 1972) takes on new significance in light of subsequent research.

More facts provoke more thinking. Perhaps a high crime rate is not as certain as thought before. Perhaps the flows of routine activities could be diverted ever so slightly to reduce crime, without sacrificing prosperity or freedom. This paper considers new metropolitan forms that alter everyday life, providing new crime prevention opportunities. But, first, this paper will examine the minimal elements of routine lawbreaking.

21.3 Crime Types and Requirements

Crime has been classified in many ways, but seldom in terms of the earthy tasks and specific interdependence it requires. From this viewpoint, there are at least four types of crime (Felson 1983). (1) The *exploitative* (or predatory) offense requires that at least one person wrongly take or damage the person or property of another. (2) The *mutualistic* offense (such as gambling or prostitution) links two or more illegal parties acting in complementary roles. (3) *Competitive* violations (such as fights) involve two illegal parties acting in the same role, usually a physical struggle against one another. (4) An *individualistic* offense is a lonely illegal act (such as solo drug use or suicide).

Although the original routine activity approach applied only to exploitative offenses, its reasoning can be extended to all four types of lawbreaking. Each type usually requires that certain minimal elements converge in space and time. Prostitute must meet john away from police and spouse. Fighters must fight without peacemakers. Suicides must avoid meddlers. Predatory violations require the offender, target, and absent guardian.

A fourth element applies to exploitative violations, also playing a role in the other types of crime: the absence of an "intimate handler" (Felson 1986b). Although some offenders may have no social bonds (hence are not subject to informal social control), other offenders are "handled," having a social bond to a parent or some other "intimate handler" who is able to "seize the handle" and impose informal social control. Unfortunately for crime victims, handled offenders can evade their intimate handlers, thus avoiding informal social control for many hours each day. This evasion links routine activities to informal social control. As Hirschi (1969) noted, social bonds prevent delinquent behavior; yet, such prevention is difficult to accomplish by remote control. Indeed, informal social control is often carried out when youths (handled potential offenders) are within sight of their parents (intimate handlers). Felson and Gottfredson (1984) offer evidence of a major dispersion of adolescent activities away from parents and other adults, including strong declines in the probability of having family meals together, with dramatic increases in the tendency to stay out late with other teenagers.

In general, a potential offender must first shake loose from parent or handler, then find a target for crime unmonitored by a guardian. The next section examines offender routines relevant to seizing criminal opportunities.

21.4 Offender Routines

If offenders were well informed, forward looking, and unrelenting, crime prevention would be very tough indeed. The current paper assumes the contrary. This section considers the earthy rules of offender activity.

We begin with Zipf's (1950) "principle of least effort," which states that people tend to find the shortest route, spend the least time, and seek the easiest means to accomplish something. Least effort means not wasting calories or time, not travelling forever to get someplace. Based on this principle, geographers and others can predict a good deal of human physical behavior from proximity and available routes. If offenders travel minimal distances and often carry out illegal activities while en route to other ones, then their routines will set the stage for the illegal opportunities that come their way. If the criminal seizes the most convenient and obvious target, using lazy reasoning and taking easy action, this leaves no dramatic challenge for Mr. Sherlock Holmes. Although crime victims normally expend no effort *aiming* to be victimized, their exposures to risk are also subject to calculation.

The principle of least effort leads to the principle of the most obvious. According to this second principle, people (including offenders) rely on ready information, including sense data. Thus, the imperfect shopper picks the best buy right under his nose, missing a better buy in small print in another aisle. She picks the best store on the main street but misses a still better store on a side street. The reasoning criminal (Cornish and Clarke 1986a) finds an interesting target on the route home from school, neglecting better targets not far from that route. The thief picks the flashiest car, the corner house, the shiniest bicycle. Even pains avoided are those most obvious and proximate: a slap in the face, a punch in the nose, a dirty look from a passerby who might summon the police. (We can expect the offender to weigh flashy car against nosy neighbor, but is he really likely to consider threats by distant courts or legislatures?)

This second principle leads to the quick risk corollary, namely, that the offender tends to expose himself to risk for very little time over very little space. This makes the risk seem small because it is over in a flash. The child who drops a cookie on the floor picks it up immediately so that it still seems safe to eat. The driver who cuts in front of your car risks your life and his for but a moment. The trespasser takes a few short steps onto dangerous turf. One man steals one pass at another man's wife. Each forbidden pleasure tempts a quick dart, puff, snort, or grab, a short detour from a safe route. Even a long visit to an illegal house can be covered with fast entry through the back door.

21.5 Systematic Accident

Yet, risk takers sometimes lose. A burglar gets caught, a daredevil breaks a leg, a drug taker has an overdose, or someone out for work or fun becomes a victim of crime. Every exploitative crime or crime prevention implies that somebody failed. Either the offender succeeded at the victim's expense or vice versa. The study of crime is a study of accidents, wreaking havoc with simple choice models. This requires a general science of surprise, applying to both pleasant and unpleasant events, such as traffic accidents, stumbling on a pot of gold, or chance encounters of old friends (Bandura 1982).

Routine activity analysis and human ecology in general offer such a science of surprise, since events that shock the victim can be collected and analyzed statistically by an outside observer and explained in terms of other activities. This leads to the principle of *systematic accident,* which states that many surprises are structured via the physical world. Systematic accident applies both to the crime victim's shock and the offender's windfall.

How can sporadic events be systematic? Although the fox finds each hare one by one, the ecologist knows that the fox population varies with the hare population upon which it feeds. Similarly, the swelling population of video cassette recorders plus the recent upsurge in property offenses rings a loud bell in the ecologist's brain. Just as lions look for deer near their watering hole, criminal offenders disproportionately find victims in certain settings or high-risk occupations (Block, Felson, and Block 1985). Similarly, a professional sports event sets the stage for nearby traffic jams and car break-ins. A convergence of picnickers helps feed neighboring insects. A convention supplies visitors to local art museums and massage parlors. Indeed, some of the principles of systematic accident are so general that they apply as well to volcanic eruptions as to criminal events (Felson 1980, 1981). This is why criminology is partly a physical science, explaining how bodies move, how they mix, and how their mixtures produce reactions, even explosions not possible when they were separate.

By engineering bodily convergences, crime prevention can be effected. One of the most important principles for understanding such sociophysical processes is urbanization.

21.6 Urban Physical Structures

For traditional urban ecologists, the local urban community was the basic unit of daily interaction, except for the important daily trip to the place of employment. The latter was contained in either the industrial zone or the central business district (CBD). People walked and used public transit, relying upon convenient community institutions. Neighborhoods covered far less area than what we call a community today, and neighborhood schools and shops were much smaller and nearer. Delinquency clustered near the industrial zone. Although sometimes rampant, crime was usually contained.

In the past three decades, the automobile and truck greatly dispersed metropolitan residence, work, schooling, shopping, and leisure. The dissipation of the CBD and the traditional industrial zone complicates urban ecology. Cars cross traditional community boundaries in a flash. The traditional notion of a city as a collection of communities is greatly strained when people can live here, work there, and shop yonder. Friends can visit one another after a short drive, not needing to rely upon a local community for daily sustenance. Commuters no longer head toward the urban core, as industry and shopping, too, disperse to suburbs and beyond.

Years after males gained automobility, females often remained housewives, keeping localism alive for a few extra decades. Subsequent increases in female employment and automobility freed women from their own communities, which were no longer the unit of daily sustenance save for children. Even the young are increasingly schooled and transported elsewhere.

In light of these facts, a new ecology of crime is required for an age of automobility. Yet, urban ecologists cling to the old urban image, partly from nostalgia, partly for want of new ideas, and partly because traditional communities never seem to die completely. Meanwhile, new suburbs adopt old communal names and facades for marketing purposes, easily fooling those who are too young to remember what a real pedestrian community was like.

How can one describe a new physical entity which seems to have no boundaries? Many geographers have put mathematics to good use for describing metropolitan spatial behavior. Yet, one still needs to know what replaced the "community." Does some other bounded entity mediate between the individual and the modern metropolis?

To answer this question, one can turn to Jacobs's (1961) classic work, *The Death and Life of Great American Cities*. Jacobs hated the suburbanized metropolis, which widened streets for autos and narrowed sidewalks. By killing pedestrian traffic, American cities undermined community life. Jacobs anticipated the crime wave that followed.

On the positive side (to depart from Jacobs), automobiles and roadways give people more choice, more nonlocal access, hence reducing the tyranny of the neighborhood. For better or worse, the modern metropolis provides new access to households, businesses, industries, schools, and places of leisure. People circulate over greater distances, gaining their sustenance in a new way. In effect, the city as a collection of neighborhoods gives way to the metropolis as a collection of buildings linked by automotive streets into a vast sociocirculatory system.

City streets are not new, but their function has changed. The world of pedestrians was a world of shortcuts, where a straight line offered the shortest route between two points. Pedestrians cut across yards and through alleys or public buildings, traversed streets, hopped over fences. The world of urban vehicles is quite different in its routines and routings from the world of pedestrian motion. Drivers enter curbed, constructed channels, going from driveway to street to the next street to freeway to side street to parking lot. They walk only the route to and from the parked vehicle. The street is the core of the sociocirculatory system linking various buildings; people, equipment, and supplies move via streets from one building to another, often several miles away. Although we are accustomed to think of streets as "outside," they might as well be inside; flanked by curbs and buildings, they impair the freedom of the great outdoors. One's home or business is an appendage to the street. If one's home burns down, this will probably affect one's neighbors only while the street is blocked by fire trucks.

Because this sociocirculatory system leads so far so quickly, internal community interaction declines, although net movement increases. One cannot rely upon the "natural" community areas, on immediate proximity, as the basis for symbiosis. Families, friendships, and businesses may still thrive, but they use streets and automobiles in so doing, as people, equipment, and supplies circulate quickly. The principle of least effort has new consequences when the only effort needed is stepping on the gas pedal.

Much of modern suburban North American housing was developed to look like a quiet, socially integrated neighborhood. After constructing streets and sewers (to attract buyers), and selling off homes one by one, developers usually deeded the common areas to municipalities for future maintenance, or even helped to form governments to perform this function. Builders wanted profits, not a century of fixing sewers, filling potholes, and providing security. Dumping sociocirculatory costs and problems, including crime, onto the public system is a fundamental fact of urban life. Municipal governments generally agree to take over these burdens on condition that streets become public. Public access in an age of automobility opens suburbs to thousands of strangers while giving residents a vast range for shopping, work, and friendship.

Via the street, one finds friend, job, and service. Via the street, one draws sustenance from the larger environment. Via the street, offender finds victim (Beavon 1985) and teenager evades parent. The street belongs to everyone, hence is supervised by no one, except for an occasional policeman who does not know who belongs there anyway. The very system that fosters easy movement and vast opportunity for good experiences also interferes with informal social control of youths and protection of person and property from intruders. And so the street system exposes people to serendipity and calamity.

Streets not only provide the means for drawing sustenance from an urban environment, but also constitute its organ of growth. In a world of pedestrians, homes may precede streets; but in a world of cars, streets precede or accompany the construction of homes, businesses, and even parks. Few North Americans will buy a home or business without adequate parking and street access at the outset. Few will patronize a business or a forest preserve lacking automotive convenience. Even backpackers drive their cars to the foot of the trail. Indeed, modern North American growth is connective growth, with streets extending outwards from existing cities, allowing new units to append themselves. Sometimes large streets are constructed first, followed by small; sometimes small streets spread first, later widened into or supplemented by large ones. In either case, each new unit must connect to the larger sociocirculatory system before it can come to life.

This pattern of sustenance and growth can be dubbed the Great Metropolitan Reef. Each home and business clings to this metroreef like coral, gaining sustenance from the street-flows of people, equipment, and supplies. The metroreef proliferates, organizing and sustaining daily life for a vast array of human activities. Young delinquents flow rather freely about the metroreef, drawing illegal sustenance readily from its rich stores and routine activities. Will the reef simply continue to grow or will the metropolis evolve into a new phase?

21.7 Metroreef to Metroquilt: The Role of Facilities

An important new urban form has emerged in recent decades. Business developers have begun to take care of sewers, sidewalks, streets, and security for a fee (Stenning and Shearing 1980). An early example of this phenomenon was the shopping center, whose developers provided member businesses a package of many services: parking, security, utilities, and (they hoped) a crowd of big spenders. If all went well, the developer made a profit and the member businesses were satisfied with services rendered.

A good word for such a setup is *facility*. Its Latin root is *facil* (meaning easy); the facility makes it easy for shoppers to shop and merchants to sell; for offices to get work done; for owners to have time to tend their own business; for people to park and feel safe.

The shopping center has been followed by other important types of facilities which, at least in southern California, are changing the urban landscape. Each development links several independent businesses or departments into a single territorial complex, offering facility management services. The condominium unites several owned apartments, providing maintenance, parking, and security for common rooms or yards, with moderate levels of privacy. The "smart" office building or office condominium provides financial and computer services, telecommunications, energy-efficient utilities, and security. The "mini-mall" assembles five to ten retailers with a parking lot in front, subject to routine informal security protection from onlookers. The industrial park unites several industrial facilities, perhaps offering food service, parking, utilities, communication, and a few trees and sculptures. The mobile home park offers hookups, landscaping, and pathways. The college or hospital campus joins several organizational functions, providing parking, security, and landscaping. The Los Angeles school district campus unites elementary, junior high, senior high, and adult school on a single site. The private recreation facility provides pool, weight room, lockers, and parking. The public recreation facility offers baseball, basketball, parking, and picnicking.

In general, these facilities attempt to draw all the benefits they can from the metroreef while trying to limit litter, crime, and extraneous traffic by privatizing internal traffic. Recent facilities developers are combining two or more activities, such as office space, hotels, homes, and apartments.* Some include child care services.† Although the apartment facility and feudal manor go back many centuries, today's facility serves without necessarily providing a community. This noncommunal symbiosis is an innovative way to provide services and protection in a dispersed metropolis, representing an important shift in the organization of routine activities.

Many people prefer single family dwellings to condominiums, or stand-alone businesses to those that are part of a larger cluster. However, the metroreef is getting too large and crowded for the urban coral to cling singly. Facilities offer wholesale access to the metroreef, providing convenience while regulating the mutual impingements of people. Were suburban communities completely safe, spacious, and clean, facilities might not be necessary. If the reef still had plenty of convenient space for self-attachment, facilities would have no niche. But the proliferation and problems of the metroreef have reached a point where facilities attract customers.

Why are modern developers so inclined to take over so many municipal functions at their own expense? Sometimes, they are compelled to do so by local authorities. Sometimes, unprofitable services draw profitable customers. Sometimes, customers pay extra for special services. Perhaps they are dissatisfied with government services. Perhaps their fear of crime is greater than before. Parking is tight. Land is more scarce, and that available has to be carved up more carefully. Those tired of time spent on the freeway may sacrifice privacy for convenience or seek to give up lawn care.

---

* The Los Angeles Times of June 4, 1987, Westside section, announces four developments being planned near the Los Angeles Airport: (1) The LAX Northside Development, designed to contain up to 4.5 million square feet of office space, plus two hotels, on 350 acres; (2) Continental City, about two million square feet of office space and two hotels on 29 acres; (3) Playa Vista, a planned community with 20 million square feet of office space, homes, and apartments for 20,000 people, and 700 to 900 new boat slips, on 957 acres near Marina del Rey; (4) Howard Hughes Center, 2.7 million square feet of office space, one hotel, on 69 acres next to the San Diego Freeway at Sepulveda Boulevard. Although these four developments have generated considerable political controversy from local residents, the growth of the metropolis and demand for their services keeps such facilities coming, opposition be damned. Los Angeles is also experiencing a proliferation of mini-malls. These, too, are generating political opposition, but grow anyway.

† One of the most interesting new facility developments is the One South Coast Place in Costa Mesa. This 16-acre site will house IBM's Orange County operation, and will include an art museum, restaurant, athletic club, shops, and two office towers. Most interestingly, it will include a 15,000-square-foot child care center to serve 120 pre-schoolers within walking distance of the offices. The project will incorporate a traffic management program, including flex-time, ride-sharing, and van-pools. The developers will spend $6 million on nearby traffic improvements to ensure no damage to local traffic flow (Los Angeles Times Pt. VIII, June 28, 1987).

A single provider may improve telecommunications and other services. In any case, one sees a growth of facilities in Los Angeles and some other parts of North America.

By taking on some new forms and increasing its share of the ecosystem, the facility can break the continuous extension of the metroreef. To be sure, today's metropolis mixes community, street, and facility. A majority of urban units continue to have their own direct hookup to the metroreef, while those facilities that exist merely attach to the much larger metroreef. Yet, urban specialists should begin to ponder whether the metropolis will become a collection of facilities rather than of communities!

How can facilities squeeze out the existing stand-alone units to transform the metroreef into something new? (1) Sometimes a university or hospital campus swallows up nearby housing like an amoeba digesting a food particle. They may bulldoze and rebuild, or simply convert the acquired property to their own uses, but the point is that facilities can spread. (2) Although facilities may begin at the edge of town, where land is vacant, the outward movement of industry and business may place them increasingly at the core rather than the periphery of daily productive activity. (3) Cities can quickly revitalize an old area by using their rights of eminent domain to clear the space, then inviting facilities to reclaim and rebuild. (4) Sometimes stand-alone units band together to form a facility. For example, single-family dwellers might get together to hire security. Sometimes local law permits them to privatize streets, but this remains rare in the United States (see Newman 1972, for a description of private streets in St. Louis, Missouri). (5) If facilities succeed in providing desirable services, stand-alone units may follow their lead, either by joining together and privatizing an area, by allowing the bulldozer in, or permitting existing facilities to gobble up surrounding turf in return for providing services.

Thus, one imagines a new metropolitan form: the Great Metropolitan Quilt, a patchwork of coterminous facilities intervening between homes, businesses, and the larger society. This metroquilt would divide urban space among a large set of corporations, whose facilities managers would be responsible for organizing everyday movements, including security.

This metroquilt would have a special sociocirculatory system, including two types of trips: those within facilities and those between facilities via boulevards and freeways. Within facilities, people would walk, drive, take elevators, escalators, and moving sidewalks. Between facilities, they would drive from the parking structure of the origin facility to that of the destination facility. All parking and walking would occur within a facility, unless a car breaks down. Public arteries would remain in the interstices, the last vestige of local government management responsibility. The evolution from metroreef to metroquilt would vastly alter the role of the police, as well as the ecological basis of lawbreaking.

Perhaps the word "evolution" is too strong, but a metropolitan "drift" seems evident. The city of the past was a collection of communities. Today's American metropolis approximates a metroreef, with vestiges of community. The metroquilt of the future may combine many facilities with a few remaining traces of community and metroreef.

All too little is known about crime production and prevention in existing facilities, but some inferences can be drawn from current spatial imbalances in crime distribution.

21.8 Imbalanced Crime Production and Occurrence

The metroreef moves offenders, targets, guardians, and handlers about so quickly that it creates tremendous imbalances in crime risk. Some spots are very risky, letting offenders find ready targets. Worse still, some spots appear to draw or assemble offenders and targets, while dumping the resulting offenses on the neighbors. For example, Roncek and Lobosco (1983) found that public high schools elevate the crime rates of nearby neighborhoods, presumably by assembling youths, who are likely to be offenders as well as victims. Brantingham and Brantingham (1982) show that local crime risk varies inversely with distance from McDonald's restaurants. Even though the restaurant itself may be safe, it draws those in prime offending and victim ages, producing high crime risk for nearby properties. On the other hand, being surrounded by intact couples tends to depress the crime risk at any point on the city map (Felson 1986a; Sampson 1987). Fewer streets leading directly to your home puts you less at risk of household victimization than many such streets (Beavon 1985).*

---

* Beavon (1985) correlates residential crime with street accessibility at the isolated edge of the Vancouver metroreef. For each street segment, he counted the number of turns through which one can enter or exit. For example, when one through street crosses two others, the block sandwiched between two can be entered six different ways. At the other extreme, a dead-end segment has one way in or out. Beavon finds that 2 percent of his sample's street segments have one turn, 18 percent have two, 17 percent have three, 34 percent have four, 21 percent have five, and less than 9 percent have six turns. (My own calculations amplify this difference, counting the combinations of routes by which an intruder can enter and exit each block. A street segment with six turns has 6×6 or 36 possible entry-exit combinations. This number increases geometrically: 1, 4, 9, 16, 25, and 36. The centers of large cities may have a few street segments with ten streets converging, thus 100 different routes in and out.) Most importantly, Beavon finds that the number of turns correlates .895 with a block's auto theft rate, .953 with theft from auto, .985 with property theft, .937 with willful damage, and .970 with breaking and entering rate per street segment. To be sure, these correlations would be lower in a study more to the center of the metroreef, but the data show the sociocirculatory system's tremendous capacity to amplify and shift crime risk from place to place (see also Newman 1972).

Detailed local analysis is the best way to learn how crime reaches people. However, large-area data sometime help. Table 21.1 sorts some 441,561 property crimes reported to police agencies in the state of Illinois in 1984 by their type of location in the sociocirculatory system. The residential category accounts for 22 percent of these offenses. Retail and trade outlets account for almost 19 percent. Public channels, vehicles, storage nodes, and gateways (including streets, parking facilities, yards, and driveways) host a full 45 percent of property crimes, as much as all residential and retail and trade categories combined.

Although industries may produce the bulk of goods stolen or damaged, very few property crimes are linked to their premises. They appear to pass most of this risk on to retail outlets, households, or places of public transit. Whatever liquor stores and bars do to lubricate property crime, they themselves suffer relatively little. If offices, hospitals, and other services assemble some offenders and targets, the resulting crime may not be "charged" to their accounts. If schools are great producers of property crime, official Illinois data indicate that very little ends up assigned to schools themselves. It appears that certain organizations suffer a fraction of the crime they probably "help" to produce, and are assigned little statistical credit for their "contribution" to crime production.*

Uneven crime risk gives uneven incentive to do something about it. For example, factories that produce lightweight durable goods suffer few thefts of what they produce. Such thefts of electronic items occur mostly in transit, in retail, or in residential settings. The industrialist has little incentive to worry about the theft of his product from customers. Even cheap and simple crime prevention is generally neglected by the manufacturer because the incentive is absent. For example, each new electronic product could easily be encoded for the owner's exclusive use, removing the thief's incentive to steal it. Similarly, 24-hour automatic bank tellers may produce a vast amount of robbery and purse-snatching, without impinging upon bankers, who save labor costs through automation.

Yet, Table 21.1 indicates that many facilities may successfully prevent crime from occurring *inside* their premises. As more transport channels, nodes, and gateways are incorporated within the walls of facilities, might one expect crime rate decreases?

---

* To be sure, these data reflect the tendencies of personal victims to report disproportionately crimes near home and the greater tendencies of some individuals and businesses to notice and report thefts. The low levels of offenses reported for airports may reflect the victim's inconvenient position for reporting. Schools may handle much of their crime without involving the police.

Table 21.1 Illinois Property Crime Frequencies by Type of Position in the Sociocirculatory System, 1984

Public Channels	
Street	43,090
Other vehicle	9,750
Highway	2,408
Sidewalk	2,399
Alley	1,977
Road	1,096
Train right-of-way	338
Trailer	146
Bus	127
Train car/train/CTA	120
Taxi	92
Bridge	44
Storage Nodes	
Parking lot, municipal	33,979
Parking lot, general use	21,468
Parking lot, business	2,155
Bike rack	1,007
Mailbox	1,016
Warehouse	552
Truck terminal	412
Train depot	333
Truck stop	265
Train yard/building	159
Bus garage	102
Airport	95
Warehouse shipping dock	85
Bus depot	57
Residential	
Private residence	68,513
Residential yard	28,660
Driveway, residential	21,327
Apartment	19,673
Garage, residential	15,923
Motel, hotel	3,034
Apartment common area	2,075
Porch	1,871
Mobile home, permanent	1,554
Mobile home park	940
Apartment storage locker	788

Continued

Table 21.1 (*Continued*)   Illinois Property Crime Frequencies by Type of Position in the Sociocirculatory System, 1984

Condominium	299
Vacation camper, trailer	136

Industrial

Construction site	2,522
Factory, manufacturing building	1,292
Junk yard, salvage yard	278
Construction company	261
Lumber yard	237
Industrial park	48

Retail and Trade

Business place, commercial	26,288
Gas station	12,834
Department store (chain)	12,511
Grocery, food store (chain)	8,235
New, used car lot	3,240
Grocery, food store (independent)	2,849
Other chain store	3,424
Bank, credit union, savings and loan, currency exchange	2,751
Drug store, pharmacy (chain)	1,906
Garage/automotive repairs	1,691
Liquor store (independent)	825
Shopping mall	794
Laundromat	783
Drug store, pharmacy (independent)	724
Department store (independent)	703
Hardware store (chain)	490
Jewelry store	314
Sporting goods store (chain)	242
Liquor store (chain)	208
Hardware store (independent)	182
Barber shop	169
Sporting goods store (independent)	152
Dry cleaner	127
Motorcycle shop	61

Urban Recreation

Bar or tavern	4,317
Restaurant (independent)	2,919
Restaurant (chain)	2,160
Church	1,900

Table 21.1 (*Continued*) Illinois Property Crime Frequencies by Type of Position in the Sociocirculatory System, 1984

Athletic club, health center, locker room, gym locker	1,482
Bowling alley	562
Golf course	555
Sports arena, stadium	425
Swimming pool	387
Movie houses, theater	223
Roller skating, ice rink	163
Educational Facilities	
School	7,202
College or university	4,282
School grounds	3,057
College or university residence hall	1,305
Library	546
Fraternity house	236
Offices and Public Facilities	
Office building	1,202
Law enforcement building	849
Public building	582
Local government building	457
Public facilities	313
Federal building	129
State building	123
Fire station	100
Penal institution	58
Medical Facilities	
Hospital	724
Medical offices	669
Cemetary	404
Nursing home	272
Rustic Recreation	
Park	1,677
Recreation or picnic area	1,335
Park building	646
Boat marina, dock, boat house	507
Lake or waterway	257
Camping grounds	226
Boat	205
River bank	185

Continued

**Table 21.1 (*Continued*)   Illinois Property Crime
Frequencies by Type of Position in the
Sociocirculatory System, 1984**

Park road or scenic drive	131
Fairgrounds	131
Wooded area	119
Forest preserve	111
Wildlife management area	29
Rural Industrial	
Farm building	1,106
Tilled farm land	572
Farm house residence	550
Farm pasture	413
Farm pen or corral	217
Grain elevator	158
Oil field	121
Historical site	31
Coal mine	18
Other	
Storage shed	2,332
Building	1,267
Vacant land	436
Coin operated machine	310
Highways, streets, alleys unspecified	33
Uncoded	8,852
Other	5,614
Unknown	2,163

Source: Illinois Law Enforcement Commission, 1984.

21.9 A New Role for Facilities

A facility has a distinct crime prevention advantage over the average street:
it can limit access and direct flows of people. Facilities can remove many
routine activities from the public domain, giving a business or corporation a
chance to make a profit selling safety to the public or enhancing security for
its own employees or property.

Victims of street crime cannot ordinarily sue their city for negligence.
However, victims of crime within private facilities are tempted to bring
such lawsuits, compelling facility managers and their insurers to consider
crime prevention.

If the metroreef gives way to the metroquilt, the facility would become
the main organizational tool for crime prevention. That formal organizations
take responsibility for large swaths of urban turf is encouraging for those

interested in crime reduction. When the parking, paths, and trees are managed by a specific suable entity, the incentive for serious crime prevention emerges. Indeed, the shift from community to street to facility as the main unit of ecological organization implies a shift in crime prevention. When community is dominant, largely unaided informal social control reigns. When streets are dominant, crime control is largely charged to hit-or-miss public policing, diluted by suburban sprawl. When facilities become dominant, architects, security planners, and facilities managers become the central actors in the crime prevention process, for better or for worse.*

Private organizations cannot guarantee protection for their own property, much less anybody else's, simply by hiring guards. Large-scale organizations have difficulty monitoring their own employees, who can easily be tempted by "inside jobs." For this reason, those organizing crime prevention efforts need to think in terms of physical design and kinetic management. Facilities designers should attempt to divert flows of likely offenders away from likely targets, or else contain these flows within limited areas which are easily monitored. Facilities designers should also consider natural informal controls, working indirectly and inadvertently to control the flows of offenders and targets. Besides, what manager wants to pay wages when surveillance can be engineered almost for free?

Such criminokinetic analysis must be more sophisticated than posting rules and demanding compliance. As an example, consider a note placed on a car by authorities in a local public park: "Please *do not* angle park. Park vertically." Since the white lines were clearly drawn for angle parking, the authorities in effect designed a violation, then appealed to thousands of patrons one-by-one not to carry it out. Had they drawn the lines vertically in the first

---

* The growth of facilities has special significance for the inequality of security. Today's metroreef probably enhances crime risk for everyone, but especially for those who live within range of many offenders. On the other hand, the modern sociocirculatory system makes it difficult to purchase true security, since some offenders can easily find their way to wealthy victims and have an incentive to do so. Nice neighborhoods are not necessarily very secure. On the other hand, a walled facility with a 24-hour doorkeeper can protect those able to pay for it. The growth of facilities may render security more a matter of supply and demand in the future than it is today (Birkbeck 1985; Cooke 1986). Some facilities will undoubtedly protect themselves, not clients. For example, shopping centers sometimes patrol inside to protect their merchants, while neglecting the parking lot vulnerabilities after the customer has paid for the goods and left. Security vendors are often more interested in selling hardware than more intricate and comprehensive crime prevention. Facilities may offer what Waller (1979) calls a "security illusion," namely conspicuous locks and alarms. Some facilities (such as schools and housing for the poor) may tolerate high crime rates rather than admitting that they have a problem. However, knowledge of environmental crime control is growing (compare Clarke 1983; Brantingham and Brantingham 1984; Poyner 1983). This subjects administrators charged with negligence to the embarrassing testimony of expert crime-prevention witnesses in courts of law. It can also provide course materials for training the next generation of crime prevention officers.

place, there would have been no need to struggle with the public about their new regulation. Similarly, if one designs products that seem to say "take me," yards that invite trespassing, and unsupervised areas that welcome intrusions, should one be surprised about what follows?

If the routines and routings of young people keep them systematically under informal supervision and away from interesting crime targets, youths will be less likely to commit crimes.* Thus, crime control must take into account the natural flows of people and things and try to guide them so that offenders and targets seldom converge in the absence of handlers and guardians, respectively. Crime control efforts must bear in mind that offenders seek quick risks and follow obvious routes. Similarly, potential victims of crime can be guided and channeled in their daily movements so as to minimize their risk. Just as unseen traffic engineers do us all a good deed by designing streets and intersections to minimize citizen danger, so can architects, planners, and facilities managers quietly and unobtrusively help prevent crime victimization. Alternatively, poor planning and management delivers crime right to the doorstep and offers ready temptation to youths.

A number of important ideas about flow management are assembled by Poyner (1983): privatizing residential streets, limiting pedestrian access, separating residential from commercial uses, limiting access to the rear of houses, blocking access from open land, arranging apartment doors and windows carefully, allocating residential child density, dispersing market facilities, favoring pedestrian overpasses, not subways, keeping schools visible from buildings serving adults, keeping school buildings compact, encouraging resident caretakers in schools.

Brantingham and Brantingham (1987) report several ideas and experiences in crime prevention planning: segregating schools from self-service stores; channeling a youth hangout within view of an all-night taxi stand; letting the recreation center caretaker live on the premises; building crime-impact planning into early design stages; in a high-rise building for the elderly, placing the recreation room on the first floor with direct view of the doors; regulating flows of adolescents by placement of fast food establishments and electronic arcades.

Wise (personal communication 1987) adds other ideas: minimizing obstructions and using bright pastel paints to protect flows through parking structures; carefully positioning bank tellers, doors, and flows of customers

---

* Similar thinking can apply to the question of displacement of crime from one setting to another. If the routes near a high school are filled with shoplifting opportunities, closing one will likely displace to another as youths continue their normal route. The principle of least effort still allows plenty of chance to break laws. However, if the entire flow of adolescents is diverted away from the shopping district, real crime reduction should result.

to discourage robberies; localizing taverns to create informal social control; providing specific crime-prevention training for facilities managers.

Clever policing in Palm Springs, California, prevented a recurrence of student holiday violence by turning all the lights green and directing the flow of automobiles right back out of town. Of course, police have less control over the metroreef than a facilities manager has over private property.

The largest sustained crime prevention research effort has been carried out by researchers connected with the British Home Office Research and Planning Unit (Clarke and Mayhew 1980; Clarke 1983; Hope 1982). Among their ideas for situational prevention are timing the arrival of football buses so spectators have no time to get drunk; keeping school plants small; and paying attention to pub size, location, and age structure. The many crime prevention successes of these British researchers were accomplished only through dozens of attempts, some of which failed. Their work showed clearly that intuition, while a valuable resource, is not foolproof. Crime prevention through social engineering can progress only through sustained experimentation and detailed collection of existing experience.

Other ideas include designing public parks and parking lots in long strips to maximize visibility from those passing by, doing away with open-campus designs, and using telecommunications and computers to reduce the size of offices and to develop "scattered site" business practices. Facilities incorporating many young males will have special problems, but even these can be reduced in size and designed for maximal inadvertent adult surveillance. The United States' pattern of several thousand students per secondary school is especially suspect.

Facilities planning and management surely deserve consideration as a tool of future crime reduction. As the metroquilt grows, it may become the only tool available.

Future Spaces
Classics in Environmental Criminology—Where Do We Go from Here?

22

J.B. KINNEY

Contents

22.1 Looking Forward 483
22.2 Problem with Praxis? 484
22.3 Looking at the Present 485

In organizing a collection of classic works in environmental criminology, we obviously feel that there is an existing critical mass of work that takes the built environment as a key element in understanding crime and its distribution in our communities and can be recognized as the beginnings of a field within criminology. Further, this pioneering literature provides the foundation for future advances in the scientific understanding of criminal events. We, of course, make many assumptions and value judgments regarding the "inclusion set" of this collection and acknowledge that other authors' works could have been incorporated. We hope though that our selection provokes healthy debate about the roots of environmental criminology. It is in this vein that we would like to conclude with a few thoughts about the pedagogical value of these earlier works, and underscore some, but by no means all, of the connections to contemporary research and future directions in environmental criminology.

Let us look now at what it means to be a "classic." Classics tend to be old. Really old. The subject of crime is as old as civilized society, but we are looking here at something that requires more than the concept of crime, or even deviance—the built environment. Situating crime in place, then, is our starting point, as one can see in Quetelet's (1842) work on the French court departments. In Quetelet, we have one of the first comparative overviews of national-level crime rated by census population and, for the time, considerable and successful effort at interpreting the meaning behind noted variations. Some years later (1856) Glyde provided a similar approach, but looked at local crime patterns for the County of Suffolk in England. Glyde's work is impressive for its early recognition that crime patterns can be differentiated by land use, and that agriculturally based areas have different crime mixes than those seen in towns and urban centers. The reader will recognize something of Quetelet and Glyde in the next generation of research. Although we claim Quetelet and Glyde to be the first classic examples of work within what we now see as environmental criminology, neither writer would have seen themselves as initiating this field. They do, however, in the course of developing their subject matter, methods, and theoretical choices, provide us with a justifiable starting point for environmental criminology. If the history of our field is young—when compared with philosophy, for example—it is mature in the sense that it can only have begun after the industrial revolutions of the nineteenth century and the flourishing of towns and recognizably "modern" urban structures. Readers with a penchant for intellectual history might find alternative start-points, and seek to identify alternative structures as essential to the inclusion of the founding members of environmental criminology. Henry Mayhew's (c. 1850–1862) multi-volume look at mid-nineteenth-century England notes geography as part of explaining crime—particularly in relation to the urban poor and their routines—and this may, for some, be a more suitable starting point; others might consider Edwin Booth's studies of the slums of London in the 1890s or Jane Adams' study of delinquency in Chicago at the turn of the twentieth century as the starting point in the historical evolution of environmental criminology. Or perhaps Burgess's (1916) study of delinquency is a safer foundation as it is counted by many to be the first study to contain many of the major elements of environmental criminology. A perusal of the references used in the original papers, or perhaps via our collected references, will, no doubt, provoke many fine essay or discussion topics.

However, if we can assume some level of agreement regarding the early contributions to environmental criminology, what, in turn, might mark the end of the "classical" period? Just as setting a true start date is subjective, so too is its end. The early 1990s can be seen as a time of reflection. An important contribution in this vein is volume 5 of *Advances in Criminological Theory*, an edition devoted to the discussion of routine activities and rational choice theories—among which environmental criminology sits comfortably. Our collection here includes a mature formulation of Brantingham and Brantingham's pattern theory from that volume. Another key contribution is a more developed discussion of the impact of nodes, paths, and edges, also from 1993, but bridging ideas are contained in their earlier co-authored works, notably the 1984 *Patterns in Crime*. Certainly, excellent work follows our "cut-off," such as one finds in the Crime Prevention Studies series. Eck and Weisburd's 1995 volume (4) *Crime and Place*, is conspicuously absent from our list of studies, and is a good first stop to pick up subsequent discussion. Another reason for winding up our collection in the early 1990s is partly a function of technology. Computational power was difficult for most academics and governments to obtain—desk top computing certainly was available, but mapping software was largely something that could only be done at large institutions, and even so, their outputs were not seen as part of the community of real-world policy discussion. During the mid- to late-1990s, software and desktop computing power became more affordable and useable. Difficult computational and visualization procedures became more accessible, and crime mapping became noticeably more mainstream. Perhaps the defining characteristic of the research and writing that follows our "classics" is the increased use of technology in support of new methodologies and analytical tests of various elements of environmental criminology.

22.1 Looking Forward

The rich intellectual tradition of crime and place work has prepared the ground for increasingly complex investigative methodologies. Rossmo's *Geographic Profiling* (1999), for example, blends academic tradition and police investigative practices, and has done much to introduce environmental criminology to a more computationally oriented research community. Indeed, a special issue of *Built Environment*, "Crime in the City" (Vol. 34:1, 2008) stands as a recent example of this intellectual "contagion." The fact that our field has grown in this way is in no small measure based on our collective ability to bridge praxis with academic rigor. Works from those included in our classics collection have been assisted greatly by a host of practitioners from both government and policing backgrounds. Ron Clarke, whose work we have included here, was once installed in the Home Office, along with Gloria Laycock, who was the first director of the Jill Dando Institute for Crime Science at the University College London. As senior members, both helped ease the acceptability of academic input into crime problems and crime prevention planning. For current examples of how situational and urgent needs of the "real world" can be met by focused, but no less academically useful, approaches, see the online resources at the Web site for the Center for Problem-Oriented Policing at http://www.popcenter.org. Environmental criminology also serves as the theoretical standard for crime and criminal intelligence analysis—two spheres with obvious practical benefits. Rachel Boba, Jerry Ratcliffe, and Spencer Chainey were all active in the police service, and have brought their experiences to bear on this rapidly growing field, and each has texts that are widely considered by police and academics alike to be essential reading.

22.2 Problem with Praxis?

There is of course a tension inherent in being known as a *practical* social science. Unlike engineering or the life sciences, praxis is often seen in the social sciences as something of an intellectual weakness. As academics who regularly teach courses on environmental criminology, we often hear comments from students such as: "This is all fine, but we already know that crime happens here more than there," or that "it is obvious that crime happens around bars or nightclubs." Some see the problem as one of simplicity: Why would anyone set out to study crime and disorder at or near an underground parking facility? What intellectual or theoretical interest or advancement could possibly stem from such a bit of "research"? As academics who also research community impacts of crime, and of methods and programs aimed at its reduction, we hear similar themes from other academics, politicians, planners, and even criminal justice professionals. We, of course, see such concerns as misplaced, and as evidence of a lack of understanding the truly complex web of social, geographic, and psychological dimensions that make up the built environment (Kinney et al. 2008). In short, environmental criminology sees crime events as complex interactions within space–time. Even superficially simple examples of crime problems, such as a hot-spot of crime around a 24/7 convenience store, is pregnant with theoretical, methodological, and epistemological interest.

However, such negative sentiment is far less common now, at the end of the first decade of the new millennium, than it was for the authors of these classic works while they contemplated the research included here. We have, it seems, turned a corner in the field of environmental criminology; we (perhaps) no longer need to continually justify the utility of exploring crime and place or the imprint of the built environment on the crime patterns in our midst. But what can be gleaned from this modest victory of theory? The central idea of environmental criminology theory is that crime is patterned. Patterns lead to predictability—or at least to the ability to forecast likely patterns. Understanding the how and where of criminal events provides for the possibility of meaningful prevention planning, and for those cases where prevention is not possible, the reduction of crime. Environmental criminology, as we have seen, bridges formal geography, psychology, and sociology in an effort to understand the spatial aspects of our day-to-day functioning. This truly multidisciplinary approach helps us deal with the complexity of social systems. Complexity, then, becomes the turf upon which crime events play out. By excavating layers of complexity surrounding and prefiguring crime events, we can do more than simply describe the obvious and move beyond the mere cataloguing of the where and when of crime, to establishing something of the why.

Let us explore one concept that captures both the complexity of the social world, of crime events themselves, and of the theoretical value of its continued study—the notion of the environmental backcloth. Perhaps more than any other construct—and hopefully many debates and papers stem from this proposition—the backcloth metaphor encapsulates the essence of environmental criminology theory and practice. Situations are deeply dynamic; no space retains its social relevancy permanently. At different times of the day, or week, or even season, places become different spaces for human activity. The backcloth is an excellent way of thinking about context in a more dynamic way. A flag is a perfect example of this: the fabric provides the physical structure (setting), yet it also has an embedded social meaning (that of nationality) (see both 1993 contributions by Brantingham and Brantingham, this volume). Flags have a purpose, like all facilities, such as a recreational park. Flags are meant to be "flown"; parks are to be visited and "used." Flags famously blow in the wind, they roll, they flop, and they bend—all without losing their material integrity. Flags change and yet do not. Land uses, or more particularly, facilities, such as a park also change their look, their feel—all the while retaining their material integrity. Parks "change" when people make alternate uses for them. Routine activities theory reminds us that we should expect a park to be used differently at different times of the day. Parents and young children, festivals and celebrations might be what city planners had in mind when designing and building an urban park, a bit of nature in the bustle of the cityscape. But the urban context is complex, and, like the wind in our flag metaphor, it changes the way we view, and ultimately use, facilities. Unassigned space nearby (perhaps a nearby block of apartments being rebuilt or demolished, awaiting new development) may lead to unwanted attention from drug dealers. Parks are known for unauthorized uses "after hours," such as underage alcohol consumption. Less obvious shifts might occur simply from time of year—some parks may be ferociously busy during summer months, but fall into complete disuse in the winter. The backcloth notion of the urban landscape reminds us that good and bad uses of space can and will occur, and that they occur not by accident, but by virtue of their material fabric. Each place is actually a complex social "space" and as such, it will likely require a specific, situational look before we can understand crime opportunity structures. The backcloth concept also reminds us that the defining features underneath our cities, towns, and communities are, nevertheless, structured and knowable, and that crime—like any set of human activities—has a pattern that in spite of its complexity is intelligible.

22.3 Looking at the Present

Work continues on themes established early on, as evidenced in this collection. By way of conclusion, let us examine a few areas that we see as representing key themes for environmental criminology in contemporary scholarship.

Neighborhood crime patterns remain a focal point for research, but researchers are looking at it in new ways (Tita and Greenbaum 2009). Groff, Weisburd, and Morris (2009) suggest that in order to capture a more accurate picture of neighborhood crime levels and their potential changes over time, smaller, micro units of analysis should be considered before making use of the more immediately available (and larger) census block boundaries. One surprising finding is the wide variability between nearby street blocks when their individual crime trajectories are considered. With Tobler's "law," as Groff, Weisburd, and Morris point out, we would expect similar patterns for similar units that are close together in space. Such findings remind us that environmental criminology is still pushing at the boundaries of our understanding of spatial patterns. The technology is clearly ready for more theory-driven organizations of local geographies. Census block boundaries contribute famously to the modifiable areal unit problem (MAUP), as Rengert and Lockwood (2009) point out, and still require investigation.

Mobility also remains a core theme for future work of activity and awareness spaces (Brantingham and Brantingham 1984) and continues to see development. Activity and awareness spaces provide researchers with a framework for generating expectations about the movements of agents in space-time, and that for most people discretionary trips are confined to places and facilities with which they are familiar. Reynald et al. (2008), for example, using data from the Netherlands, found that social barriers were strongly indicated among their offenders. They found that offenders typically live and offend in the same neighborhoods. Current work at the Institute for Canadian Urban Research Studies (ICURS) has found that offenders are willing to travel from one city to another (Frank and Brantingham 2009). This particular research is on-going, but is consistent with routine activities theory, and particularly the concept of crime in the divergent metropolis (Felson 2002). Tied to the issue of offender and victim mobility, crime events themselves have been noted to "move" or otherwise shift from one location to another. Repeat victimization has a rich literature and continues to grow (see Farrel and Pease 2008). The idea of crime contagion presents a direct link back to the early ecological concepts from the Chicago School, and is given new energy by examining the heterogeneity of local places and target suitability (Bowers, Johnson, and Pease 2005).

Perhaps the "new" area of inquiry is represented in the dramatic improvements of modeling crime events and offender movements via simulation studies. From social network analysis of illicit drug markets (Malm and Bichler [in press]) to complex social systems and simulation modeling (Brantingham et al. 2008). These research efforts, along with others (Chainey and Desyllas 2008; Johnson et al. 2009; Johnson 2009) represent a real push toward a more computationally focused criminology. A recent (2008) collection edited by Lin Liu and John Eck contains perhaps the most comprehensive collection in this vein. Computing power has not only allowed for a growth in data analysis but of visualization as well (Brantingham and Tita 2008; Breuer et al. 2008; Wang, Liu, and Eck 2008; Meenar 2008).

Works old, new, and forthcoming suggest that the field of environmental criminology has successfully established a foothold within a general criminological framework. Such a growth, in both practical and intellectual spheres, suggests it is here to stay. Courses at universities are becoming more available and more focused. The editors are fortunate to have seen this growth at our institution, but more importantly, perhaps, is the growth in public interest and in new students to the genre of criminology. Students are now actively seeking out environmental criminology—if not in name, in content. We see a similar excitement in our graduate students as well. The value of pursuing research areas that have an immediate impact on crime prevention and reduction efforts is no doubt part of this pull. But so too, we argue, is the fertile ground prepared diligently since the mid-nineteenth century. We also feel that in this rapid growth of our field, it is especially important to encourage as many of us as possible to revisit our early influences and to consider again how we have come to see space and place as necessary foci in understanding patterns in crime.

References

Adams, J. S. (1969). Directional bias in intra-urban migration. *Economic Geography*, 45, 302–323.

Adams, J. S. (1972). The geography of riots and civil disorders in the 1960s. *Economic Geography*, 48, 24–42.

Aitken, S. (1991). Person-environment theories in contemporary perceptual and behavioural geography: Personality, attitudinal and spatial choice theories. *Progress in Human Geography*, 15, 179–193.

Aitken, S., and Prosser, R. (1990). Residents' spatial knowledge of neighborhood continuity and form. *Geographical Analysis*, 22, 303–325.

Akers, R. L. (1977). *Deviant behavior: A social learning approach* (2nd ed.). Belmont, CA: Wadsworth.

Åkerström, M. (1983). *Crooks and squares*. Lund, Sweden: Studentlitteratur.

Aldrich, J., and Nelson, F. (1984). *Linear probability, logit, and probit models*. Beverly Hills, CA: Sage Publications.

Allen, F. A. (1959). Criminal justice, legal values and the rehabilitative ideal. *Journal of Criminal Law, Criminology, and Police Science*, 50, 226–232.

Allison, J. P. (1972). Economic factors and the rate of crime. *Land Economics*, 68, 193–196.

Altman, I. (1975). *Environment and social behavior: Privacy, personal space, territory, and crowding*. Monterey, CA: Brooks/Cole.

Altman, I., and Chemers, M. (1980). *Culture and environment*. Monterey, CA: Brooks/Cole.

Altman, I., and Rogoff, B. (1987). World views in psychology: Trait, interactional, organismic, and transactional. In D. Stokols and I. Altman (Eds.), *Handbook of environmental psychology*. New York: John Wiley and Sons.

American Correctional Association. (1966). *Manual of correctional standards* (3rd ed.). College Park, MD: American Correctional Association.

Amir, M. (1971). *Patterns in forcible rape*. Chicago: University of Chicago Press.

Ancel, M. (1966). *Social defence: A modern approach to criminal problems*. New York: Schocken.

Andresen, M. A. (2006). Crime measures and the spatial analysis of criminal activity. *British Journal of Criminology*, 46, 258–285.

Angel, S. (1968). *Discouraging crime through city planning*. Center for Planning and Development Research, Working Paper No. 75. Berkeley, CA: University of California Institute of Urban and Regional Development.

Appleyard, D. (1969). Why buildings are known: A predestined tool for architects and planners. *Environment and Behavior*, 1, 131–156.

Appleyard, D. (1981). *Livable streets: Protected neighborhoods*. Berkeley, CA: University of California Press.

Appleyard, D., Lynch, K., and Meyer, J. (1964). *The view from the road*. Boston: MIT Press.

Arlinghaus, S. L., and Nystuen, J. D. (1990). Geometry of boundary exchanges. *The Geographical Review*, 80, 21–31.

Athens, L. (1980). *Violent criminal acts and actors: A symbolic interactionist study*. London: Routledge & Kegan Paul.

Atkins, S., Husain, S., and Storey, A. (1991). *The influence of street lighting on crime and fear of crime*. Home Office Crime Prevention Unit Paper 28. London: HMSO.

Atkinson, M. (1974). Versions of deviance. *Sociological Review*, 22, 616–624.

Bachrach. A. J. (Ed.). (1962). *Experimental foundations of clinical psychology*. New York: Basic Books.

Bagley, C. (1965). Juvenile delinquency in Exeter: An ecological and comparative study. *Urban Studies*, 2, 33–50.

Bailey, W. C. (1966). Correctional outcome: An evaluation of 100 reports. *Journal of Criminal Law, Criminology, and Police Science*, 57, 153–160.

Baldwin, J. (1974). Social area analysis and studies of delinquency. *Social Science Research*, 3, 151–168.

Baldwin, J., and Bottoms, A. E. (1976). *The urban criminal*. London: Tavistock.

Ball, J. C. (1955). The deterrence concept in criminology and law. *Journal of Criminal Law, Criminology, and Police Science*, 46, 347–354.

Bandura, A. (1969). *Principles of behavior modification*. New York: Holt, Rinehart & Winston.

Bandura, A. (1973). *Aggression: A social learning analysis*. London: Prentice-Hall.

Bandura, A. (1977). *Social learning theory*. Englewood Cliffs, NJ: Prentice-Hall.

Bandura, A. (1982). The psychology of chance encounters and life paths. *American Psychologist*, 37, 747–755.

Barker, R. G. (1968). *Ecological psychology: Concepts and methods for studying the environment of human behavior*. Stanford, CA: Stanford University Press.

Barker, R. G., and Wright, H. (1955). *Midwest and its children*. New York: Row and Peterson.

Barlow, H. D. (1990). *Introduction to criminology* (5th ed.). Glenview, IL: Scott, Foresman.

Barnsley, M. (1988). *Fractals everywhere*. Boston: Academic Press.

Batty, M. (1991). Generating urban forms from diffusive growth. *Environment and Planning A*, 23, 511–544.

Beavon, D. J. K. (1984). Crime and the environmental opportunity structure: The influence of street networks on the patterning of property offences. Unpublished master's thesis, Simon Fraser University, Burnaby, BC.

Beavon, D. J. (1985). Crime and the environmental opportunity structures: The influence of street networks on the patterning of property offenses. Presented at the annual meeting of the American Society of Criminology.

Beccaria, Cesare. (1963). *On crimes and punishments* (H. Paolucci, Trans.). Indianapolis, IN: Bobbs-Merrill.

Becker, G. S. (1968). Crime and punishment: An economic approach. *Journal of Political Economy*, 76, 169–217.

Becker, G. S. (1973). A theory of marriage: Part one. *Journal of Political Economy*, 81, 813–846.

Becker, G. S. (1974). A theory of marriage: Part two. *Journal of Political Economy*, 82, 11–26.

Becker, H. S. (1963). *Outsiders: Studies in the sociology of deviance.* Glencoe: The Free Press.

Bell, J., and Burke, B. (1992). Cruising Cooper Street. In R. V. Clarke (Ed.), *Situational crime prevention: Successful case studies* (pp. 108–112). New York: Harrow and Heston.

Bennett, J. (1981). *Oral history and delinquency.* Chicago: University of Chicago Press.

Bennett, T. (1986). A decision-making approach to opioid addiction. In D. B. Cornish & R. V. Clarke (Eds.), *The reasoning criminal: Rational choice perspectives on offending* (pp. 83–102). New York: Springer-Verlag.

Bennett, T. (1989). Burglars' choice of targets. In D. Evans and D. Herbert (Eds.), *The geography of crime* (pp. 176–192). London: Routledge.

Bennett, T. H., and Wright, R. (1983). *Constraints and inducements to crime: The property offender's perspective.* Cambridge: Cambridge University, Institute of Criminology.

Bennett, T. H., and Wright, R. (1984a). What the burglar saw. *New Society*, 2, 162–163.

Bennett, T., and Wright, R. (1984b). The relationship between alcohol use and burglary. *British Journal of Addictions*, 79, 431–437.

Bennett, T., and Wright, R. (1984c). *Burglars on burglary: Prevention and the offender.* Brookfield, VT: Gower Publishing Company.

Bentham, J. (1789). *An introduction to the principles of morals and legislation.* London: T. Payne and Son.

Bentham, J. (1948). *An introduction to the principles of morals and legislation.* New York: Haffner.

Berelson, B., and Steiner, G. A. (1964). *Human behavior.* New York: Harcourt, Brace and World.

Berry, B. J. L., and Horton, F. E. (1970). *Geographic perspectives on urban systems.* Englewood Cliffs, NJ: Prentice-Hall.

Bevis, C., and Nutter, J. B. (1977). Changing street layouts to reduce residential burglary. Paper presented to American Society of Criminology annual meeting, Atlanta.

Birkbeck, C. (1985). The concept of opportunities for crime: Its definition and theoretical consequences. Unpublished manuscript. Merida, Venezuela: Universidad de Los Andes, Centro de Investigaciones Penales y Criminologicas.

Block, C. R. (1990). Hot spots and isocrimes in law enforcement decision making. Paper presented at the conference on Police and Community Responses to Drugs, University of Illinois at Chicago.

Block, R., Felson, M., and Block, C. R. (1985). Crime victimization rates for incumbents of 246 occupations. *Sociology and Social Research*, 69, 442–451.

BLS (Bureau of Labor Statistics). (1975). *Handbook of labor statistics 1975, reference edition.* Washington, DC: U.S. Government Printing Office.

Boggs, S. L. (1965). Urban crime patterns. *American Sociological Review*, 30, 899–908.

Bonger, W. A. (1916). *Criminality and economic conditions.* Boston: Little, Brown.

Bottoms, A. E. (1974). Review of *Defensible space* by Newman, O. *British Journal of Criminology*, 14, 203–206.

Bottoms, A., Mawby, R. I., and Xanthos, P. (1989). A tale of two estates. In D. Downes (Ed.), *Crime and the city* (pp. 36–87). London: Macmillan Press.

Bowers, K. J., Johnson, S., and Pease, K. (2005). Victimisation and re-victimisation risk, housing type and area: A study of interactions. *Crime Prevention and Community Safety*, 7, 7–17.

Bowers, W. J., and Pierce, G. L. (1975). The illusion of deterrence of Isaac Ehrlich's research on capital punishment. *Yale Law Journal*, 85, 187–208.

Box, S. (1981). *Deviance, reality and society*. London: Holt, Rinehart & Winston.

Brager, G. A., and Purcell, F. P. (1967). *Community action against poverty*. New Haven, CT: College and University Press.

Brantingham, P. J. (1991). Patterns in Canadian crime. In M. Jackson and C. Griffiths (Eds.), *Canadian criminology: Perspectives on crime and criminality* (pp. 371–402). Toronto: Harcourt Brace Jovanovich.

Brantingham, P. J., and Brantingham, P. J., Jr. (1991). Niches and predators: Theoretical departures in the ecology of crime. Paper presented at Western Society of Criminology Meeting, Berkeley, CA.

Brantingham, P. J., and Brantingham, P. L. (1975). The spatial patterning of burglary. *Howard Journal of Penology and Crime Prevention*, 14, 11–24.

Brantingham, P. J., and Brantingham, P. L. (1977). Housing patterns and burglary in a medium-sized American city. In J. Scott and S. Dinitz (Eds.), *Criminal justice planning* (pp. 63–74). New York: Praeger Publishers.

Brantingham, P. J., and Brantingham, P. L. (1978). A theoretical model of crime site selection. In M. Krohn and R. Akers (Eds.), *Crime, law and sanctions* (pp. 105–118). Beverly Hills, CA: Sage Publications.

Brantingham, P. J., and Brantingham, P. L. (1980). Crime, occupation, and economic specialization: A consideration of inter-metropolitan patterns. In K. Harries (Ed.), *Crime: A spatial perspective* (pp. 93–108). New York: Columbia University Press.

Brantingham, P. J., and Brantingham, P. L. (1981a). Introduction: The dimensions of crime. In P. J. Brantingham and P. L. Brantingham (Eds.), *Environmental criminology* (pp. 7–26). Prospect Heights, IL: Waveland Press.

Brantingham, P. J., and Brantingham, P. L. (1981c). *Environmental criminology*. Beverly Hills, CA: Sage Publications.

Brantingham, P. J., and Brantingham, P. L. (1982). Mobility, notoriety and crime: A study in crime patterns of urban nodal points. *Journal of Environmental Systems*, 11, 89–99.

Brantingham, P. J., and Brantingham, P. L. (1984). *Patterns in crime*. New York: Macmillan.

Brantingham, P. J., and Brantingham, P. L. (1991). *Environmental Criminology* (Reissued with changes). Prospect Heights, IL: Waveland Press.

Brantingham, P. J., and Tita, G. (2008). Offender mobility and crime pattern formation from first principles. In L. Liu and J. Eck (Eds.), *Artificial Crime Analysis Systems: Using Computer Simulations and Geographic Information Systems* (pp. 193–207). Hershey, PA: Information Science Reference.

Brantingham, P. J., and Brantingham, P. L. (1998). Environmental criminology: From theory to urban planning practice. *Studies on Crime and Crime Prevention*, 7, 31–60.

Brantingham, P. J., Brantingham, P. L., and Butcher, D. (1986). Perceived and actual crime risks. In R. M. Figlio, S. Hakim, and G. F. Rengert (Eds.), *Metropolitan crime patterns* (pp. 139–159). Monsey, NY: Criminal Justice Press.

Brantingham, P. J., Brantingham, P. L., and Molumby, T. (1977). Perceptions of crime in a dreadful enclosure. *Ohio Journal of Science*, 77, 256–261.

Brantingham, P. J., Dyreson, D. A., and Brantingham, P. L. (1976). Crime seen through a cone of resolution. *American Behavioral Scientist*, 20, 261–273.

Brantingham, P. J., and Faust, F. L. (1976). A conceptual model of crime-prevention. *Crime and Delinquency*, 22, 284–296.

Brantingham, P. L., and Brantingham, P. J. (1975). Residential burglary and urban form. *Urban Studies*, 12, 273–284.

Brantingham, P. L., and Brantingham, P. J. (1978). A topological technique for regionalization. *Environment and Behavior*, 10, 335–353.

Brantingham, P. L., and Brantingham, P. J. (1981b). Notes of the geometry of crime. In P. J. Brantingham and P. L. Brantingham (Eds.), *Environmental criminology* (pp. 27–54). Prospect Heights, IL: Waveland Press.

Brantingham, P. L., and Brantingham, P. J. (1981d). Mobility, notoriety, and crime: A study in the crime patterns of urban nodal points. *Journal of Environmental Systems*, 11, 89–99.

Brantingham, P. L., and Brantingham, P. J. (1984). *An evaluation of legal aid in British Columbia*. Ottawa: Department of Justice, Canada.

Brantingham, P. L., and Brantingham, P. J. (1988). Situational crime prevention in British Columbia. *Journal of Security Administration*, 1, 17–27.

Brantingham, P. L., and Brantingham, P. J. (1993a). Environment, routine and situation: Toward a pattern theory of crime. In R. V. Clarke and M. Felson (Eds.), *Routine activity and rational choice: Advances in criminological theory*, vol. 5 (pp. 259–294). New Brunswick, NJ: Transaction Publishers.

Brantingham, P. L., and Brantingham, P. J. (1993b). Nodes, paths and edges: Considerations on the complexity of crime and the physical environment. *Journal of Environmental Psychology*, 13, 3–28.

Brantingham, P. L., Brantingham, P. J., and Wong, P. S. (1990). Malls and crime: A first look. *Security Journal*, 1, 175–181.

Brantingham, P. L., Brantingham, P. J., and Wong, P. S. (1991). How public transit feeds private crime: Notes on the Vancouver "Skytrain" experience. *Security Journal*, 2, 91–95.

Brantingham, P. L., Glässer, U., Jackson, P., Kinney, J. B., and Vajihollahi, M. (2008). Mastermind: Computational modeling and simulation of spatiotemporal aspects of crime in urban environments. In Liu, L., and Eck, J. (Eds.), *Artificial Crime Analysis Systems: Using Computer Simulations and Geographic Information Systems* (pp. 252–280). Hershey, PA: Information Science Reference.

Brearley, H. C. (1932). *Homicide in the United States*. Chapel Hill, NC: University of North Carolina Press.

Brenner, H. (1976a). *Estimating the social costs of national economic policy: Implications for mental and physical health and criminal aggression*. Congress of the United States, Joint Economic Committee, Paper no. 5. Washington, DC: U.S. Government Printing Office.

Brenner, H. (1976b). *Effects of the national economy on criminal aggression, II. Final Report to National Institute of Mental Health*. Contract #282-76-0355FS.

Breuer, A., Hursey, J. J., Stroman, T., and Verma, A. (2008). Visualization of criminal activity in an urban population. In Liu, L., and Eck, J. (Eds.), *Artificial crime analysis systems: Using computer simulations and geographic information systems* (pp. 35–49). Hershey, PA: Information Science Reference.

Brotman, R., and Suffet, F. (1975). The concept of prevention and its limitations. *Annals of the American Academy of Political and Social Science*, 417, 53–65.

Brower, S., Dockett, K., and Taylor, R. B. (1983). Residents' perception of territorial features and perceived local threat. *Environment and Behavior*, 15, 419–437.

Brown, B. B., and Altman, I. (1981). Territoriality and residential crime: A conceptual framework. In P. J. Brantingham and P. L. Brantingham (Eds.), *Environmental criminology* (pp. 55–76). Beverly Hills, CA: Sage Publications.

Brown, B., and Altman, I. (1983). Territoriality, defensible space and residential burglary: An environmental analysis. *Journal of Environmental Psychology*, 3, 203–220.

Brown, B., and Altman, I. (1991). Territoriality and residential crime: A conceptual framework. In P. J. Brantingham and P. L. Brantingham (Eds.), *Environmental criminology* (pp. 55–76; reissued with changes). Prospect Heights, IL: Waveland Press.

Brown, B., and Harris, P. (1989). Residential burglary victimization: Reaction to the invasion of a primary territory. *Journal of Environmental Psychology*, 9, 119–132.

Brown, I. D. (1981). The traffic offence as a rational decision. In S. M. A. Lloyd-Bostock (Ed.), *Psychology in legal contexts: Applications and limitations*. London: Macmillan.

Bruner, J. S., Goodnow, J. J., and Austin, G. A. (1956). *A study of thinking*. New York: John Wiley and Sons.

Brunswick, E. (1956). *Perceptions and the representative design of psychological experiments*. Berkeley, CA: University of California Press.

Brunswik, E. (1962). *The conceptual framework of psychology*. Chicago: University of Chicago Press.

Buckle, A., and Farrington, D. P. (1989). An observational study of shoplifting. *British Journal of Criminology*, 24, 63–73.

Buckley, W. (1968). *Modern systems research for the behavioral scientist*. Chicago: Adline Publishing.

Bullock, H. A. (1955). Urban homicide in theory and fact. *Journal of Criminal Law, Criminology and Police Science*, 45, 565–575.

Burchard, J. D. (1977). Review of Yochelson and Samenow's *The criminal personality*, volume 1. *Contemporary Psychology*, 22, 442–443.

Burgess, E. W. (1916). Juvenile delinquency in a small city. *Journal of the American Institute of Criminal Law and Criminology*, 6, 724–728.

Burgess, E. W. (1925). The growth of the city: An introduction to a research project. In R. E. Park and E. W. Burgess (Eds.), *The city: Suggestions for investigation of human behavior in the urban environment* (pp. 47–62). Chicago: University of Chicago Press.

Burrows, J. (1988). *Retail crime: Prevention through crime analysis*. Home Office Crime Prevention Unit, Paper 11. London: HMSO.

Burt, C. (1925). *The young delinquent*. London: Appleton.

Butcher, D. (1991). Crime in the third dimension: A study of burglary patterns in a high-density residential area. Unpublished master's thesis, Simon Fraser University, Burnaby, BC.

Cahill, M. E., and Mulligan, G. F. (2003). The determinants of crime in Tucson, Arizona. *Urban Geography*, 24, 582–610.

Caldwell, R. (1965). *Criminology*. New York: Ronald Press.

Cameron, M. O. (1964). *The booster and the snitch*. New York: Free Press.

Campbell, A., and Gibbs, J. J. (1986). *Violent transactions*. Oxford: Basil Blackwell.

Canadian Committee on Correction. (1969). *The basic principles and purposes of criminal justice*. Ottawa: Queen's Printer.

Canadian Urban Victimization Survey. (1984). *Crime prevention: Awareness and practice*. Bulletin 3. Ottawa: Solicitor General of Canada.

Canadian Urban Victimization Survey. (1988). *Multiple victimization*. Bulletin 10. Ottawa: Solicitor General of Canada.

Capone, D., and Nichols, W. (1976). Urban structure and criminal mobility. *American Behavioral Scientist*, 20, 199–213.

Carroll, J. S. (1982). Committing a crime: The offender's decision. In V. J. Konecni and E. B. Ebbesen (Eds.), *The criminal justice system: A social-psychological analysis*. Oxford: Freeman.

Carroll, J. S., and Herz, E. J. (1981). Criminal thought processes in shoplifting. Paper presented at the annual meeting of the American Society of Criminology, Washington, DC.

Carroll, J., and Weaver, F. (1986). Shoplifters' perceptions of crime opportunities: A process-tracing study. In D. B. Cornish and R. V. Clarke (Eds.), *The reasoning criminal: Rational choice perspectives on offending* (pp. 19–37). New York: Springer-Verlag.

Carstairs, G. M. (1969). Overcrowding and human aggression. In H. D. Graham and T. Gurr (Eds.), *The history of violence in America* (pp. 751–764). New York: Frederick A. Praeger.

Carter, R., and Hill, K. Q. (1979). *The criminal's image of the city*. New York: Pergamon.

Carter, R., and Hill, K. Q. (1980). Area images and behavior: An alternative perspective for understanding crime. In D. E. Georges-Abeyie and K. D. Harries (Eds.), *Crime: A spatial perspective* (pp. 193–204). New York: Columbia University Press.

Cavan, R. S. (1962). *Criminology* (3rd ed.). New York: Thomas Y. Crowell.

CEA (Council of Economic Advisors). (1976). *The economic report of the president*. Washington, DC: U.S. Government Printing Office.

Chaiken, J. M., and Chaiken, M. R. (1990). Drugs and predatory crime. *Crime and Justice: An Annual Review of Research*, 13, 203–239.

Chaiken, J. M., Lawless, M. W., and Stevenson, K. (1974). *Impact of police activity on crime: Robberies on the New York City subway system*. Report No. R-1424-N.Y.C. Santa Monica, CA: Rand Corporation.

Chainey, S., and Desyllas, J. (2008). Modelling pedestrian movement to measure on-street crime risk. In Liu, L., and Eck, J. (Eds.), *Artificial crime analysis systems: Using computer simulations and geographic information systems* (pp. 71–91). Hershey, PA: Information Science Reference.

Chambliss, W. J. (1972). *Boxman: A professional thief's journey*. New York: Harper and Row.

Chapin, F. S. (1974). *Human activity patterns in the city: Things people do in time and space*. New York: John Wiley and Sons.

Chapin, V. S., and Brent, R. K. (1969). Human activity systems in the metropolitan United States. *Environment and Behavior*, 1, 107–130.

Charlesworth, J. C. (Ed.). (1967). *Contemporary political analysis*. New York: Free Press.

Choldin, H. M., and Roncek, D. W. (1976). Density, population potential and pathology: A block-level analysis. *Public Data Use*, 4, 19–30.

Churchland, P. M. (1989). *A neurocomputational perspective on the nature of mind and the structure of science*. Cambridge, MA: MIT Press.

Cimler, E., and Beach, L. R. (1981). Factors involved in juveniles' decisions about crime. *Criminal Justice and Behavior*, 8, 275–286.

Clarke, R. V. (Ed.). (1978). *Tackling vandalism*. Home Office Research Study, Number 47. London: HMSO.

Clarke, R. V. G. (1979). Defensible space and vandalism: The lessons from some recent British research. *Stadtebau und Kriminalamt (Urban planning and crime)*. Papers of an international symposium, Bundeskriminalamt, Federal Republic of Germany.

Clarke, R. V. G. (1980). Situational crime prevention: Theory and practice. *British Journal of Criminology*, 20, 136–147.

Clarke, R. V. (1983). Situational crime prevention: Its theoretical basis and practical scope. *Crime and Justice: An Annual Review of Research*, 4, 225–256.

Clarke, R. V. (1992). *Situational Crime Prevention: Successful Case Studies*. New York: Harrow and Heston.

Clarke, R. V. (1997). *Situational Crime Prevention: Successful Case Studies* (2nd ed.). Monsey, NY: Criminal Justice Press.

Clarke, R. V., and Cornish, D. B. (1983). *Crime control in Britain: A review of policy research*. Albany, NY: State University of New York Press.

Clarke, R. V., and Cornish, D. B. (1985). Modeling offenders' decisions: A framework for research and policy. *Crime and Justice: An Annual Review of Research*, 6, 147–185.

Clarke, R. V., Field, S., and McGrath, G. (1991). Target hardening of banks in Australia and displacement of robberies. *Security Journal*, 2, 84–90.

Clarke, R. V., and Hope, T. (1984). *Coping with burglary: Research perspectives on policy*. Boston: Kluwer-Nijhoff.

Clarke, R. V. G., and Hough, J. M. (Eds.) (1980). *The effectiveness of policing*. Farnborough, Hants: Gower.

Clarke, R. V., and Lester, D. (1987). Toxicity of car exhausts and opportunity for suicide: Comparison between Britain and the United States. *Journal of Epidemiology and Community Health*, 41, 114–120.

Clarke, R. V., and Mayhew, P. (Eds.) (1980). *Designing out crime*. London: HMSO.

Clarke, R. V., and Mayhew, P. (1988). The British gas suicide story and its criminological implications. *Crime and Justice: An Annual Review of Research*, 10, 79–116.

Clarke, R. V., and Weisburd, D. L. (1990). On the distribution of deviance. In D. M. Gottfredson and R.V. Clarke (Eds.), *Policy and theory in criminal justice* (pp. 10–27). Aldershot: Avebury.

Clinard, M. (1968). *Sociology of deviant behavior* (3rd ed.). New York: Holt, Rinehart and Winston.

Clinard, M. B., and Abbott, D. J. (1973). *Crime in developing countries: A comparative perspective*. New York: John Wiley and Sons.

Cloward, R. A., and Ohlin, L. E. (1960). *Delinquency and opportunity: A theory of delinquent gangs*. New York: The Free Press.

Coburn, G. (1988). Patterns of homicide in Vancouver, 1980–1986. Unpublished master's thesis, Simon Fraser University, Burnaby, BC.

Cochrane, D., and Orcutt, G. H. (1949). Application of least squares regression to relationships containing autocorrelated error terms. *Journal of the American Statistical Association*, 44, 32–61.

Cohen, A. K. (1956). *The Sutherland papers*. Bloomington, IN: Indiana University Press.

Cohen, L. E., and Cantor, D. (1981). Residential burglary in the United States: Lifestyles and demographic factors associated with the probability. *Journal of Research in Crime and Delinquency*, 18, 113–127.

Cohen, L. E., and Felson, M. (1979a). Social change and crime rate trends: A routine activity approach. *American Sociological Review*, 44, 588–605.

Cohen, L. E., and Felson, M. (1979b). On estimating the social costs of national economic policy: A critical examination of the Brenner study. *Social Indicators Research*, 6, 251–259.

Cohen, S. (1972). *Folk devils and moral panics: The creation of the Mods and Rockers*. London: MacGibbon & Kee.

Coleman, A. (1985). *Utopia on trial*. London: Hilary Shipman.

Coleman, A. (1989). Disposition and situation: Two sides of the same crime. In D. Evans and D. Herbert (Eds.), *The geography of crime* (pp. 108–134). London: Routledge.

Coleman, J. S. (1966). *Equality of educational opportunity*. Washington, DC: United States Government Printing Office.

Coleman, J. S. (1967). Toward open schools. *The Public Interest*, 9, 20–27.

Colquhoun, P. (1800). *Treatise on the police of the metropolis*. London: Baldwin.

Conger, R. D. (1978). From social learning to criminal behavior. In M. D. Krohn and R. L. Akers (Eds.), *Crime, law and sanctions*. Beverly Hills, CA: Sage Publications.

Conrad, J. (1965). *Crime and its correction*. Berkeley, CA: University of California Press.

Consumer Reports (1959). *Consumer Reports buying guide*. Mt. Vernon: Consumers Union.

Consumer Reports (1969). *Consumer Reports buying guide*. Mt. Vernon: Consumers Union.

Consumer Reports (1975). *Consumer Reports buying guide*. Mt. Vernon: Consumers Union.

Cook, P. J. (1980). Research in criminal deterrence: Laying the groundwork for the second decade. *Crime and Justice: An Annual Review of Research*, 2, 211–268.

Cook, P. J. (1986a). Criminal incapacitation effects considered in an adaptive choice framework. In D. B. Cornish and R. V. Clarke (Eds.), *The reasoning criminal: Rational choice perspectives on offending* (pp. 202–216). New York: Springer-Verlag.

Cook, P. J. (1986b). The demand and supply of criminal opportunities. *Crime and Justice: An Annual Review of Research*, 7, 1–27.

Cornish, D. B. (1978). *Gambling: A review of the literature and its implications for policy and research*. Home Office Research Study, Number 42. London: HMSO.

Cornish, D. B. (1987). Evaluating residential treatment for delinquents: A cautionary tale. In K. Hurrelmann and F. Kaufmann (Eds.), *Limits and potentials of social intervention*. Berlin/New York: de Gruyter/Aldine.

Cornish, D. B., and Clarke, R. V. (1986a). *The reasoning criminal: Rational choice perspectives on offending*. New York: Springer-Verlag.

Cornish, D. B., and Clarke, R. V. (1986b). Situational prevention, displacement of crime and rational choice theory. In K. Heal and G. Laycock (Eds.), *Situational crime prevention: From theory into practice*. London: HMSO.

Cornish, D. B., and Clarke, R. V. G. (1987). Understanding crime displacement: An application of rational choice theory. *Criminology*, 25, 933–947.

Cornish, D. B., and Clarke, R. V. (1989). Crime specialisation, crime displacement and rational choice theory. In H. Wegener, F. Lösel, and J. Haish (Eds.), *Criminal behavior and the justice system: Psychological perspectives* (pp. 102–117). New York: Springer-Verlag.

Costanzo, C. M., Halperin, W. C., and Gale, N. (1986). Criminal mobility and the directional component in journeys to crime. In R. Figlio, S. Hakim, and G. F. Rengert (Eds.), *Metropolitan crime patterns* (pp. 73–96). Monsey, NY: Criminal Justice Press.

Cotterell, J. L. (1991). The emergence of adolescent territories in a large urban environment. *Journal of Environmental Psychology*, 11, 25-41.

Covington, J., and Taylor, R. B. (1989). Gentrification and crime: Robbery and larceny changes in appreciating Baltimore neighborhood. *Urban Affairs Quarterly*, 25, 142-172.

Cressey, D. R. (1969). *Theft of a nation*. New York: Harper and Row.

Cressey, D. R. (1979). Criminological theory, social science and the repression of crime. In E. Sagarin (Ed.), *Criminology: New concerns*. Beverly Hills, CA: Sage Publications.

Cromwell, P. P., Olson, J. N., and Avary, D. W. (1991). *Breaking and entering: An ethnographic analysis of burglary*. Newbury Park, CA: Sage Publications.

Cusson, M. (1983). *Why delinquency?* Toronto: University of Toronto Press.

Cusson, M. (1989). Les zones urbaines criminelles. *Criminologie*, 22, 95–105.

Cusson, M. (1993). A strategic analysis of crime: Criminal tactics as responses to pre-criminal situations. *Advances in Criminological Theory*, 5, 295–304.

Cusson, M., and Pinsonneault, P. (1986). The decision to give up crime. In D. B. Cornish and R. V. Clarke (Eds.), *The reasoning criminal: Rational choice perspectives on offending* (pp. 72–82). New York: Springer-Verlag.

Cybriwsky, R. A. (1972). The anomic theory and the geographic study of crime. Unpublished paper read at the Annual Meeting, Association of American Geographers East Lakes Division, Indiana, PA.

Czarnowski, T. (1986). The streets as a communication artifact. In S. Anderson (Ed.), *On streets* (pp. 207–212). Boston: MIT Press.

David, P. R., and Scott, J. W. (1973). A cross-cultural comparison of juvenile offenders, offenses, due processes, and societies: The cases of Toledo, Ohio, and Rosario, Argentina. *Criminology*, 11, 183–204.

Davidson, G. C., and Neale, J. M. (1974). *Abnormal psychology*. New York: John Wiley and Sons.

DeCola, L. (1991). Fractal analysis of multiple spatial autocorrelation among point data. *Environment and Planning A*, 23, 545–556.

De Grazia, A., Handy, R., Harwood, E. C., and Kurtz, P. (1968). *The behavioral sciences*. Great Barrington, MA: Behavioral Research Council.

Decker, J. F. (1972). Curbside deterrence: An analysis of the effect of a slug rejector device, coin view window and warning labels on slug usage in New York City parking meters. *Criminology*, 10, 127–142.

De Fleur, L. B. (1967). Ecological variables in the cross cultural study of delinquency in *Ecology, Crime and Delinquency*. H. L. Voss and D. M. Petersen, Eds. New York: Appleton–Century–Crofts, 283–302.

Dentler, R. A., and Warshauer, M. E. (1965). *Big city dropouts*. New York: Center for Urban Education.

Denzin, N. K. (1977). Notes on the criminogenic hypothesis: A case study of the American liquor industry. *American Sociological Review*, 42, 905–920.

Department of the Environment. (1977). *Housing management and design*. Lambeth Inner Area Study, IAS/IA/18. London: Department of the Environment.

Ditton, J. (1977). *Part-time crime: An ethnography of fiddling and pilferage*. London: Macmillan.

Downes, D. (1966). *The delinquent solution*. London: Routledge & Kegan Paul.

Downs, R. M. (1981). Maps and mappings as metaphors for spatial representation. In L. S. Liben, A. H. Patterson, and N. Newcombe (Eds.), *Spatial representation and behavior across the life span* (pp. 143–166). New York: Academic Press.

Droettboom, T., Jr., McAllister, R. J., Kaiser, E. J., and Butler, E. W. (1971). Urban violence and residential mobility. *Journal of the American Institute of Planners*, 37, 319–325.

Duffala, D. C. (1976). Convenience stores, armed robbery, and physical environmental features. *American Behavioral Scientist*, 20, 227–246.

Durbin, J. (1970). Testing for serial correlation in least-squares regression when some of the regressors are lagged dependent variables. *Econometrica*, 38, 410–421.

Durbin, J., and Watson, G. S. (1951). Testing for serial correlation in least squares regression, II. *Biometrika*, 38, 159–178.

Durkheim, E. (1951). *Suicide: A study in sociology*. New York: Free Press.

Durkheim, E. (1966). *The division of labor in society*. New York: Free Press.

Dyos, H. J. (1957). Urban transformation: A note on the object of street improvement in Regency and early Victorian London. *International Review of Social History*, 2, 259–265.

Ebbesen, E. B., and Konecni, V. J. (1980). On the external validity of decision-making research: What do we know about decisions in the real world? In T. S. Wallsten (Ed.), *Cognitive processes in choice and decision behaviour* (pp. 21–45). Hillside, NJ: Lawrence Erlbaum.

Eck, J., and Spelman, W. (1992). Thefts from vehicles in shipyard parking lots. In R. V. Clarke (Ed.), *Situational crime prevention: Successful case studies* (pp. 165–173). New York: Harrow and Heston.

Ehrenwald, J. (1966). *Psychotherapy: Myth and method*. New York: Grune and Stratton.

Ehrlich, I. (1973). Participation in illegitimate activities: A theoretical and empirical investigation. *Journal of Political Economy*, 81, 521–565.

Ehrlich, I. (1975). The deterrent effect of capital punishment: A question of life and death. *American Economic Review*, 65, 398–417.

Ehrlich, I. (1979). The economic approach to crime: A preliminary assessment. In S. L. Messinger and E. Bittner (Eds.), *Criminology review yearbook,* volume 1. Beverly Hills, CA: Sage Publications.

Ekblom, P. (1979). *A crime-free car?* Home Office Research Unit, Research Bulletin No. 7. London: Home Office.

Ekblom, P. (1992). Preventing post office robberies in London: Effects and side effects. In R. V. Clarke (Ed.), *Situational crime prevention: Successful case studies* (pp. 66–74). New York: Harrow and Heston.

Electrical Merchandising Week. (1964, January). *Statistical and Marketing Report.* New York: Billboard Publications.

Elliot, D. S., Ageton, S. S., Huizinga, D., Knowles, B. A., and Canter, R. J. (1983). *The prevalence and incidence of delinquent behavior: 1976–1980.* Boulder, CO: Behavioral Research Institute.

Empey, L. (1974). Crime prevention: The fugitive utopia. In D. Glaser (Ed.), *Handbook of criminology.* Chicago: Rand McNally.

Engstad, P. A. (1975). Environmental opportunities and the ecology of crime. In R. A. Silverman and J. J. Teevan, Jr. (Eds.), *Crime in Canadian society* (pp. 193–211). Toronto: Butterworths.

Ennis, P. H. (1967). *Criminal victimization in the United States.* Chicago: National Opinion Research Center.

Epstein, A. (1978, September 14). In Philadelphia, odds against going to jail are good. *The Philadelphia Inquirer*, pp. B1, B3.

Evans, G. W., and Pezdek, K. (1980). Cognitive mapping: Knowledge of the real-world distance and location information. *Journal of Experimental Psychology and Memory*, 6, 13–24.

Everitt, J., and Cadwallader, M. (1972). The home area concept in urban analysis. In W. J. Mitchell (Ed.), *Environmental design: Research and practice.* Los Angeles: University of California.

Ewald, W. R. (Ed.) (1967). *Environment for man.* Bloomington, IN: Indiana University Press.

Eysenck, H. J. (1961). *Handbook of abnormal psychology.* New York: Basic Books.

Eysenck, H. J. (1964). *Crime and personality.* Boston: Houghton-Mifflin.

Eysenck, H. J. (1973). *The inequality of man.* London: Temple-Smith.

Faris, R. E. L., and Dunham, H. W. (1939). *Mental disorders in urban areas.* Chicago: University of Chicago Press.

Farrell, G., and Pease, K. (2008). Repeat victimization. In R. Wortley and L. Mazerolle (Eds.), *Environmental criminology and crime analysis* (pp. 117–135). Portland, OR: Willan Publishing.

Farrington, D. P. (1979). Longitudinal research on crime and delinquency. *Crime and Justice: An Annual Review of Research*, 1, 289–348.

Farrington, D. P. (1986). Age and crime. *Crime and Justice: An Annual Review of Research*, 7, 189–250.

Fattah, E. A. (1991). *Understanding criminal victimization: An introduction to theoretical victimology.* Scarborough, ON: Prentice-Hall.

Faust, F. L. (1973). Delinquency labeling: Its consequences and implications. *Crime and Delinquency*, 19, 41–48.

FBI (Federal Bureau of Investigation). (1967). *Uniform crime reports.* Washington, DC: United States Government Printing Office.

FBI. (1975). *Crime in the U.S.: Uniform crime report.* Washington, DC: U.S. Government Printing Office.

FBI. (1976). *Crime in the U.S.: Uniform crime report.* Washington, DC: U.S. Government Printing Office.

Feeney, F. (1986). Robbers as decision makers. In D. B. Cornish and R. V. Clarke (Eds.), *The reasoning criminal: Rational choice perspectives on offending* (pp. 53–73). New York: Springer-Verlag.

Feeney, F., and Weir, A. (1973). *The prevention and control of robbery*. Davis, CA: University of California at Davis, Center on Administration of Justice.

Feldman, M. P. (1977). *Criminal behaviour: A psychological analysis*. New York: John Wiley and Sons.

Felson, M. (1980). Human chronography. *Sociology and Social Research*, 65, 1–9.

Felson, M. (1981). Social accounts based on map, clock and calendar. In F. T. Juster and K. C. Land (Eds.), *Social accounting systems: Essays on the state of the art* (pp. 219–237). New York: Academic Press.

Felson, M. (1983). Ecology of crime. In S. H. Kadish (Ed.), *Encyclopedia of crime and justice* (pp. 665–670). New York: The Free Press.

Felson, M. (1986a). Crime at any point on the city map. In R. M. Figlio, S. Hakim, and G. F. Rengert (Eds.), *Metropolitan crime patterns* (pp. 127–136). Monsey, NY: Criminal Justice Press.

Felson, M. (1986b). Routine activities, social controls, rational decisions and criminal outcomes. In D. B. Cornish and R. V. Clarke (Eds.), *The reasoning criminal: Rational choice perspectives on offending* (pp. 119–128). New York: Springer-Verlag.

Felson, M. (1987). Routine activities and crime prevention in the developing metropolis. *Criminology*, 25, 911–931.

Felson, M. (2002). *Crime and everyday life* (3rd ed.). Thousand Oaks, CA: Sage Publications.

Felson, M. (2006). *Crime and nature*. Thousand Oaks, CA: Sage Publications.

Felson, M., and Cohen, L. E. (1980). Human ecology and crime: A routine activity approach. *Human Ecology*, 8, 398–405.

Felson, M., and Cohen, L. E. (1981). Modeling crime trends: A cumulative opportunity perspective. *Journal of Research in Crime and Delinquency*, 18, 138–164.

Felson, M., and Gottfredson, M. (1984). Social indicators of adolescent activities near peers and parents. *Journal of Marriage and the Family*, 46, 709–714.

Felson, R. B., and Steadman, H. J. (1983). Situational factors in disputes leading to criminal violence. *Criminology*, 21, 59–74.

Ferdinand, T. N. (1970). Demographic shifts and criminality. *British Journal of Criminology*, 10, 169–175.

Ferri, E. (1896). *Criminal sociology*. New York: Appleton.

Fink, G. (1969). Einsbruchstatorte vornehmlich an einfallsstrassen? *Kriminalistik*, 23, 358–360.

Fisher, B. S., and Nasar, J. L. (1991). Fear of crime in relation to three exterior site features: Prospect, refuge and escape. *Environment and Behavior*, 24, 35–65.

Flanagan, T. J., and Jamieson, K. M. (1988). *Sourcebook of criminal justice statistics 1987*. U.S. Department of Justice, Bureau of Justice Statistics. Washington, DC: U.S. Government Printing Office.

Fleisher, B. M. (1966). *The economics of delinquency*. Chicago: Quadrangle.

Flew, A. (1954). The justification of punishment. *Philosophy*, 29, 291–307.

Forrester, D., Chatterton, M., and Pease, K. (1988). *The Kirkholt Burglary Project, Rochdale*. Home Office Crime Prevention Unit, Paper 13. London: HMSO.

Fotheringham, A. (1990). What's the fuss about fractals? *Environment and Planning A*, 22, 716–718.

Fowler, E. P. (1987). Street management and city design. *Social Forces*, 66, 365–389.

Fox, J. A. (1976). *An econometric analysis of crime data*. Doctoral dissertation, Department of Sociology, University of Pennsylvania. Ann Arbor, MI: University Microfilms.

Francis, M. (1987a). Urban open spaces. In E. Zube and G. T. Moore (Eds.), *Advances in environment and behavior*, volume 1 (pp. 71–106). New York: Plenum Press.

Francis, M. (1987b). The making of democratic streets. In A. Vernez-Moudon (Ed.), *Public streets for public use* (pp. 23–39). New York: Van Nostrand Reinhold.

Francis, M. (1989). Control as dimension of public space quality. In I. Altman and E. H. Zube (Eds.), *Public places and spaces* (pp. 147–172). New York: Plenum Press.

Frank, R., and Brantingham, P. L. (2009). The effect of directionality on the activity-space of offenders. Paper presented at the Environmental Criminology and Crime Analysis (ECCA) Symposium, July 2009, Brasilia, Brazil.

Franks, C. M., and Wilson, G. T. (1975). *Behavior therapy: Theory and practice*. New York: Brunner Mazel.

Fréchette, M., and LeBlanc, M. (1978). *La délinquance cachée des adolescents montréalais*. Montreal: Groupe de recherche sur l'inadaptation juvénile, Université de Montréal.

Freeman, R. B. (1983). Crime and unemployment. In J. Q. Wilson (Ed.), *Crime and public policy*. San Francisco: Institute of Contemporary Studies Press.

Furlong, W. J., and Mehay, S. L. (1981). Urban law enforcement in Canada: An empirical analysis. *Canadian Journal of Economics*, 14, 44–57.

Gabor, T. (1981). The crime displacement hypothesis: An empirical examination. *Crime and Delinquency*, 26, 390–404.

Gabor, T., Baril, M., Cusson, M., Elie, D., LeBlanc, M., and Normandeau, A. (1987). *Armed robbery: Cops, robbers, and victims*. Springfield, IL: Charles C. Thomas.

Galle, O. R., Gove, W. R., and McPherson, J. M. (1972). Population density and pathology: What are the relations for man? *Science*, 176, 23–30.

Garber, S., Klepper, S., and Nagin, D. (1983). The role of extralegal factors in determining criminal case disposition. In A. Blumstein, J. Cohen, S. E. Martin, and M. H. Tonry (Eds.), *Research on sentencing: The search for reform*, volume 2. Washington, DC: National Academy Press.

Gärling, T. (1989). The role of cognitive maps in spatial decisions. *Journal of Environmental Psychology*, 9, 269–278.

Gärling, T., Book, A., and Lindberg, E. (1984). Cognitive mapping of large-scale environments: The interrelationships of action plans, acquisition, and orientation. *Environment and Behavior*, 16, 3-34.

Gärling, T., and Golledge, R. G. (1989). Environmental perception and cognition. In E. H. Zube and G. T. Moore (Eds.), *Advances in environment, behavior, and design*, volume 2 (pp. 203–236). New York: Plenum Press.

Gärling, T., Lindberg, E, Carreiras, M., and Book, A. (1986). Reference systems in cognitive maps. *Journal of Environmental Psychology*, 6, 1–18.

Gehike, C. E., and Biehl, K. (1934). Certain effects of grouping upon the size of the correlation coefficient in census tract material. *Journal of the American Statistical Association*, 29, 169–170.

Genereux, R. L., Ward, L. M., and Russell, J. A. (1983). The behavioral component in the meaning of places. *Journal of Environmental Psychology*, 3, 43–55.

Gerber, R. J., and McAnany, P. D. (1972). *Contemporary punishment*. South Bend, IN: University of Notre Dame Press.

Ghali, M. A. (1982). The choice of crime: An empirical analysis of juveniles' criminal choice. *Journal of Criminal Justice*, 10, 433–442.

Gibbons, D. C. (1971). Observations on the study of crime causation. *American Journal of Sociology*, 77, 262–278.

Gibbs, J. J., and Shelly, P. L. (1982). Life in the fast lane: A retrospective view by commercial thieves. *Journal of Research in Crime and Delinquency*, 19, 299–330.

Gifford, R. (1987). *Environmental psychology: Principles and practice*. Boston: Altyn and Bacon.

Glaser, D. (1964). *The effectiveness of a prison and parole system*. Indianapolis, IN: Bobbs-Merrill.

Glaser, D. (1971). *Social deviance*. Chicago: Markham.

Glaser, D. (1977). The compatibility of free will and determinism in criminology: Comments on an alleged problem. *Journal of Criminal Law and Criminology*, 67, 486–490.

Glaser, D. (1979). A review of crime-causation theory and its application. *Crime and Justice: An Annual Review of Research*, 1, 203–237.

Glasser, W. (1965). *Reality therapy*. New York: Harper and Row.

Glyde, J. (1856). Localities of crime in Suffolk. *Journal of the Statistical Society of London*, 19, 102–106.

Gold, R. (1970). Urban violence and contemporary defensive cities. *Journal of the American Institute of Planners*, 36, 146–159.

Gold, R., Murphy, E. B., and McGregor, J. (1969). Urban violence and the design and form of the urban environment. In D. J. Mulvihill and M. M. Tumin (Eds.), *Crimes of violence,* volume 11. Washington, DC: U.S. Government Printing Office.

Goldberg, S. (1958). *Introduction to difference equations*. New York: John Wiley and Sons.

Goldman. H., Dinitz, S., Lindner, L., Foster, T., and Allen, H. (1974). *Designed treatment program of sociopathy by means of drugs*. Columbus, OH: Program for the Study of Crime and Delinquency.

Goldstein, H. (1968). Police response to urban crisis. *Public Administration Review*, 28, 418–429.

Goldstein, J. (1960). Police discretion not to invoke the criminal process. *Yale Law Journal*, 69, 543–594.

Golledge, R. G. (1981). The geographical relevance of some learning theories. In K. R. Cox and R. G. Golledge (Eds.), *Behavioral problems in geography revisited* (pp. 43–66). New York: Methuen.

Golledge, R. G. (1987). Environmental cognition. In D. Stokols and I. Altman (Eds.), *Handbook on environmental psychology,* volume 1 (pp. 131–174). New York: John Wiley and Sons.

Golledge, R. G., Smith, T. R., Pellegrino, J. W., Doherty, S. E., and Marshall, S. P. (1985). A conceptual model and empirical analysis of children's acquisition of spatial knowledge. *Journal of Environmental Psychology*, 5, 125–152.

Golledge, R. G., and Specter, A. N. (1978). Comprehending the urban environment: Theory and practice. *Geographical Analysis,* 10, 403–426.

Gopal, S., Klatzky, R., and Smith, T. (1989). Navigator: A psychological based model of environmental learning through navigation. *Journal of Environmental Psychology*, 9, 309-331.

Gottfredson, M. R. (1986). Substantive contributions of victim surveys. *Crime and Justice: An Annual Review of Research*, 7, 251–287.

Gottfredson, M., and Hirschi, T. (1990). *The general theory of crime*. Stanford, CA: Stanford University Press.

Gould, L. (1969). The changing structure of crime in an affluent society. *Social Forces*, 48, 50–59.

Greenberg, D. F. (1977). Delinquency and the age structure of society. *Contemporary Crises*, 1, 189–223.

Griliches, Z. (1967). Distributed lags: A survey. *Econometrica*, 35, 16–49.

Groff, E., Weisburd, D., and Morris, N. A. (2009). Where the action is at places: Examining spatio-temporal patterns of juvenile crime at places using trajectory analysis. In D. Weisburd, W. Bernasco, and G. J. N. Bruinsma (Eds.), *Putting crime in its place: Units of analysis in geographic criminology* (pp. 61–86). New York: Springer.

Grupp, S. E. (1971). *Theories of punishment*. Bloomington, IN: Indiana University Press.

Guerry, A. M. (1833). *Essai sur la statistique morale de la France*. Paris: Crochard.

Haggett, P. (1965). *Locational analysis in human geography*. London: Butler & Tanner Ltd.

Hall, J. (1945). Criminology. In G. Gurvitch and W. E. Moore (Eds.), *Twentieth century sociology* (pp. 342–365). New York: Philosophical Library.

Halleck, S. (1974). *Crime and justice annual*. Chicago: Aldine.

Halmos, P. (1966). *The faith of the counsellors*. New York: Schaken Books.

Hampson, S. E. (1982). *The construction of personality: An introduction*. London: Routledge & Kegan Paul.

Hanawalt, B. A. (1979). *Crime and conflict in English communities: 1300–1348*. Cambridge, MA: Harvard University Press.

Handy, R., and Kurtz, P. (1964). *A current appraisal of the behavioral sciences*. Great Barrington, MA: Behavioral Research Council.

Handy, R., and Harwood, E. C. (1973). *A current appraisal of the behavioral sciences* (Rev. ed.). Great Barrington, MA: Behavioral Research Council.

Hare, R. (1970). *Psychopathy*. New York: John Wiley and Sons.

Harries, K. D. (1971). The geography of American crime, 1968. *The Journal of Geography*, 70, 204–213.

Harries, K. D. (1974). *The geography of crime and justice*. New York: McGraw-Hill.

Harries, K. D. (1976). Cities and crime: A geographic model. *Criminology*, 14, 369–386.

Harries, K. D. (1990). *Serious violence*. Springfield, IL: Charles C. Thomas

Hart, H. L. A. (1968). *Punishment and responsibility*. New York: Oxford University Press.

Harvey, M. E. (1971). The identification of developing regions in developing countries. *Economic Geography*, 48, 229–234.

Hassal, C., and Trethowan, W. H. (1972). Suicide in Birmingham. *British Medical Journal*, 1, 717–718.

Hawley, A. H. (1944). Ecology and human ecology. *Social Forces*, 22, 398–405.

Hawley, A. H. (1950). *Human ecology: A theory of community structure*. New York: Ronald.

Hayner, N. S. (1933–1934). Delinquency areas in the Puget Sound region. *American Journal of Sociology*, 39, 314–328.

Hazelwood, R. R., Reboussin, R., and Warren, J. I. (1989). Series rape: Correlates of increased aggression and the relationship of offender pleasure to victim resistance. *Journal of Interpersonal Violence*, 4, 65–78.

Hearst, E., and Jenkins, H. M. (1974). *Sign tracking*. Austin, TX: Psychonomic Society.

Heineke, J. M. (1978). Economic models of criminal behaviour: An overview. In J. M. Heineke (Ed.), *Economic models of criminal behaviour* (pp. 1–34). New York: North-Holland.

Henry, A. F., and Short, J. F. (1954). *Suicide and homicide*. New York: Free Press.

Henry, S. (1978). *The hidden economy*. London: Martin Robertson.

Hensher, D. A. (1976). The structure of journeys and the nature of travel patterns. *Environment and Planning A*, 8, 655–672.

Herbert, D. T., and Hyde, S. W. (1985). Environmental criminology: Testing some area hypotheses. *Transactions of the Institute of British Geographers*, 10, 259–274.

Hess, H. F., and Diller, J. V. (1969). Motivation for gambling as revealed in the marketing methods of the legitimate gambling industry. *Psychological Reports*, 25, 19–27.

Hinde, R. A., and Stevenson-Hinde, J. (1973). *Constraints on learning*. New York: Academic Press.

Hindelang, M. J. (1976). *Criminal victimization in eight American cities: A descriptive analysis of common theft and assault*. Cambridge, MA: Ballinger.

Hindelang, M. J. (1978). Race and involvement in common law personal crimes. *American Sociological Review*, 43, 93–109.

Hindelang, M. J., Dunn, C. S., Sutton, P., and Aumick, A. L. (1976). *Sourcebook of criminal justice statistics, 1975*. U.S. Department of Justice, Law Enforcement Assistance Administration. Washington, DC: U.S. Government Printing Office.

Hindelang, M. J., Dunn, C. S., Sutton, P., and Aumick, A. L. (1977). *Sourcebook of criminal justice statistics, 1976*. U.S. Department of Justice, Law Enforcement Assistance Administration. Washington, DC: U.S. Government Printing Office.

Hindelang, M. J., Gottfredson, M. R., and Garofalo, J. (1978). *Victims of personal crime: An empirical foundation for a theory of personal crime*. Cambridge, MA: Ballinger.

Hirschi, T. (1969). *Causes of delinquency*. Berkeley, CA: University of California Press.

Hirschi, T. (1986). On the compatibility of rational choice and social control theories. In D. B. Cornish and R. V. Clarke (Eds.), *The reasoning criminal: Rational choice perspectives on offending* (pp. 105–118). New York: Springer-Verlag.

Hirschi, T., and Selvin, H. C. (1967). *Delinquency research*. New York: Free Press.

Hirtle, S. C., and Hudson, J. (1991). Acquisition of spatial knowledge for routes. *Journal of Environmental Psychology*, 11, 335–345.

Hocker, J. L., and Wilmot, W. W. (1985). *Interpersonal conflict* (2nd ed.). Dubuque, IA: William C. Brown.

Hoffmann, H., and Catlin, G. (1985). *The 1982 urban crime survey: A report on the survey methodology*. Ottawa: Statistics Canada.

Holzman, H. R. (1983). The serious habitual property offender as "moonlighter": An empirical study of labor force participation among robbers and burglars. *Journal of Criminal Law and Criminology*, 73, 1774–1792.

Homans, G. (1964). Bringing men back in. *American Sociological Review*, 29, 809–818.

Home Office. (1979). *Criminal statistics: England and Wales, 1978*. London: HMSO.

Honig, W. (Ed.). (1966). *Operant behavior*. New York: Appleton-Century-Crofts.

Hood, R., and Sparks, R. (1970). *Key issues in criminology.* London: Weidenfeld and Nicolson.

Hope, T. J. (1982). *Burglary in schools: The prospects for prevention.* Research and Planning Unit, Paper 11. London: HMSO.

Hope, T., and Hough, M. (1988). Area, crime and incivility: A profile from the British Crime Survey. In T. Hope and M. Shaw (Eds.), *Communities and crime reduction* (pp. 30–47). London: HMSO.

Horton, F. E., and Reynolds, D. R. (1971). Effects of the urban spatial structure on individual behavior. *Economic Geography, 47,* 36–48.

Hotteling, H. (1936). Relations between two sets of variables. *Biometrika, 28,* 321–377.

Hoyt, H. (1933). *One hundred years of land values in Chicago: The relationship of the growth of Chicago to the rise in its land values, 1830–1933.* Chicago: The University of Chicago Press.

Hoyt, H. (1939). *The structure and growth of residential neighborhoods in American cities.* Federal Housing Administration, Washington, DC: U.S. Government Printing Office.

Humphreys, L. (1970). *Tearoom trade: Impersonal sex in public places.* Chicago: Aldine.

Hunter, R. D., and Jeffery, C. R. (1992). Preventing convenience store robbery through environmental design. In R. V. Clarke (Ed.), *Situational crime prevention: Successful case studies* (pp. 194–204). New York: Harrow and Heston.

ICC (Interstate Commerce Commission). (1974). *Annual report: Freight commodity statistics of Class I motor carriers of property operative in intercity service.* Washington, DC: U.S. Government Printing Office.

Illinois Law Enforcement Commission. (1984). *Crime in Illinois.* Springfield, IL: Illinois Law Enforcement Commission.

Illinois Criminal Justice Information Authority. (1989). *Spatial and temporal analysis of crime: Users manual/technical manual.* Chicago: Illinois Criminal Justice Information Authority, State of Illinois.

Inciardi, J. A. (1975). *Careers in crime.* Chicago: Rand McNally.

Inciardi, J. A. (1978). *Reflections on crime: An introduction to criminology and criminal justice.* New York: Holt, Rinehart & Winston.

Inciardi, J. A. (1979). Heroin use and street crime. *Crime and Delinquency, 25,* 335–346.

Institute for Architecture and Urban Studies. (1986). Streets in the central areas of a small American city. In S. Anderson (Ed.), *On streets* (pp. 339–375). Cambridge, MA: MIT Press.

Ittelson, W. H., Proshansky, H. M., Rivlin, L. G., and Winkel, G. H. (1974). *An introduction to environmental psychology.* New York: Holt, Rinehart & Winston.

Jackson, B. (1969). *A thief's primer.* New York: Macmillan.

Jackson, R. M. (1971). *Enforcing the law* (Rev. ed.). Harmondsworth, England: Penguin.

Jacobs, J. (1961). *The death and life of great American cities.* New York: Random House.

Jacoby, J. E. (1977). Review of Yochelson and Samenow's *The criminal personality,* volume 1. *Journal of Criminal Law and Criminology, 68,* 314–315.

Jeffery, C. R. (1956). The structure of American criminological thinking. *Journal of Criminal Law, Criminology, and Police Science, 46,* 658–672.

Jeffery, C. R. (1969). Crime prevention and control through environmental engineering. *Criminologica, 7,* 35–58.

Jeffery, C. R. (1971). *Crime prevention through environmental design*. Beverly Hills, CA: Sage Publications.

Jeffery, C. R. (1976). Criminal behavior and the physical environment: A perspective. *American Behavioral Scientist*, 20, 149–174.

Jeffery, C. R. (1977). *Crime prevention through environmental design* (2nd ed.). Beverly Hills, CA: Sage Publications.

Jeffery, C. R. (1990). *Criminology: An interdisciplinary approach*. Englewood Cliffs, NJ: Prentice-Hall.

Jeffery, C. R., and Jeffery, I. A. (1969). Delinquents and dropouts: An experimental program in behavior change. *Education and Urban Society*, 1, 325–336.

Jeffery, C. R., and Jeffery, I. A. (1975). Psychosurgery and behavior modification: Legal control techniques versus behavior control techniques. *American Behavioral Scientist*, 18, 685–722.

Jeffery, C. R., and White, J. D. (1985). Crime prevention and legal liability. In C. R. Jeffery, R. V. del Carmen, and J. D. White (Eds.), *Attacks of the insanity defense: Biological psychiatry and new perspectives on criminal behavior* (pp. 207–216). Springfield, IL: Charles C. Thomas.

Jencks, C. (1987). *Post-modernism: The new classicism in art and architecture*. London: Academy Editions.

Jencks, C., and Baird, G. (1969). *Meaning in architecture*. London: Barrie and Rockcliff.

Johnson, S. D. (2009). Repeat burglary victimisation: A tale of two theories. *Journal of Experimental Criminology*, 3 (no. 4), 215–240.

Johnson, S. D., Bowers, K. J., Birks, D., and Pease, K. (2009). Predictive mapping of crime by PorMap: Accuracy, units of analysis, and the environmental backcloth. In D. Weisburd, W. Bernasco, and G. J. N. Bruinsma (Eds.), *Putting crime in its place: Units of analysis in geographic criminology* (pp. 109–122). New York: Springer.

Joint Commission on Correctional Manpower and Training. (1968). *Offenders as a correctional manpower source*. Washington, DC: Joint Commission on Correctional Manpower and Training.

Joint Economic Committee, Subcommittee on Economy in Government. (1970). *The federal criminal justice system*. 91st Congress, 2nd Session.

Joravsky, D. (1970). *The Lysenko affair*. Cambridge, MA: Harvard University Press.

Kadish, S. H. (1962). Legal norms and discretion in the police and sentencing process. *Harvard Law Review*, 75, 904–931.

Kadish, S. H. (1967). The crisis of overcriminalization. *Annals*, 374, 157–170.

Kahneman, D., Slovic, P., and Tversky, A. (1982). *Judgment under uncertainty: Heuristics and biases*. New York: Cambridge University Press.

Kaminski, G. (1989). The relevance of ecologically oriented theory in environment and behavior research. In E. Zube and G. T. Moore (Eds.), *Advances in environment, behaviour, and design* (pp. 3–36). New York: Plenum Press.

Kaplan, L., and Maher, J. (1970). The economics of the numbers game. *American Journal of Economics and Sociology*, 29, 391–408.

Kaplan, R. (1985). The analysis of perception via preference: A strategy for studying how the environment is experienced. *Landscape*, 12, 161–176.

Kaplan, S., and Kaplan, R. (1982). *Cognition and environment: Functioning in an uncertain world*. New York: Praeger.

Kasi, S. V., and Harburg, E. (1972). Perceptions of the neighborhood and the desire to move out. *Journal of the American Institute of Planners*, 38, 318–324.

Kelling, G. L., Pate, T., Dieckman, D., and Brown, C. E. (1974). *The Kansas City preventive patrol experiment*. Washington, DC: Police Foundation.

Kennedy, L. W. (1988). Going it alone: Unreported crime and individual self-help. *Journal of Criminal Justice*, 16, 403–412.

Kennedy, L. W. (1990). *On the borders of crime: Conflict management and criminology*. White Plains, NY: Longman.

Kennedy, L. W., and Dutton, D. (1989). The incidence of wife assault in Alberta. *Canadian Journal of Behavioral Science*, 21, 40–54.

Kennedy, L. W., and Forde, D. R. (1990). Routine activities and crime: An analysis of victimization in Canada. *Criminology*, 28, 137–152.

Kennedy, L. W., and Silverman, R. A. (1984–1985). Significant others and fear of crime among the elderly. *International Journal of Aging and Human Development*, 20, 241–256.

Kennedy, L. W., Silverman, R. A., and Forde, D. R. (1991). Homicide in urban Canada: Testing the impact of economic inequality and social disorganization. *Canadian Journal of Sociology*, 16, 397–410.

Kinney, J. B., Brantingham, P. L., Wuschke, K., Kirk, M. G., and Brantingham, P. J. (2008). Crime attractors, generators and detractors: Land use and urban crime opportunities. *Built Environment*, 34 (no. 1), 62–74.

Kittrie, N. N. (1971). *The right to be different: Deviance and enforced therapy*. Baltimore, MD: Johns Hopkins University Press.

Klein, H. J. (1967). The delimitation of the town centre in the image of its citizens. In University of Amsterdam, Sociological Department (Eds.), *Urban core and inner city* (pp. 286–306). Leiden: Brill.

Klein, M. W. (1971). *Street gangs and street workers*. Englewood Cliffs, NJ: Prentice-Hall.

Kleinmuntz, B. (1968). The processing of clinical information by man and machine. In B. Kleinmuntz (Ed.), *Formal representation of human judgment* (pp. 149–186). New York: John Wiley and Sons.

Klepper, S., Nagin, D., and Tierney, L. (1983). Discrimination in the criminal justice system: A critical appraisal of the literature. In A. Blumstein, J. Cohen, S. E. Martin, and M. H. Tonry (Eds.), *Research on sentencing: The search for reform*, volume 2, (pp. 55–128). Washington, DC: National Academy Press.

Klockars, C. B. (1974). *The professional fence*. London: Tavistock.

Kobrin, F. E. (1976). The primary individual and the family: Changes in living arrangements in the U.S. since 1940. *Journal of Marriage and the Family*, 38, 233–239.

Koepsell-Girard and Associates. (1975). *Crime prevention handbook*. Falls Church, VA: Motorola Teleprogram.

Kozielecki, J. (1982). *Psychological decision theory*. Boston: Reidel.

Kreitman, N. (1976). The coal gas story: United Kingdom suicide rates, 1960–71. *British Journal of Preventive and Social Medicine*, 30, 86–93.

Kreitman, N., and Platt, S. (1984). Suicide, unemployment, and domestic gas detoxification in Britain. *Journal of Epidemiology and Community Health*, 38, 1–6.

Kretch, D., Crutchfield, R. S., and Livson, N. (1969). *Elements of psychology*. New York: Alfred A. Knopf.

Kuhn, T. (1962). *The structure of scientific revolutions.* Chicago: University of Chicago Press.

Lab, S. P. (1988). *Crime prevention: Approaches, practices and evaluations.* Cincinnati, OH: Anderson.

Lambert, J. R. (1970). *Crime, police, and race relations: A study in Birmingham.* London: Oxford University Press.

Land, K. C. (1978). Modelling macro social change. Paper presented at the annual meeting of the American Sociological Association, San Francisco.

Land, K., and Felson, M. (1976). A general framework for building dynamic macro social indicator models: Including an analysis of changes in crime rates and police expenditures. *American Journal of Sociology,* 82, 565–604.

Lander, B. (1954). *Towards an understanding of juvenile delinquency.* New York: Columbia University Press.

Langworthy, R. H., and LeBeau, J. (1992). The spatial evolution of a sting clientele. *Journal of Criminal Justice,* 20, 135–146.

Lansing, J. B., and Marans, R. W. (1969). Planner's notebook: Evaluation of neighborhood quality. *Journal of the American Institute of Planners,* 35, 195–199.

Larson, E. (1981, May 27). Saga of Joey Coyle. *Wall Street Journal,* p. 1.

Lasley, J. R. (1989). Drinking routines/lifestyles and predatory victimization: A causal analysis. *Justice Quarterly,* 6, 529–542.

Lasley, J. R., and Rosenbaum, J. L. (1988). Routine activities and multiple personal victimizations. *Sociology and Social Research,* 73, 47–50.

Lauer, B. M. (1973). The geography of disease in Summit County, Ohio. Unpublished master's thesis, Department of Geography, University of Akron, OH.

La Fave, W. (1967). *Arrest.* Boston: Little, Brown and Co.

Lawson, P. (1986). Property crime and hard times in England, 1559–1624. *Law and History Review,* 4, 95–127.

Leavell, H. R., and Clark, E. G. (1965). *Preventive medicine for the doctor in his community: An epidemiological approach* (3rd ed.). New York: McGraw-Hill.

LeBeau, J. I. (1985). Some problems with measuring and describing rape presented by the serial offender. *Justice Quarterly,* 2, 385–398.

LeBeau, J. I. (1987). Patterns of stranger and serial rape offending: Factors distinguishing apprehended and at large offenders. *Journal of Criminal Law and Criminology,* 78, 309–326.

Lejeune, R. (1977). The management of a mugging. *Urban Life,* 6, 123–148.

Lejins, P. (1967). The field of prevention. In W. Amos and C. F. Wellford (Eds.), *Delinquency prevention: Theory and practice* (pp. 1–21). Englewood Cliffs, NJ: Prentice-Hall.

Lemert, E. M. (1951). *Social pathology.* New York: McGraw-Hill.

Lentz, W. P. (1956). Rural urban differentials and juvenile delinquency. *Journal of Criminal Law, Criminology and Police Science,* 47, 331–339.

Letkemann, P. (1973). *Crime as work.* Englewood Cliffs, NJ: Prentice-Hall.

Levine, N., and Wachs, M. (1985). *Factors affecting the incidence of bus crime in Los Angeles.* Report No. CA-06-0195. Washington, DC: Office of Technical Assistance, Urban Mass Transportation Administration, U.S. Department of Transportation.

Levy-LeBoyer, C. (1984). *Vandalism: Behavior and motivations.* Amsterdam: Elsevier Science Publishing.

Levy-Leboyer, C., and Naturel, V. (1991). Neighborhood noise annoyance. *Journal of Environmental Psychology,* 11, 75–86.

Lewin, R. (1975, September). Starved brains: New research on hunger's damage. *Psychology Today,* pp. 29–33.

Lewis, C. S. (1953). The humanitarian theory of punishment. *Res Judicatae,* 6, 224–230.

Ley, D. (1974). *The Black inner city as frontier outpost.* Washington, DC: Association of American Geographers, Monograph Number 7.

Ley, D. (1983). *A social geography of the city.* New York: Harper and Row.

Ley, D., and Cybriwsky, R. (1974a). Urban graffiti as territorial markers. *Annals of the Association of American Geographers,* 64, 491–505.

Ley, D., and Cybriwsky, R. (1974b). The spatial ecology of stripped cars. *Environment and Behavior,* 6, 53–68.

Lieberson, S., and Silverman, A. R. (1965). The precipitants and underlying conditions of race riots. *American Sociological Review,* 30, 887–898.

Linedecker, C. L. (1991). *Night stalker.* New York: St. Martin's Paperbacks.

Linsky, A., and Straus, M. (1986). *Social stress in the United States: Links to regional patterns in crime and illness.* Dover, MA: Auburn House.

Liu, L., and Eck, J. (Eds.). (2008). *Artificial crime analysis systems: Using computer simulations and geographic information systems* (pp. 193–207). Hershey, PA: Information Science Reference.

Loeber, R., and Snyder, H. N. (1990). Rate of offending in criminal careers: Constancy and change in Lambda. *Criminology,* 28, 97–109.

Lombroso, C. (1911). *Crime: Its causes and remedies.* Boston: Little Brown.

Lottier, S. (1938). Distribution of criminal offenses in metropolitan regions. *Journal of Criminal Law, Criminology and Police Science,* 29, 37–50.

Lowe, J. C., and Moryadas, S. (1975). *The geography of movement.* Boston: Houghton Mifflin.

Lowman, J. (1983). Geography, crime and social control. Unpublished doctoral dissertation, University of British Columbia, Vancouver, BC.

Luedtke, G., and Associates. (1970). *Crime and the physical city: Neighborhood design techniques for crime reduction.* Springfield, VA: National Technical Information Service.

Lupsha, P. A. (1969). On theories of urban violence. *Urban Affairs Quarterly,* 4, 273–296.

Lynch, J. P. (1987). Routine activity and victimization at work. *Journal of Quantitative Criminology,* 3, 283–300.

Lynch, K. (1960). *The image of the city.* Cambridge, MA: MIT press.

Lynch, K. (1976). *Managing a sense of region.* Boston: MIT Press.

Lynch, K. (1981). *A theory of good city form.* Boston: MIT Press.

Lynch, K., and Rivkin, M. (1959). A walk around the block. *Landscape,* 8, 24–34.

Lystad, M. (1974). *An annotated bibliography: Violence at home.* DHEW Publication Number ADM 75-136. Washington, DC: U.S. Government Printing Office.

Mabe, A. R. (Ed.). (1975). Appraisal of new techniques and strategies for social control: Ethical and practical limits. *American Behavioral Scientist,* 18, 597–728.

Macdonald, J. E., and Gifford, R. (1989). Territorial cues and defensible space theory: The burglar's point of view. *Journal of Environmental Psychology,* 9, 193–205.

Mack, J. (1964). Full-time miscreants: Delinquent neighborhoods and criminal networks. *British Journal of Sociology*, 15, 38–53.

Maddala, G. S., and Rao, A. S. (1973). Tests for serial correlation in regression models with lagged dependent variables and serially correlated errors. *Econometrica*, 41, 761–774.

Maguire, K., and Flanagan, T. J. (1991). *Sourcebook of criminal justice statistics 1990*. Washington, DC: U.S. Government Printing Office.

Maguire, M. (1980). *Burglary as opportunity*. Research Bulletin, Number 10. London: Home Office Research Unit.

Maguire, M. (1982). *Burglary in a dwelling*. London: Heinemann.

Malm, A. E., and Bichler, G. (In press). Breaking the chain: Complex niches and the fragmentation of illicit drug markets. *Journal of Research in Crime and Delinquency*.

Mannheim, H. (1960). *Pioneers in criminology*. London: Stevens and Sons.

Manning, P. (1977). *Police work: The social organisation of policing*. Cambridge, MA: MIT Press.

Manosevitz, M., Lindzey, G., and Thiessen, D. (1969). *Behavioral genetics*. New York: Appleton-Century-Crofts.

Mansfield, R., Gould, L. C., and Namenwirth, J. Z. (1974). A socioeconomic model for the prediction of societal rates of property theft. *Social Forces*, 52, 462–472.

Manski, C. F. (1978). Prospects for inference on deterrence through empirical analysis of individual criminal behavior. In J. M. Heineke (Ed.), *Economic models of criminal behavior*. New York: North-Holland.

Mark, V. H., and Ervin, F. R. (1970). *Violence and the brain*. New York: Harper & Row.

Marks, A. (1977). Sex differences and their effect upon cultural evaluations of methods of self-destruction. *Omega*, 8, 65–70.

Marris, P., and Rein, M. (1967). *Dilemmas of social reform*. New York: Atherton Press.

Marris, P., and Rein, M. (1973). *Dilemmas of social reform* (2nd ed.). Chicago: Aldine.

Mars, G. (1974). Dock pilferage. In P. Rock and M. McIntosh (Eds.), *Deviance and social control*. London: Tavistock.

Marsh, P., Rosser, E., and Harre, R. (1978). *The rules of disorder*. London: Routledge & Kegan Paul.

Martin, J. B. (1952). *My life in crime*. New York: Harper.

Massey, W. S. (1989). *Algebraic topology: An introduction*. New York: Springer-Verlag.

Matulionis, M. (1971). The spatial interrelationships of morbidity and socioeconomic characteristics: Buffalo, NY. Unpublished master's thesis, Department of Geography, State University of New York at Buffalo.

Matza, D. (1964). *Delinquency and drift*. New York: John Wiley and Sons.

Maume, D. J. (1989). Inequality and metropolitan rape rates: A routine activities approach. *Justice Quarterly*, 6, 513–528.

Maurer, D. W. (1964). *Whiz mob*. New Haven, CT: College and University Press.

Mawby, R. I. (1977). Defensible space: A theoretical and empirical appraisal. *Urban Studies*, 14, 169–179.

Mayhew, H. (1861–1862). *London labour and the London poor, volume IV: Those that will not work, comprising prostitutes, thieves, swindlers and beggars*. London: Griffin Bohn.

Mayhew, P. (1977). Crime in a man's world. *New Society*, June 16.

Mayhew, P. (1979). Defensible space: The current status of a crime prevention theory. *Howard Journal of Penology and Crime Prevention*, 18, 150–159.

Mayhew, P. (1990). Opportunity and vehicle crime. In D. M. Gottfredson and R. V. Clarke (Eds.), *Policy and theory in criminal justice* (pp. 28–50). Aldershot: Avebury.

Mayhew, P., Clarke, R. V. G., Sturman, A., and Hough, J. M. (1976). *Crime as opportunity*. Home Office Research Study Number 34. London: HMSO.

Mayhew, P., Clarke, R. V. G., Burrows, J. N., Hough, J. M., and Winchester, S. W. C. (1979). *Crime in public view*. Home Office Research Study Number 49. London: HMSO.

Maynard, D. W. (1985). On the functions of social conflict among children. *American Sociological Review*, 50, 207–223.

Mazur, A., and Robertson, L. (1972). *Biology and social behavior*. New York: Free Press.

McClearn, G. E., and DeFries, J. C. (1973). *Introduction to behavioral genetics*. San Francisco: W. H. Freeman.

McClintock, F. H. (1963). *Crimes of violence*. London: Macmillan & Company.

Meehl, P. E. (1954). *Clinical versus statistical prediction: A theoretical analysis and a review of the evidence*. Minneapolis, MN: University of Minnesota Press.

Meenar, M. R. (2008). GIS-based simulation and visualization of urban land use change. In L. Liu and J. Eck (Eds.), *Artificial crime analysis systems: using computer simulations and geographic information systems* (pp. 50–69). Hershey, PA: Information Science Reference.

Menninger, K. (1968). *The crime of punishment*. New York: Viking Press.

Merchandising Week. (1973). *Statistical and marketing report, February*. New York: Billboard Publications.

Merchandising Week. (1976). *Statistical and marketing report, March*. New York: Billboard Publications.

Merry, S. E. (1982). Defining "success" in the neighborhood justice movement. In R. Tomasic and M. M. Feeley (Eds.), *Neighborhood justice: Assessment of an emerging idea*. New York: Longman.

Messinger, S., Halleck, S., Lerman, P., Morris, N., Murphy, P. V., and Wolfgang, M. E. (1973). *Crime and justice annual*. Chicago: Aldine.

Messner, S. F., and Blau, J. R. (1987). Routine leisure activities and rates of crime: A macro-level analysis. *Social Forces*, 65, 1035–1051.

Messner, S. F., and South, S. J. (1986). Economic deprivation, opportunity structure, and robber victimization: Intra- and interracial patterns. *Social Forces*, 64, 975–989.

Meyer, H. J., Borgatta, E., and Jones, W. (1966). *Girls at vocational high*. New York: Russell Sage Foundation.

Michael, J., and Adler, M. J. (1932). *Crime, law, and social science*. New York: Harcourt Brace.

Michael, J., and Wechsler, H. (1940). *Criminal law and its administration*. Chicago: Foundation Press.

Michaels, J. W. (1974). On the relation between human ecology and behavioral social psychology. *Social Forces*, 52, 313–317.

Michelson, W. H. (1976). *Man and his urban environment*. Boston: Addison-Wesley.

Miethe, T. D., Stafford, M. C., and Long, J. S. (1987). Routine activities/lifestyle and victimization. *American Sociological Review*, 52, 184–194.

Miller, A. I. (1987). *Imagery in scientific thought*. Cambridge, MA: MIT Press.

Miller, W. B. (1962). The impact of a total community delinquency control project. *Social Problems*, 10, 168–191.

Millon, T., and Millon, R. (1974). *Abnormal behavior and personality*. Philadelphia, PA: W. H. Saunders.

Mischel, W. (1968). *Personality and assessment.* New York: John Wiley and Sons.

Mischel, W. (1973). Toward a cognitive social learning reconceptualisation of personality. *Psychological Review,* 80, 252–283.

Mischel, W. (1979). On the interface of cognition and personality: Beyond the person-situation debate. *American Psychologist,* 34, 740–754.

Model School Division. (1966). *Strategy for change.* Washington, DC: U.S. Government Printing Office.

Molumby, T. (1976). Patterns of crime in a university housing project. *American Behavioral Scientist,* 20, 247–259.

Monmonier, M. S. (1972). Trends in atlas development. *Cartographica,* 18, 187–213.

Morgan, C., and King, R. (1971). *Introduction to psychology.* New York: McGraw-Hill.

Morrill, R. (1965). The Negro ghetto: problems and alternatives. *Geographical Review,* 55, 339–381.

Morris, N. (1974). *The future of imprisonment.* Chicago: University of Chicago Press.

Morris, N., and Zimring, F. (1969). Deterrence and corrections. *Annals,* 381, 137–146.

Morris, T. (1957). *The criminal area: A study in social ecology.* London: Routledge and Kegan Paul.

Morris, T. (1962). A critique of area studies. In M. E. Wolfgang, L. Savitz, and N. Johnston (Eds.), *The sociology of crime and delinquency* (pp. 191–198). New York: John Wiley and Sons.

Moynihan, D. P. (1968). *Maximum feasible misunderstanding.* New York: Free Press.

Muller, P. O. (1981). *Contemporary suburban America.* Englewood Cliffs, NJ: Prentice-Hall.

Mulvihill, D. J., and Tumin, M. M. (1969). *Crimes of violence,* volume 11. Washington, DC: U.S. Government Printing Office.

Munn, N. L., Fernald, L. D., and Fernald, P. S. (1969). *Introduction to psychology* (2nd ed.). New York: Houghton Mifflin.

Murphy, J. G. (1973). *Punishment and responsibility.* Belmont, CA: Wadsworth.

Myers, D. G., and Lamm, H. (1976). The group polarization phenomenon. *Psychological Bulletin,* 83, 602–627.

National Advisory Commission on Criminal Justice Standards and Goals. (1973). *A national strategy to reduce crime.* Washington, DC: U.S. Government Printing Office.

National Commission on the Causes and Prevention of Violence. (1969). *Crimes of violence,* Volume 13. Washington, DC: U.S. Government Printing Office.

Nettler, G. (1974). *Explaining crime.* New York: McGraw-Hill.

Newling, B. E. (1966). Urban growth and spatial structure: Mathematical models and empirical evidence. *Geographical Review,* 56, 213–225.

Newman, O. (1972). *Defensible space: Crime prevention through urban design.* New York: Macmillan.

Newman, O. (1973). *Defensible space: People and design in the violent city.* London: Architectural Press.

Newman, O. (1976). *Design guidelines for creating defensible space.* Washington, DC: U.S. Government Printing Office.

Newman, O. (1979). *Community of interest.* New York: Doubleday.

Newman, O. (1980/81). *Community of interest.* Garden City, NY: Anchor Press/Doubleday.

Nietzel, M. T. (1979). *Crime and its modification: A social learning perspective*. New York: Pergamon.

Nisbett, R. E., and Ross, L. (1980). *Human inference: Strategies and shortcomings of social judgment*. Englewood Cliffs, NJ: Prentice-Hall.

Nisbett, R. E., and Wilson, T. (1977). Telling more than we can know: Verbal reports on mental processes. *Psychological Review*, 84, 231–259.

Norrie, A. (1983). Freewill, determinism and criminal justice. *Legal Studies*, 3, 60–73.

Ohlin, L. E. (1970). *A situational approach to delinquency prevention*. Youth Development and Delinquency Prevention Administration, U.S. Department of Health, Education and Welfare. Washington, DC: U.S. Government Printing Office.

OMB (Office of Management and the Budget). (1973). *Social indicators 1973*. Washington, DC: U.S. Government Printing Office.

O'Neill, M. (1991). A biologically based model of spatial cognition and wayfinding. *Journal of Environmental Psychology*, 11, 299–320.

Orleans, P. (1973). Differential cognition of urban residents: Effects of social scale on mapping. In R. Downs and D. Stea (Eds.), *Image and environment: Cognitive mapping and spatial behavior* (pp. 115–130). Chicago: Aldine.

Orleans, P. A., and Schmidt, S. (1972). Mapping in the city. In W. J. Mitchell, Ed. *Environmental design: Research and practice*, Vol. 1. Los Angeles School of Architecture and Urban Planning, University of California.

Orsagh, T. (1983). Is there a place for economics in criminology and criminal justice? *Journal of Criminal Justice*, 99, 391–401.

Orsagh, T., and Witte, A. D. (1981). Economic status and crime: Implications for offender rehabilitation. *Journal of Criminal Law and Criminology*, 72, 1055–1071.

Packer, H. L. (1966). The courts, the police, and the rest of us. *Journal of Criminal Law, Criminology, and Police Science*, 57, 238–243.

Packer, H. L. (1968). *The limits of the criminal sanction*. Stanford, CA: Stanford University Press.

Palmer, J. (1977). Economic analyses of the deterrent effect of punishment: A review. *Journal of Research in Crime and Delinquency*, 14, 4–21.

Park, R. E., and Burgess, E. W. (1925). *The city*. Chicago: University of Chicago Press.

Parker, H. J. (1974). *View from the boys: A sociology of down-town adolescents*. Newton Abbot, England: David & Charles.

Parsons, T. (1937). *Structure of social action*. New York: McGraw-Hill.

Parsons, T. (1951). *The social system*. New York: The Free Press.

Passell, P. (1975). The deterrent effect of the death penalty: A statistical test. *Stanford Law Review*, 28, 61–79.

Payne, J. (1980). Information processing theory: Some concepts and methods applied to decision research. In T. Wallsten (Ed.), *Cognitive processes in choice and decision behaviour* (pp. 95–116). Hillsdale, NJ: Erlbaum.

Pease, K. (1992). Preventing burglary on a British public housing estate. In R. V. Clarke (Ed.), *Situational crime prevention: Successful case studies* (pp. 223–229). New York: Harrow and Heston.

Petersilia, J. (1980). Criminal career research: A review of recent evidence. *Crime and Justice: An Annual Review of Research*, 2, 321–379.

Petrovich, P. (1971). Récherches sur la criminalité à Paris dans la seconde moitié du XVIII siècle. In A. Abbiateci, F. Billacois, Y. Bongert, N. Castan, Y. Castan, and P. Petrovich (Eds.), *Crimes et criminalité en France sous l'Ancien Regime: 17e-18e siècles* (pp. 187–261). Paris: Librarie Armand Colin.

Pettiway, L. E. (1982). Mobility of robbery and burglary offenders: Ghetto and nonghetto spaces. *Urban Affairs Quarterly*, 18, 255-270.

Pipkin, J. S. (1981). Cognitive behavioral geography and repetitive travel. In K. R. Cox and R. G. Golledge (Eds.), *Behavioral problems in geography revisited* (pp. 145–181). New York: Methuen.

Piven, H., and Alcabes, A. (1969). *The crisis of qualified manpower for criminal justice.* Volume 1, *Probation/parole*; and Volume 2, *Correctional institutions.* Washington, DC: U.S. Government Printing Office.

Plant, J. S. (1937). *Personality and the cultural pattern.* New York: Commonwealth Fund.

Plint, T. (1851). *Crime in England.* London: Charles Gilpin.

Plucknett, T. F. T. (1960). *Edward I and the criminal law.* Cambridge: Cambridge University Press.

Pokorny, A. (1965). A comparison of homicides in two cities. *Journal of Criminal Law, Criminology, and Police Science*, 56, 479–487.

Pope, C. E. (1977a). *Crime-specific analysis: The characteristics of burglary incidents.* U.S. Department of Justice, Law Enforcement Assistance Administration, Analytic Report 10. Washington, DC: U.S. Government Printing Office.

Pope, C. E. (1977b). *Crime-specific analysis: An empirical examination of burglary offense and offender characteristics.* U.S. Department of Justice, Law Enforcement Assistance Administration, Analytical Report 12. Washington, DC: U.S. Government Printing Office.

Porteous, J. D. (1977). *Environment and behavior: Planning and everyday life.* Reading, MA: Addison-Wesley.

Powers, E., and Witmer, H. L. (1951). *An experiment in the prevention of delinquency.* New York: Columbia University Press.

Poyner, B. (1983). *Design against crime: Beyond defensible space.* London: Butterworths.

Poyner, B. (1988). Design modification to prevent crime in mass housing—Fallacies and realities. Paper presented to the American Society of Criminology annual meeting, Montreal.

Poyner, B. (1992a). Situational crime prevention in two parking facilities. In R. V. Clarke (Ed.), *Situational crime prevention: Successful case studies* (pp. 174–184). New York: Harrow and Heston.

Poyner, B. (1992b). Video cameras and bus vandalism. In R. V. Clarke (Ed.), *Situational crime prevention: Successful case studies* (pp. 185–193). New York: Harrow and Heston.

Poyner, B., and Webb, B. (1992). Reducing theft from shopping bags in city centre markets. In R. V. Clarke (Ed.), *Situational crime prevention: Successful case studies* (pp. 99–107). New York: Harrow and Heston.

President's Commission on Crime in the District of Columbia. (1966). *Report.* Washington, DC: U.S. Government Printing Office.

President's Commission on Law Enforcement and Administration of Justice. (1967a). *Corrections.* Washington, DC: U.S. Government Printing Office.

President's Commission on Law Enforcement and Administration of Justice. (1967b). *Science and technology.* Washington, DC: U.S. Government Printing Office.

President's Commission on Law Enforcement and Administration of Justice. (1967c). *Police.* Washington, DC: U.S. Government Printing Office.

President's Commission on Law Enforcement and Administration of Justice. (1967d). *Juvenile delinquency and youth crime.* Washington, DC: U.S. Government Printing Office.

President's Commission on Law Enforcement and Administration of Justice. (1967e). *The challenge of crime in a free society.* Washington, DC: U.S. Government Printing Office.

Pretto, R. (1991). Opportunity and occupational crime: A case study of employee property crime in the workplace. Unpublished master's thesis, School of Criminology, Simon Fraser University, Burnaby, BC.

Pribram, K. (Ed.). (1969). *On the biology of learning.* New York: Harcourt, Brace & World.

Pruitt, D. G. (1971). Choice shifts in group discussion: An introductory review. *Journal of Personality and Social Psychology,* 20, 339–360.

Prus, R. C., and Irini, S. (1980). *Hookers, rounders and desk clerks: The social organization of the hotel community.* Toronto: Sage Publications.

Pyle, D. J. (1983). *The economics of crime and law enforcement.* London: Macmillan.

Pyle, G. F. (1971). Patterns and elements of crime in Summit County, Ohio. Unpublished Report. Center for Urban Studies, University of Akron, OH.

Pyle, G. F. (1973). Measles as an urban health problem: The Akron example. *Economic Geography,* 49, 344–356.

Pyle, G. F., Hanten, E. W., Williams, P. G., Pearson A. L. II, Doyle, J. G., and Kwofie, K. (1974). *The spatial dynamics of crime.* Chicago: Department of Geography, University of Chicago.

Quetelet, L. A. J. (1842). *A treatise on man and the development of his faculties.* Edinburgh: W. and R. Chambers.

Radzinowicz, L. (1965). *The need for criminology.* London: Heinemann.

Radzinowicz, L. (1966). *Ideology and crime.* New York: Columbia University Press.

Radzinowicz, L., and King, J. (1977). *The growth of crime.* London: Hamish Hamilton.

Ramsey, M. (1991). *The effect of better street lighting on crime and fear: A review.* Home Office Crime Prevention Unit, Paper 29. London: HMSO.

Rand, A. (1986). Mobility triangles. In R. Figlio, S. Hankim, and G. F. Rengert (Eds.), *Metropolitan crime patterns* (pp. 117–126). Monsey, NY: Criminal Justice Press.

Reckless, W. C. (1933). *Vice in Chicago.* Chicago: University of Chicago Press.

Reckless, W. C. (1967). *The crime problem* (4th ed.). New York: Appleton-Century-Crofts.

Reiss, A. J. (1967). *Place of residence of arrested persons compared with the place where the offense charged in arrest.* A Report to President's Commission on Law Enforcement and Administration of Justice. Washington, DC: U.S. Government Printing Office.

Reiss, A. J. (1976). Settling the frontiers of a pioneer in American criminology: Henry McKay. In J. F. Short, Jr. (Ed.), *Delinquency, crime, and society* (pp. 64–88). Chicago: University of Chicago Press.

Rengert, G. F. (1972). Spatial aspects of criminal behavior: A suggested approach. Paper read at East Lakes Division, Association of American Geographers Annual Meeting, Philadelphia, PA.

Rengert, G. F. (1975). Some effects of being female on criminal spatial behavior. *The Pennsylvania Geographer*, 13, 10–18.

Rengert, G. F. (1980). Spatial aspects of criminal behavior. In D. Georges-Abeyie and K. D. Harris (Eds.), *Crime: A spatial perspective* (pp. 47–57). New York: Columbia University Press.

Rengert, G. F. (1988). The location of facilities and crime. *Journal of Security Administration*, 11, 12–16.

Rengert, G. F. (1989). Behavioural geography and criminal behaviour. In D. J. Evans and D. T. Herbert (Eds.), *The geography of crime* (pp. 161–175). New York: Routledge.

Rengert, G. F., and Lockwood, B. (2009). Geographical units of analysis and the analysis of crime. In D. Weisburd, W. Bernasco, and G. J. N. Bruinsma (Eds.), *Putting crime in its place: Units of analysis in geographic criminology* (pp. 109–122). New York: Springer.

Rengert, G. F., and Wasilchick, J. (1980). Residential burglary: The awareness and use of extended space. Paper read at American Society of Criminology Annual Meeting, San Francisco.

Rengert, G. F., and Wasilchick, J. (1985). *Suburban burglary: A time and place for everything*. Springfield, IL: Charles C. Thomas.

Rengert, G. F., and Wasilchick, J. (1990). *Space, time and crime: Ethnographic insights into residential burglary*. Report Submitted to U.S. Department of Justice, National Institute of Justice, Office of Justice Programs.

Report of the National Advisory Commission on Civil Disorders. (1968). Washington, DC: U.S. Government Printing Office.

Reppetto, T. A. (1974). *Residential Crime*. Cambridge, MA: Ballinger.

Reppetto, T. A. (1976). Crime prevention and the displacement phenomenon. *Crime and Delinquency*, 22, 166–177.

Reynald, D., Averdijk, M., Elffers, H., and Bernasco, W. (2008). Do social barriers affect urban crime trips? The effects of ethnic and economic neighbourhood compositions on the flow of crime in The Hague, The Netherlands. *Built Environment*, 34 (no. 1), 21–31.

Rhodes, R. P. (1977). *The insoluble problems of crime*. New York: John Wiley and Sons.

Rhodes, W. M., and Conly, C. (1991). Crime and mobility: An empirical study. In P. J. Brantingham and P. L. Brantingham (Eds.), *Environmental criminology* (pp. 167–188; reissued with changes). Prospect Heights, IL: Waveland Press.

Riessman, F., Cohen, J., and Pearl, A. (1964). *Mental health of the poor*. New York: Free Press.

Ritzer, G. (1975). *Sociology: A multiple paradigm science*. Boston: Allyn & Bacon.

Robinson, M. B. (1999). The theoretical development of crime prevention through environmental design (CPTED). *Advances in Criminological Theory*, 8, 427–462.

Roncek, D. (1975). *Crime rates and residential densities in two large cities*. Unpublished doctoral dissertation, Department of Sociology, University of Illinois, Urbana, IL.

Roncek, D., and Lobosco, A. (1983). The effect of high schools on crime in their neighborhoods. *Social Science Quarterly*, 64, 598–613.

Roncek, D., and Maier, P. A. (1991). Bars, blocks and crime revisited: Linking the theory of routine activities to the empiricism of hot spots. *Criminology*, 29, 725–753.

Roncek, D., and Pravatiner, M. A. (1989). Additional evidence that taverns enhance nearby crime. *Sociology and Social Research*, 73, 185–188.

Rose, H. M. (1971). *The Black ghetto: A spatial behavioral perspective*. New York: McGraw-Hill.

Rosenthal, D. (1970). *Genetic theory and abnormal behavior*. New York: McGraw-Hill.

Rosenzweig, M., Bennett, E. L., and Diamond. M. C. (1972). Brain changes in response to experience. *Scientific American*, 226, 22–29.

Ross, L. (1977). The intuitive psychologist and his shortcomings: Distortions in the attribution process. In L. Berkowitz (Ed.), *Advances in experimental social psychology*, volume 10 (pp. 174–221). New York: Academic Press.

Rossmo, D. K. (1999). *Geographic profiling*. Boca Raton, FL: CRC Press.

Rowe, D. C., Osgood, D. W., and Nicewinder, W. A. (1990). A latent trait approach to unifying criminal careers. *Criminology*, 28, 237–270.

Saarinen, T. F. (1969). *Perception of environment*. Association of American Geographers. Commission on College Geography. Resource Paper no. 5. Washington, DC: Association of American Geographers.

Sacks, H. (1972). Notes on police assessment of moral character. In D. Sudnow (Ed.), *Studies in social interaction* (pp. 280–293). New York: Free Press.

Sagalyn, A. (1973). *Residential security*. Washington, DC: Law Enforcement Assistance Administration.

Sagi, P. C., and Wellford, C. E. (1968). Age composition and patterns of change in criminal statistics. *Journal of Criminal Law, Criminology and Police Science*, 59, 29–36.

Samdahl, D. M., and Christensen, H. H. (1985). Environmental cues and vandalism: An exploratory study of picnic table carving. *Environment and Behavior*, 17, 445–458.

Sampson, R. J. (1987). Does an intact family reduce burglary risk for its neighbors? *Sociology and Social Research*, 71, 204–207.

Sampson, R. J., and Groves, W. B. (1989). Community structure and crime: Testing social-disorganization theory. *American Journal of Sociology*, 94, 774–802.

Sampson, R. J., and Wooldredge, J. (1987). Linking the micro- and macro-level dimensions of lifestyle-routine activity and opportunity models of predatory victimization. *Journal of Quantitative Criminology*, 3, 371–393.

Samuel, R. (1981). *East end underworld: Chapters in the life of Arthur Harding*. London: Routledge & Kegan Paul.

Sarbin, T. R. (1979). Review of Yochelson and Samenow's *The criminal personality*, volume 1. *Crime and Delinquency*, 25, 392–396.

Scarr, H. A. (1973). *Patterns of burglary*. Washington, DC: U.S. Government Printing Office.

Schachter, S., and Latane, B. (1964). *Crime, cognition, and the autonomic nervous system*. Nebraska Symposium on Motivation, Volume 12. Lincoln, NB: University of Nebraska Press.

Schafer, S. (1976). The problem of free will in criminology. *Journal of Criminal Law and Criminology*, 67, 481–485.

Schepple, K. L., and Bart, P. B. (1983). Through women's eyes: Defining danger in the wake of sexual assault. *Journal of Social Issues*, 39, 63–81.

Scheuer, J. H. (1969). *To walk the streets safely*. New York: Doubleday and Co.

Schmid, C. F. (1960a). Urban crime areas, part I. *American Sociological Review*, 25, 527–543.

Schmid, C. F. (1960b). Urban crime areas, part II. *American Sociological Review*, 25, 655–678.

Schmid, C. F., and Schmid, S. E. (1972). *Crime in the State of Washington*. Olympia, WA: Law and Justice Planning Office, Washington State Planning and Community Affairs Agency.

Schneiderman, N. (1973). *Classical conditioning*. Morristown, NJ: General Learning Press.

Schreiber, D. (1963). Juvenile delinquency and the school dropout problem. *Federal Probation*, 27, 15–19.

Schroeder, H. W., and Anderson, L. M. (1984). Perception of personal safety in urban recreation sites. *Journal of Leisure Research*, 16, 178–194.

Schuessler, K. (1962). Components of variation in city crime rates. *Social Problems*, 9, 314–321.

Schuessler, K., and Slatin, G. (1964). Sources of variation in U.S. city crime, 1950 and 1960. *Journal of Research in Crime and Delinquency*, 1, 127–148.

Schulz, D. A. (1969). *Coming up black: Patterns of ghetto socialization*. Englewood Cliffs, NJ: Prentice-Hall.

Schur, E. M. (1965). *Crimes without victims*. Englewood Cliffs, NJ: Prentice-Hall.

Scott, D. (1989, December). Graffiti wipeout. *FBI Law Enforcement Bulletin*, pp. 10–14.

Seligman, M., and Hager, J. (1972). *Biological boundaries of learning*. New York: Appleton-Century-Crofts.

Shannon, L. W. (1954). The spatial distribution of criminal offences by states. *Journal of Criminal Law, Criminology and Police Science*, 45, 264–273.

Shannon, L. W. (1988). *Criminal career continuity: Its social context*. New York: Human Sciences Press.

Shaw, C. R. (1929). *Delinquency areas*. Chicago: University of Chicago Press.

Shaw, C. R., and McKay, H. D. (1931). *Social factors in juvenile delinquency*. Washington, DC: U.S. Government Printing Office.

Shaw, C. R., and McKay, H. D. (1942). *Juvenile delinquency and urban areas: A study of rates of delinquency in relation to differential characteristics of local communities in American cities*. Chicago: University of Chicago Press.

Shaw, C. R., and McKay, H. D. (1969). *Juvenile delinquency and urban areas: A study of rates of delinquency in relation to differential characteristics of local communities in American cities* (Rev. ed.). Chicago: University of Chicago Press.

Shaw, C. R., and Moore, M. E. (1931). *The natural history of a delinquent career*. Chicago: University of Chicago Press.

Sheard, M. (1991). Burglary pattern: The impact of cul-de-sacs. Unpublished report. Police Department, Delta, BC.

Sheley, J. F. (1980). Is neutralisation necessary for criminal behaviour? *Deviant Behaviour*, 2, 49–72.

Shellow, R., Romualdi, J. P., and Bartel, E. W. (1974). Crime in rapid transit systems: An analysis and a recommended security and surveillance system. *Transportation Research Record*, 487, 1–12.

Sherman, L. W., Gartin, P. R., and Buerger, M. E. (1989). Hot spots of predatory crime: Routine activities and the criminology of place. *Criminology*, 27, 27–55.

Short, J. F., and Strodtbeck, F. (1965). *Group process and gang delinquency*. Chicago: University of Chicago Press.

Shover, N. E. (1972). Structures and careers in burglary. *Journal of Criminal Law, Criminology and Police Science*, 63, 540–549.

Simon, H. A. (1957). *Models of man, social and rational: Mathematical essays on rational human behavior in a social setting*. New York: John Wiley and Sons.

Simon, H. A. (1982) *Models of bounded rationality* (Vols. 1–3). Cambridge, MA: MIT Press.

Simon, H. A. (1983). *Reasoning in human affairs*. Oxford: Blackwell.

Skinner, F. B. (1964). Behaviorism at fifty. In T. W. Wan (Ed.), *Behaviorism and phenomenology* (pp. 79–108). Chicago: University of Chicago Press.

Skinner, F. B. (1978). *Reflections on behaviorism and society*. Englewood Cliffs, NJ: Prentice-Hall.

Skogan, W. G. (1976). The victims of crime: Some material findings. In A. L. Guenther (Ed.), *Criminal behavior in social systems* (pp. 131–148). Chicago: Rand McNally.

Skogan, W. G. (1988a). Community organizations and crime. *Crime and Justice: A Review of Research*, 10, 39–78.

Skogan, W. (1988b). Disorder, crime and community decline. In T. Hope and M. Shaw (Eds.), *Communities and crime reduction* (pp. 48–61). London: HMSO.

Skogan, W. G., and Maxfield, M. G. (1981). *Coping with crime: Individual and neighborhood reactions*. Beverly Hills, CA: Sage Publications.

Skolnick, J. (1966). *Justice without trial*. New York: John Wiley and Sons.

Sloan, J. H., Kellerman, A. L., Reay, D. T., Ferris, J. A., Koepsell, T., Rivera, F. P., Rice, C., Gray, L., and Logerfo, J. (1988). Handgun regulations, crime, assaults, and homicide. *New England Journal of Medicine*, 319, 1256–1262.

Sloan-Howitt, M., and Kelling, G. (1990). Subway graffiti in New York City: Getting up vs. meaning it and cleaning it. *Security Journal*, 1, 131–136.

Sloan-Howitt, M., and Kelling, G. L. (1992). Subway graffiti in New York City: Getting up vs. meaning it and cleaning it. In R. V. Clarke (Ed.), *Situational crime prevention: Successful case studies* (pp. 239–248). New York: Harrow and Heston.

Slovic, P., and Lichtenstein, S. (1968). The relative importance of probabilities and payoffs in risk-taking. *Journal of Experimental Psychology*, 78, 1–18.

Smith, T. S. (1976). Inverse distance variations for the flow of crime in urban areas. *Social Forces*, 25, 804–815.

Snyder, F. E. (1978). Crime and community mediation—the Boston experience: A preliminary report on the Dorchester Urban Court Program. *Wisconsin Law Review*, 3, 737–795.

Sparks, R. F. (1980). A critique of Marxist criminology. *Crime and Justice: An Annual Review of Research*, 2, 159–210.

Spilerman, S. (1970). The causes of racial disturbances: A comparison of alternative explanations. *American Sociological Review*, 35, 627–649.

SPSS Inc. (1988). *SPSS-X User's Guide* (3rd ed.). Chicago: SPSS Inc.

Stark, R. (1996). Deviant places: A theory of the ecology of crime. In P. Cordella and L. J. Seigel (Eds.), *Readings in contemporary criminological theory* (pp. 128–142). Boston: Northeastern University Press.

Stenning, P. C., and Shearing, C. D. (1980). The quiet revolution: The nature, development, and general legal implications of private security in Canada. *Criminal Law Quarterly*, 22, 220–248.

Stewart, J., and McKenzie, R. L. (1978). Composing urban spaces for security, privacy and outlook. *Landscape Architecture*, 68, 392–398.

Stokols, D. (1972). A social-psychological model of human crowding phenomena. *Journal of the American Institute of Planners*, 38, 73–75.

Stoks, F. (1983). Assessing urban environments for danger of violent crime: Especially rape. In D. Joker, G. Brimilcombe, J. Daish, J. Gray, and D. Kernohan (Eds.), *Proceedings of the conference on people and physical environment research*. Wellington, New Zealand: Ministry of Works and Development.

Sturman, A. (1978). Measuring vandalism in a city suburb. In R. V. G. Clarke (Ed.), *Tackling vandalism* (pp. 9–18). Home Office Research Study Number 47. London: HMSO.

Sussman, F. B., and Baum, F. S. (1968). *Law of juvenile delinquency* (3rd ed.). Dobbs Ferry, NY: Oceana.

Sutherland, E. H. (1924). *Criminology*. Philadelphia, PA: Lippincott.

Sutherland, E. H. (1937a). *Principles of criminology* (3rd ed.). Philadelphia, PA: Lippincott.

Sutherland, E. H. (1937b). *The professional thief*. Chicago: University of Chicago Press.

Sutherland, E. H. (1947). *Principles of criminology* (4th ed.). Philadelphia, PA: Lippincott.

Sutherland, E. H., and Cressey, D. R. (1966). *Principles of criminology* (7th ed.). Philadelphia, PA: Lippincott.

Sutherland, E. H., and Cressey, D. R. (1974). *Criminology*. Philadelphia, PA: Lippincott.

Suttles, G. D. (1968). *The social order of the slum*. Chicago: University of Chicago Press.

Szalai, A. (Ed.). (1972). *The use of time: Daily activities of urban and suburban populations in twelve countries*. The Hague: Mouton.

Szasz, T. (1963). *Law, liberty and psychiatry*. New York: Macmillan.

Szasz, T. (1965). *Psychiatric justice*. New York: Macmillan.

Tannenbaum, F. (1938). *Crime and the community*. New York: Ginn & Co.

Taylor, I., Walton, P., and Young, J. (1973). *The new criminology*. London: Routledge and Kegan Paul.

Taylor, M., and Nee, C. (1988). The role of cues in simulated residential burglary. *British Journal of Criminology*, 23, 396–401.

Taylor, R. (1988). *Human territorial functioning*. Cambridge: Cambridge University Press.

Taylor, R., and Gottfredson, S. D. (1987). Environmental design, crime and prevention: An examination of community dynamics. *Crime and Justice: An Annual Review of Research*, 8, 387–416.

Taylor, R., Gottfredson, S. D., and Brower, S. (1984). Block crime and fear: Defensible space, local social ties and territorial functioning. *Journal of Research in Crime and Delinquency*, 21, 303–331.

Theil, H. (1971). *Principles of econometrics*. New York: John Wiley and Sons.

Thiessen, D. (1972). *Gene organization and behavior*. New York: Random House.

Thompson, R. (1975). *Physiological psychology*. New York: Harper & Row.

Thrasher, F. M. (1963). *The gang: A study of 1,313 gangs in Chicago* (Abridged). Chicago: University of Chicago Press. (Original work published 1927.)

Timms, D. W. G. (1971). *The urban mosaic: Towards a theory of residential differentiation*. Cambridge: Cambridge University Press.

Tita, G. E., and Greenbaum, R. T. (2009). Crime, neighborhoods, and units of analysis: Putting space in its place. In D. Weisburd, W. Bernasco, and G. J. N. Bruinsma (Eds.), *Putting crime in its place: Units of analysis in geographic criminology* (pp. 145–170). New York: Springer.

Tittle, C. R., and Logan, C. H. (1973). Sanctions and deviance: Evidence and remaining questions. *Law and Society Review*, 7, 371–392.

Tizard, J. (1976). Psychology and social policy. *Bulletin of the British Psychological Society*, 29, 225–233.

Tobias, J. J. (1967). *Crime and industrial society in the nineteenth century*. New York: Schocken Books.

Tobias, J. J. (1972). *Urban crime in Victorian England*. New York: Schocken Books.

Todorovich, A. (1970). The application of ecological models to the study of juvenile delinquency in Belgrade. *International Review of Criminal Policy*, 28, 64–71.

Toomey, B. G., Simonsen, C. E., and Allen, H. E. (1975). Right to treatment: Issues and prospects. *Proceedings of the 20th Annual Southern Conference on Corrections*. Tallahassee, FL: Florida State University.

Trasler, G. B. (1973). Criminal behavior. In H. J. Eysenck (Ed.), *Handbook of abnormal psychology* (pp. 273–298). London: Pitman Medical Publications.

Trasler, G. B. (1979). Delinquency, recidivism, and desistance. *British Journal of Criminology*, 19, 314–322.

Tremblay, P. (1986). Designing crime. *British Journal of Criminology*, 26, 234–253.

Tseloni, A., Osborn, D. R., Trickett, A., and Pease, K. (2002). Modelling property crime using the British Crime Survey: What have we learnt? *British Journal of Criminology*, 42, 109–128.

Tuck, M. (1979). Consumer behaviour theory and the criminal justice system: Towards a new strategy of research. *Journal of the Market Research Society*, 21, 44–58.

Turner, C. B., and Cashdan, S. (1988). Perception of college students' motives for shoplifting. *Psychological Reports*, 62, 855–862.

Turner, S. (1969a). Delinquency and distance. In M. E. Wolfgang and T. Sellin (Eds.), *Delinquency: Selected studies* (pp. 11–26). New York: John Wiley and Sons.

Turner, S. (1969b). The ecology of delinquency. In M. E. Wolfgang and T. Sellin (Eds.), *Delinquency: Selected Studies*, (pp. 52–58). New York: John Wiley and Sons.

Tversky, A., and Kahneman, D. (1974). Judgment under uncertainty: Heuristics and biases. *Science*, 185, 1124–1131.

Ulrich, R., Stachnik, T., and Mabry, J. (Eds.). (1966). *Control of human behavior*. New York: Scott, Foresman and Co.

USCB (U.S. Census Bureau). (1971). *U.S. census of population: 1970. Number of inhabitants, Final report, PC(1)-A1 United States Summary*. Washington, DC: U.S. Government Printing Office.

USCB. (1973a). *Census of transportation, 1972. U.S. summary*. Washington, DC: U.S. Government Printing Office.

USCB. (1973b). *Who's home when*. Working Paper 37. Washington, DC: U.S. Government Printing Office.

USCB. (1975–1976). *Statistical abstract of the U.S.* Washington, DC: U.S. Government Printing Office.

USCB. (1947–1976). *Current population studies*. Washington, DC: U.S. Government Printing Office.

USDJ (U.S. Department of Justice). (1974a). *Preliminary report of the impact cities, crime survey results*. Washington, DC: Law Enforcement Assistance Administration (NCJISS).

USDJ. (1974b). *Crime in the nation's five largest cities: Advance report*. Washington, DC: Law Enforcement Assistance Administration (NCJISS).

USDJ. (1974c). *Crimes and victims: A report on the Dayton-San Jose pilot survey of victimization*. Washington, DC: Law Enforcement Assistance Administration.

USDJ. (1976). *Criminal victimizations in the U.S., 1973*. Washington, DC: Law Enforcement Assistance Administration (NCJISS).

USDJ. (1977). *Criminal victimizations in the U.S.: A comparison of 1974 and 1975 findings*. Washington, DC: Law Enforcement Assistance Administration (NCJISS).

United States Commission on Civil Rights. (1967). *Racial isolation in the public schools*. Washington, DC: U.S. Government Printing Office.

U.S. Senate, Select Committee on Small Business. (1969). *Crime against small business*. 91st Congress, 1st Session, Senate Document No. 91-14.

Van de Voordt, T. (1986). Le Corbusier, C.S. in the dock. *Netherlands Journal of Housing Environmental Research*, 1, 83–85.

Van Den Berghe, P. (1974). Bringing beasts back in: Toward a biosocial theory of aggression. *American Sociological Review*, 39, 777–788.

Van Den Berghe, P. (1975). *Man in society: A biosocial view*. New York: Elsevier.

Van Dijk, J. J. M., Mayhew, P., and Killias, M. (1990). *Experiences of crime across the world: Key findings from the 1989 International Crime Survey*. Deventer: Kluwer Law and Taxation Publishers.

Van Soomeran, P. (1989). The physical urban environment and reduction of urban insecurity: A general introduction. In *Local Strategies for the Reduction of Urban Insecurity in Europe* (pp. 219–233). Urban Renaissance in Europe Study Series, Volume 35. Strasbourg: Council of Europe.

Van Vliet, W. (1983). Exploring the fourth environment: An examination of the home range of city and suburban teenagers. *Environment and Behavior*, 15, 567–588.

Vetter, H. J., and Silverman, I. J. (1978). *The nature of crime*. Philadelphia, PA: W. B. Saunders Company.

Vidler, A. (1986). The scenes of the street: Transformation in ideal and reality, 1750–1871. In S. Anderson (Ed.), *On streets*, (pp. 28–111). Boston: MIT Press.

Vold, G. B. (1958). *Theoretical criminology*. New York: Oxford University Press.

Vold, G. B. (1979). *Theoretical criminology* (2nd ed.). New York: Oxford University Press.

Von Hentig, H. (1949). *The criminal and his victim: Studies in the sociobiology of crime*. New Haven, CT: Yale University Press.

Voss, H. L., and Petersen, D. M. (1971). *Ecology, crime and delinquency*. New York: Appleton.

Waldo, G. P. (Ed.). (1983). *Career criminals*. Beverly Hills, CA: Sage Publications.

Walker, N. D. (1979). The efficacy and morality of deterrents. *Criminal Law Review*, March, 129–144.

Waller, I. (1979). What reduces residential burglary: Action and research in Seattle and Toronto. Paper presented at the Third International Symposium on Victimology, Munster, West Germany.

Waller, I., and Okihiro, N. (1978). *Burglary: The victim and the public*. Toronto: University of Toronto Press.

Wallis, C. P., and Maliphant, R. (1967). Delinquent areas in the County of London: Ecological factors. *British Journal of Criminology*, 7, 250–284.

Walsh, D. P. (1978). *Shoplifting: Controlling a major crime*. London: Macmillan.

Walsh, D. P. (1980). *Break-ins: Burglary from private houses*. London: Constable.

Walsh, D. P. (1986). Victim selection procedures among economic criminals: The rational choice perspective. In D. B. Cornish and R. V. Clarke (Eds.), *The reasoning criminal: Rational choice perspectives on offending* (pp. 38–56). New York: Springer-Verlag.

Wanderer, J. J. (1969). An index of riot severity and some correlates. *American Journal of Sociology*, 74, 500–505.

Wang, X., Liu, L., and Eck, J. (2008). Crime simulation using GIS and artificial intelligent agents. In L. Liu and J. Eck (Eds.), *Artificial crime analysis systems: Using computer simulations and geographic information systems* (pp. 209–225). Hershey, PA: Information Science Reference.

Warr, M., and Stafford, M. (1991). The influence of delinquent peers: What they think or what they do? *Criminology*, 29, 851–866.

Warr, P. B., and Knapper, C. (1968). *The perception of people and events*. Chichester: John Wiley and Sons.

Washnis, G. J. (1976). *Citizen involvement in crime prevention*. Lexington: Heath.

Webb, B., and Laycock, G. (1992). *Tackling car crime: The nature and extent of the problem*. Home Office Crime Prevention Unit, Paper 32. London: HMSO.

Webber, M. J., and Rigby, D. L. (1996). *The golden age illusion: Rethinking postwar capitalism*. New York: Guilford Press.

Weinstein, D., and Deitch, L. (1974). *The impact of legalized gambling: The socio-economic consequences of lotteries and off-track betting*. New York: Praeger.

Weisburd, D. L. (1992). Contrasting crime general and crime specific theory: The case of hot spots of crime. *Advances in Criminological Theory*, 4, 45–70.

Weisburd, D. L., Wheeler, S., and Waring, E. (1991). *Crimes of the middle classes*. New Haven, CT: Yale University Press.

Wellford, C. F. (1973). Age composition and the increase in recorded crime. *Criminology*, 11, 61–70.

West, D. J. (1963). *The habitual prisoner*. London: Macmillan.

West, D. J. (1982). *Delinquency: Its roots, careers and prospects*. London: Heinemann Educational Books.

West, W. G. (1978). The short term careers of serious thieves. *Canadian Journal of Criminology*, 20, 169–190.

Wheeler, S., Weisburd, D. L., Waring, E., and Bode, N. (1988). White collar crimes and criminals. *American Criminal Law Review*, 25, 331–357.

White, R. C. (1932). The relation of felonies to environmental factors in Indianapolis. *Social Forces*, 10, 498–509.

Whitman, I. L., Davis, R. M., and Goldstone, S. E. (1971). Measuring impacts of urban water development. *Water Resources Bulletin*, 7, 667–668.

Whyte, W. (1988). *City: Rediscovering the center*. New York: Doubleday.

Wiggins, J. S. (1973). *Personality and prediction: Principles of personality assessment*. Reading, MA: Addison-Wesley.

Wikstrom, P.-O. H. (1991). *Urban crime, criminals, and victims: The Swedish experience in an Anglo-American comparative perspective*. New York: Springer-Verlag.

Wilcox, S. (1973). The geography of robbery. In F. Feeney and A. Weir (Eds.), *The prevention and control of robbery,* volume 3 (pp. 27–93). Davis, CA: The Center of Administration of Justice, University of California at Davis.

Wiles, P., and Costello, A. (2000). The "road to nowhere": The evidence for travelling criminals. Home Office Research Study 207. London: Research, Development and Statistics Directorate, Home Office.

Wilkins, L. T. (1964). *Social deviance.* London: Tavistock.

Wilkins, L. T., and Chandler, A. (1965). Confidence and competence in decision making. *British Journal of Criminology,* 5, 22–35.

Wilkinson, P. (1977). *Terrorism and the liberal state.* London: Macmillan.

Wilks, J. A. (1967). Ecological correlates of crime and delinquency. In *Crime and its impact: An assessment* (pp. 138–156). Task Force on Assessment, the President's Commission on Law Enforcement and the Administration. Washington, DC: U.S. Government Printing Office.

Williamson, H. (1968). *Hustler!* New York: Doubleday.

Willmer, M. A. P. (1970). *Crime and information theory.* Edinburgh: Edinburgh University Press.

Wilson, E. (1975). *Sociobiology.* Cambridge, MA: Harvard University Press.

Wilson, J. Q. (1968a). *Varieties of police behavior.* Cambridge, MA: Harvard University Press.

Wilson, J. Q. (1968b). Dilemmas of police administration. *Public Administration Review,* 28, 407–416.

Wilson, J. Q. (1975). *Thinking about crime.* New York: Basic Books.

Wilson, J. Q., and Herrnstein, R. J. (1985). *Crime and human nature.* New York: Touchstone Books.

Wilson, J. Q., and Kelling, G. (1982). Broken windows: The police and neighborhood safety. *Atlantic Monthly,* March, 29–38.

Wilson, S. (1978). Vandalism and "defensible space" on London housing estates. In R. V. G. Clarke (Ed.), *Tackling vandalism* (pp. 41–65). London: HMSO.

Winchester, S., and Jackson, H. (1982). *Residential burglary: The limits of prevention.* Home Office Research Study Number 74. London: HMSO.

Wise, J., and Stoks, F. (1981). *Correlates of environmental behaviors in subsidized housing or design and vandalism: Three case studies for the Seattle housing authority.* Seattle, WA: School of Architecture.

Witmer, H. L., and Tufts, E. (1964). *The effectiveness of delinquency prevention programs.* Washington, DC: Children's Bureau.

Witte, A. D. (1980). Estimating the economic model of crime with individual data. *Quarterly Journal of Economics,* 94, 57–84.

Wolf, C. P. (1975). *Environmental sociology.* Washington, DC: Ad Hoc Committee on Environmental Sociology.

Wolfgang, M. E. (1958). *Patterns of criminal homicide.* Philadelphia, PA: University of Pennsylvania Press.

Wolfgang, M. E. (1970). Urban crime. In J. Q. Wilson (Ed.), *The metropolitan enigma* (pp. 270–311). New York: Anchor Books.

Wolfgang, M. E. (1977). Real and perceived changes in crime. In S. F. Landau and L. Sebba (Eds.), *Criminology in perspective.* Lexington, MA: Lexington Books.

Wolfgang, M. E., and Ferracuti, F. (1967). *The subculture of violence: Towards an integrated theory in criminology.* London: Social Science Paperbacks.

Wolfgang, M. E., Figlio, R. M., and Sellin, T. (1972). *Delinquency in a birth cohort.* Chicago: University of Chicago Press.

Wolfgang, M. E., Thornberry, T. P., and Figlio, R. M. (1987). *From boy to man, from delinquency to crime.* Chicago: University of Chicago Press.

Wolpert, J. (1964). The decision process in spatial context. *Annals of the Association of American Geographers,* 54, 537–558.

Wootton, B. A. (1959). *Social science and social policy.* New York: Macmillan.

Wootton, B. A. (1963). *Crime and the criminal law.* London: Stevens.

Yochelson, S., and Samenow, S. E. (1976). *The criminal personality* (Vols. 1–2). New York: Aronson.

Zeisel, J. (1975). *Sociology and architectural design.* New York: Russell Sage Foundation.

Zimbardo, P. G., and Ruch, F. L. (1975). *Psychology and life.* Glenview, IL: Scott, Foresman.

Zimring, F., and Hawkins, G. (1973). *Deterrence: The legal threat of crime control.* Chicago: University of Chicago Press.

Zipf, G. K. (1949). *Human behavior and the principle of least effort: An introduction to human ecology.* Cambridge, MA: Addison-Wesley.

Zipf, G. K. (1950). *The principle of least effort.* Reading, MA: Addison-Wesley.

Index

A

Action spaces, 238
Activity spaces, 238–239, 259, 287–288, 309, 375
Akron crime analysis. *See* Urban crime, Akron
Allen, Francis, 413
Antisocial acts, 173
Awareness space model, 238, 239, 240, 247, 258–259, 287

B

Backcloth, activity, 388
Backcloth, environmental, 280–282, 284–285, 295, 365, 372
Backcloth, template/activity, 374–379
Becker, Howard, 315
Behavior therapy, 417
Behavior, models of
    biogenic model, 433, 435
    learning theory model, 433, 434–435
    overview, 432–433
    psychogenic model, 433
    sociological, 433
Behaviorism, 322
Boggs, Sarah, 412, 426, 443
Booth, Edwin, 482
Bounded rationality, 23
Brantingham, P.J., 1, 2, 6, 19, 20, 26, 184, 185, 317, 326, 348, 444, 482
Brantingham, P.L., 1, 2, 6, 19, 20, 26, 184, 185, 317, 326, 348, 444, 482
British Crime Survey, 219
British Mental Health Act of 1959, 397
Burgess, Ernest, 2, 10, 83–86, 173
Burglary, suburban. *See* Property crimes; Suburban burglary
Burnside gang, 238–239

C

California v. Robinson, 419
Canadian Urban Victimization Survey, 217, 219–220
    activity variables, 221
    classifications of victimization, 220–221
    overview of research, 220
    personal crime, 224
    property crime at home, 222, 224, 227
    robberies, 224
    social context, 222
    urban structure, impact of, 225–228
    vehicle theft, 222, 227
Capital punishment, 446–447
Center for Problem-Oriented Policing, 25, 483
Chicago Area Project, 119–123
Chicago School, 2, 486
Clarke, Ronald, 22, 24, 185, 393–394
Clustering, ethnic, 306
Cocooning, 305–306
Cognitive psychology, 322–325
Cohen, Lawrence, 183, 184, 218
Colquhoun, Patrick, 195
Community action programs, 422–424
Conformity, 432
Conrad, John, 420
Convergence, 191, 214–216, 348–349, 349–350
Cornish, Derek, 22, 24, 185
Correctional system, 421–422
CPTED. *See* Crime prevention through environmental design (CPTED)
Cressey, Donald, 411, 412
Crime. *See also* Criminals
    causes, 32
    complexity of, 366
    conventional theories of, 214

convergence of circumstances, 191,
      214–216, 348–349, 349–350
effects, 32
etiology of, 278, 279–285
feedback loops of, 378
high-risk, low-reward, 7
juvenile (*See* Juvenile delinquency)
legal dimension, 6
offender dimension, 6
persons, against (*See* Violent crime)
physical opportunities, 453–456
place/situational dimension, 6
poverty, link to (*See* Socioeconomic
      factors of crime)
prevention (*See* Crime prevention)
property (*See* Property crimes)
rates (*See* Rates of crime)
socioeconomic factors, relationship
      between (*See* Socioeconomic
      factors of crime)
spatiotemporal component, 6, 214–216
target selection, 290–291
templates (*See* Crime templates)
transactional nature of, 274
triggering events, 381
types, impact on criminal readiness, 381
victim dimension, 6
Crime patterns, intraurban. *See* Intraurban
      crime patterns
Crime prevention
   choice model, implications of, 452–453
   community organizations and agencies
      for, 398–399
   crime prevention through
      environmental design (CPTED)
      (*See* Crime prevention through
      environmental design (CPTED))
   defining, 395–396
   deterrence, 413–141
   dispositional theories, 450–452
   environmental design (*See*
      Environmental design)
   experiments, 319
   facilities, relationship between, 471
   governmental regulations, 276–277
   increasing chances of being caught,
      456–457
   juvenile crime, of, 118–119
   mission of, 395
   neighborhood characteristics, 178–180
   objections to rehabilitative intervention,
      457–458

physical environment modifications,
      275
physical opportunities, reducing,
      453–456
policy, 336–338, 340, 363, 407
public health model (*See* Public health
      model of crime prevention)
punishment (*See* Punishment)
situational, 25
surveillance, 180, 309, 456–457
urban design, through (*See* Crime
      prevention through urban design
      (CPTUD))
vigilante groups, 305
Crime prevention through environmental
      design (CPTED), 245
Crime prevention through urban design
      (CPTUD), 179–180, 425–426
Crime templates, 26
   criminals' expectations, 291–292
   housing models, 292–294
   Newman's areal template, 292–293
   research, 295–296
   surveillance, impact of, 295
   target choice, 291
   variations in crime, 294–295, 370–371
Criminal justice system
   correctional system, 421–422
   courts, 419
   model of, 417–418
   parole, 420
   police, role of, 418, 419, 425
   probation, 420
   reform measures, 419–420
Criminals. *See also* Crime
   age of, 300
   decision making (*See* Decision making,
      offenders')
   experienced, traits of, 247
   goals of, 380–381
   impulsive acts, 316
   motivations of, 369
   network of peers/associates, 335
   noncriminal spatial activity, 267
   novice, traits of, 247
   ordinary behaviors of, 238
   readiness of, 285, 330–331, 369,
      379–382
   risky behavior, 324, 464
   social networks of, 249
   suburban residential burglars (*See*
      Suburban burglary)

target selection of, 249
thinking patterns of, 324
triggering events/situations, 285–286
Criminologists, 428
Criminology, 316–319
  biological theories, 411
  classical school of, 409–410
  Freudian psychology, influence of, 442
  psychological theories, 411
  purpose of discipline, 365
  sociological theories, 411
  theoretical, 410–411
Critical density, 178
Critical intensity zones, 180

D

Death penalty, 446–447
Decision making, offenders', 208
  background factors, 330*f*, 331
  continuance, 332, 334–335
  crime-specific, 328–329
  desistance, 335
  end points of, 367–368
  flowchart of decision, 331–332
  geographic impingements on, 348
  lifestyle-based, 348
  network of peers/associates, 335
  overview, 312–314
  rational choice framework, 325–326
  readiness factor, 330–331
  relevance for policy decisions, 336–338
  sequence of, 368–369
Defensible space, 7–8, 9, 459
Density. *See* Population density
Deterrence-punishment model, 6–7
Deviance, sociology of, 314–316
Displacement, crime
  assumptions regarding choice, 352–353
  choice structuring of criminal acts,
    357–360
  choice structuring of offender
    perceptions, 360–362
  properties, choice structuring of,
    353–354, 356–357
Distance decay, 234
  crime-distance gradients, 145–147, 154
Durham v. U.S., 419

E

Easter v. District of Columbia, 419

Eck, John, 486
Ecological analysis of crime, 191–193
Economic models of criminal behavior,
    319–322
Economy and crime, relationship between,
    16
Edges, 301–302. *See also* Urban mosaic
Environment, conceptualization of, 7
Environmental backcloth. *See* Backcloth,
    environmental
Environmental criminology
  aggregate patterns of criminal behavior,
    276–277
  classic works, defining, 481–482
  current scholarship, 485–486
  development of, 1, 3
  future trends, 483
  long-range interventions, 277
  meta-theory, 185
  origin of term, 6
  overview, 308–310
  praxis, 484–485
  routine activity theory (*See* Routine
    activity theory)
  terminology, 6
Environmental design, 9
  crime prevention and control through,
    432
  organism-environment interaction,
    440–441
  physical environment, relationship
    between, 444
Environmental engineering
  behavioral science, application of, 424,
    426–428
  prior to offense, 424
  technology, use of, 425
Environmental psychology, 437–440,
    443–444
Environmental sociology, 436–437
Ethics of punishment, 396–397

F

Facilities, 468–471, 476–479
Faust, Frederick, 393
Felson, Marcus, 14, 15, 183, 184, 185, 218,
    378, 394
Female crime, 452
Ferri, Enrico, 276
Forde, David, 17, 184
French code, 34, 40

G

Gangs and delinquency, 114–115. *See also*
    Juvenile delinquency
Gault, The Matter of, 419
Geographic profiling, 21–22
Geometric theory of crime, 6
    activity patterns, 19, 238–239
    activity spaces, 19, 21
    applications, 21–22
    awareness spaces, 19
    crime, geometry of, 19–20
    edge, concept of, 20
    nodes, 19, 20, 26, 238, 239, 240
    overview, 18–19
    pathways, 19, 26, 238, 239
    predictions, 184
    testing of, 20–21
Glyde, John, 2, 482
Gold, R., 180–181
Gould, Leroy, 195
Guardians, 191, 196, 225, 345, 378
Guerry, André-Michel, 1, 231, 411

H

H statistic, 210
Harries, Keith, 3, 231
Hawley, Amos, 190
Hirschi, Travis, 343, 346, 366
Hooliganism, 319
Household activity ratio, 208–210
Human ecology
    rhythm, 15
    tempo, 15 (*See also* Tempo [of
        violations])
    timing, 15

I

Immigration
    language/communication issues, 11–12
    population turnover, impact on, 11–12
Importance-beliefs, 323
Income and crime, relationship between, 16
Infanticide, 59
Intraurban crime patterns, 3
    Belgrade study, 166–167, 169–170
    Birmingham, England analysis, 161–162
    Chicago, Shaw and McKay analysis,
        156–158, 174–175
    crime control, 178–180

defensive environment, creating,
        180–181
    diminishment outward, 172–173
    Irish immigrants, Birmingham, 161–162
    Irish immigrants, England, 159
    location of crime, 174–175, 177
    London analysis, 158–161
    overview, 155–156
    population density, relationship
        between, 178–179
    property crimes, 177
    Seattle studies, 170, 172
    types of crime, 174–175
    Washington, D.C. 1966 report, 162–166

J

Jeffery, C. Ray, 6, 7, 8, 9, 18, 393, 407
Jill Dando Institute for Crime Science, 483
Juvenile delinquency
    activity patterns, 376–377
    Belgrade study, 166–167, 169–170
    Burgess study, 1916, small city, 83–86
    causes, 88
    Chicago analysis, 156–158
    community action, 119–123
    conventional controls, 346–347
    education of, 424
    employed *versus* unemployed teens, 283
    episodic, 316
    ethnicity, relationship between, 158
    gangs (*See* Gangs)
    genetic factors, 346
    geographical correlations, 89, 115
    government assistance, relationship
        between, 92, 97
    handles, 343, 344, 345, 347
    home ownership rates, relationship
        between, 94, 97–98
    housing issues, 453
    immigrant youth, relationship between,
        98, 99, 102, 103, 107–108, 118, 157
    indirect controls, 424
    industrial land use, relationship
        between, 160
    London, England, study, 160
    median rentals, relationship between,
        92, 94, 97–98
    motivation of offenders, 347
    nodes of youth, analyzing, 300, 376–377
    policy decisions, 336–338
    population density variables, 90–92

poverty, relationship between, 105
prevention, 118–119
race, relationship between, 98, 99, 103,
        105, 107–108, 157, 158
rates of, 88–89
recidivism, 157
social controls, informal, 343–345
socioeconomic status, relationship
        between, 116–117
technological factors, 346
treatment, 119
urban community characteristics,
        relationship between, 88
value systems, relationship between,
        115–116, 117–118
zones in 1969 Chicago, statistics for, 109

K

Kennedy, Leslie, 17, 184
Kent v. U.S., 419
Kinney, J. Bryan, 394

L

Laycock, Gloria, 483
Learning theory model of behavior, 433,
        434–435
Liu, Lin, 486
Lynch, Kevin, 19

M

Mayhew, Henry, 275
McKay, Henry, 2, 10, 11, 12, 13, 14, 87, 156,
        158, 160, 218, 231, 236, 243, 442
Medical geography, 130–131
Metroquilt, 476
Metroreef, 468, 470, 471, 476
Morris, Norval, 413, 443–444
Morris, T., 160, 237
Motivation, criminal, 16

N

National Commission of Law Observance,
        243
National Commission on the Causes and
        Prevention of Violence, 188
Neurological intervention of criminals,
        446–447
Newman, Oscar, 7–8, 9, 292, 293, 294

Nodes
    geometric theory of crime, as part of, 19,
            20, 26
    rationality, chosen through, 26

O

Operant conditioning, 432

P

Packer, Herbert, 397
Paley, William, 414
Pathways
    geometric theory of crime, as part of,
            19, 26
    rationality, chosen through, 26
Pattern theory, 6
    aggregated, 375, 378
    basic search area for cluster of offenders,
            236–237
    basic search area for single offender,
            234–236
    benefits, 27–28
    burglaries, application to, 384–386
    complex search area for multiple
            offenders, 241–242
    complex search area for single offender,
            237–240
    complexity of, 28
    concentric zone cities, 250
    crime site selection, 232, 233
    criminal event process, 373–374
    development, 26–27
    dispersed development urban areas,
            251–252, 253
    distance decay (*See* Distance decay)
    dynamic search area for multiple
            offenders, 248–249
    dynamic search area for single offender,
            246–247
    flexibility of, 372
    fringe areas, 253
    grid networks, 252–253
    limitations of, 372
    mobility, 232
    mosaic form cities, 250–251
    motivation, 232
    multidisciplinary nature of, 388–390
    office supply pilfering, example of,
            383–384
    opportunity, 232

overview, 26–27, 371–372
perception, 232
routine activities, relationship between, 375–376
rubrics, 232
selective search area for multiple offenders, 242–243, 246
selective search area for single offender, 243–246
serial rape, application to, 387–388
template backcloth, 374–375
temporal variations, 381–382, 386
Patterns, crime
geometric theory of crime, as part of, 20
pattern theory (See Pattern theory)
Plant, James S., 122
Policing patterns, 259
Population density
crime, relationship between, 178–179
Positivists, 409
Poverty. See Socioeconomic factors of crime
Poyner, Barry, 294
President's Commission on Law Enforcement, 418
Propensity to crime
age, differences by, 63–67, 69–72
change, impact of, 32–33
classes/curves, France in 1800s, 47–48
climate, influence of, 40, 46–47, 53, 73
education, influence of, 50–51
education, relationship between, 52–53
gender, differences by, 57, 59–60, 61, 73
intellect of accused, relationship between, 36
morality, relationship between, 59, 60
overview, 29–30, 29–31
poverty, relationship between, 52, 74
prejudices, relationship between, 49–50
probability statistics, 33–34
profession of the accused, 61, 74
race, relationship between, 51–52, 53, 55
repression of, 35–36
seasonal influences, 55–57, 73
social class, relationship to, 74
Property crimes
crime-specific studies of, 318
decision making regarding (See Decision making, offenders')
gender differences in accused, 57, 59–60
intellect of the accused, relationship between, 36
point of entry, 177

protecting property, 455
rational approach, 24
residential burglary, 329–330
type of establishment, 177
Public health model of crime prevention
dangers to society, dealing with, 402
goals of criminal justice system, 402–403
levels of prevention, 399–400
primary prevention, 403–404
rehabilitation, 405–406
secondary prevention, 403, 406
tertiary prevention, 402–403, 405–406
treatment, 404–405
Public housing
London analysis of crime patterns, 160–161
Punishment
behavioral control, 414–415
brain chemistry in reaction to, 445–446
correctional agencies, 398–399
culpability, 397–398
ethics of, 396–397
role of, in criminology, 414–415
threat of, 445–446
utilitarian justification of, 396
Pyle, Gerald, 3

Q

Quetelet, Adolphe, 1, 2, 411, 482

R

Rates of crime
activity pattern, 204–205
Akron crime analyses (See Urban crime, Akron)
burglary rates, 203
business establishment trends, 206–207
ecological fallacies of, 126
family activities, relationship between, 200, 203
multivariate analyses, 126, 128–129
property trends, 206
reporting reliability, 209–210
robbery rates, 203
spatial analysis, 190
temporal independence of criminal acts, 190–191
trends, routine activity, 189–190, 196, 207

unemployment, relationship between, 209

urban structure, relationship between (*See* Urban structure)

victimization data, 203

Rational choice theory, 6, 184–185

applications, 25

choice structuring criminal acts, 357–360

choice structuring of offender perceptions, 360–362

choice structuring of properties, 353–354, 356–357

crime-control policies, use in determining, 363

criminal decision making, 24

defining, 24

offenders, assumptions regarding, 352–353

overview, 22–23

prevention implications, 452–453

refinement of, 314

synthesis of, 325–326

Rational crime theory, 343

Reality therapy, 417

Recidivism, 398, 420–421

Red light districts, 254–255

Reduced-form relationship, 13

Rehabilitation. *See also* Punishment

court support for, 419

goal of, 398

ideal of, 413–414, 419

rhetoric of, 405–406

therapeutic approaches to, 415–417

Reiss, Albert, 194

Rengert, George, 21, 184, 288, 348

Report of the President's Commission on Crime in the District of Columbia, 162–166

Report to the King (Rapport au Roi), 38–39

Reppetto, Thomas, 193, 445

Rookeries, criminal, 236, 243, 275–276

Rossmo, D. Kim, 21

Rouse v. Cameron, 419–420

Routine activity theory, 6

activity patterns, 206

activity spaces, 287–288, 309

awareness spaces, 288

context of activities, 219

descriptive analyses, 193–194

elements of crime, 462

exposure to crime, 224–225

household activity ratio, relationship between, 208–211, 214

location of offenses/crime, 197, 199

macro testing of, 17

micro testing of, 17

microlevel assumptions, 196–197

nodes, 286–287, 298–300

offender routines, 463, 464

overview, 14–15

pathways, 300–301

prediction abilities of, 17

property crime, 229

road networks, 289

systematic accident, 464–465

target suitability, 199–200

travel patterns, 286–287

trends in crime rates, 189–190

types of crime involved, 15–16, 463

types of offenses, relationship between, 207

urban mosaic, 296–298

victimization, relationship between, 218, 219

violent crime, in context of, 229

S

Sampson, Robert, 13

Schmid, C.F., 170, 172, 231

Schmid, S.E., 170, 172

Search and seizure, 418

Sexual offender laws, 413

Shaw, Clifford, 2, 10, 11, 12, 13, 14, 87, 156, 158, 160, 190, 218, 231, 236, 243, 442

Simon, Herbert, 23

Skinner, B.F., 432, 434

Social area analysis, 443

Social change, 348

Social control

ineffectiveness of, 215

Social definitionist paradigm, 433–434

Social disorganization theory, 2, 3, 22

analyses of, 13

city growth/expansion, 10–11

competition over space, 10–11

crime, link to, 11–12

description of, 9–10

economic deprivation, 12

ethnic heterogenity, 12

family disruption, 12

overview, 10–11

population turnover, 11–12
prediction abilities of, 17
residential land use classifications, 10
social deprivation, 12
Social factist paradigm, 433–434
Social learning theory, 322
Socioeconomic factors of crime
    affluence, 154
    awareness space, relationship between,
        288
    low-income areas' inability to combat
        crime, 272
    poverty, 74, 105, 152, 188, 283–284
    relationship between, 195
    urban mosaic, 296–298
Sociopaths, 445, 447
Spatial clustering of offenders, 236–237, 309
Spatial criminology, 1, 3, 232
    crime site selection, 233–234
    red light patterning of crime, 254–255
    social disorganization theory (See Social
        disorganization theory)
Spatial learning, 264–265
Spatial perception, 264
Spatiotemporal component of crime, 6,
    214–216
Spatiotemporal impact of crime, 194
Stereotypes, 181
Suburban burglary
    activity path extension, 265–266
    assumptions, false, 271
    awareness space of criminal, 258–259,
        261
    chance location, 265–266
    characteristics of, 257
    criminal activity space, 259
    evaluation of space by burglar, 262–264
    location, burglar's choice of, 258
    opportunity, 258–259
    recreation sites, link of crime sites to,
        269
    search space, 259, 264
    secondary information sources, link of
        crime sites to, 269–271
    workplace, link of crime sites to,
        268–269
Suffolk, England, 1856 crime statistics,
    77–82
Surveillance, 8, 295, 309, 456–457
Survival needs, crime tied to, 282, 283
Sutherland, E.H., 442
Systematic accident, 464–465

T

Tannenbaum, Frank, 115, 120
Target selection, 249, 290–291, 318,
    369–370, 373, 376, 377–378, 380
Technology, impact on crime, 192
Tempo (of violations), 191, 215
Temporal independence of criminal acts,
    190–191
Territoriality
    crime, relationship between, 307–308
    insiders, crimes committed by,
        306–307
    outsiders, reaction to, 304–306
    residential areas, 302–302
Thomas, W.I., 442
Thrill crimes, 295–296
Tobias, J.J., 195, 231, 243
Transportation arteries, impact on crime,
    252, 260, 289
Treatment-rehabilitation model, 6–7
Triggering events, 285

U

Unemployment
    crime, link to, 13, 282, 283
Uniform Crime Report, 188–189
Urban crime, Akron
    aggravated assault, 140
    burglary, 144
    canonical analysis, 132–134, 140–141
    crime rates/numbers, 126, 128–129, 138,
        139
    crime-distance gradients, 145–147, 154
    Factor I analysis, 134, 138, 141, 143
    Factor II analysis, 138
    Factor III analysis, 138–139, 143–144,
        144
    Factor IV analysis, 139, 144–145
    Factor V analysis, 140
    medical geography analysis, 130–131
    overview, 126
    physical environment, 138
    poverty coefficients, 129, 138
    race coeffcients, 129, 138
    rape, 140
    robbery, 140
    social environment, 138
    variables, 129
    violent crimes, 154
Urban design, 8

Urban fringe, 253
Urban mosaic
    crime, impact on, 296–298
    edges, 301–302
    pattern theory, 250–251
    residential areas, 302–303
    territories, 301–302
Urban planning, 425–426
Urban structure
    crime rates, relationship between, 219,
        465–468
    facilities, 468–471, 476–479
    routine activities variables, relationship
        between, 227, 228
    victimization, relationship between, 226

Canadian Urban Victimization
        Survey (*See* Canadian Urban
        Victimization Survey)
context of crime, in, 26
demographic patterns, 217–218
predictors of victimization, 226
public exposure, risks of, 218
selection of, 290–291
target selection of, 249
vulnerability studies, 318
Violent crime
    gender differences in accused, 57, 59,
        61–63
    intellect of the accused, relationship
        between, 36–38

V

Victims
    affluence of, 154

W

Wasilchick, John, 21, 184, 288, 348
Watchers, 306